Travel, Travel Writing, and British Political Economy

"Brian Cooper unearths the hitherto neglected connections between economics and travel writing to successfully shed fresh light on each of these arenas. The book is an important addition to our knowledge of the history of political economy."

– **Robert J. Mayhew**, Dept. of Geographical Sciences, University of Bristol, UK

The book draws on the history of economics, literary theory, and the history of science to explore how European travelers like Alexander von Humboldt and their readers, circa 1750–1850, adapted the work of British political economists, such as Adam Smith, to help organize their observations, and, in turn, how political economists used travelers' observations in their own analyses.

Cooper examines journals, letters, books, art, and critical reviews to cast in sharp relief questions raised about political economy by contemporaries over the status of facts and evidence, whether its principles admitted of universal application, and the determination of wealth, value, and happiness in different societies. Travelers citing T.R. Malthus's population principle blurred the gendered boundaries between domestic economy and British political economy, as embodied in the idealized subjects: domestic woman and economic man.

The book opens new realms in the histories of science in its analyses of debates about gender in social scientific observation: Maria Edgeworth, Maria Graham, and Harriet Martineau observe a role associated with women and methodically interpret what they observe, an act reserved, in theory, by men.

Brian P. Cooper is an independent scholar whose research explores the boundaries of economics past and present. His publications include *Family Fictions and Family Facts: Harriet Martineau, Adolphe Quetelet, and the Population Question in England, 1798–1859* (2007) and "Social Classifications, Social Statistics and the 'Facts' of 'Difference' in Economics", in *Toward a Feminist Philosophy of Economics* (2003).

Routledge Research in Travel Writing

Edited by Peter Hulme, University of Essex
Tim Youngs, Nottingham Trent University

Travel Writing from Black Australia
Utopia, Melancholia, and Aboriginality
Robert Clarke

Travel Writing in Dutch and German, 1790–1930
Modernity, Regionality, Mobility
Edited by Alison E. Martin, Lut Missinne, and Beatrix van Dam

French Political Travel Writing in the Interwar Years
Radical Departures
Martyn Cornick, Martin Hurcombe, and Angela Kershaw

Travelling Servants
Mobility and Employment in British Fiction and Travel Writing 1750–1850
Kathryn Walchester

The Desertmakers
Travel, War and the State in Latin America
Javier Uriarte

Time and Temporalities in European Travel Writing
Paula Henrikson and Christina Kullberg

Revisiting Italy
British Women Travel Writers and the Risorgimento (1844–61)
Rebecca Butler

Travel, Travel Writing, and British Political Economy
"Instructions for Travellers," circa 1750–1850
Brian P. Cooper

For more information about this series, please visit: https://www.routledge.com/Routledge-Research-in-Travel-Writing/book-series/RRTW

Travel, Travel Writing, and British Political Economy
"Instructions for Travellers," circa 1750–1850

Brian P. Cooper

NEW YORK AND LONDON

First published 2022
by Routledge
605 Third Avenue, New York, NY 10158

and by Routledge
2 Park Square, Milton Park, Abingdon, Oxon, OX14 4RN

Routledge is an imprint of the Taylor & Francis Group, an informa business

© 2022 Taylor & Francis

The right of Brian P. Cooper to be identified as author of this work has been asserted by him in accordance with sections 77 and 78 of the Copyright, Designs and Patents Act 1988.

All rights reserved. No part of this book may be reprinted or reproduced or utilised in any form or by any electronic, mechanical, or other means, now known or hereafter invented, including photocopying and recording, or in any information storage or retrieval system, without permission in writing from the publishers.

Trademark notice: Product or corporate names may be trademarks or registered trademarks, and are used only for identification and explanation without intent to infringe.

Library of Congress Cataloging-in-Publication Data
Names: Cooper, Brian P. (Brian Philip), 1958- author.
Title: Travel, travel writing, and British political economy : "instructions for travellers," circa 1750-1850 / Brian P. Cooper.
Description: New York, NY : Routledge, 2021. | Series: Routledge research in travel writing | Includes bibliographical references and index.
Identifiers: LCCN 2021023115 | ISBN 9781138019508 (hardback) | ISBN 9781032125770 (paperback) | ISBN 9781315778952 (ebook)
Subjects: LCSH: Travelers' writings, European--History and criticism. | European prose literature--18th century--History and criticism. | European prose literature--19th century--History and criticism. | Economics and literature--England. | Economics in literature. | Economists--Great Britain--History. | LCGFT: Literary criticism.
Classification: LCC PN56.T7 .C69 2021 | DDC 809/.9332--dc23
LC record available at https://lccn.loc.gov/2021023115

ISBN: 9781138019508 (hbk)
ISBN: 9781032125770 (pbk)
ISBN: 9781315778952 (ebk)

DOI: 10.4324/9781315778952

Typeset in Sabon
by Deanta Global Publishing Services, Chennai, India

To Margueritte

Contents

	List of Figures	viii
	Acknowledgments	ix
	List of Abbreviations	x
	A Note to Readers	xi
1	Introduction	1
2	"Instructions for Travellers"	29
3	Travels with Malthus: The Population Principle in the Field	92
4	Travelers in Search of Malthus's "Authenticated *Facts*": The Case of Ireland	135
5	Travel Accounts of Spanish America and British Political Economy, circa 1800–1823	168
6	"To Give This Country Its True Value": British Travelers in La Plata and Chile, and the Financial Crisis of 1825–6	211
7	Travels with Harriet Martineau	256
	Bibliography	323
	Index	355

Figures

1.1	Milk-Boys of Buenos Ayres, circa 1820. Harvard University	2
1.2	East India Company painting of cashew tree branch and fruit, circa 1825. Personal collection of the author. Photo: Karen Hatch	8
1.3	East India Company painting of pineapple tree branch and fruit, circa 1825. Personal collection of the author. Photo: Karen Hatch	9
2.1	The "mixture of castes, under their common or distinguishing names", Lima, Peru, circa 1825. Harvard University	42
2.2	The "drollest and most diverting kind of conveyance" in Dublin. Kress Collection, Baker Library, Harvard Business School	63
5.1	Statistical analysis of the Kingdom of New Spain. Territorial extent and population. Harvard University	183
5.2	The size and population of constituent parts of New Spain. Harvard University	184
5.3	Statistical analysis. Intendancy of Mexico, 1803. Harvard University	185
5.4	Rio slave market, early 1820s. University of Michigan	189
5.5	Pernambuco Gate and slave market, early 1820s. University of Michigan	190
6.1	Population estimates for the provinces of the La Plata Federal Union, circa 1815–1825. Harvard University	223
6.2	Population and territorial extent of the provinces of Chile, circa 1825. Harvard University	224
7.1	Man returning from the market in Cincinnati, circa 1830. Yale University	258

Acknowledgments

This study of the interaction between travel, travel writing, and British political economy in the eighteenth and nineteenth centuries represents an attempt to combine several long-standing interests of mine. These range from research on the early histories of observation and objectivities in the social sciences, the relationships between economy, domestic economy, and political economy, to exchanges between and among self-identified political economists and everyone else questioning the boundaries of the emerging science. Tim Alborn, Silvana Collela, Diana Strassmann, Drucilla A. Barker, Edith Kuiper, Ulla Grapard, Jean Shackelford, Robert W. Dimand, Heather Boushey, Valerie Sanders, Deborah A. Logan, Deborah Valenze, Lorraine Daston, Peter Galison, and the late Louise A. Tilly, all encouraged my initial forays into these areas. More recently, Tim and Deborah provided valuable feedback on draft chapters of this manuscript; Karen Hatch, Thomas Ligner, Robert Zinck, and Melissa Murphy assisted in the preparation of the images. Many thanks to them all, and to Mitchell Manners and Jayanthi Chander, my editors who shepherded this book through to completion.

Travel helped shape the trajectory of this project. A few instances stand out: a meeting with Carl Thompson in London in 2011; a two-minute conversation with Rob Langham of Routledge at the ASSA meetings in Chicago in 2012; my participation in a November 2016 NACBS panel in Washington, D.C. organized by Tim; conversations during a June 2018 INCS conference planned by Silvana in Rome; and, in 2020, exchanges with Mary Morgan and other participants in a 2020 Zoom conference, "Roads to Knowledge: Travel in the History of Economics," put together by Harro Maas and Mauro Boianovsky. I am indebted to them all, as I am to the many others in academics who have assured me that space was available for my work, and who have opened spaces for it. Discussions on the theory of knowledge with two former travel writers, my dearest friends, Philip Benson and Deirdre Ball, during trips on five continents helped as well. As always, immeasurable thanks to Margueritte Murphy for her love and support.

Abbreviations

DOMESTIC MANNERS	Frances Trollope. *Domestic Manners of the Americans*
EASTERN LIFE	Harriet Martineau, *Eastern Life, Present and Past*
ESSAY	T.R. Malthus, *Essay on the Principle of Population*
HOW TO OBSERVE	Harriet Martineau, *How to Observe. Morals and Manners*
JOURNEY	Joseph Andrews, *Journey from Buenos Ayres: Through the provinces of Cordova, ... etc.*
JRC	Maria Graham, *Journal of a Residence in Chile, during the Year 1822; and a Voyage from Chile to Brazil, in 1823*
JVB	Maria Graham, *Journal of a Voyage to Brazil, and Residence There, during Part of the Years 1821, 1822, 1823*
REPORTS	Francis Bond Head, *Reports relating to the failure of the Rio Plata mining association*
RETROSPECT	Harriet Martineau, *Retrospect of Western Travel*
ROUGH NOTES	Francis Bond Head, *Rough Notes Taken during Some Rapid Journeys across the Pampas and among the Andes*
SOCIETY	Harriet Martineau, *Society in America*
TCP	John Miers, *Travels in Chile and La Plata*
TMS	Adam Smith, *Theory of Moral Sentiments*
WN	Adam Smith, *An Inquiry into the Nature and Causes of the Wealth of Nations*

References for Smith's *Wealth of Nations*, *Theory of Moral Sentiments*, *Lectures on Jurisprudence*, and Malthus's 1798 edition of *Essay* are in the following order: book, chapter, part, article, and paragraph. Not all elements appear every time.

A Note to Readers

I forgo, as much as possible, using quotation marks for categories and terms such as savage and barbarian. Readers should understand that the meanings of words conform to those common to the periods in question rather than present-day usage.

1 Introduction

> There is scarcely any history or any account of voyages or travels that does not abound with facts or opinions, the bearings of which cannot be understood without some previous acquaintance with the principles of political economy.
>
> Jane Haldimand Marcet, *Conversations on Political Economy* (1816)[1]

The epigraph indicates growing confidence among British political economists at the beginning of the nineteenth century that knowledge of their craft created a pathway to understanding the world. According to Marcet, familiarity with principles of political economy was necessary for readers of her educational work to come to terms with the myriad "facts or opinions" generated in the popular literary genre of voyages and travels. By the early nineteenth century, the link between the principles of British political economy, travel, and travel writing may have appeared self-evident. British merchants eager to hunt out new markets overseas needed to calculate and broadcast the costs, benefits, and profits of potential investments; diplomats and functionaries abroad filed reports on what they saw and did, and how these affected the fortunes of the home country. In fact, numerous travelers, both prominent and obscure, went into the field intent on organizing and publicizing at least some of their observations using insights from British political economists.

Or not. Colonel William Duane, traveling through Colombia with his daughter and stepson in 1822 and 1823, concerned himself with matters, both small and large, germane to the science. He interceded "on behalf of persons in the United States, having claims against the government, of which other agents had not procured the liquidation", and took note of Colombia's "commerce, domestic and foreign".[2] Yet, Duane, in his only mention of the new science, ridicules political economy and political economists. Duane writes of the first report by the Minister of Finance that

> the ideas of a fiscal kind are such as have been prevalent in Europe for the last half century, or what in common discourse is called *political*

DOI: 10.4324/9781315778952-1

2 Introduction

economy; in which the fancies of Rousseau, the illusions of the French economists, or school of Quesnay, and the perplexity and contradictions of the English school of Smith, and of Say, who may be called the Economistics, are the sources of scientific absurdity.[3]

Other travelers felt the need to at least explicitly acknowledge political economy, even as they relegate it to a minor role in their accounts. E.E. Vidal, in *Picturesque illustrations of Buenos Ayres and Monte Video, consisting of twenty-four views* (1820), remarks, in the text accompanying his illustration of "Milk-Boys", on how cheap it is to produce milk for Buenos Ayres, and observes how the "urchins" who bring it into the city adulterate it by replenishing their bottles in the river.[4] See Figure 1.1. Vidal goes no further, however, in his market analysis; he has informed readers at the outset of his account that he chose to leave "those more abstruse topics" of the politics and commerce of Buenos Aires and Montevideo "to the professed historian and political economist" in favor of reporting on "such peculiarities in the habits, manners, and customs of the people as appeared to him most striking during a residence of three years in the country".[5] Political economy had gained enough currency that it could serve as a handy trope in travel

Figure 1.1 Milk-Boys of Buenos Ayres, circa 1820. Harvard University.

writing. Even those who trod well-beaten paths in the burgeoning tourist trade saw fit to use political economic terms to comment, in published works and unpublished letters and journals, on the lands they visited: the vicar J.W. Cunningham concludes, in *Cautions to Continental Travellers* (1818), "Let the traveler remember that *he is called not to import the principles or habits of foreign nations into his own, but to export to those less favoured countries the principles and practices he has learned at home*".[6]

But we can stand Marcet's observation on its head. If she urges armchair travelers not to leave home without a firm grounding in the principles of political economy, what instructions did political economists follow as they sifted through travel accounts, or themselves undertook trips which figured in their works? If travelers faced the prospect of having to observe and explain a potentially overwhelming number of unfamiliar phenomena, political economists were subject to this same dilemma. Travelers' "facts or opinions" shed light on the uncertain epistemological and methodological boundaries of political economy, and place in stark relief the struggles of British political economists of this period to claim the discipline, a branch of moral philosophy, was a science. And the facts were themselves suspect sources for evidence. Both the provenance and legacy of the literature of travels and voyages made it more difficult for those in the late eighteenth and early nineteenth century to claim verisimilitude for travelers' observations: travel accounts, already saddled with a reputation for dubious veracity, also helped birth the English novel; sharing a family relationship with a genre associated with adventures, drama, and, above all, fiction, cast doubt on the credibility of travel accounts.[7] In addition, in early modern usage, the "term 'science' had meant 'certain knowledge,' and referred to a wider body of knowledge rather than specific disciplines"; fine arts, including fictions, were acceptable means for producing knowledge, and travel narratives provided a vehicle where literature and science could meet.[8] By the beginning of the nineteenth century, science had only begun to clearly detach itself from literature as an all-encompassing descriptor of prose in English. Further, as more and more travelers sought to circulate their accounts, publishers and audiences demanded that they both instruct and entertain readers. This imperative clashed with the desire of political economists to promote their work as a science. After all, how reliable could facts be if found in a literature quite possibly riddled with lies meant to amuse or titillate?

Those who wished to mine the literature of voyages and travels to help stabilize the boundaries of political economy, and to clarify when and where political economy principles applied, faced still another challenge: travelers were all too happy to tap into other forms of knowledge to make and explain their observations. These alternatives include, among others, history, natural history, geology, botany, ethnology, political arithmetic, statistics, antiquarianism, and mercantilism, each with a wealth of iterations.[9] We should add to this list individuals' knowledge of economic relationships derived from experience but not disciplined by an understanding of the work of Adam Smith and other political economists. Form informs content, too: many travel writers employ the conventions of multiple literary genres, from letters to Gothic and Romantic novels, in their accounts; and, as in the case of Vidal's *Picturesque*, traveler-observers from the late eighteenth century forward could also apply the aesthetic ideal developed by William Gilpin, and become one of his "picturesque travelers".[10] Political economy thus faced stiff competition as contemporaries searched for means to comprehend unfamiliar lands and peoples through both actual and armchair travel.

I confront a similarly wide set of choices. There is no universally accepted scholarly definition for travel writing. According to eighteenth and nineteenth century English convention, voyages and travels covered texts written by a diverse set of characters in a diverse set of genres: letters, diaries, guides to customs and manners, scientific reports, fantasy narratives, and rewrites of accounts by others. Adventurers and explorers, missionaries, merchants residing overseas, company agents recounting rapid passages through foreign lands, naturalists, sailors and soldiers, literary travelers, armchair travelers, engineers, colonial administrators, plantation owners, and, much more infrequently, (former) slaves, make up a partial roster of those who penned accounts. Accounts themselves traveled, were assembled, packaged, edited, published, distributed, interpreted, reinterpreted, and translated from and into foreign tongues; there is no necessary correspondence between an account as written and an account as published.

Academic research on the variegated histories of travel and travel writing has exploded in the past twenty years. This work encompasses disciplines running the gamut from A to Z, including, but not restricted to, anthropology, art history, cultural history, geography, history of science, leisure and tourism studies, legal history, literary history and criticism, maritime history, political history, sociology, transatlantic studies, and zoology. Researchers have mounted art exhibits, organized conferences, published articles and books, and established professional associations, journals, and a research center devoted to the field.[11] Driven by insights on the production and transmission of knowledge from literary analyses, especially poststructuralist and postmodern theory, cultural history, postcolonial studies, and gender studies, as well as work in the history of science, analysts of travel and travel writing have pondered the relationship between literary and material culture, epistemological and ethical concerns, and questions of national, ethnic, and religious boundaries that arise from encounters between peoples from different geographical spaces. Scholars reexamine the histories of earlier episodes of globalization, particularly European scientific and commercial exploration from the early modern period forward. Researchers explore as well imperial and colonial expansion, and the rise of nationalist ideologies in light of the experiences of travelers, actual and imagined, and the representations of travel literature, both factual and fictional.

Given the range of available options, I've chosen to draw on three principal approaches to consider the relationship between travel, travel writing, and the work of British political economists: feminist history of economics, literary history, and the histories of observation and scientific objectivity. Feminist economics places gender at the center of economic analyses, including critiques of the methodologies, epistemologies, normative assumptions, and conclusions of the discipline. I explore a central, gendered tension apparent in British political economy from the late eighteenth through the first half of the nineteenth century as it unfolds in travel literature: political economists routinely sought to distinguish the science from the art of political economy, roughly a distinction between the discovery and description of the principles of political economy and acting on those principles. Legislation formed part of the art of political economy; so too did activities grouped under the heading "economy" or "domestic economy", work increasingly associated with women. Acting with economy or as an "economist" entails prudent spending and consumption by a household and its individual members. Tending to domestic economy in this period also meant educating children of the middle classes, and, increasingly, the lower ranks and classes, to emulate these patterns of behavior. British women readily took on many educational activities, and some achieved international prominence by doing so. *Conversations*, for example, was just one of a series of didactic works in fiction on topics in the sciences published by Marcet.[12] British political economists, however, downplayed the significance of household activities to their science. As a result, women and children play only token parts as subjects and agents, that is, consumers and producers, in the science of political economy, a status consistent with what became by the 1830s the ideal of separate public and private spheres for men and women in Great Britain.

This was the theory, at least. In practice, neglect of domestic economy by political economists proved untenable. They believed the principles of political economy gained value when they took hold in real life, and individuals, families, households, and the state embodied them. Hence the significance of the epigraph, in which Marcet casually introduces a methodological principle; ideally, her readers, once familiar with the tenets of political economy, would read travel literature as would a political economist. But Marcet did not just use *Conversations* to creatively repackage the ideas and principles of Smith, her friend David Ricardo, and T.R. Malthus, and do so in a form more palatable than pamphlets and treatises for her imagined audience, women and girls of the middle and upper classes. She also used *Conversations* to originate the concept of the wage fund, which remained a bedrock doctrine for British political economists until the second half of the nineteenth century. Thus, Marcet employed the art of political economy to introduce a new principle in the science of political economy.

Travelers did not necessarily take a doctrinaire approach to political economy, hence trotted out their own versions of economic principles in which domestic economy formed an integral part of political economy. They even literally observed this relationship on display on native bodies. British travelers to India in the first half of the nineteenth century, for instance, registered their distaste at the penchant of Indians to adorn themselves with gold and coins that could otherwise be used as circulating currency to enrich the country. The continued resistance of Indians to British prodding them to use savings banks meant that they were effectively turning up their expensively ringed noses at European fashion and finance.[13] This meant that they also dismissively waved away theories of political economy (with bejeweled hands?). The British were not amused.

But Alborn indicates that Orientalism also offered British travelers a way to approve of such ornamentation on women in Europe and the Near East. To travelers in lands which lacked the security of property and the institutions for savings available in Britain, these ornaments served variously as inheritance, savings, and collateral for loans. In Genoa, they constituted "an essential part of the hymeneal dower" for married women, and, overall, "*necessary* adjutants to Genoese domestic economy".[14] In Ischia, John George Francis surmised that the passion of women "for articles of jewelry; especially earrings of the largest size, wrought in solid gold and after fantastic patterns" countered the "islanders' improvident character". Jewelry serves as heirlooms, too, evoking passions beyond self-love or self-interest. Francis empathizes with his wife's servant, Teresa, who recalled taking to bed after pawning her mother's earrings: "Questo mi ha fatto molto male!" ("This made me very ill!").[15] British travelers in parts of Europe and the Near East observed that women and domestic economy proved indispensable for the functioning of political economy, with the proof plain to see in the public sphere, and hard to overlook in the private sphere. For those travelers who chose not to fence off domestic economy from political economy in their accounts, the science of British political economy stopped at the waters' edge.

Literary historians have pored over how literature fostered the development and mobilization of the ideology of separate spheres. They continue to do so in part by mapping out contradictions and lacunae in texts, and how authors use rhetorical devices such as tropes, litotes, and metonymy to produce meaning. Two other critical terms in use in present-day literary analyses, excess and defect, often recur in travel accounts, too. Analyses of excess in literary history touch on ethics and norms of limits, and the ways in which excess unsettles attempts to classify and explain objects and phenomena. Travel writers acknowledge the challenge of trying to make sense of the multitudinous phenomena they witness, with both observation and representation producing, in their words, both excess and defect. A surfeit of new sensations can paralyze a traveler's ability to observe and represent, even if the traveler commits to a particular epistemological framework for observation: excess produces defect.

Publishers and copy editors weigh similar concerns when they decide what to include in the travel accounts they prepare for press. They, typesetters, proofreaders, and translators, may divide the text into separate volumes, books, chapters, or sections, add or delete punctuation, and harmonize spelling. All these individuals, as well as the authors themselves, may add paratext. Paratext includes cover art, titles, front matter such as dedications, prefaces (Vidal explained his exclusion of political economy from his work on Buenos Aires and Montevideo in one), introductions, material within the main body of the text such as chapter headings, illustrations, statistical and other tables, maps, footnotes, and back matter such as glossaries, appendixes, or endnotes, even advertisements for other publications.[16] Authors and their allies use paratext to guide readers, to prepare them for reading the text or alert them to certain features of the narrative; these "borderlands of the text" help contextualize it.[17] In return, context helps determine the meaning of paratext; in Genette's (translated) words, *its being depends upon its site*.[18] Prefaces and introductions sometimes include authors' apologia for a lack of editing to meet the demands for timely publication; the subsequent appearance of expanded, abridged, or translated editions of books can significantly change the meanings of texts.

Literary historians specialize in detecting the traces of earlier systems of thought in texts, too. One method travel writers use to authenticate their accounts is to cite the work of earlier authorities. Following the protocols of literary historians helps me avoid anachronistic readings, and hew closer to contemporary usages. The practice of locating meaning in its specific historical context, even if that reference hearkens back to an earlier period, is hardly restricted to those toiling in literature departments. Alborn, a (cultural) historian, for instance, indicates that British travelers, dazzled by the amount of gold, silver, and jewelry held by churches on the Continent, believed stealing such treasure, or the act of "plunder", would represent a fitting secular conversion into cash and credit of all the riches the Church had closeted away.[19] Samuel Maunder, a popular mid nineteenth century historian, captures a sentiment common to these travelers when he concludes that a similar episode of despoliation from England's own history, Henry VIII's seizure of Catholic Church properties, put to productive purposes that which the Church had "abstracted from the wealth of the nation and made perpetually inconvertible and unproductive". Furthermore, even the "paltriest smattering of true political economy" would lead one to conclude that, had Henry not grabbed the baubles and cash, a "most sanguinary revolt", driven by the "hunger" of the poor, would have resulted.[20] From the vantage point of present-day economics, however, Weingast reminds us that plunder represents the antithesis of the security of property, which Smith identifies as essential for commercial society to flourish.[21] Travelers could carry with them popular versions of political economy which, although anointed "true political economy", could contradict the principles political economists actually espoused.

Literary historians examine the means by which travelers turn "facts and opinions" into text. They do the same for objects. Travelers shipped

8 *Introduction*

off samples of manufactured products, flora and fauna, crafts, and art objects to their home countries. A native artist or artists commissioned by the British East India Company in the early 1820s painted the cashew and pineapple fruits depicted in Figures 1.2 and 1.3. These particular representations of India's bounty were sent to England, either for collectors or perhaps to entice viewers to move to the colony; they speak to the potential power of objects that travel, a focus of material culture studies. Objects have subjectivity and agency. Obviously, no perfect correspondence exists between word and thing, and though language helps form objects out of things, sometimes words fail and things remain things, eluding or pushing at the limits of naming, classification, and systematic knowledge.[22] Keeping in mind that things are not entirely reducible to objects, objects are not just constructed by humans but construct people as well. This is just as true of absent objects. Travelers' tales are replete with incidences of objects lost, swept overboard in storms or away by raging rivers, and lamentations for the stories these fellow travelers could have told. But, even found objects could experience limited subjectivity and agency, as they often travel without their customary baggage. The cashew and pineapple portraits display no hint of the historical, political, institutional, social, and environmental contexts from which they are drawn, or who drew and painted them. They even lack names; fellow human travelers presumably supplied British viewers these and other pertinent facts about the things represented in the paintings.

Figure 1.2 East India Company painting of cashew tree branch and fruit, circa 1825. Personal collection of the author. Photo: Karen Hatch.

Figure 1.3 East India Company painting of pineapple tree branch and fruit, circa 1825. Personal collection of the author. Photo: Karen Hatch.

Historians also recognize the importance of the world of objects and how their journeys contribute to making or losing knowledge.[23] These objects include books, letters, and essays, the chief subjects of this book, as well as scientific and commercial samples and any accompanying sketches, drawings, paintings, and written descriptions; but think of bacteria, bibles, bills of exchange, and bank notes, too. The materiality of objects helps constitute relations of knowledge and power. Individuals of different status, varying in respectability, credibility, authority, and power, negotiated the meanings of objects that traveled. They did so through multiple filters: with books these include the forms of address (in dedications, prefaces, the body of the texts, and so on) and the critical reception of the texts.[24]

Just as not every travel object reaches its intended destination, not every travel experience makes it into writing, and not every traveler's recorded observation into publication. Individuals' choices, enmeshed in the workings of social networks, and all tangled up with commercial considerations, combine to help determine what writing sees the light of day.[25] Travelers, publishers, editors, and typesetters took pains to exclude anything thought likely to put off readers, material deemed too disgusting, inflammatory, or simply boring.[26] Authors and their allies tried to fashion different audiences by couching accounts in different literary formats. The prices and means of distribution of various types of publications mattered for potential audiences as well.

The location, identity, and social status of those responsible for each of these steps were important in this regard. Timing mattered, too. If travelers were first to visit a country, had something new to offer readers about an oft-visited locale, or if they visited places in the news, they would have greater incentive to publish than would otherwise be the case. Maria Graham, John Miers, Francis Bond Head, and Joseph Andrews, whose works I cover in Chapters Five and Six, fit this mold: each quickly turned out material about South America in the mid-1820s, slaking a thirst in Great Britain for information about a region whose mines featured prominently in popular narratives about the economic boom and bust of 1825–6. If a book sold well, an author could effectively change identity and become a travel writer. Nonetheless the profit motive appears not to have been a major motivating factor for British travel writers in this period. According to Davies, who examined the publisher John Murray's publication ledger, social and academic status concerns may have provided more compelling reasons than mere money for travelers publishing accounts in the 1820s, though writing for pay became more frequent as the nineteenth century progressed.[27]

Authors, publishers and editors shaped texts to create not just audiences, but to establish trust in accounts; a travel writer's authority could be fleeting, and was always at risk of refutation. Graham, for instance, became embroiled in controversy over the massive earthquake in Chile of 19 November 1822. She recorded detailed descriptions of the tremors and subsequent tsunami, and contemporaries initially found her account accurate and compelling. When a dispute over her interpretations of the event erupted among geologists in 1834, however, Graham found her credibility at stake. She mustered a vigorous and, unusual for a woman at the time, deliberately public defense of her observations, an effort which proved ultimately successful.[28]

Insights from the histories of observation and objectivity have helped me focus my examination of these debates about the credibility of travel accounts. Contemporaries like Andrews registered doubts about whether other travelers, such as Francis Bond Head, had in truth made unprejudiced and unbiased observations, thereby rendering their narratives "an impartial investigation into facts".[29] The fact that travelers often had to secure the trust of readers in the absence of supporting witnesses or physical evidence for their representations made this process no easier.[30] Historians and historians of science have indicated the historicity, contingency, and shifting meanings of objectivity.[31] Beginning in the early modern period, Europeans increasingly linked the credibility of eyewitness accounts to standard procedures and methods of observation and representation, rather than the reputation of observers. Discussions on what and how travelers should observe included, for example, those sparked by several British men in India who, inspired by Adam Smith's moral philosophy, briefly adopted the stance and viewing procedures of Smith's impartial spectator in order to make nonjudgmental observations and representations of the practice of sati (widow burning) during the last half of the eighteenth century.[32] Contemporaries also clearly focused on who should observe. Travelers increasingly questioned or discounted altogether testimonies from natives, including Indigenous elites whose status had previously lent authority to their accounts. The work of producing scientific knowledge also relied in part on a division of labor between observers and interpreters, part of a set of debates over whether observation and representation should be split between amateurs and experts, respectively. That these divisions were gendered, with women relegated to subordinate roles in theory and (largely in) practice, has been well documented in gender studies, cultural studies, and more recently in the history of science.[33]

We can see in travel accounts and their reception in this period what Keighren, Withers, and Bell term "the sociology of credibility".[34] European scientists only fully embraced objectivity as a cardinal virtue for scientific practice in the mid nineteenth century, if by objectivity we mean, for instance, the desire "to knowledge that bears no trace of the knower … Objectivity is blind sight, seeing without inference, interpretation, or intelligence"; one should clarify that objectivity takes on a number of guises, from the just-noted aperspectival objectivity to mechanical objectivity, and, that participants in the births of social sciences also evinced no little concern about detecting and rooting out bias and prejudice in their work.[35] This embrace occurred after "observation" emerged as both epistemic genre and category, where texts containing observations conformed to "recognizable conventions of style and content", and an observation was subject to reflection "as an essential method for gaining knowledge", respectively.[36] Debates about the credibility of the science contained in travel accounts therefore form part of the early history of observation and the prehistory of objectivity in the social sciences.

The histories of observation and credibility described here intertwine; stabilizing observations is a precondition for conceiving of and achieving credibility. During the eighteenth century the aforementioned changes in testimony and observation had occasioned an epistemological shift.[37] Historical epistemology, dubbed by Daston, "traces the social and cultural roots of such new early modern categories as 'facts', 'experiments', and 'objectivity'".[38] To which we should add "observation". Historical epistemology raises questions about the subjectivity of observers, their sense of self, and their relationships with others. The histories of observation and prehistory of objectivity raise ontological questions as well. These involve the process of discovery, the role of scientific communities in the creation and stabilization of scientific objects and categories, and the accurate description of such objects and classes. The shift from credible eyewitnesses to credible procedures was gradual and partial: not all eyewitness accounts lacked credibility. Habitual training in observational practices is critical to establishing objectivity: with time and practice, training produces "cultivated perception", which enables researchers to forge "stable kinds out of confused sensations", thereby "generating order out of chaos".[39]

British political economists' use of travel accounts forms part of the histories of observation and objectivity.[40] They certainly assumed that their own testimonies were unimpeachable, or at least not patently false. And, when perusing travel literature in this period, they were quite happy to accept the veracity of authorities they agreed with. Those whose observations could not be turned into supporting evidence for principles of political economy were another matter. Different epistemologies turn identical facts into different types of evidence: "Question and evidence are ... 'correlative' in the strong sense that facts can only become evidence in response to some particular question."[41] British political economy is no different; political economists agreed that facts joined with theory produced "evidence", whereas facts without theory did not.

Observations from travelers highlighted this distinction. In an exchange of letters between Malthus and Ricardo in the summer of 1814, for instance, Ricardo complains that the "Evidence" section of the House of Lords' Report into the Corn Laws, which presented information from witnesses who had traveled throughout the United Kingdom (Great Britain and Ireland), contained little actual evidence. Ricardo expresses his disappointment that the publication "discloses some important facts, but how ignorant the persons giving evidence appear to be of the subject as a matter of science". Political economy would be the science in question here. Malthus concurs with his friend, although he credits the witnesses with producing some evidence, however dubious: "It [the report] contains as you observe some very curious information. The evidence is a little suspicious, though it is a good deal such as I expected from Theory."[42] The report's authors express skepticism about the value of the testimony, too, though not about the credibility of the facts they collected; the committee members note that their charge included "collecting information in the most impartial manner" on the matters suggested by petitioners to the House of Lords. They conclude, however, that they had not been altogether successful in gathering evidence:

> They [the committee] have, therefore, endeavoured to ascertain whether any of the petitioners might be disposed to give evidence in support of any of the allegations contained in the petitions, or upon any points connected with this important subject. In this, however, your Committee have not been so successful as they could have wished, which has, perhaps, arisen from the petitioners themselves having no defined opinions upon the subject, so far as relates to general policy; a circumstance which the Committee consider the more probable, as on examination of their petitions it is evident that the prayer of them rather expresses a desire for delay, with a view to further investigation, than any precise opinion on the system which it might be most expedient for the Legislature to pursue.[43]

The committee members and petitioners cite the lack of "defined opinions" or "any precise opinion" on policy among the petitioners. Questions of policy speak to the art of political economy. Without naming political economy as such, both the committee and petitioners concede the futility of further investigation absent a foundation in the science: this would simply set loose more facts in the pursuit of theory.

The testimony before the committee of Edward Wakefield, a farmer and land-agent from Suffolk who had traveled extensively throughout the rural districts of the United Kingdom, also exemplifies the gap between common notions on agriculture and the understanding of political economists. When asked "From your information on this subject, do you believe that this country is capable of producing a much greater quantity of grain", Wakefield who, in his own words, had "devoted the whole of my time to no other object but inquiries upon this subject [the present state of agriculture in the United Kingdom]", replies, "*Infinitely*, certainly". A curious conjecture, and, if not rising to the level of Malthus's "curious information", a clear refutation of the population principle. Wakefield, not content to demonstrate how at odds he is with the principles of political economy, quickly proceeds to cast doubt on whether farmers even understand the principles of domestic economy. When queried whether cultivation he had observed in England "carried on with as much economy as might be", Wakefield demurs: "I think it is very seldom that farmers understand the term economy as the question means to apply it; I should call it economical, liberally to supply a farm with the capital wanted." Pressed on this point, Wakefield supplies examples where farmers do not in fact act with economy.[44]

Research into travel and travel writing allows us to explore how political economists collected travelers' "facts and opinions", and shaped these into evidence or rejected them. But present-day economists are largely missing from the recent ferment about travel writing. This despite the hallowed place that Daniel Defoe's *Robinson Crusoe*, or at least the title character, occupies in economic storytelling. Studies in other disciplines on the relationships between travel, travel writing, and economics are also few and far between.[45] Such examinations promise to be fruitful, however, simply because of the sheer volume of travel writing from this era. Voyages of discovery by Europeans, for commercial, scientific, military, and tourism purposes, increased markedly from 1750 to 1850. Travel accounts thus occupied an increasing proportion of the rapidly rising volume of reading material available to Britons, ranking second to devotional material in subjects published, purchased, and read during the latter part of the eighteenth into the early nineteenth century.[46] As the number of accounts increased, so too did the means of their dissemination in books and journals, subscription and circulating libraries, and reading and scientific societies.

Again, travel observations highlight contemporary disagreements about what exactly constituted the facts, evidence, methods, and ends pertinent to the science of political economy. Some believed travel accounts off-limits, tout court. The poet Samuel Taylor Coleridge, for instance, caustically points to Malthus's use of travel narratives as an indication of the political economist's lack of seriousness and methodological rigor. Coleridge, exasperated by the length of the second edition of *Essay on Population* (1803), writes in manuscript notes that, after the mathematical formula expressing the population principle appears, "all that follows to the three hundredth and fifty-fifth page may be an entertaining farrago of quotations from books of travels, &c., but surely very impertinent in a philosophical work ... three hundred and fifty pages to prove an axiom!"[47] Travel accounts do not count as evidence for or against the population principle, in Coleridge's estimation; entertaining, yes, but unnecessary. Coleridge considered *Essay* a "philosophical work". The published review drawn from his marginalia repeats this charge:

> From page 17 to page 355, Mr. Malthus retails and details from others' travels, and from his own, facts of all nations, and of all ages, in all states of society, to prove that men have suffered, and are suffering, from ignorance, filth, famine, diseases, large cities, unwholesome employment, superstition, bad passions, bad habits, bad laws, and bad government; that all these have made men wicked, and poor, and miserable.[48]

All this ink to prove a point that "no one individual in Europe would have felt the least inclination to contradict", that is, that wicked, poor, and miserable men "do not rear, even if they beget, as large families as happy and good people would do". As Coleridge sputtered, "It is neither more nor less than book-making!"[49] Book-making of what kind? The review appears in *The Annual Review, and History of Literature; for 1803* under the heading "General Politics", as part of the genera of "History, Politics, and Statistics". Political economy, in the journal's accounting, had yet to successfully earn its own separate classification; it still fell under the rubric of literature, which at the time, in English, still covered all written literature.

The combination of approaches I use leads me, again, to emphasize how examining travel and travel writing helps us sketch details of the permeable borders of British political economy from 1750 to 1850. Robust institutions and formal credentialing of political economists did not appear until late in this period; travelers participated in the discussions about what political economy was and should be, the means by which to observe and classify phenomena, produce evidence, and, crucially, to practice its art, in this disciplinary absence. Women writers, engineers, speculators, poets, and others all contributed to these debates as the British empire expanded and applications of the principles of political economy affected the lives of peoples around the globe.

An Itinerary

The remainder of the book proceeds in roughly chronological order. Chapter Two spans the period from the sixteenth century into the beginning of the nineteenth. During this time Europeans witnessed two interrelated phenomena: an increasing volume of travel, which generated new observations, facts, and questions; and heightened communication which reflected and facilitated shifts in the ethos and philosophy of science. Investigations and descriptions of far-flung events and objects began to supplement and sometimes supplant discussion and debate between individual scientists. But, how could travelers and travel writers establish their credibility if their observations and representations could not be certified by a single reputable eyewitness or adjudicated by learned argument?

Members of the Royal Society of London attempted to answer this question. Spurred by efforts by Spanish authorities in the late sixteenth century to begin systematically gathering facts about their imperial possessions, as well as attempts by Richard Hakluyt and others to direct, collect, and disseminate material in order to further English colonization, Society members sought to codify instructions for travelers on how to observe, what to observe, and how to represent in the second half of the seventeenth century. The directives, meant in part to foster the development of Baconian science, represent one of a number of new secular templates for European travelers to mold their accounts. Geographers and cartographers improvised in the field, for instance, by enlisting translators and other locals offering expertise to direct their observations.[50] Or misdirect: Indigenous interpreters could and did selectively use and withhold information, as when Don Luis de Velasco led Cristóbal Colón on a wayward course through the Caribbean for three weeks during the fall of 1492.[51]

When European travelers and writers, aiming their works at travelers, put into print their versions of Indigenous tongues, which were often nonwritten, they did so to serve a variety of important functions. Bigelow traces mistranslations of native descriptions of mining practices into "vernacular scientific writing" in an attempt to recover "Indigenous technical literacies" in early modern Spanish colonial America. Andean miners and metallurgists employed techniques following a spatial logic, where the depth at which metals were found proved crucial for classification according to the color properties of ores. Spanish translations from Quechua resulted in a hybrid written technical language which Bigelow, following present-day convention, calls "Quechuañol". The Spanish mistranslated the Indigenous systems of knowledge, taking color properties of "castas de metalles" and "metalles mulatos" to mean colors, thereby mixing in and highlighting racialized connotations the colonizers associated with the colors. More mistranslations followed, from Spanish into English, German, and French; one German edition, published in Pennsylvania, even ended up in George Washington's personal library. Following the trails of the various mistranslations helps reveal not only how different "classifications of race and color" were applied by readers of different European polities to people in "sistema de castas", categories used by colonial and revolutionary authorities and their subjects to attempt to delineate the mixes of different peoples – European, Indian, and African – and their offspring in parts of the Spanish New World in the eighteenth and nineteenth centuries, but the legal, political, economic, and social consequences thereof.[52]

The alliance of travel writing with the "new philosophy" in England helped usher in a rise of European interest in the scientific uses of travel literature; printed instructions directed travelers to systematically make new observations and generate new knowledge that would be available to others.[53] European designs to standardize methods of observation and reporting by travelers to shore up the credibility of accounts ran into a number of obstacles, aside from the translation issues just cited. National and multinational expeditions emphasizing scientific collection, and maritime and terrestrial discovery involved both common and uniquely national styles of exploration, observation, and reporting. While compilers of educational itineraries for the Grand Tour drew on classical philosophy and humanistic teachings, literature, and aesthetics, cosmopolitan elites failed to fully commit to an Enlightenment ideal that appreciated national differences and reduced if not entirely banished national prejudices from observations and representations of foreign peoples and places. And natural histories, to cite a last example, neither constituted a unitary body of thought nor set of practices: they attracted "Swedish cameralists, British neo-mercantilists, French physiocrats, and even republican figures such as Humboldt and Thomas Jefferson".[54]

Travelers and their readers helped create or reexamine classifications of race, skin color, nation, civilization, savage, and barbarian; they grappled with questions of bias, prejudice, credibility, and the relationship of travel accounts with commercial, colonial, and imperial ambitions. Travelers' use of a mix of epistemologies could lead to a jostling among them for preeminence. Still, as Jonsson notes, "beneath the diversity of political opinion was a common assumption that expertise about natural systems should have a central place in the making of modern polities and economies" (Jonsson, "Rival Ecologies", p. 1346). Joseph Banks, as president of the Royal Society in the late eighteenth century, pushed colonial policy toward exploiting natural resources by promoting agricultural improvement. Closer to home, political arithmeticians such as Arthur Young and John Marshall delivered instructions for travelers in agricultural districts in order to pursue information on similar endeavors in Europe.

The remainder of the chapter covers how British political economists joined these conversations starting in the second half of the eighteenth century. They used stadial histories as the principal method to organize observations from travelers' accounts and turn them into evidence, as well as to make conjectures about societies in the past for which there were no observations. Anyone who reads Smith's *Wealth of Nations* or Malthus's *Essay on Population* will recognize these histories. They typically assign a society to either three or four of the following classes: savage, barbarian, pastoral, and commercial. Stadial histories allow political economists, travelers, and others to gather facts and assemble evidence on how control over property and production determined the following: material progress; mental progress; civilization and civility; and, subjectivity and agency at both the individual and societal level. Contemporaries wielded them to describe and explain how institutional, racial, status, and gender differences could arise across space and time among humans presumably governed by similar physiological needs and psychological drives: neither constant material progress nor the linear ascendancy of the intellect and moral behavior, however, necessarily characterized movement through the stages. The histories both shaped and were shaped by contemporary understandings of rank, race, and gender. On this last point, though the improved status of women coincided with societal progress, stadial users differed in how this correlation came about.[55]

A quick note on usage, then and now. Present-day researchers often use the terms stadial and conjectural interchangeably; I use the term stadial, while also noting how eighteenth and nineteenth century users made conjectures based on stadial histories. This is an international genre exhibiting both commonalities and differences across German, French, and British histories.[56] Stadial histories serve as a foundation for British political economists and others, including many travelers, to speculate about the status of societies by largely, though not completely, reducing comparative analysis to comparative economics. The dynamic is self-reinforcing: stadial analyses were based in part on travelers' observations that themselves rely on stadial histories.

Historians of economics typically held that stadial histories appeared in Europe around 1750 only to peter out soon after 1800. Sockwell, for example, maintains that James Mill was probably the last to use the method, in his *History of British India* (1818).[57] But, prior to the advent of evolutionary theory, stadial histories remained the framework of choice for British political economists who wished to classify societies by type and degree of civilization. This remained true even as they began to focus more narrowly on the operation of the laws of political economy within commercial societies, which were marked by a moderation and channeling of desires for sex and goods into more acceptable venues such as companionate marriage and trade.[58] Palmeri argues that the histories retained significant influence throughout the nineteenth and into the twentieth century on evolutionary theorists such as Darwin, on political economists like Marx, the founders of sociology and anthropology, and even on Freud and the beginnings of psychology. Thus, the conjectural history of Smith and Malthus "helped shape the emerging discipline of political economy in the first two-thirds of the nineteenth century" as proto-anthropological accounts of British society.[59]

Walter Bagehot alluded to this in 1876 when he joked that in Adam Smith's hands, political economic analysis showed man's progress, or how "from being a savage, man rose to be a Scotchman".[60]

Stadial histories prove very malleable in practice, and allowed for new historical narratives, characteristics that most likely contributed to their longevity. Historians, beginning with Dugald Stewart, in his "An Account of the Life and Writings of Adam Smith", a 1793 lecture to the Royal Society of Edinburgh, credit Sir James Steuart for bringing the term "conjectural history" into English in 1767, in *Inquiry into the Principles of Political Economy* (Palmeri 2016, 61).[61] According to O'Brien, eighteenth century Scottish writers widely rejected the term "conjecture"; Stewart, a student and biographer of Smith, perhaps engaging in a bit of polemics about method, however, characterizes Smith's use of historical analysis, where societies progress through successive stages, as "*Theoretical* or *Conjectural History*; an expression which coincides pretty nearly in its meaning with that of *Natural History*, as employed by Mr. Hume" in *The Natural History of Religion* (1757).[62] Stewart puns that travelers' accounts and facts, while insufficient in and of themselves as evidence of regularities, nevertheless serve as "land marks" for conjectures:

> long before that stage of society when men begin to think of recording their transactions, many of the most important steps of their progress have been made. A few insulated facts may perhaps be collected from the casual observations of travellers, who have viewed the arrangements of rude nations; but nothing, it is evident, can be obtained in this way, which approaches to a regular and connected detail of human Improvement. In this want of direct evidence, we are under a necessity of supplying the place of fact by conjecture; and when we are unable to ascertain how men have actually conducted themselves upon particular occasions, of considering in what manner they are likely to have proceeded, from the principles of their nature, and the circumstances of their external situation. In such enquiries, the detached facts which travels and voyages afford us, may frequently serve as land marks to our speculations; and sometimes our conclusions *a priori*, may tend to confirm the credibility of facts, which, on a superficial view, appeared to be doubtful or incredible.[63]

Stewart takes a gimlet-eyed view of the credibility of travelers as observers of "rude nations". Their facts do not count as evidence unless joined to speculations. In fact, facts gathered by travelers may only be judged credible in light of deductive reasoning, or, in what reads as more wordplay on Stewart's part, "conclusions *a priori*". The chapter concludes with several examples of how travel accounts mixing political economy, stadial histories, and other frameworks work, and how, in particular, they contribute to speculations about the qualities of economic man.

Malthus's successive editions of *Essay on Population* form the focal point for Chapter Three. *Essay* offers a new twist to ruminations on nature and human nature by combining political economy, the population principle, and stadial histories, all supported by the observations of travelers. Malthus had conjectured in the anonymously published 1798 edition that man was a "compound being" whose "corporal propensities" could act as "disturbing forces" that would overpower decisions of a "rational being".[64] The population principle constitutes a universal principle, but evidence from travelers, including Malthus himself in Scandinavia, indicated the principle could manifest itself in "compound beings" in a dizzying variety of ways. Thus, analysts sought out institutional, historical, environmental, and political facts gathered by travelers to tease out the different causes in different societies that affected the operation of the population principle.

Some of these facts had to do with household behavior; the population principle erases the line between political economy and domestic economy. When Malthus introduces the concept of moral restraint in the greatly expanded 1803 edition of *Essay*, he casts it in the following terms: if individuals prudently formed households, their choices offered a means to potentially avoid misery and/or vice in the aggregate. This mirrors contemporary British literature on morals and manners, written principally by women, such as Hannah More, for women. More uses observations from contemporary travelers as object lessons on prudence, economy, and charity to make clear that the responsibility for household economy fell principally on women. Thus, home and empire, and economy and political economy mutually constitute one another through the consumption choices of households.[65]

Chapter Four chronicles efforts by travelers who responded to Malthus's plea for "authenticated *facts*" regarding early nineteenth century Ireland. The give and take between British political economists and travelers occurred as causal analysis took its place alongside description and classification at the close of the eighteenth century in the European human sciences. Puzzlement over how to differentiate natural from accidental causes, and to trace effects from causes troubled political economists and travelers alike. Correspondence between the political economist David Ricardo and Maria Edgeworth from 1822 to 1823 attests to this search for methods and observations that would help answer the epistemological and ontological questions generated by the need to classify objects and identify causes.

The two friends spar over one of Malthus's facts, the relative security of food production in Ireland and England. They offer contrasting visions of happiness, and differ over the question whether the English or the Irish are happier. Both propose answers founded on numerical estimates of the riskiness of potatoes as a food crop. Their correspondence offers details culled from travelers, and (apparently) include a scientific sample. Both types of facts shed light on the meanings the two writers ascribe to the potato in the political economy of Ireland. Their letters indicate that women could demonstrate expertise in political economy, in observation, and interpretation, based on experience in domestic economy. The correspondence, when viewed through the histories of observation, exemplifies the permeability of the gendered boundaries between domestic and political economy, and observation and interpretation.

Their debate forms part of the legacy of the Republic of Letters. The rapid rise in the number of paper and other objects exchanged between members of intellectual communities in Europe and America in the seventeenth and eighteenth centuries presents present-day readers tantalizing but partial evidence concerning travel, observation, and interpretation. Corresponding circles would sometimes circulate letters from members, including travelers, or read them aloud among assembled members.[66] Letters take on a number of guises; Lady Mary Wortley Montagu's *The Turkish Embassy Letters*, for instance, are not the actual letters, but transcriptions most likely made between her return to England from Constantinople in 1718 and 1724; these circulated as a fair-copy manuscript until publication in 1763. Letters represent information technologies that scientists use as they seek to provide evidence for their work. Crucial tools for collecting, stabilizing, and disseminating observations, letters help stabilize subjects, too, through the affirmation of acceptable styles of investigator behavior. Correspondents could combine within individual letters testimony, numbers, copies of statistical tables, drawings, scientific and commercial samples (such as textile swatches), or curios, with or without accompanying descriptions. Then as now, the (re)presentation of information can change as it moves from letters to other genres, and to other rhetorical situations and audiences.[67]

Letters provide one answer to the question of how to establish trust at a distance. They facilitate the movement of information across space, and could help forge and maintain strong ties among communicants as they exchange pleasantries, work through scientific questions, all while trying to avoid the taint of personal or party prejudice.[68] They could also help establish protocols for assessing the reliability of correspondents and accounts. In sum, they could promote the ideals of credibility. Yet, facts and observations transmitted in informal, private correspondence cannot necessarily so easily be stabilized and turned into evidence.[69] The fact that eighteenth and nineteenth century correspondents frequently destroyed or lost letters also ran counter to desires among those wishing to establish scientific norms of shared information and transparency.

Chapter Five surveys the interlacing of British political economy and other contemporary epistemologies in several books, travel accounts of Spanish America, circa 1800 to 1823. Alexander von Humboldt's version of natural history, which he termed physique générale, or "general natural science", centers on the interaction of physical and cultural forces.[70] Humboldt's writings challenged political economists to rethink the importance of features of the human landscape to the wealth and civilization of societies and nations. These features included the distribution of wealth and property, laws on the use of land, and other factors that shape the interaction of humans with their environments, and, over time, shape environments themselves. European travelers observed that what little was known to Europeans of South American geopolitical spaces and national identities was difficult to classify, hence analytically unstable. European travelers inconsistently characterized the peoples of the new nations as variously part savage, part barbarian, and part civilized.

Along with their luggage and provisions, travelers to Spanish America in the first decades of the nineteenth century like Maria Graham packed a variety of epistemologies to help them try to comprehend the people, places, and phenomena they encountered. The work of Humboldt offered a daunting guide for travelers wishing to fashion credible accounts of the region, with its demand that travelers collect comprehensive historical, institutional, environmental, political, and, above all, statistical information. Statistics – stable, compact, and therefore more easily transportable information – could transform questions of difference into numerically measurable degrees of sameness. There were epistemological and ontological problems with enumeration, however, as well as practical ones. The term "statistics" carried a variety of connotations, for one. British political economists debated whether they pointed merely to statistical regularities, or whether one could actually divine causal relationships from the numbers, for another. Stock-in-trade of merchants, writers, and readers of travel accounts hoped statistics, when expanded to include population and other measures of national resources, would reveal the true value of South America. Yet contemporary statistical accounts point to both a lack of observations and, conversely, too many facts for observers to easily absorb, prompting oft-contradictory interpretive speculation.

But observe they did. And represent. Pratt draws a distinction between men and women traveling in and writing on South America in the 1820s, the former a "capitalist vanguard", and the latter *"exploratrices sociales"*.[71] Pratt assumes separate spheres of observation, based on a dichotomy between women and men's interests. But, as evidenced by the writings of Graham, the epistemological foci of female travelers and their male counterparts overlap. Both women and men needed to establish the credibility of their accounts, and both women and men employ multiple, often similar means to do so. Hence the gendered lines between the two sets of epistemological concerns blur.[72]

Chapter Six covers travel writing produced on South America in the 1810s and early 1820s from another angle. As the Spanish American colonial empire collapsed, a flood of British speculation in mining ventures followed, with British joint stock companies sending representatives to the region to scout out prospects for investments. To Pratt, the writings of travelers such as Miers, Bond, and Head, chief protagonists in the chapter, part of her "capitalist vanguard", reflect a confident, commercial people filled with visions of the productive possibilities of the revolutionary republics.

If these travelers focused British attention toward investment opportunities overseas, the gaze was directed inward, too: the postmortems of the 1825–6 investment boom and bust in Britain make clear that any investment scheme was threatened not only by the cupidity and irrationality of others, but by the British themselves. The growing popularity of statistical facts as evidence for travelers, be they actual or armchair, appears as a theme in the chapter. Once on the ground in South America, company agents went beyond mundane calculations of profits and loss. They sized up the willingness of South Americans to engage in free trade, took in population estimates when possible, assessed the degree to which the division of labor had spread, and gauged the wealth and material condition of the people they came across, all phenomena of concern to political economists, all measures of the progress of civilization.

Seen through the lens of political economy, the representatives of English mining companies and their contemporaries faced unique challenges when judging whether their observations and representations were unbiased and credible. Political economy was predicated on the individual exercise of self-interest, and interests can clash when principals are unable to directly monitor the performance of agents, instances present-day economists call principal-agent problems. Add to this the fact that European travelers encountered novel modes of industrial organization in the mining industries of the new republics.[73] They puzzled too over the casta classifications which Spanish colonial authorities had devised in order to facilitate political and economic control. The multiple, sometimes indeterminate, or plainly nonsensical names and meanings of the castas indicated to travelers a lack of governance, even a lack of civilization. All this led the agents and their readers to question the applicability as well as the premises of British political economy. They queried, for instance, the links between civilization, wealth, and happiness; greater wealth did not always translate to greater happiness, or even to greater material comfort.

The final chapter focuses on reflections made by the British writer Harriet Martineau from the mid-1830s to the 1850s on the connections between travel, observation, and social analysis. Martineau achieved international fame on the basis of *Illustrations of Political Economy* (1832–4), a set of short novels meant to instruct readers in the principles of political economy. Martineau's stories drew in large part on work by political economists, including the population principles of Malthus, who became a close friend during the course of the series, but also in part from contemporary travel writings. Martineau went on to publish numerous travel accounts herself, and several works resulting from her journey to the United States in 1834–6 form the core of the chapter.[74] These include *Society in America* (1837), which she had originally sought to title *Theory and Practice of Society in America*, *Retrospect of Western Travel* (1838), as well as *How to Observe. Morals and Manners* (1838), which she dashed off during the Atlantic crossing to America, but published only after her return to England. Martineau forthrightly tackles in *How to Observe* questions that had arisen among Europeans in the previous three centuries on bias, prejudice, and credibility in travelers' observations of human behavior in different regions. She proffers methodologies which would allow travelers to make comparative analyses of different societies. In retrospect, Martineau succeeded. *How to Observe* has been designated the first systematic methodological treatise in both anthropology and sociology. Martineau attempts to put these precepts into practice in *Society* as well as in other works such as *Eastern Life, Present and Past* (1848), her account of her journey to Egypt, Palestine, and Syria in 1846. I conclude with a look at Martineau's essay "Travel during the Last Half Century" (1858), an overview of European scientific exploration, and commercial and imperial expansion. Contemporary readers clearly did not passively consume travel writing, no matter how informative or entertaining the accounts.[75] Martineau examines what the European reading public gleaned from travel writing, delivering both a lesson on how to observe readers' reactions to travel literature, and a gloss on the sciences best suited to analyze different societies. If travelers produced new facts associated with new social sciences, for Martineau the timeless principles of political economy nonetheless remain the starting point for social analysis.

Notes

1 Jane Haldimand Marcet, *Conversations on Political Economy; in Which the Elements of That Science Are Familiarly Explained* (London: Longman et al., 1816), p. 10.
2 William Duane, *A Visit to Colombia: In the Years 1822 & 1823, by Laguayra and Caracas, Over the Cordillera to Bogota, and Thence by the Magdalena to Cartagena* (Philadelphia, PA: T.H. Palmer, 1826), pp. iii, iv.
3 Duane, *A Visit to Colombia*, 547, emphasis in original.
4 Emeric Essex Vidal, *Picturesque Illustrations of Buenos Ayres and Monte Video, Consisting of Twenty-Four Views: Accompanied with Descriptions of the Scenery, and of the Costumes, Manners, &c., of the Inhabitants of Those Cities and Their Environs* (London: R. Ackermann, 1820), pp. 33–4.
5 Vidal, *Picturesque Illustrations of Buenos Ayres and Monte Video*, p. iii.
6 John William Cunningham, *Cautions to Continental Travellers* (London: Ellerton and Henderson, 1818), p. 94, emphasis in original.
7 Marcet herself faced this challenge in *Conversations*, a fictionalized account of a young woman's education in the principles of political economy.
8 Judy A. Hayden, "Intersections and Cross-Fertilization", in Judy A. Hayden, ed., *Travel Narratives, the New Science, and Literary Discourse, 1569–1750* (Burlington, VT: Ashgate, 2012), pp. 1–21, (at pp. 1–2, 16).
9 Innes M. Keighren, and Charles W.J. Withers, "Questions of Inscription and Epistemology in British Travelers' Accounts of Early Nineteenth-Century South America", *Annals of the Association of American Geographers*, 101, no. 6 (2011): 1331–46 (at p. 1335); John V. Pickstone, "Working Knowledges before and after Circa 1800: Practices and Disciplines in the History of Science, Technology, and Medicine", *Isis*, 98, no. 3 (2007): 489–516 (at pp. 491–2); Lars Magnusson, *Mercantilism: The Shaping of an Economic Language* (New York: Routledge, 2002).

10 Giorgia Alù, and Sarah Patricia Hill, "The Travelling Eye: Reading the Visual in Travel Narratives", *Studies in Travel Writing*, 22, no. 1 (2018): 1–15 (at p. 6).
11 These include: Nottingham Trent University's Centre For Travel Writing Studies; *Studies in Travel Writing*; *The Journal of African-Travel Writing*; *Annals of Tourism Research*; International Society for Travel Writing; The Society for American Travel Writing, a member society of the American Literature Association; the annual Borders & Crossings / Seuils et Traverses Conference; and compendiums such as Peter Hulmes and Tim Youngs, eds., *The Cambridge Companion to Travel Writing* (Cambridge: Cambridge University Press, 2002), and Jennifer Speake, ed., *Travel and Exploration: An Encyclopedia*, 3 vols. (London: Routledge, 2003).
12 She wrote the first, *Conversations on Natural Philosophy*, which covered physics, mechanics, astronomy, the properties of fluids, air, and optics, in 1805, although it was not published until 1819. She published her second, *Conversations on Chemistry, Intended More Especially for the Female Sex*, anonymously in 1806, This, her most popular work, inspired the young Michael Faraday to pursue chemistry.
13 Timothy L. Alborn, *All that Glittered: Britain's Most Precious Metal from Adam Smith to the Gold Rush* (New York: Oxford University Press, 2019), pp. 118–9.
14 ["M.L.B."] "The Genoese", *Mirror of Literature, Amusement, and Instruction*, 14, no. 390 (1829): 178–80 (at pp. 178, 179, emphasis in original).
15 John George Francis, *Notes from a Journal Kept in Italy and Sicily* (London: Longman, Brown, Green, and Longmans, 1847), pp. 187–9.
16 Genette defines paratext as consisting of peritext, material located inside a book, and epitext, letters, journals, diaries, and the like located outside the book. Gérard Genette, *Paratexts: Thresholds of Interpretation* [1987], trans. Jane E. Lewin (Cambridge: Cambridge University Press, 1997), pp. 4–5.
17 Richard Macksey, "Foreword", in *Paratexts: Thresholds of Interpretation* [1987], trans. Jane E. Lewin (Cambridge: Cambridge University Press, 1997), pp. xi–xxii (at pp. xii, xx).
18 Macksey, "Forward", p. xvii, emphasis in original.
19 Alborn, *All That Glittered*, pp. 132–5.
20 Samuel Maunder, *The Treasury of History*, 2nd edn. (London: Longman, Brown, Green, and Longmans, 1844), p. 295.
21 Barry R. Weingast, "Adam Smith's Theory of Violence and the Political-Economics of Development", *National Bureau of Economics* (2017). www.nber.org/chapters/c13509.pdf [29 March 2017].
22 Bill Brown, "Thing Theory", *Critical Inquiry*, 28, no. 1 (2001): 1–22; John Plotz, "Can the Sofa Speak? A Look at Thing Theory", *Criticism*, 47, no. 1 (2005): 109–18 (at p. 110).
23 Steven Shapin, *A Social History of Truth: Civility and Science in Seventeenth-Century England* (Chicago, IL: University of Chicago Press, 1994); David Philip Miller and Peter H. Reill, eds., *Visions of Empire: Voyages, Botany and Representations of Nature* (Cambridge: Cambridge University Press, 1996); David Lux and Harold Cook, "Closed Circles or Open Networks: Communicating at a Distance during the Scientific Revolution", *History of Science*, 36, no. 112 (1998): 179–211; Felix Driver, *Geography Militant: Cultures of Exploration and Empire* (Oxford: Blackwell, 2001); and Marie-Noëlle Bourguet, "A Portable World: The Notebooks of European Travellers (Eighteenth to Nineteenth Centuries)", *Intellectual History Review*, 20, no. 3 (2010): 377–400.
24 Miles Ogborn, "Writing Travels: Power, Knowledge and Ritual on the English East India Company's Early Voyages", *Transactions of the Institute of British Geographers*, 27, no. 2 (2002): 155–71 (at p. 156).

Introduction 25

25 Ogborn, "Writing Travels"; Ogborn, *Indian Ink: Script and Print in the Making of the English East India Company* (Chicago, IL: University of Chicago Press, 2007); David N. Livingstone, "The Moral Discourse of Climate: Historical Considerations on Race, Place and Virtue", *Journal of Historical Geography*, 17, no. 4 (1991): 413–34; Nicholas Thomas, *Entangled Objects: Exchange, Material Culture, and Colonialism in the Pacific* (Cambridge, MA: Harvard University Press, 1991).
26 MacLaren models the process by which explorers and travelers become authors in I.S. MacLaren, "In Consideration of the Evolution of Explorers and Travellers into Authors: A Model", *Studies in Travel Writing*, 15, no. 3 (2011): 221–41.
27 Mark Davies, *A Perambulating Paradox: British Travel Literature and the Image of Sweden, c. 1770–1865* (Lund: Lunds Universitet, 2000), p. 31.
28 Carl Thompson, "Earthquakes and Petticoats: Maria Graham, Geology, and Early Nineteenth-Century 'Polite' Science", *Journal of Victorian Culture*, 17, no. 3 (2012): 329–46.
29 Joseph Andrews, *Journey from Buenos Ayres: Through the Provinces of Cordova, ... etc.*, vols. 1 and 2 (London: John Murray, 1827), vol. 1, p. xix.
30 Charles W.J. Withers, "Mapping the Niger, 1798–1832: Trust, Testimony and 'Ocular Demonstration' in the Late Enlightenment", *Imago Mundi: The International Journal for the History of Cartography*, 56, no. 2 (2004): 170–93; Innes M. Keighren, Charles W.J. Withers, and Bill Bell, *Travels into Print: Exploration, Writing, and Publishing with John Murray, 1773–1859* (Chicago, IL: University of Chicago Press, 2015), pp. 72 ff.
31 See, for example, Steven Shapin, "The Sciences of Subjectivity", *Social Studies of Science*, 42, no. 2 (2012): 170–84.
32 Norbert Schürer, "The Impartial Spectator of Sati, 1757–84", *Eighteenth-Century Studies*, 42, no. 1 (2008): 19–44.
33 Lorraine Daston and Elizabeth Lunbeck, "Introduction: Observation Observed", in Lorraine Daston and Elizabeth Lunbeck, eds., *Histories of Scientific Observation* (Chicago, IL: Chicago University Press, 2011), pp. 1–9.
34 Keighren, Withers, and Bell, *Travels into Print*, p. 69.
35 Lorraine Daston and Peter Galison, *Objectivity* (New York: Zone Books, 2007), p. 17. On aperspectival objectivity, see Thomas Nagle, *The View from Nowhere* (Oxford: Oxford University Press, 1986), and Daston, "Objectivity and the Escape from Perspective", *Social Studies of Science*, 22, no. 4 (1992): 597–618. See also: Daston, and Peter Galison, "The Image of Objectivity", *Representations*, no. 40 (1992): 81–128. On the early history of objectivity in the social sciences, see Daston, "The Moral Economy of Science", *Osiris*, 10 (1995): 1–24 (at pp. 18–23), and Brian P. Cooper and Margueritte S. Murphy, "The Death of the Author at the Birth of Social Science: The Cases of Harriet Martineau and Adolphe Quetelet", *Studies in History and Philosophy of Science*, 31, no. 1 (2000): 1–36.
36 Lorraine Daston and Elizabeth Lunbeck, "Framing the History of Scientific Observation, 500–1800. Introduction", in Lorraine Daston and Elizabeth Lunbeck, eds., *Histories of Scientific Observation* (Chicago, IL: Chicago University Press, 2011), pp. 11–14 (at pp. 11–12).
37 Lorraine Daston, *Classical Probability in the Enlightenment* (Princeton, NJ: Princeton University Press, 1995b), pp. 306–420.
38 Jorge Canizares-Esquerra, *How to Write the History of the New World: Histories, Epistemologies, and Identities in the Eighteenth-Century Atlantic World* (Stanford, CA: Stanford University Press, 2001), p. 6.
39 Lorraine Daston, "On Scientific Observation", *Isis*, 99, no. 1 (2008): 97–110; see also, Michael Friedman, "History and Philosophy of Science in a New Key", *Isis*, 99, no. 1 (2008): 125–34 (at p. 130).

26 Introduction

40 Cooper and Murphy, "The Death of the Author"; Bert Mosselmans, "Adolphe Quetelet, the Average Man and the Development of Economic Methodology", *European Journal of the History of Economic Thought*, 12, no. 4 (2005): 565–83; Harro Maas, "Sorting Things Out: The Economist as an Armchair Observer", in Lorraine Daston and Elizabeth Lunbeck, eds., *Histories of Scientific Observation* (Chicago, IL: Chicago University Press, 2011), pp. 206–29.
41 James Chandler, Arnold I. Davidson, and Harry Harootunian, eds., "Editors' Introduction: Questions of Evidence", *Critical Inquiry*, 17, no. 4 (1991): 738–40, (at p. 738).
42 David Ricardo, *The Works and Correspondence of David Ricardo, Vol. 6 Letters 1810–1815*. Ed. Piero Sraffa with the Collaboration of M.H. Dobb (Indianapolis, IN: Liberty Fund, 2005), pp. 130, 132; Mary S. Morgan, "Experimental Farming and Ricardo's Political Arithmetic of Distribution", Working Papers on the Nature of Evidence: How Well Do 'Facts' Travel? No. 03/05 (Department of Economic History: London School of Economics, 2005), p. 12.
43 Great Britain, Parliament. House of Lords, *First and Second Reports from the Committees of the House of Lords, Appointed to Inquire into the State of the Growth, Commerce, and Consumption of Grain, and All Laws Relating Thereto: To Which Were Referred the Several Petitions Presented to the House in the Session of 1813–14, Respecting the Corn Laws* (London: J. Ridgway, 1814), pp. 6–7.
44 Great Britain, Parliament. House of Lords, *First and Second Reports*, pp. 40 (emphasis added), 44.
45 The Allied Social Sciences Association annual meetings hosted a session on travel writing and economics in 1998. More recently a mini-conference hosted by the University of Lausanne, "Roads to Knowledge: Travels in the History of Economics", held in June 2020, focused principally on late nineteenth and twentieth century travel and travelers.
46 See: Richard D. Altick, *The English Common Reader: A Social History of the Mass Reading Public, 1800–1900* [1957] (Columbus, OH: Ohio State University Press, 1998); J. Paul Hunter, *Before Novels: The Cultural Contexts of Eighteenth-Century English Fiction* (New York: W.W. Norton, 1990), chapter 3; Jan Fergus, *Provincial Readers in Eighteenth-Century England* (Oxford: Oxford University Press, 2006).
47 Quoted in John Bonar, *Malthus and His Work* (London: Macmillan, 1885), p. 375.
48 [Southey, R.], "Malthus on Population", *The Annual Review, and History of Literature; for 1803*, 2 (1804): 292–301 (at p. 293). Bonar credits the review to Coleridge's friend, the poet Robert Southey in Bonar, *Malthus and His Work*, p. 374.
49 Quoted in Bonar, *Malthus and His Work*, p. 375.
50 Michael T. Bravo, "Precision and Curiosity in Scientific Travel: James Rennell and the Orientalist Geography of the New Imperialist Age (1760–1830)", in Jás Elsner and Joan-Pau Rubiés, eds., *Voyages and Visions: Towards a Cultural History of Travel* (London: Reaktion Books, 1999), pp. 162–83.
51 Anna Brickhouse, *The Unsettlement of America: Translation, Interpretation, and the Story of Don Luis de Velasco, 1560–1945* (New York: Oxford University Press, 2015), pp. 17–25.
52 Allison Margaret Bigelow, "Transatlantic Quechañol: Reading Race through Colonial Translations", *PMLA*, 134, no. 2 (2019): 242–59 (at pp. 243, 248–50).
53 Michael McKeon, *Origin of the English Novel 1600–1740* (Baltimore, MD: Johns Hopkins University Press, 1987), p. 101; Justin Stagl, "The Methodising of Travel in the 16th Century: A Tale of Three Cities", *History*

and Anthropology IV (Amsterdam: Harwood Academic Publishers, 1990), pp. 303–38 (at p. 324).
54 Fredrik Albritton Jonsson, "Rival Ecologies of Global Commerce: Adam Smith and the Natural Historians", *American Historical Review*, 115, no. 5 (2010): 1342–63 (at p. 1346). Further references to Jonsson, "Rival Ecologies", are included parenthetically in the text.
55 Richard Olson, "Sex and Status in Scottish Enlightenment Social Science: John Millar and the Sociology of Gender Roles", *History of the Human Sciences*, 11, no. 1 (1998): 73–100.
56 George Stocking, *Victorian Anthropology* (New York: Free Press, 1987); Robert Wokler, "Conjectural History and Anthropology in the Enlightenment", in Christopher Fox, Roy Porter, and Robert Wokler, eds., *Inventing Human Science: Eighteenth-Century Domains* (Berkeley, CA: University of California Press, 1995), pp. 31–52; Larry Wolff and Marco Cipolloni, eds., *The Anthropology of the Enlightenment* (Stanford, CA: Stanford University Press, 2007); Frank Palmeri, "Conjectural History and the Origins of Sociology", *Studies in Eighteenth Century Culture*, 37 (2008): 1–21, and *State of Nature, Stages of Society: Enlightenment Conjectural History and Modern Social Discourse* (New York: Columbia University Press, 2016), pp. 4–6.
57 W.D. Sockwell, "Contributions of Henry Brougham to Classical Political Economy", *History of Political Economy*, 23, no. 4 (1991): 645–73 (at p. 647).
58 Pat Moloney, "Savages in the Scottish Enlightenment's History of Desire", *Journal of the History of Sexuality*, 14, no. 3 (2005): 237–65.
59 See also H.M. Höpfl, "From Savage to Scotsman: Conjectural History in the Scottish Enlightenment", *The Journal of British Studies*, 17, no. 2 (1978): 19–40 (at p. 32).
60 William Bagehot, "Adam Smith as a Person", *Fortnightly Review*, 26 (1876): 18–42 (at p. 23).
61 Höpfl, "From Savage to Scotsman", p. 19.
62 Dugald Stewart, "Account of the Life and Writings of Adam Smith, LL.D.", *Transactions of the Royal Society of Edinburgh*, 3 (Part 1) (Edinburgh: Royal Society of Edinburgh, 1794), pp. 55–137 (at p. 86). Karen O'Brien, *Narratives of Enlightenment: Cosmopolitan History from Voltaire to Gibbon* (Cambridge: Cambridge University Press, 1997), p. 133. See also Silvia Sebastiani, *The Scottish Enlightenment: Race, Gender, and the Limits of Progress* (New York: Palgrave, 2013), pp. 6–8. Further references to Sebastiani, *The Scottish Enlightenment*, which appear in Chapter Two, are included parenthetically in the text.
63 Stewart, "Account of the Life and Writings of Adam Smith, LL.D.", pp. 85–6.
64 [Thomas Robert Malthus], *An Essay on the Principle of Population, As It Affects the Future Improvement of Society, with Remarks on the Speculations of Mr. Godwin, M. Condorcet, and Other Writers* (London: J. Johnson 1798), chapter 13, paragraph 3.
65 Felix Driver and David Gilbert, "Imperial Cities: Overlapping Territories, Intertwined Histories", in Felix Driver and David Gilbert, eds., *Imperial Cities: Landscape, Display and Identity* (Manchester: Manchester University Press, 1999), pp. 1–20 (at p. 3); Megan A. Nocia, "The London Shopscape: Educating the Child Consumer in the Stories of Mary Wollstonecraft, Maria Edgeworth, and Mary Martha Sherwood", *Children's Literature*, 41 (2013): 28–56 (at p. 37).
66 Peter Burke, "The Philosopher as Traveller: Bernier's Orient", in Jaś Elsner and Joan-Pau Rubiés, eds., *Voyages and Visions: Towards a Cultural History of Travel* (London: Reaktion Books, 1999), 124–37 (at p. 130).
67 Jeanne Fahnestock, "Accommodating Science: The Rhetorical Life of Scientific Facts", *Written Communication*, 3, no. 3 (1986): 275–96.

28 *Introduction*

68 S. Irving, "Public Knowledge, Natural Philosophy, and the Eighteenth-Century Republic of Letters", *Early American Literature*, 49, no. 1 (2014): 67–88.
69 J.M. Ziman, "Information, Communication, Knowledge", *Nature*, 224, no. 5217 (1969): 318–24 (at pp. 320–1).
70 Laura Dassow Walls, *The Passage to Cosmos: Alexander von Humboldt and the Shaping of America* (Chicago, IL: University of Chicago Press, 2009).
71 Mary Louise Pratt, *Imperial Eyes: Travel Writing and Transculturation*, 2nd edn. (New York: Routledge, 2008), chapter 7.
72 Keighren, Withers, and Bell, *Travels into Print*, pp. 68–9.
73 John Mayo, "The Development of British Interests in Chile's Norte Chico in the Early Nineteenth Century", *The Americas*, 57, no. 3 (2001): 363–94 (at pp. 375–6).
74 Martineau wrote up her travel observations across several different genres: books, numerous letters and newspaper articles, illustrated guides (*Guide to Windermere* (1850), *A Complete Guide to the English Lakes* (1855), the definitive guide to the Lake District for a quarter of a century, *A Description of the English Lakes* (1858), and *Suggestions towards the Future Government of India* (1858), instructions from an armchair traveler for future travelers and administrators to India.
75 Robin Jarvis, "William Beckford: Travel Writer, Travel Reader", *The Review of English Studies*, 65, no. 268 (2014): 99–117.

2 "Instructions for Travellers"

> this is a subject I by no means profess to be a competent judge of, and have only thrown together a few observations on the subject, as they were suggested to me from a general view of the state of things in the country.
> John Bush, *Hibernia Curiosa*, 1769[1]

Bush's subject is political economy. This chapter charts developments, beginning in the early modern period, that led European travelers to comment extensively on issues relevant to political economy, even if they, like Bush, felt incompetent to judge what they observed. Soon after its birth, European travelers gravitated toward British political economy as a means to make sense of what they observed. And, again from the very beginnings of the science, political economists used facts drawn from travel accounts to query their own work, ranging from how to define the scope and methods of the discipline, to exploring more specific questions about production, consumption, population, and value.

Travel guide and travel account writers from the early modern period up to the beginning of the nineteenth century attempt to instruct readers on what to observe, how to observe, and how to represent. While readers and travelers drew on a number of literary genres, I chiefly report on three: natural history, stadial histories, and political economy. Whatever the genre, writers promote activity which would allow them to claim the veracity of their representations. Their texts stress accuracy, for instance. Thus, Spanish surveys of its New World empire beginning in the sixteenth century emphasize the systematic production of information on the geography, resources, and people of a region. From the late sixteenth through the seventeenth century other secular instructions for European travelers began to supplant discourses around religious crusades and pilgrimages which had promoted salvation and the tailored development of individual personality. Commercial, scientific, colonial, and imperial interests often overlapped in these texts. Richard Hakluyt, for example, provided advice, in *Divers Voyages Touching the Discoverie of America* (1582) and *The Principal Navigations, Voiages, Traffique and Discoueries of the English Nation* (1589–1600), on trade, colonization, diplomacy, and exploration to

DOI: 10.4324/9781315778952-2

travelers who gathered information from regions hitherto unexplored by the English. Hakluyt's works form part of a genre which served as one template to advance the interests of English colonial and imperial expansion.[2]

The Royal Society of London serves as a key institution in this regard, and as a linchpin for the first part of this chapter. Soon after its founding in 1660, members, prompted by Spain's example, spearheaded English efforts to standardize observations and reports by travelers. Travelers would follow the precepts of the new science of Francis Bacon and Robert Boyle, which grounded natural philosophy in natural history.[3] Developments in both the new science and in English common-law for the establishment of impartial and verifiable testimony helped establish a "discourse of fact" in Restoration England, and contemporaries appealed more and more frequently to "matter[s] of fact" to settle disputes about evidence.[4] The Royal Society early on allied the new science with commerce, colonial, and imperial purposes. When the Society began to push for queries on skin color later in the seventeenth century, these helped usher in an outpouring of work vital to the early ventures in the European sciences of race, inquiries tied to the growth of the global slave trade.

An individual's social status was positively associated with one's credibility, reliability as an eyewitness, and the truth of the facts related to an audience as testimony.[5] English gentleman, assumed free of economic pressure, were judged more reliable and trustworthy than merchants or laborers.[6] Gentlemanly status was not, however, determinative. Though the value of singularities in the "economy of curiosity" encouraged polite conversation among gentlemen in the Society, the Society also "accepted reports from authors of varying social status and occupation, including non-Fellows", as well as contributions from outside the metropolis and from foreigners. By the mid eighteenth century, "the management of testimony" by members of the Royal Society "continued to be based mainly on the social status, occupation, and the number of witnesses of the occurrences"; yet members increasingly valued expertise and competence when assessing the credibility of observers, especially in cases beggaring belief, such as monstrous births, or where multiple witnesses contradicted one another.[7]

Directives on how to comport oneself in order to observe new matters of fact formed an important part of the new travel guides and reports. Sailors, merchants, colonial administrators, and others, gentlemen or not, could fulfill these instructions, the better to drum up commerce and serve colonial and imperial purposes. Nor did Europeans believe they held exclusive claim to credibility in this regard. Pursuit of accurate information often meant recruiting native subjects and agents to divulge knowledge specific to their region. By the mid eighteenth century,

> The recognition that accurate cartographic knowledge could be forthcoming from native informants, and that local navigational systems (e.g. those of the Polynesians) could rival those of His Majesty's Royal Navy, contributed to the ferment of travel literature in overlapping with

political discussions about a wide range of topics such as liberty, empire or colonialism.[8]

Travelers did not necessarily follow Royal Society (or others') instructions, however, or even read them.[9] They had wide latitude in choosing how they would observe and represent what they had experienced, and in choosing whether to explicitly acknowledge the frameworks which shaped their texts.

Editors of collections of travels and voyages such as Hakluyt also took an active role in translating and compiling accounts; these collections began to emerge in the early modern period as their own authoritative genre, joining mercantile and humanistic educational interests, distinct from but allied with cosmography, geography, and history, and inflected by the different religious and commercial concerns of the different nations of Europe. Hakluyt, for example, gathered empirical information to further English colonial projects by joining the cosmopolitanism of the Republic of Letters and national interest, grounding the combination in Protestant evangelism.[10] By the eighteenth century, editors began to consciously trim and more systematically arrange accounts to suit a broader readership, one that desired less scattershot, more credible, and less boring accounts, texts that both entertained and contained useful information on topics ranging from matters of state to controversies over the credibility of eyewitness observations.[11] The culling of excess led to a move away from a "faithful reproduction of authentic narratives" and the "most authentic evidence", relayed in the observer's own words, toward conveying what was most essential in an account. This impulse reflected a cosmographical principle that the exposition of ideas through interpretation of the facts can lead to better explanations of the world, while bypassing the question of eyewitness credibility.[12]

British political economists, who desired both systematic knowledge and authenticated facts, had by this time joined the ferment. The second part of this chapter opens with an examination of Josiah Tucker's *Instructions for Travellers* (1757), part of his planned-for but never composed comprehensive treatise on political economy. Tucker professes to offer a standard methodology for studying and judging any society, and asks his travelers to pay particular attention to any encounters with singularities, a focus which the Royal Society also emphasizes at this time. But *Instructions* was only printed for private circulation and, although published in Dublin in 1758, never widely distributed during Tucker's lifetime.[13] As a consequence, *Instructions* had no influence on his contemporaries, including fellow political economists such as Adam Smith.

Smith and others developed stadial histories instead. These offer a comparative approach to understanding similarities and differences between human populations across time and space. Stadial histories work as explanatory devices par excellence, vague enough to accommodate contradictions in both classifications and causes: the histories were both conjectural, designed to fill in for the lack of evidence in the historical record, and empirical, buttressed by travel accounts. Users, however, pondered whether these were universal histories or not. Moreover, the histories tempted users to hierarchically rank civilizations, peoples, and races, a normative approach at odds with Enlightenment cosmopolitanism.

Enlightenment philosophers did develop means other than stadial histories to describe and explain social phenomena. Montesquieu, for example, in *De l'Esprit des Loix* (1748), speculated that the political and economic needs produced under three different forms of government, republican, monarchic, and despotic, shape behavior. Montesquieu drew his ideas from historical records and from close study of contemporary Europe, including travelers' accounts such as his own short visit to Naples in 1729. Contemporaries on the Grand Tour repeated Montesquieu's reports on the political and economic mismanagement there. This exemplifies how travelers' accounts and analysts' development of systematic knowledge operated in a feedback loop: facts fed systems, and systems produced facts supporting systems. But the loops were not airtight. When Adam Smith borrowed travel observations from natural historians as he sought evidence to support his stadial history based political economy, he did so by omitting facts which contradicted his suppositions. And natives, when possible, wrote back, as Neapolitan intellectuals did in protesting dismissive depictions of their city and their efforts at administrative reform.

The final sections of the chapter illustrate how a number of European travelers in Ireland, South Africa, and England in the latter half of the eighteenth century and the beginning of the nineteenth century deploy doctrines of British political economy and other vehicles for observation, including natural history and political arithmetic. In their work we find hints of different versions of economic man as they query, in text and paratexts, questions of excess and defect, and the methodological and epistemological guidelines and ontological implications of observation and reporting. Smith presents readers a vision of an ideal traveler, a subject outfitted with knowledge of both stadial history and political economy, a character who looks suspiciously like a political economist. Arthur Young and William Marshall, who was Young's most vociferous contemporary critic, on the other hand, both promote farmers and farm agents who travel, make careful, comparative observations and measurements, and are capable of efficient management of agricultural estates. These works map the still-amorphous boundaries of political economy, tracing some of its many possible definitions, its relationships to economy, oeconomy, and natural economy, and highlighting the polysemy of contemporary sciences of society.

Early Modern European Travel Accounts: Science, Commercial Interests, Cosmopolitanism

The prime markers of difference for Europeans in foreign encounters in the early modern period were not economic, but religion and the presence or absence of European notions of civility. The ancient Greeks had invented "barbarian" as a pejorative to describe Scythians and others who did not subscribe to their ideas of behavior. Early modern Europeans initially redefined barbarianism as a combination of the absence of Christianity and the lack of European-style civility. Barbarian also represents the term of choice in translations of demeaning descriptions by Japanese, Chinese, and other non-European commentators of uncouth others, such as European travelers, traders, and missionaries. The epithet savage took on life as a floating signifier for Europeans, too.

> Even though there was from the beginning a tendency to equate the contents of the good and truthful Christian life with the specific conventions of European morality, this assumption was repeatedly shattered. Christians could be savages, as the English thought of the Irish, and Native American could be preferable to bad Christians as the papist Catholics would have been defined by radical Protestants. On the other hand, the behaviour of fully rational Indigenes could be contrasted with the effective brutality of sinful Christians ... Finally, the not-yet-Christian Chinese could become models of a superior civilization in the eyes of the very Jesuits who sought to convert them, while the Japanese presented the most puzzling case of a sophisticated civilization which could fully compare with Europe and yet was like a subtle, even perverse, inversion of its values.[14]

The first extensive contacts between Europeans with peoples of the New World in the sixteenth century reminded Europeans not only that there were varying degrees of barbarity and savagery, but that each could coexist, peaceably, with civilization within a given people or nation. Europeans found themselves unable to universally and definitively assign peoples to one category or another.

Among the English, this epistemological and ontological uncertainty reflected and amplified anxieties about native threats to the security of overseas colonies. This is evident in comments by Captain John Smith, in *The Generall Historie of Virginia* (1624). Smith contrasts the failure of the English to deal with Powhatan "Salvages" with the achievements of the Spanish conquerors of Mexico, "where thousands of Salvages dwelled in strong houses". To Smith, the inhabitants of Mexico "were civilized people" and "had wealth". The Powhatan "Salvages", on the other hand, "meere Barbarians as wilde as beasts, have nothing".[15] While all savages were not alike, apparently, and wealth represented a key marker of difference, Smith could not find the words to clearly distinguish between savages: some were barbarians, others civilized.

The English could themselves represent a similar classificatory puzzle. In the sixteenth century, English commercial, diplomatic, religious, and recreational travelers adopted a particular mode of action to navigate their way among peoples in Mediterranean climes. Englishmen and the occasional Englishwoman were circumspect in their day-to-day interactions in the region, their behavior characterized by politeness, watchfulness, and accommodation.[16] England was relatively weak in the early modern period compared to its regional rivals, Catholic Europe and the Ottoman Empire. The Ottomans, with whom England initially formed an alliance, presented to English travelers and diplomats a complicated entity. The English acted cautiously in order to cultivate opportunities among the mostly peaceful mixing of Jews, Christians, and Muslims, and the numerous nationalities joined together in a thriving commercial, intellectual, and artistic empire. All this while some English traveler writers, recognizing sectarian differences within Islam, argued for diplomatic alliances with Safavid Persia as a bulwark against the Ottomans.[17]

Games terms this pattern of adaptable subjectivity and agency on the part of English travelers toward foreigners in the Mediterranean cosmopolitanism. Even dissimulation played a role, with travelers sometimes feigning an inability to speak English. These habits enabled the English to more easily move about, and to establish and maintain trading outposts and networks. They also helped English merchants establish and burnish reputations at home and expand patronage networks in England by demonstrating commercial success abroad. The English were more judgmental, however, in their writings, with merchants freely criticizing their Muslim and Catholic hosts in correspondence.[18]

This flexible behavior held for English commercial travel elsewhere, too. In the "Ordinances for the direction of the intended voyage for Cathay, dated May, 9, 1553", for example, Sebastian Cabot advises sailors and traders intending to travel with the expedition of the Cathay Company that "every nation and region is to be considered advisedly, and not to provoke them by any disdain, laughing, contempt, or such like, but to use them with prudent circumspection, with all gentleness, and courtesy". Cabot also cautions members of the company "Not to disclose to any nation the state of our religion, but to pass over it silence, without any declaration of it, seeming to bear with such laws and rites, as the place hath, where you shall arrive".[19] The Company did not receive a royal charter, probably reflecting the religious and political uncertainty prevailing in England under Edward VI, Henry VIII's son and successor. Hence, the polite fiction of "our religion"; Cabot sought as much to paper over sectarian differences among the English members of the expedition, tensions which had been brought to a boil by Henry VIII's break with the Catholic church, as to hedge against trespassing against the spiritual beliefs and practices of potential trading partners.[20]

Cabot tasks expedition members with presenting a common, areligious front to foreigners. An earlier item in his list directed, however, that morning and evening prayers "with other common services appointed by the king's majesty and laws of this realm" be read by an officer or officers of the expedition.[21] This instruction could potentially create or exacerbate religious conflict between expedition members. Edward VI introduced two evangelical Prayer Books, abolished the Catholic Mass, required services be held in English, and ordered the remaining Catholic paraphernalia stripped from the churches, all prior to the issuance of "Ordinances". After Edward's death in July 1553, his successor, Queen Mary, reversed the changes. Cabot calls for "prudent and worldly policy" to mediate relationships among the travelers themselves; the stance he desires the English take toward foreigners would only work if the English applied such standards to one another.[22] The "Ordinances, instructions, and advertisements" asks for cooperation among disparate members, harnessing their individual interests to achieve a common interest, the success of the Company.

Cabot's directive to treat those they encountered with respect and caution had its limits. When members of the Cathay expedition were advised to seek out natives

> it is to be considered, how they may be used, learning much of their natures and dispositions, by some one such person, as you first either allure, or take to be brought aboard your ships, and there to learn as you may, without violence or force; and no woman to be tempted or intreated to incontinence, or dishonesty.
>
> 24. Item, the person so taken, to be well entertained, used, and appareled, to be set on land, to the intent that he or she may allure others to draw nigh to shew the commodities: and if the person taken may be made drunk with your beer, or wine, you shall know the secrets of his heart.[23]

The instructions direct members of the Company to act hospitably, employing friendly persuasion by means couched in the language of the arts of seduction, on first contact, in order to entice natives to trade. The orders hint at coercion as well. One person should be used; no matter how weak or divided the Company might be, a single individual would not represent a threat, especially once aboard a Company vessel. That one person should be used in such a manner as to divulge information useful for trade, though one can question whether secrets of one's heart translate into trade secrets. The suggestion that the Company should resort to getting their contact drunk, if necessary, acknowledges that natives might not willingly give up what the English desired.

European commercial travelers and colonial administrators had clear incentives to get details right about geography and valuable resources in non-European lands, despite religious intolerance and uncertainty about how to classify and treat people. Among the English, Hakluyt corresponded over several decades with cosmographers, merchants, fishermen, and other travelers to gather accurate material on the new regions and peoples they visited. He in turn provided advice and instructions for the pursuit of exploration, diplomacy, trade, colonization, and evangelization. Hakluyt imagines

Englishmen establishing self-sufficient colonies in North America. Colonists would primarily support themselves by raising crops for export, while England would gain new markets for English goods, especially cloth, new employment for England's poor, and new sources for goods provided at the moment by England's European competitors. Colonization of the Americas would be a boon to English commerce in another sense: not only would the English seek to convert Virginia natives to Christianity, the Indigenous were also envisioned as potential trading partners.

By the latter half of the seventeenth century, with England firmly established as a European power, English attitudes and actions had shifted toward aggressive and coercive efforts to remake rather than to accommodate to the worlds overseas, as in the case of Ireland.[24] This occurred as individuals and institutions in Europe experienced a push and pull between a desire for transparency and sharing of information for the advancement of knowledge, and the recognition that secrecy could confer advantages to those who had proprietary information. The spread of the printing press helped effect a break from the tendency of medieval practitioners of scientific pursuits to zealously guard the knowledge they obtained and share it only with a privileged few; publication of travel writing and guides for English and other Europeans increased substantially during the sixteenth and seventeenth centuries. But barriers to openness remained significant. Colonial administrators needed to keep some material under lock and key for reasons of state, merchants held exclusive information close at hand, and other individuals were reluctant to reveal their observations to the public simply for fear of embarrassment.[25]

Spain became the first European country to use printed instructions to direct exploration, administration, and exploitation of the resources of its colonies when authorities circulated questionnaires throughout parts of its New World empire to collect information in the early sixteenth century.[26] Administrators aimed to systematically determine the commercial value of Spanish possessions; the inquiries included questions on natural resources and people, "the political, moral, and natural history" of the territories, with accurate chorographic information facilitating the transport of goods to markets. The surveys speak to centralized Spanish colonial administration, but also to the creative means by which authorities sought to assemble information to guide policy: some questions allowed for open-ended responses, while others supplied the possible range of responses.[27]

While Spanish authorities restricted circulation of the questionnaires throughout the rest of Europe, word of their efforts inspired members of the Royal Society of London in the 1660s to develop instructions for travelers to assist the cause of natural history and experimental philosophy. The founding of The Royal Society in November 1660 marks a break in European scientific practice which had previously featured discussion and debate between individuals. The new philosophy highlighted systematic investigations of nature centered on new "matters of fact". Descriptions of phenomena that made up these matters of fact were often so strange and unpredictable that learned argument and reason alone were deemed insufficient to determine the truth or falsity of reports about them. Veracity could only be established by developing and agreeing upon new standardized procedures for observations and scientific investigations: "Establishing new knowledge about nature therefore depended upon multiple and sometimes ambiguous ways of judging the reliability of testimony about matters of fact."[28]

Travelers and their observations took natural history, hence natural philosophy, in a variety of directions, as is evident in discussions about "philosophical travel" in early proceedings of the Royal Society.[29] Philosophical travel produced a type of cosmopolitanism as travelers struggled to reconcile assumptions about the unity of man with the recognition of differences based on particular political, economic, customary, environmental, and climatic contexts. François Bernier's reflections personified philosophical travel. His *Travels in the Mogul Empire* (1670) chronicles his residency in India where he served, briefly, as personal physician to the Mughal prince Dara Shikoh. Bernier embraces a lack of prejudice and more detached, systematic observation in and through travel. He employs his experiences abroad in radical self-reflection on European mores and politics, criticizing Europe and rejecting barbarism and despotism both abroad and at home in favor of a vision of "civil progress founded upon criticism, tolerance and rationality".[30]

The expansion of travel by Europeans allowed for the collection of new matters of fact, sparked curiosity, facilitated the growth of scientific networks, spurred yet more travel, and enabled interested parties to more easily test the reliability of previous accounts. The Royal Society sought to harness the observations and analyses of mariners and other travelers to the cause of science by joining Bacon's natural history to Spanish systematizing élan. The effort tapped into English roots, too. Cabot's instructions for the proposed expedition to China included the admonition that all merchants "and other skillful persons in writing" on the expedition capable of doing so make and record navigational and astronomical observations, compare the same, and make good any discrepancies.[31] The subtitle of *Profitable Instructions* (1633), "*Describing what speciall Observations are to be taken by Travellers in all Nations, States and Countries; Pleasant and Profitable*", indicates the universal nature of the instructions. The address to the reader argues for actual travel; while armchair travel allows one to see the entire world while avoiding its corruption, the authors contend that "it is a good way to keepe a man innocent; but withall as Ignorant", and that "Experience added to learning, makes a perfect Man." Observation represents one of the three paths to civil knowledge, and, along with "Study" and "Conference", is necessary, when combined with religious knowledge, for administration. What is more, "The use of Observation is in noting the coherence of causes, effects, counsels, and successes, with the proportion and likenesse betweene

Nature and Nature, Fortune and Fortune, Action and Action, State and State, Time past and Time present."[32]

Bacon called for information which would enable readers to gauge the plausibility of travel accounts, and discussions about the guides underscore the importance of testimony and fact to science. Members of The Royal Society hoped that equipping travelers with standardized lists of questions would discipline observation and help produce credible knowledge for the new science at a moment when contemporaries viewed eyewitness accounts with increasing skepticism. Travelers' reports mimicked experiments since they "involved careful observation and were in principle repeatable".[33] Boyle, in *General Heads for a Natural History of a Countrey, Great or Small* (1665–6), proposed a set of general inquiries, directions on what objects and phenomena travelers should observe. These objects included people: "there must be careful account given of the Inhabitants themselves". Economic production, such as "by what particular Arts and Industries the Inhabitants improve the Advantages and remedy the Inconveniences of their Soyl", mattered as well. The directives asked travelers to keep a daily journal in which they should record observations in a clear, plain style, while abstaining from moral judgment. "Observations" even included answers to specific questions travelers were to ask of themselves and those they met abroad. Once back in England, they should rewrite the journal as a scientific history. All this would help build "a good Natural History", and "the improvement of *True Philosophy*, and the welfare of *Mankind*".[34]

Travel guide writers and scientific researchers cultivated a symbiotic relationship. Prior to the publication of the first of these guides, members of the Society published "Directions for Sea-men, bound for far Voyages", in January 1666 in order to take advantage of the fact that mariners could gather new information from around the globe. Mariners quickly embraced the spirit of directives and began to shape sea journals into tools for scientific inquiry into all manners of subjects, including natural and moral history.[35] Further, when the Royal Society published William Dampier's *A New Voyage Around the World* (1697) it set off an early eighteenth century boom in the market for literature on voyages among educated readers in Europe. *A New Voyage* joined the new science of the Royal Society to the established genre of voyage literature; the hybrid forced authors, editors, and publishers working in a literature which had traditionally embraced the fantastic and fictitious, such as sea monsters, cannibals, and two-headed beings, to adopt and adapt to new standards of authenticity and credibility, from the keeping of sea logs, to translating those logs into journals, and, eventually into print.

Contemporaneously, as the result of the establishment of new trade routes and colonies, European states and scientific institutions began enlisting travelers into efforts to systematically observe and classify physical differences between peoples, especially skin color. The Royal Society put together questions on skin color for travelers from 1660 to 1700, and these queries in natural history "had a far reaching effect in evoking commentaries on Blackness from European travelers and colonists". Reports led to new queries, which gave rise to new reports, and observations on skin color became a regular feature of narratives of travelers who wished to capture the attention of the Royal Society. These "allowed Western witnesses to fix any instability of power into a contrast between an 'impartial,' 'indifferent' observer, and the observed, often known solely in terms of a physical body".[36]

This perspective values exceptional cases witnessed through "observation and experience". Singularities were reported to the Society as if divorced from context as "deracinated particular[s]", cases that required further scientific explanation, even though they were "events so strange and singular as to defy induction, much less deduction".[37] Boyle's chief work on color theory, *Experiments and Considerations touching Colours* (1664), contains a chapter, "Experiment XI", on "The Blackness of the Skin, and Hair of Negroes", in which he, after "consulting with Authors, and with Books of Voyages, and with Travellers, to satisfie my self in matters of Fact", transforms "The Blackness of the Skin, and Hair of Negroes" from a natural fact to an anomaly.[38] Inconvenient, irregular facts would, in theory, check the tendency of natural historians and philosophers to make innumerable generalizations or too hastily theorize, and curb the growth of political controversies that often ensued as a result.[39]

Yet colonial economic interests of Royal Society members that helped prompt these inquiries into singularities produced regularities around the theme of Blackness. These include Royal Society investments in the slave-trading Royal African Company from 1682 to 1696.[40] By 1700, solicitations from the Royal Society for information on peoples' skin color, from travelers, ambassadors, and colonists, as well as "conversations about the issue at the meetings of the Society focused on black Africans".[41] As Europeans began to seek more information on skin color, they simultaneously began to enlist attributes associated with Blacks' skin color as justifications for slavery. The developing scientific discussions on race cast Blackness as a negative attribute in other ways. The Royal Society helped nurture the shift away from classical humoral theories on the effect of regional climate and environment on behavior. These had placed England, much of Europe and Africa, the "north" and "south", respectively, in positions normatively inferior to the "center", Greece and Rome. The new racialist theories cast English whiteness in a more positive light and left Africa as the remaining negative region. This was one of the many factors that helped justify the heightened exploitation of Africans in the slave trade: the status of Africans in English New World colonies declined as plantation systems expanded.[42]

The burgeoning interest in the science of skin color in Europe abetted the invention of racial classification by Europeans. Present-day scholars cite a number of men as the inventors of racial classification, including Carl

Linnaeus, Bernier, John Locke, Immanuel Kant, G.-L. Leclerc de Buffon, Johann Friedrich Blumenbach, and Thomas Hobbes.[43] Linnaeus, in *Systema Naturae* (1735), for example, classifies man as belonging to four varieties according to skin color, red, white, black, and yellow. His work helped shift previous, fluid European conceptions of non-Europeans: "Chinese, described in the sixteenth and seventeenth centuries as whiter than Europeans, became yellow in the eighteenth; and in the same period the Amerindians, also previously seen as white or mulatto, took on a red color."[44] Europeans hardly settled on a single epistemology to categorize the subjects of racial classification.[45] Thus, while English writers of the period for the most part start from the premise that humans form a single species, accepting the Biblical assumption of the common origin of mankind, or monogenesis, French writers consider more seriously the possibility of polygenesis, the idea that different races represented different species. Moreover, by the late eighteenth century the French shifted from designating Africans as savages and barbarians to calling them primitives.[46]

By the beginning of the eighteenth century, skin color and its association with race stood as key markers of identity and difference for Europeans; British travelers could use race as a proxy to judge the value of other peoples and societies around the globe.[47] Race retains a number of different meanings for the British well into the eighteenth century and beyond, however, interlacing notions, along with judgments, of national heritage, religion, language, blood and family, occupation, gender, and status. Tucker, for instance, alludes to "a customary Prepossession entertained against Projects of all kinds; And that Projectors are looked upon as a Race of Beings who have something very singular and whimsical in their Composition".[48] And some seventy-five years later, an anonymous reviewer of Robert Proctor's account of his travels in South America writes of the Pampas that the "natives of these wilds are called Gauchos; a race little superior to Indian savages".[49]

Away from learned discussions on skin color and race set off by reports of travelers, Europeans openly borrowed and incorporated Indigenous knowledge and ways of thinking about difference between peoples into their sciences. Even when explicitly tied to the goal of furthering commercial interests and political control, however, these ventures into previously unknown epistemologies could go awry. For example, Spanish colonial authorities deployed "sistema de castas" beginning in the seventeenth century in order to identify and impose order on the polyglot populations in their New World possessions.[50] The "sistema" would mark an individual as belonging to this caste and not that, and would enhance administrative control, including determining where one could live and how much tax one paid. Placement in the hierarchical classification system of the "castas" depended principally on your place of birth, family, appearance or color, and the ethnic and/or racial group you lived with, though other more intangible factors, such as honor, reputation, and quality ("calidad") could come into play as well.[51] The whiter the lineage, the higher the status. Those born in Spain to Spanish parents and who had traveled to the New World occupied the top caste because Spanish notions of the purity of blood, prevalent since the reconquest of Spain from the Moors, emphasized ties to the soil of the mother country. Those born in the colonies to Spanish parents who had traveled there, "mestizos", had lesser status, those of pure Indigenous groups, with the exception of nobility, typically lower status still, and for those unfortunate individuals involuntarily transported to Spain's New World empire, pure African ancestry landed an individual on the lowest rung of the "sistema de castas". Any ancestral presence of Blackness irredeemably stained individuals; they and their descendants could never attain the purity of Whiteness, at least in theory.

Colonial authorities did not, however, apply "sistema de castas" consistently across the empire. A traveler to the different American viceroyalties would observe differences in the number of official "castas" and their names: "castas" hardly appeared in Nueva Granada, while elsewhere the number of categories in circulation ranged from fourteen to sixteen, to sixty-four or even more.[52] And translating and conveying to readers the meanings of the classifications proved elusive to European travelers and residents in the early nineteenth century. The Englishman W.B. Stevenson, who lived in and traveled throughout South America from 1803 to 1823, and published his three-volume *A Historical and Descriptive Narrative of Twenty Years' Residence in South America* as British interest in the republics was reaching fever pitch, produces a table on "the mixture of castes [in Lima], under their common or distinguishing names". See Figure 2.1. Readers can detect traces of the history of local resistance to Spanish colonial authority in the assertion by Stevenson that the table does not exhaust the list of possible "castas": "This table, which I have endeavoured to make as correct as possible, from personal observation, must be considered as general, and not including particular cases."[53] Stevenson strives to create in his imaginative rendering of the "castas" of Lima what Ricoeur calls "a supposed equivalence" in translation rather than an exact rendering of the categories.[54] Stevenson's later observation, for example, that, "In the suburbs of San Lazaro are *cofradias* or clubs belonging to the different castes or nations of the Africans," indicates that the translation of "casta" in the table conveys but one meaning of caste.[55]

Stevenson mixes prior beliefs and an openness to the effects of first-hand observations when he ascribes scientific meaning to the "sistema de castas". He modifies the table based on his belief that the "sistema" should be read as a classification system categorizing people by color, yet another European permutation of the original Spanish mistranslation of the Indigenous system for classifying the color properties of metallic ores. Stevenson uses the "sistema" to convey a concise description of how parents transmit traits to children: "I have classed the colours according to their appearance, not according to the mixture of the castes, because I have always remarked,

FATHER.	MOTHER.	CHILDREN.	COLOUR.
European......	European	Creole	White.
Creole	Creole	Creole	White.
White	Indian	Mestiso	5/8 White, 3/8 Indian—Fair.
Indian	White	Mestiso	4/8 White, 4/8 Indian.
White	Mestiso	Creole.........	White—often very Fair.
Mestiso	White	Creole.........	White—but rather Sallow.
Mestiso	Mestiso	Creole.........	Sallow—often light Hair.
White	Negro	Mulatto	7/8 White, 1/8 Negro—often Fair.
Negro	White	Zambo	4/8 White, 4/8 Negro—dark copper
White	Mulatto	Quarteron ...	6/8 White, 2/8 Negro—Fair.
Mulatto	White	Mulatto	5/8 White, 3/8 Negro—Tawny.
White	Quarteron ...	Quinteron......	7/8 White, 1/8 Negro—very Fair.
Quarteron	White	Quarteron......	6/8 White, 2/8 Negro—Tawny
White	Quinteron ...	Creole.........	White—light Eyes, fair Hair.
Negro	Indian	Chino	4/8 Negro, 4/8 Indian.
Indian	Negro	Chino	2/8 Negro, 6/8 Indian.
Negro	Mulatto	Zambo	5/8 Negro, 3/8 White.
Mulatto	Negro	Zambo.........	3/8 Negro, 4/8 White.
Negro	Zambo	Zambo	15/16 Negro, 1/16 White—Dark.
Zambo	Negro	Zambo.........	7/8 Negro, 1/8 White.
Negro	Chino	Zambo-chino	15/16 Negro, 1/16 Indian.
Chino	Negro	Zambo-chino	7/8 Negro, 1/8 Indian.
Negro	Negro	Negro	

Figure 2.1 The "mixture of castes, under their common or distinguishing names", Lima, Peru, circa 1825. Harvard University.

that a child receives more of the colour of the father than of the mother"; as Bigelow notes, "[t]he localized meaning of an individual's *casta* classification ... was always nuanced, contingent, and relational rather than fixed or absolute."[56] The table and Stevenson's immediate commentary both fail, however, to indicate the inflections of economic meaning, pertaining to gender and status differences, within individual "casta". The category "Black", for instance, encompasses both free and enslaved Blacks, and women, men, and children. The groups endure very different economic circumstances and face very different economic prospects; Stevenson later observes that the free Black man "considers himself as better than the *bozales*, the name given to African slaves, and will rarely intermarry with them".[57]

Clearly colonial inhabitants imbued the "castas" with a healthy degree of untidiness. They resisted the desire by authorities to wield them to impose strict epistemological, political, and economic order, developing and insisting upon their own caste identities, comingling and occupying spaces beyond the official definitions. Indios in early colonial Peru, for instance, created new classifications for themselves and used them in wills and real estate contracts.[58] Employing more subterfuge, other individuals claimed false genealogies, purchased certificates of Whiteness, and whimsically invented and used nonsense names for categories. While efforts to change or obscure caste typically involved moving up the "casta" hierarchy, some individuals claimed membership in an Indian caste, seeking haven in Indigenous communities beyond easy reach of colonial authorities.

The ways in which non-Europeans conceive of and classify skin color and race from early modernity into the beginning of the nineteenth century provide lessons on the non-deterministic nature of such processes, and exemplify the capacity for subjects to evade certain categorization whether or not travelers came armed with the latest scientific guidance on the topic. English colonists drawing on natural philosophy interpreted the rapid decline of Amerindian populations in North America, decreases caused by lack of immunity to Old World contagious diseases, as evidence of the greater vigor, hence superiority of their own bodies.[59] Amerindian tribes in the southeastern United States coming into contact with European travelers in the early eighteenth century, however, not only developed their own skin color classification schemes, they began to self-identify as red, prior to Europeans' descriptions of them as such, to distinguish themselves from white Europeans and their Black African slaves.[60] The color signifiers took on different meanings according to the political, diplomatic, and economic context, but "Indian and European similarities enabled them to see their differences in sharper relief and, over the course of the eighteenth century, construct new identities that exaggerated the contrasts between them while ignoring what they had in common".[61] This process involved occasional dissimulation on the part of Native Americans who denigrated Whites in communication among themselves, while adapting an inferior position for diplomatic relations when recognizing they occupied a weaker economic or military position.[62] Different tribes on the continent adopted the term at different times; similarly, among Europeans in the southeast, the English began using the term prior to the French. Tribes did adapt attitudes about the skin color of others from European settlers. Recognizing the status accorded Black Africans, tribes too grafted these sets of beliefs into their classifications, and black became an inferior color in the hierarchy of skin tones among the Native Americans Shoemaker studies. Yet, this is only part of the story in the English colonies, as intermarriage between Native Americans and Blacks was becoming common in southern New England and Virginia during this period.[63]

By way of contrast, travelers who traveled in Europe on the Grand Tour composed reports focusing on art, ruins of classical architecture, and life at European courts. Their accounts form part of the response to an outpouring of advice literature, *Ars apodemica*, literally the "art of travel", between the mid sixteenth and the late eighteenth century. *Ars apodemica* authors sought to ennoble travel by clothing it as an educational mission, based on classical philosophy, which would assist the traveler as he learned new languages, and acquired courtly refinement and political experience. These cosmopolitan goals evolved from work in the sixteenth century of Theodor Zwinger, Hugo Blotius, and others concerned about the reams of new information coming to light from contemporary travels and voyages. *Ars apodemica* authors crafted guidelines that would enable travelers and readers to organize and make sense of these new observations.[64]

The Grand Tour guides and resulting travelers' accounts were deemed less credible, and certainly less informative with respect to natural knowledge than those informed by the new science. Grand Tourists came in many types and from many nations. But the guidebooks they consulted often varied little in content, whatever the language of the original edition. Writers borrowed freely from one another, suggested standardized itineraries, and in so doing felt no compunction describing sites they had not visited. Such homogeneity demanded little more of a traveler than "a passive assent, at most by which what he saw conformed simply to what he read".[65] These informal generic constraints helped ingrain in travelers dutifully following the guides a tendency to see natives as mere backdrop on display at the various stops of the Tour.

Late seventeenth century contemporaries recognized other shortcomings. William Petty proposed a course of travel and travel instruction with a decidedly economic bent as a direct alternative to the Grand Tour. Petty sketched plans for a school for young men from respectable families who could not afford the Tour.[66] Rather than go overseas to acquire further refinement, young men could journey to London to rub shoulders with those who had gained wide experience of the world, that is, men of the Royal Exchange. Students would observe and interact with these men, absorbing lessons on how to search out commercial possibilities from those "who have fresh concerne & correspondance with all parts of the known world & with all the Commodityes growing or made within the same". Instruction would include natural history, too: the young men would take in singularities, "faire Collections of all natural and artificiall rarities, with com[m]ents upon them and the applications upon them".[67] The costs of the students' combined travel (to London) and armchair travel would be cheaper than the Grand Tour.

Grand Tour guides nonetheless specified the means by which knowledge gained through travel could be systematized in order to benefit the learned community. The Grand Tour could provide useful economic information, sometimes evoking responses from travelers that hearkened to principles of a more barbaric age. Joseph Addison's visit to Italy at the beginning of the eighteenth century prompted him to marvel at the gold, silver, and other riches at the small chapel of Santa Casa de Loreto, on the Adriatic coast. He speculated that plundering the treasure and turning it into specie would do much to alleviate the poverty and misery in the region: "If these Riches were all turn'd into Current Coin, and employ'd in Commerce, they would make *Italy* the most flourishing Country in *Europe*."⁶⁸

By the mid eighteenth century, as the frontiers of the Grand Tour expanded further south, writers evinced greater interest in the people they observed, noting their customs and manners, commerce, and trade. The trips offered travelers with opportunities for observations and conversations that helped shape the foundations of British political economy. When Adam Smith accompanied Henry Scott, the 3rd Duke of Buccleuch, as his tutor on a continental tour, from 1764 to 1767, he was beginning work on *The Wealth of Nations*; while in France he met the Physiocrats François Quesnay, Turgot, and Jacques Necker. Smith believed the spread of commercial travel, and the resulting positive contact and interaction with others wrought constructive changes in societies; in his case, travel and trade in ideas helped shape *The Wealth of Nations*. Smith was not totally sanguine, however, about the effects of travel on subjectivity and agency. While both he and Scott benefited from the Grand Tour, Smith believed wealthy young men traveling the continent too often behaved badly, and were hardly fit to make unbiased, sober observations and reflections (*WN* V. 1.164).⁶⁹

For the natives' part, intellectuals on the European periphery protested negative depictions of locals that crept into the Grand Tour literature. Some chafed in particular at representations of local political economies. By the second half of the eighteenth century, intellectuals from Naples, for example, began to cavil against the view, expressed particularly in French travel guides, that all Neapolitans fit the prevalent description of the "lazzari" (or "lazzarone"), the poor and homeless.⁷⁰ Foreign guidebooks routinely portrayed the "lazzari" as idle and dissolute, living and begging in squalor amid the beauties of the city. Calaresu locates the source for travelers' caricatures about Neapolitans in theories, popularized by Montesquieu in *De l'esprit des loix* (1748), on how the environment and climate affect the character of a people. Montesquieu conjectures that people from cold climates tend to be industrious and orderly, and those from hotter climes idle and chaotic; different systems of government were best suited to curb and channel the desires of people in different regions. Montesquieu's two-week sojourn in Naples, in 1729, along with the accounts of contemporary travelers in Persia and Turkey, most likely strongly influenced the tenor of *De l'esprit*.⁷¹ To Calaresu, "It was the vulgarization of this theory [of Montesquieu's] which made its ways into the guidebooks of the later eighteenth century. In this way, travellers' views informed theories and then the theories substantiated prejudiced observation [by travelers]."⁷²

Neapolitan intellectuals found the guides irksome. Contrary to the spirit of cosmopolitanism, the guides threatened to exclude them from interacting with intellectual circles throughout the rest of Europe. Foreign guide writers elided the work of a sizeable group of Neapolitans actively devoted to Enlightenment principles, ignoring attempts by Antonio Genovesi and Ferdinando Galiani to press for urgent economic and political reforms which would address the causes of the very issues that foreign travelers cited as bedeviling the city, a feudal economic system and weak government.[73] The Neapolitans took to letters and literary journals to counter the caricatures of Naples and even wrote their own travel guides as ripostes. Reflections by Neapolitans on their travel throughout Europe and experiences as foreign residents in major cities in Europe, where they mingled with cosmopolitan elites, formed the foundation for many of their calls for civic transformation. Travel enabled them to both approach the ideal of observations without national prejudice and value national differences within a shared, enlightened, European heritage: why, they asked, were foreigners unable to replicate this feat?[74]

Josiah Tucker: a political economist's "Instructions for Travellers"

While Neapolitans and foreigners turned to travel writing as they tangled over political and economic developments in Naples, British writers began to associate the independence and wealth of their own kingdoms with the benefits of free trade. As in the Neapolitan case, this development arose out of the international trade in ideas: the British adapted notions borrowed from others, such as the Dutch, as they moved from mercantilist debates in the seventeenth century, to free trade eventually becoming an article of faith in British political economy in the late eighteenth and early nineteenth centuries.[75] But, what, exactly, was free trade? The British mooted this question and the possibility of creating an "empire of free trade" during debates on a proposal put forward by William Pitt in 1785 for a commercial treaty with Ireland. Livesey presents a useful typology of three varieties of free trade afloat during these discussions.[76] He denotes as "imperialist" or "neo-mercantilist" those who were critical of monopolies, but who nonetheless favored a reorganization of trade for "the benefit of the imperial metropole".[77] Smithian free traders, on the other hand, supported open markets because they exerted a discipline which could increase efficiency, hence output, prosperity, and happiness if buttressed by institutional features such as the security of property, political and juridical stability, a free press, and freedom of conscience. Advocates of a third strand of free trade, dubbed "neo-Machiavellian", promoted "the right of every political community to organize its trade according to its interests".[78]

Tucker, a Welsh cleric and political economist, fervently advocated for free trade. He first established his reputation as an expert on things economic with the publication of *A Brief Essay on the Advantages and Disadvantages, Which Respectively Attend France and Great Britain* (1749). Translated into French, *A Brief Essay* had enormous influence on Physiocrats such as

Quesnay, and Tucker was particularly well known for articulating the benefits of both free trade and the division of labor prior to Smith's *Wealth of Nations*. Passionately anti-war, he expressed the view as early as 1749 that the American colonies would and should become independent. Tucker traveled little outside of his postings aside from a brief trip to France sometime prior to 1757. Though they did not meet during this journey, Turgot translated two of his works into French, and they later carried on a correspondence. Conversations with merchants among his Bristol parishioners, as well as from his observations of goings-on at Bristol's waterfront and manufactories comprise the principal sources of inspiration for Tucker's work.[79]

To Tucker, Great Britain could only fully reap the benefits of free trade by allowing free travel within its borders, and by allowing foreigners to establish residency and become naturalized citizens in England. He took up the relationships between travelers and natives, and trade and commerce, in part one of *Reflections on the Expediency of a Law for the Naturalization of Foreign Protestants* (1751). Tucker first felt it necessary to answer, in the preface, questions about his credibility in offering opinions on affairs not directly related to his clerical responsibilities. Tucker argues that he does no harm to his credibility as a cleric so long as his writings do not interfere with his religious duties, and he renders his opinions in an "inoffensive Manner".[80] He ventures that

> it may not be reckoned absurd in a Clergyman, to form a judgment (and to deliver it modestly) on Subjects; by which, not only national Wealth and Prosperity, and the external Blessings of Life are increased; but, by which, Industry, Frugality, and Sobriety are promoted.[81]

Tucker adopts the character of a modest, inoffensive, and credible commentator untainted by partisan passions. Having claimed this persona, Tucker asserts that his professional practice demands he inquire into the commercial life of the nation. Measures that encourage sobriety, justice, and frugality not only form an integral part of his calling, the last virtue represents the source of the "Fund for Charity". To deny clerics the opportunity to address commercial concerns would deny them the opportunity to do good.

Tucker points to harm caused to the English who travel within England by freeman oaths enforced in various towns and cities. In the oaths, designed to ban commerce by foreigners, "the word *Foreigner* denotes not only an *Alien*, or one born out of the *King's Obeysance*, but every *Englishman*, not free of their Corporation."[82] The oaths hamper economic integration within England by restricting the free movement of labor. They create a category mistake, alienating English men and women, turning them into foreigners in their native land.

Tucker warms to the theme of the relationships between commerce, travel and alienation in "Important Queries occasioned by the Rejection of the late

Naturalization Bill", the second part of his 1751 essay, where he again criticizes regulations that curb commerce. He starts the essay by voicing his objections in the context of considerations about prejudice in observation, asking, rhetorically, if foreigners contribute value to the country, and questioning "Whether popular Prejudices are to be considered as the Test of Truth". He proceeds to query how commerce, if viewed from the perspective of political economy, blurs the legal, epistemological, and, ultimately, ontological status of both foreign travelers and natives in England. Tucker asks "Whether those Natives, who pursue Measures pernicious to their country, should not be ranked as Aliens? And those Foreigners, who conduce by their Industry and Virtue to the Publick Good of this Kingdom, be respected as Natives?"[83]

Tucker provides a novel take on travel, current English identity, and commerce in his essays on naturalization; in *Instructions for Travellers* he seeks to mold the identity of future travelers. Tucker wrote *Instructions* for all prospective travelers, and particularly those undertaking the Grand Tour, who, if following the guide, were open to being shaped into ideal observers of all they witness. He sorts contemporary English travelers into groups according to their reasons for journeying abroad: to collect objects for studies in natural philosophy and antiquarianism; to improve in the arts, such as painting and architecture; to gain a reputation for virtue and "elegant taste"; and to acquire "foreign airs", new clothes, and fashions. A fifth group sought to "to rub off local prejudices (which is indeed the most commendable Motive, though not the most prevailing) and to acquire that enlarged and impartial View of Men and Things, which no single one Country can afford"; and a sixth set undertook the equivalent of pilgrimages to ancient sites in Italy and Greece.[84] While Tucker considers a quest to rid oneself of prejudice and partiality the most praiseworthy reason for travel, he embeds this desire in a list of other worthy motives for journeying abroad. He thus acknowledges some of the earlier instructional literature for travelers, such as natural history and Grand Tour guides, and works for philosophical travelers, and the ways they address the diverse motives of their reader-travelers.

He does not direct his work toward the immediate use of travelers seeking to fulfill these objectives, though all could make use of what he proposes. In his scheme, a traveler will derive the greatest benefit through pursuit of a narrower purpose, one expressed in the subtitle, "A Plan for improving in the moral and political Theory of Trade and Taxes, by means of Travelling". Tucker summarizes the plan as one directed toward

> tracing such secret, though powerful Effects and Consequences, as are produced by the various Systems of Religion, Government, and Commerce in the World: he must observe, how these Systems operate on different People, or on the same People in different Periods, *viz.* Whether they enlarge, or contract the active Powers in human Nature, and whether they make those Powers become useful, or pernicious to Society. For in Fact the human Mind is in some Sense but as Clay in

the Hands of the Potter, which receives its Figure and Impression, if I may so speak, according as it is moulded or formed by these different Systems: So that the Political, the Religious, and Commercial Characters of any People, will be found, for the most Part, to be the Result of this three-fold Combination of Religion, Government, and Commerce on their Minds.

(Tucker 1758, pp. 4–5)

Tucker calls for divining systematic causes, to make visible their effects on people in different societies at different times. At other points in *Instructions*, Tucker indicates that the system of taxation forms the principal basis for a nation's prosperity or poverty. For instance, a traveler should observe

whether they [taxes] make the Passion of Self-Love (that ruling Principle of human Nature) subservient to the Public Good, or detrimental. In short, That State or Kingdom which by means of proper Taxes converts Drones into Bees, will be Rich: But every Community which turns Bees into Drones, must be Poor.

(Tucker 1758, p. 14)

Tucker converts the notorious questions about whether private vice leads to public virtue raised in Bernard Mandeville's *The Grumbling Hive* (1705) and *The Fable of the Bees* (1714) into a bland lesson on virtuous public policy. But commerce and trade do not represent the sole movers of society according to Tucker; nor does the "three-fold Combination of Religion, Government, and Commerce" complete the list. Rather, the "grand Maxim" is that "the Looks, Numbers, and Behaviour of the People, their general Cloathing, Food, and Dwelling, their Attainments in Agriculture, Manufactures, Arts and Sciences", are effects of four types of causes.

Therefore let him consider, whether, and how far, the said Effects may be ascribed to the natural Soil and Situation of the Country. – To the peculiar Genius and Singular Inventions of the Inhabitants. – To the Public Spirit and Tenor of their Constitution, – or to the Religious Principles established, or tolerated among them. For certain it is, that every considerable Effect must be ascribed, and may be traced up to, one or more of these Causes; which for the Sake of greater Distinction I will term Natural, –Artificial, –Political, –and Religious.

(Tucker 1758, p. 15)

Tucker adds the non-human environment, the "Natural", to systems of religion, commerce, and government as an element that helps produce "secret, though powerful Effects and Consequences" in different lands. He instructs travelers to file observations under these categories, suggests that queries under these heads will best guide the traveler's inquiries, and provides examples to "illustrate the Nature of the Plan, and at the same Time give a Sample or Specimen of the intended Manner of Proceeding". Tucker also subscribes to the belief that the traveler can use the same questions anytime and anywhere: his heads and queries represent a uniform and universal methodology for observation. He thus notes that, "Though the Scene is laid in *England*, yet the same Questions, *mutatis mutandis*, may serve for any Country or Climate whatever" (Tucker 1758, p. 15, emphases in original).

Tucker concedes that a traveler faces an overwhelming number of possible observations under each head. He suggests that the traveler deal with this excess by valorizing singularities:

> It is next to impossible that any Traveller could note down all that can be said on each of these Heads; and it would be a mere Waste of Time to attempt it. Nevertheless when a judicious Traveller meets with any thing very *singular*, curious or remarkable, he would do well to pay a more peculiar Attention to it, and to enter down the whole Process of the Affair. If nothing singular or striking occurs, there is no harm done; but if something should appear worth his Notice and Regard, the present System of Queries will serve both to fix his Attention, to Improve his Reasoning, and to arrange his Thoughts and Ideas in their proper Order.
> (Tucker 1758, p. 23, note, emphasis in original)

Taking note of singularities, a foundational preoccupation of members of the Royal Society writing on natural philosophy and natural history in the previous century, will not only reduce the possibility of observational excess, it will sharpen the skills of observers, producing new and better observing subjects. The queries will lead to happier agents, too. Though they enforce a discipline, or "*Labour*", pursuing the questions "will turn to an *Amusement*", transforming work into play, once the traveler becomes habituated to them (Tucker 1758, p. 95, emphases in original).

Tucker also proposes to provide travelers with information that would enable them to make normative judgments about observations having to do with, among other matters, political economy. Under "*Queries relating to the Nature and Tendency of the National Taxes*", Tucker asks, as the first question: "As Taxes must be levied in all Countries for the Defence and Support of the State, – What constitutes a good Tax and what a bad one?" His answer:

> A good Tax is that which tends to prevent Idleness, check Extravagance, and promote Industry: a bad Tax, on the contrary, falls the heaviest of all upon the industrious Man, excusing, or at least not punishing the Idle, the Spend-thrift, or the Vain. Taxes therefore when properly laid on, must enrich a Country; but when improperly, will as certainly impoverish it.
> (Tucker 1758, pp. 54–5)

Tucker claims that his instructions, which limit travelers' observations to four categories, constitute an entirely new method of answering the questions posed at the beginning of the work: what systems of commerce, religion, and government characterize a country, and what determines how they work (Tucker 1758, p. 94)? Whatever their novelty, Tucker's *Instructions* proved, however, a road not taken.

Contributions to the Birth of British Political Economy: Stadial Histories and Travel Writing

Stadial histories, on the other hand, served as the foundation for speculations by British political economists on what information gleaned from travelers in their encounters with new societies implied for understanding the diversity of humankind and the progress of civilizations. Smith's version, which first appeared in his unpublished *Lectures on Jurisprudence* (1762–3), typifies the Scottish approach to stadial history. He posited four types of societies or four stages of growth arrayed around the different modes of production, consumption, and subsistence that predominated in each stage: hunting and gathering societies; nomadic and pastoral life, which included shepherding and cattle grazing societies; feudal agricultural societies; and commercial and manufacturing civilizations. Transitions through these different stages, synonymous with the transition from savagery to barbarism to civility, were, in turn, associated with distinct forms of property relations. The stages offer users the opportunity to make systematic analyses of the sources of differences across contemporary societies, and represent a decisive break with European providentially-based world histories. The travel accounts Smith cites, "fairly representative" of the material available to his contemporaries, provide him with examples of how his stadial analysis operates in the real world, including regions only recently explored by Europeans.[85] His work was therefore not only conjectural, but empirical. Stadial historians also assumed that, absent historical documentation for ancient civilizations, facts gathered by contemporary travelers could, by analogy, stand in for this lack of evidence, and analysts could conjecture about past civilizations.

In theory, stadial histories offer a teleological account of development and the progress of civility. But they suggest what could have happened in the past rather than provide proof of what did happen, and "many conjectural histories [sic] regard progress and improvement as discontinuous, inconsistent, and noncumulative".[86] Nor did stadial historians adhere to an unbending belief in the superiority of European societies. Thus Jean-Jacques Rousseau, David Hume, John Millar, Adam Ferguson, Henry Home (Lord Kames), William Robertson, Smith, and Malthus put their histories to widely different uses. Robertson, in *History of America* (1777 and 1796), a work that helped popularize stadial histories, posits potentially unstable and non-teleological processes, captured by the term "adventurism", as keys to the development of "commercial character".[87] Robertson effectively rejects the premise that transitions through the stages effect fundamental and predictable changes in the mental dispositions of peoples. Malthus, on the other hand, speculates that the population principle is universal, operating and having operated at all times, in all societies, in all stages. He nonetheless proceeds to search, through his own travels, in travel literature, and the armchair speculations of others, especially Robertson, for facts that would allow for less speculative and more rational conjectures about the past.[88]

Joining travel accounts to political economy erected on a stadial foundation generated no single explanation of what led to contemporary outcomes. Like Captain John Smith, some of Malthus's contemporaries who traveled in North America concluded that Indigenous civilizations there contained characteristics of both savage and civilized societies; others rolled the savage and barbarian stages into one.[89] Still others found that some human societies exhibited characteristics of barbarian, savage, and commercial civilizations all mixed together. Nonetheless, by the early nineteenth century the stadial histories used by British political economists exhibited the common feature that a given society's development was assumed to be typically static. Savage or barbarian societies, for example, could only shift into a higher stage of civilization, or even simply to a higher, more civilized savage or barbarian state, if compelled by two interlocking causes: contact with a trading nation; and a solution, however, temporary, to the population problem.

We might attribute the strength and durability of the stadial histories to their combination of simplicity and suppleness. Still, there were significant and significantly confounding singularities that generated questions about progress and civilization and the capacity of stadial histories as explanatory devices. Russia, an international power, long considered both European and Asian by Western Europeans, perplexed French and British analysts who noted the coexistence of stirrings toward modernization with the institution of serfdom.[90] Contemporary China, about which Europeans knew little, presented another set of puzzles to users of stadial histories, not least due to the diversity of conditions there reported by travelers over the centuries. Analysts cited its stagnant civilization.[91] But Europeans also mulled evidence of Chinese success in agriculture and commerce; taken as a body, the accounts illustrated that a universal comparative perspective could lead a philosopher astray. As an "advanced alternative system" to that of much of Europe, especially France and Britain, many Europeans found China "sui generis".[92] The European hunt for causes of China's peculiar position involved circulating observations gathered and written up by travelers, mostly Jesuit missionaries, as well as a smattering of merchants, sailors, soldiers, and emissaries. European-based writers and publishers packaged and published these reports in more accessible forms, giving readers like Smith an opportunity to formulate ideas about the administration of China. Smith expressed disdain about some of the

"Instructions for Travellers" 53

travelers and their reports. He writes, on earlier Jesuit accounts praising the high quality of Chinese navigable canals and high roads, infrastructure which they claim "exceed very much everything of the same kind which is known in Europe":

> The accounts of those works, however, which have been transmitted to Europe, have generally been drawn up by weak and wondering travellers; frequently by stupid and lying missionaries. If they had been examined by more intelligent eyes, and if the accounts of them had been reported by more faithful witnesses, they would not, perhaps, appear to be so wonderful.
>
> (WN V.1.III.1.14)

Smith speculates that the Chinese had erected and maintained works close to the centers of power in order to impress, "as in France, where the great roads, the great communications which are likely to be the subjects of conversation at the court and in the capital, are attended to, and all the rest neglected". The spectacle fooled unfaithful witnesses such as the Jesuits. Yet Smith concluded that the Jesuits' observations were most likely correct. The "revenue of the sovereign" in China depended on land taxes or rents. The government would have a strong incentive to encourage as much and as valuable agricultural production as possible. This outcome would only be realized by fostering as extensive a market as possible by building and maintaining a network of high-quality roads and canals.

For Smith, increased commerce produced positive effects beyond an enhancement of state revenues. In "Of Police", published in *Lectures on Jurisprudence* (1762–3), Smith claims that, "'whenever commerce is introduced into any country probity and punctuality always accompany it.'".[93] He wrote, earlier, in *Theory of Moral Sentiments* (1759):

> Among civilized nations, the virtues which are founded upon humanity, are more cultivated than those which are founded upon self-denial and the command of the passions. Among rude and barbarous nations, it is quite otherwise, the virtues of self-denial are more cultivated than those of humanity. The general security and happiness which prevail in ages of civility and politeness, afford little exercise to the contempt of danger, to patience in enduring labour, hunger, and pain. Poverty may easily be avoided, and the contempt of it therefore almost ceases to be a virtue. The abstinence from pleasure becomes less necessary, and the mind is more at liberty to unbend itself, and to indulge its natural inclinations in all those particular respects.
>
> (TMS V.I.18)[94]

Trade and commerce set off a virtuous cycle. People become more their natural selves, truly civilized once freed from the strictures on behavior occasioned by poverty. True, Smith famously frets about how a single-minded application of the division of labor produced dull workmen, "as stupid and ignorant as it is possible for a human creature to become" (*WN* V. 1.178). These "creatures", in addition, lacked the time and motivation to cultivate the martial spirit (*WN* V.1.14). Higher up the social scale, luxury bred corruption. Ferguson, in *An Essay on the History of Civil Society* (1767), asserts that while the pursuit of commercial interests might offer a welcome substitute for war,

> if the individual, not called to unite with his country, be left to pursue his private advantage; we may find him become effeminate, mercenary, and sensual; not because pleasures and profits are become more alluring, but because he has fewer calls to attend to other objects; and because he has more encouragement to study his personal advantages, and pursue his separate interests.[95]

And greedy capitalists, when not tripped up by self-deception, a natural vice fed by the endless artificial wants created by commercial society, lied and conspired against the interests of others. Dishonesty also eroded faith in the credibility and accuracy of observations and representations by merchants and capitalists. Travelers' observations that Confucian ritual and morality ruled the Chinese empire, yet its people appeared unable or unwilling to govern themselves enough to stop cheating, took place against the backdrop, reflected in Ferguson's remarks, of European struggles to similarly reconcile commerce and virtue.[96]

In the main, stadial historians consider societal feminization produced by trade a tonic for men. Smith and others note that another sort of commerce, the more frequent mingling between the sexes through conversation, also serves to soften the manners of men. National progress through the stages improves the status of women as well, as they escape from servility and bondage into companionate marriage. The status of women, serves, in turn, as a marker of civilization. Distinctions between European commercial civilizations and barbarous and savage societies also opens the possibility for the "[e]ntwining of race and nation around the conception of progress as feminization".[97] This marker had a class component, too. Smith considers the households of middling class families "where love and esteem for one another reigned", the sites "that gave shape to the man of perfect virtue, who united self-control with a greater sensitivity toward others", a conclusion consistent with late eighteenth century morals and manners literature.[98]

In this conception women in commercial societies become visible principally in relation to men: "the process of the improvement of women was seen, first of all, as a function of the completion of the humanity of men".[99] The ideal woman was able to civilize men through her dual identities as mother and wife; women had roles to play in (domestic) economic and social spheres, but not the political. The enmeshed institutions of private property and marriage, which secure women's freedom from slavery, nonetheless limit the emancipatory promise of progressive development for women through the stages. But stadial historians worried that intercourse between the sexes, through conversation in salons, at home, or in schools, presented opportunities for women to trespass into the public sphere, bringing its own threats to virtue. It risked confusing natural roles, as in France, where, according to the British, women dominated men. When women act, and are not just acted upon, they imperil existing hierarchies.

If the status of women emerged among stadial historians as one of the primary differences between stages, another coalesced around how societies used resources. Smith draws on the work of travelers to search for facts about how populations use the resources at their disposal; and the travelers Smith references rely on natural history to make their observations (Marouby, "Adam Smith", p. 87). These include the Finnish naturalist Pehr Kalm, one of nineteen acolytes Linnaeus dispatched to scour the world for plants to augment Sweden's wealth and power. Kalm fetched up in North America, where he traveled from 1748 to 1751, making his way north from Philadelphia, where he met Benjamin Franklin, and eventually ending up in Quebec. Linnaeus and other cameralists in northern Europe, trained in the science of police, the contemporary European science of public administration, sought improvement through internal colonization and active political management of people and things, by experts, to harness "the divine utility of nature". Kalm consequently paid special attention to the state of agriculture in each area he visited. He and other like-minded travelers sought to document, classify, and profit from the fruits of new (to them) botanical and agricultural products, and from knowledge gained by experimentation in soil and forestry management (Jonsson, "Rival Ecologies", p. 1344).

Smith had a copy of Kalm's recollections in his library and refers to it in his ruminations on North American agriculture in *Wealth of Nations*. Smith balks, however, at completely embracing the methods and interpretations of Kalm and his ilk; he and natural historians ultimately disagreed about the means by which humans and non-human nature would harmoniously resolve their many relationships. Smith's partial rejection of natural history stems from at least two sources. First, while both Smith and Kalm judge the behavior of farmers newly arrived in North American wasteful, they differ over the solution to this problem. Smith express faith in the power of self-interested individuals in markets. Changes in market prices ensure smooth flows of resources from suppliers to users; increasing demand for food in North America would drive up prices, and, in response, farmers would implement agricultural improvements through better soil and crop management, and better animal husbandry. Thus, market prices quickly gravitate to natural prices (Jonsson, "Rival Ecologies", pp. 1343–4). Moreover, laissez fare would ensure equilibrium in nature, not just markets, as the rise and fall of prices dictate the direction of technological innovation, resource substitution, and conservation. Smith looks to nature and observes self-regulating processes which justify his faith in market exchange; in turn, markets serve as the best means to manage the balance of nature.

Kalm advocates the intervention of experts, as did Linnaeus, other natural historians, assorted writers on forestry matters, and sundry others. Though they also endorse the expansion of commerce, they support regulation of the natural order that underlay markets. Valuable resources such as water, fertile agricultural land, and forests form parts of systems too complex and ultimately too fragile to be left to the devices of nature or the dictates of laissez faire. In its stead, cameralists and the like lobbied states to employ their expertise to shape policy and law. Active interventions in markets were sometimes, even often necessary to ensure the health and wealth of a nation and its natural resources.

Smith and political economists argue, instead, that anti-laissez faire experiments could not successfully force nature into unnatural channels (Jonsson, "Rival Ecologies", pp. 1351–2). Smith does acknowledge exceptions in *Wealth of Nations*. Though these were chiefly due to "regulations of police", natural, non-human singularities, "natural productions" of "peculiarly happy soil and situation", like certain vineyards in France, also produce unnatural market outcomes. The lack of quantity to meet effectual demand may result in prices remaining well above that necessary to pay rent, wages, and profits at their natural rates for centuries (*WN* I.7.24). Indeed, "Such enhancements of the market price are evidently the effect of natural causes which may hinder the effectual demand from ever being fully supplied, and which may continue, therefore, to operate *for-ever*" (*WN* I.7.25, emphasis added).

Smith did not waver in his particular use of stadial histories, the assumptions that lay behind it and the conclusions it entailed, despite evidence from travelers, and the dinner table, to the contrary. He described a universal model of development where regional variation simply did not matter. For example, Smith held the same forces of demand and supply that drove the market for Scottish beef would operate in North America, no matter the differences in local grasses, population size and so forth (Jonsson, "Rival Ecologies", pp. 1354–5). The union of Scotland and England in 1707 prompted agricultural innovation in the Scottish Lowlands, increasing productivity and production; demand for Scottish beef from English consumers rose sharply as a result. Smith calls the rise of the manufactures of Leeds, Halifax, Sheffield, Birmingham, and Wolverhampton and their populations "the offspring of agriculture". That is, provision of capital to the countryside led to agricultural surpluses, supplying the food necessary to feed urban populations, leading in turn to the growth of towns and cities. For stadial historians and political economists this process represented the natural transition from an agricultural to a commercial society. Jonsson concludes that Smith "simply adopted a universal stadial model of natural growth" (Jonsson, "Rival Ecologies", p. 1355).

Yet the term "natural" takes on a wide variety of meanings in the works of Smith and other political economists (Marouby, "Adam Smith",

p. 87).[100] Following Smith himself, we can read this story of British growth instead as a model of *unnatural* growth, with cause and effect reversed in the transition through the last two stages. Smith notes that the rise of the towns cited above "have generally been posterior to those which were the offspring of foreign commerce". Though their growth "could not take place but in consequence of the extension and improvement of agriculture", this was but "the last and greatest effect of foreign commerce, and of the manufactures immediately introduced by it" (WN III.III.19). When Smith muses over the historical development discernible across most of Europe, including England, he observes that the production of an agricultural surplus did not drive the growth of towns and cities, leading to a growing urban population. Rather, "the commerce and manufactures of cities, instead of being the effect, have been the cause and occasion of the improvement and cultivation of the country" (WN III.IV.18). The rise of cattle grazing in Scottish Lowlands merely continued this process: growth in England, Great Britain, and the greater part of Europe was "contrary to the natural course of things" (WN III.IV.19).

Stewart later wrote, in considering Smith's conjectures, "it is more important to ascertain the progress that is most simple than the progress that is most agreeable to fact; for paradoxical as the proposition may appear, it is certainly true, that the real progress is not always the most natural".[101] Smith would not, however, let the fact of what actually took place get in the way of a good conjectural (hi)story.[102] His use of information gleaned from travel writers "reveals a pattern of selections, of misreadings or interpretive moves, and of outright omissions" (Marouby, "Adam Smith", p. 87). Marouby emphasizes how Smith remains wedded to a vision in which the struggle for subsistence serves as the initial impetus that drives societies to trade, innovate, and advance through the successive stages of stadial history. Thus, Smith consistently downplays the size of the populations of hunter-gatherer or savage societies: "the point is for Smith that the mode of subsistence corresponding to the first stage *cannot* sustain anything but a tiny population without threatening its own resources" (Marouby, "Adam Smith", p. 89, emphasis in original). According to the Smith's sources, however, not all or even most societies in the first stage suffered from constant want or necessity, nor were they thinly populated.

Smith's sustains his vision in part by omitting the category of "gatherer" from hunter-gatherer societies (Marouby, "Adam Smith", p. 89). The omission has a clear gendered effect, as his chief sources agree that women do the vast bulk of collecting food, while men typically hunt. By excluding this women's work, Smith wittingly or not, constructs a reductive view of production in savage societies, where he "recognizes the division but rejects the labor" of women (Marouby, "Adam Smith", p. 93).[103]

Further, Smith either elides, or acknowledges only to quickly dismiss, evidence from his sources which point to the presence of agriculture, the defining characteristic of the third stage, in the first stage.[104] Travelers who report that many civilizations relied on more than one mode of production represents nothing new. But, critically, the accounts Smith cites indicate that for Native North Americans the fruits of agriculture constitute the chief portion of their diets, with hunting providing a supplement. Labeling these societies as hunter-gatherer represents a category error: these are primarily agricultural societies.

Even relabeling these societies, say, "first-stage agricultural societies", which would make visible the taxonomic illegibility, would obscure as much as it reveals. In truth, Smith did not have access to information on contemporary societies whose members did in fact subsist almost entirely by hunting. Those travelers whose accounts Smith did collect and read report that: women perform the bulk of agricultural work and provide most of the subsistence in savage societies; and, as detailed in long passages, while men hunted, they actually performed little discernible labor, spending most of their time at leisure. Smith bends available facts to gendered system when he represents almost all work as physical activity by men and men alone.

Smith's sources also report that some savage nations had sizeable populations, and that none teetered perpetually on the brink of subsistence disaster. Quite the contrary, they thrived. Women's work evidently more than suffices to feed a population. Smith's sources routinely decry the idleness of the native Americans and the tendency of Native North Americans to do little but feast or sleep, or do nothing at all. Yet these unproductive Indigenes live lives of abundance, even excess. They express no need, no desire to acquire more, and choose leisure over more labor. The logic of Smith's stadial history, where individuals within societies work to escape food insecurity, activity that advances societies through the stages, collapses (Marouby, "Adam Smith", pp. 95–6).

The apparently unproductive nature of Native North Americans places these savage societies at or near the bottom of the scale of civilization. Smith notes, in the first chapter of Book V of *Wealth of Nations*, "On the Expense of Defense", that each successive stage is characterized by less leisure. What he observes has been verified in part by evidence of an industrious revolution, where the working classes in northwestern Europe began to devote more hours to paid work in the long eighteenth century in order to purchase more consumer goods.[105] This partially recuperates the logic of Smith's system and his insistence, at the opening of *Wealth of Nations*, that even "the very meanest person in a civilized country" possessed impressive if humble "accommodation" including shoes, woolen coat, and linen shirts, eating utensils, and "comfortable habitation". For Smith, the possessions of an "industrious and frugal peasant" lay beyond "many an African king, the absolute master of the lives and liberties of ten thousand naked savages" (*WN* I.I.39). Data from travel writings available to Smith would suggest that his conjecture lacked universal application. But to acknowledge them would violate the epistemological and ontological order of his stadial histories. Smith grounds his political economy partly on travelers' observations that represent projections of the very theories he desires they support.

From Natural History to Political Economy: John Bush and George Cooper on Ireland

John Bush's *Hibernia Curiosa* (1769), the source of this chapter's epigraph, represents a generic hodgepodge. Bush mixes observations from the perspectives of natural history, touristic enthusiasm, aesthetics, and political economy in his epistolary account of a brief visit to Ireland in 1764. For instance, Bush adds touches of the romantic and sublime to his natural history observations, writing that "I never rode through a valley where there was such a mixture of beauty, of grandeur, of *sublimity*, if you will allow me the use of the expression here, and of something really awful, as is exhibited in this most enormous Glyn of the Mountains" (Bush, *Hibernia Curiosa*, p. 74, emphasis in original). In paratext, his opening address "TO THE READER", Bush describes his purpose as "not so much to write a natural history of the kingdom, as to exhibit a view of what may be expected from one". If the Latin title beckons readers to peruse the textual equivalent of a curiosity cabinet, the extended title promises much more: "a general View of the Manners, Customs, Dispositions, &c. of the Inhabitants of Ireland", "occasional Observations on the STATE of TRADE and AGRICULTURE", as well as an account of some of Ireland's "most remarkable NATURAL CURIOSITIES". Bush emphasizes the amusement value of natural history, calling it "a science, perhaps, of all others, the most generally pleasing, and fertile of entertainment" (Bush, *Hibernia Curiosa*, p. vi). And, he follows the conclusion "TO THE READER", where he refers to his work as a "specimen of Hibernian entertainment", by asserting that he will satisfy his reader's thirst for information on the "curious and romantic subjects of nature" (Bush, *Hibernia Curiosa*, pp. xv and 1).

Bush presents *Hibernia Curiosa* as offering useful, if less entertaining information as well; it is, after all, based on a science, as is evident in the title. His eyewitness observations, source of a limited "view" of natural history "carefully taken from nature itself", while partial, nonetheless hew truer to nature than wonder cabinets full of "spurious, unnatural pictures of it, collected into a *fifth story* for the sedentary, domestic traveler to draw his copy from" (Bush, *Hibernia Curiosa*, p. vi, emphasis in original). Bush includes in his letter a sample of a branch and fruit from a cane-apple (or strawberry) tree, along with a few acorns, all from Killarney; he asks his friend to plant the seeds from the fruit and nuts in his garden in Kent and provides detailed instructions on how to do so. If the transplantations succeed, living plants, rather than a display in a curiosity cabinet, will produce "one of the greatest curiosities, of the kind, in the county of Kent" (Bush, *Hibernia Curiosa*, pp. 126–7).

Further, Bush believes his observations prove more accurate than the paucity of already-published Irish natural histories. These are chiefly narratives pieced together by armchair travelers, and "the greatest part of these appear to have been wrote [sic] implicitly from tradition or the hear-say of other people" (Bush, *Hibernia Curiosa*, p. vii). Bush, by way of contrast, claims to have taken pains to make his own observations, and to transcribe them without unnecessary embellishment: "I assure you, I have taken nothing of importance on trust, but the whole is the result of my own observations, in every case in which it was possible for me to get at them, and to which I have kept as nearly as possible in the descriptive" (Bush, *Hibernia Curiosa*, p. 129). He professes no slavish adherence to method, while acknowledging the challenges to representation presented by those involved in the steps between the writing of a travel account and its publication. Method, whether expressed in paratexts added by others or deletions from an account, comprises one of the possible obstacles thrown up between a writer's draft of a natural history and its actual appearance as text:

> You gentleman, in the paper and calf-skin trade, have a little patience, and you shall have an *original* natural history, or tour, to work upon, to pick out, stick in, curtail, transpose, digest, *methodize*, or however you please, according to the art and mystery of your profession. We assure you, Sirs, by This is not meant the following production, for though 'tis perfectly original, and therefore should be one of the best subjects in your shops to work upon, yet it is beyond your profoundest art to *methodize*.
>
> (Bush, *Hibernia Curiosa*, p. viii, emphases in original)

Bush's own paratextual address assures readers that he has fended off the inclusion of paratexts (and paratextual practices) of others. Bush forsakes these and the impulse to follow a "foolish attachment to what is called order and method" in order to shape a natural history narrative that both informs and amuses or is at least not "dull and unentertaining" (Bush, *Hibernia Curiosa*, p. viii). Devotion to method "not naturally adapted to" the material at hand can produce exhaustive and, to the reader, exhausting detail. And, yet another aesthetic scandal can ensue from methodizing; Bush will report on what is "really curious" in order to avoid what is "nauseating" and "against good sense and taste" (Bush, *Hibernia Curiosa*, pp. viii–ix).

When Bush opposes "travelling *methodically*", he does so because he believes it forces a traveler to make too many observations and representations, an "endless task" if one were to carefully describe the beauties of Irish lakes, for instance (Bush, *Hibernia Curiosa*, pp. x, emphasis in original, and 89). If devotion to method contributes to observational excess, pursuing a systematic tour through a countryside with the charge to take every possible thing into account would also prevent a traveler from taking in as many sights, "a diversity of prospects", over as many miles as he or she would like to observe (Bush, *Hibernia Curiosa*, p. x). That is, a traveler constantly runs the risk of creating observational defect, too.

Bush may rail against method, but he is not anti-method. A traveler should adapt the perspective of natural history to one's own inclination, taste, and pleasure. By doing so, a traveler will "gratify his curiosity". Thus the "most natural method for keeping up the entertainment of his reader, should be the same with the most eligible plan of a journey" (Bush, *Hibernia Curiosa*, pp. ix and x). Presumably, this will mitigate against the prospect that a traveler will suffer fatigue from having to make too many observations.

The prospect of defect still looms over Bush's representations, however, despite, or perhaps because of this method of fending off observational excess. Introducing a description of the lake of Killarney, he laments, "I despair, indeed, of giving you an adequate description of this aqueo-insular paradise, for it is impossible for any expressions to convey the conceptions of the delighted spectator on the spot." An excess of beauty, an aesthetic overload, can bring about representational defect when Bush attempts to render features of the landscape he admits are "beyond description" (Bush, *Hibernia Curiosa*, pp. 90 and 91).

Still, Bush urges readers to trust that his account represents a more accurate description of Ireland than previous natural histories. Bush affects modesty, both in his persona (despite his earlier catty remarks about the methods of publishers and booksellers), and in his purpose. He purports to take care to report only "a sketch of some, amongst many" of the phenomena a fellow traveler might observe in Ireland and to "represent no more than the general out-lines of the appearance of things". He thus takes on the characteristics of a subject willing to let facts which "naturally engage his notice" do the same for the reader. When he views Ireland through the lens of natural history, a "species of natural entertainment" engrosses him and, again, presumably his readers, too (Bush, *Hibernia Curiosa*, p. xiii). If *Hibernia Curiosa* satisfies demands of readers of travel narratives that they both inform and amuse, that fulfillment arises naturally, out of conditions on the ground in Ireland itself.

Bush avows that his representations "are wrote [sic] with candour and ingenuity, untinctured with prejudice or partiality; such as the originals appeared to him with an honest freedom, and without respect of persons, he has endeavoured to depicture them to his readers" (Bush, *Hibernia Curiosa*, p. xiii); and "In the descriptive, he has copied immediately from nature" (Bush, *Hibernia Curiosa*, p. xiv). In rendering his observations into prose, Bush promises only mimesis, not a perfect correspondence between Irish nature and his representations. In the midst of portraying the wonders of Powerscourt Waterfall in county Wicklow, for example, Bush concedes that the "highest description must fall short of the beauty of the original" (Bush, *Hibernia Curiosa*, p. 69). Alongside his modesty, his shrinkage of self in the face of the curiosities of nature, Bush tries to convince readers that he embodies other qualities that establish a traveler's credibility as an eyewitness giving testimony; his representations are candid, unprejudiced, impartial, honest, unconstrained, and not tainted by the status of his interlocutors.

When Bush turns to the question of what to observe, he employs the language of natural history. His "out-lines" suggests capturing regularities in natural phenomena, a goal of natural historians. But Bush also observes "such objects or curiosity ... that should be supposed naturally to engage his notice and attention" (Bush, *Hibernia Curiosa*, p. x). This too evokes a Baconian legacy, enshrined in the Royal Society instructions calling on travelers to take singularities seriously. Bush finds The Giant's Causeway striking enough to catch and hold his attention for some fifteen pages, during which he denotes the formation a "singularity" (Bush, *Hibernia Curiosa*, pp. 48–62 and 61). The salmon-leap at Leislip [Leixlip] constitutes another such singularity:

> Tis almost incredible, to a stranger, the height to which these fish will leap: I assure you, that I have often seem them, at this very fall, leap near 20 feet: you may think, perhaps, that I shall want more credit for this than the generality of my readers will believe I have a right to; but, upon my honour, 'tis no less than matter of fact.
> (Bush, *Hibernia Curiosa*, p. 65)

Bush acknowledges the fantastic nature of his observations. To allay readers' concerns about his credibility, he offers one interpretation of the instructions to travelers promulgated by the Royal Society: he reports his observations as matters of fact.

Hibernia Curiosa hardly lacks for treatment of political economy, even though the subject had not yet entered the English lexicon during his journey. Bush covers, in cursory fashion, topics ranging from the provisioning of Dublin, the "rate of hackney-coaches, and sedans" in the city, prices for sheep and cattle; the commerce of Cork, the "prodigious sums" brought in by rentals for the salmon fisheries, and the prices of the fish for export and for the domestic market (Bush, *Hibernia Curiosa*, pp, 21, 23–6, 27–8, 41–2, 62, and 62–3).

Bush's political economy almost entirely lacks entertainment value, however, thus failing to achieve a goal deemed increasingly necessary for European travel accounts. His description of the chaise-marine, a horse-drawn contraption in Dublin, serves as a notable exception. Bush finds this "drollest and most diverting kind of conveyance for your genteel and ungenteel parties of pleasure", and notes that "These simple constructions are almost the only kind of carts, in common use, for the carrying or moving of goods, merchandize of every kind, hay, straw, corn, dung, turf, &c., throughout the kingdom" (Bush, *Hibernia Curiosa*, pp. 24–5). See Figure 2.2. The chaise-marine stands out as the only example in *Hibernia*

Figure 2.2 The "drollest and most diverting kind of conveyance" in Dublin. Kress Collection, Baker Library, Harvard Business School.

Curiosa where Bush could be said to convey matters of political economy in a manner that both informs and entertains.

In fact, when Bush ventures out of Dublin and into the Irish countryside, he openly declares his observations, heavily weighted toward the political economic, devoid of amusement. The visible immiseration of the mass of the rural population, the pervasiveness of "poverty, and want of employment" among them, leads him to confide, "Too much, indeed, of this is seen throughout the kingdom to be pleasing to an English traveller" (Bush, *Hibernia Curiosa:*, pp. 15 and 29). Still, he marvels at the almost universal hospitality and civility of the Irish. This despite the fact that

> Poverty and oppression will naturally make man sour, rude and unsociable, and eradicate, or at least, suppress all the more amiable principles and passions of mankind. But it should seem unfair and ungenerous to judge of, or decide against the natural disposition of a man reduced by indigence and oppression almost to desperation. For a peasant of Ireland to be civil and engaging is a work of supererogation.
> (Bush, *Hibernia Curiosa*, p. 26)

From Bush's observations, few in Ireland match the stereotype of the wild Irish. He attributes what wildness there is, which is to be found principally among the peasants in Connaught, to the despotism of landlords there.

These "absolute tyrants" constitute a law unto themselves. They extract exorbitant rents and their oppressive measures "have almost depopulated this province of Ireland" (Bush, *Hibernia Curiosa*, p. 29). Bush himself did not witness this state of affairs, having avoided Connaught as "the least inviting to a traveller of any part of the kingdom" (Bush, *Hibernia Curiosa*, p. 27). He instead relies on the testimony of local experts, "some of the more sensible people of the very province", to attest to this fact (Bush, *Hibernia Curiosa*, p. 29).

Natural history and political economy sit uncomfortably together in *Hibernia Curiosa*. For one, Bush's venture into the epistemological territory of political economy departs from one of the chief norms of natural history initially established by the Royal Society, a skittishness to move beyond observing facts to indulging in theoretical speculation. Bush describes causal relationships between landlords, poverty, and population in Connaught without hesitancy; the systems of landownership and tenancy share primary responsibility for the misery and, as a result, a scanty population. Bush happily adds more causes to the list, including the tithes exacted by the Church of England and the Catholic Church, and crippling restrictions on Irish trade (Bush, *Hibernia Curiosa*, pp. 30–4). But, again, the chief source of Irish wretchedness is the state of agriculture, where land is "cultivated in the vilest manner, by a set of abject, miserable occupiers that are absolutely no better than slaves to the despicably lazy subordinate landlords" (Bush, *Hibernia Curiosa*, p. 39). Bush's political economy thus appears to be unconstrained by concerns about the snares of speculative reasoning.

This marks a stark contrast to his natural history. Here, Bush does not entirely shy away from searching for causes. Recounting the "most generally prevailing opinion here [in Ireland]" on the origin of the numerous drowned trees found at the bottom of bogs, Bush deploys key words from natural history as well as law on the credibility of testimony and evidence. He writes that locals believe the trees "were originally thrown down by the universal deluge in the time of Noah. There may be truth in this opinion, but 'tis certain, at best, 'tis altogether conjectural, though not altogether improbable" (Bush, *Hibernia Curiosa*, p. 75). He disputes the prevailing native accounts about the source of the peat cut from the bogs, believing them "erroneous"; he tests, to his satisfaction, an alternative theory against facts "universally observable" such as observations on vegetative growth and decay (Bush, *Hibernia Curiosa*, pp. 77–83).

His version of political economy, on the other hand, informs readers in a fundamentally different manner. Bush ignores questions about matters of fact, probability, conjecture, certainty, and theory. His method when taking up questions central to the new science consists of first rapidly making definitive casual claims, and only then explaining his reasoning behind the claims, the precise opposite from his natural history. This is exemplified at the conclusion of *Hibernia Curiosa* in Bush's account of the ongoing Whiteboys disturbances, "a piece of the civil history" distinct from the general view of natural history that prevails through most of his account (Bush, *Hibernia Curiosa*, p. 132). Bush quickly concludes that the rural oppression he described earlier in his narrative formed the prime cause of the riots:

> The severe treatment and oppression of the lowest class of the inhabitants, in some parts of this kingdom have met with from their priests and subordinate landlords, was the principal cause of those disturbances I have met with. I have but too much reason to believe that this remark was well grounded, from the observations I had an opportunity of making in the midst of the country where these insurgents have given the greatest disturbance.
> (Bush, *Hibernia Curiosa*, p. 133)

Bush relies on his own observations here, including taking testimony from representatives of the various classes about the causes of the disturbances, and weighing them against "the obvious appearance of things in the country". Not for him the evidence of things unseen. After canvassing the opinions of the poorer classes, he "soon had sufficient reason to believe that their disquiet arose, in general, from the severe mistreatment they met with from their landlords, and the lords of the manors, and principally from their clergy" (Bush, *Hibernia Curiosa*, p. 134). Bush offers a succinct summary of his analysis, clocking in at three sentences. Compare this to the seven pages Bush devotes to weighing alternative theories before proving, to his satisfaction at least, the vegetative source and processes that produce peat.

Bush does in fact close *Hibernia Curiosa* with a lengthy section on the reasoning that led to his conclusions about the sources of poverty and distress in Ireland. He takes seriously the complaint of the Irish poor about the loss of their rights to common land, while noting that landowners and the clergy insist on the enforcement of their own customary rights to tithes, much to the detriment of the poor (Bush, *Hibernia Curiosa*, p. 137). Even so, he endorses the enclosure movement, which he recognizes as controversial in both England and Ireland: "On an impartial and altogether disinterested view of the case, and favourable as I have appeared to the poor of this, and as I would ever appear to the same class in both kingdoms, were I to decide on the case, I should give it against them." Bush combines the discourse of impartiality and that of disinterest; later, self-professed political economists deemed any person who could act with disinterest an ideal observer.[106] As to the merits of enclosures, Bush insists that, although he is sympathetic to the case against them, the transformation of commons into private property allows owners to make improvements on the land. This leads to greater efficiency in agricultural production, greater employment, and less distress among the population (Bush, *Hibernia Curiosa:*, pp. 138–40).

Too fine a division of privately-owned land in Ireland also had deleterious effects on the production of food, and adversely affected the subjectivity and agency of the rural Irish poor. Bush again characterizes these poor as no better than slaves, subject to "subaltern landlords". The shift in management of land and people from customary to contractual relations meant that tenants no longer understood themselves as stewards of the land under life-tenancy but as renters. As a result, they no longer saw a need to care for the property they would, under customary usage, have passed on to their family; as subjects liable to rackrenting, they let the land and buildings they occupied deteriorate. Bush maintains that if a landlord "understood his business, he might make double the present produce, and employ to advantage three times the hands that now work upon the lands". Workers would then obtain "a much better subsistence than [from] the fortuitous benevolence of travellers" or from their previous use of common lands (Bush, *Hibernia Curiosa*, pp. 141–2).

Natural history and political economy, still listed here as an unnamed element of civil history, share little actual space in the text of *Hibernia Curiosa*. The two sciences do, however, find some common epistemological ground. For one, Bush repeatedly makes statements assessing the credibility of his and others' observations both on objects of concern to natural history and to those having to do with political economy. For the latter, Bush concludes, on the veracity of the testimony given by representatives of the lower classes about the grievances that gave rise to the White-boys, that "I cannot but acknowledge, in favour of them, that the general civility of the people, with the apparent honesty and candour of their accounts, gave the greatest credit to their representations" (Bush, *Hibernia Curiosa*, p. 137). The calm manner of the witnesses testifies to their civility. This marker of civilization, in turn, offers proof that the poor Irish peasants are civilized, an attribute which lends credibility to their statements.

If Adam Smith departs from natural historians on the relationships between human ecology, food supply, and population, Bush sees human intervention to improve the landscape as an aesthetically pleasing union of nature and domestic economy. He praises the transplantation of the "native [English] taste and genius for rural design" into Ireland by one of the famous Lennox sisters, Lady Louisa Conolly. Lady Louisa, to whom Bush dedicated *Hibernia Curiosa*, successfully improved "a spot, by nature infertile of beauty or elegance" at Castletown House in county Kildare, a Palladian-style country house built in 1722. The improvements she oversaw before and after Bush's visit inscribe a visible, benign, and beneficent sign of the union of England and Ireland on the landscape, a union embodied in the person of Lady Louisa herself. Born in England, she resided in Ireland from the age of eight, and married, at age fifteen, the Irish politician Thomas Conolly. Bush invites the English to extend Lady Louisa's efforts to transform the landscape, even to areas of the Kilkenny district blessed by natural wonders: "what an inimitably rural and romantic paradise would the peninsula I have been describing be made, if to the infinite beauties it has from nature, a little art was introduced by the most elegantly designing lady" (Bush, *Hibernia Curiosa*, p. 121). Bush's prose is ripe with suggestive imagery. The harsh criticism Bush lays against the management of Irish lands and agriculture (implicitly) applies principles of political economy to relations between humans and non-human nature in Ireland. But Bush's appreciation of the efforts of Lady Lucy remind us that, by applying a still more prosaic science, with an ancient lineage, domestic economy, an Englishwoman can improve on even the most beautiful of nature's works in Ireland, too.

By the turn of the nineteenth century, if travelers to Ireland and elsewhere could list political economy as one of the sciences they employed to make and report observations, they did not necessarily do so, at least not automatically. When, after a visit of a few weeks to Ireland in autumn 1799, George Cooper published *Letters on the Irish Nation* (1800), he admits in "Introduction" that he had threatened to abandon publication "a hundred times", and, worse, he "even proceeded to tear my papers".[107] Excess and defect haunted Cooper:

> [H]ad I done justice to the attempt [to promote good understanding between Ireland and Great Britain], ... I should have been carried far beyond those bounds which I had prescribed for myself. The torrent would have carried me away from all my professional avocations, instead of filling up a chasm in them. The more I thought of my subject, the more I found the difficulties of it increase. I may truly say, that, like a tired traveller, I found "Alps on Alps arise," without the consolation of any visible limit or boundary. I was forced to pause, and leave it unfinished. I have therefore done little more than the merely sketching an outline, which I have filled up with equal haste and imperfection.
> (Cooper, *Letters* (1800), pp. xxvii–xxviii)

The passage captures the dizzying torrent of sensations that can overwhelm travelers attempting to represent what they have observed. In quick succession Cooper presses into service three allusions to the sublime to express the travails of the writer. The prospect of representational failure appears both as defect, an unfilled "chasm", and excess, the lack of "any visible limit or boundary".

Cooper prepares the reader for disappointment in the "Introduction" to *Letters*. His travels constitute "a personal examination into the state and condition of the Irish nation", and, while other visitors to Ireland were free to focus on "other interesting objects", such as "natural curiosities", *Letters* involves the sober "study of the government, the religion, the commerce, and the manners of a great nation". No small task, this; Cooper concludes that it comprises "a large portion of the whole circle of human science", the mastery of which "is only within the scope of such talents as must be combined to form both the statesman and the metaphysician". Tellingly, political economists and political economy fail to make an appearance in Cooper's "whole circle of human science" (Cooper, *Letters* (1800), pp. xii–xiii). Not only does Cooper claim to lack the powers to fulfill the task he has set out for himself, but, he "cannot aspire to be considered as more than a superficial observer". At least one reader of the 1800 edition concurred. A reviewer for *The Anti-Jacobin Review and Magazine* found Cooper's struggle to wrest sense out of his observations unsuccessful, complaining that "Many of the author's observations respecting government are just and judicious, but we are not sure that we always comprehend his meaning."[108]

Far from abandoning his work, Cooper published a second edition of *Letters* in 1801 following the "very flattering reception" to the first (Cooper, *Letters* (1801), "Advertisement", p. iii). Where the 1800 octavo edition lacks explicit reference to political economy, and runs a brisk two hundred pages, the second edition is three-quarters longer. Cooper's incorporation of insights derived from the work of Adam Smith contributes significantly to the "fresh matter" that he "thought would tend to remove every possible obscurity" in the second edition (Cooper, *Letters* (1801), "Advertisement", p. v). This may have helped Cooper tamp down excess; in the "Introduction" to the second edition, Cooper drops the following lines that had featured in the first: "The more I thought of my subject, the more I found the difficulties of it increase. I may truly say, that, like a tired traveller, I found 'Alps on Alps arise,' without the consolation of any visible limit or boundary. I was forced to pause, and leave it unfinished." Rather than suffering near paralysis at the prospect of the sublime, Cooper steps back from the chasm in the second edition:

> [H]ad I done justice to the attempt, ... I should have been carried far beyond those bounds which I had prescribed for myself. The torrent would have carried me away from all my professional avocations, instead of filling up a chasm in them. Had I stepped still more out of the way, I should like Atalanta have lost the race, and that too, perhaps, without picking up the golden apples. For, the more I thought of my subject, the more, I confess, I found the difficulties of it increase. I have therefore done little more than the merely sketching an outline.
>
> (Cooper, *Letters* (1801), p. xl)

How does Cooper sketch his "outline"? He claimed little original or new in his observations. Still, Cooper declares his "historically descriptive" method of "personal observation of the facts" superior to the "abstract reasoning" which dominated debate swirling about the proposed union between Ireland and England from contemporary armchair travelers in England (Cooper, *Letters* (1800), p. xiv; (1801), p. xxi). Cooper does gesture toward a natural history of Ireland. The table of contents promises an account that begins with a "Short Sketch of the Climate of Ireland, and of the General Physical Appearance of that Kingdom". But Cooper demurs from actually writing about these elements or making many observations of the "picturesque" in *Letters*; "I could not persuade myself to fill my letters with descriptions of that sort" (Cooper, *Letters* (1800), p. xiii; (1801), p. xix). In fact, Cooper limits his descriptions of the climate, soil and "natural beauties" to a mere one and one-half pages in both editions (Cooper, *Letters* (1800), pp. 3–5; (1801), pp. 4–6).

Yet Cooper is not averse to principles. Methods key to the work of contemporary British political economists, such as a focus on commercial society and trade, and the use of stadial histories to construct a hierarchy of societies, appear in both editions. Cooper, like Bush, named Irish tenancy as the chief source of poverty and unrest in Ireland. In the first edition of *Letters* Cooper is at a loss to understand why commercial policy has kept the Irish poor when the obvious remedy is at hand; "Foreign trade alone can create opulent mercantile communities and corporations. The example of England has shewn the advantages which these produce both to the cause of liberty and of civilization." The advantages are twofold: "Commerce, which affords subsistence to a great number of subjects, ... increases the population of the country, and the wealth of the revenues." Cooper conflates the wealth of a nation's subjects with their happiness, for, "There is no truer maxim of policy than that to make a people richer is the way to make subjects happier, and the state more powerful" (Cooper, *Letters* (1800), pp. 180, 182, 183; (1801): 321, 323–4, 325).

For Cooper, union and commerce would spread benefits to the Irish more widely than heretofore among the mass of the people, not just by reducing poverty but by softening manners. Irish national character would be transformed; the Irish would no longer be barbaric. Reviewers in fact focused on Cooper's discourses on Irish character in Letter 1, observations which they found, in general, enlightening. One reviewer of the first edition in *The monthly magazine, or, British register* asserts Cooper's "letters impart a great deal of information, relative to the real character of the inhabitants of Ireland".[109] Another, in *The New London Review; or, Monthly Report of Authors and Books*, writes that "To the author, it seems that the principle of passion bears a more than equal sway, with this people, than reason", and agrees with Cooper's "judicious reflections" on Irish national character that conclude Letter 1.[110]

Cooper favors the metaphysics of Hume over Montesquieu, and posits moral as opposed to physical causes as the dominant factors determining national character. Analysts could rank societies and nations as more or less civilized according to the extent to which their population was governed by passion or reason. Thus,

> Perhaps it will be found, that all national characters differ in proportion to the degrees in which these two principles of reason and passion are found to preponderate. They constitute all the intermediate gradations between the civilized state and the inhabitants of New Zealand. They form even the extremes themselves.
>
> (Cooper, *Letters* (1800), pp. 11–12; (1801), p. 15)

Cooper relies here on stadial histories, with Letter 1 headings including "3. Lower Class considered– have long been stationary– Resemblance in Manners of all uncivilized Nations". The lower classes exist in a state of barbarity; Cooper calls the Irish Aborigines. Cooper leans on repeated observations by previous travelers to claim impartiality in his description of Irish national character, and further ventures "I shall have little difficulty in describing this character, as it may be depictured in the same few words with that of all nations that have been seen in a state of ignorance and barbarity" (Cooper, *Letters* (1800), p. 37; (1801), p. 55). Apparently, all barbarians suffer the same lack of refinement of manners, no matter when and where they are found. For Cooper, universal causes in stadial histories produce universal effects; these can be changed by universal causes, too, especially the expansion of trade and commerce. Thus, union with England will remedy Irish stationarity, in the same way "Russia has emerged from barbarity in proportion as commerce has extended there. The same effects must arise from similar causes in Ireland" (Cooper, (1800), p. 184).[111]

While Cooper resorts to political economy to frame his observations in the first edition, without saying so in so many words, he openly calls on the authority of Adam Smith in the second. When Cooper pairs a description of Ireland drawn from stadial histories with Smithian political economy he illustrates just how supple the union can be; the combination allows him to assume and derive both universal and locally and historically specific causes. Put another way, the pairing allows Cooper to explain observations as manifestations of synchronic or diachronic phenomena, or as completely non-temporal ones. For instance, Cooper finds the fact that one can "discover almost the same traits of character in the poor peasantry of Ireland, which distinguishes every uncivilized people" unworthy of notice, except for the "extraordinary" circumstance that Ireland does not fit the main criterion for an uncivilized country in Smith's stadial taxonomy. That "Africa, Tartary, and Siberia, have always been countries in a state of barbarism" Smith attributes to their nature as "inland countries"; Ireland is not (Cooper, *Letters* (1801), pp. 59–60). Cooper explains this paradox by a focus on Irish tenancy, oppressive religious practices, and poor government policy. The insecurity of renters' property holds back investment in rural holdings, forcing capital from its natural channels. Cooper simultaneously uses stadial histories as universal histories, and explains deviations from such histories through the application of political economy.

Economic Observations, Economic Policies, and Economic Men

Travelers to Ireland could use the combination of stadial histories and political economy to make both observations and policy recommendations. This was also true of European travelers who ranged through regions as varied as South Africa and the English Home Counties. When commissioner-general of the Dutch Cape Colony Jacobus Abraham De Mist traveled to the interior of South Africa in 1803, he carried copies of the authoritative travel narratives of the day, including the first volume of Englishman John Barrow's popular *An Account of Travels Into the Interior of Southern Africa* (1801); these taught administrators "lessons in observation". In De Mist's reports, natural history, the picturesque, the pastoral, the beautiful, and the sublime, all jostle for space alongside merely "utilitarian, political and economical points of view". These went well beyond previous administrative reports from the Dutch East India Company (VOC) which had focused on routes through the land, the types of soils composing it, and its agricultural potential.[112]

De Mist treats the published travel narratives on the colony with caution, warning that they are rife with misconceived statements, expressions of national prejudice or, as in the case of Barrow's almost unremittingly negative views of the settlers, outright xenophobia (Huigen, *Knowledge and Colonialism*, 172, 184). The statesman Gijsbert Karel, Count van Hogendorp, who similarly sifted through travel accounts as basis for his 1802 proposal advocating new policies in the Cape, points, in paratext, to another trap that armchair travelers cum policymakers need to avoid, that of excess and defect:

> From all the known reports of the Cape of Good Hope, I have had to choose some and then again I had to confine myself to those that coincided with the perspective from which I view these colonies. The Botanist attaches great value to all kinds of plants which are relatively unimportant to Political Economy [Politijke Economie], while he mentions others that serve as food to the inhabitants or have substantial trading value. The Geologist pores over the mountain layers, without finding anything that is important to the Statesman, but he may also indicate the suitability of the soil for use, or for prospecting for useful minerals, or the position of mountains and rivers, as defences against the enemy. I have therefore neither overlooked a single traveler, nor used any one in its entirety as the basis of my work.
> (Quoted and translated in Huigen, *Knowledge and Colonialism*, p. 173)[113]

Lacking access to VOC archives, van Hogendorp draws on the few extant accounts of the colony, using, however, only selective information from them. When venturing out as an armchair traveler to the Cape, one should understand the different viewpoints of these authors. Van Hogendorp's perspective, shaped by the scientific foundations of his craft as a statesman, guides his selection of materials from the accounts; he combines useful elements from other sciences in order to formulate and pursue policies for the benefit of the nation.

Note that political economy plays a central, named role in van Hogendorp's statement on method. In contrast, though Barrow specifically refers, once, to domestic economy in *Travels*, political economy fails to appear in either volume. His opening remarks on conditions in the Colony, however, includes a statement on population that could have been penned by Malthus, as he observes that "The progress of the population ..., like some of the provinces of North America, has nearly doubled itself in every twenty years."[114] Van Hogendorp executes a neat rhetorical turn with political economy, one that balances its importance to statesmanship: political economy subsumes botany; statecraft subsumes geology. Political economists and statesmen perform similar functions, drawing and culling observations from other sciences. If not actually commensurate, van Hogendorp suggests that as a means to fashion policy the fledgling science of political economy exists on nearly equal footing with the science of legislation.

What might these Dutch colonial administrators mean when they refer to political economy? De Mist seeks to integrate the commerce of the Cape with that of the Dutch Republic by allowing them to begin trading with one another; residents of both the Colony and Netherlands would prosper, and the tax revenue of the state increase (Huigen, *Knowledge and Colonialism*, pp. 171–2 and 210). This required securing property rights in the colony. Frequent clashes between European residents and their descendants and the Khoikhoi, San, and Xhosa cost precious resources. Commercial society could take root in the Cape Colony only by stabilizing borders between communities. When De Mist suggests shrinking the size of the colony, thus allowing the San more space and the settlers less, he proposes this expediency as a means to end the war between the two sides (Huigen, *Knowledge and Colonialism*, pp. 184–5). Scholars in the colony at the beginning of the nineteenth century, consisting mostly of independent gentlemen, mixed with a smattering of colonial administrators, representing a number of European polities and a similarly diverse set of mentors and influences such as Linnaeus, Buffon, and Rousseau, issued reports that challenged stereotypical representations of the Indigenous population (Huigen, *Knowledge and Colonialism*, chapter eight). Barrow writes that the Xhosas deserve a place alongside "the first Europeans", the highest rank of the barbaric (Barrow, *Travels*, I, p. 206). De Mist portrays the Indigenous sympathetically as well, and protection of their population from the brutish behavior of the settlers forms a key part of his plans for reform (Huigen, *Knowledge and Colonialism*, p. 171).

Sympathy for the plight of the Indigenous had its limits, though. Huigen identifies only one Batavian writer, Robert Jacob Gordon, who considered not just the Xhosas of the Eastern Cape, but the San, too, as his equals (Huigen, *Knowledge and Colonialism*, p. 93). Gordon, commander of the Dutch East India Company garrison in the Cape from 1780 until he took his own life in 1795, after the British invasion, undertook six trips in southern Africa, more than any other European in the eighteenth century. His journals reveal an individual who treats different peoples as simply different, perhaps due to his training as a naturalist, reinforced by his observations while mediating conflicts between local peoples and colonists. For example, recording sightings of different species of birds during the fourth trip, on 23 July 1779, Gordon writes that the crows of Europe and those of southern Africa are the same bird, despite superficial differences in markings and calls. He extrapolates, "It is the same with the sparrow found in this country, which differs slightly from ours; as also with the people."[115] Moreover, while he refers to unidentified communities that do not fit into any of the known European classifications, the San, Xhosa, Nama, Amaquas, and other Khoikhoi peoples, as savages ("de wilden"), an encounter with one such group from 20 to 22 August 1779, reveals caution (both his party and the Indigenous are armed), and ultimately, mutual respect.[116] Gordon's exceptionalism stands out, however, notwithstanding other administrators' occasional outbursts of anti-colonialist sentiment, criticism of hybrid populations, and not unsympathetic remarks on Indigenous populations (Huigen, *Knowledge and Colonialism*, p. 171).

In fact, the published travel accounts scramble the typical assignment of colonial signifiers to the Colony's population, painting settlers and their hybrid descendants, offspring of Europeans and Khoi, as economically superior but morally inferior to the local peoples because of their cruelty toward them. The economic transformations called for by travelers and administrators invariably involved moral transformations. In an 1803 memorandum, De Mist insists that the farmers on the border bear responsibility for the war with the Xhosa, and condemns them as "indolent, lazy, and cowardly"; the settler population had degenerated to the lowest rank of the civilized (Huigen, *Knowledge and Colonialism*, p. 183).

This reads as a faint echo of Barrow's remarks on the domestic and political economies and stadial histories of the different populations in the Colony. In his first description of the Colony's Europeans and their descendants, Barrow starts off mildly enough. The Dutch find the living too easy and are too isolated in South Africa. A mild climate, the exploitation of African slaves and colonial policy, which keeps settlers uneducated and farm households distant from one another, all combine to stifle "the spirit of industry" and independence among colonists who might otherwise bridle at the "shackles imposed on it [the colony] by the parent state" (Barrow, *Travels*, I, p. 7). But Barrow eventually damns the Dutch men in the colony, judging them

> Unwilling to work, and unable to think; with a mind disengaged from every sort of care or reflexion, indulging to excess in the gratification of every sensual appetite, the African peasant grows to an unwieldy size, and is carried off the stage by the first inflammatory disease that attacks him.
>
> (Barrow, *Travels*, I, pp. 77–8)

Dutch men and their male descendants play multiple characters in the theater of the Cape Colony, cast by Barrow as a shifting array of nationalities and occupations. This idealized but hardly ideal character appears: first, as one among the "planters of Africa"; alternatively, as an African peasant; next, as "a true Dutch peasant, or boor as he styles himself"; then, as a Dutch farmer; and, finally, as an African farmer (Barrow, *Travels*, I, pp. 77, 78, 80, 81, 80, 83, and 84). Dutch females appear, initially, as something worse yet, registering as inert, hardly human: "The women of the African peasantry pass a life of the most listless inactivity. The mistress of the family ... seems fixed to her chair like a piece of furniture" (Barrow, *Travels*, I, p. 84). Barrow faults the "wilds of Africa" and an education among "slaves and Hottentots" for her lack of delicacy.

De Mist also speculates that the manners of the settlers had been "bastardised" by lack of contact with "civilised" people and adds their constant consumption of meat to the list of baneful environmental influences responsible for their degeneration. Travel to South Africa and residency there transforms the Dutch into a population no longer Dutch. They have not turned into savages, although Barrow inscribes them with signifiers that might mark them as such. De Mist and other Batavian travel writers on the other hand tempered their disgust for the farmers, and even note their positive attributes on occasion (Huigen, *Knowledge and Colonialism*, p. 184). For De Mist, colonial policy should work toward civilizing the settlers, through religion and education, so "that even the Capetonians become Dutch again" (quoted in Huigen, *Knowledge and Colonialism*, p. 182).

Barrow excludes the Dutch in the Cape Colony from the fervor for agricultural innovation gripping segments of Europe at the time, asserting that "Hitherto there have been few speculators among the Dutch planters; the spirit of improvement and experiment never entered their minds" (Barrow, *Travels*, I, p. 67). Alexander Gillespie, a major in the British Royal Marines who took part in an expedition that captured the colony in 1806, relates that authorities actively discouraged at least one such experiment; when the colony was restored to the Dutch, they annulled a contract with an agriculturalist sent specifically from England to conduct scientific trials and implement improvements "around a considerable district".[117] European promoters of agricultural improvement such as Adam Smith's friend, the 3rd Duke of Buccleuch championed experimentation, innovation, the introduction of new crops, and new methods of farm management.[118] Quantification would allow them to gauge the effectiveness of these measures. The peripatetic Arthur Young looks to political arithmetic, the British offshoot of cameralism, to inform his quantitative methods in works such as *Political Arithmetic: Containing Observations on the Present State of Great Britain; and the Principles of Her Policy in the Encouragement of Agriculture* in 1774. Young's work also reflects the influence of physiocratic thinking he acquired during travels in France; the fruits of the land and sea, agriculture, mining, and fisheries represent the chief sources of national wealth.

Critics, then and now, have questioned Young's observations and representations, contesting his knowledge, the accuracy, reliability, and methodological quality of his surveys, and his lack of adherence to theory.[119] They charge him as well with a penchant for hyperbole, and for encouraging prejudiced commentary from his witnesses. Contemporaries griped that Young's verbosity belied his "just the facts" narratives and produced little of use. For example, in the lapse between the completion of his third and final trip to France, which concluded in January 1790, and the publication of *Travels in France* (1792), Young shaped his raw materials into a hybrid literary form, lumping together elements associated with fictions with those derived from political essays, the latter to better answer Edmund Burke's *Reflections on the Revolution in France*, which had been published in November 1790. Young added paratext to his diary and an agricultural survey, including an autobiographical sketch, a preface, two introductions, and two epilogues. And he acquiesced to the demands of his publisher to cut this material for *Travels*; in order to make it viable for commercial publication, he jettisoned much of the survey material. At one point, Young confesses that he uses a schoolmaster to check and correct his "figures", a gesture of modesty also designed to add to the impression of accuracy of *Travels*. Young adopts a number of different identities and voices in the text, contradicts himself, and passes judgment on the French. All these changes, including his digressions, lend immediacy to his account, enhancing its authenticity, if not his attempt to convey impartiality.[120]

Young's changes violated the contemporaneous publication guidelines and suggested practices of the Royal Society. And they did little to move William Marshall. Marshall compiled observations from those who traveled through England's rural districts at the behest of the Board of Agriculture in *The Review and Abstract of the County Reports to the Board of Agriculture* (1818), a five-volume set of texts that first started appearing in 1808. Young had been appointed secretary to the Board in 1793, soon after its formation, and helped direct the General View of Agriculture surveys. Without naming Young in the completed version of *The Review and Abstract*, Marshall criticized the lack of system of many of the surveys, carping that they deliver little useful information.

Marshall's sniping at Young begins in the table of contents. "Natural Economy", the first major heading of the table, only arrives after two sub-headings, "Natural Districts" and "Reporters". Natural economy claimed roots deep in the past, based on the Aristotelian ideal of *oikonomia*, or domestic economy, where a manager (*oikonomos*) of a rural estate tailors production to consumption for the purposes of biological and social reproduction, carefully husbanding natural resources to obtain necessities for the household via "thrift, regularity, and efficient dispensation".[121] Early modern users referred to natural economy as "oeconomy", which emphasizes a focus on necessities and the domestic space rather than the excesses engendered in markets, natural limits rather than artificial limitlessness.

Many early modern Europeans idealized economy as a moral, political, and aesthetic exemplar for administration of the "national oeconomy" aimed at increasing the wealth and happiness of the people; they found emerging practices of production, consumption, and distribution located in merchant capitalism, foreign trade, and joint-stock trading, as opposed to the still predominant household economies, troubling as a result.[122] Roberts also "stresses the need to consider oeconomy as a set of practices (including conceptualization and communication), rather than as a prior concept or theory [of "the economy"] which could be applied to shape or explain activity" in the latter half of the long eighteenth century.[123] Oeconomy also serves as the common root of political economy and ecology. The "oeconomy of nature", first formulated by Kenelm Digby in 1644, and which came into widespread use soon thereafter, represents an application of Baconian natural philosophy to the concept of natural economy, and "became foundational to the history of ecology in subsequent centuries".[124] British political economy, on the other hand, developed in part by shedding the concepts and language of natural philosophy.[125]

Natural economy therefore presents Marshall and his contemporaries with yet another alternative to the methods and assumptions of political economy as a means to measure and ensure the growth and happiness of human populations. Natural economy potentially places non-human nature at the center of analyses and practices, with non-human subjects and agents on equal footing with their human counterparts. At *least* on par with human nature: provocatively, if Marshall's table of contents reflects both ontological and epistemological orderings, natural economy takes precedence over political economy, which appears later in the table. Regardless, humans and the rest of nature form a set of relationships governed by interdependence rather than discrete principles applicable to human and non-human realms, respectively.[126]

Natural economy also offered the prospect of improved empirical observations. It represents the "material interface between humanity and [the rest of] the natural world".[127] Marshall sought to wrestle the work of the Board of Agriculture into systematic reports imparting legible and useful information to a reader. He announces as much in the "Contents" of *A Review (and Complete Abstract) of the Reports to the Board of Agriculture from the Midland Department of England* (1815), one of the preliminary volumes that preceded *The Review and Abstract*: the contents are "SYSTEMATICALLY ARRANGED".[128]

But the table of contents in *The Review and Abstract*, which Marshall had "prefixed" to the text, and which he considers "an appropriate arrangement (as being at once both natural and practical), ... intelligible at sight, and easily to be referred to", signifies that his attempt was not entirely successful.[129] The table indicates where topics can be found in the text rather than what follows, successively, in the text; it reads like an index, albeit one lacking any alphabetical order within the headings or subheadings. The subheadings within "Natural Economy" announce, for example, the initial page for the "Extent" of various counties, followed by the same for the "Elevation" of each county, "Turn of Surface", "Climature", "Waters", "Soils", and so on of each county whose surveyor covered that subject. What are we to make of an index, haphazardly arranged, masquerading as a table of contents? Marshall was stymied from the beginning of this project, actually, driven at one point to adding a footnote to the table of contents to express his exasperation:

> On the Winter Management of Store Cattle, – on the Thrashing or Dressing of Corn, on the Expenditure of Hay or Straw, or on the raising of Manure therefrom, – not a word! (excepting the item here referred to, and excepting what may have been incidentally mentioned under other heads). Indeed, those very important concerns of the arable Farmer, appear not to have been thought of, by the framer of the plan of the Board's Reports.
> (Marshall, *The Review and Abstract*, p. x, note)

Marshall continues his critique of the work of the Board of Agriculture throughout the "Advertisement". He nonetheless boasts that he has "furnished an ample field of substantial natural facts, which cannot fail to become of the first utility" (Marshall, *The Review and Abstract*, "Advertisement", p. 15).

Marshall's system displays a surfeit of attention to "natural and economical FACTS". Four other major headings follow "Natural Economy" in the table of contents: "Political Economy" and "Rural Economy", trailed by "Woodlands" and "Agriculture". Marshall explains in the introduction that he has sorted the material into "the principal branches into which the main subject before us, naturally separates" (Marshall, *The Review and Abstract*, xxxviii). This natural ordering closely follows the ordering of the table of contents:

> The GENERAL ECONOMY of a country, – which is under efficient government, and whose lands are appropriated, – is composed of three obviously differential parts, or separable subjects: namely,
>
> 1. The NATURAL ECONOMY of the country itself; – its situation, extent, and conformation; – the materials of which it is formed, – their arrangement and natural characters.
> 2. Its POLITICAL ECONOMY; – comprizing whatever relates to public concerns, connected with
> 3. Its RURAL ECONOMY; – including what belongs to private property and its management, relative to rural concerns. (Marshall, *The Review and Abstract*: xxxix)

General economy, which depends on the security of private property and "efficient government", subsumes the other categories of economy. Marshall lists natural economy prior to political economy in each of his arrangements, which suggests a consistent hierarchical ordering of the two. Domestic economy, though entirely absent from the text, traditionally forms an essential feature of natural economy, with households managing natural resources. Political economy rests cushioned between natural economy and rural economy; how Marshall believes it is "connected" to rural economy remains unclear. The connection probably reflects the organizing principles of a text devoted largely to agricultural concerns, as Marshall later introduces a section of the report on Lancashire by calling the relationship between agriculture and manufacturing an "unsettled point in political economy" (Marshall, *The Review and Abstract*, p. 255).

Marshall describes what it takes to put together the ideal agricultural survey, based on a plan he submitted to the Society of Arts in London in February 1780. Surveyors would meld theory and experience, where "experience of Agriculture is acquired through adequate observation, either on self-practice, or the practice of others". They must "collect and compress the useful information which is at present widely scattered in almost numberless volumes; – and to reduce these joint accumulations of agricultural knowledge to systematic science" in a work to be entitled "SYSTEM OF ENGLISH AGRICULTURE" (Marshall, *The Review and Abstract*, xviii, xxi). Surveyors, then, are also reporters who winnow and comment on earlier surveys, some of which had never been published, to extract, condense, and impart valuable information and to correct errors. Marshall calls on observers to tame the unruliness of information too dispersed and almost too prolific.

Marshall's ideal observer needs, however, to *stop traveling*. He should take up residence on a farm for (at least) a year in the district that best excels at a particular branch of agriculture, "if possible in the house of the best-informed farmer in the district pitched upon". The traveler, now temporary resident, should "minutely observe and register the living practice which surrounds him: not the practice of theoretical, but of professional farmers". Marshall's "plan is [not] confined merely to observation" of inputs, crop yields and prices; the observer should become familiar with the tools used in agricultural operations, and take "a complete REVIEW OF WRITTEN AGRICULTURE, from Fitz-Herbert, in 1534, to the present time". Ideal observers would both "receive and … offer information", the latter to communicate details of agricultural practice to the public. Observers are ideally participant observers who can provide "useful information" to farmers and the government alike (Marshall, *The Review and Abstract*, pp. xx and xxi).

Marshall dedicates an entire section of the introduction to spell out the sundry other "qualifications that are requisite to the twofold task of Surveying, and Reporting, the rural practices and improvement of a country". He calls for a practical knowledge of farming techniques "in all its branches, and in different districts", not simply for the sake of familiarity, but for the observer "to mature his judgement, dispel local prejudices, and prepare his mind, by due expansion, to form just conceptions of the varying methods and proceedings of other men". Other requisites for the surveyor include woodland management skills, knowledge of the laws governing private property, and an understanding of the "MANAGEMENT OF TENANTED LANDS, and the proper GOVERNMENT of their OCCUPIERS". In addition, the observer should have a "competent knowledge" of the sciences relevant to agriculture, including mathematics and mechanics. Natural history will especially help the observer make discoveries and assimilate them to facts already known, and "practical knowledge" of composition will aid his reporting (Marshall, *The Review and Abstract*, pp. xxx–xxxii).

Yet all this is not enough. To report on a particular county or district, one needs to have "maturely studied, and to have become fully acquainted with, the natural and economical FACTS which belong" to it (Marshall, *The Review and Abstract*, p. xxxii). Hence Marshall's insistence, again, that his ideal observer-reporter stop traveling. Without repeated, on-the-spot observations of a district, an observer-reporter will not acquire enough knowledge of the local ecology and microeconomy to fulfill his task.

Marshall models a particular form of masculine subjectivity and agency in his rural travelers. His ideal expertly observes and reports on agricultural developments and does so without prejudice. He can manage farms, too. Tobin maintains that Young had previously drawn on his own travel observations to develop a new ideal, which she labels "economic man".[130] This new economic man, a farmer, would fluently tabulate both the costs and benefits of farm operations, and observe and represent all the other minutiae of farm operations accurately so that others, including passing travelers or resident observers, could trust their observations. Farmers, like merchants who engage in travel and trade abroad, need to establish creditworthiness with strangers. Merchants did so by using people, institutions and technologies such as agents, letters of credit, and bills of exchange. Farmers should be able to do the same: credible accounting lent credit to accounts.

These men would act with prudence and economy, which contemporaries identified as quintessentially middle-class features. Indeed, identification as British increasingly meant aping fellow natives endowed with economy. Yet this commercial virtue had failed to establish itself as a universal ideal among famers and farm agents by the second decade of the nineteenth century, if we are to believe the testimony from Edward Wakefield quoted in the previous chapter. Young attempted to act with prudence and economy in his status as a sometime estate agent and owner of an experimental farm of modest size. He fit snugly between and was firmly opposed to the stereotypically thoughtless excesses of aristocratic landowners, who had little interest beyond hunting, drinking, and carousing, and then again the stereotypical ignorance of many tenant farmers.

Both Young and Marshall sought to establish and signal their credibility by promoting prowess and probity in observing, reporting, and actually farming. But, again, Marshall's ideal traveler travels, then stops. Marshall issues a scathing, thinly veiled criticism of Young in this regard. Any traveler who follows Young's method will fail as an observer fit to make a *"general Report"* on agriculture in the district thus passed over,

> For what a man, even of such acquirements, can collect from enquiries, is beneath public attention. An ENQUIRING TOURIST ... must be liable to be led into error at every step, and to be imposed upon by every one with whom he may happen to converse.
> (Marshall, *The Review and Abstract*, p. xxxiii, emphasis in original)

The epithet refers to Young, who labels some of his travels tours, such as *A six weeks tour, through the southern counties of England and Wales* (1768), and *A six months tour through the north of England* (1771). Neither account would satisfy Marshall's methodological prescription for a general report on a single district.

Adam Smith envisions yet two more types of economic men on view in commercial society in the sixth and final edition of *Theory of Moral Sentiments* (1790). He writes, in a new chapter on propriety, that character and conduct, subjectivity and agency, reflect not individual, innate moral virtue, but are malleable, the result of both individual desires and social factors, the play of passions and the desire to seek approbation in the theater of public life.[131] Economic inequality activates self-interested behavior, and thus stimulates commercial activity. But this "is, at the same time, the great and most universal cause of the corruption of our moral sentiments", because applause is proffered for wealth and power, in contradistinction to poverty and weakness, which people are too often prone to despise (*TMS*, I. iii. 3. 1). If the "great objects of ambition and emulation" are to "enjoy the respect and admiration of mankind",

> Two different roads are presented to us, equally leading to the attainment of this so much desired object; the one, by the study of wisdom and the practice of virtue; the other, by the acquisition of wealth and greatness. Two different characters are presented to our emulation; the one of proud ambition and avidity; the other, of humble modesty and equitable justice. Two different models, two different pictures, are held out to us, according to which we may fashion our own character and behaviour; the one more gaudy and glittering in its colouring; the other more correct and exquisitely beautiful in its outline; the one forcing itself upon the notice of every wandering eye; the other, attracting the

> attention of scarce any body but the most studious and careful observer. They are the wise and the virtuous chiefly, a select, though I am afraid, but a small party, who are the real and steady admirers of wisdom and virtue. The great mob of mankind are the admirers and worshippers, and what may seem more extraordinary, most frequently the disinterested admirers and worshippers of wealth and greatness.
>
> <div align="right">(<i>TMS</i>, I. iii. 3. 1)</div>

Only a rare observer of society had the skills to discern both true beauty and true virtue, and avoid distraction from the displays of the wealthy. Moreover, while disinterest constituted a necessary attribute for credible travel observations, this was not necessarily true for observations at home. Smith tempers his pessimistic assessment of human nature and capacity for aesthetic and moral judgment by concluding that men in commercial society, in the main, were virtuous. Attitudes and behavior that typified virtue were almost always synonymous with those that characterized successful fortune seeking by men in stations below the highest ranks:

> In the middling and inferior stations of life, the road to virtue and that to fortune, to such fortune, at least, as men in such situations can reasonably expect to acquire, are, happily, in most cases, very nearly the same. In all the middling and inferior professions, real and solid professional abilities, joined to prudent, just, and temperate conduct, can very seldom fail of success ... Men in the inferior and middling stations of life, besides, can never be great enough to be above the law, which generally must overawe them into some sort of respect for, at least, the more important rules of justice. The success of such people, too, almost always depends upon the favour and good opinion of their neighbors and equals; and without a tolerably regular conduct these, can seldom be obtained. The good old proverb, therefore, that honesty is the best policy, holds, in such situations, almost perfectly true. In such situations, therefore, we may generally expect a considerable degree of virtue; and, fortunately for the good morals of society, these are the situations of by far the greater part of mankind.
>
> <div align="right">(<i>TMS</i>, I. iii. 3. 2)</div>

Smith derives his empirical results, where the real economic man closely approaches the ideal, from his fine-grained interpretation, neither wholly deductive nor inductive, of observable social interactions in what contemporaries were beginning to categorize as typical attributes of commercial societies, viewed through a stadial lens. Respect for the law and sociability constrain the "greater part of mankind" to behave virtuously in such societies. The capacity for and use of language was key to sociability. For Smith the play of language over the course of history had enabled not just the exchange of an increasing volume of goods, but also the increased circulation of sentiments and sympathy. Increasingly complex and sophisticated conversations help establish "a sense of propriety that would socialize and individuate simultaneously". Propriety, internalized as self-approval, served as a firmer foundation for individual contentment and virtue than the approbation of others.[132]

The versions of economic man outlined above, while hardly the only models available in this period, align with ideals of femininity and childhood pushed, chiefly by women writers, from the mid eighteenth into the early nineteenth centuries in conduct books and educational treatises.[133] Authors of conduct books sought to shape both readers and their charges in order that they emulate proper behavior. Women and children were urged to carefully measure the costs and benefits of household production and consumption in these works. Economy constitutes one of the many attributes that make up virtuous behavior; paired with prudence, it helps women and children economists accumulate more for Christian charity. Smith, too, is aware of the necessity to provide young people with proper models to emulate in order that children can embrace charity as the ultimate aim of economy. Writing to Lord Shelburne from Glasgow on 29 October 1759, about Thomas Petty-Fitzmaurice, student and charge of Smith's, Smith notes Lord Shelburne's "very laudible anxiety that your son should be held to Oeconomy not that he might hoard, but that he might be able to give". Smith also assures Lord Shelburne that he had taken Thomas on a trip with him to Edinburgh rather than leave him behind in Glasgow; though Edinburgh was "a very dissolute town", and Smith was at times obliged "to sup or dine at places where it was improper to carry him"; he had provided Thomas fitting models for emulation, having "ordered a small entertainment at our lodgings and invited two or three young lawyers to keep him company".[134]

Political economists paid little heed to the conduct and methods proposed by Marshall for his ideal travelers. They also took issue with the new economic man put forth by Young: no matter how well-versed in observing and reporting, and how prudently he managed farms, if he aped other aspects of political arithmetic, he was unpalatable to political economists. They blanched at what they regarded as an unhealthy tendency for political arithmeticians to support policies that would increase not just the revenue of the state, but state control. They also decried what they saw as the undisciplined exuberance of political arithmeticians for counting without apparent end. Stewart, for instance, argues that political arithmeticians focus too readily on facts:

> The facts accumulated by the statistical collector are merely particular results, which other men have seldom an opportunity of verifying or of disproving; and which, to those who consider them in an insulated state, can never afford any important information ... If these observations be just, instead of appealing to political arithmetic as a check on

the conclusions of political economy, it would often be more reasonable to have recourse to political economy as a check on the extravagancies of political arithmetic.[135]

Stewart indicates that individual facts hold little scientific value for political economists unless tethered to systematic analyses. Like those offered by political economy. Hence Stewart notes, "In general, as Mr. Smith remarks, little stress ought to be laid to the results of what is commonly called Political Arithmetic."

While Smith expressed the opinion that "I have no great faith in political arithmetick", he acquired twelve volumes by Young and works by other political arithmeticians for his library (*WN*, IV. V, note 26).[136] In the preface to the second edition of *Essay* Malthus credits Young as well for helping prepare the ground for his work on the "poverty and misery arising from a too rapid increase in population".[137] But that is getting ahead of our story. Malthus's first *Essay on Population* (1798) dropped like a grenade into long running discussions on the size of England's population and whether it had increased, stagnated, or decreased since the Glorious Revolution of 1688. The basic facts were in dispute. The British had not conducted a population census in modern times for fears that census takers would trench on civil liberties, strengthen the hands of revenue takers (a goal of political arithmeticians), and allow the state to snoop into the most intimate details of individual households. The increasingly costly conflict with revolutionary France helped overturn such sentiment in England; the nation needed facts about the manpower at her disposal. In late 1800, the British Parliament agreed to the first population census for England, Scotland, and Wales, to be conducted on 10 March 1801.

Prior to the census one could only stitch together population estimates based primarily on local parish registers of baptism and deaths, and no one dared to claim that the ensuing numbers were definitive. The debate had mixed religious and moral concerns with state policy regarding trade, food prices, and wages. Had the rise of commerce and the consequent increase in consumption of imported luxuries, principally from Catholic France, so sapped the moral and physical energies of Protestant England that population had not increased? Should food be cheap so English families could more easily rear up an abundance of workers, thus making English exports inexpensive? Or should food prices be dear so as to support the agricultural sector, a suggestion that held sway in a Parliament largely run by rural landholders? Malthus asserted that the population principle was universal, and uses botanical examples from natural history to argue against human perfectibility in *Essay*.[138] For more proof, he packed his trunks, bags, and notebooks to travel to Scandinavia in 1799, in order to see for himself if that were the case in a land with topography, climate, history, and institutions very different from those in England. His trip forms the point of departure for the next chapter.

Notes

1 John Bush, *Hibernia Curiosa* (London: W. Flexney, 1769), p. 34. Further references to *Hibernia Curiosa* are included parenthetically in the text.
2 Daniel Carey, "Inquiries, Heads, and Directions: Orienting Early Modern Travel", in Judy A. Hayden, ed., *Travel Narratives, the New Science, and Literary Discourse, 1569–1750* (Burlington, VT: Ashgate, 2012), pp. 25–51.
3 John Gascoigne, "The Royal Society, Natural History and the Peoples of the 'New World(s)', 1660–1800", *The British Society for the History of Science*, 42, no. 4 (2009): 539–62 (at p. 540).
4 Barbara J. Shapiro, *A Culture of Fact: England, 1550–1720* (Ithaca, NY: Cornell University Press, 2000), and Joseph M. Levine, "Review [of Shapiro, Barbara J. (2000) *A Culture of Fact: England, 1550–1720*, Ithaca, NY: Cornell University Press]", *Albion*, 33, no. 1 (2001): 102–3 (at p. 102). See also Steven Shapin and Simon Schaffer, *Leviathan and the Air-Pump: Hobbes, Boyle, and the Experimental Life* (Princeton, NJ: Princeton University Press, 1985); Shapin, *A Social History of Truth*.
5 Hayden, "Intersections and Cross-Fertilization", pp. 10–1.
6 Shapin, *A Social History of Truth*. This mirrors contemporary discussions in England about political representation. Gentleman depended more on fixed capital, typically land, than did merchants, capitalists, projectors, and speculators. Hence the interests of rural landowners aligned more closely to the fate of the state on account of the immobility of their capital.
7 Palmira Fontes da Costa, *The Singular and the Making of Knowledge at the Royal Society of London in the Eighteenth Century* (Cambridge: Cambridge Scholars, 2009), p. 147.
8 Bravo, "Precision and Curiosity in Scientific Travel", p. 165.
9 Jason H. Pearl, "Geography and Authority in the Royal Society Instructions", in Judy A. Hayden, ed., *Travel Narratives, the New Science, and Literary Discourse, 1569–1750* (Burlington, VT: Ashgate, 2012), pp. 71–83.
10 Joan-Pau Rubiés, "From the 'History of Travayle' to the History of Travel Collections: The Rise of an Early Modern Genre", in Daniel Carey and Claire Jowitt, eds., *Richard Hakluyt and Travel Writing in Early Modern Europe* (New York: Ashgate, 2012), pp. 25–41 (at pp. 26–8, 30–3); David Harris Sacks, "'To Deduce a Colonie': Richard Hakluyt's Godly Mission in Its Contexts, c. 1580–1616", in Daniel Carey and Claire Jowitt, eds., *Richard Hakluyt and Travel Writing in Early Modern Europe* (New York: Ashgate, 2012), pp. 197–218.
11 Ashley Eva Millar, *A Singular Case: Debating China's Political Economy in the European Enlightenment* (Montreal, QC: McGill-Queen's Press, 2017), pp. 55–8; Robert Mayhew, "The Character of English Geography c. 1660–1800: A Textual Approach", *Journal of Historical Geography*, 24, no. 4 (1998): 385–412.
12 Rubiés, "From the 'History of Travayle' to the History of Travel Collections", pp. 40–1.
13 *Instructions* represents an expanded version of "General Directions for Travellers, etc.," part of *The Elements of Commerce and Theory of Taxes*, which Tucker had privately printed and distributed in 1755. George Shelton, *Dean Tucker and 18th-Century Economics and Political Thought* (New York: Macmillan, 1981), pp. 89, 105.
14 Joan-Pau Rubiés, "Christianity and Civilization in Sixteenth Century Ethnological Discourse", in Henriette Brugge and Joan-Pau Rubiés, eds., *Shifting Cultures: Interaction and Discourse in the Expansion of Europe* (Münster: Lit Verlag, 1995), pp. 35–60 (at pp. 42–3).
15 John Smith, *The Generall Historie of Virginia* (1624), p. 158. http://docsouth.unc.edu/southlit/smith/smith.html [27 January 2013].

16 Allison Games, *The Web of Empire: English Cosmopolitans in an Age of Expansion, 1560–1660* (New York: Oxford University Press, 2008).
17 Chlöe Houston, "'Thou Glorious Kingdome, Thou Chiefe of Empires': Persia in Early Seventeenth-Century Travel Literature", *Studies in Travel Writing*, 13, no. 2 (2009): 141–52.
18 Games, *The Web of Empire*, pp. 12, 79.
19 Sebastian Cabot, "Ordinances for the Direction of the Intended Voyage for Cathay, Dated May, 9, 1553.", [n.d.] Reprinted in John Pinkerton, *A General Collection of the Best and Most Interesting Voyages and Travels in All Parts of the World: Many of Which Are Now First Translated into English; Digested on a New Plan*, vol. I (London: Longman, Hurst, Rees, and Orme, 1808), pp. 1–7 (at p. 5).
20 Robert K. Batchelor, *London: The Selden Map and the Making of a Global City, 1549–1689* (Chicago, IL: Chicago University Press, 2014), pp. 34–8.
21 Cabot, "Ordinances for the Direction of the Intended Voyage for Cathay", p. 3.
22 Cabot, "Ordinances for the Direction of the Intended Voyage for Cathay", p. 6.
23 Cabot, "Ordinances for the Direction of the Intended Voyage for Cathay", p. 5.
24 Games, *The Web of Empire*, pp. 255–87.
25 William Eamon, "From the Secrets of Nature to Public Knowledge", in David C. Lundberg and Robert S. Westman, eds., *Reappraisals of the Scientific Revolution* (Cambridge: Cambridge University Press, 1990), pp. 333–66.
26 Hayden, "Intersections and Cross-Fertilization", p. 17; Daniel Carey, "Inquiries, Heads, and Directions: Orienting Early Modern Travel", in Judy A. Hayden, ed., *Travel Narratives, the New Science, and Literary Discourse, 1569–1750* (Burlington, VT: Ashgate, 2012), pp. 25–51.
27 Carey, "Inquiries, Heads, and Directions", pp. 27–31.
28 Lux and Cook, "Closed Circles or Open Networks", p. 179.
29 Daniel Carey, "Compiling Nature's History: Travellers and Travel Narratives in the Early Royal Society", *Annals of Science*, 54, no. 3 (1997): 269–92.
30 Burke, "The Philosopher as Traveller"; Jaś Elsner, and Joan-Pau Rubiés, "Introduction", in J. Elsner and Joan-Pau Rubiés, eds., *Voyages and Visions: Towards a Cultural History of Travel* (London: Reaktion Books, 1999), pp. 1–56 (at p. 50).
31 Cabot, "Ordinances for the Direction of the Intended Voyage for Cathay", p. 2.
32 William Davison, Robert Devereux, and Philip Sidney, *Profitable Instructions Describing What Special Observations Are to Be Taken by Travellers in All Nations, States and Countries; Pleasant and Profitable* (London: Benjamin Fisher, 1633), pp. 58–9, 64–5.
33 Carey, "Inquiries, Heads, and Directions", pp. 283, 285–6.
34 Robert Boyle, "General Heads for a Natural History of a Country, Great or Small, Imparted Likewise by Mr. Boyle", *Philosophical Transactions of the Royal Society*, 1 (1665–6): 186–9 (at pp. 188, 186, 189, emphasis in original). See Hayden, "Intersections and Cross-Fertilization", pp. 9–10.
35 James Kelly, "Bordering on Fact in Early Eighteenth-Century Sea Journals", in Dan Doll and Jessica Munns, eds., *Recording and Reordering: Essays on the Seventeenth- and Eighteenth-Century Diary and Journal* (Cranbury, NJ: Bucknell University Press, 2006), pp. 158–84 (at pp. 164–5).
36 Cristina Malcolmson, *Studies of Skin Color in the Early Royal Society: Boyle, Cavendish, Swift* (Burlington, VT: Ashgate, 2013), pp. 2, 63, 30.
37 Malcolmson, *Studies of Skin Color*, p. 58; Daston, Lorraine, "The Ideal and Reality of the Republic of Letters", *Science in Context* 4, no. 2 (1991): 367–86 (at pp. 338, 342).
38 Robert Boyle, "*Experiments and Considerations Touching Colours*", London (1664) http://www.gutenberg.org/files/14504/14504-h/14504-h.htm#Page_151 [13 April 2020]; Malcolmson, *Studies of Skin Color*, pp. 31–7.

39 Lorraine Daston, "Baconian Facts, Academic Civility, and the Prehistory of Objectivity", in Alan Megill, ed., *Rethinking Objectivity* [1991] (Durham, NC: Duke University Press, 1994), pp. 37–63 (at pp. 49–50).
40 Malcolmson, *Studies of Skin Color*, pp. 22–3; Mark Govier, "The Royal Society, Slavery and the Island of Jamaica: 1660–1700", *Notes and Records of the Royal Society of London*, 53, no. 2 (1999): 203–17 (at pp. 204, 206–7).
41 Malcolmson, *Studies of Skin Color*, p. 4.
42 Ira Berlin, *Many Thousands Gone: The First Two Centuries of Slavery in North America* (Cambridge, MA: Harvard University Press, 1998), pp. 15–177; Mary Floyd-Wilson, *English Ethnicity and Race in Early Modern Drama* (Cambridge: Cambridge University Press, 2003), p. 140.
43 See Siep Stuurman, "François Bernier and the Invention of Racial Classification", *History Workshop Journal*, 50, no. 1 (2000): 1–21, and Thierry Hoquet, "Biologization of Race and Racialization of the Human: Bernier, Buffon, Linnaeus", in Nicolas Bancel, Thomas David, and Dominic Thomas, eds., *The Invention of Race: Scientific and Popular Representations* (New York: Routledge, 2014), pp. 17–32.
44 Sebastiani, *The Scottish Enlightenment*, p. 14.
45 Nicholas Hudson, "From 'Nation' to 'Race': The Origin of Racial Classification in Eighteenth-Century Thought", *Eighteenth-Century Studies*, 29, no. 3 (1996): 247–64; Michael Keevak, *Becoming Yellow: A Short History of Racial Thinking* (Princeton, NJ: Princeton University Press, 2011); Andrew S. Curran, *The Anatomy of Blackness: Science and Slavery in an Age of Enlightenment* (Baltimore, MD: Johns Hopkins University Press, 2011).
46 T.C. Jacques, "From Savages and Barbarians to Primitives: Africa, Social Typologies, and History in 18th-Century French Philosophy", *History and Theory*, 36, no. 2 (1997): 190–215.
47 Bronwen Douglas, *Science, Voyages, and Encounters in Oceania, 1511–1850* (New York: Palgrave Macmillan, 2014); Roxanne Wheeler, *The Complexion of Race: Categories of Difference in Eighteenth-Century British Culture* (Philadelphia, PA: University of Pennsylvania Press, 2000).
48 Josiah Tucker, *A Brief Essay on the Advantages and Disadvantages, Which Respectively Attend France and Great Britain, with Regard to Trade* (1749), 2nd edn. (London: Printed for T. Tyre, 1750), p. 137.
49 Anon., "Proctor's *Journey across the Cordillera of the Andes*", *Monthly Review, or Literary Journal Enlarged*, 107 (1825): 128–40 (at p. 130).
50 David Cahill, "Colour by Numbers: Racial and Ethnic Categories in the Viceroyalty of Peru", *Journal of Latin American Studies*, 26, no. 2 (1994): 325–46; Stuart B. Schwartz, "Colonial Identities and the sociedad de castas", *Colonial Latin America Review*, 4, no. 1 (1995): 185–201; Karen B. Graubart, "The Creolization of the New World: Local Forms of Identification in Urban Colonial Peru, 1560–1640", *Hispanic American Historical Review*, 89, no. 3 (2009): 471–99.
51 Douglas R. Cope, *The Limits of Racial Domination: Plebeian Society in Colonial Mexico City, 1660–1720* (Madison, WI: University of Wisconsin Press, 1994), pp. 53–6; Maria Elena Martínez, *Genealogical Fictions: Limpieza de sangre, Religion, and Gender in Colonial Mexico* (Palo Alto, CA: Stanford University Press, 2008), pp. 143–6.
52 Joanne Rappaport, *The Disappearing Mestizo: Configuring Difference in the Colonial Kingdom of Granada* (Durham, NC: Duke University Press, 2014); Ilona Katzew, *Casta Paintings: Images of Race in Eighteenth-Century Mexico* (New Haven, CT: Yale University Press, 2004), p. 40; Bigelow, "Transatlantic Quechañol", p. 245.

53 William Bennet Stevenson, *A Historical and Descriptive Narrative of Twenty Years' Residence in South America*, vol. 1 (London: Hurst, Robinson, 1825), pp. 285–6.
54 Paul Ricoeur, *On Translation*, trans. Eileen Brennan (New York: Routledge, 2014), p. 22.
55 Stevenson, *A Historical and Descriptive Narrative*, vol. 1, p. 304.
56 Stevenson, *A Historical and Descriptive Narrative*, vol. 1, p. 286; Bigelow, "Transatlantic Quechañol", p. 245.
57 Stevenson, *A Historical and Descriptive Narrative*, vol. 1, p. 307.
58 Graubart, "The Creolization of the New World".
59 Joyce E. Chaplin, "Natural Philosophy and an Early Racial Idiom in North America: Comparing English and Indian Bodies", *William Mary Quarterly*, 54, no. 1 (1997): 229–52.
60 Nancy Shoemaker, "How Indians Got to Be Red", *The American Historical Review*, 102, no. 3 (1997): 625–44, and *A Strange Likeness: Becoming Red and White in Eighteenth-Century North America* (Oxford: Oxford University Press, 2004).
61 Shoemaker, *A Strange Likeness*, p. 3.
62 Shoemaker, "How Indians Got to Be Red".
63 Daniel Mandell, "Review" [of Nancy Shoemaker. *A Strange Likeness: Becoming Red and White in Eighteenth-Century North America* (New York: Oxford University Press, 2004)], H-Atlantic, H-Net Reviews (April 2005), www.h-net.org/reviews/showrev.php?id=10476 [13 March 2018].
64 Justin Stagl, "The Methodising of Travel in the 16th Century: A Tale of Three Cities", *History and Anthropology* 4, no. 2 (Amsterdam: Harwood Academic Publishers, 1990), pp. 303–38, and *A History of Curiosity: The Theory of Travel, 1550–1800* (Amsterdam: Harwood Academic Publishers, 1995), pp. 47–95.
65 Melissa Calaresu, "Looking for Virgil's Tomb: The End of the Grand Tour and the Cosmopolitan Ideal: Neapolitan Critiques of French Travel Accounts (1750–1800)", in Jás Elsner And Joan-Pau Rubiés, eds., *Voyages and Visions: Towards a Cultural History of Travel* (London: Reaktion Books, 1999), pp. 138–61 (at p. 141).
66 Margaret Hunt, "Racism, Imperialism, and the Traveler's Gaze in Eighteenth-Century England", *The Journal of British Studies*, 32, no. 4 (1993): 333–57 (at pp. 333–4).
67 William Petty, *The Petty Papers: Some Unpublished Writings of Sir William Petty*, vol. 1, ed. Marquis of Lansdowne (London: Constable & Company, 1927), pp. 40–2.
68 Joseph Addison, *Remarks on Several Parts of Italy, &c in the Years 1701, 1702, 1703* [1705] (London: J. and R. Tonson, and S. Draper, 1745), p. 94 (emphases in original).
69 Adam Smith, *An Inquiry into the Nature and Causes of the Wealth of Nations* (1776), 2 vols., *Glasgow Edition of the Works and Correspondence of Adam Smith*, vol. 3., R.H. Campbell, A.S. Skinner, and W.B. Todd, eds. (Oxford: Oxford University Press, 1978b). References to *Wealth of Nations* are included parenthetically in the text as WN with citations in the following order: book, chapter, part, article, and paragraph. Not all elements appear every time.
70 Calaresu, "Looking for Virgil's Tomb", especially pp. 150–6.
71 Calaresu, "Looking for Virgil's Tomb", pp. 146–7; David Young, "Montesquieu's View of Despotism and His Use of Travel Literature", *The Review of Politics*, 40, no. 3 (1978): 392–405.
72 Calaresu, "Looking for Virgil's Tomb", p. 149.

88 *"Instructions for Travellers"*

73 John Robertson, *The Case for the Enlightenment: Scotland and Naples, 1680–1760* (Cambridge: Cambridge University Press, 2005).
74 Calaresu, "Looking for Virgil's Tomb", p. 161.
75 Sophus Reinert, *Translating Empire: Emulation and the Origins of Political Economy* (Cambridge, MA: Harvard University Press, 2011).
76 James Livesey, "Free Trade and Empire in the Anglo-Irish Commercial Proposition", *Journal of British Studies*, 52, no. 1 (2013): 103–27 (at pp. 103, 104, 106).
77 Based on Bernard Semmel, *The Rise of Free Trade Imperialism: Classical Political Economy the Empire of Free Trade and Imperialism 1750–1850* (New York: Cambridge University Press, 1970).
78 Derived from István Hont, *Jealousy of Trade: Competition and the Nation State in Historical Perspective* (Cambridge, MA: Harvard University Press, 2005).
79 Walter Ernest Clark, *Josiah Tucker, Economist: A Study in the History of Economics* (New York: Columbia University, 1903), p. 40.
80 Josiah Tucker, *Reflections on the Expediency of a Law for the Naturalization of Foreign Protestants: In Two Parts*, Part 1 (London: Printed for T. Tyre, 1751), p. iii.
81 Tucker, *Reflections on the Expediency of a Law*, p. iv.
82 Tucker, *Reflections on the Expediency of a Law*, p. v, note.
83 Josiah Tucker, "Important Queries Occasioned by the Rejection of the late Naturalization Bill", in *A Brief Essay on the Advantages and Disadvantages Which Respectively Attend France and Great Britain, with Regard to Trade: With Some Proposals for Removing the Principal Disadvantages of Great Britain. In a New Method* (London: Printed for T. Tyre, 1753), pp. 1–48 (at pp. 1–2).
84 Tucker, *Instructions for Travellers* (1757) (Dublin: William Watson, 1758), pp. 3–4. A seventh category, which Tucker includes in a bracketed aside, indicates the rise of English power and self-confidence in Europe: only the English are prosperous and free enough to travel as fools who return no wiser, and certainly poorer, than when they left. Further references are included parenthetically in the text.
85 Christian Marouby, "Adam Smith and the Anthropology of the Enlightenment: The "Ethnographic" Sources of Economic Progress", in Larry Wolff and Marco Cipolloni, eds., *The Anthropology of the Enlightenment* (Stanford, CA: Stanford University Press, 2007), pp. 85–102 (at p. 87). Further references are included parenthetically in the text.
86 Palmeri, *State of Nature*, p. 52.
87 Neil Hargraves, "Enterprise, Adventure and Industry: The Formation of 'Commercial Character' in William Robertson's History of America", *History of European Ideas*, 29, no. 1 (2003): 33–54.
88 Palmeri, *State of Nature*, pp. 61–9.
89 Ronald L. Meek, *Social Science and the Ignoble Savage* (Cambridge: Cambridge University Press, 1976); Nathaniel Wolloch, "The Civilizing Process, Nature, and Stadial Theory", *Eighteenth-Century Studies*, 44, no. 2 (2011): 245–59 (at p. 253).
90 Ezequiel Adamovsky, "Before Development Economics: Western Political Economy, the "Russian Case", and the First Perceptions of Economic Backwardness (from the 1760s Until the Mid-nineteenth Century)", *Journal of the History of Economic Thought*, 32, no. 3 (2010): 349–76.
91 Anthony Pagden, "The Immobility of China: Orientalism and Occidentalism in the Enlightenment", in Larry Wolff and Marco Cipolloni, eds., *The Anthropology of the Enlightenment* (Stanford, CA: Stanford University Press, 2007), pp. 50–64.
92 Millar, *A Singular Case*, pp. 25, 30.

93 Adam Smith, *Lectures on Jurisprudence* (1762–3), *Glasgow Edition of the Works and Correspondence of Adam Smith*, vol. 5. R.L. Meek, D.D. Raphael, and P.G. Stein, eds. (Oxford: Oxford University Press, 1978a) (at II.17).
94 Adam Smith, *The Theory of Moral Sentiments* (1759), D.D. Raphael, and A.L. Macfie, eds., *Glasgow Edition of the Works and Correspondence of Adam Smith*, vol. 1 (Oxford: Oxford University Press, 1976) (at V.I.18). References to *The Theory of Moral Sentiments* are included parenthetically in the text as TMS with citations in the following order: book, chapter, part, article, and paragraph. Not all elements appear every time.
95 Adam Ferguson, *An Essay on the History of Civil Society* (Edinburgh: A. Millar & T. Caddel, 1767), p. 384.
96 Millar, *A Singular Case*, chapter 2.
97 Sebastiani, *The Scottish Enlightenment*, pp. 21, chapter 5.
98 Sebastiani, *The Scottish Enlightenment*, p. 146.
99 Sebastiani, *The Scottish Enlightenment*, p. 134.
100 See also Edward Puro, "Use of the Term 'Natural' in Adam Smith's Wealth of Nations", *Research in the History of Economic Thought and Methodology*, 9 (1992): 73–86, and Margaret Schabas, *The Natural Origins of Economics* (Chicago, IL: The University of Chicago Press, 2005).
101 Dugald Stewart, *Elements of the Philosophy of the Human Mind* [1792]) vols. 1 and 2 (Albany, NY: E. and E. Hosford, 1822), p. 296.
102 Palmeri, *State of Nature*, p. 7.
103 On Smith's tendency to systematically undervalue women's production see Kathryn Sutherland, "Adam Smith's Master Narrative: Women and the *Wealth of Nations*", in Stephen Copley and Kathryn Sutherland, eds., *Adam Smith's Wealth of Nations: New Interdisciplinary Essays* (Manchester: Manchester University Press, 1995), pp. 97–121.
104 Palmeri, *State of Nature*, p. 41.
105 Jan de Vries, "The Industrial Revolution and the Industrious Revolution", *The Journal of Economic History*, 54, no. 2 (1994): 249–70, and *The Industrious Revolution: Consumer Behavior and the Household Economy, 1650 to the Present* (New York: Cambridge University Press, 2008).
106 Whether any political economist would actually ever believe in such a creature, given the paeans to self-interest in their work, remains doubtful.
107 George Cooper, *Letters on the Irish Nation: Written during a Visit to that Kingdom, in the Autumn of the Year 1799* (London: J. Davis for J. White, 1800). p. xxv. Cooper came out with a revised and expanded second edition in 1801, also published by J. White. Further references to *Letters* are included parenthetically in the text by publication date.
108 Anon., "Cooper's *Letters on the Irish Nation*", *The Anti-Jacobin Review and Magazine*, 7 (1801): 173–8 (at p. 176).
109 Anon., "Retrospect of Domestic Literature. – Irish Politics.", *The Monthly Magazine, or, British Register, Supplementary Number to the Monthly Magazine*, 10, no. 68 (1800): 597 (at p. 597).
110 Anon., "Cooper's Letters on the Irish Nation", *The New London Review; or, Monthly Report of Authors and Books*, 3 (1800): 49–56 (at pp. 51, 52).
111 Cooper omits this sentence from the 1801 edition.
112 Siegfried Huigen, *Knowledge and Colonialism: Eighteenth-Century Travellers in South Africa* (Leiden: Brill, 2009), pp. 178 and 179–81. Further references to *Knowledge and Colonialism* are included parenthetically in the text.
113 From "Inleiding", in *Verhandelingen over den Oost-Indischen Handel*. Amsterdam: Weduwe Doll. Iii–iv. "Inleiding" translates variously as "Preface" or "Introduction".

114 John Barrow, *An Account of Travels into the Interior of Southern Africa, in the Years 1797 and 1798*, vol. 1 (London: T. Cadell, junior and W. Davies, 1801), p. 6. Further references to *Travels* are included parenthetically in the text.
115 Robert Jacob Gordon, "Fourth Journey" [From 27 June 1779 to 13 January 1780], trans. Patrick Cullinan (Johannesburg, SA: Brenthurst Library), MSS 107/3/1, from 27 June 1779 to 21 October 1779, pp. 1–59 (at p. 6). (14 February 2017) https://www.robertjacobgordon.nl/travel-journals/fourth-journey/fourth-journey [4 June 2018]
116 Gordon, "Fourth Journey", pp. 18–22.
117 Alexander Gillespie, *Gleanings and Remarks: Collected during Many Months of Residence at Buenos Ayres, and within the Upper Country* (Leeds: B. Dewhirst, 1818), p. 17.
118 Brian Bonnyman, *The Third Duke of Buccleuch and Adam Smith: Estate Management and Improvement in Enlightenment Scotland* (Edinburgh: Edinburgh University Press, 2014).
119 Robert Carson Allen and Cormac Ó Gráda, "On the Road Again with Arthur Young: English, Irish, and French Agriculture during the Industrial Revolution", *The Journal of Economic History*, 48, no. 1 (1988): 93–116; Liam Brunt, "Rehabilitating Arthur Young", *The Economic History Review*, 56, no. 2 (2003): 265–99; Terry Reilly, "Arthur Young's *Travels in France*: Historicity and the Use of Literary Forms", in Dan Doll and Jessica Munns, eds., *Recording and Reordering: Essays on the Seventeenth- and Eighteenth-Century Diary and Journal* (Cranbury, NJ: Bucknell University Press, 2006), pp. 122–36.
120 Reilly, "Arthur Young's *Travels in France*", pp. 122–3, 124, 126–8.
121 Peter Remien, "Oeconomy and Ecology in Early Modern England", *PMLA*, 132, no. 5 (2017): 1117–33 (at p. 1118).
122 Remien, "Oeconomy and Ecology", pp. 1121–3; Keith Tribe, "Oeconomic History", *Studies in the History and Philosophy of Science*, Part A, 36, no. 3 (2005): 586–97 (at pp. 592–3).
123 Lissa Roberts, "Practicing Oeconomy during the Second Half of the Long Eighteenth Century: An Introduction", *History and Technology*, 30, no. 3 (2014): 133–48 (at p. 133).
124 Remien, "Oeconomy and Ecology", pp. 1119, 1120.
125 Schabas, *The Natural Origins*.
126 Remien, "Oeconomy and Ecology", pp. 1120–1.
127 Remien, "Oeconomy and Ecology", pp. 1118, 1119.
128 William Marshall, *A Review (and Complete Abstract) of the Reports to the Board of Agriculture from the Midland Department of England* (York: Thomas Wilson and Sons, 1815), p. iii.
129 William Marshall, *The Review and Abstract of the County Reports to the Board of Agriculture* [1808], 1st edn. (York: Thomas Wilson and Sons, 1818), "Advertisement": pp. 14, 15. Further references to *The Review and Abstract* are included parenthetically in the text.
130 Beth Fowkes Tobin, "Arthur Young, Agriculture, and the Construction of the New Economic Man", in Beth Fowkes Tobin, ed., *History, Gemder, and 18th-Century Literature* (Athens, GA: University of Georgia Press, 1994), pp. 179–97.
131 E.J. Hundert, "Sociability and Self-Love in the Theatre of Moral Sentiments: Mandeville to Adam Smith", in Stefan Collini, Richard Whatmore, and Brian Young, eds., *Economy, Polity, and Society: British Intellectual History* (Cambridge: Cambridge University Press, 2000), pp. 31–47 (at pp. 32, 41–6).
132 Nicholas Phillipson, "Language, Sociability, and History: Some Reflections on the Foundations of Adam Smith's Science of Man", in Stefan Collini, Richard Whatmore, and Brian Young, eds., *Economy, Polity, and Society: British*

Intellectual History (Cambridge: Cambridge University Press, 2000), pp. 70–84 (at p. 80); Brian P. Cooper, *Family Fictions and Family Facts: Harriet Martineau, Adolphe Quetelet, and the Population Question in England, 1789–1859* (London and New York: Routledge, 2007), pp. 46–8.

133 Cooper, *Family Fictions and Family Facts*, chapter 3.
134 The letter was advertised by The 19th Century Rare Book and Photograph Shop in August 2020.
135 Stewart, *Elements*, pp. 228–9.
136 Robert W. Dimand, "'I Have No Great Faith in Political Arithmetick'": Adam Smith and Quantitative Political Economy", in Ingrid H. Rima, ed., *Measurement, Quantification and Economic Analysis: Numeracy in Economics* (London: Routledge, 1995), pp. 22–30.
137 Thomas Robert Malthus, *An Essay on the Principle of Population*, 2nd edn. (London: J. Johnson, 1803), p. iv.
138 J. Marc MacDonald, "Malthus and the Philanthropists, 1764–1859: The Cultural Circulation of Political Economy, Botany, and Natural Knowledge", *Social Sciences*, MDPI, Open Access Journal, 6, no. 1 (2017): 1–33 (at p. 11).

3 Travels with Malthus
The Population Principle in the Field

The geographical references in the 1798 *Essay* range far and wide, but it contains scant evidence on the population principle. So, in the late spring of 1799, Malthus and three companions headed to Scandinavia. Fresh off the notoriety of *Essay*, he sought real-world confirmation of the workings of the population principle and the peninsula, while a remote, little-visited region at the time, remained one of the few areas of war-torn Europe still accessible to English travelers. Malthus incorporated details from his trip, the first outside of England for the thirty-three-year old, as well as evidence from other travelers on the operation of the population principle in the greatly expanded post-1798 versions of *Essay*.

The first section of the chapter addresses the apparent lack of discussion among political economists about an important aspect of the division they posited between the art and science of political economy. When Malthus relates in his notes how the population principle works in Norway, he exposes the split between political and domestic economy, one marker of the boundaries of British political economy, as a divide more apparent than real.[1] True, British political economists ignored domestic economy as matter of epistemology if not ontology. The nascent discipline's subjects and agents were almost universally masculine as a consequence. Malthus's Norwegian experiences signify, however, how household management and women occupied central, if little acknowledged places in his political economy: the dynamics of family formation and behavior governed how the population principle operated in real life.

The second section of the chapter addresses work by two well-known English contemporaries of Malthus, who also draw on travel observations to comment on the relationship between domestic and political economies: Edward Daniel Clarke and Hannah More. Clarke traveled with Malthus to Scandinavia, and borrowed and adapted Malthus's Norwegian notes in *Travels in Various Countries of Europe, Asia and Africa* (1810–23). Clarke's adaptations are of interest for two reasons. First, his observations about Norwegian household labor call into question his credibility as an observer in a manner that Malthus's did not. Second, Clarke was no unabashed free

DOI: 10.4324/9781315778952-3

trade supporter; he decried the fact that travel and trade had contaminated manners and morals in Christiania (present-day Oslo), Norway.

More, a prominent religious writer, abolitionist, philanthropist, and member of the Blue Stockings Society, also rails against travel and trade, indicting them as polluters of morals and manners in Christian England. In the opening pages of *Moral Sketches of Prevailing Opinions and Manners, Foreign and Domestic: With Reflections on Prayer* (1819), More presents readers with evidence of what she saw as the harm caused by hordes of English traveling to France after Waterloo. Her plaint sheds light on the interlocking ties between English domestic economy, political economy, and national, especially religious, character. More points to the reality and necessity of wage work for working-class Englishwomen. She calls on upper class women to limit their travel and confine their spending to domestically produced items, in order to buttress the earnings of their poor "sisters". Wealthy women's purchases could thus extend the boundaries of women's sphere from family to factory, and across the Channel to France. More's tract and the discussion it set off in the British periodical press on bias and prejudice in observations and the nature of evidence in economic analysis allows us another glimpse at debates about the contours of political economy: More supports a consciously Christian political economy emphasizing female consumption in the service of spirituality, forged from her religious belief and many years of experience in the politics and economics of charity and abolition.

The third section of the chapter returns to Malthus, and pivots to post-1798 versions of *Essay*, where he presents observations from his Norway excursion and his 1817 trip to Switzerland. His analysis underscores again the intertwined relationship of domestic and political economies; Malthus finds that the preventive check predominates in both countries, and he posits that it is because habits of prudence, cleanliness, and foresight have taken hold in poor households. His recounting of conversations from his travels in Switzerland details as well how peasants derive knowledge from experience which nearly replicates expert knowledge in political economy. As Malthus notes, however, political economists will know and use social statistics; readers of *Essay* will assume that Swiss peasants will not. The acquisition of such expertise was one way to wall off political economy from other forms of knowledge such as domestic economy.

Malthus and other political economists hoped to gather evidence from travelers about the relationship between economic principles and real life. They also sought, most vociferously in debates over free trade, to bring about the day when those principles would fully operate in real life. The chapter concludes with an examination of two cases where Malthus issued instructions for travelers to India which illustrate these two imperatives. For the first, Malthus asked Sir James Mackintosh to conduct statistical inquiries relevant to determining the operation of the population principle in India. For the second, Malthus tried to mold the conduct of graduates of the East India College to be consistent with his principle of moral restraint, which recast the traditional Christian virtue of prudence as a marker and driver of material progress.

Malthus gathered observations in order to see how the population principle operated in environments very different from England. It's important to emphasize that Malthus does not question *if* the principle works, rather *how* it works. His own observations from Norway and Switzerland take up parts of one chapter each in *Essay*. The bulk of Malthus's translations of travel accounts that made it into *Essay* have to do with how he uses the criteria of the principle of population as well as that of stadial histories to turn the travel writings of others who are not political economists into evidence. The various couplings of the population principle, stadial histories, and observations generated by, but not restricted to, natural histories, missionaries' reports, and statistical accounts do not, however, always end happily in *Essay*. Some travelers cited by Malthus in *Essay* locate happiness in societies that Malthus would classify as being wracked by misery. That Malthus resolves these epistemological and ontological conflicts in favor of the population principle throughout the successive editions of *Essay* should come as no surprise. He simply sticks to his principle.

Malthus on Norway: Observations on the Boundaries of Political Economy

By the close of the eighteenth century, travel accounts had helped shape a common set of British perceptions about Norway; it was vast, sparsely peopled, cold, and dotted with lofty peaks. Few Britons had actually visited Norway, though they were unexceptional foreigners in this regard.[2] Nonetheless, despite the paucity of first-hand accounts, what was clear to Britons was just how different Norway was from their home kingdoms. Unlike Britain, the combined kingdoms of Denmark-Norway hardly qualified as a military power. And, compared to England, Norway was a commercial weakling. It had little in the way of manufacturing; isolated on the periphery of Europe, Norway's population, composed mainly of farmers and fisherman, traded primary goods from its mines, forests, and coastal waters in international markets.

These British visions of Norway had been in circulation long before Malthus took his trip. Mary Wollstonecraft's *Letters Written During a Short Residence in Sweden, Norway, and Denmark* (1796), immediately popular among English readers, would seem a possible resource for Malthus in preparation for his journey. In her own words, Wollstonecraft, who had published more than twenty reviews of travel books in the *Analytical Review*, was considered during her trip as a "woman of observation" who asks "*men's questions*".[3] Wollstonecraft draws on her own body of work, natural history, and the writings of Rousseau, to relay, in twenty-five letters, observations on the rights of women in Scandinavia, and, more generally, the often-fraught relationships between self and others in commercial society. Malthus knew of Wollstonecraft's work, having read Godwin's *Memoirs* of her, published in January 1798, and her *Posthumous Works*; he used the same publisher as Wollstonecraft had for *Vindication of the Rights of Women*. But, like many of his contemporaries, Malthus recoiled in disgust from Godwin's forthright revelations of the sexual egalitarianism of Wollstonecraft and their circle; he objected as well to its explicit tie to the French Revolution at a time when British military fortunes against France were at their bleakest. Bederman suggests that Malthus's alarm at Wollstonecraft's sexual freedom was the principal, if unintended, spur for him to put the population principle in the first edition of *Essay*; if all women took the same opportunities to cohabit outside of marriage, population would explode.[4]

Whatever the reason, Malthus apparently did not avail himself of *Letters*, despite its initial popularity. He instead relied on two other guides. *Natural History of Norway* (1755), by Erich Pontoppidan, a Danish bishop, historian, and antiquary, was one. The other, which Wollstonecraft also consulted, was William Coxe's *Travels into Poland, Russia, Sweden, and Denmark* (1791).[5] The tenor of travel writing on Norway, and the North generally, shifted in the decades between *Natural History* and *Travels*, a change partially reflected in the titles. *Natural History* was just that, a natural history, a straightforward representation of Norway's air, water, minerals, flora, fauna, etc. Though Pontoppidan does observe the "Dispositions, Customs, and Manner of Living of the Inhabitants", as announced on the title page, he chose to limit his discussion of the social life of the Norwegians to their effects on subjects of natural history.

Coxe's *Travels* appears to have more direct influence on Malthus's note-taking than Pontoppidan's account. Coxe, an English priest and historian, opens his chapters on Norway by claiming to first offer "a few general observations on the history, geography, climate, and productions" of the kingdom.[6] This range of topics hearkens back to the information The Royal Society and Josiah Tucker asked travelers to gather, especially if they were interested in improving theories of trade and taxation. As promised, Coxe provides only a very brief, two-page summary of Norway's political history and geography. His first contemporary observation draws the reader directly into the pre-Malthusian debates on population. Coxe notes that Norway's "population is by no means adequate to its extent", a common enough sentiment. He supports this conclusion, however, with statistical facts, a table on Norway's births and deaths, "which may assist us in forming a probable statement of the population of Norway". Coxe proceeds to do just that, estimating the population of Norway by using the data in the table in two different ways. With the first, Coxe assumes that "one in 35 dies annually" in the kingdom; with the second, he adapts Richard Price's method, which Coxe refers to as "the usual mode of calculation", and multiplies the annual number of births by 30 (Coxe, *Travels*, pp. 189 and 190–1).

Coxe fills much of the remainder of his account on Norway with descriptions of Norway's natural scenery and towns, apart from a lengthy digression on the centuries-long speculation on the cause of death of Charles XII of Sweden at the fortress of Fredriksten (Coxe, *Travels*, pp. 211–7). But Coxe follows his speculations on population with observations focused primarily on Norwegian commerce and frequently imparts facts useful to merchants, analysts, and policy makers. These include statistics on employment, production, costs, and revenues of forest products and mines, the price of "milch" cows, bulls, and horses, and the like (Coxe, *Travels*, pp. 245–6). He does not shy away from assigning causes for these facts. Some of the causes are natural, such as Norway's soil and climate. Others Coxe terms artificial. He ascribes increases in agricultural productivity, for example, to the efforts of the "patriotic society, which gives premiums for the best improvements and instructions in every part of farming" (Coxe, *Travels*, p. 203).

Coxe did not support completely unfettered free trade. He cites with approval, for example, the continued operation of silver mines and works outside Kongsberg, sites that often lose money and generate, at best, little revenue, but ensure much employment of those "who would be otherwise incapable of gaining their livelihood". The works have the added benefit of producing a supply of specie in a land where currency is scarce (Coxe, *Travels*, p. 235). Coxe also endorses, in mercantilist terms, the recent establishment of a cobalt mine near Fossum. He hails it as "a great acquisition to Denmark, as besides giving employment to so many hands, it prevents the importation of Prussian blue" (Coxe, *Travels*, p. 240). Coxe applies political economy unsystematically in *Travels*, however, and offers no detailed suggestions on how to observe while traveling.

Malthus's notes on Norway appear similarly fragmented. But we can deduce something of Malthus's stance on observational methods from the recollections of his travel companion Clarke, a clergyman, mineralogist and antiquarian. Clarke had a reputation as a less than credible author of travel accounts; James attributes Malthus's reticence to lend Clarke his own notebooks to Clarke's history of altering and embellishing the work of others when he incorporated them into his own narratives. Malthus's fears were realized when Clarke mangled his diary entries in the fifth volume of *Travels*.[7] In his "Authors Preface" to the posthumously published ninth volume, however, Clarke avers that

> In his descriptions, he has scrupulously endeavoured to present the Reader with the whole of what he saw; not to select according to his own fancy, but to report faithfully every thing as it appeared; because it is often from a body of evidence, that accurate conclusions are deduced. It is also this kind of evidence which places beyond dispute the *autopsy* of a traveller; and distinguishes him from the mere writer of Travels, who never himself saw what he relates.[8]

Putting his sullied reputation aside, this reads as standard paratext, testifying to the credibility of the author and what follows. But Clarke could not possibly have seen everything that Malthus did. By borrowing Malthus's eyewitness observations to craft his own account, Clarke has identified, if not named, a position he himself occupies, somewhere between a "mere writer of Travels" and a "traveller".

Malthus would most likely be a "traveller", not a "mere writer of Travels" in Clarke's estimation; why else use Malthus's journals for his own work? For the most part Malthus jotted a record of the day's happenings each evening of the trip. His journal entries approach unmediated *in media res* recordings of his observations; he adds few rhetorical flourishes or details garnished from his readings of Pontoppidan and Coxe. He had little opportunity or even incentive to frame his observations as unbiased. Yet, according to Clarke, Malthus's method of recording observations in a daily journal was much preferred to that of "Those who, without any notes of this kind, make up a book of Travels after their return home; attempting, perhaps, by the aid of invention, to supply the deficiencies of actual observation".[9]

Coxe laces his prose with elements of both the romantic and the picturesque when describing the country between Fredericstadt and Christiania. The sights include a "beautiful" cataract, "very picturesque objects", a "most delightful prospect", a scene "prettily sprinkled with numerous lakes and rivulets", one "situation ... exceedingly romantic", and another "most delightful" (Coxe, *Travels*, pp. 217–8, 220, and 221). He invokes the aesthetics of the sublime as well. Two miles from a town "we came to the top of a mountain, and burst upon as fine a view as I ever beheld", a view "on which we stood in raptures". The physical sensation literally rivets Coxe and his companions who only "at length forced ourselves from this enchanting spot" (Coxe, *Travels*, pp. 222–3). On the other hand, he recalls the landscape viewed from a summit near Dahlin as "dreary but sublime scenery". A similar sensibility leaches into his description of the peaks around the silver mining district of Kongsberg, where "the leading features of the circumjacent scenery are ruggedness and horror" (Coxe, *Travels*, pp. 249 and 233).

Malthus, in contrast, does not indulge in romantic reveries when contemplating Norway's scenery. But the form of the texts, one, Coxe's publication, polished for style, the other diary notes, quickly composed, also drives this difference. Malthus records features of the landscape in a mostly matter of fact voice, taking regular notice of the daily temperature, types and qualities of crops in the fields he passes, and fineness of the mineral deposits at the mines he and his companions visit. Malthus experiences no hairbreadth escape from wolves, who remain safely off-page, no threat of frostbite, no risk of tumbling off a precipice into an abyss, not even a quiet conversation on Norwegian sea monsters, the last a topic the credibility of which the good Bishop Pontoppidan had speculated about over the course of an entire chapter in his *Natural History*.[10] Little more was at stake than the threat of an overturned cart, meager or dirty fare, an uncomfortable night's sleep, and price-gouging by opportunistic natives.

When it came to the natives, Malthus observes their work in the aforementioned fields and mines, and docks, as guides and university professors. He relishes attending dinners and dances offered by Norwegian high society; unlike Wollstonecraft, he was quite taken with the wealthy Anker family. He guesses at the relative prosperity of Norway's population by the quality and cleanliness of their housing, dress, and appearance; he takes special interest, as had Coxe, in the custom of women to do their tasks dressed only in light shifts and petticoats, revealing more flesh than their contemporaries in England.[11] He pays particular attention to whether those he observes appear well- or ill-fed, and is also mindful to inquire about wages and occupations, and the types and prices of provisions available for inhabitants of the regions he travels through.

While Malthus does not observe Scandinavia solely through the lens of the population principle, he was quite intent to learn how it operates there. Accordingly, he devotes much ink in the journals to what he saw as the small number of marriages in Norway. He attributes the relative strength of the preventive as opposed to positive check on population in part to a system of required military service. This, he believes, leads to later marriages. Malthus most likely highlights this institutional feature in his journal because his hosts, many of whom were military officers, frequently brought it up in conversation. That the policy had recently been abolished contributed to its currency.[12] Present-day statistical analysis does not bear out Malthus's belief that Norwegians would marry earlier as a result of the abolition of compulsory military service, and consequently increase Norway's population and population growth rates. The terms appear to have had no effect on marriage or fertility rates.[13] Malthus's experience indicates that repeated, uniform observations from multiple, apparently reliable sources may not be objective so much as objectively wrong. A mechanical procedure of aggregating and deeming identical observations accurate could easily prove faulty.

Malthus combed through the Danish statistician Frederik Thaarup's *Versuch einer Statistik der Dänischen Monarchie* (first published 1795) to find the most up-to-date information on Norway. He uses the statistics on life and death as a quick, rough and ready way to measure the happiness of a society's inhabitants. His contemporaries were not necessarily so diligent.[14] Yet Malthus takes liberties as he sifts through Thaarup's data; he omits the fertility rate calculated by Thaarup, "most likely because it implied that the population of Norway would double in the lamentably short span of 77 years; he also cited mortality rates that applied only to the years 1775–84".[15] Skipping over the fertility rate and the considerable difference in mortality rates between the north and south of the country allows Malthus to arrive at the happy, if incorrect conclusion, that the preventive as opposed to the positive check prevailed in Norway.[16] He takes the population principle as his guide.

But this may be too harsh. The links between military conscription and population, for instance, were not established facts but conjectures by like-minded eyewitnesses, and statistics were often scanty. Drake cites the brief duration of Malthus's travels, his unsystematic itinerary, the character of his sources, and his "somewhat cavalier approach" to statistical evidence as reasons for his faulty statistical reasoning.[17] The so-called avalanche of printed numbers, the explosive growth in social statistics from the 1820s on, was barely a rumble at this point, and the rise of probabilistic thinking an even more distant murmur.[18] Malthus's accounting thus suffers not only from a lack of statistics, but an error in determining whether the conscription policy would constitute an "accidental," "constant", or no cause of early marriages in Norway.

Malthus's fact-gathering in Scandinavia hints at another only partially successful effort by British political economists to define the scope and objects of their pursuits as a science. Again, present-day commentators note how British political economists, from Smith to his followers in the early nineteenth century, tended to ignore or devalue women's activities, including glossing over the not-insignificant participation of women in the paid labor market.[19] Domestic economy manifestly did not come under the purview of the science of political economy, but, like policy and administration, formed part of the art of political economy. If British political economists and their supporters noted the similarities between domestic economy and political economy at all in texts, it was only briefly and in passing, in introductory remarks on the science. Jane Marcet, for instance, in the introduction to *Conversations on Political Economy* (1816), has her main character, Mrs. B, answer a hypothetical query about what political economy is all about:

> I once heard a lady ask a philosopher to tell her in a few words what is meant by political economy. Madam, replied he, you understand perfectly what is meant by household economy, you need only extend your idea of the economy of a family to that of a whole people – of a nation, and you will have some comprehension of the nature of political economy.[20]

But "household" and "domestic" make only few and minor appearances elsewhere in *Conversations*. Malthus himself contributes to the absence of women's sphere in the science. "Domestic" and "woman" do not appear in *Definitions in Political Economy* (1827), a book on what Malthus proclaims were key terms in political economy, their meanings, and the rules which should govern their use. The gendered division of labor between household and market activities constituted a gendered division of knowledge. Marcet and other British women writers did play important public roles in promoting education in political economy during the first decades of the nineteenth century. Though handsomely remunerated for this work, their presence as financially independent women in the paid labor force could be accommodated as logical if somewhat discomfiting extensions of women's role as educators within the family.

Malthus invites social analysts to take the bonds between political economy and domestic economy seriously, however, in part because of what he observes during his travels in Norway. It was clear, if not clearly stated, that the population principle is predicated on an intimate relationship between domestic economy and political economy both in practice, and, implicitly, in theory. This is evident in the operation of moral restraint, which Malthus adds as a mediating factor to the population principle in the 1803 *Essay*. Thus, the capacity to manage resources prudently within a household proves critical for family formation and sustenance. Proper or improper household management determines if family members and, in aggregate, populations would suffer misery or famine, or engage in vice.

His Scandinavian account illuminates another facet of the relationship between domestic economy and the population principle, one relevant to the histories of social scientific observation: Norwegian women were expert observers on political economy. The production of scientific knowledge in the nineteenth century relied in part on a gendered division of labor between observers and interpreters, as has been well documented in gender studies, cultural studies, and studies in the history of science. Malthus praises the observational prowess of Norwegian women. After a month and a half of travel, for instance, he dined at the Ankers in Christiania on 4 July 1799, and jotted down a journal entry in which he succinctly expands on the significance of the conversations of the evening:

> Dined at Mr Ancher's [sic] – after dinner in the garden had some conversations with Mrs Collet whom I found the best person for examination that I had yet met with. In general I have found the gentlemen either unable or unwilling to answer the questions I have asked; but very willing to run on into long discussions of their own.[21]

Malthus does not specify what questions he asked of Mrs. Collet. But we can infer that she provided useful information on the population principle, and the imbrication of state policies, domestic, and political economies. If so, Mrs. Collet proved superior to Norwegian men when it came to conversations with Malthus on political economy.

Norwegian women could serve as better eyewitnesses than their menfolk. Or, at least those in the circles that Malthus socialized in; the Ankers, the most prominent commercial family in Norway at the time, had been the first to introduce Malthus to the subject of the effect on marriages of the change in Norwegian policy on military service.[22] Yet Norwegian women of means lacked an essential ingredient necessary to fully participate in the burgeoning European domestic and international scientific communication networks of the period: time. They had little leisure because of the unusual demands placed on them to maintain their households. Malthus writes that at the Ankers' party,

> Mrs. Collett told me that the housekeeping in Norway, from its peculiar nature, & the largeness of the establishments necessary, took up so much time, that the ladies had not leisure for many other employments after marriage. In their house in the country they make up eleven servants' beds. We have heard from many authorities that the servants are very idle, & never like to do any thing out of their peculiar department, so that more are required for the same work in England.[23]

Specialization can entail either breaking down tasks into ever more minute sub-routines, or assigning a "peculiar department" to separate individuals whose jobs do not represent intermediate steps in a production process. Adam Smith observed the former, in his famous anecdote about the division of labor in a pin factory, and emphasized the greater productivity that resulted. The servants in wealthier Norwegian households illustrate the latter meaning of specialization; they remain idle once they finish their tasks, unlike the busy ladies who had to supervise them.

That domestic labor is subject to task orientation, a focus on completion of chores and production for consumption within the household as opposed to the time discipline of factory work geared to ceaseless labor, more production, and more efficient production for sale, has long been a staple of historical analyses.[24] Among present-day economists, Becker famously integrated domestic economy and political economy by positing an efficient working of the division of labor where individuals work at home or in the market based on their comparative advantage in producing in one sphere or the other. The household and paid labor markets function as separate sites in a trading regime.[25]

British political economists evinced little interest in treating domestic economy as part of the science of political economy, however much the division labor applied to household labor. This was true even when taking into account that the peculiar nature of arrangements in wealthy Norwegian households lay in the fact that servants, not the ladies of the household, enjoyed the most leisure time. The ladies could not, therefore, emulate their English sisters by taking up occupations outside the household such as charitable pursuits or writing. According to Smith, the spread of the division of labor helps spur growth of commercial civilizations by encouraging the production of goods outside of households. Not so in Norway. This would suggest, to any contemporary analyst paying attention, the absence of universal models of domesticity or of the transition to the highest stage of civilization. Could Norway really belong to the roster of commercial societies?

Edward Daniel Clarke and Hannah More: Foreign Associations, Domestic Arrangements, and Political Economy

Malthus remained mum in the journal about this consequence of the high degree of specialization within Norwegian households. He does, however, see fit to quote Mrs. Collett to note that the ladies of the household could take up few additional employments as a consequence of household workplace arrangements. He was not the only one of his traveling party to remark on this effect. Clarke observes that in Norway, "literary female characters are unknown".[26] Norwegian authorities, including Mrs. Collett, informed Malthus of an all-consuming domestic economy that limited women's agency in Norway in one important respect: if they made observations vital to political economy, they could do but little to represent such matters.

The dearth of Norwegian female authors stood in sharp contrast to the work of their British sisters. That no universal model characterized all the possible ways to divide domestic and political economy was hardly revelatory. Contemporaries recognized that identical social objects, households in this case, could produce radically different effects in societies as different as Norway and England. A little reflection, however, reminds them and us of a potential paradox. To make real the emerging British ideal of separate spheres required households to accumulate enough resources to keep women out of the public sphere. But that same freedom from want could give women the leisure to do the opposite, to become "literary female characters", public figures in real life.

Clarke weighs in on what he sees as incorrect notions of Norwegian domestic life in vogue at the time. He disagrees with the sentiment that household relations between Norwegian wives and husbands were analogous to those between master and slave:

> It has been said, that the women of *Norway* are domestic slaves, and their husbands domestic tyrants. Some truth, we are ready to allow, may be found in the former part of this sweeping assertion; although there may be none whatsoever in the latter. But the slavery of a *Norwegian* wife is voluntary; she delights in her labour, because it is "the labour of love;" and if this be a "domestic slavery," it is well repaid by domestic happiness; by a full measure of reciprocal regard and affection in the fidelity and increasing attachment of her husband: for "as the sun when it ariseth in the high heaven, so is the beauty of a good wife in the ordering of her house."[27]

If Clarke refers to Wollstonecraft here, he misreads her. Wollstonecraft criticizes what she calls the drudgery and slavery of servants and wives not in Norway, but in Sweden (Wollstonecraft, *Letters*, pp. 27–8 and 194). She also claims Danish, not Norwegian, "men of business are domestic tyrants", and Danish, not Norwegian, mothers are "slaves of infants" because they spoil their children (Wollstonecraft, *Letters*, p. 202). Regardless, Clarke assumes

Norwegian women accept emotional rather than monetary compensation for their domestic work. Norwegian husbands, in return, repay their wives with greater love and fidelity. According to Clarke, both men and women are happy with this exchange; it epitomizes the ideal of Christian domestic economy.[28]

Clarke frets that a different sort of exchange, foreign trade, produces vice in Christiania. Inhabitants of the Norwegian port city have acquired unsavory manners from foreigners:

> From the more frequent intercourse which here takes place with other countries, the ill effects of what is called *refinement* become daily visible, while the *Christianians* retain a number of barbarisms which might well be laid aside. The good old virtues of this country are making hourly sacrifices to the follies and caprices of other nations.[29]

Foreign trade exposes countries to different ways of being. Political economists, again, tended to cast the expansion of trade in positive terms, with increased intercourse between nations softening manners. Clarke, however, observes that trade can and has introduced undesirable habits into Norway. Not only that, some homegrown barbarisms were successfully maintaining their market share against foreign virtues. The mere fact that a nation could participate in the trade for goods did not guarantee progress in manners.

Clarke fails to identify the countries and refinements contaminating Norwegian identities and virtues. His contemporary Hannah More shows no such compunction when she meditates on the dangers travel and contact with foreigners, foreign habits, and foreign goods pose to English spiritual and economic life, and masculine and feminine identities in *Moral Sketches*. More was hardly the first British religious writer to decry the effect of post-Napoleonic continental travel on British economic and spiritual well-being. John W. Cunningham published *Cautions to Continental Travellers* (1818) to warn British travelers who "might catch something of the spirit and manners of the countries which they visit" of just such effects, with the travelers, in numbers "beyond all previous calculation", calculated as "likely to exercise a considerable influence on the English national character". The young and females, "on the whole, more susceptible of impression than males", are especially vulnerable to continental influence.[30]

More focuses, as had Cunningham, on travel to and from France; Colbert cites estimates that "some 15,512 British tourists and residents were present in Paris alone during 1815".[31] *Moral Sketches* explores the economic steps More suggests to resist what she sees as peacetime threats posed by France. The title, which promises the reader a book of morals and manners, only hints at these economic themes, which More addresses in the preface, and in "Foreign Associations", which opens the main body of the text. This apparent discrepancy between form and content nicely captures the tension between More's dual personas; she was both a writer who upheld conservative values of church and state, and an Evangelical activist who, increasingly critical of the established order, espoused a wide range of reforms to alleviate poverty. Beginning in 1789 More and her sister Martha, with an assist of funds from William Wilberforce and others, began traveling throughout their neighborhood of Mendip Hills to launch a set of initiatives aimed at helping the poor. The sisters established Sunday and day schools, founded mutual savings societies for women, implemented schemes to increase employment in cottage industries, and pressed parish officials to improve workhouse conditions, among many other activities. Some of their work proved controversial, most notoriously during the Blagdon Controversy at the turn of the century. Though the flare-up eventually fizzled out, at its height critics charged that the sisters and their schools challenged High Church and aristocratic paternal authority, encouraged not just Evangelicalism but Methodism, and, most sensationally, promoted the rise of radicalism and revolutionary sentiment in the Mendips.[32]

The Blagdon Controversy had led some Britons to question More's religiosity. Nearly two decades later, however, in *Moral Sketches*, she assumes that her spirituality was not at issue. More attempts to convince her intended audience, wealthy Englishwomen, to reflect on and change their behavior, a standard theme in devotional literature of the period. The collection proved popular. Though More had feared that its first edition of 1500 copies would fail to sell, her memoirist William Roberts claimed that it sold out on the day of its appearance, and by November 1819 More herself wrote that her publisher, Thomas Caddell, was pressing her to put out a fourth edition.[33]

More's questioning of the risk of spiritual damage incurred when her compatriots traveled across the Channel marks the literal point of entry for her audience. More does acknowledge that readers of *Moral Sketches* might find her prejudiced, a troubling attribute for one making observations on travel in order to reflect on spirituality. She first apologizes for and then plays down the effect that her anti-French and pro-English beliefs, which some reviewers found off-putting and, in the case of an American review, "hardly to be believed", might have on her credibility.[34] She writes in *Moral Sketches* that "she yet believes that there are to be found worse prejudices than those national attachments, which in her are irreclaimable".[35] Further, she argues that "national attachments" and prejudice are actually distinct. She reminds readers of the definition of prejudice, and then explains why this should not be applied to "the more enlightened Britons" who hold national attachments. More, in one of the few instances in *Moral Sketches* where she refers to the more inclusive "Great Britain" rather than to "England" or things "English", lists the reasons Britons hold their nation in such high esteem: the constitution, "the best that mortal man has ever yet devised"; the Church of England; "a system of religious and civil liberty" imitated by some and envied by all foreign countries; and institutions "which promise to convey the chief of these blessings to foreign lands" (More, *Moral Sketches*,

p. xii). For More, a native's fondness for Britain is self-evident if one compares these glories with those of other nations.

An individual's capacity to judge the value of each nation's institutions depends on travel, through exchanges of ideas and people. These reflections sharpen insight. If they lead to partiality, it is an understandable preference for the British way of life, not reflexive prejudice. More acknowledges that foreign associations can diminish this partiality. But she frets that travel can prove costly if it leads travelers to become too enamored with searching for novel pleasurable sensations. Habits acquired during travel change tastes, and changes in tastes can harm morals; thus,

> if once the rightness of an action should come to be determined by its pleasantness, an entirely new system of morals must be introduced amongst Christians; the question then would be no longer, what *ought* we to do, but what should we *like* to do?
> (More, *Moral Sketches*, p. xiv; emphases in original)

More's opposition of duty and pleasure may sound like a dig at utilitarian thinkers such as James Mill and Jeremy Bentham. More likely she references her own Evangelical awakening in the previous century when she, one of the leading figures in English poetry and theater in the 1770s, chose to withdraw from the pleasures of fashionable London society to embrace her religious calling.[36] More admits that Britons traveled for a variety of necessary, even noble reasons. They went abroad for health or business, or "the meritorious desire, of doing moral and religious good" (More, *Moral Sketches*, pp. xiv–xv). Travelers may return less biased as a result. But, again, they also ran the risk of returning as less religious beings.

More's own wish to do "moral and religious good" had moved her to travel throughout the Mendips in the 1790s. She and her sister identified profiteering, the negligence of the rich, which led to low wages and inadequate employment, and defective state institutions as chief causes of poverty in rural England.[37] Her resulting prescriptions, born out of observations of rural distress similar to those which had so provoked Malthus, nevertheless stand in marked contrast to his. Malthus came to believe that raising wages and funding charitable efforts like the Speenhamland system of poor relief exacerbated the very problems they were meant to solve. More acted, however, on the premise that these measures could help rather than harm the poor.

More warns that "the excess of continental intercourse", specifically exposure to French morals, manners, and goods, pollute English life (More, *Moral Sketches*, p. viii). She mines familiar themes, working the fear of travel's effects on desire into an argument against free trade, sauced with a helping of anti-French sentiment. English commentators had, again, long raised alarms about the baneful effects the import of foreign goods could have on English specie, jobs, masculinity, and economic and political order.

They pointed in particular to the risk faced by English manufactures, but also feared that well-to-do men faced emasculation if they consumed too many foreign luxury goods, particularly of the French variety.

Moral Sketches was hardly More's first intervention in the politics, economics, and morals of travel, and lessons from her work with the abolitionist movement are instructive. She famously denounced Britons who traveled to Africa to purchase slaves in *Slavery, A Poem* (1788): "They are *not* Christians who infest thy shore."[38] More accused the slave traders of being motivated by one of the seven deadly sins:

> And thou, WHITE SAVAGE! whether lust of gold,
> Or lust of conquest, rule thee uncontrol'd![39]

Inordinate desire for wealth or power fueled the brutality of the trade. It also turned White Britons, civilized travelers, into savages. More points out the availability of alternative models of travel for the British, prototypes consistent with religious doctrine. For example, she contrasts slave traders unfavorably with Captain Cook and his "gentle mind", and love of "arts" and "humankind".[40] And, for those who would go so far as to permanently emigrate and seek to establish an empire overseas, she cites the Quakers, who had freed their slaves throughout North America.[41]

More and other abolitionists pursued a host of strategies as they sought to abolish the slave trade. They wrote anti-slavery tracts. They formed anti-slave trade societies, such as the Society for Effecting the Abolition of the African Slave Trade, whose members included Wilberforce and More. They produced goods, such as cameos and medallions crafted by Josiah Wedgewood which women and men wore to advertise their support for the movement. And they turned to Parliament with bills and petitions to abolish the trade. After the defeat of one such bill in 1791, abolitionists redoubled efforts to undercut the profitability of the trade through widespread consumer boycotts of slave-produced sugar, Britain's most valuable import at the time. Women, chief purchasers of food for families, played a key role in organizing these boycotts; consumption choices of households mutually constituted home and empire.[42]

More had joined some of the first notable boycotts, in 1778, the same year she published "Slavery". Some four decades later, in *Moral Sketches*, she revisits the tactic of directing British women's spending toward moral ends, but focuses on Channel rather than Atlantic crossings of people and goods. In the interim, the recognition that the spending power of girls and women, harnessed by prudent domestic economy, could be put to spiritual ends had been given widespread currency in numerous conduct books and texts on morals and manners. Wollstonecraft, for instance, uses the conceit of travel to promote such ends in *Original Stories from Real Life; with Conversations, Calculated to Regulate the Affections, and Form the Mind to Truth and Goodness*, originally published in 1788. She imagines a tour of London conducted by a Mrs. Mason, with two young relatives, Mary and Caroline, ages fourteen and twelve, in tow; Mrs. Mason instructs her charges on how to navigate the whys and wherefores of developing proper female subjectivity. In relating this fictional tour Wollstonecraft

> lobbies for a mindful consumerism which will reserve funds for the practicing of charity; she also urges a responsible patronage of carefully selected shops, arguing that frivolous spending and failing to pay bills defrauds the working poor and strengthens foreign markets.[43]

Thoughtless spending on foreign goods by girls can cause factories in England to close and drive unemployed male workers to crime; some "unhappy creatures" even end up at the gallows, pushed by "accidental idleness".[44] Wollstonecraft depicts a nation where domestic economy and political economy intertwine, where political economy is decidedly a Christian political economy.[45]

More scrutinizes actual travel, and gives the arguments against engaging in certain types of foreign trade a slightly different twist than Wollstonecraft. She acknowledges how excessive travel and the influence of specifically French habits threaten English masculinity and a paternalistic social order, all the while emphasizing the deleterious effects these create for English femininity and female workers. More ultimately imagines a world where rich and middle-class Englishwomen forsake travel to foreign shores; instead, these women purchase goods and services produced by poor Englishwomen. As with her own experience in the Mendips, she touts a model of female philanthropists who dedicate their travels, and money, to improving the lot of the less fortunate at home.

More bemoans the decline of a type of domesticity embodied by a "country gentleman of rank and fortune" who does not travel too far. The farther this paragon of masculinity strays out of his rural ambit, the less cohesive his own sense of self and the larger moral order. His influence, importance, usefulness, and dignity all diminish "in proportion to the distance he wanders from his proper orbit" (More, *Moral Sketches*, p. viii). This form of paternalism, with "each at his natural and appropriate station" had withered in post-Napoleonic England (More, *Moral Sketches*, p. 5). Thus,

> instead of each centinel remaining at his providentially appointed watch, – at this crucial moment, a very large proportion of our nobles and gentry, an indefinite number of our laity, and not a few of our clergy, that important part of our community, of which the situation is peculiarly local, – all these ... important portions of our country at once abandoned it.
>
> (More, *Moral Sketches*, p. 6)

In fact, the sentinels had traveled to France. More criticized the eagerness of the wealthy and clergy to visit their vanquished enemies. By doing so, they had abandoned the English poor. They failed to spend money on domestic goods, robbing the poor of jobs; the charity of the wealthy, when called for, had disappeared as well. The absent English and their missing spending contributed to the post-war misery, discontent, and criminality of the poor in the home country.

Travel by English both to and from France put England in spiritual peril, too; More marvels that "France was made a scene for the education of English, of Protestant children!" (More, *Moral Sketches*, p. 8). Returnees threatened to import French principles along with French habits; furthermore, the forces of emulation in English society meant that French manners and morals could and did spread throughout the population. More cites one egregious example of a woman aping her betters: "It is almost too ludicrous to assert, that the wife of a reputable farmer being asked lately what she had done with her daughter, replied, 'I have *Frenched* her and *musicked* her, and shall now carry her to France'" (More, *Moral Sketches*, p. 9, note; emphases in original). Worse still, More feared that travel to and from France by the English put English "national character" at risk. She foresaw "the decline of religion in the domestic arrangements of the great", which she deemed a calamitous turn of events for the spiritual life of the nation (More, *Moral Sketches*, pp. 10 and 11).

A reviewer in *The British Review, and London Critical Journal* wrote approvingly of More's "censure" of the "the unfortunate tendency of the present times towards French journeys, French manners, and French indifference to moral and religious principles. We feel fully sensible of the truth and importance of every one of her remarks on this painful subject."[46] An essayist in *The Monthly Review*, on the other hand, criticized More for her anti-travel sentiments, reasoning that most English travelers spent too little time and had too little intimate contact with the natives to be contaminated by French manners and principles. Plus, travel by individuals between Britain and France, aside from the benefit of adding to the stock of knowledge, produced one good that outweighed all the possible minor negative consequences: contact reduced antipathies between the two nations, lessening the probability that another war would break out between them.[47]

More had declaimed earlier in *Moral Sketches* that, "We only refuse to imitate our continental neighbours, in the very point in which they are respectable: *They stay at home*" (More, *Moral Sketches*, pp. xv–xvi; emphasis in original). She advanced a pair of economic arguments for emulating this aspect of French domesticity, noting that "*They* prudently augment the resources of their own country in two ways, by spending their own money in their own land, with the additional profit of holding out to us those allurements, which cause ours to be spent there also" (More, *Moral Sketches*, p. xvi; emphasis in original). *The Gentleman's Magazine* agreed with More's economics, and even supplied an estimate of the damages that would be sustained by British shops and manufactures if the then-current 30,000 English residents in Paris stayed abroad for a one quarter of a year: 3,600,00*l*. Such a "loss" would throw many English shops into "beggary" and many poor into unemployment. Cunningham had declared it "no small evil that two millions and a half of the national property have been now for two years annually consumed in foreign countries, and at a moment when our looms and our labourers have been standing still for want of employment".[48] *The Gentleman's Magazine* reviewer suggests of the expatriates, "There is nothing left for them now than to return, and to sell all that they have, and to give to the poor – the condition of many of whom is their own creation!"[49]

The Monthly Review essayist fails to address, much less dispute, More's neo-mercantilist logic. Rather, the reviewer caviled that the reluctance by the French to travel could be attributed to two economic factors: they lacked the means, and, lacking the number of merchants and traders that England had, they were less of a commercial nation.

> a commercial nation, like the English, will always produce a greater number of travellers than a nation in which commerce is less generally prevalent; the former being likely to contain the largest quantity of wealth, or of what may be called the material for travelling, and the enterprizing spirit being stronger among a nation of traders and merchants.[50]

More and her reviewers were debating how to interpret the relationship between national and economic character in England and Britain. *The British Review* essayist reads More as calling for a British femininity consistent with a vision of the emerging ideology of separate spheres which would leave little room for female agency. Women should remain at or very close to home.

> Nothing can be more just, and at the same time, more discriminative and delicate, than the disapprobation expressed by Mrs. More of that desertion of home, and its various appropriate and delicate duties, which some well-intentioned females are apt to be guilty of for the sake of paying a more conspicuous part in the field of active benevolence or piety. Charity, in its true sense, she seems to think, should begin at home, with our British ladies; and we are quite sure, that if the exercise of charity within this limited range were, in general, to form their leading task and occupation, their labours would in the end have a much wider spread; for of what is the community formed but of an aggregation of homes, of hearths, of families, and neighbourhoods.[51]

More challenges this stricture on female domesticity, however, when she introduces yet another economic reason to support English wealth remaining with the English. When the wealthy and middle classes rambled to France or purchased French goods at home, they directly threatened the livelihoods of many poor English women. More notes that her contemporaries frequently fail to observe or represent this gender-specific effect of imports of French "articles of dress and decoration"; *The Gentleman's Magazine* offers proof of this absence when it omits any mention of More's concern about this aspect of cross-Channel trade. Nonetheless it constitutes to More "a grievance not the less serious because it is overlooked, and because it affects only a subordinate class in society". She pleads

> the distress of those unfortunate females who used to procure a decent support by their own industry, and of whom thousands are now plunging into misery. We would fervently but respectfully advocate the cause of this meritorious and most pitiable class.
> (More, *Moral Sketches*, p. 13)

More plays on the fluidity of the concepts of female domesticity and Evangelical activism. One could, a la *The British Review*, restrict the sphere of female charitable activity to homes, hearths, neighborhoods, and individuals personally touched by the philanthropist. This form of maternalism would mirror More's ideal of paternalism. Or one could touch the world, even while, literally speaking, remaining at home. The sugar boycotts provided proof that spending by women could affect multitudes beyond the confines of the female philanthropists' respective neighborhoods.

More endorses a buy-English campaign to aid poor women under threat from French products. She invokes British patriotism, British laws, "the sensibilities of a well-regulated heart, the tenderness of an enlightened conscience", justice, and charity, all to sway her female readers to question their behavior and to refrain from purchasing French goods (More, *Moral Sketches*, p. 14). More's call for solidarity between wealthy and poor women rests on two key assumptions. First, that women of the upper-classes had independent command over consumption, a conjecture borne out by the experiences of the sugar boycotters. Second, that they could actually use this spending power to purchase goods produced by poor English women.

Alarmingly, failure to purchase English goods made by poor women would force many to resort to crime in order to gain "a scanty, precarious, and miserable support". More's call to conscience assumes a preexisting solidarity between rich and poor Englishwomen; perhaps, she muses, readers had helped individual poor women get "taught better principles at school", or given them assistance to learn a trade. Think, she asks, of the degradation that would follow if the reader did not buy poor women's goods: "If by crushing that trade I now drive her to despair, if I throw her on a temptation which may overcome those better principles she acquired through my means" (More, *Moral Sketches*, p. 15). These women have "been bred to no other means of gaining their support", and "will probably, if these fail, throw themselves into the very jaws of destruction" (More, *Moral Sketches*, p. 16).

More implores readers to imagine the pain they might cause women they know and have helped. She then asks readers to expand this vision of female sympathy, beyond the limits espoused by *The British Review*, to imagine untold (and unknown) thousands of women in similar predicaments. More advises readers to exercise prudence in spending in order to shield these poor women workers from harm:

> Think, then, with tenderness, on these thousands of young women of your own sex, whom a little self-denial on your part might restore to comfort – might snatch from ruin ... Consider, then, once more we beseech, consider that it is not only their bread, but their virtue, of which you may be unintentionally depriving them.
> (More, *Moral Sketches*, p. 16)

More emphasizes, again, how travel and travelers' spending have not just economic but moral and spiritual dimensions. Consumption by the well-to-do can produce either a vicious or a virtuous circle of and for women. (Im)prudent buying by wealthy women produces (im)prudent behavior by poor women workers. More also appeals to the reader's self-interest:

> Spare yourself, then, the pain of feeling that, if you hear of any of these unfortunate beings having, previously to entering other sinful courses, been tempted by famine to commit a robbery – spare yourself the pain of reflecting, that you, perhaps, by a thoughtless gratification of your taste, first robbed her of that subsistence, the failure of which has driven her to a crime she abhorred.
> (More, *Moral Sketches*, p. 17)

Self-denial, pain, famine, and subsistence were all key concepts for contemporary political economists schooled in the teachings of Bentham and Malthus. Political economists primarily imagined men, not women, as subjects and agents operating in the realms governed by these terms. More not only recognized that women existed who by nature had to earn wages, but maintained that assistance must be directed toward them in order to aid England's families. More's observations, then, unveil a version of English domesticity driven by women who feel, spend, and earn, a political economy that those who call themselves political economists, men, almost universally fail to represent.

Travel Observations by Malthus: From Journals to *Essay*

Malthus did not transform his notes on the domestic economy of the well-to-do in Norway into political economy in *Essay*. But, what did he choose to represent? If we turn to the sixth edition (1826), the last to appear during Malthus's lifetime, Norway held pride of place, the first country in Book II,

"Of the Checks to Population in the Different States of Modern Europe". Malthus adds material when he moves from his raw but already edited diary entries for the Scandinavian journey to the more refined style of the post-1798 editions of *Essay*. Some additions, such as punctuation, are minor; others, such as Malthus's use of new information that had come to light since 1799 are not. Malthus cuts material as well; he omits, for example, any elements of the natural history perspective which lend some semblance of daily rhythm to his halting, fragmentary notes on Norway. He also drains his account of the glimpses of what his friends agreed was a cheerful personality, and gives no taste of the voices of his Norwegian informants, either. Gone too are any traces of the division between observation and literary representation, a gendered split engendered by the demands placed on women by domestic economy in Norway. This is not a case of Malthus deferring to female modesty; the voices of all those he met in Norway are absent from *Essay*. We meet no named people at all with the exception of authors of published articles.

These elisions form part of the translation of travelers' accounts Malthus performs in *Essay*. His authoritative voice, however, remains. He conveys, mostly in third-person narration, observations on Norway in a manner cool, affectless, and impersonal. These gestures toward an unbiased voice follow what would become one of the credos of scientific objectivity. Malthus does not, however, always adopt a flat tone. For instance, he comments that

> In summer of the year 1799 ... I particularly remarked, that the sons of housemen and the farmers' boys [in Norway] were fatter, larger, and had better calves to their legs, than boys of the same age and in similar situations in England.[52]

And the following chapter, "Of the Checks to Population in Sweden" contains the following charged statement: "Yet notwithstanding this constant and striking tendency to overflowing numbers, strange to say! the government and the political economists of Sweden are continually calling, out for population! population!"

Malthus silences individual voices when moving from his journal to *Essay*. He also writes out whole peoples. Valenze argues that the journals show just how much the methods of subsistence food production by the Sami people, especially their interdependence with their reindeer, unsettled Malthus. In 1803 he still chose to confine most of his analyses of food to developments in grain and cattle production, pushing to the margin forms of provisioning such as fishing, hunting, and foraging. If Malthus and his contemporaries had to adapt their narratives to accommodate the widespread use of the potato in Europe as a subsistence food source, he more or less faithfully reproduces the story of development told in stadial histories, which typically depict humans as becoming fully human, *civilized*, only when pursuing the cultivation of plant foodstuffs on private property.[53] At any rate, the cozy, nay domestic relations, between the Sami and reindeer, did not fit these stadial histories.

Malthus appears to effectively write out as well observations detailing how women and domestic economy were integral to political economy. Yet compare Malthus's treatment of Norwegian observers and observations with the prominence he gives to the voices of a Swiss peasant woman and her husband in the sixth edition of *Essay*.

> The party had scarcely arrived at a little inn at the end of the lake, when the mistress of the house began to complain of the poverty and misery of all the parishes in the neighbourhood. She said that the country produced little, and yet was full of inhabitants; that boys and girls were marrying who ought still to be at school; and that, while this habit of early marriages continued, they should always be wretched and distressed for subsistence.
> (*Essay*, 1826, I, pp. 357–8)

Malthus continues, "The peasant, who afterwards conducted us to the source of the Orbe, entered more fully into the subject, and appeared to understand the principle of population almost as well as any man I ever met with". The shift from woman to man jars, but Malthus does mean the husband of the "mistress of the house" here. Reasoning like a political economist, the peasant, as did his wife, identifies a combination of low earnings, early marriages, and consequent high birth rates as the source of redundant population and distress in the canton of Jura.

Still, Malthus found that the peasant fell just short of a complete understanding of the population principle:

> The only point in which he failed, as to his philosophical knowledge of the subject, was in confining his reasonings too much to barren and mountainous countries, and not extending them to the plains. In fertile situations, he thought, perhaps, that the plenty of corn and employment might remove the difficulty, and allow of early marriages. Not having lived much in the plains, it was natural for him to fall into this error; particularly, as in such situations the difficulty is not only more concealed from the extensiveness of the subject; but is in reality less, from the greater mortality naturally occasioned by low grounds, towns, and manufactories.
> (*Essay*, 1826, I, p. 359)

Malthus corrects the peasant's erroneous conception about how the population principle operates where food is more plentiful than in Jura. But the mildness of Malthus's critique undercuts it; the peasant commits only a single error after all. Readers may well question the claims of expertise about the population principle on the part of Malthus and his fellow political economists as a result. The peasant and others Malthus converses with in his travels in Switzerland and Savoy achieve a nearly complete philosophical understanding of the subject; Malthus praises "the great philosophical precision" of one of the peasant's explanations (*Essay*, 1826, I, pp. 359). Despite their low rank on the socioeconomic scale, and lack of formal instruction in political economy, the peasants need only observe what went on around them to become nearly as proficient as political economists in reasoning about one of the key principles of the science. And, Malthus concludes, they would become even more expert were they able to travel, to witness how the population principle worked in different environments.

Malthus's travels in Switzerland led him to conclude that, for many peasants, not just the innkeeper and his wife, experience leads to a nascent understanding of political economy, a nearly correct sense of how to achieve prosperity and happiness for themselves and those around them.

> In other conversations which I had with the lower classes of people in different parts of Switzerland and Savoy, I found many, who, though not sufficiently skilled in the principle of population to see its effects on society, like my friend of the Lac de Joux, yet saw them clearly enough as affecting their own individual interests; and were perfectly aware of the evils which they should probably bring upon themselves by marrying before they could have a tolerable prospect of being able to maintain a family.
>
> (*Essay*, 1826, I, p. 360)

Contemporaries were quick to charge that the toxic combination of self-interest, politics, and money produced biased observers and observations in political economy. But Malthus insists here that self-interest begets useful knowledge about the population principle.

If poor people remain unable to generalize correctly about population, indicating the limits to their ability to reason scientifically or philosophically when relying on individual experience alone, they could still bring about the day when the preventive check took hold in real life. All they needed to do was change their behavior. Put another way, peasants could learn the principle of population and then embody it in ways that enhanced their well-being. Malthus concluded that this had already occurred in Switzerland, where

> the improving habits of the people with respect to prudence, cleanliness &c., had increased gradually the general healthiness of the country, and, by enabling them to rear up to manhood a greater proportion of their children, had furnished the requisite population with a smaller number of births.
>
> (*Essay*, 1826, I, pp. 338–9)

And Malthus expresses the belief that knowledge of the principle of population could be readily diffused among those of the lower classes who had yet to comprehend it:

> From the general ideas which I have found to prevail on these subjects, I should by no means say that it would be a difficult task to make the common people comprehend the principle of population, and its effect in producing low wages and poverty.
> (*Essay*, 1826, I, p. 360)

If present-day economists not only try to describe the world, but make the world fit their descriptions, the same held true for political economists of Malthus's vintage who, though maintaining the distinction between the art and science of political economy, believed putting their principles into practice would be the best way to enhance the wealth and happiness of a society. Malthus's statement also acknowledges moves afoot to educate the masses, regardless of age, status, or gender, in Great Britain. The first Mechanics' Institute was established in Edinburgh, in 1821; Henry Brougham hustled the Society for the Diffusion of Useful Knowledge into existence in 1826. That year, 1826, also marked the tenth anniversary of the appearance of the influential *Conversations on Political Economy*, by Marcet.

If the poor could mimic the reasoning of political economists on the population principle, or could be easily taught the principle as part of the period's rage for political economy, what role would remain for those who actually called themselves political economists? Malthus suggests that he and others should augment their work with statistics on births, deaths, and marriages, if the numbers prove trustworthy:

> In reviewing the states of modern Europe, we shall be assisted in our inquiries by registers of births, deaths, and marriages, which, when they are complete and correct, point out to us with some degree of precision whether the prevailing checks to population are of the positive or preventive kind.
> (*Essay*, 1826, I, p. 259)

Few poor people would have ready access to such information, whether by dint of illiteracy or lack of access to networks such as the Economical Society of Berne, whose members had vigorously debated the possible depopulation of Switzerland some thirty-five to forty years earlier (*Essay*, 1826, I, pp. 337ff). The Scandinavian trip confirms for Malthus that the foresight of men in Norway has led to a healthier and happier population than the densely populated commercial civilization of England. Statistics on materials used in shelter and clothing, quantities of different foodstuffs, the weight and salubrity of youth, and so on, could serve as evidence to support or even supplant eyewitness accounts on the operation of the population principle. Even absent these statistics, Malthus concludes that few positive checks operate in Norway. The population increased slowly despite a low mortality rate: "in common years, the mortality is less than in any other country in Europe, the registers of which are known to be correct" (*Essay*, 1826, I, p. 260). Note, however, that statistics represent no panacea for Malthus. He inserts a note: "The registers for Russia give a smaller mortality; but it is supposed that they are defective."

Malthus also cites extensively from others' travel accounts in post-1798 versions of *Essay*. These include histories based on travel accounts, such as Jesuit histories of the Americas and Asia, and accounts that traveled, that is, the increasing volume of publications on vital statistics and population censuses from the states of Europe. Sometimes Malthus translates passages written in foreign languages into English; in other places, he quotes foreign works verbatim. In the latter, readers who read only English had to do the work of translation. We can speculate that Malthus took some observations of other travelers at face value, initially, at least, simply because of the authority and credibility of the authors. Abbé Raynal, Cook, and Pérouse were travelers and eyewitnesses whose veracity was widely accepted. Yet the fact that different travelers repeatedly made the same observation did not necessarily lend credence to an account for Malthus. Malthus assures the reader, without elaboration, that he has attempted to verify the truthfulness of the narratives he invokes, even those observations made by or cited by authorities like Robertson.[54]

If marrying his own travel accounts to the principle of population took work, using the accounts of others to verify the principle proved to be a balky process, too, even as he sought to reaffirm the universal nature of the principle. *Essay* indicates, unsurprisingly, that travelers' accounts, stadial histories, and the population principle did not necessarily fit seamlessly with one another. One impediment lay in the porous boundaries of the stages. Malthus used stadial histories in *Essay* to argue that the successive stages of civilization were characterized by fewer and fewer instances of savage or barbaric behavior, reading the stages as both a moral taxonomy and a moral hierarchy. But it was not necessarily clear that some societies, like Norway, were wholly in one stage or another, even putting the Sami aside: "The Norwegians, though not in a nomadic state, are still in a considerable degree in a pastoral state" (*Essay*, 1826, I, p. 272).

Despite stadial ambiguity, Malthus told and retold a tale that as a society progressed through stages, its morals and manners improved, as did the happiness of its inhabitants. Or, at least its misery decreased. But Malthus did not ignore a competing narrative, cited in some of the travel accounts he relied on in *Essay*, that a state of nature was more conducive to happiness than contemporary commercial civilization in Europe. Invoking and simultaneously rejecting the authority of Raynal, for example, he repeats evidence from travelers attesting to the brevity of savage life:

> The missionaries speak of the Indians in South America as subject to perpetual diseases for which they know no remedy. Ignorant of the use of the most simple herbs, or of any change in their gross diet, they die of these diseases in great numbers. The Jesuit Fauque says, that, in all the different excursions which he had made, he scarcely found a single individual of an advanced age. Robertson determines the period of human life to be shorter among savages than in well-regulated and industrious communities. Raynal, notwithstanding his frequent declamations in favour of savage life, says of the Indians of Canada, that few are so long lived as our people, whose manner of living is more uniform and tranquil. And Cook and Pérouse confirm these opinions in the remarks which they make on some of the inhabitants of the north-west coast of America.
>
> (*Essay*, 1826, I, p. 44)[55]

Malthus finds the principle of population a useful counter to the conclusion other Europeans had reached when interpreting travel accounts, that savage life, if brief, was still happy. This pairing, happiness and a short life span, constituted a taxonomic scandal in an epistemology that wed stadial history and the population principle.

Happiness may be difficult to detect, hence compare, the claims of authorities notwithstanding. Absent a device similar to Bentham's hypothetical utilometer, happiness was impossible to measure. Malthus focuses here on statistical facts, and sets aside the question of whether the savage or the civilized is the happier society. Bodies could be made visible in statistical tables on marriages, births and deaths, notwithstanding difficulties in the actual practice of enumeration. Statistics could be more stable than states of mind, if the classifications and their meanings remained fixed. Statistics also offer multiple combinatorial possibilities for analyses. If, according to travel accounts, savages rarely achieved the natural span of life while living in a state of nature, this fact allows analysts to weigh the natural if mutable effects of the principle of population. Its operation could be deduced from the measurable facts of life and death, in ways that happiness could not.

Sir James Mackintosh and Statistical Accounts of India: "Something Like Data"

Malthus also requested other travelers gather and send population statistics to him. Shortly before Sir James Mackintosh left England in 1804 to take up the position as Recorder (chief judge) of Bombay, Malthus asked his friend to conduct a survey there using a series of queries he had drawn up. Almost all of these concerned vital statistics.[56] These comprise one set of Malthus's instructions for travelers. Mackintosh had more than a passing familiarity with the tenets of political economy when he left for India; aside from Malthus, he counted as friends Samuel Romilly, Francis Horner,

Jeremy Bentham, and Étienne Dumont, a key figure in translating, editing, and making Bentham's works known in Continental circles. On 29 June 1804, barely a month after his arrival in India, Mackintosh expressed his eagerness, in a letter addressed to a "Mr. [Richard] Sharp", to receive books he had ordered on political economy; in August he informed Sharp that he had

> engaged the Government in a statistical survey of this Island [Bombay], with bills of births, marriages, deaths, &c. which I shall publish, when it is ready for me, as the first fruits of economical observation within the tropics.[57]

Mackintosh had, in fact, lost Malthus's list of questions, and sought Sharp's assistance to replace them, as he believed "They may really help us a great deal." Moreover, while he wrote Sharp that "I am bound to profess my gratitude to Bentham and Dumont, not only for the instruction which I have received from them, but perhaps still more for the bent which they have given to my mind", Mackintosh was most interested in Bentham's penal reforms, expressing his disappointment that he would not be able to introduce the panopticon into the Bombay penal system.[58] And his major publication during his stint in India, *Plan of a Comparative Vocabulary of Indian Languages* (1806), reflected his Orientalist taste for philology; political economy faced stiff competition for his time and attention.

Nor did Mackintosh limit his statistical passions to tabulating the births, deaths, and marriages so desired by Malthus. He offered to direct several members of the Literary Society of Bombay, which he headed as its first president, in collecting materials for a statistical account of Bombay.[59] Though his plans came to naught, Mackintosh composed a preliminary set of "Queries", published as "Appendix A.", in the first volume of *Transactions*. The questions illuminate the considerable leeway that travelers in this period had to make "economical observation[s]" and then embed them into a statistical account replete with other forms of knowledge. Mackintosh's list begins with more than two dozen questions on topics of natural history, followed by a set on "Political Arithmetic" which include the vital statistics Malthus so eagerly sought.[60] Nowhere does Mackintosh allude to the prevailing hostility toward political arithmetic among political economists; nor does he posit a competition between natural history and political economy. Other queries came under the headings "In the Different Religions", "Earlier History", and "During the English Government".[61] His account would mix political arithmetic, political economy, natural history, and much else into a harmonious whole, useful knowledge to advance both science and British administration of India.

Mackintosh's suggestion to undertake a statistical account formed a principal theme of his 26 November 1804 address, "A Discourse at the Opening of the Literary Society of Bombay". He begins his remarks by praising the shared purposes of the small yet occupationally diverse group gathered before him:

> I hope that we agree in considering all Europeans who visit remote countries, what ever their separate pursuits may be, as detachments from the main body of civilized men sent out to levy contributions of knowledge, as well as to gain victories over barbarism.[62]

The civilized reside principally in Europe. And European men (Mackintosh leaves women out of the equation for the moment) had two goals when traveling to far-flung regions: to bring knowledge to the uncivilized, and to triumph against barbarism. The latter required the acquisition of knowledge about the barbarous, which would facilitate the rule of civilized nations over uncivilized ones. In an age where, again, all written works in English could still be denoted "literature", Mackintosh envisioned the Literary Society reporting on a wide range of topics, including explorations in both the physical and moral sciences as part of their remit. To Mackintosh, the "beautiful science of *natural history*" formed the foundation of all physical knowledge; "*moral* [science] … will chiefly comprehend the past and present condition of the inhabitants of the vast country which surrounds us" (Mackintosh, "A Discourse", p. xviii; emphases in original).

Political economy occupied a central place in both Mackintosh's proposed statistical account and his vision of the moral sciences. He urged his listeners to take up political arithmetic and statistics in order to make the observations necessary to determine "present condition[s]" which were so vital to moral science (Mackintosh, "A Discourse", p. xxi). Political arithmetic and statistics, in turn, formed "part of the foundation of the science of political economy". While he remains unnamed, Malthus's influence appears in Mackintosh's call for "permanent tables" of vital and demographic statistics. These include population, births, deaths, marriages, the age distribution of the population, infant and child survival rates, and the occupational distribution of the population.

Mackintosh notes as well the opportunity to study population phenomena peculiar to India, including whether polygamy had its origin in the sex ratio between males and females. Statistics on wages, prices, particularly of provisions, and interest rates, which give insight into the "subsistence of the people" should follow, as well as information on the "laws and customs which regulate such great objects". Mackintosh calls for historical perspective here, asking for investigations into how any or all of India's laws and customs have changed "under different times and under different circumstances" (Mackintosh, "A Discourse", pp. xxi–xxii).

Mackintosh assured his audience that such observations make up the warp and weft of political economy. Facts were easy to come by for "all men of good sense", requiring nothing on the part of the observer "but a resolution to observe facts attentively, and to relate them accurately". These observations were actually woven into the fabric of daily life in British India. If one wished to move beyond mere observation and gathering facts to principles, that was easy, too: "[he] will in general find aid to his understanding in the great work of Dr. Smith, the most permanent monument of philosophical genius which our nation has produced in the present age." Knowledge of the population, industry and wealth of a district governed by the East India Company form part of the duties "of every Englishmen who fills a civil office" in India, thus constitute the stuff of the "very science of administration" (Mackintosh, "A Discourse", p. xxii).

Making observations in the name of the "science of administration" was the work of political arithmetic; again, these observations also form part of the foundation of the science of political economy. Mackintosh outlines, however, a distinction between the two sciences. Mackintosh calls for research to be made publicly available, a departure from previous practice in political arithmetic and statistics. These two sciences, when not neglected entirely, produced information solely for governments (Mackintosh, "A Discourse", p. xxi). While governance called for some "secrecy", a science typically only flourishes when facts are freely communicated and exchanged. This is true even for political arithmetic; if administrators fail to publish information they gather, it will be "effectually secured from all useful examination by the mass of official lumber under which it is usually buried". This not only keeps knowledge useful for the pursuit of science from the public, it reduces the effectiveness of public administration. Rather than exhume buried paperwork, public servants fall back on inferior, but more easily accessible, already published material to perform their tasks (Mackintosh, "A Discourse", pp. xxiii–xxiv).

Allowing information to see the light of day through publication also serves "as the best security to a government that they are not deceived by the reports of their servants; and where these servants act at a distance the importance of such a security for their veracity is very great" (Mackintosh, "A Discourse", p. xxiii). Thus, for Mackintosh, transparency and information sharing by public administrators in India would reduce principal-agent problems in British administration of India. Principals allow others, agents, to represent them and act on their behalf. Principal-agent problems in economics occur for two reasons. First, principals must trust agents who often have more information about matters at hand than principals. Second, principals cannot directly observe and monitor agents in order to ensure that agents carry out their instructions, and not shirk or steal.[63] Both problems, information differences, or what economists refer to as asymmetric information, and lack of effective monitoring arose when individuals traveled to India to work on behalf of parties back home in Britain. According to a published "Note on 'Preliminary Discourse'", likely written by Mackintosh, the monitoring problems presented themselves within India, too, as "native officers, subject to no very efficient check", produced erroneous population counts.[64]

Another set of his instructions for travelers meant that Malthus himself was keenly aware of principal-agent problems at the Company. The year after he pressed Mackintosh to conduct inquiries in India, Malthus took up the first-ever professorship in political economy, a post as Professor of History and Political Economy at the East India College at Haileybury. The College had been created to prepare boys for civil service positions with the Company in India by providing them an education both practical and vocational.[65] For Malthus, writing in defense of the institution in *Statements Respecting the East-India College* (1817), the college would, in addition, ideally teach its students masculine virtues; the "specific object" was "to inculcate, gradually, manly feelings, manly studies, and manly self-controul, rather earlier than usual".[66] The goal was to transform the students before they traveled, to inoculate them against the temptations that awaited them in India. That is, Malthus tried to instill moral restraint in his charges. Haileybury would provide an education where students would gradually learn, through their own choices, to regulate their desires: self-management would assist the management of empire.[67]

Malthus and Haileybury only partially succeeded in this endeavor. Student riots in 1811 and 1816 forced Malthus to take pen in hand in two pamphlets to rebut criticisms of the College. *Statements* was the second; in the first, *A Letter to the Rt. Hon. Lord Grenville* (1813), Malthus seeks to allay fears expressed by Lord Grenville in explaining his opposition to the extension of the Company's charter, that the college would bring about the wrong kind of transformation among students. Malthus characterizes Grenville as worrying that the students would be "formed ... into a class resembling an Indian caste", and that, instead, the "young should be drawn from "the public schools of the country, where they would learn British feelings and British habits".[68] In Malthus's reading, Grenville wished to ensure that students would become British in a traditional way, at British public schools. The alternative, education offered at Haileybury, might turn the students into Indians before they left British soil; they could go native without even traveling abroad.

Malthus's reply sidesteps the question of how travel or even the prospect of travel overseas can affect national identities; he effectively assumed those trained would retain a British identity. Malthus argues instead that the College would further reforms suggested and implemented by Marquis Wellesley, governor-general in India between 1798 and 1805. He endorses Wellesley's argument that Company and British interests would be best served by effecting a different sort of shift in Company-men identities. Wellesley had noted that previous modes of preparing civil servants for British administration of India had resulted in critical shortages of skilled statesmen, hence Haileybury should help raise up statesman rather than merchants.

Malthus concurred, maintaining that the great expansion of the British Empire in India and its administrators' duties had necessitated "for many years ... making a great change in the qualifications necessary for its civil servants". Wellesley established a college at Fort William (Calcutta) on 10 July 1800, to "combine the usual studies of a European university with a knowledge of the oriental languages" to address this need. Malthus writes that "this education, the marquis says, should neither be exclusively European nor Indian, but of a mixed nature". He quotes the Marquis: the education's "foundation must be judiciously laid in England, and the superstructure systematically completed in India".[69] The directors of the Company soon closed the college at Fort William, but recognizing the needs it served, opened the college at Haileybury. Still, a traveler set to take up duties in India for the Company would be only partially outfitted on departure by his instruction at the college; he would acquire the rest of the training necessary for his tasks, instruction in Indigenous languages, once on Indian soil.

Malthus encountered resistance among most Company shareholders to disciplinary expulsions and competitive exams at Haileybury, actions akin to the workings of the "positive check" of the population principle.[70] These measures were directed at increasing the efficiency of company operations, as were others such as the costs of tuition. The costs of attending Haileybury and the risk of expulsion would serve as economic incentives for prudent behavior by students and share-holder patrons; these in turn would produce prudent graduates, who, once graduated as proper civil servants, would help bring the principles of political economy to life in India. Malthus concluded, however, that shareholders had little desire to abide by "those general rules, the gross violation of which cannot be passed over without a sacrifice of much greater and more general interests than those of an individual and his connexions".[71]

In general, the disputes which pitted interested parties against one another within the Company do not easily reduce to principal-agent relationships. Former students exercised considerable discretion in carrying out their duties as the company lacked means to effectively monitor them once in India. But it is sometimes difficult to differentiate between principals and agents. Shareholders were owners of the company in their own right, college officials tried to act as more than rubber stamps, and company directors often deferred to the desires of shareholders.

Haileybury offers evidence of just how hard the project of making the world, or just its travelers, in the image of political economy could prove to be. Some students may have learned the lesson; rioting students clearly did not. The students may have been too young, and the personal and economic disincentives of patronage too strong for the lessons to take hold. What pupil would act against the desires of his parents or patrons, or his own self-interest, to take advantage of the opportunities for plunder that awaited him in India? The college may have groomed the students to become prudent agents, but they retained their own agency: the subjects of political economics felt free to ignore the instructions of political economists.[72]

Notwithstanding the difficulty principal-agent relationships presented in real life to the Company, Mackintosh believed India would provide a test of whether political economy was a science of truly universal laws:

> the principles of political economy have been investigated in Europe, and the application of them to such a country as India must be one of the most curious tests which could be contrived of their truth and universal application. Everything here is new; and if they are found here to be also the true principles of natural subsistence and wealth, it will be no longer possible to dispute that they are the general laws which everywhere govern this important part of the movements of the social machine.
> (Mackintosh, "A Discourse", p. xxiv)

Mackintosh does not assume the universality of the laws of political economy; whether they apply to India, which he classifies as new rather than new to Europeans, remains to be seen. He implies, however, that political economists have already acquired the observations and knowledge to correctly discern and describe the laws governing subsistence and wealth for the nations of Europe. Apparently, this is true even in European nations like Norway, whose stadial status Malthus deemed indeterminate.

Mackintosh did arrange for a compilation of documents "upon the subject of the population for Bombay" for the years 1800 to 1808. His aim was to bring to the public "authentic information respecting the population of tropical countries". Mackintosh acknowledges the crude nature of the count of deaths in Bombay, an enumeration based on the number of bodies burned or buried on the island: "These returns being made by native officers, subject to no very efficient check, may be considered as liable to considerable errors of negligence and incorrectness, though exempt from those of intentional falsehood." Before delving into more detailed information on the Muslim population, the writer concludes that "we have only conjectural estimates of the whole population of the island, which vary from a hundred and sixty to a hundred and eighty thousand souls".[73] The returns for births and deaths among the Christian part of the population, while theoretically more accurate than those for Muslims due to the use of baptismal records for births, and registers of burials for deaths, prove, however, no less problematic. In the different parishes "the proportion of births and deaths to population differ very considerably from each other, and some of them deviate widely from the result of the like inquiries in most other places". While the writer does not know how much simple inaccuracy contributes to the deviations, he cites as the first possible cause of error the enumerators' lack of familiarity with political arithmetic.[74]

Yet the results did allow Mackintosh to settle one question, on the prevalence of polygamy in India and, by extension, elsewhere; he concludes that it is rarely practiced. To prove this, Mackintosh engages in a comparative exercise, pitting observations gathered by different travelers about the sex ratio between men and women against one another. On one side stood the famed explorer of Africa and the Middle East, the Scot James Bruce, who "attempts to support [the] theory" of the "illustrious philosopher" Montesquieu that polygamy is pervasive in Eastern nations. Mackintosh speculates that travelers "too much disposed to make general inferences from a few peculiar cases" had "misled" Montesquieu into believing that warm climates produce a "superabundance of women". Bruce "attempts to support this theory" with spurious evidence, a "statement of a most extraordinary nature" on the sex ratios he had observed during his travels.

Mackintosh employs both other travelers' facts and general principles, assumptions about the nature of economic behavior and the nature of observation, to refute Bruce and Montesquieu. Bruce makes an easy target. While celebrated, contemporaries contested his more outlandish claims, and Mackintosh is no exception. Bruce insists that he traveled through countries with sex ratios of two females to one male, and that a ratio of four to one prevailed "from Suez to the Straits of Babelmandel ... as far as the Line and 30° beyond it". Mackintosh strenuously, and perhaps jokingly, objects:

> The confidence with which a private traveler makes a statement so minute is sufficient to deprive it of all authority. Without imputing intentional falsehood to Mr. Bruce (which seems foreign to his character), this statement may be quoted as an instance of that dogmatism, enterprising credulity, ostentation, and loose recollection which have thrown an unmerited suspicion over the general veracity of one of the most enterprising travellers as well as amusing of writers.

Bruce may be innocent of the charge of bias, but his personal idiosyncrasies cast doubt on his credibility. Returning to the matter at hand, Mackintosh speculates that the poor in Africa and the Middle East most likely behave as do their peers in Europe. If men can barely feed one family, much less have the resources to maintain three or four in Europe, to expect an "Egyptian fellah" to be able to do so "would be the height of extravagance". Polygamy derives from bad government, not physical causes. Thus, "facts are more important than any reasonings, however conclusive".[75]

Bruce and Montesquieu statements on population lack authority according to Mackintosh; they rested on too few and too faulty travelers' observations. Vital statistics and accurate enumerations could serve as tools to help arbitrate disputes about travelers' facts and philosophers' principles. Political economists did fret, however, about the apparent lack of boundaries in statistical accounts, and the uses government might have for such information, criticisms they had earlier leveled at political arithmeticians. Malthus certainly endorses statistical accounts in principle, though. Mackintosh sides with Malthus on their utility; he cites the numbers drawn from parts of India with "accurate enumerations" on population, which

Francis Buchanan, working on behalf of the Company, included in *A Journey from Madras* (1807), as evidence that the sex ratio was close to one to one. But even the relatively inaccurate reports for Bombay helped establish the fact to Mackintosh's satisfaction.

The Bombay vital statistics collected by Mackintosh for 1800–08 may be unbiased, "exempt from those [errors] of intentional falsehood". They may help settle a question about the prevalence of polygamy in India. They may even help refute the observations of a famous traveler and the conjectures of a renowned armchair traveler. But they remain, again, inaccurate. Nor did they circulate in a particularly timely fashion. No enumeration existed for the Hindu population of Bombay for this period, as the reviewer in *The Quarterly Oriental Magazine, Review, and Register* lamented, in 1824, twenty years after Mackintosh first set foot on the subcontinent. This is part of a piece; though the "Advertisement" for the first volume of the *Transactions of the Literary Society of Bombay* carries the date of 23 September 1815, the first three volumes were not published until 1819, in London. The *Quarterly Oriental* reviewer concludes that the registers upon which the extrapolated estimates for the Hindu population are based are likely to be inaccurate. Mackintosh's note and tables do not yet measure up to the promise of statistics as compact, concise, credible, and complete summaries of easily and quickly transportable, that is, useful information: "although they are perhaps not very incorrect: at any rate, they furnish something like data" on the condition of the population of Bombay.[76]

This may explain why Malthus did not use any of his friends' statistics in the 1826 edition of *Essay*. Malthus did not use Buchanan's more "accurate enumerations", either. Indeed, the section on India lacks any vital statistics altogether. Instead, Malthus relied on material assembled by the famed orientalist philologist Sir William Jones, posthumously published in *Collected Works* (1799). Jones wrote extensively on the manners, customs, status of women, laws, and other institutions of the peoples of the subcontinent. Malthus used Jones's ethnological work for almost all the evidence he cites on India in *Essay*.

James Mill dismissed the possibility of credible travelers' observations altogether when he composed the three-volume *British History in India* in 1817. He had not traveled to the subcontinent, nor did he know any Indigenous languages; he was only appointed an Assistant Examiner of correspondence at the East India Company in 1819. *History* and the reactions it evoked among British residents in India illustrates how, again, political economists could simply choose to ignore what travelers and residents wrote if their accounts did not square with how political economists thought the principles of their science operated. Yet, the dispute between Mill and his critics in British India was as much about the principles governing observation and analysis as Mill's attempt to apply his particular flavor of political economy to governing India.

Mill had studied at the University of Edinburgh where Dugald Stewart had introduced him to stadial histories. Mill believed Indians were less civilized than the British, thus unprepared for self-rule. He opens *History* with a description of the problems he encountered when he tried to gather information on British experiences in India. One set lay in separating fact from opinion. Much of the literature he perused consisted, he claims, of "a body of statements, given indiscriminately as matters of fact, ascertained by the senses, the far greater part was in general only matter of opinion, borrowed, in succession, by one set of Indian gentlemen from another".[77] Shapiro notes that seventeenth century appeals to matters of fact rested in part on the development, by John Locke especially, of a philosophical defense of induction in terms of probability. Shapiro teases out how Locke's contemporaries wrestled with the implications of the distinction between scientific facts, verifiable by replication, and one-time events, the truth of which were testified to by historical witnesses.[78] How was one to discern the differences for establishing a unique fact, as in history or law, and a general fact, as in philosophy or science?[79]

Mill provides an answer to this question. He touts discrimination as the key to filtering the factual and the significant from the myriad of materials available on British India.[80] Having belittled Indigenous testimony, Mill proceeds to argue against placing too much value on eyewitness observation by Europeans in the region, too. In addition to the aforementioned risk that "Indian gentlemen" might simply adopt and repeat the opinions of others, an individual on the scene versed in Indian languages

> can treasure up the facts, which are presented to his senses; he can learn the facts which are recorded in such native books, as have not been translated; and he can ascertain facts by conversation with the natives, which have never yet been committed to writing. This he can do; and I am not aware he can do any thing further.[81]

Mill cautions the reader, "But, as no fact is more certain, so none is of more importance, in the science of human nature, than this; that the powers of observation, in every individual, are exceedingly limited." Thus, for Mill, better than an observer is an interpreter who aggregates accounts:

> an account of India complete in all its parts, at any one moment, still more through a series of ages, could never be derived from the personal observation of any one individual, but must be collected from the testimony of a great number of individuals, of any whom the power of perception could extend but a little way.[82]

Mill could not claim credibility as an eyewitness to events in British India; nonetheless, he tries to make a virtue out of armchair travel. Distance from the scene guarantees his ability to observe and understand more than any traveler or resident: "A duly qualified man can obtain more knowledge of India in one year in his closet in England than he could obtain during the course of the longest life, by the use of his eyes and ears in India."[83] Presumably a polymath like Mill could perform this work, though he remains silent here about the exact qualifications of his ideal virtual traveler.

British residents in India initially reacted quite negatively to *History*. They objected to Mill's methods, facts, and interpretations. One of the critiques appears in a review in *The Quarterly Oriental Magazine, Review, and Register* of a paper by a member of the Literary Society of Bombay variously referred to as Capt. Kennedy or Major Kennedy. Mill makes clear that he writes a judgmental history; he characterizes Indian peoples, institutions, politics, laws, and culture as all long-running failures. The review contains remarks on the role of taste, prejudice, and bigotry in making and reporting observations. The reviewer acknowledges the limits to an individual's capacity to understand the manners and customs of Indian peoples. But we also find sympathy for Hindus and Muslims, their religious beliefs and practices, as well as their literatures, albeit mixed with open condescension toward those same groups when the subject of the wisdom of British rule arises.[84] Anyone working on Orientalists and Orientalism during this period will find this mix of contradictory elements familiar.

The reviewer only reluctantly considers Mill's text, and cautions other British residents against spending much time on *History*. There's the question of audience:

> The third volume breaks a spear with the author of the *History of British India* in favour of the national character of the Hindus. As long as there are no other vehicles of conveying to the public the sentiments of enlightened men in India on publications in Europe, they may be permitted occasionally to occupy the pages of the Bombay Transactions and similar miscellanies. They are, however, not properly admissible, as the research of the societies instituted in the east are directed to describe and explain what they discover here, and not to contend with the error and prejudice that spring up at home. If such were their object, they would be fully employed, and with no writer more legitimately than Mr. Mill.[85]

The Quarterly Oriental Magazine speaks chiefly to British residents in India, on works produced about India in India. The formation of the Literary Society and the launch of the journal and similar India-based publications helps establish a public sphere in British India, one with local members, a foreign node of knowledge production separate from British or continental European circles. Distance, time really, affects the ability of travelers and resident foreigners to exchange information with interested parties overseas, and also can exacerbate barriers to establishing common parameters for making unbiased observations. The reviewer's critique of Mill's methods provides evidence of this epistemological gap between British India and Britain. The political economist uses only one standard to select among the observations made by Indians and resident foreigners, and "solely estimated his guides by their conformity to his preconceived opinions". The reviewer concludes that "we think that we have never encountered volumes more strongly characterised by prejudiced judgment and imperfect investigation".[86]

Can One Measure the Comparative Happiness of a Population?

Meanwhile, Mackintosh spoke for many of his contemporary travelers who compiled statistical accounts when he declared that political economy could prove to be a useful branch of knowledge for making and interpreting observations. He concludes "Discourse" by asserting that

> of all kinds of knowledge, political economy has the greatest tendency to promote quiet and safe improvement in the general condition of mankind; because it shows that the improvement is in the interest of the government, and that stability is in the interest of the people.

Mackintosh felt confident that in a world convulsed by war,

> in all possible cases the counsels of this science are at least safe. They are adapted to all forms of government; they require only a wise and just administration. They require as the first principle of all prosperity that perfect security of persons and property which can only exist where the supreme authority is stable.
>
> (Mackintosh, "A Discourse", p. xxv)

For this traveler, then, political economy was the most important framework through which to make observations, even in statistical accounts which would include information on languages, literature, religion, and sundry other topics. Mackintosh reiterates the first principle of political economists, that security is necessary for material progress and prosperity. It is unclear, however, whether he has dropped his belief, expressed earlier in the essay, that the principles of political economy may not necessarily operate in non-European societies. Here, when he claims that these principles "are adapted to all forms of government", does he refer to all principles, or only those related to security?

Mackintosh hardly had last word on the significance of political economy in statistical accounts, or the significance of statistical accounts in political economy, whatever his stance on the universality of the science. Nor the first word. Just prior to the above passage, he quotes from *Tableau historique et politique des pertes* (1799), by Francois d'Ivernois, to the effect that

> If the various states of Europe kept and published annually an exact account of their population, noting carefully in a second column the exact age at which the children die, this second column would show the relative merits of the governments and the comparative happiness of their subjects. A simple arithmetical statement would then be perhaps more conclusive than all the arguments that could be produced.
> (Mackintosh, "A Discourse", p. xxiv)[87]

Vital statistics, most notably historical series of the infant mortality rate, would allow one to determine at a glance the relative merit of a European society's government and its inhabitants' happiness. Malthus included and approvingly cited this passage, too, in the second edition of *Essay*. He sought confirmation of his own speculations, but his commentary on the passage shades into conjecture based on belief and hope rather than actual proof. He added to the political arithmetical of d'Ivernois by reiterating his belief that infant mortality would be lowest where the birth rate was lowest. England ranked third in this respect, after Switzerland and Norway. This he declares not only "an extraordinary fact", given the "great towns and manufactories" in England, but testimony that England has passed the "surest test of happiness and good government" (*Essay*, 1803, p. 314). The reviewer of *Essay* in *The British Critic and Quarterly Theological Review* agreed, and expressed the hope that "further investigation will corroborate such a favourable statement of the superior happiness we enjoy above the other states of Europe".[88]

According to Mackintosh a simple calculation could bring to a close endless speculation on the subjects of governance and happiness. This did not occur of course. Like Malthus, the enhancement of health and the preservation of life formed the chief objects of later studies and reform efforts by devotees of social medicine and the sanitary movements, though they would part ways with political economists over both the means by which to study society and the ends of these studies.[89] Citing vital statistics gathered from his Scandinavian tour, Malthus criticized Sweden for state support of hospitals and the provision of free medical care, likening the results of such policies to the pernicious effects of the English poor laws. The Swedish authorities were too focused on treating misery rather than preventing it, and state policies lessened individual responsibility for care of the self, thus dampening preventive checks to population growth.[90] For their part, doctors felt political economists placed too much emphasis on prosperity and paid too little attention to health as a marker of happiness. In India, as in England, individual subjects, households, and entire populations, proved hard to measure and refashion as the material of political economists' and others' policies.[91] British beliefs that food production and distribution should be based on work, and that money incomes rather than need would suffice to fight famines, resulted in additional harm. The stories of these policies and the periodic catastrophes that ensued, which persisted until the end of

British rule, have been told elsewhere. The next chapter revisits representations of early nineteenth century Ireland where, once again, the relationship between food, prosperity, and happiness helped shape the observations of travelers and political economists.

Notes

1. Norway was at that time part of the Kingdom of Denmark, and the Swedish portion of the journal was lost.
2. British writers composed some two hundred travel accounts on Norway from the close of the eighteenth to the beginning of the twentieth century. But the bulk of these were written in the latter half of the nineteenth century. Most accounts appeared in books; others were published in journal and magazine articles. Peter Fjågesund and Ruth A. Symes, *The Northern Utopia: British Perceptions of Norway in the Nineteenth Century* (Amsterdam: Rodopi, 2003), pp. 13–4, 18.
3. Mary Wollstonecraft, *Letters Written during a Short Residence in Sweden, Norway, and Denmark* (London: J. Johnson, 1796), p. 13 (emphases in original); Ingrid Horrocks, "Creating an 'Insinuating Interest': Mary Wollstonecraft's Travel Reviews and *A Short Residence*", *Studies in Travel Writing*, 19, no. 1 (2015): 1–15. Further references to *Letters* are included parenthetically in the text.
4. Gail Bederman, "Sex, Scandal, Satire, and Population in 1798: Revisiting Malthus's First Essay", *Journal of British Studies*, 47, no. 4 (2008): 768–95 (at pp. 776, 795).
5. Thomas Robert Malthus, *The Travel Diaries of Thomas Robert Malthus*, Patricia James, ed. (London: Cambridge University Press, 1966), p. 25. Coxe's narratives were first published in two volumes in 1784; volume 2 concludes with Books VII and VIII, on Sweden and Denmark, respectively. Coxe added volumes over time: volume 5, published in 1791, contained information from a second journey which included countries he did not visit in the first. Norway is covered in this edition, in Book X "Travels into Sweden," chapters v–vii.
6. William Coxe, *Travels into Poland, Russia, Sweden, and Denmark*, vol. 5 (London: T. Cadell, 1791), p. 187. Further references to *Travels* are included parenthetically in the text.
7. Malthus, *The Travel Diaries*, pp. 18–21.
8. Edward Daniel Clarke, *Travels in Various Countries of Europe, Asia and Africa*, vol. 3 Part 1 (London: T. Cadell and W. Davies, 1819), p. vii (emphasis in original).
9. Clarke, *Travels in Various Countries*, Part 1, p. vii.
10. Erich Pontoppidan, *Natural History of Norway* [1751], vols. 1 and 2 (London: A. Linde, 1755), pp. 183–210. Wollstonecraft inquired into the existence of sea monsters during her visit to Norway, and concluded that there was no proof to be found:

    > I did not leave Norway without making some inquiries about the monsters said to have been seen in the northern sea; but though I conversed with several captains, I could not meet with one who had heard any traditional description of them, much less had any ocular demonstration of their existence. Till the fact be better ascertained, I should think the account of them ought to be torn out of our Geographical Grammars. (Wollstonecraft, *Letters*, pp. 176–7)

11. Malthus, *The Travel Diaries*, p. 134.
12. Malthus, *The Travel Diaries*, pp. 89, 103,119, 152, 169, 173, 178.

13 Michael Drake, "Malthus on Norway", *Population Studies*, 20, no. 2 (1966): 175–96 (at pp. 176–7).
14 Fjågesund and Symes, *The Northern Utopia*, pp. 236–7.
15 Drake, "Malthus on Norway", p. 181; Deborah Valenze, "Malthus among the Laplanders: Reindeer Herders in the Crucible of Civilization" (Unpublished paper, 2016), p. 23.
16 Drake, "Malthus on Norway", p. 180–2.
17 Drake, "Malthus on Norway", p. 186.
18 Ian Hacking, "Biopower and the Avalanche of Printed Numbers", *Humanities in Society*, 5 (1982): 279–95; Theodore Porter, *The Rise of Statistical Thinking, 1820–1900* (Princeton, NJ: Princeton University Press, 1986).
19 Michèle Pujol, *Feminism and Anti-Feminism in Early Economic Thought* (Northampton, MA: Edward Elgar, 1992).
20 Marcet, *Conversations on Political Economy*, pp. 17–8.
21 Malthus, *The Travel Diaries*, p. 117.
22 Malthus, *The Travel Diaries*, p. 89.
23 Malthus, *The Travel Diaries*, p. 120.
24 E.P. Thompson, "Time, Work-Discipline, and Industrial Capitalism", *Past and Present*, no. 38 (1967): 56–97 (especially pp. 78–9).
25 Gary S. Becker, *A Treatise on the Family* (Cambridge, MA: Harvard University Press, 1981).
26 Edward Daniel Clarke, *Travels in Various Countries of Europe, Asia and Africa*, vol. 3 Part 2 (London: T. Cadell, 1823), p. 76.
27 Clarke quotes Ecclesiasticus 26:16; Clarke, *Travels in Various Countries*, Part 2, p. 30.
28 Sylvia Bowerbank, "The Bastille of Nature: Wollstonecraft versus Malthus in Scandinavia", in Anka Ryall and Catherine Sandbach-Dahlström, eds., *Mary Wollstonecraft's Journey to Scandinavia: Essays* (Stockholm: Almqvist & Wicksell International, 2003), pp. 165–84 (at p. 174).
29 Clarke, *Travels in Various Countries*, Part 2, p. 31 (emphasis in original).
30 John William Cunningham, *Cautions to Continental Travellers* (London: Ellerton and Henderson, 1818), pp. vi, 2, 3, 12–6. A statement of the Chancellor of the Exchequer before Parliament cited by Cunningham indicates "that more than 90,000 persons had embarked, in little more than two years, from one port alone, of whom 12,700 remained abroad" (*Cautions*, p. 3).
31 Benjamin Colbert, "Bibliography of British Travel Writing, 1780–1840. The European Tour, 1814–1818 (excluding Britain and Ireland)", *Cardiff Corvey. Reading the Romantic Text*, 13 (2004): 5–44 (at p. 5), www.cf.ac.uk/encap/corvey/articles/cc13_n01.pdf [21 November 2016].
32 The controversy has been variously dated 1799–1802, 1800–1803, and 1799–1803. Mitzi Myers, "'A Peculiar Protection': Hannah More and the Cultural Politics of Blagdon Controversy", in Beth Fowkes Tobin, ed., *History, Gender, and 18th-Century Literature* (Athens, GA: University of Georgia Press, 1994), pp. 227–57; Jane Nardin, "Hannah More and the Problem of Poverty", *Texas Studies in Literature and Language*, 43, no. 3 (2001): 267–84 (at pp. 267–8); Anne Stott, "Hannah More and the Blagdon Controversy, 1799–1802", *The Journal of Ecclesiastical History*, 51, no. 2 (2000): 319–46.
33 William Roberts, ed., *Memoirs of the Life and Correspondence of Mrs. Hannah More*, 2nd edn. (London: R.B. Seeley and W. Burnside, 1839), p. 378; Arthur Roberts, ed., *Letters of Hannah More to Zachary Macaulay, Containing Notices of Lord Macaulay's Youth* (London: James Nisbet and Co, 1860), p. 142.
34 Anon., "Hannah More's New Work", *The Analectic Magazine*, 14 (1819): 429–33 (at p. 430).

132 *Travels with Malthus*

35 Hannah More, *Moral Sketches of Prevailing Opinions and Manners, Foreign and Domestic: With Reflections on Prayer* (London: T. Cadell & W. Davies, 1819), p. xi. Further references to *Moral Sketches* are included parenthetically in the text.
36 Her friends during this period included Joshua Reynolds, Dr. Johnson, David Garrick, and her fellow Bristolian Josiah Tucker, by then Dean of Gloucester.
37 Nardin, "Hannah More and the Problem of Poverty", pp. 272–4.
38 Hannah More, *Slavery, A Poem* (London: T. Cadell, 1788), line 188 (emphasis in original).
39 More, *Slavery*, Lines 211 and 212.
40 More, *Slavery*, Lines 235 and 236.
41 More, *Slavery*, Lines 244–8.
42 Driver and Gilbert, "Imperial Cities", p. 7.
43 Nocia, "The London Shopscape", p. 29.
44 Mary Wollstonecraft, *Original Stories from Real Life; with Conversations, Calculated to Regulate the Affections, and Form the Mind to Truth and Goodness* (1788) (London: J. Johnson, 1796), p. 149.
45 Nocia, "The London Shopscape", pp. 35–6.
46 "Anon., Review of Hannah More's *Moral Sketches of Prevailing Opinions and Manners, Foreign and Domestic*", *The British Review, and London Critical Journal*, 14, no. 28 (1819): 458–74 (at p. 461); see also Anon., "Review. More's *Moral Sketches, &c.*", *The Investigator*, 1 (1820): 131–41 (at pp. 134–6).
47 Anon., "Review of Hannah More's *Moral Sketches of Prevailing Opinions and Manners, Foreign and Domestic*", *The Monthly Review*, 91 (1820): 164–74 (at p. 167). *The Monthly Review* had earlier criticized Cunningham's publication as the work of "one alarmed beyond all fair bounds at the hazards of continental travelling": Anon., "Review of J.W. Cunningham's *Cautions to Continental Travellers*", *The Monthly Review*, 89 (1819): 445–6 (at p. 446).
48 Cunningham, *Cautions*, p. 78.
49 Anon., "[Review of] *Moral Sketches of Prevailing Opinions and Manners, &c., With Reflections on Prayer*", *The Gentleman's Magazine*, 89, Part 2 (1819): 434–5; 532–4 (at p. 434).
50 Anon., "Review of Hannah More's *Moral Sketches ...*", *The Monthly Review*, p. 168.
51 Anon., "Review of Hannah More's *Moral Sketches ...*", *The British Review*, p. 469.
52 Thomas Robert Malthus, *An Essay on the Principle of Population*, 6th edn., 2 vols. (London: John Murray, 1826), vol. 1, p. 268. Further references to *Essay* are included parenthetically in the text by year of publication and volume and page numbers.
53 Valenze, "Malthus among the Laplanders".
54 Malthus writes:

> In the course of this chapter ['Of the Checks to Population among the American Indians'] I often give the same references as Robertson; but never without having examined and verified them myself. Where I have not had an opportunity of doing this, I refer to Robertson alone.
>
> (*Essay*, 1826, I, 37)

55 Malthus cites a 1780 edition of Robertson's *History of America*, which was published in two separate sets of volumes, in 1777 and 1796, and Bruce's five-volume *Travels to Discover the Source of the Nile* (1790).
56 Jonsson, "Rival Ecologies", pp. 1360–1.

57 James Mackintosh, *Memoirs of the Life of the Right Honourable Sir James Mackintosh*, vol. 1, ed. Robert James Mackintosh (London: Edward Moxon, 1835), pp. 209, 215.
58 Mackintosh, *Memoirs*, p. 215.
59 Anon., "Advertisement", *Transactions of the Literary Society of Bombay*, vol. 1, [1819], ed. Vishvanath Narayan Mandlik (Bombay: Bombay Education Society Press, 1877), pp. v–ix (at p. vi).
60 James Mackintosh, "Appendix A.", [1819] in Vishvanath Narayan Mandlik, ed., *Transactions of the Literary Society of Bombay*, vol. 1 (Bombay: Bombay Education Society Press, 1877), pp. 305–8 (at pp. 305–7).
61 Mackintosh, "Appendix A.", pp. 307–8.
62 James Mackintosh, "A Discourse at the Opening of the Literary Society of Bombay" [1819], in Vishvanath Narayan Mandlik, ed., *Transactions of the Literary Society of Bombay*, vol. 1 (Bombay: Bombay Education Society Press, 1877), pp. xii–xxvi (at p. xiii). Further references to "A Discourse" are included parenthetically in the text.
63 Academic economists only began to investigate principal-agent problems in earnest in the 1970s. Economists tend to deal with principal-agent and monitoring issues separately, as they seek to tease out the causes and consequences of imperfect information both in markets and in the internal structures of economic organizations.
64 [James Mackintosh?], "Note on 'Preliminary Discourse'" [1819], in Vishvanath Narayan Mandlik, ed., *Transactions of the Literary Society of Bombay*, vol. 1 (Bombay: Bombay Education Society Press, 1877), pp. xxvii–xli (at p. xxvii).
65 Keith Tribe, "Professors Malthus and Jones: Political Economy at the East India College 1806–1858", *European Journal of the History of Economic Thought*, 2, no. 2 (1995): 327–54 (at p. 330).
66 Thomas Robert Malthus, *Statements Respecting the East-India College, with an Appeal to Facts, in Refutation of the Charges Lately Brought against It, in the Court of Proprietors* (London: John Murray, 1817), p. 102.
67 Timothy L. Alborn, *Conceiving Companies: Joint-Stock Politics in Victorian England* (London: Routledge, 1998), p. 33; "Boys to Men: Moral Restraint at Haileybury College", in Brian Dolan, ed., *Malthus, Medicine and Morality: "Malthusianism" after 1798* (Amsterdam: Editions Rodopi, 2000), pp. 33–55.
68 Thomas Robert Malthus, *A Letter to the Rt. Hon. Lord Grenville* (London: J. Johnson, 1813), p. 3.
69 Malthus, *A Letter*, pp. 4, 5, 10.
70 Alborn, "Boys to Men", pp. 44–5.
71 Malthus, *Statements Respecting the East-India College*, p. 80; see Patricia James, *Population Malthus, His Life and Times* (London: Routledge & Kegan Paul, 1979), pp. 216–8, 241–2.
72 The present-day subjects of economics feel free to do much the same.
73 [Mackintosh?], "Note", p. xxvii.
74 [Mackintosh?], "Note", pp. xxvii–xxviii.
75 [Mackintosh?], "Note", p. xxxi.
76 Anon., "Transactions of the Literary Society of Bombay", *The Quarterly Oriental Magazine, Review, and Register*, 2 (1824): 17–53 (at p. 18).
77 James Mill, *The History of British India*, vol. 1. (London: Baldwin, Cradock and Joy, 1817), p. vii.
78 Barbara J. Shapiro, *A Culture of Fact: England, 1550–1720* (Ithaca, NY: Cornell University Press, 2000).
79 Joseph M. Levine, "Review" [of Shapiro, Barbara J. (2000) *A Culture of Fact: England, 1550–1720*, Ithaca, NY: Cornell University Press], *Albion*, 33, no. 1 (2001): 102–3 (at p. 102).

80 Mill, *History*, p. ix.
81 Mill, *History*, p. xiv.
82 Mill, *History*, p. xiv.
83 Mill, *History*, p. xv.
84 Anon., "Transactions of the Literary Society of Bombay", *The Quarterly Oriental Magazine, Review, and Register*, 1, no. 2 (1824): 177–235 (at pp. 210–1).
85 Anon., "Transactions", p. 211.
86 Anon., "Transactions", pp. 211, 212.
87 Si les divers États de l'Europe tenaient & publiaient un régistre annuel & exact de leur population, en y indiquant avec soin les époques précises de la vie où meurent les enfans; cette seconde colonne du register servirait á prononcer comparativement sur le mérite des souverains & sur le bonheur des sujets. Une simple formule arithmétique en dirait peut-être davantage que tous les raisonnemens. [François d'Ivernois, *Tableau historique et politique des pertes* (London: Baylis, 1799), p. 16, note].
88 Anon., "Malthus on the Principle of Population", *The British Critic and Quarterly Theological Review*, 23 (1804): 59–69 (at p. 69).
89 Christopher Hamlin and Kathleen Gallagher-Kamper, "Malthus and the Doctors: Political Economy, Medicine, and the State in England, Ireland, and Scotland, 1800–1840", in Brian Dolan, ed., *Malthus, Medicine and Morality: "Malthusianism" after 1798* (Amsterdam: Editions Rodopi, 2000), pp. 115–40.
90 Brian Dolan, "Malthus's Political Economy of Health: The Critique of Scandinavia in the *Essay on Population*", in Brian Dolan, ed., *Malthus, Medicine and Morality: "Malthusianism" after 1798* (Amsterdam: Editions Rodopi, 2000), pp. 9–32 (at pp. 21–5).
91 Timothy L. Alborn, "Age and Empire in the Indian Census, 1871–1931", *The Journal of Interdisciplinary History*, 30, no. 1 (1999): 61–89.

4 Travelers in Search of Malthus's "Authenticated *Facts*"
The Case of Ireland

If people travel, so too do objects. This chapter examines correspondence between the English political economist David Ricardo and the Anglo-Irish author Maria Edgeworth in 1822 and 1823 in which the two friends dilate on the use of the potato in Ireland and population growth on the island; they amicably disagreed on the question – for or against the potato? Their letters formed part of the increasing number of objects that traveled among and between scientists in this period. Another object that traveled took center stage in their correspondence when Edgeworth apparently sent Ricardo a scientific sample, a package of potato flour given to her during one of her trips to France.

Their letters are informed by the disputes over methods that roiled the world of British political economists during the first half of the nineteenth century. Ireland had been well-trod for centuries by the British, and travelers' observations play a crucial role in the two friends' discussions. Edgeworth's reflections on her own travel and bias in travelers' observations, and their shared passion for using statistical facts, drawn from experimental agriculture, provide additional context to their give and take over potatoes and population. The epistolary exchange occurred against the backdrop of a rising number of accounts by English travelers to Ireland in the early decades of the nineteenth century. These visitors sought to organize observations to satisfy the curiosity of Englishmen and women who, despite hundreds of years of nonstop, frequently bloody engagement, remained woefully ignorant about the island. Travelers attempted to balance objective observations against the desire to recommend remedies for the political, religious and economic ailments of the kingdom, a standard theme of earlier English travel writing on Ireland.

Edgeworth's exchange with Ricardo also offers a glimpse at a set of discussions among British political economists, their followers and their critics in the first half of the nineteenth century on the meanings and measures of value. This is not the much-belabored debate on the meaning of the labor theory of value. Rather, British travelers and political economists faced quandaries about how to gauge the well-being and happiness of a society.

DOI: 10.4324/9781315778952-4

Ireland and England: The Politics and Economics of "Family" Relationships

What tales did visitors tell of their time in Ireland? How were the early nineteenth century observations of Malthus and other British political economists on Ireland related to these travel accounts? As Hooper and others have noted, extant travel writings from the early modern period were composed almost exclusively by English men who had accompanied soldiers tramping through the countryside or who were soldiers themselves. These accounts, unsurprisingly, are replete with references as to how best to secure one's safety from the Irish. Their accounts also included analysis and suggestions for political reform which would stabilize Ireland for economic development.[1]

What was not so clear in these accounts was how to stabilize the Irish population, natives who appear frequently as primitives, barbarians, or wild Irish. Some writers proposed extreme measures to remedy Irish behavior, and thus stamp out Irish disorder and poverty. This was true even as the practical issues of the security of travelers and their palpable sense of fear had subsided later in the seventeenth century.[2] These proposals included a radical plan put forth by William Petty, who as physician-general to Oliver Cromwell's army in Ireland surveyed the island and acquired vast land holdings on it as partial payment for his services. Drawing on facts gleaned in part from his travels, Petty suggested in *Treatise of Ireland* (1687) that the English remove a million inhabitants from Ireland, out of an estimated population of "1300 Thousand People", and resettle them in England.[3] The Irish would become English; the Irish Catholics who remained in Ireland would be those "such as can all speak English", and would be forced to take English names, while "The Transplanters into England may do the same". The Irish landscape itself would be transformed into an English one; "The Lands upon the down-Survey, may also have English Names put upon them."[4] Those resettled in England would become more productive, as productive, in fact, as Englishmen, because they would, in effect, *become Englishmen.*[5]

Petty's plan was meant, in his words,

> To cut up the Roots of those Evils in Ireland, which by Differences of Births, Extractions, Manners, Languages, Customs, and Religions, have continually wasted the Blood and Treasure of both Nations for above 500 Years; and have made Ireland, for the most Part, a Diminution and a Burthen, not an Advantage, to England.[6]

Petty's political arithmetic was a branch of natural philosophy designed to bring matters to account in terms of number, weight, and measure. Political arithmetic would discipline observations and representations, including those by travelers; observations would be "thereby made capable of Demonstrations" and useful to policy.[7] Petty's plan would effectively extinguish Ireland as a separate political entity, and the Irish as a separate people. But the effective conversion of all Irish people and things into English people and things would deliver measurable benefits to England beyond pacification; it would enhance the revenues of the king, the public and the Church of England. Political arithmetic was ultimately at the service of the state.

If the beginning of the eighteenth century ushered in a more peaceful if not pacific period in Anglo-Irish relations, the 1798 rebellion and the Acts of Union saw out the century. The Acts of Union of 1800 changed Ireland's status, as it became part of a new political entity, a United Kingdom of Great Britain and Ireland. The two nations failed, however, to coalesce into a single unambiguously identifiable national identity; while the English considered Ireland more foreign country than home, Union "estranged home space itself".[8] Ireland was now simultaneously home and away, domestic and foreign. This represented a challenge to British identity; politically, at least, they were part Irish, represented by Irish representatives in the British parliament.

Thus, while travelers continued to observe Ireland in the light of English colonial subordination, past and present, they now also dwelled on both Ireland's exoticism and the new ambiguity embodied in its familial relations with her sister nations, especially England. Those who did venture to the Emerald Isle in this period included a number of women. Anne Plumptre, for instance, who inspired by Wollstonecraft's account of her travels in Scandinavia, published *Narrative of a Residence in Ireland during the Summer of 1814, and that of 1815* (1817). English travelers at the time of the Union, women and men, tried foremost to redress English ignorance about Ireland and its people. George Cooper introduces the first edition of *Letters* by noting that, while Ireland has been much discussed, very few British had actually traveled to and observed the country. He cannot account "why the sister kingdom has been so strangely overlooked" (Cooper, *Letters on the Irish Nation* (1800), ix–x; xi). Cooper was responding to an English public eager for information about Ireland. Too eager, perhaps. George III, William Pitt, and others considered Edgeworth's fictional *Castle Rackrent* (1800) "a valuable source of facts concerning present-day Ireland"; the *Monthly Review* listed the tale under the heading "Ireland", in the "company of texts and pamphlets debating the Union", rather than under "Novels".[9] Cooper grounds his account in political history and analysis rather than natural history, prompted by a desire to promote political harmony between the two kingdoms still absorbing the aftershocks of 1798. Yet in this he and others actually remain faithful to the previous century's accounts, which routinely depart from natural history descriptions to address Ireland's religious and political history, as well as the efficacy of policy recommendations designed to ameliorate Irish poverty and sectarian strife.

Those who did venture to travel to the island in the first decades of the nineteenth century still tended to begin their reports on Ireland with natural history observations under the presumption that understanding the Irish landscape and climate would provide crucial insights into Irish character and poverty. According to John Bush and many other contemporaries, Lady Louisa Conolly applied the arts of domestic economy to beautify the landscape; early nineteenth century visitors' landscape descriptions veered, however, toward an aesthetic stemming from political economy, specifically the divergent agricultural histories of the two kingdoms. English travelers viewed Irish agriculture, with its lack of trees, hedgerows, and tidy villages, as disorganized and ugly. The roots of these differences lay in climatologically-based differences in crops, and the stark differences in rates of enclosure in the two kingdoms; "British travelers found it difficult to visually organize, to literally *see*, much less comprehend and appreciate, much of the Irish landscape they encountered."[10] English travelers' aesthetic visions, honed in England, both reflected and prompted desires to turn the foreign into the domestic, and to make the Irish landscape more like England.

English travelers had already begun to transcribe the aesthetics of the landscape onto the inhabitants of rural Ireland late in the eighteenth century. Arthur Young, touring through Mitchelstown in County Cork, concludes that, in a country transitioning from barbarity, the locals were still no better than savages, or wild animals:

> In a country changing from licentious barbarity into civilized order, building is an object of perhaps greater consequence than may at first be apparent. In a wild, or but half cultivated tract, with no better edifice than a mud cabbin, what are the objects that can impress a love of order on the mind of man? He must be wild as the roaming herds; savage as his rocky mountains; confusion, disorder, riot have nothing better than himself to damage or destroy.[11]

Human markings on the landscape signify the degree of civilization, or the lack thereof. Metonym gives way to simile as Young answers his own question on what his observations about the Irish landscape reveal about the Irish people.

The Union led visitors to Ireland to reconsider comparisons of the Irish customs, manners, and economic fortunes with those of the English, as well as renew reflections on what it meant to be English. To Plumptre, writing in "Preface", judging the relative merits of each country will help bind them closer together.

> If we are anxious to be introduced to a knowledge of the face of their country, to understand its natural advantages and disadvantages, its customs and manners, its civil and political state, that we may be enabled to compare them with our own, and judge between them and ourselves – a much deeper interest will surely be excited when these injuries, these comparisons, relate to an object so near to us as a SISTER.[12]

Plumptre continues, with a nod toward the demands of contemporary readers of travel narratives, by asserting her identity as an authoritative source of facts: "my constant aim has been to examine every object with accuracy, to pursue every inquiry with impartiality". Her goal, to convey information, truthfully, supersedes, but does not entirely extinguish the imperative to entertain:

> In narrating the results of my investigations, I have looked to fidelity as my polar star, – that has never been sacrificed at the shrine of embellishment and amusement; though ... I have been at the same time very ambitious that truth should be dressed in an amusing garb.[13]

The same process of comprehension, comparison, and judgment of England and Ireland, driven by impartial and accurate assembling of facts, but lacking the necessity to entertain, animated the work of British political economists; "One might have thought that Ireland was the inspiration for the Malthusian population models which played such a crucial role in nineteenth-century political economy."[14] Certainly Malthus, Nassau Senior, J.R. McCulloch, and other political economists who paraded before Parliamentary committees saw fit to pose as expert witnesses on all things Irish. They typically applied a strict application of political economic principles to the Irish situation in their testimony, citing, for instance, the lean years of 1821 and 1822 as an example of the positive check in action.[15]

If this is the political economists' gaze, it is Malthusian, or at least a response to the population principle. Turned toward Ireland in the 1820s, users of this perspective focused chiefly on the land tenure system and the potato, and mirrored the general attitude of visitors to Ireland, who held that both shaped the fortunes and the very character of the Irish. When we turn to Malthus, a cursory glance at the table of contents of the 1826 *Essay* confirms that view, as Ireland has literally the last word in the first volume on the population principle. Malthus and readers' long tour of countries in different time periods concludes with a return home to the contemporary United Kingdom, England, Scotland, and Ireland.[16]

But Malthus actually knew or professed to know very little of Ireland, and had no first-hand knowledge of the island until he visited Westmeath and the Lake of Killarney in July 1817. In a letter to Ricardo on 17 August of that year, Malthus remarks that he had "been both gratified and instructed by my tour". His comment on the relative "comfort and safety" of the trip echoes a motif of previous English visitors to the island. He organizes what he has observed in light of the population principle:

> the predominant evil of Ireland, namely a population greatly in excess above the demand for labour, though in general not much in excess above the means of subsistence on account of the rapidity with which

potatoes have increased under a system of cultivating them on very small properties rather with a view to support than sale.

This excess, Malthus concludes, is excessive, as

> The *Land* in Ireland is infinitely more peopled than in England; and to give full effect to the natural resources of the country, a great part of this population should be swept from the soil into large manufacturing and commercial Towns.[17]

Malthus implies that England's ratio of people to land complies with a natural order consistent with the highest stage of civilization. For Ireland to achieve a similar degree of commercial civilization as England, the rural Irish poor must be herded into cities like so many cattle. Malthus reminds us that political economists had difficulty maintaining a distinction between the science and art of their discipline. He is no Petty to be sure. But his remarks reflect a similar impulse to achieve wholesome English ends by noxious means inflicted on subject peoples.

Malthus's Irish sojourn had no discernible impact on subsequent editions of *Essay*. Malthus did not actually refer to Ireland at great length or with much subtlety in the sections on individual nations in the post-1798 editions, despite its prominent position in the text. Beginning with the second edition Malthus cites a general lack of "details of the population of Ireland", yet fails to avail himself of the growing number of contemporary accounts of English travelers to the kingdom. And he only drops his reference to the inhabitants as barbarous, a glaring taxonomical inconsistency under his classification of Ireland as a modern European state, in the sixth. He does conclude the section on Ireland in that edition with the addition of new material, a reference to statistics from the 1821 population census, but only in two brief paragraphs that had otherwise remained essentially unchanged since 1803. In total, the three short paragraphs on Ireland in the sixth edition consist of a little over 300 words (312 to be exact), including statistics. While this represents a substantial increase over the approximately 200 words devoted to the one paragraph on Ireland in the fourth edition in 1807, it's dwarfed by the nearly 4,500 Malthus dedicates to Scotland in the same chapter.[18] Thus, Ireland looks like an afterthought in *Essay*. This does not prevent Malthus from venturing his opinions on Irish policy. The population principle, again, underwrote his prescriptions; in the fifth (1817) edition of *Essay*, he objects to the overwhelming reliance of the Irish on the potato. To Malthus, any policy which encouraged population growth in the absence of demand for the resulting supply of workers would result in low wages, condemning the poor to misery.

Malthus is not exceptional among British political economists in his relative neglect of Ireland and the Irish. In the main, British political economists had little or no direct knowledge about Ireland, despite their avidity to testify about Irish policy in parliament. Still, contemporaries queried what they took as Malthus's incuriosity about Ireland. One, the Rev. William Richardson, noted in 1811 that Malthus "seemed quite alive to the pursuit of information" on population into the most obscure corners of Europe, yet appeared to almost entirely neglect Ireland.[19] Another contemporary puzzled, "Ireland's case affords so striking an illustration of the doctrines which Mr. Malthus has advanced in the late *Essay on Population*, that we are surprised he did not enter into it in more detail."

This second quote turns out to be from Malthus himself.[20] It appears in the first of two essays on Ireland he published in 1808 and 1809 in *The Edinburgh Review*.[21] These essays are armchair travel accounts of Ireland. But they still tell us something about Malthus's engagement with the emerging norms of openness in science, especially discussions on the need for impartiality in gathering facts in order to lend credibility to accounts. First, this anonymous essay might not have been so anonymous after all. Publishers and editors certainly knew who wrote for them, and passed along this information to friends. Readers outside of these networks might still correctly guess the authorship of certain pieces; journals like *The Edinburgh Review* tended to draw on a limited roster of writers, which was even more limited for specialized topics like political economy during this period. Essayists could also initial their pieces in some journals, thus disclosing important clues to their identities to discerning readers. Yet, misattributions did occur, with authors mistakenly and publicly tarred by a controversial essay. In terms of openness, anonymous essays could be freer in content, style, and tone than signed ones. Thus, anonymity could allow political economists to more frankly weigh in on matters of policy, the art of political economy. On the other hand, anonymity could lead to less openness and less discussion if a writer was unwilling to publicly stand by what she or he wrote.

Ó Gráda calls the tone of the 1808 and 1809 essays "more moderate and sympathetic" on the issue of the potato and Irish population than anything in *Essay* or other texts publicly acknowledged as Malthus's own, but concludes that they illustrate "a rather superficial knowledge of Irish history and conditions".[22] Malthus foresees a gradual, not jarring adjustment process for an Irish population sustained by potatoes, as the supply of food inevitably grew less abundant. Thus, while speculating that seasons of hunger will still stalk the Irish, Malthus predicts that they will eventually develop habits consistent with the preventive check, chiefly later marriages: "as the gradual diminution of the real wages of the laboring classes of society, slowly, and almost insensibly, generates the habits necessary for an order of things in which the funds for the maintenance of labour are stationary". Here he explicitly, if speculatively rules out an event like the Great Famine ("Newenham and Others on the State of Ireland" (1808), 345).[23]

The prospect Malthus presents is not all rosy, though, and he makes several highly critical remarks about the Irish in the review essays. In the 1808 review, he called on the authority of Young to note that the Irish subsisted like domesticated animals.

> But though it is certainly true that the Irish peasant has hitherto been able to command a greater quantity of the food to which he is accustomed, than the English labourer can of bread, yet it by no means follows that his general condition should be proportionably better. Something else besides food is required to make life comfortable; and the surplus potatoes of the Irishman, when converted into money, will have but a small power in purchasing other articles. Owing to the deficiency of manufacturing capital in Ireland, and the indolent habits of workmen in general, the conveniences of clothing, furniture, &c. are as dear as in England; while the pecuniary wages of the Irish labourer are not equal to half the earnings of the Englishman. Hence arises the unsparing meal of potatoes noticed by Mr. Young, at which the beggar, the pig, the dog, the cat, and the poultry, seem all equally welcome; while the cabin that affords shelter to all their various inhabitants, is hardly superior to an English pigstye; – its furniture confined almost exclusively to the pot in which the potatoes are boiled; and the clothing of its human inmates as deficient in quantity as it is wretched in quality. Mr Young observes, that an Irishman and his wife are much more solicitous to feed than to clothe their children, but the fact is, that they have the power of doing the one, and not that of doing the other.
>
> ("Newenham and Others on the State of Ireland" (1808), pp. 339–40)

Malthus acknowledges the chief merit of the potato is that it allows the Irish to be better fed, in fact, than English laborers subsisting on bread. Future Irish laborers might be able to adequately feed their families. But having enough to eat does not suffice as the sole measure of well-being. Potatoes may have great value as food for the Irish, but little exchange value for other goods. Add in the inadequate wages earned by the Irish, and the Irish would be unable to procure some of the necessities of life, such as clothing, an eventuality which, Malthus concludes, "could never present very flattering prospects of happiness" ("Newenham and Others on the State of Ireland" (1808), p. 340).

Malthus acknowledges that Newenham's work raises questions about observation and credibility when he asserts in the second essay that "What we want with regard to Ireland, is a collection of well authenticated *facts.*"[24] Let us ignore for the moment, as does Malthus, his own contribution to the lack of the observations necessary to obtain these facts. Malthus opens the 1808 essay by wholeheartedly endorsing a longstanding

> complaint with the public, that, among the few persons whose situations and habits have led them to an intimate knowledge of the state

of Ireland, and who are daily compelled to contemplate what *is*, and to contrast it with what *might* be, that there has been hitherto so little anxiety either to collect or to circulate correct information.

Malthus's irritation reflects a shift in attitude toward British ignorance about Ireland, a shift fostered by the political union between the two kingdoms. He goes on to claim that more accurate knowledge of "what *is*" would facilitate the "one great object needful on this subject – *discussion*", the object being Catholic Emancipation ("Newenham and Others on the State of Ireland" (1808), p. 336; emphases in original).

For Malthus, collecting correct information was necessary but insufficient to generate knowledge useful for comparison with "what *might* be". Obtaining such knowledge involved a three-stage process. The first, collecting facts, exposed travelers to the risk of biased observations due to the political or economic interests or lack of interest on the part of the observer or the observed. Even statistical facts were subject to this risk. Malthus repeats the charge made by contemporaries that Protestant prejudice led to biased Irish population estimates. Protestant clergy collected numbers at the parish level, and saw political advantage in downplaying both the numbers of Catholics and the growth of their population in their parishes ("Newenham and Others on the State of Ireland" (1808), p. 337).

The next two stages, arranging facts in order to generate useful information, and subsequent interpretation, both call for skill and sound judgment on the part of the analyst. Malthus commends Newenham for his diligent efforts to gather information to ascertain the "whole truth" on the subject of Irish population. He

> has collected all the *data* respecting the population of Ireland, at different periods, furnished by previous inquiries; has enlarged and extended them by his own personal researches, and those of his friends; and has strengthened the whole by a variety of collateral information, all bearing upon the main question.
> ("Newenham and Others on the State of Ireland" (1808), p. 337, emphasis in original)

Yet Newenham's method compares unfavorably with Young's; where

> Mr Newenham states very distinctly, that the wages of labour in husbandry have risen, since the time of Mr Young's tour, from 6 ½ d. to 10 ½ d. a day, yet he has not given us, as Mr Young did, a list of prices with which to compare these earnings.

Statistics are not enough, nor are historical comparisons, unless the comparisons are placed in the correct context ("Newenham on the State of Ireland" (1809), p. 164).

In the 1803 *Essay*, Malthus credited Young as one who, "in most of his works, appears clearly to understand the principle of population" (*Essay*, 1803, p. 570). Still, Malthus was quick to criticize what he took to be a lack of methodological consistency in Young's travel accounts. He objected to a scheme proposed by Young to give allotments of land to the English poor precisely because he had observed the negative effects produced by a similar system in Ireland. Malthus quotes Young: "If each had his ample potatoe-ground and a cow, the price of wheat would be of little more consequence to them than it is to their brethren in Ireland" (*Essay*, 1803, p. 572).[25] For Malthus, the provision of one or two cows and half an acre for grass for potatoes to families with three or more children "must result in complete indigence to those who cannot find employment, and an incomplete subsistence even to those who can". This was true because

> [t]he obvious tendency of Mr. Young's plan is, by encouraging marriage and furnishing a cheap food, independent of the price of corn, and of course of the demand for labour, to place the lower classes of people exactly in this situation.
>
> (*Essay*, 1803, p. 574)

Malthus points out that Young himself, in his account of his travels in France, had observed and argued against an arrangement similar to his proposal for England. France encouraged peasants to subdivide property into increasingly small slivers of land. The population fared badly, with "numbers dying of diseases arising from insufficient nourishment" (*Essay*, 1803, p. 571). In contrast, he claims the largely landless agricultural poor in England still earned enough through wage labor to live a comfortable life. Malthus, hardly a reticent armchair traveler, invites Young to travel through rural England, an undertaking Young had already famously pursued:

> When you are engaged in this political tour, finish it by seeing England, and I will shew you a set of peasants well clothed, well nourished, tolerably drunken from superfluity, well lodged and at their ease; and yet amongst them, not one in a thousand has either land or cattle.
>
> (*Essay*, 1803, p. 571)

The anonymous Malthus of the 1808 and 1809 essays was not reluctant to wade into the political and religious controversies dogging Anglo-Irish relations. Malthus named political and religious institutions, not the soil or the potato, as the key determinants of the size and condition of the Irish population. Thus, Catholic Emancipation was necessary to give the Irish something to live for other than subsistence. Malthus expects that expert observation and representation would offer both description and prescriptions, both "what *is*" and what "*might* be".

Malthus's criticism implies the substitution of "*should* be" for "*might* be" in Ireland. He charges that "what *is*" has "frustrated the natural advantages of Ireland". Malthus minces no words in condemnation of the pernicious effects on the Irish of legislation, "commercial regulations, aided by penal laws", shoved through a "servile" parliament by British traders to advance their own narrow interests. Malthus judges these acts as "among the worst that ever came from such suspicious advisers" ("Newenham on the State of Ireland" (1809), p. 158). Though he demurs from entering into "the disgusting detail of the various commercial regulations" befouling Anglo-Irish relations, Malthus decries English measures to stifle competition from Irish woolen manufactures. And he expresses amazement that the King would embrace the English manufacturers' cause, citing the promise by the sovereign, in reply to an address to the Commons, "*Gentlemen, I will do all that in me lies to discourage the woolen manufacture of Ireland.*" For Malthus, this

> was spoken not of an enemy's country, as from the language one might naturally suppose, nor even of a distant colony likely to be separated from the parent state, – but of a part of the dominions of the crown of England, so situated, that its loss would at all times endanger the safety of the whole.
> ("Newenham on the State of Ireland" (1809), pp. 158–9; emphases in original)

Malthus's rhetoric does not recall the language of sister nations, employed by Plumptre and others, that accompanied the Acts of Union. He finds the analogy comparing the relationship to that between mother country and colony, or that between a parent and child, unconvincing as well. Malthus assumes Ireland and Great Britain constitute a unified whole. The action of Parliament and King threaten to produce an unnatural and dangerously disunified Union.

English legislation against Irish wool manufacturers threatened the political and social bodies of the United Kingdom by stymieing the natural advantages of Ireland. But the population principle illustrated the fallacy of automatically associating natural processes with health. The natural fecundity of the potato in Ireland appears to both enact and generate the paradox that so shocked Malthus's contemporaries: it produces too many healthy bodies and these eventually enfeeble the social body.[26] Was Ireland's natural advantage in potato production in reality a disadvantage? The next section looks at how travel and travel writing shaped the contours of the correspondence between Edgeworth and Ricardo as they debated whether this was in fact true.

Maria Edgeworth: Economic Lessons from Travels

The correspondence on Ireland between Edgeworth and Ricardo was triggered by a lack of facts gathered during travel. In a 9 July 1822 letter,

Edgeworth sought to communicate thoughts and questions to Ricardo on subjects in political economy she regretted not bringing up when she had visited him in London in 1821. Edgeworth recalls to Ricardo:

> Now that I am three hundred miles from you I regret however that I did not make still better use of my time when I was with you – that I did not make more advantage of your kind readiness to explain and discuss and of that candid mild truly philosophic temper in discussion of which, tho' I call it philosophic, there are so few living or dead examples even among philosophers.[27]

Chief among these subjects was the potato. Famine stalked Ireland during the early 1820s, and, not for the first time, the reliance of the Irish on the potato came under question. Edgeworth expresses her "wish" that Ricardo "would come to poor little Ireland and see and judge of it [the merits of the potato] for yourself": she was "for", and he was "against" the "potatoe". By mid-December, Ricardo had accepted Edgeworth's invitation, declaring "I should be glad to accept your summons and go to Ireland to judge for myself".[28] But he passed away before he could fulfill his promise.

Edgeworth's writings prior to this exchange shed light on how she conceived of the relationship between political economy and travelers' observations. Edgeworth and her father, Richard Lovell, corresponded extensively with domestic and foreign literati, scientists, and the scientifically inclined. British correspondents included Sir Joseph Banks, Anna Letitia Barbauld, Clarke, Sir Walter Scott, Josiah Wedgwood, Lindley Murray, a best-selling textbook author, James Watt, and Erasmus Darwin, who passed away midway through writing a letter to Richard Lovell.[29] The Edgeworths visited many of these individuals, trading on both her father's scientific and her own literary reputation to garner letters of introduction. When Edgeworth met Dr. George Birkbeck, a founder of the London Mechanics Institute, in Glasgow in 1803, for instance, she noted of Birkbeck, who lectured on mechanical and chemical subjects, that "He is going to give a lecture on purpose to children, and he says he took the idea for doing so from [our] 'Practical Education.'"[30]

The reputations of Maria and her father also opened many doors on the Continent. They met Joseph-Michel Montgolfier, the chemist Claude Louis Berthollet, the Swiss watchmaker Abraham-Louis Breguet, and Étienne Dumont there. During an extended stay in France in 1802 they also encountered André Morellet, known as Abbé Morellet, a *philosophe* and author of several works on political economy and statistics. That this last was a political economist hardly marked him as an unusual host for the Edgeworths. Maria and her father both visited and entertained a number of prominent British political economists, including Ricardo, Malthus, James Mill, Marcet, Henry Brougham, Francis Horner, and Dugald Stewart.

Edgeworth had been familiar with the ideas of political economists since her youth; the first major work her father gave her to read when she returned from England to live permanently in Ireland, in 1782, at age fourteen, was *Wealth of Nations*, and she incorporated philosophical aspects of it throughout her writings.[31] Her short story for children, "The Cherry Orchard" (1801), on the merits of the division of labor, is often cited as a one of the first attempts to popularize political economy. In fact, Edgeworth had already attempted to explain real-life applications of political economy doctrines in *Practical Education* (first published in 1798) in the chapter "Prudence and Economy".[32] Edgeworth fails to use the term "political economy" in this chapter, and neither she nor her father uses it anywhere else in *Practical Education*; this may reflect, however, the sexual division of knowledge in political economy, which Edgeworth elsewhere acknowledges. In a letter to her aunt, Mrs. Ruxton, she jests about her visit to Stewart, Edinburgh, in March 1803:

> I have not heard him lecture; no woman can go to the public lectures here, and I don't choose to go in men's or boy's clothes, or in the pocket of the Irish giant, though he is here and well able to carry me. Mrs. Stewart has been for years wishing in vain for the pleasures of hearing one of her husband's lectures.
> (Edgeworth, *The Life and Letters*: I, 143)

Edgeworth makes light of how political economists in Edinburgh impeded public efforts by women to learn the new science. The division between domestic and political economies is textual in *Practical Education*, but it also erects a boundary outside the text which Edgeworth chooses not to transgress, either through cross-dressing or trespass. It splits the social body in two, and hampers women's efforts to become political economists.

Or so it appears. Domestic and political economy overlap in *Practical Education*, where Edgeworth rolls out example after example of how to educate girls and boys to become economists, adepts at household management, in "Prudence and Economy", the penultimate chapter of the book.[33] Prudence and economy are necessary for proper domestic economy, and boys and girls were made, not born, economists. This was also true for the ideal subjects and agents of British political economists: they agreed that men, women, and children would have to learn and then act with prudence and economy in order for the universal principles of political economy to take hold in real life. Hence the importance of Edgeworth's educational work. If readers of her lessons and tales emulated the behavior of those characters who acted with prudence and economy, then they and the nation would approach the ideals of political economy. If women and children could not attend lectures on political economy, then the lectures would have to go to them. And women like Edgeworth could do the lecturing, too, by the way.

Edgeworth did not claim that the political economy principles she espoused in her works always produced identical effects in real life. This was true even within a given society at a given point in time. For example, while lessons in *Practical Education* apply to both girls and boys in any British family of but modest means or more, Edgeworth delineates economic subjects sharply differentiated by gender. Women and men, and girls and boys were each subject to societal norms which placed dissimilar constraints on their economic agency. Again, girls and boys did not immediately emerge as fully-fledged economic agents; the Edgeworths sought to teach children how to manage one's desires.

Since children could emulate behavior learned through reading, the Edgeworths and other writers of the period carefully considered the place of travel narratives, including fictional ones, in educational curricula; we encountered Wollstonecraft's tales of fictional travels from a decade earlier, *Original Stories from Real Life*, in the previous chapter. Travel accounts, like travel, could educate and transform individuals. But travel accounts include numerous depictions of desire gone awry. Travelers lost their heads, figuratively, by going native, or literally, in violent encounters with less pacific Indigenous peoples.

As a result, parents had to exercise caution when introducing children to travel narratives. Take Daniel Defoe's *Robinson Crusoe*. It enjoyed new popularity in Europe at the end of the nineteenth century, thanks to adaptations directed toward children.[34] The Edgeworths, like other educators and conduct book writers of the period, however, believed that *Crusoe* should not be read by young women and men of middle and upper classes, or should only be included as part of an educational curriculum as a cautionary tale. The reason? The novel would have a deleterious effect on children's desires. The Edgeworths argue in *Practical Education* that travel adventures, including *Crusoe*, along with fictions and popular novels, inflamed the imaginations of young people. The effect, however, differed by gender, according to the occupational expectations for the young men and women in question. The Edgeworths warn that young males of an "enterprising temper" should not read these tales lest they be tempted to run off to sea and travel the world in ships. Unless, that is, they are expected to take up a career in the army or at sea. Young women, on the other hand, would rapidly conclude that they could not "go rambling about the world in quest of adventures, even if they so desired" (*Practical Education*, pp. 335–7). While less cautious about subjecting young women than men to travels and voyage literature, parents nevertheless need to exercise more caution with young girls than young boys when it came to inculcating attitudes and behaviors consistent with prudence and economy. Young women have less scope for experimentation, failure, or transgressions than boys; society is less forgiving.

If the Edgeworths express doubt about the value of tales of travels and voyages for young people, Maria nonetheless borrows piquant details from reports on life abroad to illustrate important observations about economic subjectivity and agency, and domestic economy and political economy in "Prudence and Economy", similar to those of Wollstonecraft's *Real Life*. Edgeworth's examples, however, change as the children become older. The first attitude children should learn is respect for the property rights of others. Maria asks parents of younger children to "teach them a love for exactness about property; a respect for the rights of others, rather than a tenacious anxiety about their own". Laws, regulations, and institutions spelling out property rights are all well and good for society. But Maria insists that adults teach the youngest individuals to adopt certain attitudes about property in their behavior. For older children, Edgeworth focuses on how parents' actions can help children develop proper attitudes with respect to income and property they receive from their parents. Parents should not only give these to young people only "when they are of the proper age to manage money and property of their own", they must do so in precise quantities and at regular intervals which are clearly spelled out in advance. Edgeworth points out the consequences of failing to heed this warning: "all persons who have a fluctuating revenue are disposed to be imprudent and extravagant" (*Practical Education*, p. 709).

Edgeworth demonstrates what happens when these precepts about property are violated by immediately asking the reader to compare the behavior of different classes and races in different outposts of the empire, a brief journey both informative and entertaining. Edgeworth first marshals evidence from Bryan Edwards's influential two-volume *History, Civil and Commercial, of the British Colonies in the West Indies* (1793) to identify the source of imprudence, extravagance, and speculation among both West Indies planters and slaves. Edwards, a planter and outspoken foe of abolition who had been elected as a Fellow of the Royal Society in 1794 and member of parliament in 1796, observed that both transplanted groups suffer from "uncertainty as to the tenure of property, or as to the rewards of industry". If the planters' behavior was deranged by uncertain prospects for staggering wealth or abject ruin due to the caprices of the weather, according to Edwards, the ability of the planters to seize property set aside for their gardens deprived slaves of the capacity to even imagine or speak of economy. Edgeworth, an abolitionist, quotes Edwards:

> Prudence is a term that has no place in the negro vocabulary ... When they earn a little money, they immediately gratify their palate with salted meats and other provisions, which are to them delicacies. The idea of accumulating, and of being economic to accumulate, is unknown to these poor slaves, who hold their lands by the most uncertain of all tenures.
>
> (*Practical Education*, pp. 709–10)

Edgeworth remains silent on the obvious, if cruel, irony that the property of slaves is insecure by definition because they themselves are property.

Instead, she asks the reader, "Is it wonderful that the term prudence should be unknown in the negro vocabulary?"

Edgeworth immediately relocates the reader-traveler from the West Indies to London. There she adapts Patrick Colquhoun's observations from *A Treatise on the Police of the Metropolis* (1796) to fit the lessons at hand. Colquhoun had drawn on the utilitarianism of Bentham when he founded the Thames River Police, the first regular preventive police force in England. He also visited Adam Smith on a number of occasions, and adapted his views on policing, crime, and crime prevention both from Smith and from his observations of the effectiveness of the system of police in France.[35] In *A Treatise*, Colquhoun takes the reader on a tour through the ways and byways of criminality in the metropolis, and proposes to explain phenomena painfully familiar to readers. He promises in the address "To the Reader" that he will flesh out the details of what is "too obvious to require elucidation" to the public, "the present insecurity with regard to *property*, and in some instances with respect to *life* itself".[36] For Colquhoun, improvident behavior represents a chief cause of criminal behavior

> and even the luxurious mode of living which prevails too generally among various classes of the lower ranks of the people in the metropolis, leads to much misery and to many crimes. [They are] [a]ccustomed from their earliest infancy to indulge themselves in eating many articles of expensive food in season, and possessing little or no knowledge of that kind of frugality and care which enables well-regulated families to make everything go as far as possible, by a diversified mode of cookery and good management.[37]

Edgeworth's gloss on Colquhoun's observations in *Practical Education* elides the link between improvidence and crime. Her readers presumably do not commonly appear in the criminal courts as suspects. She simply remarks that the "very poorest class of people in London, who feel despair, and who merely live to bear the evil of the day, are, it is said, very little disposed to be prudent". Quoting Colquhoun, Edgeworth notes that the poor constitute the chief consumers of seasonal luxury goods, "oysters, crabs, lobsters, pickled salmon, &c", when they first appear on the market, while "The middle ranks, and those immediately under them, abstain generally from such indulgencies until the prices are moderate" (*Practical Education*, p. 710).

Edgeworth uses observations from what contemporaries would have considered authoritative travel accounts to establish similarity as well as difference across geopolitical space. The conditions of the poorest of the working classes in London, though based on labor relations fundamentally dissimilar to that of West Indian slaves, can create material deprivation and behavior similar to that of the slaves. That the insecurity of property produces similar effects in dissimilar places proves for Edgeworth the existence of universal causes; the comparisons "shew that the same causes act upon the mind independently of climate" (*Practical Education*, p. 710).

Edgeworth rejects a belief popular among contemporaries that different climates and environments suffice to explain differences in human behavior around the globe. Scarcity, on the other hand, does act as a universal cause. Scarcity refers to more than the lack of material means of support. It includes sensory deprivation, an intemperate craving, an insatiable desire, even, for luxury goods; a defect which produces excess. Both West Indies slaves and London's poor spend, imprudently, to awaken their tastes, to feel.[38] According to Edgeworth, the very poor cannot wait until prices moderate to purchase luxury goods. They lack the foresight and self-discipline to check their desires; they fail to exercise prudence and economy, unlike the middle classes and those immediately beneath them who can and do wait until prices have fallen to purchase desired goods. Despite her admission that the illustrations are "far fetched", by equating the behavior of the West Indies planters and slaves to that of the poorest class in the metropolis, she literally brings home lessons about the security of property learned in the empire, placing them in the streets of London.

Edgeworth returns the reader from virtual travel within the empire to deliver the final lesson in *Practical Education*: charity is a chief object of economy and political economy. The lesson is reminiscent of Wollstonecraft, who concludes in *Real Life* that "Œconomy and self-denial are necessary in every station, to enable us to be generous, and to act conformably to the rules of justice".[39] When parents help children cultivate habits of foresight and prudence, the children have more money to donate to the poor. Thus, the higher purpose of cultivating habits of accumulation in children is not to enhance the wealth of the household, and, by extension, nation. These were children after all. Notably, however, Edgeworth voices her recommendations on the attitudes and behaviors for children in the rhetoric of commerce. Hence, the above passage from *Practical Education* concludes, "the little *revenue* of young people ought to be fixed and certain" (*Practical Education*, p. 710, emphasis in the original). This reiterates their warning from a page earlier that "fluctuating revenue" produces individuals prone to improvidence and extravagant spending. Revenue is an odd word choice for a child's allowance. Maria's lesson on prudence and economy may be for the benefit of children, but its value would be readily apparent to adults and the nation as well.

The Political Economy of the Potato in Ireland: Theories and Observations from the Field

Travel writing could impart important lessons to children and adults about economy and political economy. Edgeworth believed travel itself would, ideally, turn her into a more objective observer, one who might recognize local, regional, societal, even racial differences without bias. Recounting a trip to England with her father in 1799, Edgeworth quotes him as frequently saying, "Travelling ... was from time to time necessary, to change the course of ideas, and to prevent the growth of local prejudices."[40] The question was not just how to observe without prejudice when traveling. Since travel transformed the self, travelers had to ensure the changes led them to make unbiased observations both at home and abroad.

Edgeworth's travel writings reflect her embrace of this ideal of observation without prejudice. In letters from her family's trips in Britain and France in 1802 and 1803, she recalls the scenery, as well as visits to hotels, castles, and commercial works. She rarely references political economy in her letters from this trip; she brings instead a puckish tone and an eye for physical oddity to her correspondence. She describes traveling in the countryside in quick and broad strokes, fitting for representations of what are essentially fugitive glances of landscapes and people.

Some of her descriptions invoke regional or national types. She writes in October 1802 of a glimpse of the Poissardes of Calais, "with their picturesque nets, ugly faces and beautiful legs" (Edgeworth, *The Life and Letters*, I, p. 89). She also indulges in the contemporary vogue to link character to physiognomy. At Dunkirk,

> all things and persons began to look like Dutch prints and Dutch toys ... Even when moving the people all looked like wooden toys set in strings – the strings in Flanders must be of gold; the Flemings seem to be all a money-making, money-loving people; they are fast recovering their activity after the Revolution.
>
> (Edgeworth, *The Life and Letters*, I, pp. 90–1)

Even human traces on the countryside conform to regional or national identities. "The road to Bruges, fifty feet broad, solidly paved in the middle, seems, like all French and Flemish roads, to have been laid out by some inflexible mathematician; they are always right lines, the shortest possible between points" (Edgeworth, *The Life and Letters*, I, 91). Her commentary speaks to her inability to closely observe and distinguish differences among people and in the landscape while literally on the road, peering from a moving carriage. Nonetheless, she claims to heed her father's dictum when she writes of the "pretty" countryside in the approach to Brussels, "The English who can see nothing worth seeing in this country must certainly pass through it with huge blinkers of prejudice" (Edgeworth, *The Life and Letters*, I, p. 100).

She confesses, however, that even when she has sustained and intimate conversations during visits with the best of French society, she is prone to hasty observations and ultimately chauvinistic judgments about the observed. She concludes an involved recounting of an unpleasant visit with Madame de Genlis in March 1803, during the last week of her family's residency in Paris, with the lament, "But you know, my dear aunt, that I am not famous for judging sanely of strangers on a first visit" (Edgeworth, *The Life and Letters*, I, p. 139). Edgeworth alludes to the irreducible otherness of the traveler. Even when she has settled in Paris, the peripatetic nature of salon visits ensures an ongoing series of first encounters which test her ability to rationally judge the natives.

Edgeworth laces her letters from this trip with literary allusions, sketching some people and places she encounters as real-life embodiments of well-known fictional characters and locations. She does so to gothic, if often comic, effect. While describing the road to Bruges, Edgeworth writes:

> The post-houses are often lone, wretched places, one into which I peeped, a *grenier*, like that described by Smollett, in which the murdered body is concealed. At another post-house we met with a woman calling herself a *servante*, to whom we took not only an aversion but a horror; Charlotte said that she should be afraid, not of that woman cutting her throat, but that she would take a mallet and strike her head flat at one blow. Do you remember the woman in "Caleb Williams," when he wakens and sees her standing over him with an uplifted hatchet? Our *servante* might have stood for this picture.
> (Edgeworth, *The Life and Letters*, I, p. 91)

Edgeworth considered anecdotes such as the above, often recounted in private letters and diaries, a valuable mode of historical reportage that leads us closer to the truth. Or, so she asserts in "Preface" to *Castle Rackrent*. Edgeworth argues that we should value the private utterances of the unknown as well as the famous.

> We are surely justified ... to collect the most minute facts relative to the domestic lives, not only of the great and good, but even of the worthless and insignificant, since it is only by a comparison of their actual happiness or misery in the privacy of domestic life that we can form a just estimate of the real reward of virtue or the real punishment of vice.[41]

Unlike the great and their biographers, the unknown do not have the sagacity to shape and polish their narratives. They do have their prejudices and report events with bias, but "we never bow to the authority of him who has no great name to sanction his absurdities".[42] Apparently, the lack of authority of the vulgar allows us to more easily separate truth from falsity in their accounts. Gamer suggests that Edgeworth's argument constitutes a brief "for an alternative history based in private, domestic lives", and that Edgeworth "effectively relocates 'historical fact' and 'real character' in what she defines as private and domestic spheres, opening them to voices formerly unauthorized either by education or occupation to write factual, historical narrative".[43] Everyone has a life; anyone can observe and represent. Lovers of truth needed to pay attention to the words of great and insignificant alike.

Anecdotes constitute at once a source and type of evidence for Edgeworth and a method of analysis; she uses anecdotes to highlight local, regional, and national differences. Yet anecdotes could be difficult to recover and to make public, hardly obvious candidates for Malthus's authenticated *facts*. Edgeworth also expresses grave doubts about how well her anecdote-based lessons traveled. In a letter to Dumont, an Edgeworth literary confidant, she cites the tension caused by her dual preferences for the anecdote and her desire to convey universal truths. Anecdotes simply might not translate as illustrations of a general truth. Or travel. Edgeworth asks Dumont of her novels, "Ennui – what can they make of it in French? ... L'Absent, The Absentee, – it is impossible that a Parisian can make any sense of it from beginning to end. But these things teach authors what is merely local and temporary" (Edgeworth, *The Life and Letters*, I, p. 233).[44] Present-day critics influenced by New Historicism, who emphasize the value of anecdotes as points of departure for their works in intellectual history, resist the temptations of grand narratives, opting instead to accept the "[in]accessibility of a social-historical whole determining individual lives or events".[45] Edgeworth nonetheless implies that historical analysis would enable one to recover universal and timeless truths. She had expressed this belief explicitly, again, in *Practical Education* when she illustrated through virtual travel that "the same causes act upon the mind independently of climate". Thus, the insecurity of property produces improvident behavior no matter the time or place.

Anecdotes play a prominent role in the amicable disagreement between Edgeworth and Ricardo over the merits of the potato in Ireland, a dispute in which the friends wrangled over the use of theory, method, and the interpretation of facts in political economy. Fundamentally, the two differed over whether Malthus's principle of population necessarily entailed a universal theory of agricultural rent or one that was "merely local and temporary". Ricardo took Malthus's principle as the basis for his work on diminishing returns in agriculture. An increase in population led to less fertile land being taken into cultivation, and rents rose as a result. For Ricardo's theory of distribution, these rising rents squeezed out capitalist profits, and, consequently, the interests of landlords were opposed to those of other members of society.

Edgeworth supported the views on rent of one of Ricardo's critics, the political economist Richard Jones.[46] Jones, who advocated a thorough and ongoing inductive testing of maxims of political economy by facts, believed that rents, historically, were not necessarily related to the quality of soil brought under cultivation. The link between soil quality and rents, which Ricardo assumed was universal in nature, "would affect the progress of a very limited division of rents" and was applicable only to "one very peculiar state of society".[47] For Jones and Edgeworth, rents could and did rise with agricultural improvements; productivity could be improved so much that diminishing returns did not take hold. Edgeworth articulated this perspective in her fictions, such as *Castle Rackrent* and *The Absentee* (1812).

Idle, ill-informed landlords, or landlords who were simply absent, not the operation of a universal principle of political economy, were at the root of mismanaged estates and the resulting agricultural troubles in Ireland. When Edgeworth argues for rational agricultural reform and the overall improvement of Irish estate management, she does so at least partially on the accumulation of anecdotal evidence peculiar to Ireland.

Edgeworth's expressed views on Irish agriculture to Ricardo that were grounded in the facts of daily life she encountered as she helped her father manage the family estate in Edgeworthstown. The exchange between Edgeworth and Ricardo also devolved from principal-agent problems. When Maria and her father returned to Ireland, in 1782, Richard Lovell dismissed agents from his lands to manage the properties on his own behalf, a step he took because the agents had allowed it to fall into disrepair. Her father reveled in the active management of the estate. In his *Memoirs*, Maria reproduces a letter he sent to Erasmus Darwin in 1798, in which he asks Darwin, "Are you still bent upon agriculture?" He continues:

> If you are, here is a note and query for you. In 1787 I rented a farm of thirty acres, at a rack rent of half a guinea per acre. I improved it, was never any one time one hundred pounds out of pocket; and in five years had seventeen pounds clear profit to balance of accounts. I let it at a long lease, at one guinea and a half per acre, to a rich tenant. – Query: how was it improved? A most exact account was kept of profit and loss.[48]

Maria would have thus been well acquainted with the benefits of active rather than absentee landlordism. And these benefits could and should be judged on the basis of quantification. The Edgeworths embraced measurement, where accurate accounting of costs, profits, and losses produced more precise, accurate, and useful information that would facilitate comparison and judgment than did vague terms such as "better" or "worse", or "more" or "less".

Edgeworth had firsthand knowledge as well of the contemporary vogue for agricultural experimentation from her father's management of the family estate, as is clear from the quote above. Experimental farming involved efforts to increase food production by bringing former wastelands into production, increasing the fertility and yields of land already under cultivation through refinements in drainage, testing new machinery, introducing new fertilizers and new, more nutritious food crops, crop rotation trials, innovations in animal husbandry and breeding, and more. Travelers duly noted that ideas and information on crops and innovative farming techniques circulated throughout Europe. Coxe, for instance, writes that Peter Anker had introduced "various species of English husbandry" in the use of clover and turnips on the outskirts of Christiania (Coxe, *Travels*, p. 229). Richard Lovell enthusiastically turned his hand to agricultural inventions and experiments. According to the *Dictionary of National Biography*, "The Society of Arts gave him a silver medal for a new 'perambulator' or land-measuring machine in 1768, and he invented a 'turnip-cutter'" as well.[49] He deployed his penchant for inventiveness to experimentation on his own estate. In the letter to Darwin, cited above, he continues:

> I propose to heat hot-houses by pipes laid through dung-hills, and communicating with the open air at one end, and opening into the house at the other. Such pipes, in common stable-dung, continue to give out air at a regular heat of 95° Fahrenheit for many days, as Lovel and I have tried in a pipe six inches diameter.[50]

Edgeworth's father did not restrict his penchant for agricultural improvement to the areas around Edgeworthstown. Maria would have observed talk of her father's "schemes for the reclamation of bogs and improvement of roads" in Ireland, which included a report he made to an Irish commission in 1810.[51]

Edgeworth derives her political economy of the potato from an understanding of the principles of political economy tempered by her own firsthand observation. The accumulation and distillation of facts gathered by others, including travelers such as Arthur Young, was important to her political economy as well. Edgeworth concludes *Castle Rackrent* with an editor's statement that begins by praising Young's *A Tour in Ireland* as "the first faithful portrait of its inhabitants".[52] This mix of philosophical principle and real-life knowledge is similar to the lessons Edgeworth tried to impart in her educational writings.

In contrast, historians of economics have until recently characterized Ricardo's theorizing about the laws of income distribution, which determined the share of output going to the different classes, landowners, capitalists, and workers, as abstract and deductive. In describing his methods, Ricardo cites a set of conundrums familiar to contemporary social analysts; there are too many facts and too many causes, and many of these causes may be invisible. In an 7 October 1815 letter to Malthus, Ricardo cautions that

> [T]here are so many combinations, – so many operating causes in Political Economy, that there is a great danger in appealing to experience in favor of a particular doctrine, unless we are sure that all the causes of variation are seen and their effects duly estimated.[53]

To rely on the evidence of experience could prove dangerous. Even facts should be viewed with suspicion; those who rely too heavily on them as opposed to theory are prone to bias. Thus, in an 1811 commentary on the work of the Bullion Committee, Ricardo lambasted men who were "all for fact and nothing for theory. Such men can hardly ever sift their facts.

They are credulous, and necessarily so, because they have no standard of reference."[54]

Ricardo's work on money and banking, the source of the passage just quoted, and where he drew on his extensive knowledge of stockbroking, is often cited as an exception to his dislike for fashioning theories based on experience. Edgeworth trades on this expertise on occasion in their correspondence. His responses to her questions in her 7 January 1822 letter demonstrate that, at least in this realm, mastery of institutional details gained from experience proves useful for understanding. Edgeworth asks questions both speculative, about the timing of investments, and practical, as when she asks advice about technical details attending a purchase of "French funds", such as whether the power of attorney should be drawn up in London or Dublin.[55]

Morgan adds experimental agriculture to the list of empirical examples that Ricardo drew on as he developed his notions on distribution. Ricardo wholeheartedly supported the population principle of his friend Malthus, and endorsed the view that knowing how much food was available to feed workers and at what price lay at the heart of understanding the prosperity and happiness of a society. Advancements in experimental farming offered hope that productivity increases in agriculture could keep pace with or even outstrip population growth. Ricardo paid close attention to accounting data on inputs, outputs, costs, and revenues generated from these experiments, as well as reports from Edgar Wakefield, who became his land agent in 1815.[56] Thus, his "model-building was a mixture of inductive and deductive work, and not a process of abstraction".[57]

On the other side of the equation, experimental farmers mixed theory derived from "book learning" with lessons drawn by travelers such as Young and Alexander von Humboldt from their comparative observations on agriculture and farming methods in lands near and far. Farmers in Britain, Ireland, and on the Continent would report the results of their experiments in contemporary farming newspapers and journals, and other publications. Crucially, these reports did not always include information on the costs and profits of farm experiments:

> Experimental reports were sometimes reported in financial terms, and if farmers ... did not provide the monetary arithmetic that demonstrated increased profit as well as productivity, they found their claims of "improvement" open to question.[58]

Thus, the reports helped enforce a new moral discipline with respect to published information about farming methods and experiments. Eyewitness accounts, even augmented with statistical information about production no longer sufficed as evidence. One needed to include facts on costs and profits, placed on a consistent and comparable basis. These produce useful knowledge, or Malthus's authenticated *facts*.

Ricardo made few remarks on farming in his work and letters.[59] Yet, Ricardo's familiarity with the empirical work in experimental farming may have helped smooth his correspondence with Edgeworth on the potato and population in Ireland. They clearly shared a common vocabulary of theories derived from political economists, including those from Ricardo himself, and would be at ease discussing the detailed facts of agriculture, too.[60] They clashed, however, over how to interpret the facts.

Edgeworth assumed that if Ricardo traveled to Ireland, he would be a credible and expert witness, able to see and interpret what he observed without bias. Edgeworth claims that the evidence of experience would help them judge the potato. Yet Edgeworth's argument about what system of agriculture would best secure sustenance for the Irish did not rest solely on the prospect of a visit and observations by Ricardo. Edgeworth relied, in part, on nonhuman objects that traveled and transmitted information, letters and a scientific sample. Each of these traveling objects could "speak" in Edgeworth's absence. In her 9 July 1822 letter, Edgeworth refers to an enclosed sample of potato flour, though it is not clear whether the sample consisted of potato flour or potato starch. It is not even clear that Edgeworth actually sent Ricardo the sample; in a 28 December 1822 letter, she refers to having sent it or intending to send it in her next.[61]

Regardless, Edgeworth clearly intended that Ricardo could see for himself that potatoes could be stored as a flour, evidence that the plant was a less uncertain and risky crop than political economists since at least Smith commonly believed, both in absolute and relative terms: Smith noted that potatoes, unlike wheat, could not be stored for years in granaries.[62] Failing a visit by Ricardo, the potato flour would visit him. The long-term viability of the potato would testify to the reality that it could be a secure staple food stock.

In one sense, the exchange between Edgeworth and Ricardo is a banal example of European scientific correspondence in the 1820s. European scientific explorers and armchair travelers alike, such as Humboldt and Cuvier, both of whom Edgeworth met in Paris in 1819, collected, shipped and received soil, rocks, flora and fauna, and other things, with accompanying written descriptions, illustrations, maps and instruments, and, increasingly, scientific articles, reports, and statistics. These traveled across national borders following routines established years earlier. Edgeworth's potato flour came from a French nobleman, Charles Philibert Comte de Lasteyrie-Du Saillant, a noted writer on agriculture, and was probably obtained by Edgeworth when she visited France from 1802 to 1803 during the brief Peace of Amiens.[63] Twenty years on, the sample had surely lost its viability as a foodstuff, but had gained value as a debating point.

This period was marked by the continuation of disputes over whether the work of observation and interpretation in science should be split between amateurs and experts, respectively.[64] Those involved in the discussions argued over whether to apportion observation to women, less educated men, even children, and reserve interpretation for men formally trained in the sciences. The status of Edgeworth and Ricardo vis-á-vis the production and exchange of knowledge in political economy is not equivalent, of course. But their relationship is not strictly hierarchical, either. If Ricardo is the renowned theorist, Edgeworth has honed her knowledge of political economy as an educator. She also possesses and offers to Ricardo her expert knowledge of local conditions. Such expertise might smack of experience, which Ricardo roundly criticized and was wary of employing, even in the case of agriculture. Yet Edgeworth stands her ground methodologically. Her invitation to Ricardo bears witness to her belief that, only if he were to travel to Ireland and observe first-hand the Irish and the potato, under the watchful eye of one both Indigenous and English, would he be able to produce Malthus's authenticated *facts*.

Their letters mix topics both professional and personal. Edgeworth's read as playful at times, even occasionally drifting into more stereotypically feminine topics and voice – she recalls "Mrs. Ricardo's fur tippet!" from her London visit, for instance – than do Ricardo's. In taking up political economy and the potato, Edgeworth combines an informal, conversationally casual tone with methodological rigor. She couches her question on the potato in terms of a philosophical debate broached by eminences such as Bishop Berkeley, in *The Querist* – "Whether it is possible Ireland should be well improved while our beef is exported while our labourers live upon potatoes" – and by James Mill, in the article "Cottagers", in *Encyclopedia Britannica*.[65] She then raises and quickly ticks off answers to each of the major "Malthean" objections to the potato. Her list is simply that, a list, and she quickly refutes or acknowledges the merits of each objection. Further, she asks whether these "Malthean" objections "do not all ... apply to machinery to manufactures to all that tends to save time and labor and encrease the wealth of a country?"[66] She acknowledges, however, that, even if potato flour could be stored long term, it was still an open question, as Ricardo himself noted, whether it could be stored in bulk, and at a cost reasonable enough to ensure a profit to merchants.[67] In sum, Edgeworth cites relevant literature, and alludes to evidence, including the existence and viability of the potato flour sample. If Edgeworth and Ricardo share political economy and agricultural experimentation as starting points for answering the potato question, Edgeworth also assumes they are on familiar methodological ground in discussing the relevance of Malthus's population principle to the question.

This does not mean that they agreed on the answer, or, ultimately, even the means, the theories and evidence, to answer the question. Scientific practices of observation, interpretation, and representation were clearly not yet standardized in early nineteenth century Europe, and certainly not for British political economists. The lack of consensus among them was so glaringly obvious, even those who sympathized with the predicament of the *savants* felt free to make them the butt of jokes. Edgeworth notes in her diary in 1822 that "a gentleman answered very well the other day when asked if he would be of the famous Political Economy Club, that he would, whenever he could find two members of it that agree on any one point" (Edgeworth, *The Life and Letters*, II, p. 65).

Ricardo was a keen participant in the Club, which had been founded in London in 1821, and no doubt would have appreciated the joke about an organization riven by dissension; the quip even made it into the centenary history of the club.[68] In their correspondence, however, Edgeworth considered the inclusion of the potato flour and her comments on its meaning and import as steps consistent with good scientific practice. She consciously fashions her method after a prominent pair of British political economists, teasingly assuring Ricardo that, "You see I set formally to work at the argument as your own dear Bentham or Mill would do."[69] Joking aside, she does conduct a formal analysis, as Ricardo acknowledges.[70] In a 22 December 1822 letter, Edgeworth also offers a preliminary analysis of the causes of the recent crop failure in Ireland and the suffering that followed.

> The distress which arose last year in Ireland it has been asserted arose from the *general* failure of the potatoe crop. But it could not have arisen from that cause for this plain reason the failure was not general – Potatoes were plentiful and good in many parts of this country though bad in others – The distress as far as I have been able to learn arose partly from want of communication and information between the places where there was plenty and places where there was scarcity – and partly from want of money. Where there was sufficient information there was plenty of food appeared, both potatoes and corn, but there was actual want of money to purchase this food or there was a want of exchangeable value or commodities among the lower classes – All the money they had went for rent and did not fully pay the rent – Remember I am now merely stating facts –
>
> Where the potatoes did fail this, as I am informed arose in great measure from the improvidence of the people who did not plant them in time –[71]

Variations in local conditions loom large in Edgeworth's description of the previous year's hardships. The event Edgeworth refers to was actually not a single event, and the causes of the distresses were multifold, a lack of information, the failure of communication between parts of the country where the crop was plentiful and those where it failed, and a lack of money among the lower classes to purchase food all contributed to the suffering. Edgeworth refuses to reduce the Irish peasantry to a homogeneous, undifferentiated mass. As a result, Edgeworth rejects the impulse to name improvidence the sole or even the main contributing factor in the distress.

Edgeworth reminds Ricardo of the methodological and epistemological work at hand: "Remember I am now merely stating facts –". Multiple types of evidence figure in her account: statistics on crop prices and yields; the testimony of "a clear headed man who has had much experience in farming land and in living among the lower classes of people here so as to know their habits"; and a brief review of the forms of land tenure in Ireland.[72] Though she refers to her evidence as facts, they represent something more. They provide source material for a narrative of Irish woe more complicated than a story based on a single cause, a general failure of the potato crop.

Edgeworth goes so far as to calculate what she terms "the comparative advantages of corn and potatoes", to determine whether corn was a viable alternative to potatoes as a food crop. In using "comparative advantages", Edgeworth resorts to an expression and concept that, thanks in part to Ricardo, had only recently emerged as part of the formal technical vocabulary of political economists.[73] This term can also be easily confused, in the vernacular, with the concept of absolute advantage. Edgeworth is not simply playful here. She compares data on costs, yields, and prices for potatoes and corn (wheat), and notes that planting potatoes is considerably more profitable than cultivating wheat in Ireland. But, in the correspondence she does not perform the calculations necessary to determine that Ireland possesses a comparative advantage with respect to England in producing potatoes instead of wheat. It does, because of its climate.[74] Ricardo does not press Edgeworth on her logic in his reply. Nor do the two pursue the possibility that trade in foodstuffs might lessen the frequency of famine in Ireland.

To what end her inquiries? She asks Ricardo:

> In fact you in England who do not live upon potatoes and who have gone through all the prosperity and adversity of manufactures are you better off – are you happier – I don't ask whether you are richer than we are in Ireland. Take an average of years – don't fix your eye upon this dreadful time of famine.[75]

Edgeworth does not omit the population principle in her reckoning. But her calculation that the Irish are happier than the English hinges on the infrequency of famines in Ireland; an analysis of the state of the two peoples must be taken over "an average of years". Edgeworth adapts a critique of manufacturing common in England at the time. Increasing wealth could paradoxically leave the poor wealthier but less happy, due to the cycles of boom and bust in manufacturing industries. These swings could hamper the ability of the poor to save enough to marry prudently. The Edgeworth of *Practical Education* would suggest that something else would retard moral restraint in manufacturing England: the fluctuating revenue of wage workers will lead directly to imprudent behavior.

Ricardo, in response to Edgeworth, asserts that "my motto, after Mr. Bentham, is 'the greatest happiness to the greatest number.'" To determine whether a society has achieved this goal, Ricardo also relies on Malthus's principle. In reply to a letter from Malthus describing his trip to Ireland in 1817, Ricardo concurs with his friend's conclusion that the potato lay behind the "predominant evil" that stalks the land, a population in excess of the demand for labor. It was no less than Ricardo expected. Humboldt had found the same during his travels in New Spain.

> Humbold [sic] in his account of New Spain points out the very same evils as you do in Ireland, proceeding too from the same cause. The land there yields a great abundance of Bananas, Manioc, Potatoes and Wheat with very little labour, and the people having no taste for luxuries, and having abundance of food, have the privilege of being idle … Happiness is the object to be desired, and we cannot be quite sure that provided he is equally well fed, a man may not be happier in the enjoyment of the luxury of idleness than in the enjoyment of the luxuries of a neat cottage, and good clothes. And after all we do not know if these would fall to his share. His labour might only increase the enjoyments of his employer.[76]

Humboldt, the most celebrated scientific traveler of the first half of the century, appears as a principal subject in the next chapter. His presence here underscores the importance of travel accounts for the comparative analyses of British political economists. Though it is not clear how what Humboldt observes in New Spain can be construed as "evil", Ricardo reads Humboldt as positing that happiness depends not only on material well-being, but also the ability to have and choose how to spend leisure time. Still, subsistence remains the linchpin of any analysis of happiness. Ricardo asks Edgeworth to not minimize the effects of the probability of famine, an ever-present threat, on the happiness of the Irish population, writing

> I think we are not only richer but happier in England than in Ireland, and for the reasons I have before given, we are never so near actual famine as you are; what can you put in the scale against this dreadful evil?[77]

The two friends assign different weights to the probability of prosperity or adversity occurring in England, the risk of famines in Ireland, and the relationship of each to happiness. Their exchange reflects questions about the boundary between expert and lay knowledge of political economy. These questions became more urgent as accounts by travelers, many of whom did not self-identify as political economists, revealed that, above subsistence levels of consumption, people took many different paths in the pursuit of happiness. Some were happier choosing leisure rather than multiplying desires and goods, even comforts such as a snug house and decent clothing. But how would an analyst know who would choose which option, and who were happiest? If everyone, travelers and the sedentary included, had intimate experience and knowledge of what made them happy, political economists could hardly claim exclusive knowledge about how to achieve happiness.

Risk and Security: Beyond the Population Principle

The correspondence between Edgeworth and Ricardo on the political economy of the potato in Ireland signals the importance of travel and travel accounts for accumulating, organizing, and judging evidence about Malthus's population principle in the early 1820s. Edgeworth and Ricardo agreed that the key to answering their questions about the potato and Irish and English happiness lay in directing their gaze toward what could be measured. This would enable them to determine the "relative security or risk associated with heavy reliance upon either crop [wheat or potato]".[78] Both focus on monoculture, and exclude alternative, customary means some English and Irish used to acquire food, such as keeping farm animals, gleaning, foraging, hunting, fishing, etc. If we skip the anachronism of expecting Edgeworth and Ricardo to apply a staple from present-day financial portfolio theory, they both overlook the ways in which diversification reduces risk. Both nonetheless gesture towards probabilistic assessments as the primary means to compare the well-being of the Irish to the English, a full decade before the Belgian astronomer, statistician, and social scientist Adolphe Quetelet proposed to apply the law of error to analyze social phenomena.

Food security referred not only to the riskiness of depending on one crop for subsistence, but to the reliability of the means to secure it. English landowners had purchased the security of property for their agricultural holdings through enclosures and consolidations in the seventeenth and eighteenth centuries. The resulting greater food production and productivity came, however, at the price of monetizing what we call food insecurity for much of the population in both nations.

Ricardo's concerns foreshadow the apprehensions expressed by Malthus in his 5 May 1827 testimony before the Select Committee on Emigration of the House of Commons. Malthus drew on observations from his 1817 trip to Ireland to voice alarm at the continued population increase there, and recommended the mass emigration of Irish from the United Kingdom as a curative measure. The influx of redundant Irish into England threatened to reduce the wages of the English laboring poor, force many to seek relief, and turn the English poor into potato eaters, all of which would be "most fatal to the happiness of the labouring classes of England". Specifically, if the English poor were to adopt Irish manners and switch to eating potatoes rather than the more expensive wheat, they would have, in the committee's summation of Malthus's testimony, "no recourse in a time of scarcity; whereas in the case of a population habitually living on wheat, there is always the resource of potatoes to compensate for the failure of an average crop". Malthus referred to this as "a pernicious effect"; the English poor, like the Irish, would run the risk of food insecurity "if their wages are determined by the price of potatoes".[79]

Similar questions about security and risk haunted the British in a very different set of locales in the 1820s, as investors rushed to invest their savings overseas, including in speculative ventures in post-colonial Spanish America. Travelers sought to ascertain the value of what they observed in the region, and used the insights of British political economists and of others, like Humboldt, to frame their observations. Statistics and quantitative analysis took increasingly important roles in these assessments; looking further ahead, Chapter Six has as one of its centerpieces the British response to the collapse of South American mining shares in the bursting of the financial bubble from 1825 to 1826. Security, risk, and investment, like happiness and value, have multiple meanings. As a consequence, travelers and political economists alike struggled to find the tools and language adequate to the task of defining and stabilizing these meanings when they contemplated the new worlds of post-revolutionary Spanish America.

Notes

1 Glenn Hooper, "Preface", in Glenn Hooper, ed., *The Tourist's Gaze: Travellers to Ireland, 1800–2000* (Cork: Cork University Press, 2001), pp. xiii–xxx (at pp. xvi–xvii).
2 Hooper, "Preface", pp. xvii–xviii.
3 William Petty, "A Treatise on Ireland, 1687", ed. Charles Henry Hull, *The Economic Writings of Sir William Petty, Together with the Observations upon Bills of Mortality, More Probably by Captain John Graunt*, vol. 2 (Cambridge: Cambridge University Press, 1899), pp. 545–621 (at p. 555). The manuscript was not published in Petty's lifetime. King James had Petty's friend Samuel Pepys examine the proposal, but did not act on it.
4 Petty, "A Treatise on Ireland", p. 568.
5 Theodore Porter, *The Rise of Statistical Thinking, 1820–1900* (Princeton, NJ: Princeton University Press, 1986), pp. 19–20.
6 Petty, "A Treatise on Ireland", p. 549.
7 Petty, "A Treatise on Ireland", p. 558.
8 On the former, see William H.A. Williams, *Tourism, Landscape, and the Irish Character: British Travel Writers in Pre-famine Ireland* (Madison, WI: University of Wisconsin Press, 2008), p. 4; on the latter, see Ina Ferris, *The Romantic National Tale and the Question of Ireland* (Cambridge: Cambridge University Press, 2002), p. 18.
9 Michael Gamer, "Maria Edgeworth and the Romance of Real Life", *Novel*, 34, no. 2 (2001): 232–66 (at p. 250); see also Marilyn Butler, *Maria Edgeworth: A Literary Biography* (Oxford: Clarendon, 1972), pp. 358–60.
10 Williams, *Tourism*, pp. 133–8, 138 (emphasis in original).
11 Arthur Young, *A Tour in Ireland; with General Observations on the Present State of that Kingdom: Made in the Years 1776, 1777, and 1778. And Brought Down to the End of 1779*, vol. 2 (London: T. Cadell, 1780), p. 59.
12 Anne Plumptre, *Narrative of a Residence in Ireland during the Summer of 1814, and That of 1815* (London: Henry Colburn, 1817), p. v.
13 Plumptre, *Narrative*, p. vi.

Malthus's "Authenticated Facts" 165

14 Joel Mokyr, "Review" [of Murphy, Antoin, ed. *Economists and the Irish Economy from the Eighteenth Century to the Present Day*. Dublin: Irish Academic Press], *The Journal of Economic History*, 45, no. 3 (1985): 731–2 (at p. 731).
15 Cormac Ó Gráda, "Malthus and the Pre-famine Economy", in Antoin Murphy, ed., *Economists and the Irish Economy from the Eighteenth Century to the Present Day* (Dublin: Irish Academic Press, 1984), pp. 75–95.
16 But not Wales. His analysis of the United Kingdom begins with England, in Book II, Chapter IX, followed by Ireland, lumped together with Scotland, in Chapter X. Malthus did not separate Wales from England, a practice consistent with the decennial British population censuses which had commenced in 1801.
17 David Ricardo, *The Works and Correspondence of David Ricardo*, Vol. 7 *Letters 1816–1818* [1951], ed. Piero Sraffa, with the collaboration of Maurice H. Dobb (Cambridge: Cambridge University Press for the Royal Economic Society, 1973b), p. 175 (emphasis in original).
18 James, *Population Malthus*, pp. 145–6.
19 Quoted in James, *Population Malthus*, p. 147.
20 [Thomas Robert Malthus], "Newenham and Others on the State of Ireland", *The Edinburgh Review*, 12 (1808): 336–55 (at p. 339). Further references to "Newenham and Others on the State of Ireland" (1808) are included parenthetically in the text.
21 These reviews are chiefly on two of Thomas Newenham's works, *A Statistical and Historical Inquiry into the Progress and Magnitude of the Population of Ireland* (1805) in the first, and *A View of the Natural, Political and Commercial Circumstances of Ireland* (1809) in the second. Newenham's works review many of the contemporaneous accounts on Irish population. See James, *Population Malthus*, pp. 149–56, and Ó Gráda, "Malthus and the Pre-famine Economy", pp. 79–80.
22 Ó Gráda, "Malthus and the Pre-famine Economy", p. 79.
23 Ó Gráda, "Malthus and the Pre-famine Economy", pp. 79–80.
24 Thomas Robert Malthus, "Newenham on the State of Ireland", *The Edinburgh Review*, 14 (1809): 151–70 (at p. 152; emphasis in original). Further references to "Newenham on the State of Ireland" (1809) are included parenthetically in the text.
25 Arthur Young, *The Questions of Scarcity Plainly Stated and Remedies Considered* (London: W.J. and J. Richardson and J. Wright, 1800), p. 77.
26 Catherine Gallagher, "The Body Versus the Social Body in the Works of Thomas Malthus and Henry Mayhew", *Representations*, 14 (1986): 83–106 (at p. 83).
27 David Ricardo, *The Works and Correspondence of David Ricardo*, Vol. 9 *Letters 1821–1823* [1951], ed. Piero Sraffa, with the collaboration of Maurice H. Dobb (Cambridge: Cambridge University Press for the Royal Economic Society, 1973c), p. 230.
28 Ricardo, *Works*, Vol. 9, pp. 232, 239–40.
29 Richard Lovell Edgeworth, and Maria Edgeworth, *The Memoirs of Richard Lovell Edgeworth*, 3rd edn. (London: Richard Bentley, 1844), pp. 396–7.
30 Letter from Maria to Miss Honora Edgeworth, 4 April 1803, in Maria Edgeworth, *The Life and Letters of Maria Edgeworth*, ed. Augustus John Cuthbert Hare, vols. 1 and 2 (New York: Houghton Mifflin, 1895), vol. I, p. 144. Further references to *The Life and Letters*, by volume, are included parenthetically in the text.
31 Butler, *Maria Edgeworth*, pp. 28 ff.
32 Richard Lovell Edgeworth, and Maria Edgeworth, *Practical Education* (London: J. Johnson, 1798). The contents list the chapter as "Prudence and Economy"; the first page of the chapter in the main body of the text titles it "On Prudence

and Economy", p. 691. Further references to *Practical Education* are included parenthetically in the text.
33 A summary chapter and appendix follow "Prudence and Economy".
34 Artur Blaim, *Robinson Crusoe and His Doubles: The English Robinsonade of the Eighteenth Century* (Frankfurt am Main: Peter Lang, 2016).
35 David G. Barrie, "Patrick Colquhoun, the Scottish Enlightenment and Police Reform in Glasgow in the Late Eighteenth Century", *Crime, Histoire & Sociétiés/Crime, History & Societies*, 12, no. 2 (2008): 59–79.
36 Patrick Colquhoun, *A Treatise on the Police of the Metropolis* (London: H. Fry, 1796), p. iii (emphases in original).
37 Colquhoun, *A Treatise on the Police*, p. 38.
38 Christopher Herbert makes a similar argument about the rhetoric used by Henry Mayhew and other mid nineteenth century reformers to describe the state of London's poor. Christopher Herbert, *Culture and Anomie: Ethnographic Imagination in the Nineteenth Century* (Chicago: University of Chicago Press 1991), chapter 4.
39 Wollstonecraft, Mary, *Original Stories from Real Life*, pp. 151–2.
40 Edgeworth, and Edgeworth, *The Memoirs of Richard Lovell Edgeworth*, p. 393.
41 Maria Edgeworth, *Castle Rackrent* [1800] and *Ennui* [1809] (New York: Penguin Classics, 1992), p. 61.
42 Edgeworth, *Castle Rackrent*, p. 62.
43 Gamer, "Maria Edgeworth", pp. 244–5.
44 Saba Bahar, "The "Value of a NAME:" The Representation of Political Economy in Maria Edgeworth's *The Absentee*", *Genre*, 35, no.2 (2002): 283–308 (at p. 291).
45 David Simpson, "Touches of the Real" [Review of *Practising New Historicism* by Catherine Gallagher and Stephen Greenblatt], *London Review of Books*, 23, no. 10 (2001): 25–6. On New Historicism, see Catherine Gallagher and Stephen Greenblatt, *Practicing New Historicism* (Chicago: University of Chicago Press, 2000).
46 William Kern, "Maria Edgeworth and Classical Political Economy" (n.d.). American Economic Association: Committee on the Status of Women in the Economics Profession. https://web.archive.org/web/20110725212131/http://www.cswep.org/edgeworth.html [10 May 2015].
47 Richard Jones, *An Essay on the Distribution of Wealth, and on the Sources of Taxation* (London: John Murray, 1831), p. vii.
48 Edgeworth, and Edgeworth, *The Memoirs of Richard Lovell Edgeworth*, p. 356.
49 Leslie Stephen, "Edgeworth, Richard Lovell", *Dictionary of National Biography, 1885–1900* [1888], vol. 16 (London: Smith, Elder & Co. (1885–1900), pp. 383–5 (at p. 384).
50 Edgeworth, and Edgeworth, *The Memoirs of Richard Lovell Edgeworth*, p. 356.
51 Stephen, "Edgeworth, Richard Lovell", p. 384.
52 Edgeworth, *Castle Rackrent*, p. 121.
53 David Ricardo, *The Works and Correspondence of David Ricardo, Vol. 6 Letters 1810–1815* [1951], ed. Piero Sraffa, with the collaboration of Maurice H. Dobb (Cambridge: Cambridge University Press for the Royal Economic Society, 1973a), p. 295.
54 David Ricardo, *The Works and Correspondence of David Ricardo, Vol. 3 Pamphlets and Papers, 1809–1811* [1951], ed. Piero Sraffa, with the collaboration of Maurice H. Dobb (Cambridge: Cambridge University Press for the Royal Economic Society, 1962), p. 181.
55 Ricardo, *Works, Vol. 9*, p. 144.
56 Mary S. Morgan, *The World in the Model: How Economists Work and Think* (New York: Cambridge University Press, 2012), p. 51.

57 Morgan, *The World in the Model*, p. 45 (note 2); see also Christophe Depoortière, "William Nassau Senior and David Ricardo on the Method of Political Economy", *Journal of the History of Economic Thought*, 35, no. 1 (2013): 19–42, especially p. 31.
58 Morgan, *The World in the Model*, p. 55.
59 Mary S. Morgan, "Experimental Farming and Ricardo's Political Arithmetic of Distribution", Working Papers on the Nature of Evidence: How Well do 'Facts' Travel? No. 03/05 (Department of Economic History: London School of Economics, 2005), p. 11.
60 "Ricardo had presented her with a copy of [his *On*] *Protection to Agriculture*, 2nd edn., 1822". Ricardo, *Works*, Vol. 9, p. 203, note 2.
61 Ricardo, *Works*, Vol. 9, p. 253.
62 Jonsson, "Rival Ecologies", p. 1353.
63 Ricardo, *Works*, Vol. 9, p. 231, note.
64 Daston and Lunbeck, "Introduction: Observation Observed", pp. 3–5.
65 Ricardo, *Works*, Vol. 9, pp. 230–1.
66 Ricardo, *Works*, Vol. 9, p. 232.
67 Ricardo, *Works*, Vol. 9, p. 238–9.
68 H[enry] H[iggs], "Introduction", *Political Economy Club. Founded in London, 1821. Minutes of Proceedings, etc.*, vol. 6 (London: Macmillan and Co, 1921), pp. vii–xxvi (at p. xii).
69 Ricardo, *Works*, Vol. 9, p. 253.
70 Ricardo, *Works*, Vol. 9, p. 259.
71 Ricardo, *Works*, Vol. 9, pp. 254–5.
72 Ricardo, *Works*, Vol. 9, pp. 254–5.
73 Jane Marcet first introduced the concept of comparative advantage to the public in 1816, in *Conversations on Political Economy*.
74 Cormac Ó Gráda, *Black '47 and Beyond: The Great Irish Famine in History, Economy, and Memory* (Princeton: Princeton University Press, 1999), p. 9.
75 Ricardo, *Works*, Vol. 9, p. 232.
76 Ricardo, *Works*, Vol. 7, pp. 184–5.
77 Ricardo, *Works*, Vol. 9, p. 239.
78 Kern, "Maria Edgeworth and Classical Political Economy".
79 Great Britain, House of Commons Select Committee on Emigration, *Third Report from the Select Committee on Emigration from the United Kingdom, 1827* (London: House of Commons, 1827), pp. 9–10, 313, 314.

5 Travel Accounts of Spanish America and British Political Economy, circa 1800–1823

> Within the last thirty years, a great revolution has taken place in the maxims of the Spanish government with regard to its colonies; and in no particular has its change of policy been more remarkable, than in the dereliction of its antient system of secrecy and concealment, in all that related to its American possessions. [John Allen], *The Edinburgh Review* 1810[1]

Spanish governments had zealously closed off their American possessions to outsiders, and stymied efforts of travelers and armchair travelers alike to gain information about their American colonies for centuries. When a steady trickle of foreigners finally began to visit the territories starting late in the eighteenth century, and issued reports to readers in Europe, their accounts raised a number of questions. What phenomena were important enough to observe and represent, and how were these observations and representations to be made? What role did the concerns of British political economists, their focus on population, births, deaths, and marriages, and, of course, trade and commerce, as well as on the degree to which this part of the New World and its inhabitants were savage or civilized, moral or amoral, miserable or happy, play in these observations and representations? Should foreign observers in Spanish America adopt or adapt Indigenous systems of knowledge? Could they rely solely on eyewitness accounts, or, if they used Indigenous ones, had these travelers identified Indigenes to observe, represent, and translate without bias or prejudice? And, were the same techniques and epistemologies of observers applicable throughout the whole of Spain's American possessions?

This chapter and the following touch on how these questions played out in the work of travelers who crisscrossed parts of Spanish America at the turn of the century through the early and mid-1820s. Their reports and British reaction to their texts during this period highlight the key role played by principles of political economy in helping Europeans make and interpret observations about Spanish America. This chapter opens with an account of the work of François Joseph de Pons, who journeyed through parts of present-day Venezuela and Colombia in the first years of the new century. The British

DOI: 10.4324/9781315778952-5

translated de Pons's observations on the untapped commercial potential of the region into an account framed by both political and domestic economies.

Humboldt, de Pons's more famous contemporary, journeyed through the same territory at the same time. But here I focus on *Essai Politique sur la Royaume de la Nouvelle-Espagne* (1808–11) and its first English translation, *Political Essay on the Kingdom of New Spain* (1811), volumes which first brought Humboldt international renown. Each illustrates in exhaustive detail Humboldt's wide-ranging vision of social analysis; they forced political economists and other Britons keen to sniff out facts about Spanish America to pay close attention to how the environment interacts with human institutions and policy to shape the fortunes and happiness of a population. How Humboldt reimagines the myriad forms of these interactions as well as contemporary reception by British political economists and other British readers to his methodological, epistemological, and ontological innovations form the next part of this chapter.

Almost two decades after de Pons and Humboldt traversed the northern reaches of the continent, Maria Graham stepped ashore in Valparaiso, Chile. The second section of this chapter deals with her observations during the nine months she spent in Chile, as detailed in *Journal of a Residence in Chile, during the Year 1822; and a Voyage from Chile to Brazil, in 1823* (1824).[2] Pratt includes Graham as part of the "exploratrices sociales", females who traveled in South America during the revolutions against Spain and the tumult of the period immediately following the success of those struggles. According to Pratt, the writings and other activities of these women form a "political and personal" discourse distinct from yet ultimately wedded to that of male travelers to the continent who sought primarily to further European commercial interests.[3]

Graham grounds her narrative of the recent revolutionary history of Chile in the language of political economy in *JRC*. She asserts that knowledge and practice of its principles, especially free trade, will guarantee the progress, prosperity, and happiness of the residents of Chile. Yet Graham's use of local interlocutors to explain phenomena lead her to reflect on the nature of observation. Her musings, like Humboldt's, stem from a vision of the analysis and ends of economic life radically different from the methodological bent of most contemporary British political economists. Graham illustrates how the concept of the domestic could sanction, even demand, women's participation in the political economic analysis of what is and what should be. Because women teach others how to observe, they actively shape economic life and political economy itself.

Travelers on the Political and Domestic Economy of Spain's New World Colonies, c. 1800

The Seven Years' War spurred Spain's Bourbon rulers to extensively reorganize colonial administration in her New World Empire in order to increase production, and, ultimately, the tax revenue and authority of the state. These efforts intensified at the close of the century as Spain teetered near bankruptcy after the war with revolutionary France; Spain and its colonies moved to ease mercantilist policies, in some instances directly inspired by the work of Adam Smith.[4] Early nineteenth century British political economists sharply criticized these efforts at liberalization, however, for being insufficiently liberal. The reformers conceived of their work as entailing a union rather than a separation between economics and politics; hence, to use their terminology, the identification of political with civil economy in a "science of the state".[5] Thus, Charles III in the preamble to the 1778 Free Trade Act (Reglamento para el comercio libre) declared that "only a free and protected Commerce between European and American Spaniards can restore Agriculture, Industry, and Population in my Dominions to their former vigour".[6] Still, the focus on commerce helped to continue a shift in British discourse about Spanish America; the territories now represented areas for possible trade, investment, and, above all, rational governance instead of simply sites of the Black Legend.

During this period Spanish America had opened, if only just a crack, to foreign travelers. Most foreigners allowed to travel in Spanish America in this period were scientists or diplomats, as was de Pons, an agent from the French government to Caracas. A planter in French Hispaniola, de Pons fled the slave revolt there and took up residence in Spanish Hispaniola, moving on to Caracas in 1801. He traveled through territory he called Eastern Terra Firma from 1801 to 1804 and published a three-volume account of his journeys, *Voyage à la partie orientale de la terre-ferme dans l'Amérique Méridionale*, in 1806. Two English translations of *Voyage* appeared soon thereafter, an abridged version in 1806, and a full-length, two-volume one in 1807, both titled *Travels in South America, during the Years 1801, 1802, 1803, and 1804*.[7]

The translations and the three reviews covered here, one of *Voyage* and two of the 1807 *Travels*, testify to the eagerness with which the British received de Pons's information about the commercial potential of the region. *The Edinburgh Review* applauds *Voyage* in July 1806, noting that readers "will find very ample details" on the "natural resources and productions" of the region in the volumes.[8] Two years later *The Gentleman's Magazine* similarly hails *Travels*: "Perhaps no work published within the last year has been so well calculated to gratify public curiosity".[9] Public curiosity and praise could be traced to the twists and turns of British entanglements in South America. While British expeditionary forces unsuccessfully invaded Rio de la Plata in 1806 and 1807, the outbreak of the Peninsular War transformed the Spanish from foes to allies, and further whetted the appetite of the British for news of the area.[10] What had been an inchoate British policy forged principally in steel – was the goal of the military expeditions to establish trading posts or full-blown colonies, or were they vanguards for an attempt to conquer the entire continent? – began to turn toward ways to incorporate South America into what has been termed Britain's "informal empire" or "empire of free trade".[11] Thus, British recognition of Mexico, Buenos Aires, and Colombia as independent states all came in the form of commercial treaties.[12] And customs data from Valparaiso and Santiago indicates that of the top forty merchants in Chile in the 1820s, the British, with sixteen, made up the largest national group.[13] As a result of Great Britain's dominant position in world financial and manufactured goods markets, as well as its trading and military might, the British were soon to exercise significant influence in the region through loans, investment, and a commitment to the expansion of trade, all as an accompaniment to diplomacy.[14]

The layout of *Voyage* makes clear that de Pons's focus is in fact commerce. He devotes four of the eleven chapters to describing the products, commerce, fiscal administration, and customs and manners of the peoples of the area. The other chapters cover the history, geography, and civil, religious, and military administration of the region. De Pons uses these chapters to examine how the combination of Spanish policy and the environment contributed to the shortfall in production and tax revenue from a region where the natural environment was, in many respects, quite fertile.

British translators and reviewers of *Voyage* made explicit the connection between analysis of the commerce of the region and contemporaneous British political economic thought. The term "économie politique" actually appears in only a handful of places in *Voyage*, and the 1806 *Travels* entirely omits the term political economy. But reviewers argued, as did de Pons himself, that boosting output from the region would result from a freer flow of people, information, investment, and trade, all driven by the relaxation of stringent government control. These prescriptions would be familiar to British followers of political economy. Yet the 1807 translation further suggests that the British read *Voyage* as a description of both the political and domestic economy of the region:

> The Spaniards are, literally, speaking, beyond every other people jealous of inquisitive strangers. There are very few of them who will cordially assist his inquiries concerning their political and domestic economy; but there are many who, under the appearance of zeal and friendship, will, upon the most grave and important subjects, give as facts, relations the farthest removed from the truth.[15]

The phrase "political and domestic economy" is not an exact translation of the original's "régime politique et domestique". Still, *The Gentleman's Magazine* reviewer of the 1807 *Travels* maintains that the "new and happy prospect of trading with that country ... will make the study of Depons' work, in some measure, a matter of necessity to those likely to be concerned in it".[16] Those likely to be concerned included not just merchants, but policymakers, political economists, and other analysts. Reviewers, like de Pons, ponder and judge the work habits and innate capacities of Indigenes, their degree of civilization, and the ineffectiveness of government in the colonies, matters of both political and domestic economy. *The Gentleman's Magazine* reviewer bemoans, for example, the total or near-total absence of trade in certain plant products: the reviewer blames the "indolence universally prevailing".[17]

The review concludes, however, on a hopeful note. If the Spanish should succeed in triumphing over the French invaders in Europe,

> It is to be hoped they will remember the frank and disinterested assistance we have afforded them, and open the gates to the full tide of rational thought and wealth that may flow to this part of America, by the enterprize of our Merchants.[18]

The reviewer embeds the commercial motives driving British interest in the colonies in a larger project, the worldwide expansion of rationality and prosperity. Commercial interests are therefore disinterested. This assertion would appear to be highly questionable, even laughable given both the longstanding association of profit-seeking with self-interested behavior, and recent British military operations on the continent. The statement stems, however, from commonplace assumptions and conclusions by supporters of Smithian political economy. Free trade spreads wealth, prosperity, and happiness; it helps diffuse knowledge, too, leading to better governance by the state and self-governance by individuals and households. Correct principles of political economy and domestic economy, embodied by British merchants, could help initiate the virtuous cycle that will create more wealth, happiness, and rationality in South America. The force of ideas trumps the force of arms in this accounting.

The British commentators saw Bourbon reforms as leading to neo-mercantilist free trade, and pled instead for the establishment of Smithian free trade. British efforts to promote such a shift went beyond pleading, however disinterested. They took actions which were hardly in accord with the ideals of Smithian free trade, often working assiduously to protect existing trade barriers, or even erect new ones. For example, after French troops invaded Portugal in 1807, the British helped the Portuguese government flee to Brazil. Lord Strangford subsequently pushed through a trade treaty in 1810 that stipulated that the British would pay a lower tariff on exports into Brazil than would Portugal. The treaty also forbade Brazilian exports of tobacco and sugar, a provision included to protect British Caribbean producers of these goods. And, as a final stroke, the language of the treaty implied that in theory the terms could apply *forever*: "the Present Treaty shall be unlimited in point of duration, and that the obligations and conditions expressed or implied in it shall be perpetual and immutable."[19]

Voyage arrived on British shores just as these debates about commercial policies had begun to percolate, and accurate observations were at a premium. De Pons, however, encountered difficulties with the Spanish who would, in his words, dissemble to any seeker of information, even in the context of a reformed colonial administration which encouraged greater openness, more and more accurate information about the colonies and their resources, and freer trade. Yet *Voyage* opens with de Pons claiming that his work fits two of the most important criteria of objectivity, truthfulness and accuracy: "The work ... has no foundation but truth, nor any ornament besides its accuracy" (*Travels* (1807), I, p. xvii).[20] If the Spanish and Creoles are untrustworthy, de Pons happily supplies his own authority as a ready substitute for European readers skeptical of reports emanating from residents about their American possessions. His testaments to his credibility include eight years' residence in San Domingo, and nearly four additional years in the provinces he describes in *Travels*. De Pons also claims to have diligently checked public records and archives, and, in the end, sought to "soumettre au témoignage de mes yeux", or "submit everything to the inspection of my own eyes".[21] He is his own expert eyewitness.

According to British reviewers, *Voyage* measures up well against previous accounts, but still falls short of being authoritative. *The Edinburgh Review* essayist aims at "extracting whatever to us seems most new or valuable in his observations". To economize on words, the reviewer proposes, to cite one example, to note "those particulars" about the government of Caracas only where de Pons "differs from Robertson['s *History*], or where he has added facts or observations of importance to the account of that elegant historian".[22] The implicit message is that, in the main, de Pons account conforms to Robertson's. Yet neither the overall agreement of *Voyage* with *History*, nor a recitation of his own bona fides insulates de Pons from criticism of his observations. He omits pertinent information, for one. The reviewer of the 1807 translation for *The Monthly Review, Or, Literary Journal* points to several instances where de Pons fails to deliver promised facts:

> In his chorographical particulars, the author introduces an account of timber for building, &c. but it is conveyed in too general terms for specific information ... M. Depons does not insert the respective latitudes of some of the ports, mouths of rivers, &c. in his chorography of these provinces; – a material omission, which he ought to have particularly avoided, since he tells us that no tolerably correct account of them had ever been published.[23]

De Pons does detail the many different types of goods produced in the region, the quality of these goods compared to those produced elsewhere, as well as statistics on output and revenues. But he fails to provide accurate geographical information authorities would need to establish infrastructure, public works which would serve to enhance trade in these goods as well as, again, tax revenue; thus, his account lacks certain facts vital for the expansion of commerce.

British reviewers also charge de Pons with bias. *The Edinburgh Review* points out that in his "picture of the character and manners of the Creoles, some allowance must be made for the prejudices of a stranger, and for the dislike of the Frenchman for every thing Spanish". The reviewer ventures that "[i]f they would but give up their *siesta*, or afternoon nap, he [de Pons] seems not unwilling to hope that they might yet attain to some degree of civilization".[24] The complaint, using a national stereotype to tweak de Pons for the same, undercuts itself, but does not vitiate it entirely. The passage also indicates how easily *Voyage* could bear a message about the blurry distinction between two principal contemporary English definitions of civilization. Civilization could describe the cultivation of manners by an individual such as a Spanish gentleman, or, as a noun to which analysts could attach an adjective and define the principal means of production by a society. De Pons observes the Spanish of the region, and finds them wanting as potential leaders of a new commercial civilization. The jibe about "degree of civilization" would remind British readers of both Spain's relative weakness as a commercial power, and that Spanish indolence, a lack of manners, was as much a cause as a symptom of that weakness.

The reviewer indicts de Pons's views on Spanish propensities and capacities for useful labor, but does not extend the same sympathy or gentle humor to the Indians de Pons reports on. The reviewer notes without comment de Pons's opinion that the "Indians subject to the Spanish government are as remarkable for the indolence and weakness of their character, as for the mildness of their disposition." The review concludes, as had de Pons, that the Indians have "a natural propensity to indolence".[25] The reviewer for *The Monthly Review*, on the other hand, takes issue with this conclusion:

> M. Depons also seems to conclude too precipitately that the Indians are destitute of intellectual powers. Their indolence, inactivity and apparent passiveness, arise out of their having but few desires to be indulged, and but few wants to be satisfied. Their natural capacities are equal to those of other men; and the instances of Joseph Brant, and others, clearly shew that, when they are accustomed to social life, they are not deficient in either activity or talents.[26]

The Monthly Review invokes the standard equation of activity with commercial civilization. It baldly declares that, while Indians possess capacities for activity and intellectual power equal to those of other men, they lack "social life", which would awaken those same capacities. The reviewer, however, encapsulates a stance toward fellow Europeans that is also both liberal and judgmental. De Pons fails to observe the Indians correctly and consequently misjudges their innate abilities, and the Spanish fail to incorporate Indians into their social interactions. The failure of Spanish governance means that the Indians cannot as yet capitalize on the benefits, fulfilling their natural capacities, that increasing commercial activity encourages.

Spanish authorities took a huge step to "open the gates to the full tide of rational thought", however, when they allowed Humboldt free rein to roam through Spanish possessions in the New World. Traveling at roughly the same time as de Pons, Humboldt, and the botanist Aimé Bonpland visited Cuba, parts of present-day Colombia, Venezuela, Peru, and Ecuador, and then the Kingdom of New Spain (present-day Mexico, Texas, and California) between 1799 and 1804. It is hard to overstate the impact of Humboldt and the numerous writings he poured forth about his travels in Spanish America. During the first half of the nineteenth century, reading Humboldt's published work, copies of numerous letters plus some twenty-three volumes in French which appeared between 1805 and 1834, proved de rigueur for European and American scientists such as Charles Darwin, and profoundly influenced ways of observation and representation by subsequent explorers in Mexico, Central and South America, and the United States as well. The British diplomat Henry G. Ward, for one, in *Mexico in 1827* (1828), acknowledged his debt to Humboldt by concluding that "to write a book upon Mexico, without referring to Baron Humboldt at almost every page, is nearly impossible".[27]

Humboldt's volumes received more widespread notice among British readers once they had been translated into English; crucially, these versions were less costly than the originals. *Essai Politique* had been published in expensive folios, a two-volume quarto edition and a five-volume octavo edition.[28] In 1810, John Allen concluded his piece in *The Edinburgh Review* on the still-incomplete quarto edition of *Essai* by calling for a less expensive release; "we are persuaded it might be published for one fifth of the price of the original, which has been made most unnecessarily splendid, and most exorbitantly dear".[29]

British translators also made Humboldt's works more accessible by placing his analyses, in part, in a stadial history framework readily comprehensible to contemporaries. John Black who translated the first English edition of *Essai Politique*, opens his preface, for instance, by asking readers to consider that travel literature allows them to observe the world from a stadial point of view: "We see the human race before us in every stage of civilization, from the refinement and enterprise of the inhabitants of the west of Europe, down to the stupid savage of New Holland or the Terra del Fuego."[30] Black compares *Essai Politique* favorably to the "numerous productions which have appeared of late without adding any thing to our stock of information". Humboldt's extensive use of first-hand observation, measurements, statistics, and material gleaned from colonial archives form the foundations for *Essai Politique*. For Black, Humboldt's wealth and status removed obstacles to travel and observation in two ways: he could move freely in lands under "arbitrary government"; and they allowed Humboldt to "provide himself with every thing which could most advance his pursuits". Both advantages allow Humboldt to capitalize on his vast breadth and depth of knowledge (Black, "Preface", p. v.).

Black anoints "M. de Humboldt" an authority, and compares his reports favorably to the "specious paragraphs of our celebrated countryman Robertson" (Black, "Preface", p. v). While Robertson sometimes imparts "little specific information", Humboldt "furnishes us with precise data on a very great variety of important subjects" (Black, "Preface", pp. vii–viii). Black's repeated use of "us" and "we" recruits the reader to join in his approbation. If Black believes that Humboldt's reports nicely match some of the emerging criteria for objective observation and representation (specificity, precision, and vast amounts of data, for example), he also voices some caveats. Chief among these is the fact that Humboldt's work was vetted by the "natives of New Spain" and the Spanish government, a process which may have raised doubts among readers about "the accuracy and fullness of the information" in *Essai Politique* (Black, "Preface", v–vii). Humboldt, in Black's words, "is exceedingly prone to give favourable accounts of all the individuals whom he has occasion to mention" as a consequence (Black, "Preface", p. vii). Humboldt is also prolix, occasionally repetitive, and sometimes includes inessential material, all of "which have a necessary tendency to fatigue the attention of the reader". Black acknowledges, however, that Humboldt shares these shortcomings, as well as a failure to underscore "the more important and leading features of an object", with many other authors, especially his fellow Germans (Black, "Preface", p. viii).

Black's preface is but the first of several paratextual items that follow the title pages of volume one of *Political Essay*. To read that volume is to mimic a long voyage away from home, with its extended preparation for the reader before the journey, the main body of the text, actually begins. Black's remarks run twelve pages; a three page "Dedication" by Humboldt to the King of Spain, Charles IV, follows. Humboldt's encomium to the king alerts the reader to the purpose of his travels; Charles asked him to compose a "statistical essay on the kingdom of New Spain" to fulfill the king's desire to obtain "accurate information" on areas subject to his rule (Humboldt, *Political Essay*, I, p. xvi). Humboldt closes his dedicatory remarks (before a formal sign-off) by claiming that his efforts

> breathe the sentiments of gratitude which I owe to the government who protected me, and to the noble and loyal nation who received me, not as a traveler, but as a fellow-citizen. How can we displease a good king, when we speak to him of the national interest, of the improvement of social institutions, and the eternal principles on which the prosperity of nations is founded?
>
> (Humboldt, *Political Essay*, I, p. xvii)

After a blank page, a two-page "Contents" follows which sheds light on Humboldt's conceptions of the national interest and "the eternal principles on which the prosperity of nations is founded". Geography takes center stage. The contents indicate, for instance, that a reader must traverse a

"Geographical Introduction" before arriving at the main body of the text. And when the reader finally reaches that body, the "Contents" announce that the first book addresses both "General considerations on the extent and physical aspect" of New Spain, and "The influence of the inequalities of soil on climate, agriculture, commerce, and military defence of the country".

"Geographical Introduction" runs a daunting 145 pages in *Political Essay*, and "Introduction Géographique" an even more staggering 199 pages in *Essai Politique*.[31] The introduction locates New Spain for readers by offering a systematic account of the geographical observations taken by Humboldt and his company, as well as measurements by other explorers. It also illustrates a methodological, epistemological, and ontological model of how scientific observation and representation should proceed. Humboldt invites readers to not only observe his observations and methods, but, implicitly, to reproduce or refine his measurements. Humboldt's openness foreshadows what would become an ideal of scientific objectivity; if readers had the wherewithal to retrace his route, they could theoretically gauge the accuracy of his account. Humboldt's meticulously detailed reporting stands in stark contrast to de Pons, whose occasional lapses in identifying the most basic geographic particulars irritated the reviewer for *The Monthly Review*. Humboldt, however, considers de Pons in a more generous spirit than *The Monthly Review*. In one of the few instances where he mentions his contemporary, he concludes, in *Personal narrative of travels to the equinoctial regions of the New continent during the years 1799–1804* (1814–29), a never-to-be-finished collaborative effort with the Romantic poet Helen Maria Williams which repackaged Humboldt's account for a wider audience, that de Pons "has in general collected very accurate notions during his stay in Caracas".[32]

Once the main text commences, Humboldt informs readers that he sought to understand the causes of the stark variation in economic performance in the different parts of Spanish America he had observed. In Black's abridged version, Humboldt writes:

> I arrived in Mexico by the South Sea in March 1803, and resided a year in that vast kingdom. I had recently visited the province of Caracas, the banks of the Orinooko, the Rio Negro, New Granada, Quito, and the coast of Peru, and I could not avoid being struck with the contrast between the civilization of New Spain, and the scanty cultivation of those parts of South America which had fallen under my notice. This contrast excited me to a particular study of the statisticks of Mexico, and to an investigation of the causes which have had the greatest influence on the progress of the population and national industry.
> (Humboldt, *Political Essay*, I, p. 1)[33]

Witness some of the key words Humboldt uses: civilization, cultivation, causes, progress, population, industry. These are all standard terms used by political economists. Civilization, along with "contrast", recalls stadial histories, too. Progress does double duty, as both stadial referent and, in Humboldt's concern over the population of Mexico, a clear nod to Malthus. Humboldt also signals the importance of population in his work in the opening to *Personal narrative*, writing that he aims to reach more readers "than the details of observations merely scientific, or than my researches on the population, the commerce, and the mines of New Spain".[34]

These allusions to political economy are no mere bagatelles. The relationship between political economists and Humboldt is best described as one of mutual influence. Humboldt fulsomely praises Malthus and Smith – in a footnote he calls Malthus's 1798 essay "one of the most profound works in political economy which has ever appeared" ("ouvrage d'économie politique des plus profonds qui aient jamais paru") – and consciously incorporates the insights of both to craft his account of New Spain (Humboldt, *Political Essay*, I, p. 107).[35]

Humboldt does not express unqualified admiration of political economy in *Political Essay*. He points to what he sees as flaws in the reasoning of contemporaries, especially political economists, on the sources of riches, or their absence, in New Spain. The lack of first-hand observations from the region put the shortcomings of reductionism with respect to causes and effects on full display. Thus, a traveler will recognize the fertility of the soil in Mexico; an armchair traveler, on the other hand, a reader of "vague and uncertain notions hitherto published" on the interior of the colonies, "will have some difficulty believing that the principal sources of the Mexican riches are by no means the mines, but an agriculture which has gradually been ameliorating since the end of the last century". Humboldt refutes those who contend that a slavish devotion to mining has led the Spanish and Mexicans to neglect the agricultural sector. Those who have "inferred that it is to the working of the mines that we are to attribute the small care bestowed on the cultivation of soil in other parts of the Spanish colonies" incorrectly reason from a small sample (Humboldt, *Political Essay*, II, Book IV, pp. 404–5).

Humboldt admits that, while this inference may be just for insignificant patches of territory, "this reasoning cannot now explain why in countries of three or four times the extent of France agriculture is in the state of languor". He locates the sources of this torpor elsewhere, speculating that the "same physical and moral causes which fetter the progress of national industry in the Spanish colonies have been inimical to a better cultivation of the soil". Humboldt believes, instead, that mining can promote the fortunes of agriculture, that "under improved social conditions the countries which most abound with mineral productions will be as well if not better cultivated than those in which no productions are to be found" (Humboldt, *Political Essay*, II, Book IV, pp. 405–6).

What perpetuated incorrect inferences on the relationship between mining and agriculture in the Spanish colonies? Humboldt places the blame on the works of political economy, which promote another type of laziness:

"the desire natural to man of simplifying the causes of every thing has introduced into works of political economy a species of reasoning which is perpetuated, because it flatters the mental indolence of the multitude" (Humboldt, *Political Essay*, II, Book IV, p. 406). Humboldt ridicules the notion that an "abundance of gold and silver" are solely responsible for depopulation, the neglect of agriculture and the moribund state of manufacturing in Spanish America. It is as if, Humboldt continues, one were to claim that "all the evils of Spain are to be attributed to the discovery of America, or the wandering race of the merinos, or the religious intolerance of the clergy!" (Humboldt, *Political Essay*, II, Book IV, p. 406). Humboldt may be dealing with a set of straw men here since Allen asserts in *The Edinburgh Review* that Ulloa had long since disproved the "vulgar error" that mine labor was the principal source of depopulation in Spanish America.[36]

Humboldt's sarcasm also provoked a tart response from the translator of *Political Essay*, who points to a methodological divide between Humboldt and contemporary British political economists. They part company when it comes to causes; Humboldt insists that analysts pay attention to the multiple causes of phenomena, while political economists, according to Black, focus on the principal causes. Black cites no less an authority than "an acute political economist, M. Brougham" to rebuke Humboldt. Brougham, in *Colonial Policy of the European Powers* (1803), had delineated how the unique confluence of institutions, resources, and the stage of growth of nations could determine the policies appropriate to promote economic development.[37] In a note, Black writes that Humboldt "surely does not mean that they [America, merinos, and the clergy] are not among the principal causes of the present state of Spain". In addition, Black finds the implication that the targets of Humboldt's ridicule do not know "that there are other causes in abundance" itself demeaning (Humboldt, *Political Essay* II, Book IV, p. 406, note).

Some British political economists responded quickly to Humboldt's writings. While Smith had already noted the poor economic performance of some nations blessed with rich resources in *Wealth of Nations*, *Essai Politique* provided fresh evidence to political economists about the possible institutional sources for this paradox, as well as a cautionary note on inferential reasoning.[38] Clearly political economists appreciated the role institutions play in the economy prior to Humboldt. This was especially true after Malthus questioned the relationship between systems of poor relief and population growth. He believed Norway, where he observed the apparently baneful influence on early marriages, hence births, of a change in the terms of military service, provided additional evidence on this score. Thus, political economists would have been particularly receptive to Humboldt when he ascribes the differences in economic and population growth between North America and Mexico to the respective "degrees of perfection of their social institutions" (Humboldt, *Political Essay*, I, p. 14).[39]

Malthus only learned about Humboldt's work and its relevance to political economists in 1817, as a result of correspondence with Ricardo cited in the previous chapter.[40] He made little mention of Humboldt in any of the editions of *Essay on Population* that appeared during his lifetime, and limits most of his references on Spanish America in *Essay* to quotes from Roberston, Raynal, various Jesuit missionaries, and the like in the chapter "Of the Checks to Population among the American Indians". Yet, once he was made aware of Humboldt's volumes, Malthus quickly adapted one of his insights to make a key point of the fifth edition of *Essay* (1817). Malthus claims that "experience" proves that if a laborer can easily obtain subsistence with only two or three days of work, but will need to work "three or four days more" to be able to afford conveniences and comforts, he will "therefore often prefer the luxury of idleness to the luxury of improved lodging and clothing" (Malthus, *Essay* (1817), III, p. 23). Malthus notes that that this situation "is said by Humboldt to be particularly the case in some parts of South America". According to Malthus, echoing Ricardo, the situation prevails elsewhere, too, in India, Ireland, and anywhere else where "food is plentiful compared with capital and manufactured commodities".

Malthus's use of these observations by Humboldt raises two questions. First, did the relationship between resource availability and economic growth unfold in the same way in different societies? Ricardo thought so in his letter to Malthus: "Humbold [sic] in his account of New Spain points out the very same evils as you do in Ireland, proceeding too from the same cause." Second, if political economists wished to go so far as to say that whole societies choose to go without comforts that the English would deem necessities, what exactly drives that choice? Political economists did not dispute the observed facts; a combination of easily produced staple foodstuffs, bananas in the lowlands and maize in the Cordillera, a radically unequal distribution of income and land, political instability, and a population typically indolent and improvident, produce slow economic growth. Malthus fashions these facts into an attack on what he believed to be Ricardo's naïve belief that a straightforward positive relationship between natural resource availability and economic growth could only be thwarted by "a vicious government". Malthus names a different cause when he proposes that a lack of effective demand rather than a lack of capital could be the primary reason for food-rich societies to choose the paradoxical pairing of the luxury of leisure with material privation. Malthus quotes extensively from *Essai* as he constructs a causal chain in *Principles of Political Economy* which ran from rich national resources to institutions to un-industrious character, and extends it to explain poor economic growth.[41]

Humboldt characterizes his work as directed toward "a particular study of the statisticks of Mexico" which would enable one to divine the causes that influence population and industry. "Statisticks" is an old word, though it may be a translator's or typesetter's typo for the original French "statistique", or a neologism melding the English "statistics" and the German "statistik". Regardless of the word's origin, Humboldt does present the reader with analysis strikingly different from contemporary political economy. Walls suggests that it bears a close resemblance to the much older version of economy, "oikonomia", and calls the essay a broad epistemological and ontological challenge to political economists.[42] Where might these challenges lie? Lesham concludes that the ancient Greek texts on "oikonomia" stress the need for the head of the household or "oikos" to cultivate a prudent disposition. Prudence, in turn, would generate the theoretical and practical knowledge necessary to ethically manage, outside the "oikos", the surplus generated over and above man's needs.[43] Thus, "oikonomia" emphasizes an excess of means rather than Malthusian scarcity, and focuses on the prudent household head rather than population as the principal unit of analysis. As a final challenge to political economy, "oikonomia" embeds prudence in a decision-making domain explicitly ethical and purposefully social, as opposed to that of a political economy where individual self-interest, even if not vicious, is at a remove from any intentional furthering of the social good.

The practice of "oikonomia" would include performing types of analyses similar to those undertaken by Humboldt in the Kingdom of New Spain and, not coincidentally, reminiscent of Edgeworth's gloss on the West Indies. These include examination of how the climate and environment, the degree of political and juridical stability, as well as that of the security, physical condition, and distribution of property, and, not least, political history all conduce to the production and population of the kingdom. Readers would find information on all these, as well as much more in *Essai Politique* and *Political Essay*.

Alternatively, Humboldt's contemporaries may have more readily linked his statistical essay to the contemporary German science of state referred to as cameralism than to "oikonomia". Cameralism, in its analysis and practice, represented another alternative to political economy. We've previously encountered a British variant, political arithmetic, which supporters and detractors also called both "police", or public administration for the common good, Bourbon reformer's "science of the state", as well as "statistik"; James Mackintosh's description of a "statistical account" that would further a more publicly transparent "science of administration" represents yet another possibility.[44] Late eighteenth and early nineteenth theorists and practitioners of cameralism, while retaining the desire to measure everything that could possibly assist the science, had leavened its statist proclivities by adapting the work of French Physiocrats in the 1770s and the liberalism of Smith in the 1790s.[45] Present-day commentators have touched on its links and debts to "oikos" and "oikonomia"; the cameralist prince runs the state like a well-regulated household, prudently managing both non-human resources and relationships among people.[46] As a final clue to possible sources for Humboldt's work, Lindenfed notes that German universities and academies taught cameralism not as "a 'scientific method' or even an in-depth investigation of a particular subject", but emphasized "comprehensiveness and systematic knowledge".[47]

Whether contemporaries thought of *Essai Politique* as an exercise in "oikonomia", cameralism, "statistik", or a "sui generis" science, Humboldt sought to illustrate the necessity for prudent management by both households and the state. Prudence would promote both the well-being and happiness of the inhabitants of New Spain and enhance the ability of the state to garner tax revenue. Prudential management by the state meant paying careful attention to how policies affected the condition of the land, water, and other elements of the environment.

Prudential policies in New Spain would, in turn, be based on statistics. The first page of Volume II of *Political Essay* (drawn from Book III, Chapter VIII) presents a strikingly different account than does the opening of the second volume of *Essai* (which begins with Book III, Chapter VIII): *Political Essay* presents in sparse words and numbers three summary statistics, "Territorial extent," "Population", and inhabitants per square league. See Figure 5.1. If one reading in English wanted a succinct, stand-alone statement of a "Statistical Analysis of the Kingdom of New Spain", the title of this page, these four lines of text swimming in a large expanse of blank white space represent just that. The next page includes statistics on the territorial extent and population of constituent parts of New Spain. See Figure 5.2. These are estimates, and the data don't add up to the totals displayed on the previous page. This discrepancy serves as a reminder to readers about the parlous nature of population statistics in New Spain. Yet they may have also bolstered Humboldt's authority by demonstrating that he possessed the confidence to report measurements that might be precise, but inaccurate.

The top borders of the following 187 pages illustrate the types of challenges *Essay* represents to political economists. The borders are identical; each displays the principal result of Humboldt's statistical analyses for the "Intendancy of Mexico". See Figure 5.3. Like the tables at the beginning of the volume, this table fixes the reader's gaze. It depicts the fruit of two sets of observations by Humboldt and those who assisted him: one set maps the geography of Mexico; the other counts the Indigenous and European population of the intendancy. The tables convey information necessary, though hardly sufficient, for a monarch to conduct statecraft and manage a nation imagined as a collection of people and resources. The interplay between tables and text reinforces the primacy of Mexico to the administration of New Spain; the province not only comes first in the text, less-populated intendancies such as Puebla and Guanaxuato have similar tables only at the beginning of each section. The tables also restate Malthus's population principle, or, so much land produces so many people and a geopolitical space more thinly or densely populated. They embody an attractive feature of statistics; no reader need travel to New Spain to determine the extent of its territory and size of its population in 1803; instead, the tables transport this information to the reader. But the tables also ask the reader to consider

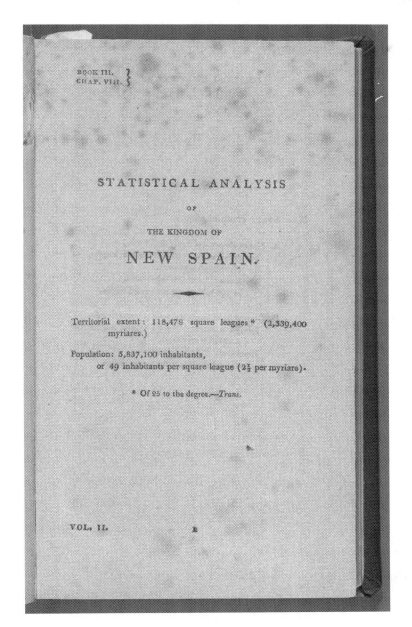

Figure 5.1 Statistical analysis of the Kingdom of New Spain. Territorial extent and population. Harvard University.

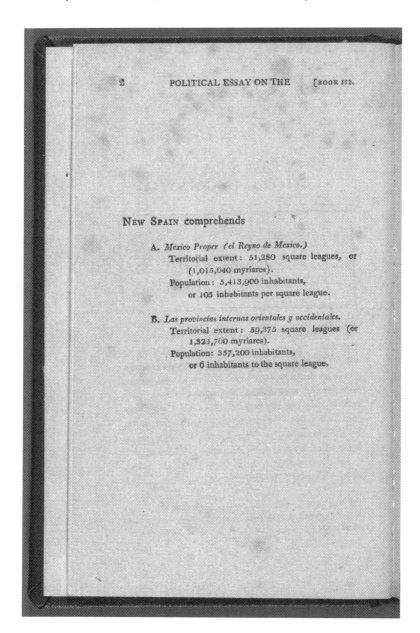

Figure 5.2 The size and population of constituent parts of New Spain. Harvard University.

STATISTICAL ANALYSIS.	Population in 1803.	Extent of Surface in square Leagues.	No. of Inhabitants to the square League
I. Intendancy of Mexico.	1,511,800	5,927	255

Figure 5.3 Statistical analysis. Intendancy of Mexico, 1803. Harvard University.

what lies behind them. These aggregates beg the question of causes; how did *this* number of people come to populate *that* amount of land in *this* particular year?

The table bluntly emphasizes the dual nature of its summary statistics, both end and beginning of serious statistical analyses of New Spain. Each page reminds readers of the paucity of actual narratives and plentitude of possible narratives in the discourse of statistics. The text on the remainder of the pages provides explanation. And what does the text tell us? Humboldt deluges the reader with historical and contemporary facts, from the quality of the soils and waters, which had been degraded by deforestation after the Spanish Conquest, to the abundance or scarcity of flora and fauna, to property laws that concentrated the wealth of New Spain in the hands of a few families, to the too often baneful operations of the Catholic Church, etc. These all combine to produce population, the middle cell of the table. Humboldt's account dares British political economists and other armchair analysts to observe Malthus's authenticated *facts* for New Spain, much less disentangle their causes, by reading a book in a cozy sitting room in London or Haileybury.

"They Wanted the Principles of Political Economy": Maria Graham and the "Art of Seeing" in Chile

Humboldt was expert on the northern reaches of Spanish America. With the notable exception of Molina's *The Geographical, Natural, and Civil History of Chili*, which first appeared in English translation in 1808, authoritative work on the more southerly Spanish colonial possessions in the Americas began to emerge only in the 1820s. The revolutionary and immediate post-revolutionary period opened the territories to foreign soldiers and sailors, diplomats, commercial speculators, and others, mostly, but not exclusively, men, few of whom published accounts of their travels. One who did was Maria Graham. Born Maria Dundas in Cumberland in 1785, Graham received an education including instruction in writing, languages, and painting. When her family moved to Edinburgh in 1803, she met Dugald Stewart, who walked her through the intricacies of conjectural and stadial histories, and other theories of social development. At age twenty-three, Maria traveled to India with her father, an admiral, and, while voyaging out, met and fell in love with Thomas Graham, a naval officer whom she married in India in 1809. Upon their return to England two years later, Graham was taken under wing by James Mackintosh, the jurist, politician, historian, and friend of Malthus, who had met Graham in India. Mackintosh introduced her to London intellectual circles where she became friends with the publisher John Murray, Mary Somerville, and Jane Marcet, among others.

While in England, Graham wrote travelogues on India (she was only the third British woman and the first in the nineteenth century to do so) and Italy, as well as translating and other work for Murray, including the first biography in English of Nicholas Poussin. She took to sea again in 1821 with her husband, now Captain Graham, who had assumed command of the *HMS Doris* and was tasked with helping to protect British mercantile interests along the Pacific coast of South America. According to letters she sent to Murray, Maria departed fully intent on writing up an account of her time in South America.[48] Graham penned two volumes on her experiences in Brazil and Chile in 1824, the first of the dozen books on South American commissioned and published by John Murray II between 1824 and 1839. Murray hoped to capitalize on the British public's thirst for travel literature in general, which the firm had helped foster, and for works on South America in particular.[49]

Graham's previous travel accounts, *Journal of a Residence in India* (1812), *Letters on India* (1814), and *Three Months Passed in the Mountains East of Rome, during the Year 1819* (1821), had established her authority in the genre. Praise for her works on India was not, however, unstinting. *The Critical Review* objected to Graham's sweeping condemnations in *Journal* of the morals and manners of the Hindus and English she observed, and concluded "Those, who go abroad, are too apt to measure the right and wrong of every thing by the standard of right and wrong in their own country; but to do this must often lead to false estimates and erroneous conclusions."[50] The reviewer insists that the "standard of right, as far as it respects moral duties" is universal, and that one must see past what are only "exterior" differences in what people in different regions of the globe consider right and wrong. These latter are not "immutably fixed, or universally the same, but vary with the climate and other circumstances".[51] In *Letters*, Graham herself wondered if she "was not once liable to the reproach of European prejudice" in *Journal*.[52]

The Quarterly Review rolled out another form of "European prejudice" in its review of *Journal* when its reviewer denigrated Graham's status as a woman. The essayist, probably John Barrow, ventured that Graham had traveled to India, "like most ladies, to procure a husband instead of information". Nonetheless, the reviewer called her work "a literary curiosity, which we are not disposed to overlook", deemed her descriptions of peoples and places "correct" and her prints, derived from her drawings, authentic and accurate.[53] Graham sought to achieve credibility in part by larding her books on India with references to the works of contemporary Orientalists, but also through detailing the care she took in making her observations of people and places. For example, Graham not only extensively quoted texts on the botany of India, she was able to check and bolster the quality of her observations by visiting the Calcutta Botanic Gardens, which the British East India Company had established in 1787.[54]

Graham faced a different set of issues for her South American narratives. For one, she wished to position herself as a "philosophical traveler", a desire which would require a modicum of preparation on her part. Though Graham could draw on no set of texts or botanical repositories like those available for India, prior to her trip she did read what were closest to the authoritative works then in print. These included the available volumes of Humboldt's *Personal Narrative*, as well as Robert Southey's *History of Brazil* (1810–9), though Graham was not reticent about challenging Humboldt, even before her arrival in South America. On the voyage out, the *Doris* made a stop in Tenerife. Graham's hikes around the island convinced her that Humboldt was somewhat wanting as an observer; he had overlooked many details of life on the island, especially those having to do with domestic arrangements and social organization, and in other instances he had simply made mistaken observations. She wrote John Murray II that Humboldt's observations were "too fine & philosophical".[55] While Akel reads this as Graham attempting to set herself above Humboldt, Keighren, Withers, and Bell consider her critique as an effort to set herself apart from the famous traveler and to validate her own methods of "sensate empiricism … and her own interpretations – truth to nature and truth to self".[56]

Graham directly addresses readers in a manner that spoke to her desire to establish her believability in the "Preface" to *Journal of a Voyage to Brazil, and Residence There, during Part of the Years 1821, 1822, 1823* (1824), the first of her South American volumes to appear in print.[57] She strikes a modest tone. She acknowledges the imperfections and limitations of her account, which was based on letters in which she indulged in the contemporary vogue for adopting a Romantic subjectivity. Graham writes that, while she has purged the published account of many "pages recording both public and private occurrences", she confides there may yet remain "too much of a personal nature". Nonetheless, she assures readers that "what is said is at least honest". She promises no new information on Brazil, rather a compilation of already available facts, and her viewpoint on the events she herself observed and recorded.

As to public events, all that can be new in the Journal is the bringing together facts which have reached Europe one by one, and in recording the impression produced on the spot by those occurrences which might be viewed in a very different light elsewhere. Some have, no doubt, been distorted by the interested channels through which they have reached the public; some by the ignorance of the reporters; and most by the party spirit which has viewed either with enthusiasm or malignity the acquisition of freedom in any quarter of the globe.

(*JVB*, p. iii)

Interest and ignorance bias accounts of recent events in Brazil. Interested parties in Britain distort them further by viewing them according to their own party interests. Graham, as a woman, might well claim to have no such interest.

Graham admits, however, that her account is prejudiced, too. Yet, she asserts that partiality may not lessen the value of what she imparts; "The writer does not pretend to perfect impartiality; for in some cases, impartiality is no virtue" (*JVB*, p. iii). Graham does not provide examples of occasions when impartiality would be less objective than partiality; she does, however, hint at the ethical dimensions and costs to her subjectivity of observing, representing and interpreting facts about Brazil. Graham writes that, "knowing that no human good can be obtained without a mixture of evil, she trusts that a fair picture of both has been given, although it has cost some pain in the writing" (*JVB*, pp. iii–iv).

Pain is evident in her written and pictorial accounts of her first encounter in Recife of a sight which "absolutely sickened" the abolitionist. Graham relates that "whatever strong and poignant the feelings may be at home, when imagination pictures slavery, they are nothing compared to the staggering sight of a slave-market" (*JVB*, p. 105). Eyewitness observations prove truer than the imagination. Graham calls on two forms of representation, drawings and words, to portray the suffering of slaves in Brazil. See Figures 5.4 and 5.5. The frontispiece of *JVB*, which depicts the slave market in Rio, is consistent with most iconography of slavery in the Americas in this period. It portrays slaves in an urban setting, not in the rural areas where they performed most of their work.[58] Graham appeals to the reader's imagination by quoting Shakespeare:

> about fifty young creatures, boys and girls, with all the appearance of disease and famine consequent upon scanty food and long confinement in unwholesome places, were sitting and lying about among the filthiest animals in the streets. The sight sent us home to the ship with the heartache and resolution, "not loud but deep," that nothing in our power should be considered too little, or too great, that can tend to abolish or to alleviate slavery.

(*JVB*, p. 105)

Spanish America, British Political Economy 189

Figure 5.4 Rio slave market, early 1820s. University of Michigan.

Onshore, Graham found the English merchants in Bahia incurious and unobservant, and guided solely by self-interest, thus ignorant as to "all matters of general science or information. Not one knew the name of the plants around his own door". Exasperated, she ventures that, in her interactions with these men of commerce, her status as a woman may have further hurt her ability to observe things Brazilian.

> I was completely out of patience with these incurious money - makers. I was perhaps unjust to my countrymen: I dare say there are many who *could* have told me these things, but I am sure none *did* tell me, and equally sure that I asked information of all I met with. But a woman is not, I believe, considered as privileged to know any thing by these commercial personages.
>
> (JVB, p. 148, emphases in original)

To the reviewer in *The London Literary Gazette*, however, all Graham's efforts at impartiality and, when called for, as in her consideration of Brazilian slavery, partiality, came to naught. The review offers the harsh and sweeping judgment that "we hardly think it merited publication at all". To

190 Spanish America, British Political Economy

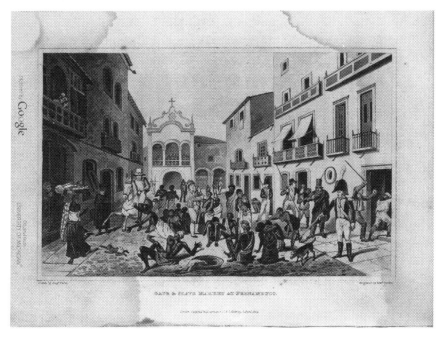

Figure 5.5 Pernambuco Gate and slave market, early 1820s. University of Michigan.

the reviewer, Graham offers little new information beyond what Southey, who had not visited Brazil, and others had already written, and "not good entertainment, either for man or beast". And, quoting a passage in which Graham muses on the nature of truth, the reviewer sneers at "the absurdity into which this class of female philosophers plunge when they write about what they do not understand".[59]

Graham attempted to gain readers' trust in her volume on Chile through a different route. She did so in part by providing readers with new and important information, filling in gaps in the historical record of the Chilean revolution. Her husband, now dead, had introduced Graham to Lord Cochrane, the former British naval officer who enlisted in the revolutionaries' service as commander of the naval forces of Chile. Through Cochrane, Graham was able to secure meetings with political and military leaders of the revolutions, a rare privilege, rarer still for a woman. So, she begins *JRC* not with the journal, but with a long "Introduction", almost one-fifth of the entire book, on the military and political maneuvering that brought Chile independence. Graham informs readers that this is "perhaps, its [the volume's] most important part" (*JRC*, p. iii). An even longer "Appendix", containing reprints of documents Graham uses to supplement her journal entries, concludes the book. Sandwiched in between, Graham's journal, which contains dated entries of her residency in Chile, starts on 28 April 1822, as the *HMS Doris* enters the harbor of Valparaiso. Graham mourns the death of her husband, who had passed away earlier that month, shortly after the *Doris* rounded Cape Horn, but resists entreaties to return to England, and ends up residing in Chile from April 1822 through January 1823.

Polyvocality marks *JRC*, and Thompson calls Graham's narrative approach encyclopedic.[60] Graham writes at times as a grieving widow, her comments leavened by still fresh sorrow, at other times as an opinionated censor of the behavior of the natives and resident foreigners, and still elsewhere as a detached and skilled observer of nature who spices her descriptions with scientific terminology and citations. On some of the occasions when she admits the limits of her knowledge she defers to others' voices, including local political and Creole elites, and foreign authorities alike. Graham veers from passages on botany and other environmental elements, which would not be out of place in a natural history, to transcripts of conversations with political and military leaders, to musing about her own fitness to observe and comment on what she sees of Chile. And she added her own illustrations to *JRC*, too. Throughout, Graham intersperses fragments of verse, from Shakespeare to Byron, and a smattering of footnotes.

The one constant in this swirling mix of voices and narrative approaches is how Graham filters her observations on Chile's past, present, and future prospects through contemporary doctrines of political economy, intensifying and enlarging a focus she had taken with respect to free trade in *JVB*.[61] This is true even for "Introduction", though her guiding object for the chapter is to explain recent political events in Chile. *The Quarterly Review* criticized this part of *Journal* for that very reason. The reviewer confesses that if he has spent more time in the review on the issue of trade in Chile than is perhaps warranted, it is "because it is the freedom of trade in which, according to the views of Captain Hall and Mrs. Graham, the great benefit of the revolution is to be felt".[62] Graham does in fact frame much of her narrative on the revolution in terms of economic performance and the benefits of free trade. Graham even represents the efforts of Cochrane as exploits that would allow Chileans to act according to the principles of political economy. Free from the fetters of Spain, they could now choose to curb the power of monopolists. Competition and free trade would redound to their benefit; they would become more prosperous and happier.

Graham sums up the role of the state in Spanish America during the pre-revolutionary period by concluding that "The whole system of Spain, while the colonies were kept close, was, with regard to them, commercial, and not political." Specifically, the viceroys presided over monopolies in the Americas, were only "bounded by their sordid and mercantile interests", and ran the colonial system of Spain as a mercantile system (*JRC*, pp. 14–5). *The Quarterly Review* deemed this unexceptional, asserting that Spain's reliance on monopolies in its New World possessions differed little from their use in the colonial systems of other European nations, including England.[63] According to Graham, the revolutionary government had shaken off some, but not all of the vestiges of this system. For example, in 1818 the Chilean senate was forced to take up the question of how to finance both the regular functions of government and pay and provision the revolutionary military. They partially succeeded despite a lack of guiding, that is, political economic principles. "The first labours of the senate were naturally directed to the improvement of the finances, which, in spite of a total want of knowledge and principle in political economy, did advance considerably." On the other hand, a similar lack of principled behavior effectively hamstrung attempts by San Martin and the senate to raise revenues necessary to prosecute the war: "Since the departure of the expedition from Chile, the director and senate had been uniformly engaged in endeavours to increase the revenue: but they wanted the principles of political economy, and were never able to effect more than temporary supplies" (*JRC*, pp. 75–6). The principles of political economy constitute the foundation for sound public finance for Graham. A government that fails to adhere to these principles runs the risk of running into unsustainable debt.

Graham asserts that knowledge of political economy is also prerequisite for Smithian free trade. Though one of the first decrees of the new government in 1811 opened Chile to free and equal trade with all countries, the act also called for taxes on commerce to generate revenue for the government and to protect industries deemed to be of national importance.[64] Graham includes, translates, and endorses Cochrane's address "To the worthy and independent inhabitants of Guayaquil" on his departure from that city on 20 November 1821 (*JRC*, pp.100–3). In Graham's recounting, Cochrane devotes almost the entire speech to denouncing monopoly, and touting free trade and competition as the best and surest means to achieve prosperity and happiness:

> It is very gratifying to me to observe the change that has taken place in your ideas concerning political oeconomy, and to see that you can appreciate and despise as it deserves the clamour of the few that still perhaps desire to interrupt the general prosperity, although I cannot believe that any inhabitant of Guayaquil can be capable of placing his private interest in competition with the public good.
>
> (*JRC*, p. 101)

Cochrane congratulates the residents of Guayaquil on the shift in "public opinion" on matters "concerning commerce and manufactures" in the year since independence. A free press prompted the turn against the policies of monopoly promoted by the Spanish. Cochrane applauds the effect this has had; a correct understanding of political economy will enhance the fortunes of the public.

The *Monthly Review*, which calls Graham "this observing and accomplished traveler", judges her eyewitness account of the revolution invaluable, owing to the fact that much of the archival record had been destroyed during the fighting.[65] *The Quarterly Review*, however, refused to be swayed by these arguments. For one, the reviewer acknowledges that, "We are not advocates for freedom of trade in its fullest extent." In addition, the reviewer believed that Chile did not represent a good site for free trade to flourish. The new nation lacked goods to exchange, which meant it lacked the currency to purchase European goods. *The Quarterly Review* foresaw ruin for European merchants whose goods currently crowded Chile's harbors: "We must think that trade cannot be long beneficial to Chili, by which the countries with whom it trades are losers." This analysis does not take into account the possible expediency of Chile printing money, copper coin, or paper currency, to pay for the goods. Great Britain had just recently resumed the gold standard, and most Britons were in no mood to countenance any currency not backed by gold.

The reviewer also mocks one of the dreams of political economists, the economically rational peasant. Would the Chilean peasant quickly grasp the benefits of free trade through a process of reflection about what best furthered his self-interest? Graham and Cochrane both speak of the rapid diffusion and assimilation of correct ideas on the principles of political economy in Chile. But, according to *The Quarterly Review*, the ratiocinating Chilean peasant may merely be the figment of the imagination, and

> when we are seriously told of a peasant being zealous for independence, because, by the freedom of trade which it has introduced, he buys his shirt cheaper than he did formerly, we must be allowed to hesitate before we admire his inductive powers.[66]

The reviewer reasons that the evidence of experience contradicts the straightforward equation of free trade with prosperity and happiness. The leaders of new governments in Chile and elsewhere in South America have simply substituted the old trade barriers with new ones in order "to suit their own party or personal advantage".[67]

Journal bears out some of the qualms expressed in *The Quarterly Review* about the exercise of the art of political economy and its effect, expressed in stadial terms, on Chile. A duty on copper leads Graham to complain that "[t]his is a direct and most oppressive tax on industry, and by its effects retards the population of the country, as well as its civilization" (*JRC*, p. 174). And on early maneuverings by the revolutionary government, Graham sardonically remarks,

> the minister Rodriguez, acting, I presume, upon the principle, that individual riches make public prosperity, is making private speculations jointly with his friend Arcas the merchant, and purchasing with the government-money all the tobacco and spirits now in the market, in contemplation of the heavy duties he means to lay on these articles by the new *reglamento*.
>
> (*JRC*, p. 182)

In sum, Chile's new tax and trade policy, according to Graham, "will, of course, at once retard civilization and rob the revenue" (*JRC*, p. 275, see also p. 288). Political economists would applaud Graham's rejection of a simple-minded equation of private vices with public virtue. For one, it echoes their misgivings about Mandeville. Further, when Chileno merchants and officials conspire to create and enjoy the benefits of monopolies at public expense, the anecdote reads like a real-life instance of the kind of capitalist conspiracy Smith warned readers to be on guard against in *Wealth of Nations*.

Political economists might have found other elements of Graham's political economy unsettling, though. In an entry on newly issued commercial regulations for Chile she confesses "I understand not much of these things; but there are passages so opposite to common sense, that a child must be struck with them" (*JRC*, p. 287). Was political economy so easy a subject that an otherwise uncomprehending woman or even a child could comprehend it? Marcet had based *Conversations on Political Economy* on her belief that children could *learn* political economy, and met with the support and approval of Ricardo and his kind. But, appeals to common sense lay queasily close to using the evidence of experience to validate principle. And political economists fond of universal principles such as free trade might recoil at the prospect of having to delve into the commercial codes of each country, of each region, of each locality, in a detailed institutional analysis that a Humboldt might undertake, in order to discern whether the regulations in question were accidental or constant causes affecting how the principles operated in real life.

We've returned to some of the questions that opened the book. What elements of travel writing constituted useful knowledge for political economy, and how and by whom were they best transmitted? A reviewer in *The Philomathic Journal* questioned whether Graham had chosen the most appropriate way to relate the facts of her time in Chile, as "the form of a journal necessarily facilitates the introduction of much, which, though it may be of interest to the individual, can have little claim upon the public".[68] Still, *The Philomathic Journal*, like most other contemporary reviews, praised Graham for her observations, concluding that "the author has arrived at the best means of observation, and has intimately mixed with the highest circles. She appears to have been an attentive observer of what was passing around her, and a diligent collector of facts."[69]

Graham does not hesitate to question or correct the observations of others as she goes about collecting facts in Chile. She notes, for example, after an extended ramble on the outskirts of town just two weeks into her residency, on 11 May 1822, that "the old maps and travels" showing Valparaiso at the mouth of a river are incorrect (*JRC*, p. 123, note). On 31 May, she writes that, on reaching home after a long and exhausting day, "I roused myself to my daily task of study, and of writing down the occurrences of the day" (*JRC*, p. 145). Graham continues:

> I have often thought a collection of faithful journals might furnish better food to a moral philosopher for his speculations, than all the formal disquisitions that ever were written. There are days of hurry and happy disposition, that also leave a hurry of spirits, that permits but the shortest and most concise entries; others there are, where idleness and the self-importance we all feel, more or less in writing a journal, swell the pages with laborious trifling; and some, again, where a few short sentences tell of a state of mind that it requires courage indeed to exhibit to another eye. A copied journal is less characteristic: it may be equally true, it may give a better, because more rational and careful account of countries visited; and the copying it, may awaken associations and lead the writer to other views, – to descant with other feelings on the same occurrences. And though there be no intentional variation, some shades of character will be kept under by fear, some suppressed, it may be through modesty, and there are feelings for others which will blot out many more: yet the journal is true; true to nature, true to facts, and true to a better feeling than often dictates the momentary lines of spleen or suffering. This truth I solemnly engage myself to preserve. I cannot give, and I trust no one will demand more.
>
> (*JRC*, pp. 145–6)

Thus, "the [copied] journal was a medium not simply for recording Graham's impressions but also for reflecting on and making sense of them".[70] That Graham adds material to her journal here and excises it there before publication is unremarkable, and repeats a process she used to write *Journal of a Residence in India* and *Letters on India*. Of the former, compiled from letters sent to a friend, Graham kept a private diary of her time in India, distinct from the published journal; Hagglund speculates that Graham had yet another manuscript journal, also dissimilar from the published journal, which she may have discarded after the publication of the book.[71] Thus, "[t]he regulated journal as the basis to a travel account presented a tension, then, between its private and quotidian composition and its hoped-for public and systematic expression".[72] Temporal and spatial distance, and distance from the emotions occasioned by immediate observation, reflect and represent to the reader the correct "moral decorum" necessary to asserting the credibility of a scientific author and her account. As Graham pointed out in a letter to Murray, "what use is it to tell [the] truth if it looks like a fib".[73] Graham's reflection on how she produces a copied or regulated journal reveals to the reader that she does so methodically, to manufacture an account adhering more closely to the dictates of reason, one that, while mediated and partial, represents truth.

The term "political economy" had been entirely absent from *Journal of a Residence in India*, even though one of Graham's first observations concerns the masses of jewelry adorning men and women of all classes in Bombay. Other British travelers to India were quick to critique the waste of potential circulating medium represented by all the gold and silver ornaments they witnessed, as well as question the savings propensities or prudence of Indians. Though Graham subjects the issue to a political economic analysis of sorts, she does so without judgment. She attributes the plentitude of body ornamentation both to the cheapness of food, lodging, and clothing and the long-prevalent insecurity of property in India; though the threat of plundering "barbarous armies" had receded, residents clung to the custom of keeping what wealth they possessed on their persons, the easier to flee with it.[74] Graham critiques this predilection, however, on aesthetic rather than economic grounds. When Graham and her sister visit a harem she relates that her host Fatima's "earrings were very beautiful", but admits that she does "not like the custom of boring the hem of the ear, and studding it all around with joys, nor could even Fatima's beautiful face reconcile me to the nose-jewel".[75] Further, while Graham uses the language of stadial theory in *Letters on India*, and took note of the potential economic value of botanical subjects in India, "economy" merits only a single mention.[76] She uses it in reference to Mughal emperor Akbar and employs it in terms that sound like the sciences of police or "statistik". Thus, Akbar, "with his minister, the learned Abul Fazil, was employed in regulating the economy of the state; in procuring information regarding the different provinces, with their produce and revenue, and in framing regulations of public justice and utility". [77]

These absences are notable given Graham's "careful and painstaking research" for the work, with the "almost certainly fictional" letters covering topics such as "languages, literature, music, fine arts, architecture, theology, philosophy, law, history and manners and customs".[78] But Graham made a conscious choice to omit "details and suggestions upon its [India's] trade and commercial speculations", or the political and military history of the country. She notes that almost all the works available to her contemporaries already cover these topics. She opts instead to fill a gap in the literature by writing a "more popular work ... – a work which, without entangling its readers in the thorny walk of politics or commercial speculation, should bring before them much of what strikes the eye and the mind of an observant stranger".[79] Travel writings for the general reader, like Graham's, occupy a separate niche and contain observations that differ from those designed for the specialist, be they statesmen, soldiers, or traders.

In her Chile journal, however, Graham often tries to make sense of what she sees of daily life through the lens of political economy. She quickly notes, for example, the lack of consumption by Chilenos of the most up-to-date consumer products. The ones available at the port of Valparaiso are coarser versions of their European models, and the residents need to transform their tastes before they adapt European fashions. Graham suggests they should emulate people such as Frey, the German blacksmith and farrier in Valparaiso, "whose beautifully neat house and workshop, and his garden, render him an excellent model for the rising Chilenos" in order to effect such a shift in manners (*JRC*, p. 130).

In her early journal entries on Chile Graham cautions readers that she needed to spend more time there so she could observe without bias, an approach she applies to her speculations on political economy. Thus, on 27 May, when she notes the waste of fertile land, Graham also admits that it lacks people and that "it is too early to judge of these things yet" (*JRC*, pp. 137–8). She believed her first impressions of Valparaiso were colored by distance from home and by the absence of her husband. She missed him, but also missed his ability to bring out her less selfish, more cheerful side, where she did not dwell on the "sad realities of life", and where the "poetry of life" was closer to Byron's than Crabbe's (*JRC*, p. 134).

Graham's reflections on her own observations and those of others lead her to consider the value of travel. She does so in a digression that assumes the cross-fertilization of political and domestic economies, and, coincidentally, demonstrates what she means by a "copied journal". She labels "adventurers" all who come to South America

> whose only aim has been to accumulate wealth in these rich provinces, without either ... philanthropic or chivalrous views ... To all whose views have been so bounded, disappointment must be the consequence. Mere gold and silver scarcely render individuals rich; and nations they have in many cases rendered poor.
>
> (*JRC*, p. 138)

True value lies not in gold but in service to others. This sentiment reads, as in Edgeworth's "Prudence and Economy", like an economy whose practitioners value charity above all else, as opposed to purely self-interested behavior that only unintentionally enhances the greater good. Graham, echoing her plaint about English merchants in Brazil, concludes that travelers and foreign residents who do operate solely on the narrow basis of self-interest often make faulty observations. "I had an opportunity to-day of observing how carelessly even sensible men make their observations in foreign countries, and on daily matters concerning them" (*JRC*, p. 139). In her 30 May entry, she quotes a physician who suggests that *culen* (*Cytisus Arboreus*), a plant known for its medicinal properties, be brought to Chile to cultivate for export. She hesitates to correct him; she is a newcomer, and he has resided in the country for "some years". But she recalls being shown a plant by the same name by people on the outskirts of the city. He, in turn, demurs and "said it could not be because he never heard of it here". After going home, she takes a walk and finds *culen* in abundance.

This episode reminds Graham of one of Mrs. Barbauld's well-known tales for young people, "Eyes and No Eyes; or, the Art of Seeing". In the tale, a teacher quizzes two children who have returned from walks through the countryside. One professes that he has seen nothing worthy of note; the other excitedly recounts the various plants, animals, and landscapes he has observed, as well as the working people he has conversed with during his stroll. He's collected samples, too. The teacher in "Eyes and No Eyes; or, the Art of Seeing" delivers the moral of the lesson, that

> one man walks through the world with his eyes open, and another with his eyes shut; and upon this difference depends all the superiority of knowledge the one acquires above the other ... [T]he observing eye and inquiring mind find matter of improvement and delight in every ramble in town or country.[80]

The "Art of Seeing" leads Graham to muse about why there will always be a role for women and her nation as educators teaching universal values, "forming the minds of the young, and leading them to proper objects of pursuit". They will educate not just British parents and their children, but the world.

> I am proud to belong to the sex and nation, which will furnish names to engage the reverence and affection of our fellow-creatures as long as virtue and literature continue to be cultivated. As long as there are parents to teach and children to be taught, no father, no mother will hear with indifference the names of Barbauld, Trimmer, or Edgeworth. The first stone is laid; schools are established, and their works are preparing to form and enlighten the children of another language and another hemisphere.
> (*JRC*, p. 140)

Women do not remain mute bystanders, but transmit to others knowledge they glean from the world. Graham assumes, first and foremost, that her readers believe that educational authorities like Barbauld, Trimmer, and Edgeworth take pains to teach anyone, young or old, how to observe, no matter what object they pursue, no matter where they were in the world.

This speaks to Graham's own catholic yet careful methods of observation and reporting. Women observe with their eyes, but sometimes they need to do more to understand what they observe. Graham includes several episodes in which she herself was a participant-observer in Chile, both engaged and slightly detached, thus apparently authoritative.[81] The day after her successful search for *culen*, 31 May, for instance, she set out for the Rincona, an obscure spot in the Almendral, to see the production of coarse pottery commonly used for carrying water, cooking, and other everyday purposes. Puzzled, at first, as she spies no manufactory or its furnaces on her walk, Graham adjusts her perspective, and confides

> I found that I must look for no regular manufactory, no division of labour, no machinery, not even the potter's wheel, none of the aids to industry which I had conceived almost indispensable to a trade so artificial as that of making earthenware.
> (*JRC*, p. 141)

Manufacturing without a "regular manufactory" or a division of labor is almost, but not totally inconceivable to Graham. She must shed her expectations of what she will observe in order to observe. But Graham finds the factory easily enough, happening upon a "family of manufacturers" in the open, at the door of one of the poorest huts in the Rincona.

Graham proceeds to radically rework Smith's famous example in WN on the division of labor, the nail workshop. Smith, who most likely retells a tale long in circulation, adopts a disembodied vantage point in his account, where the observer need not engage the workers. This viewing position fulfills his vision of the role of "philosophers or men of speculation, whose trade it is not to do any thing, but to observe every thing", men whose own work is subject to the division of labor (WN, I, 1, 9). Smith employs the rhetoric of statistics to tell his tale about the gains in production obtained from the division of labor. A prodigious increase in output of nails results from grouping workers together and subdividing their tasks into "about eighteen different operations" for making each nail. Compared to an individual, ten workers produce anywhere from two hundred forty to four thousand eight hundred times more nails, even though the workmen he watches are "very poor, and therefore but indifferently accommodated with the necessary machinery" (WN, I, 1, 3).

Graham, by way of contrast, fashions a first-person narrative to relate her discovery of where and how the pottery is made. She joins her fellow potters, the better to observe and understand their work as "the shortest way of learning is to mix at once with those we wish to learn from". She starts by seeking to imitate a girl making a simple saucer; her action reads as innocent enough that the "chief directress" does not throw her out. Instead, she corrects Graham's clumsy efforts. Graham's workers are, like Smith's, very poor, and lack capital. Graham forgoes quantitative detail on the effects of the division of labor, however, stating only that the subdivision of tasks for creating small, inexpensive "jars, plates, and dishes" occurs according to age and ability.

The sexual division of labor prevails in both accounts. Only men make Smith's pins; only women and girls make Graham's pottery. Thus, "family of manufacturers" is a misnomer in Graham's tale; she believes that "no man condescends to employ himself" in making such small wares. The factory represents a space open to women and girls, but closed to men by custom. After the posthumous publication in 1763 of Lady Mary Wortley Montagu's *The Turkish Embassy Letters*, which opens with the provocation, in the "Preface by a Lady. Written in 1724.", "that the world should see how much better purpose the LADIES travel than their LORDS", and that "a lady has the skill to strike out a new path" regarding the truth of a travel account, European readers thrilled at the idea that women travelers could gain access to spaces, like harems or Turkish baths, forbidden to men.[82] Montagu unlearns her assumptions about Turkish and British society in order to be able observe and learn from her experiences, most famously with the women in the hamam or "bagnio". Montagu names this private sphere after a public space reserved exclusively in England for men to exchange information and conduct their business: she calls it "the women's coffee-house, where all the news of the town is told, scandal invented, &c.".[83] Graham went through a similar expérience some sixty years later in Chile; she may tease readers with her long walk to an obscure portion of the Rincona to espy secret goings-on, but her revelations, like her visit to the harem in India, and unlike Montagu's frank mentions of women's nudity, hardly titillate. The women and girls of the Rincona produce essential and ubiquitous, if humble goods for everyday use, hardly a fitting subject for Orientalist or anti-Orientalist daydreams.

Graham's ulterior motive for visiting the site is in fact to discover the secret polishing process for the pottery. Yet she also observes women's paid work hiding in plain sight. Again, British political economists among Graham's contemporaries choose to overlook many women's economic activities, whether paid or unpaid. The labors of the female potters not only form part of the public sphere, they occur *in public*; observers will fail to see and account for such activities only if they fail to exercise Barbauld's art of seeing. Though she does not proselytize about the merits of supporting poorly paid women's work, like Hannah More in *Moral Sketches*, Graham offers readers a similar lesson, that they should be included as part of what to observe while traveling. The lesson the elderly Chileno teaches Graham, for instance, produces both valuable observations for Graham, and, given that Graham's saucer passes muster, an object of monetary value for the factory.

For Graham, education in Chile also serves a recognizably Smithian political economic purpose. "The immediate wants of Chile are education in the upper and middling classes, and greater number of working hands. I ought, I suppose, to say productive labourers; but hands, both indirectly and directly productive, are wanting" (*JRC*, p. 157). By the beginning of the nineteenth century elites and politicians in the Southern Cone had adapted political economy as the administrative discourse of choice. They borrowed and mixed principles derived from French and British political economists among others, employing mechanical and physiological metaphors in their descriptions of colonial societies. Members of "Tribunal del Real Consulado", institutions organized in Chile and the United Provinces and "envisaged by Spanish authorities to solve commercial conflicts and to study means to improve agriculture, commerce, industry", jostled over proposals for public administration that would go beyond the modest reforms of the Bourbons.[84] Representing competing, often quarreling interests, they united around promoting through discussions and publications the spread of commerce through free trade within and between the colonies and Spain, argued against monopolies, supported agricultural experiments and innovations, denounced slavery, lamented the lack of population in the region, and stressed the need for more education of residents, all in the cause of civilization.⁸⁵ Members believed the causes of regional decline to be interrelated. In a 10 January 1796 memoir, for instance, the Chilean educator and politician Manuel de Salas asks for the cultivation of people to transform agriculture; more educated people produced more and better cultivated land.⁸⁶ In turn, efforts to improve agriculture "helped to educate and discipline the population in working and patriotic habits", and "helped to fix in the people ideas of citizenship and vassalhood".⁸⁷ Overall, Salas observed "an urgent need to develop local industry, and to instruct the population in useful knowledge to find out local resources and new industrial uses for them".⁸⁸

Travel and travel writing by Europeans also played key roles in Southern Cone education, for both good and ill, according to Salas and other Southern Cone pre-revolutionary elites. Salas, who had traveled in Europe during his youth, claimed in the same 1796 piece that "idleness … was not an influence of Chilean climate, as foreign travellers had stated, but a consequence of the lack of useful occupation". His compatriot José de Cos Iriberri added, in 1798, that to attribute national indolence to local climate was a "superstition" diffused, in part, by travelers, among others.⁸⁹ On the other hand, Salas and Anselmo de la Cruz both "directly called for foreign immigrants to teach the population" of Chile.⁹⁰ While Salas criticized scientific expeditions whose members left nothing of value to the region, he envisioned the gains to be had from the labor of "enlightened travellers who remained in the country, contributing to its development, bringing useful knowledge in natural history and the laws and principles of commerce".⁹¹ Foreign travelers would prove useful if only they stopped traveling and became residents. An education in political economy would prove key to understanding the laws and principles of commerce. It would assist those crafting policies to address the causes of economic backwardness in the Southern Cone. And it would aid those seeking to observe these factors. Iriberri writes that success in administration hinges on equipping observers with a profound understanding of political economy.⁹² Three years later, another member of the Chilean Consulado, Tomás Lurquín, would call political economy a "science that teaches men to reach their happiness".⁹³

Colonial authorities in the Southern Cone and their counterparts in Spain did not stint, either, in promoting economy as part of their reforms. For over a decade, starting in 1797, they undertook a major publishing effort, supporting the distribution of a weekly magazine, *Semanario de Agricultura y Artes dirigido á los Párrocos* (The Magazine of Agriculture and Arts for Parish Rectors), to parish priests in order to instruct people in oeconomy.⁹⁴ *Semanario*, as indicated by its title, introduced readers and correspondents to the latest work on agricultural innovations, including prudent measurement and accurate accounting of costs and benefits in farming. The magazine specifically directed articles toward female readers, potential "oeconomic women", as well, making good the promise, announced in paratext to the first volume, that domestic economy ("Economía doméstica") would take its place as a key topic for articles in the series, among other topics such as natural history and rural architecture.[95] Reformers hoped that if readers embraced a wide range of meanings and practices entailed by oeconomy, they would help increase both the wealth and moral condition of populations in Spain and its colonies, and stabilize the politics of the Empire.

After the revolutions, in Chile and the United Provinces, "political economy was assumed to be the best tool available" for public administration. Hence, "Most newspapers and learned journals published in Buenos Aires and Santiago de Chile announced that political economy would be a prominent feature of their pages." As debates raged over the dimensions of free trade in the new republics, Jean Baptiste Say's *Treatise on Political Economy* proved the most popular work on political economy in the region in the first half of the nineteenth century; Southern Cone elites absorbed ideas of Smith and other British political economists, too.[96]

But some in the United Provinces accused officials in Buenos Aires, the capitol, of too blunt an application of political economy, that is, inattention to detail in performing its art. The debate led one writer in 1825, in the Mendozan journal *Eco de los Andes*, to claim that the central government had not only failed to adequately adjust policies to local conditions, but that the policies led to the destruction of local interests; the writer called the silently suffering provinces ("Si hemos sufrido en silencio la ruina de nuestro comercio") victims of theories ("víctima de las teorías").[97] The writer asked the government to do "as Great Britain, which does not follow its own economists who denounce those commercial restrictions in which that country has based its prosperity".[98] In turn, a rebuttal from a correspondent who adopted the non de plume "El economista" denigrated him as "an ignorant writer who knows nothing of political economy" (es un ignorante que nada entiende de economía política).[99]

Foreign supplies to satisfy demands of one of the arts of political economy, the educational needs Graham writes of, which would instill as well principles of economy in Chileans, were already being addressed by disciples of Joseph Lancaster who spread his educational project into South America in the early 1820s. They considered his schools to be incubators of a Christian education which would produce virtuous and useful members of society. Further, by assisting the reform of South American ideas, manners, and customs, the schools would promote the rise of commercial civilization. Graham praised in particular the establishment of Lancaster-style schools in Chile by "Mr. Thompson [sic]" (*JRC*, p. 157). Graham refers to the Baptist reformer James Thomson, a native of Edinburgh and fervent advocate of education for girls and women. Better known in South America as "Diego" Thomson, Thomson found employment in Buenos Aires beginning in 1818 as an adviser to the government on education, and left to do the same in Chile in 1821.[100] Reflecting on his experiences in South America, Thomson writes, "Female education in my opinion, is the thing most wanted in every country; and when it shall be properly attended to, the renovation of the world will go on rapidly."[101] The renewal Thomson writes of covers both the sacred and the secular; when he traveled to Santiago in 1821, the *Public Gazette* there trumpeted his arrival, and touted public education as "the basis of solid prosperity".[102]

Similar educational efforts spanned the Atlantic. In London, the German publisher Rudolph Ackermann joined with the Spanish liberal educator and politician José Joaquín de Mora and others to produce reading materials for the instruction of girls and young women in South America. The works aimed to mold women into good wives and mothers who would, in turn, help produce good citizens. In *Cartas sobre la educación del bello sexo por un señora americana* (1824), supposedly written by an anonymous "señora americana", Mora argues for an education in the English mode, calling it "one of the most effective ways to modernize Spanish America"; the only chapter devoted to a national educational model is Letter VIII, "Educacion del Bello Sexo en Inglaterra".[103] Bernardino Rivadavia, Rio de la Plata's ambassador to London, ordered copies of the epistolary conduct book, and had them shipped to the Sociedad de Beneficencia, the chief women's organization in Buenos Aires which he had founded in 1823 and to which the book was dedicated.[104]

According to its supporters, the English model of education instilled the value of activity, hard work, and productivity, while other European nations, including Spain, taught girls to be indolent and useless.[105] South American commitment to more liberal European-style schooling in the first half of the nineteenth century was fitful at best. While Rivadavia took inspiration from the utilitarian philosophy of Jeremy Bentham, whom he met on a number of occasions from 1818 to 1824, he and others apparently did so largely on the basis of simplified versions of Bentham's work translated into French by Etienne Dumont; moreover, Bentham and Rivadavia abruptly broke off all contact in 1825.[106] In the early 1820s, however, British travelers like Graham could point to the support given by Rivadavia's government in Rio de la Plata and that of Bernardo O'Higgins in Chile to the diffusion of education through Lancaster-type schools as evidence that a transformation in South American customs and manners was already at hand. Could prosperity be far behind?

Graham hesitates, however, when attempting to gauge the interaction of two of the main indicators of civilization favored by political economists, the material well-being and happiness of those she observed in Chile:

> It is impossible to conceive a greater degree of *apparent* poverty than is exhibited in the potters' cottages in Rincona ... [T]he hamlet ... is the most wretched I have yet seen. Its natives, however, pointed out to me their beautiful view, which is indeed magnificent, across the ocean to the snow-capped Andes, and boasted of their pleasure of walking on their hills of a holiday evening: then they showed me their sweet and wholesome stream of water, and their ancient fig-trees, inviting me to

go back "when the figs should be ripe, and the flowers looking at themselves in the stream." I was ashamed of some of the expressions of pity that had escaped me. – If I cannot better their condition, why awaken them to a sense of its miseries?

(*JRC*, pp. 143–4; emphasis added)

With her remark on the "apparent poverty" of Rincona, Graham confronts the same paradox that had forced political economists to more closely examine the relationship between wealth and happiness. How could Graham, or a political economist for that matter, reconcile the two conflicting facts of Rincona? Graham does not play the role of the detached observer when she writes that material poverty does not produce unhappiness in Rincona. Graham mixes condescension with a sense of the impropriety, shame even, of practicing the art of political economy when she asks the natives about their condition and takes their answers at face value. Domestic economy may have allowed women to act, as teachers, anywhere in the world. But Graham's question indicates that one of the very real limits to this part of the art of political economy is that students may not be receptive to the lesson at hand. Her friend John Miers writes in *Travels in Chile and La Plata* (1826) that when Graham donated "a number of useful and valuable books, in history and the fine arts" to the national library in Santiago, she received "not a single line of thanks".[107] And, even if Graham and other women could educate people outside of their households, what good would it do if they could not effectively act to ameliorate their material condition?

Notes

1 [John Allen], "Humboldt- *Essai Politique sur la Nouvelle Espagne*", *The Edinburgh Review*, XVI, no. XXI (1810): 62–102 (at pp. 62–3). The attribution of authorship to John Allen is in Frank Whitson Fetter, "The Authorship of Economic Articles in the *Edinburgh Review*, 1802–47", *Journal of Political Economy*, 61, no. 3 (1953): 232–59 (at p. 245).
2 Maria Graham, *Journal of a Residence in Chile, during the Year 1822; and a Voyage from Chile to Brazil, in 1823* (London: Longman, Hurst, Rees, Orme, Brown, and Green; John Murray, 1824). Hereafter referred to as *JRC*.
3 Pratt, *Imperial Eyes*, pp. 152–70; Adriana Méndez Rodenas, *Transatlantic Travels in Nineteenth-Century Latin America: European Women Pilgrims* (Lanham, MD: Bucknell University Press and Rowman & Littlefield, 2014), p. 6.
4 P. Molero Hernández, "Translation and Reception of *The Wealth of Nations* by Spanish and Latin American Authors during Eighteenth and Nineteenth Centuries", *Open Journal of Social Sciences*, 3, no. 5, (2015): 46–57. < http://dx.doi.org/10.4236/jss.2015.35008> [6 November 2018].
5 Ricardo D. Salvatore, "The Strength of Markets in Latin America's Sociopolitical Discourse, 1750-1850: Some Preliminary Observations", *Latin American Perspectives*, 26, no. 1 (1999): 22–43 (at p. 26).
6 John Fisher, "Imperial 'Free Trade' and the Hispanic Economy, 1778-1796", *Journal of Latin American Studies*, 13, no. 1 (1981): 21–56 (at p. 21).

7 F[rançois Raimond Joseph] De Pons, *Voyage à la partie orientale de la terre-ferme dans l'Amérique Méridionale* (Paris: F. Buisson, 1806); Depons (sic), F.[R.J.] *Voyage à la partie orientale de la terre-ferme dans l'Amérique Méridionale: fait pendant les années 1801, 1802, 1803 et 1804*, 3 vols. (Paris: Chez Colnet, 1806). The English translations: *Travels in parts of South America, during the years 1801, 1802, 1803 & 1804; containing a description of the captain-generalship of Carraccas, with an account of the laws, commerce, and natural productions of that country : as also a view of the customs and manners of the Spaniards and native Indians*. An abridged English translation of *Voyage à la partie orientale de la terre-ferme dans l'Amérique Méridionale* (London: Richard Phillips, 1806); *Travels in parts of South America, during the years 1801, 1802, 1803 & 1804; containing a description of the captain-generalship of Carraccas, with an account of the laws, commerce, and natural productions of that country : as also a view of the customs and manners of the Spaniards and native Indians*, 2 vols. (London: Longman and Co., and Hurst, Rees, and Orme, 1807).
8 Anon., "Depons [sic]- *Voyage dans l' Amerique Meridionale*", *The Edinburgh Review: Or Critical Journal*, 8, no. 16 (1806): 378–99 (at p. 379).
9 Anon., "M. Depons' Travels in South America", *The Gentleman's Magazine*, 78, Part 2 (1808): 808–15 (at p. 809).
10 The first British invasion was a filibuster, the second, officially sanctioned. France and Spain invaded Portugal on 27 October 1807; war broke out between France and Spain on 2 May 1808.
11 For classic statements on informal empire and its relationship to formal empire, see John Gallagher and Ronald Robinson, "The Imperialism of Free Trade", *Economic History Review*, 6, no. 1 (1953): 1–15; H.S. Ferns, "Beginnings of British Investment in Argentina", *The Economic History Review*, 4, no. 3 (1952): 341–52; Peter Winn, "British Informal Empire in Uruguay in the Nineteenth Century", *Past and Present*, no. 73 (1976): 100–26; and Matthew Brown, ed., *Informal Empire in Latin America: Culture, Commerce, and Capital* (Malden, MA: Blackwell; John Wiley & Sons, 2009). For a contestation of the notion of informal empire, see W.M. Mathew, "The Imperialism of Free Trade: Peru, 1820–70", *The Economic History Review* 21, no. 3 (1968): 562–79.
12 Great Britain recognized Buenos Ayres on 2 February 1825, Colombia on 18 April of the same year, and Mexico on 26 December 1826. Britain and Chile did not agree to a treaty of friendship, commerce, and navigation until 4 October 1854.
13 John Mayo, "The Development of British Interests in Chile's Norte Chico in the Early Nineteenth Century", *The Americas*, 57, no. 3 (2001): 363–94 (at p. 367).
14 David Rock, "Porteño Liberals and Imperialist Emissaries in the Rio de la Plata: Rivadavia and the British", in Matthew Brown and Gabriel Paquette, eds., *Connections after Colonialism: Europe and Latin America in the 1820s* (Tuscaloosa: The University of Alabama Press), pp. 207–22 (at p. 208).
15 F.[R.J.] Depons, *Travels in parts of South America, during the years 1801, 1802, 1803 & 1804; containing a description of the captain-generalship of Carraccas, with an account of the laws, commerce, and natural productions of that country : as also a view of the customs and manners of the Spaniards and native Indians*, 2 vols. (London: Longman and Co., and Hurst, Rees, and Orme, 1807), vol. 1, p. xxxix. The original:

> Les Espagnols, plus que toute autre nation, sont, littérairement parlant, jaloux de tout étranger observateur. Il est fort peu qui se prêtent franchement à

faciliter des recherches sur leur régime politique et domestique; mais il en est beaucoup qui, sous le voile du zèle et de l'affection, donnent pour positives, et sur les maitières les plus graces, des reseignemens diamétralement opposes à la vérité. Depons, *Voyage*, vol. 1, pp. 30–1.

16 Anon., "M. Depons' Travels", p. 809.
17 Anon., "M. Depons' Travels", p. 810.
18 Anon., "M. Depons' Travels", p. 815.
19 Quoted in Gallagher and Robinson, "The Imperialism of Free Trade", p. 8. The treaty was written to be in effect only until 1825, unless renewed; it expired in 1844.
20 Depons, *Travels*, vol. 1, p. xvii; "L'ouvrage que je présente au public n'a pour base que la vérite, pour ornament que l'exactitude", Depons, *Voyage*, vol. 1, p. 1.
21 Depons, *Travels*, vol. 1, p. xxxix; Depons, *Voyage*, vol. 1, p. 32.
22 Anon., "Depons [sic]- *Voyage dans l' Amerique Meridionale*", *The Edinburgh Review: Or Critical Journal*, 8, no. 16 (1806): 378–99 (at pp. 379, 388).
23 Anon., "Depons's *Travels in South America*", *The Monthly Review, Or, Literary Journal*, 54 (1807): 351–62 (at p. 353).
24 Anon., "Depons [sic]- *Voyage*", p. 384.
25 Anon., "Depons [sic]- *Voyage*", p. 387.
26 Anon., "Depons's *Travels*", pp. 361–2.
27 Henry G. Ward, *Mexico in 1827*, vols. 1 and 2 (London: Henry Colburn, 1828), vol. 2, p. 706.
28 Andrea Wulf, *The Invention of Nature: Alexander von Humboldt's New World* (New York: Alfred A. Knopf, 2015), p. 433.
29 [Allen], "Humboldt- *Essai Politique*", p. 68. I use the 1811 octavo edition of *Essai*. Alexander von Humboldt, *Essai Politique sur la Royaume de la Nouvelle-Espagne* (Paris: F. Schoell, 1811).
30 John Black, "Preface by the Translator", in Alexander von Humboldt, *Political Essay on the Kingdom of New Spain* 3 vols. (London: Longman et. al, 1811), vol. 1, pp. iii–iv. Further references to "Preface" and *Political Essay* are included parenthetically in the text.
31 "Introduction Géographique" follows an editor's advertisement in the 1811 *Essai Politique*. For comparison, "Geographical Introduction" runs a comparatively brief 115 pages in the New York edition: *Political Essay on the Kingdom of New Spain*, trans. John Black (New York: I. Riley, 1811).
32 Alexander von Humboldt and Helen M. Williams, *Personal Narrative of Travels of the Equinoctial Regions of the New Continent during Years 1799–1804*, trans. Helen Maria Williams, vol. I (London: Longman, et. al, 1814), vol. 1, p. 15. *Personal Narrative* was a translation of part of the seven-volume quarto edition *Voyages aux regions équinoctiales du Nouveau Continent fit en 1799, 1800, 1801, 1802, 1803 et 1804* (1814–31). On the important role played by translators, especially women, in shaping the reception of Humboldt's work in Britain, see Alison Martin, *Nature Translated: Alexander von Humboldt's Works in Nineteenth-Century Britain* (Edinburgh: Edinburgh University Press, 2018).
33 The original reads:

> Arrivé au Mexique par la mer du Sud, en mars 1803, j'ai résidé dans ce vaste royaume pendant un an. Après avoir fait des recherches dans la province de Caraccas, aux rives de l'Orénoque et du Rio Negro, dans la Nouvelle-Grenade, à Quito et sur la côtes du Pérou, où je m'tois rendu pour observer dans l'hémisphère austral le passage de Mercure sur le soleil, le 9 novembre 1802, je devoir être frappe du contraste qu'offre la civilisation de la Nouvelle-

Espagne avec le peu de culture des parties de l'Amérique méridionale que je venois de parcourir. Ce contraste m'excoitit à la fois et à l'étude particulière de la statistique Mexique, et à la recherche des causes qui ont le plus influé sur les progrès sur la populatión et de l'industrie nationale. (*Essai Politique*, I, pp. 203–4)

34 Humboldt and Williams, *Personal Narrative*, vol. 1, p. xx.
35 Humboldt, *Essai Politique*, I, p. 339, note.
36 [Allen], "*Humboldt- Essai Politique*", p. 68.
37 Sockwell, "Contributions", pp. 647–8.
38 Boianovsky, "Humboldt and the Economists", pp. 58–9.
39 "le degré de perfection les institutions sociales"; Humboldt, *Essai Politique*, I, p. 220.
40 Ricardo, in relating to James Mill on 12 September 1817 that he had been "reading without plan or order" works of travel and voyages including "Humbold's [sic] New Spain", and claimed that "My object is only amusement". Ricardo, *Works, Vol. 7*, pp. 189–90. Mill, however, makes only passing reference to Humboldt in *The History of British India* (1817), and fails to broach the subjects of statistical accounts or political economy in his notes on *Essai Politique*. See Robert A. Fenn, ed., "Literature", in *James Mill's Common Place Books*, Vol. IV, Ch. 18 (2010). <http://intellectualhistory.net/mill/cpb4ch18.html> [10 January 2017].
41 Malthus first published *Principles* in 1820, but made many changes to the text throughout the 1820s; these were incorporated into a posthumously published version, in 1836. Already in the 1820 edition Malthus cites Humboldt's observations in New Spain as evidence that effective demand, not a lack of capital leads to slow growth in a fertile country. See, for example, an American reprint, Thomas Robert Malthus, *Principles of Political Economy* [1820] (Boston: Wells and Lilly, 1821), pp. 304 and 409. See, in the posthumously published version, *Principles of Political Economy*, 2nd edn. [1820] (London: William Pickering, 1836), pp. 336–44; 344–5. See also Boianovsky, "Humboldt and the Economists", pp. 58–9.
42 Walls, *The Passage to Cosmos*, p. 122.
43 Dotan Lesham, "Oikonomia Redefined", *Journal of the History of Economic Thought*, 35, no. 1 (2013): 43–61 (at p. 59).
44 To complicate matters further, cameralism has also been called the German version of mercantilism: David F. Lindenfeld, *The Practical Imagination: The German Sciences of State in the Nineteenth Century* (Chicago: University of Chicago Press, 1997), p. 12.
45 Keith Tribe, *Governing Economy: The Reformation of German Economic Discourse, 1750–1840* (Cambridge: Cambridge University Press, 1988); David A.R. Forrester, "Rational Administration, Finance and Control Accounting: The Experience of Cameralism", *Critical Perspectives on Accounting*, 1, no. 4 (1990): 285–317.
46 Lindenfeld, *The Practical Imagination*, pp. 11–12; Keith Tribe, "Cameralism and the Science of Government", *The Journal of Modern History*, 56, no. 2 (1984): 263–84; Tribe, *Governing Economy*, chapter 3; Hermann Rebel, "Reimagining the *Oikos*: Austrian Cameralism in its Social Formation", in Jay O'Brien and William Roseberry, eds., *Golden Ages, Dark Ages: Imagining the Past in Anthropology and History* (Berkeley: University of California Press, 1991), pp. 48–80; Cooper, *Family Fictions*, pp. 39–40.
47 Lindenfeld, *The Practical Imagination*, p. 14.
48 Keighren and Withers, "Questions of Inscription", p. 1335; Thompson, "Earthquakes", p. 332.

49 Keighren and Withers, "Questions of Inscription", p. 1334.
50 Anon., "Maria Graham's *Journal of a Residence in India*", *The Critical Review*, 3, no. 4 (1813): 337–46 (at p. 344). I use the second edition of *Journal*, which came out in 1813: Maria Graham, *Journal of a Residence in India* [1812] (London: Longman, Hurst, Rees, Orme, and Brown, 1813). The majority of the second edition is identical to the first. In the second, Graham added a glossary of words used in British India and included a long extract from an anonymous correspondent commenting on her discussion of the Dutch in South Africa in the first edition of the book: see Betty Hagglund, "From Travel Diary to Printed Book: The Indian Travel Writings of Maria Graham", *Itinérances Féminines* (2008), n.p. <www.crlv.org/viatica/septembreoctobre-2008-itin%C3%A9ra nces-f%C3%A9minines/travel-diary-printed-book> [30 April 2015].
51 Anon., "Maria Graham's *Journal*", pp. 344–5.
52 Maria Graham, *Letters on India* (London: Longman, Hurst, Rees, Orme, and Brown, 1814), p. 85.
53 Anon., "Graham's *Journal of a Residence in India*,", *The Quarterly Review*, 8, no. 16 (1812): 406–21 (at pp. 406–7). The attribution is from Jonathan Cutmore, ed., "The Quarterly Review Archive", *Romantic Circles* (2015). <https://www.rc.umd.edu/reference/qr/index/16.html> [12 October 2015].
54 Betty Hagglund, "The Botanical Writings of Maria Graham", *Journal of Literature and Science*, 4, no. 1 (2011): 44–58 (at p. 47).
55 Quoted in Keighren, Withers, and Bell, *Travels into Print*, p. 69.
56 Regina Akel, *The Journals of Maria Graham (1785–1842)* (2007), p. 97. <wrap .warwick.ac.uk/2585/> [18 April 2015]; Keighren, Withers, and Bell, *Travels into Print*, p. 70.
57 Maria Graham, *Journal of a Voyage to Brazil, and Residence There, during Part of the Years 1821, 1822, 1823* (London: Longman, Hurst, Rees, Orme, Brown, and Green; John Murray, 1824). Hereafter referred to as *JVB*.
58 John E. Crowley, "[Review of] *Witnessing Slavery: Art and Travel in the Age of Abolition*", *Journal of British Studies*, 59, no. 4 (2020): 966–7.
59 Anon., "[Review of] *Journal of a Voyage to Brazil*", *The London Literary Gazette*, 377, (1824): 227–8 (at p. 227, and note).
60 Thompson, "Earthquakes", p. 334, and Akel, *The Journals of Maria Graham*.
61 Nicolás Barbosa Lopez, "The Exiled Insider: The Ambivalent Reception of Maria Graham's Journal of a Voyage to Brazil (1824)", *e-Journal of Portuguese History*, 16, no. 1 (2018). <http://www.scielo.mec.pt/scielo.php?script=sci_art text&pid=S1645-64322018000100005> [16 August 2020].
62 Anon., "Chili, Peru, &c.", *The Quarterly Review*, 30, no. 60 (1824): 441–72 (at p. 465). The essay also covers Captain Basil Hall's *Extracts from a Journal Written on the Coasts of Chili, Peru, and Mexico in the Years 1820, 1821, 1822* (1824), and Peter Schmidtmeyer's *Travels into Chile, over the Andes, in the Years 1820 and 1821* (1824).
63 Anon., "Chili, Peru, &c.", p. 464.
64 Mayo, "The Development of British Interests", p. 366.
65 Anon., "Mrs. Graham's *Voyage to Brazil*", *Monthly Review, or Literary Journal Enlarged*, 106 (1825): 180–89 (at p. 180); Anon., "Mrs. Graham's *Residence in Chile*", *Monthly Review, or Literary Journal Enlarged*, 106 (1825): 189–200 (at pp. 189–90). Graham pointed to another reason for the lack of records: "sometime in 1821" the "political speculations" and "commercial schemes" of the "Protector of Peru" and the "ministers in Chile", respectively, combined to greatly reduce the number and quality of public papers about the region. Graham interviewed both royalists and revolutionaries to corroborate her information, and the former "agreed in all facts with that as told by the patriots" (*JRC*, pp. iii–iv).

66 Anon., "Chili, Peru, &c.", p. 464.
67 Anon., "Chili, Peru, &c.", p. 466.
68 Anon., "Graham's *Journal of a Residence in Chile*", *The Philomathic Journal*, 1 (1824): 410–21 (at p. 421).
69 Anon., "Graham's *Journal*, p. 420.
70 Keighren and Withers, "Questions of Inscription", p. 1336.
71 Hagglund, "From Travel Diary to Printed Book", n.p.
72 Keighren and Withers, "Questions of Inscription", p. 1337.
73 Quoted in Keighren and Withers, "Questions of Inscription", p. 1337.
74 Graham, *Residence in India*, p. 3.
75 Graham, *Residence in India*, p. 18.
76 On Graham sizing up the potential value of Indian flora, see Hagglund, "The Botanical Writings", p. 47.
77 Graham, *Residence in India*, p. 239.
78 Hagglund, "From Travel Diary to Printed Book", n.p.
79 Graham, *Residence in India*, p. vi.
80 Anna Laetitia Barbauld, "Eyes and No Eyes; or, the Art of Seeing," in John Aikin and Anna Laetitia Barbauld, *Evenings at Home; or, the Juvenile Budget Opened: Consisting of a Variety of Miscellaneous Pieces*, vol. 4 (London: J. Johnson, 1794), pp. 93–109 (at pp. 108–9).
81 Adriana Méndez Rodenas, *Transatlantic Travels in Nineteenth-Century Latin America: European Women Pilgrims* (Lanham, MD: Bucknell University Press and Rowman & Littlefield, 2014), pp. 146–9.
82 Anon., "Preface", in *Letters of the Right Honourable Lady M—y W—y M—e Written during Her Travels in Europe, Asia and Africa to Persons of Distinction, Men of Letters, &c. in Different Parts of Europe*, by Lady Mary Wortley Montagu, vol. 1 [1724] (London: P. Becket and P.A. De Hondt, 1763), pp. v–xi (at p. viii).
83 Lady Mary Wortley Montagu, *Letters of the Right Honourable Lady M—y W—y M—e Written during Her Travels in Europe, Asia and Africa to Persons of Distinction, Men of Letters, &c. in Different Parts of Europe*, vol. 1 [1724] (London: P. Becket and P.A. De Hondt, 1763), p. 163. Teresa Heffernan and Daniel O'Quinn, "Introduction", in Teresa Heffernan and Daniel O'Quinn, eds., *The Turkish Embassy Letters* [1763] by Lady Mary Wortley Montagu (Peterborough, Ontario: Broadview Press, 2013), pp. 11–34 (at p. 30).
84 Marcelo Somarriva, "'An Open Field and Fair Play': The Relationship between Britain and the Southern Cone of America between 1808 and 1830", PhD Thesis (Department of History, University College London, 2013), p. 48.
85 Somarriva, "An Open Field", pp. 45–7.
86 Somarriva, "An Open Field", p. 49. Manuel de Salas, "Representación hecha al ministerio de Hacienda 10 de enero 1796", in Miguel Cruchaga, ed., *Estudio sobre la organización i la hacienda pública de Chile*, vol.1 (Santiago: "Los Tiempos", 1878), pp. 274–90.
87 "Emplearan alegremente las manos en la labor, sus discursos en educar sus hijos, fijando en ellos las ideas de ciudadanos i vasallos." Salas, "Representación", p. 290.
88 Somarriva, "An Open Field", p. 49; Salas, "Representación", p. 275.
89 José de Cos Iriberri, "Segunda Memoria leida por el mismo señor secretario en Junta de Posesión de 1ero de octubre de 1798", in Miguel Cruchaga, ed., *Estudio sobre la organización i la hacienda pública de Chile*, vol. 1 (Santiago: "Los Tiempos", 1878), pp. 303–8 (at p. 303); Somarriva, "An Open Field", p. 49.
90 Somarriva, "An Open Field", p. 50.
91 Salas, "Representación", p. 289; Somarriva, "An Open Field", p. 50.

92 Los golpes felices de combinación con que de repente se ha detenido alguna vez el curso de todos los males i se han hecho nacer al mismo tiempo los mayores bienes en algunos ramos de administracion, estan reservados para aquellos que despues de haber recorrido un pais, despues de haber visto mucho con observadores i armados con la lente de un profundo estudio de la economía política, se hallan surtidos de los elementos necesarios para haceria con acierto. Iriberri, "Segunda Memoria", p. 303.

93 "La economía política, esta ciencia que enseña a conducir los hombres a su felicidad". Tomás Lurquín, "Cuarta Memoria leida por el secretario sustituto don Tomás Lurquín en Junta de Posesión de 12 de enero de 1801", in Miguel Cruchaga, ed., *Estudio sobre la organización i la hacienda pública de Chile*, vol. 1 (Santiago: "Los Tiempos," 1878), pp. 314–9 (at p. 315).

94 Elena Serrano, "Making *Oeconomic* People: The Spanish *Magazine of Agriculture and Arts for Parish Rectors* (1797–1808)", *History and Technology*, 30, no. 3 (2014): 149–76.

95 Anon., "Carta", *Semanario de Agricultura y Artes: dirigido á los párrocos*, vol. 1 (Madrid: Real Jardin Botanico, 1797), pp. XII–XIV.

96 Somarriva, "'An Open Field", pp. 66, 67, 73–7.

97 Anon., Continuan las Observaciones de la Víctima de las Teorías", *La Década Araucana*, 13, (1825): 320-2 (at p. 320).

Los principios de los economistas que tanto han deslumbrado a Buenos Aires, apenas pueden ser ciertos en teorías, pero en la aplicación no son exactos: los intereses locales que
indispensablemente deben combinarse exigen alteraciones en la práctica de esos principios, sin
las que no pueden uniformarse. Ningún economista exige la destrucción de los intereses locales.

98 Somarriva, "An Open Field", p. 78.

99 "El economista", "Remitido al señor editor del eco de los andes "víctima de las teorías", *La Década Araucana* 15 (1826): 350–2 (at p. 351).

100 Webster E. Browning, "Joseph Lancaster, James Thomson, and the Lancasterian System of Mutual Instruction, with Special Reference to Hispanic America", *Hispanic American Historical Review*, 4, no. 1 (1921): 49–98.

101 James Thomson, *Letters on the Moral and Religious State of South America: Written during a Residence of Nearly Seven Years in Buenos Aires, Chile, Peru, and Colombia* (London: J. Nisbet, 1827), p. 129.

102 Thomson, *Letters*, p. 10.

103 Iona Macintyre, *Women and Print Culture in Post-independence Buenos Aires* (Woodbridge: Tamesis Books, 2010), p. 183.

104 Macintyre, *Women and Print Culture*, p. 113.

105 Macintyre, *Women and Print Culture*, pp. 183–5.

106 Jonathan Harris, "Bernardino Rivadavia and Benthamite 'Discipleship'", *Latin American Research Review*, 33, no. 1 (1998): 129–49 (at pp. 131–2).

107 John Miers, *Travels in Chile and La Plata*, vols. 1 and 2 (London: Baldwin, Cradock, and Joy. 1826), vol. 2, p. 257.

6 "To Give This Country Its True Value"

British Travelers in La Plata and Chile, and the Financial Crisis of 1825–6

> The numbers of our intelligent countrymen who are engaged in different parts of this immense continent will afford us the necessary observations and matters of fact, and enable us to give this country its true value, and to appreciate its actually existent available resources.
> John Miers, *Travels in Chile and La Plata* (1826)[1]

Humboldt had presented a sprawling template for analysts and policy makers, both in Europe and South America, seeking to measure and extract value from the New World. Humboldt's approach involved detailed observations of an areas' history, politics, institutions, and the interactions between peoples and environments. Careful observation, according to Graham, also included observing oneself, to detect and shake off prejudice, and thus see unfamiliar and important phenomena that might otherwise be overlooked. Graham presented women's paid labor as one such phenomenon.[2] Graham offered another women's occupation, education, which she tendered as an essential handmaiden to both economy and economics, as a prescription for both observing and creating value in South America and beyond. Pre-revolutionary Southern Cone elites located value in agriculture. In 1798, Iriberri, for instance, declared the sector the most essential of the arts, the most fertile, nurturing mother of humankind, and the true wellspring of public happiness; any other source was artificial and risky.[3] Consequently, members of the elite Chile and the United Provinces had all called for a shift in resources away from mining toward agriculture.

Complicating contemporary British efforts to identify and locate value in South America in 1826 was the fact that the nation continued to be convulsed by the aftershocks from the collapse of what John Barrow, in anonymous post in *The Quarterly Review*, successively called an "age of speculation", a "mania for speculation", and a "rage for speculation".[4] The boom had seen men and women of the wealthy and middle classes eagerly seeking outlets for their money. Some, like Maria Edgeworth, parked their cash in French funds; others had looked to more distant lands. British investors snapped up bonds issued to finance government operations and mines in the new Central and South America republics, unfazed by warnings from Barrow,

DOI: 10.4324/9781315778952-6

Francis Place as well as by members of the House of Commons who debated the merits of mining investments; all invoked the works of Humboldt and other travelers in their cautions.[5] Nor were investors deterred by the unraveling, in 1823, of the Poyais fraud of Gregor MacGregor, the epitome of the lying traveler. Despite these tocsins and the earlier criticisms of the mining sector by South American elites, numerous mining companies sprang up, enticing investors with prospectuses promising to turn rumors of fabulously valuable deposits of metals in the new nations into extraordinary profits (English 1825 and 1827; Schwartz 1999: 10–12; Costeloe 2003 and 2011).[6] A few adventurous souls like Miers traveled to the region to both invest in and work the mines. Demand for information on South America continued to surge in Great Britain and the rest of Europe, with the publication of travel accounts about the continent peaking between 1815 and 1830.[7]

The chapter opens by taking up the work of Miers, who had befriended Graham in Chile. Miers sought out investment opportunities in Spanish America during and after the speculative fever, and devotes considerable space in the two volumes of *TCP* to sizing up the costs and benefits of investing in mines in the region.[8] Like Graham, Miers draws on a hodgepodge of established and emerging scientific disciplines, including political economy, and the conventions of several literary genres to organize his observations. Miers, also like Graham, questioned the credibility, indeed the very purpose of observations by Europeans who traveled to South America brimming with commercial knowledge, but who were motivated solely by self-interested profit-seeking rather than a devotion to charity.

Miers, again like Graham, writes both as a foreign traveler and foreign resident in Chile. His accounts in the second volume of *TCP* exemplify how foreign residents may have an observational advantage over travelers from Britain. Resident aliens can take the time to make more frequent and more informed observations than can their traveling compatriots. They also have more opportunities to cast aside the national prejudices that could lead to biased accounts. If Miers initially believed Chile a space populated by barbarous people who knew little of mining, he later disabused himself of this perspective and urges readers not to repeat his failings in observation. Thus, Miers offers readers a vision of what economic analysis could look like when one is transformed by the experience of travel. If he left England ready to deploy a recognizably British political economy to help organize his observations, he returned a changed man, arguing for a more expansive vision of the epistemological and ontological possibilities of social analyses and business praxis.

Miers's volumes appeared in a year that ushered in numerous bankruptcies and widespread unemployment in England. The chapter concludes with an examination of travel reports from 1826 and 1827 by Francis Bond Head and Joseph Andrews, who also undertook trips to South America on behalf of English mining associations. Head and Andrews sought to answer a question similar to Miers's: what was the true value of mines in

South America? Like Miers, Head and Andrews were not businessmen, a status which left them open to charges that they lacked a businessman's observational and operational acuity. Nevertheless, as commercial travelers they found it necessary to convince readers that they engaged in unbiased reporting, even as they delved into matters that directly concerned their own financial interests.

Miers, Head, and Andrews all drew on the work of political economists to try to answer questions on value. They consider the lack of the division of labor and population in Rio de la Plata and Chile crucial impediments to prospects for future investments in the mines. The travelers had more catholic concerns, though. They needed to identify the causes behind the failures of specific mines, as well as speculate about whether and how company projects might be profitably revived. They measured what costs and benefits they could for the mines by taking assays and surveys to ascertain the prevalence and quality of ores, and they calculated costs for inputs such as labor, fuel, and transportation. These calculable elements underlay the assessment of what present-day economists call risk, allowing analysts to estimate the probability of success for an investment as well any profits a mine might generate.

The travelers also wrestled with what economists today designate as uncertainty. These were features of the landscape in Rio de la Plata and Chile that affected the value of the mines yet were not calculable. These factors include purely random events, but particularly the combustible political instability in the new republics. The distance between England and South America contributed to the lack of timely information, of course, and, where credible information was available, those South Americans with exclusive access to it stood to gain enormous profits from their privileged position.[9] The travelers reported instances where individuals and groups acted to further their own self-interest to the detriment of the interests of companies and their shareholders. Head called this "knaves riding fools"; these principal-agent problems hampered the calculation of risk for the mining investments, and turned them, in the parlance of the day, from investments to speculations, and from speculations to gambles.[10]

Political economists were also interested in how investments could be transformed into speculations, and speculations into gambles. But the observations and interests of political economists diverged from those of the travelers when it came to the financial crisis. Political economists ignored the work of the commercial travelers and their explorations of the economic questions raised by the ambiguous legal and political status of joint-stock companies, as well as the clash of interests engendered within the companies. And political economists resolutely kept their focus domestic. Their gaze traveled little further than Threadneedle Street and England's counties, as they concluded that imprudent currency issues by the Bank of England and private banks had sparked the speculative boom and bust. Uncertainty began at home.

John Miers and the Limits of Political Economy in Rio de la Plata and Chile

Miers is best known today for his work on the botany of Argentina and Chile, for which he provided significant and new, to Europeans, details, including recording previously unknown species and genera. More generally, his Royal Society obituary claims that Miers "was for long regarded as a standard authority on the geography of the countries and the customs of the people with which it dealt" in the English-speaking world.[11] Born in London in 1789, Miers initially entered his father's jewelry business, but pursued interests in mineralogy and chemistry during his leisure hours. He married Anne Place, eldest daughter of the radical reformer Francis Place and governess for James Mill in 1818. Soon thereafter he and his wife went to South America, at the behest of Cochrane, to explore the possibility of investing in the mining, refining, and milling of copper and other minerals in Chile. After landing at Buenos Aires, Miers crossed the Pampas and Cordillera Andes into Chile, and ended up staying in South America for seven years.

He returned to England in June 1825, and began work on *TCP*. He left the work with his father-in-law, who, during his absence, had published *Illustrations and Proofs of the Principle of Population* (1822), a work in which Place not only embraced the arguments of Malthus, but advocated the use of contraception. Place apparently had "a profound influence" on *TCP* through his proofreading, revisions, additions, all assisted by consultations with British travelers who had returned from the Southern Cone.[12] The volumes appeared in print in 1826, shortly after Miers had traveled back to Buenos to establish a national mint.[13] The reviewer for *The London Magazine* informs readers that Miers appears to have assigned the dual functions of travel writing – entertainment and information – to either of the two volumes; the first "contains the writer's personal travels, and his observations in the course of them; the second volume is the historical part, and contains a historical and statistical account of Chile".[14] The volumes impart a taste of how different Miers's experiences were in traveling through Rio de la Plata compared to his residency in Chile, as he offers descriptions with much more institutional detail, in the manner of Humboldt, when writing about his years in Chile. His experience was not the norm. British residents were more numerous and on much firmer footing in Rio de la Plata than in Chile, having begun to establish themselves in Buenos Aires shortly after the May Revolution in 1810. When Great Britain recognized the independence of the United States of La Plata in 1825 with the signing of the commercial treaty, a key feature enshrined guarantees that British residents could freely exercise their religion.

By comparison, the British failed to recognize Chile until 1831 even though revolutionaries there had proclaimed independence from Spain in 1818. As previously noted, by that time a small group of Chileans knew of the work of classical economists, including Smith and Say, on basic principles of political economy and topics such as trade, and monetary policy. These Chileans, including a few high government officials, rejected, however, the notion that principles of political economy could be applied universally.[15] The far different conditions in Chile meant that policies designed for Great Britain were not appropriate for the new republic without modification, a sentiment echoed by our British travelers.

Chile may have been less well documented than Rio de la Plata, but Rio was not really that well known among the British, either. Events of 1825 further spurred efforts by the British to gain and circulate information about both countries. Miers confides to readers that he published his volumes in order to correct the "numerous misconceptions which were entertained, and the incorrect accounts which had been published relative to these countries" which he found on his return to England in 1825 (*TCP*, I, p. iv). He admits, however, that errors and omissions mar *Travels*. For one, his brief stay in England meant that he was unable to revise the manuscript as carefully as intended. His abrupt return to South America led Miers to "claim the indulgence of the reader, for such inaccuracies and defects of style and arrangement as he is conscious pervades it" (*TCP*, I, p. iv). In the first volume Miers combines observations from his two trips through Rio de la Plata, in 1818 and 1825. Though he often marks the passage of time in this volume with a specific date, or a reference to changes in appearance of the places and people he revisited, a reader may be forced to backtrack to determine exactly where Miers is in space and time. This mimics how Miers retraces his own steps, and impresses upon the reader the truth of his apology for failing to carefully edit the work. When he writes that, "It was the intention of the Author to have given some account of the natural history of Chile, but he found it impossible from want of time", he acknowledges that his account of past travels suffers, ironically enough, from the press of his current travel commitments (*TCP*, I, p. v).

In the words of *The Monthly Review*, Miers "looks at matters generally with an eye to business". The reviewer approves of the maps and other information Miers provides on the logistics of land travel between Buenos Aires and Chile, all apparently accurate; these include instructions for the novice traveler on items to take for travel in the pampas (*TCP*, I, pp. 345–6). The reviewer likewise commends Miers's detailed report "on the present condition and future prospects of the mines and Chile".[16] An essayist in *The Westminster Review* echoes both these sentiments; further, Mier's views are "generally enlightened, and always liberal", and, "his observations, though a little embittered by failure in some of his projects, and by personal circumstances arising out of them, are judicious and important".[17] The *Monthly Review* essayist takes Miers to task, on the other hand, for what the writer deems exaggerated, prejudiced, and ultimately inaccurate observations about the manners and customs of peoples he encounters; Miers writes, for example, that the Chilenos to possess no virtues whatsoever (*TCP*, II,

p. 223). The reviewer feigns astonishment and notes that prior accounts by British travelers such as Robert Proctor, Graham, and Captain Basil Hall, and Miers's own text flatly contradict this assertion. The writer sarcastically asks whether any of the positive attributes Miers finds in the behavior of the Chilenos should be struck off the list of virtues altogether.[18]

Miers speaks in a number of other voices aside from the man of business in *Travels*. Though he consciously pushes away references to the sublime, he occasionally invokes the "romantic", as in his recollection of the post-house at Portozuelas, where

> The verdure and luxuriance of the vegetation, contrasted with the bare weather-beaten masses of rock, the wretchedness of the huts, and the miserable appearance of the inhabitants of this beautifully sheltered spot, gave to the whole an air of the romantic.
>
> (*TCP*, I, p. 86)

The Monthly Review concludes that "the mere *general* reader who takes up this work as 'a book of travels' will be disappointed if they expect to find amusing anecdotes".[19] A reviewer in *The London Magazine*, while averring that each volume "is full of instruction", took a different tack, maintaining that Miers's "adventures have put him into the way of compiling an excellent book", and that the "two volumes abound in passages which will amuse as much as they inform".[20] As if to illustrate this point, *The London Magazine* includes a lengthy extract drawn from *TCP* in which Miers adopts the styles and conventions of at least two genres of contemporary fictions.[21] The two-and-a-half week crisis of Anne's difficult labor and delivery in the Cordillera, and subsequent illness and recovery reads like a shipwreck tale; as his wife goes into labor, Miers's party lands in a location "forty-five miles from any habitable spot", lacking adequate shelter and desperately short of supplies (*TCP*, I, p. 170). Miers chronicles his wife's life-threatening puerperal fever, and the subsequent struggle to find accommodations for his "charges", Anne and his infant son, who will have to fend for themselves for a period in Mendoza. The episode also features elements of domestic fiction. But Miers's retelling comes with a twist on the genre, as he portrays an inversion of expected gender roles; Miers nurses his wife and son, and he and the doctor in his party "were obliged to do the office of washerwomen" as part of their care (*TCP*, I, p. 175).

Miers also draws on sciences and pseudo-sciences to make and explain his observations. These include his botanical observations and those on climate, which "produces a remarkable effect" on the landscape. He makes physiognomic observations; of the governor of Mendoza he concludes that "there was nothing in his physiognomy indicative of a mind above a common cast" (*TCP*, I, pp. 237, 151). Miers is able to conduct rudimentary experiments, but only when he has leisure time to do so. In one case, he collected water from mineral springs in the Cordillera but had to wait some two and a half years before he could subject the sample to several reagents he had at his house in Concon, Chile (*TCP*, I, pp. 311–2). Miers disputes some previous observations made by foreigners, finds that locals could be variously reliable and unreliable in their observations, and does not hesitate to correct what he sees as mistaken observations, whatever the source (for examples, see *TCP*, I, pp. 23, 279–81).

Miers does not spare himself from charges of ignorance of whole branches of particular sciences, and admits that his general knowledge may prove erroneous. With respect to geognosy,

> Never having either travelled in mountainous countries, or had opportunities for gathering practical information relative to mountain formations otherwise than from books, I may be excused if the views I have given of the structure of the Cordillera do not prove correct; an acquaintance with the science of geognosy can only be derived from actual observations of mountain formations. It would be unpardonable were I to mislead others by pretending to a full acquaintance on subjects of which I have no more than a general knowledge.
>
> (*TCP*, I, pp. 306–7)

Miers, previously only an armchair traveler in mountainous terrain, equipped exclusively with knowledge gathered from reading, represents himself to readers of *TCP* as an inferior observer compared to any traveler with first-hand experience of mountains. He suffers from the additional disability that, if he observed partly to satisfy his "curiosity", he also did so as a diversion from his "gloomy reflexions" over traveling without his wife and child. Miers acknowledges "uncertainty" as to whether his observations in geognosy were "scientifically correct" as a result (*TCP*, I, p. 307).

Miers questions his own qualifications as a scientific observer; what about his qualities as an observer of social phenomena? Miers deploys a stadial framework to gauge the state of civilization of the South Americans, linking modes of production to the behavior and appearance of the region's inhabitants. When he traverses the same ground, years later, Miers notes little change in their conditions and manners. The credibility of his observations of post-house life is undercut, however, by his exhausting use of a few select adjectives. He repeatedly employs "wretched" and "miserable" in his descriptions, with "filthy" and "dirty" coming in for only slightly less frequent abuse. Miers uses these words interchangeably to describe most post-houses and their residents as his party treks through the Pampas and Cordillera, though he reserves "hovel" for the post houses and "savage" and "barbarian" for people, respectively. At the very first post-house he encounters, Miers searches for a suitable referent for his readers and finds, unsurprisingly, the Irish. The post house resembles "in every thing, except its size, an Irish mud cabin" (*TCP*, I, p. 14). At times, Miers concedes that he cannot adequately represent what he observes. He recollects the travelers' room at the post-house in San Luis as a "hole ... filthy and dirty beyond description" (*TCP*, I, p. 99). On other occasions he fails to even observe much less represent the economic phenomena in question. In Mercedes he

> could discover no regular employment that any of the people here followed; ... from all I could see, and all I could learn, there was no sort of regular employment; I could not make out from them how they contrived to live.
>
> (*TCP*, I, p. 44)

And Miers indulges in category mixing when describing some people whose work he does observe. Oxen carts carry most of the commercial traffic between Mendoza and Buenos Ayres, and the "carriteros, or drivers, are generally natives of Santiago del Estero, men bred up to this business; they are a barbarous and savage race, but trustworthy" (*TCP*, I, p. 245). There are stages within stages, too. The Pampas Indians he met while in town in Mendoza and Buenos Ayres "are still in an early stage of a savage life" (*TCP*, I, p. 257). The essayist in *The Westminster Review* chimes in, adding that the environment, the primitive hut which "imperfectly covers him" and "the wild and uncultivated plains on which he dwells", exert a curious effect on the character of a post-house keeper: "The habits of the savage are oddly engrafted on the courtesy and hauteur of Old Spain."[22]

Stadial histories and British political economy have no exclusive claims to observational and representational blind spots, or fuzzy classifications when it comes to describing peoples, productions, or objects abroad. Or the use of pejoratives. Robert Proctor, who fails to use the terms "civilization", "economy", or political economy" in *Narrative of a Journey across the Cordillera of the Andes, and of a Residence in Lima, and Other Parts of Peru, in the Years 1823 and 1824* (1825), also generously sprinkles "miserable" and "hovel" throughout his descriptions of peoples and places in the pampas. Miers likewise does not use "economy" or any of its cognates in the first volume of *TCP*. When he finally refers to political economists, well into the second volume, he does so as a joke at the expense of the Chileans. He writes of an "augmentation duty", a new tariff introduced in Chile in 1822: "This financial invention, hitherto unheard-of in the civilized countries of Europe, is due only to the genius of the sage political economists of Chile" (*TCP*, II, pp. 201–2).

Yet no reader could escape noticing the pervasive presence of topics in political economy in *Travels*, or Miers's familiarity with its fundamental tenets. For instance, he points to the restocking of herds of cattle that followed the restoration of public order and "from the security afforded to private property" in Buenos Aires; he contrasts this with Santa Fè which, "from the insecurity which still prevails, is destitute of cattle" (*TCP*, I, p. 196). Miers also chose "Division of labour" as title for the final section in the second volume's chapter on "Agriculture.–Tenures." (*TCP*, II, p. 341).

"To Give This Country Its True Value" 219

The chapter title announces the importance of laws on property for agriculture in Chile. Thus, while the Chilenos are "profligate and improvident", the "fault is not so much inherent in them as in the whole system reigning throughout the country". The system of landholding places so much power in the landowner that this discourages "habits of frugality and forethought in the tenant" (*TCP*, II, p. 357). But Miers goes beyond blaming the system of tenure. He conducts his analysis in a Humboldtian vein, explaining how the land, climate, and the past and present history of property laws and rights of inheritance, which lead to a lack of secure property rights, combine to cause agricultural backwardness in Chile and leave almost all of its resident tenants and laborers impoverished.

Malthus, morals, and manners matter for Miers's political economy as well, as reflected in Miers's diatribe against the Catholic Church in Chile. The church holds unseemly power over Chileans according to Miers, influence, he implies, that affects the operation of the population principle; "The act of confession discloses connexions that are but too common among a people bound by no moral restraint; no sooner is this discovered by the priest than he obliges the parties to marry" (*TCP*, II, p. 223). Like his compatriots and fellow travelers, Miers applauds the introduction of Lancasterian schools in Rio de la Plata and Chile (for the latter, see *TCP*, II, p. 257). Local Creoles and the British educator "Dr. Gillies" had erected schools in Mendoza in part to improve the status of women. Miers believed that these schools would produce "a material change in the moral conduct of the people", and were necessary for commerce to thrive (*TCP*, I, pp. 226–8).

For the present, however, Miers notes a general lack of good moral behavior in commercial dealings in Chile. This lack results in the usual corruption, including but not limited to mendacity, thievery, bribery, and, Chile's inordinately numerous, opaque, and lengthy lawsuits. Miers reports he has

> found no one in Chile disposed to sacrifice his views of gain to motives of philanthropy, all are alike eager to secure as extensive an advantage from their competitors in the market as their influence can command, or their money can purchase.
>
> (*TCP*, II, p. 380)

Miers refers not only to Chilean corruption here. Smuggling specie and bullion out of the country deserved its own subheading as a principal reason so little of the output of Chilean mines ended up at the mint. The smuggling, with the collusion of British naval officers and British and other foreign merchants, was so widespread that "it is only wonderful how *any* bullion has found its way to the mint" (*TCP*, II, p. 453, emphasis added). By definition, the trafficking represents activity not officially observed, at least until members of the public witness the off-loading of bullion in English ports, or officials at the Bullion Office at the Bank of England examine the bills of lading against the actual cargo.

Miers feels no compunction about moving from describing to judging the people he observes. Nor does he hesitate to do so in terms of the principles of political economy. At Zanjon, he witnesses unproductive people occupying productive land and concludes

> The dirtiness, wretchedness, and laziness of these people are beyond all belief. In any exertion on horseback they are surprisingly agile; but dismounted, they appear in an element foreign to their nature. How easy with a little labour would it be to procure from their rich but useless lands, an abundance of food! how delightful would be the shade, and how delicious the fruit of trees which might be produced in great abundance! But these people are not willing to avail themselves of such advantages, preferring an idle vagabond listless existence, subsisting on half raw flesh, and leading the life of mere savage Indians.
> (*TCP*, I, pp. 213–4)

Miers, once past observations of phenomena beyond belief, addresses the combination that had vexed political economists familiar with Humboldt's work, an account of a region rich in resources, but poorly populated by a people materially poor. He employs the familiar cast of dismissive signifiers, including the summary, if contradictory, "idle vagabond listless existence".

No surprises here. But Miers's observations point to still another contradiction brought to the notice of political economists by travelers, one hardly addressed much less contained in the discourse of political economy. He unearths pockets of South America where the inhabitants were, in his words, degenerate yet contented, and, more confounding still, prosperous yet living with a bare minimum of comforts, simultaneously wealthy and poor. The postmaster at Coral de Cuero, for one, was given a large piece of land, and "still owns", despite the depredations of Indians, "400 capital horses, 1,000 sheep, a large flock of goats, and several hundred horned cattle". Yet the postmaster and his family are ill-clothed, dirty, and live in a hovel "open to the entrance of the wind on all sides". They have no furniture, hence sleep on the ground, "and yet all are fat, healthy, and contented". Miers admits that

> It is impossible for any one, who has never witnessed such scenes, to form an adequate conception of the very degraded existence of these people. This is a fair specimen of a great part of the inhabitants of these provinces, who, possessed of the most ample and abundant riches, enjoy nothing but the extreme of poverty and misery.
> (*TCP*, I, pp. 125–6)

Jokes about whether "capital horses" represent mobile or fixed capital aside, even an inattentive reader might interject here "but the post-master and his family are not poor, they own a good deal of (live)stock!" Similarly, the postmaster at Coral de Barrancas, "though leading the life of a perfect gaucho, which both his appearance and mode of living bespoke, cannot be worth less than 60,000 dollars, an immense property in these provinces" (*TCP*, I, p. 220). Thus, just as abundant resources may not lead to monetary wealth, and greater wealth to greater happiness, greater monetary wealth need not be reflected in greater material comfort. The latter combination adds up to a taxonomic scandal: how can people who are not, by the way, unsociable misers, be simultaneously rich and poor?

This leads Miers to yet another puzzle, one more readily considered by political economists. Parts of Rio de la Plata yielded abundant food yet few people. Miers fixes on government policy as a principal cause for this outcome, even in the population center of Mendoza. Local governance ensures that irrigation canals reach each home in the city. As a result, each household in Mendoza produces food sufficient for "family, labourers, and servants". What is more, for the Mendozan household head, "his wants are few, and these the climate supplies and renders little clothing necessary" (*TCP*, I, p. 224). The typical Mendozan household is nearly autarkic, not chafed by the goad of necessity. Little or no trade stifles the development of the division of labor, and the absence of both would retard the growth of population:

> Whatever the resources of these provinces may someday become, they cannot be forced onwards beyond the ordinary pace observed in other countries, which must be quick or slow in proportion to the wisdom and liberality, or the bigotry and tyranny of its government: under the most favorable circumstances its riches can only be brought into light, and made productive of power and influence by the increase and illumination of its population. The progress of population must necessarily be very slow, unless assisted by emigration.
>
> (*TCP*, I, p. 266)

The progress of population, a combination of population growth, and the diffusion of knowledge, signifies the growth of civilization.[23] Causality could run in both directions between economic and population growth. European travelers and South Americans alike asserted that more people were needed in order to absorb investment in the South American republics. Capital investment, in turn, would promote economic growth, and economic growth would lead to population growth. Population growth could lead to yet more economic growth by increasing the density of population. An increasing density of population would do more than foster the spread of the division of labor; it would increase effective demand and multiply desires beyond subsistence needs, setting off a virtuous cycle of, again, economic and population growth. Population, population density, and population growth thus served as both markers and essential determinants of the growth of civilization in South America.

At least one British traveler, Alexander Gillespie, had earlier reported South Americans initiating policy changes along these lines. Gillespie was sent into the countryside after being captured in Buenos Aires on 12 August 1806, in the aftermath of the first, failed British incursion into Rio de la Plata. He confesses the limits to his observations in "Introduction" to *Gleanings and remarks: collected during many months of residence at Buenos Ayres, and within the upper country* (1818), admitting that, as a military traveler, his "records too must be more various than compleat, when they are noted upon little scraps of paper, and his deductions neither positive nor sure, when he is precluded from every source of scientific reference".[24] Gillespie, who had retired to Leeds by 1818, praises in "Conclusion" the policies of Juan Martín de Pueyrredón, elected Supreme Director in of the United Provinces of the Rio de la Plata in 1816, in terms of political economy and population:

> The most benign and sensible enactment of this administration has been evinced, in giving industry with its implements to the tenants of the plains, who have already been supplied with lands on which to fix their habitations; thus encouraging the social connexions, increasing the population, civilizing their manners, and condensing the varied hues of the human race into more definite classes and colours.[25]

His last remark anticipates the concern expressed by Stevenson in the following decade that untidy classifications of people signify statistical and, ultimately, produce epistemological uncertainty. Stevenson expressed irritation at casta classifications in Peru; Gillespie speculates that the advance of commercial civilization would make clear, would stabilize, class and color distinctions in the neighboring republic.

But what exactly was the population in the new republics? Miers writes that the "population of the provinces of the La Plata Federal union has been greatly exaggerated" (*TCP*, I, p. 263). He reports three widely varying sets of numbers for cities and provinces of the La Plata Federal Union. See Figure 6.1. The tables reproduce official estimates, those from an unnamed "recent traveller"; and a set compiled by Miers himself, "from the best information [he] could obtain" (*TCP*, I, p. 264). Miers has even fewer resources to draw on when he presents population statistics for Chile. He provides one estimate for each of the thirteen provinces comprising the non-Indian territory of Chile, and for the country as a whole, as well as estimates for square miles and population density for the same. See Figure 6.2. These are numbers of a very rough sort. Miers rounds his statistics for population to the nearest ten thousand people, and, while more precise with his estimates for territory encompassed by each province, even these he rounds to the nearest fifty miles (*TCP*, I, p. 481). Miers provides no additional information that would allow a reader to independently assess the veracity of the different estimates.

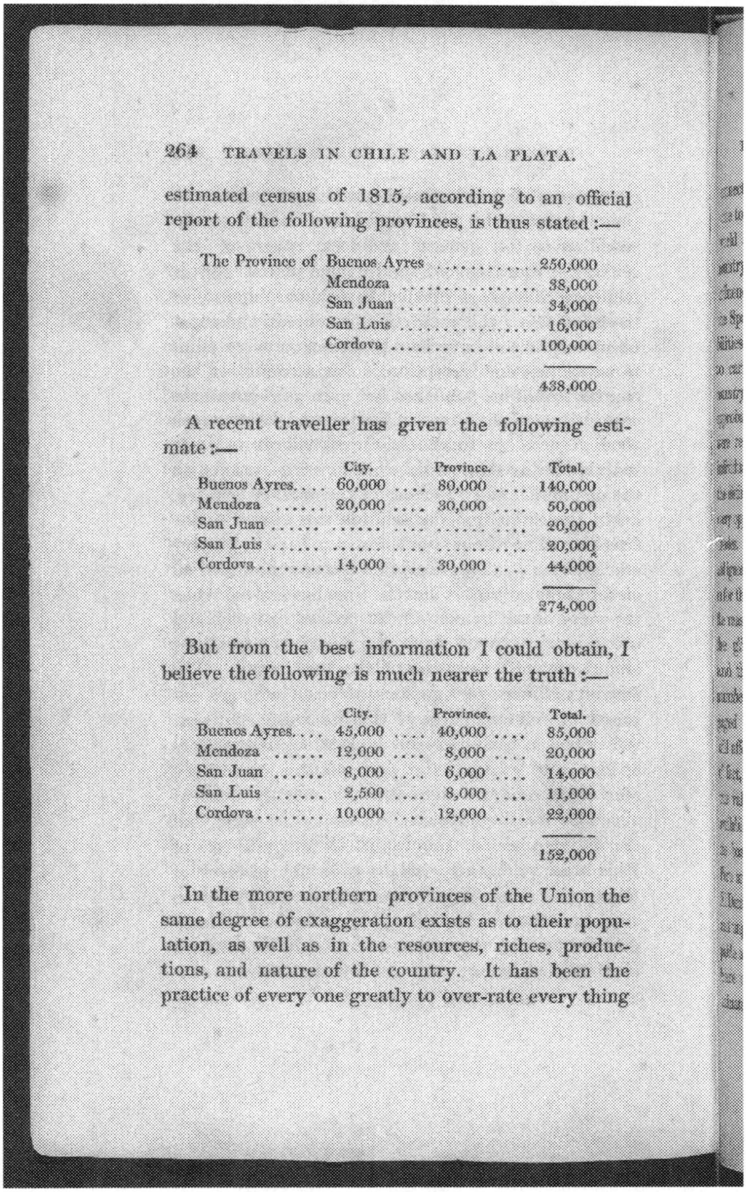

264 TRAVELS IN CHILE AND LA PLATA.

estimated census of 1815, according to an official report of the following provinces, is thus stated:—

The Province of Buenos Ayres	250,000
Mendoza	38,000
San Juan	34,000
San Luis	16,000
Cordova	100,000
	438,000

A recent traveller has given the following estimate:—

	City.	Province.	Total.
Buenos Ayres	60,000	80,000	140,000
Mendoza	20,000	30,000	50,000
San Juan			20,000
San Luis			20,000
Cordova	14,000	30,000	44,000
			274,000

But from the best information I could obtain, I believe the following is much nearer the truth:—

	City.	Province.	Total.
Buenos Ayres	45,000	40,000	85,000
Mendoza	12,000	8,000	20,000
San Juan	8,000	6,000	14,000
San Luis	2,500	8,000	11,000
Cordova	10,000	12,000	22,000
			152,000

In the more northern provinces of the Union the same degree of exaggeration exists as to their population, as well as in the resources, riches, productions, and nature of the country. It has been the practice of every one greatly to over-rate every thing

Figure 6.1 Population estimates for the provinces of the La Plata Federal Union, circa 1815–1825. Harvard University.

224 "To Give This Country Its True Value"

> TRAVELS IN CHILE AND LA PLATA. 481
>
> The number of square miles, and the amount of the population of each of the provinces, may be estimated as follows:
>
> | Provinces. | Square Miles. | Population. |
> |---|---|---|
> | Copiapo | 18,750 | 10,000 |
> | Coquimbo | 13,300 | 20,000 |
> | Quillota | 4,600 | 40,000 |
> | Aconcagua | 4,400 | 60,000 |
> | Santiago | 3,830 | 90,000 |
> | Melipilli | 850 | 20,000 |
> | Rancagua | 3,830 | 70,000 |
> | Colchagua | 4,400 | 80,000 |
> | Maule | 3,750 | 50,000 |
> | Chillan | 2,200 | 30,000 |
> | Itata | 1,800 | 20,000 |
> | Rere | 3,250 | 30,000 |
> | Puchacal | 2,000 | 40,000 |
> | Total | 66,960 | 560,000 |
>
> About 8½ to each square mile.
>
> VOL. I. 2 I

Figure 6.2 Population and territorial extent of the provinces of Chile, circa 1825. Harvard University.

"To Give This Country Its True Value" 225

Lack of accurate facts on population hampered British calculations of the risks to investments in Spanish America. Too low (high) population estimates would under (over)state the readiness of the new nations to absorb new capital. The state of population statistics themselves serves as an index of civilization. The extreme range in estimates reported by Miers thus argued against the presence of the knowledge and infrastructure necessary to absorb domestic and foreign investment.

South American elites agreed that a dearth of accurate statistics constituted an unwanted barrier to flows of capital to the continent. The Secretary of State of the United Provinces of Rio de la Plata, Ignacio Nuñez, for instance, claimed in *An Account, Historical, Political, and Statistical, of the United Provinces of Rio de la Plata* (1825), published simultaneously in English and Spanish, that "Europe knows not my country".[26] He asserts that "statistical data" on the Americas would indicate "what they are intrinsically worth, and what they actually know". Political economy, on the other hand, merits little formal consideration in Nuñez's account, even though he assigns its absence an important role in the post-revolution chaos in the republics. Squabbling among the revolutionaries arose in part from the fact that "the only complete notions of political economy which they [the revolutionaries] possessed" were from the previous colonial government, which Nuñez describes as unreformed.[27]

Statistical knowledge about population would help secure new European investment for the republics; it would also promote population growth through the encouragement of emigration. South Americans like Nuñez were keen to attract people to the continent in stark recognition that the population problem they faced was one of too few people rather than too many. An influx of immigrants would "essentially be serviceable to a country where population is wanting, and every thing else superabundant".[28] The statistics on population in Rio de la Plata in *An Account* read, however, as slapdash and, frankly, not terribly valuable. Nuñez turns to population statistics only after he duly considers the state of building materials in the region in "Measurement for the Materials on Masonry, Carpenters' Work, and other similar objects", a passage in which he conveys his irritation at the oft-indeterminate nature of the measures.[29] The population statistics prove to be similarly rough-hewn. Nuñez provides data on deaths and births from the Buenos Ayres *Statistical Register* in the curiously titled "Incidents Among the Population in 1823", and explains that the editor of the *Register*, "[d]oubtful of the accuracy of the census of population", adjusted these to estimate population for the province. The editor did not, however, resort to the "indirect means, which the most celebrated writers on statistics [such as Price] have established" for adjusting the statistics because Buenos is "not a city of the first rank".[30] As was the case with capital investment, statistical uncertainty marks Rio de la Plata as relatively uncivilized, of a lower order, and thus hurts efforts to attract emigrants to the new republic.

But South Americans did not consider an influx of Europeans an unambiguous good. True, immigrants would deploy much needed skills; for those of a liberal bent, emigrants could also bring civilization in the guise of British manners and educational principles. Many feared, however, that they had shrugged off one colonial power only to risk falling prey to another; they might go "British", even in the absence of a British military invasion.

British political economists did not necessarily assuage the unease of South Americans on this issue. While Bentham proposed establishing a small agricultural colony in Chile and enlisted Miers in his botanical interests, J.R. McCulloch proposed massive emigration by the British to Spanish America.[31] Some 50,000 Anglo-Saxon colonists, McCulloch conjectures, would constitute, through the process of emulation, a kind of informal British education for South Americans. They would form a bulwark for the reform of South American morals and manners necessary to promote commercial progress. The colonists would "propagate *their* habits and improvements through the whole mass". They would in all probability also propagate themselves. Combined, these would gradually render "the greater part of South America *essentially British*".[32] McCulloch's use of the modifier *essentially* calls into question how much British or Anglo-Saxon identity the emigrants would actually retain, and how much the natives would be transformed.

For South Americans already forced to accommodate the palpable influence of British residents, manners, trade, capital, and arms as they struggled to shape the identities of their newly independent nations and their peoples, the prospect of waves of British immigrants flooding their nations offered a vision of questionable value, especially if these newcomers intent on fulfilling a civilizing mission were Protestants. Nonetheless, writers in newspapers and journals welcomed immigrants who could contribute to the economic development of the new republics; what mattered, crucially, were the skills and useful knowledge immigrants would introduce.[33]

Miers's commentary on population forms a counterpart to political economists' struggles to shape what they and others observed into knowledge. We can pair his skepticism with the question about the population principle posed by the evangelical cleric John Bird Sumner in 1817, as he reviewed the fifth edition of Malthus's *Essay* for *Quarterly Review*:

> The first survey of the subject affords a striking problem. It presents us with a view of men essentially the same in their passions, constitutions, and physical powers, yet, in different countries, or in the same country at different times, varying in the rate in which they increase their numbers through every degree of a very exhaustive scale ... How are we to account for these striking variations?[34]

Identical underlying facts of human psychology and physiology did not lead to identical outcomes. Many contemporaries, including political economists, did, of course, try to identify the specific factors driving population growth, stagnation, or decline in given geopolitical spaces. Miers, as we've seen, took careful note of the different pro- and anti-natal effects of laws and institutions in Rio de la Plata and Chile.

Answering Sumner's query required statistics. Political economists, however, were hardly universal supporters of statistics. This was true whether they considered statistics a simple compilation of numerical facts, a mode of analysis, and guide to policy such as political arithmetic, statistik, or Humboldtian statistical accounts, or something else entirely. James Mill, for instance, disparaged statistics as mere facts, and disputed the premise of reasoning about the population principle from population statistics. For Mill, absent information on causes, statistics on population could neither confirm nor refute the population principle, and were almost useless as a result. Writing in *Elements of Political Economy* (1821), Mill harrumphed that

> The reasoning from these tables evades the point in dispute. I know no tables which exhibit any thing, even if we give them, what they never deserve, credit for exactness, except the mere fact with regard to the state of increase. They show, or pretend to show, whether a certain population is increasing or not increasing, and if increasing, at what rate. But, if it appeared, from such tables, that the population of every country in the world were stationary, no man, capable of reasoning, would infer, that the human race is incapable of increasing. Every body knows the fact, that in the greater number of countries, the population is stationary, or nearly so. But what does this prove, so long as we are not informed, by what causes it is prevented from increasing? We know well, that there are two causes, by which it may be prevented from increasing, how great soever its natural tendency to increase. The one is poverty; under which, let the number born be what it may, all but a certain number undergo a premature destruction. The other is prudence; by which either marriages are sparingly contracted, or care is taken that children, beyond a certain number, shall not be the fruit. It is useless to inform us, that there is little or no increase in population in certain countries, if we receive not, at the same time, accurate information of the degree in which poverty, or prudence, or other causes, operate to prevent it.[35]

Mill objects to statistics on population due, in part, to their failure to meet the ideal of exactness. They thus lack creditworthiness, a lack which, coincidentally may extend to any travel account that includes them. Nor do numbers directly speak to causes. They may appear to show an increase or decrease in what they measure. Yet, statistics cannot tell us how an object such as population arrived at a certain point, or how it will proceed.

Mill's "other causes" could be too innumerable to count. This presented a difficulty for those who wished to perfect the science of political economy or contribute to its art. Thomas Carlyle, who was soon to earn a reputation as an acerbic critic of Mill and other utilitarian political economists, spoke to these points a few years later, in 1829. In a famous passage from "Signs of the Times", published anonymously in *Edinburgh Review*, Carlyle writes:

> the wise men, who now appear as Political Philosophers, deal exclusively with the mechanical province; and by occupying themselves in counting-up and estimating other men's motives, strive by curious checking and balancing, and other adjustments of Profit and Loss, to guide them to their true advantage; while, unfortunately, those same "motives" are so innumerable, and so variable in every individual, that no really useful conclusion can be drawn from their enumeration.[36]

Carlyle goes beyond disputing the methods of political economy, and the science's susceptibility to excess. He admits that Mechanism, including the utilitarianism of Mill, Bentham, "wisely contrived, has done much for man". But "in a moral and social point of view, we cannot be persuaded that it has ever been the chief source of his worth or happiness". He denies the possibility that political economy can actually guide us to what is of value and what makes us happy.

John Miers Learns to "Unlearn his Knowledge"

Mill and Carlyle were free to retire to their closets and speculate on how poverty, prudence, and other causes determined population and whatever else was of value to a society. Speculations of a different sort underwrote Miers's account. He made his initial voyage to South America in 1818 while in the grip of a copper mania. He admits as much in the opening chapter of *TCP*: "I embarked with a friend a very considerable capital in the speculation" due to the fact that "The inducements were powerful and alluring". *The Monthly Review* essayist concludes that Miers writes as "a disappointed speculator", whose "personal misfortunes ... give, here and there, a gloomy and fretful character to his narrative".[37]

Miers's confession that visions of profits warped his perspective might lead readers to question his credibility. His description of his speculative activity at the opening of *TCP* is in fact unstable, marked by rapid shifts in tone. Miers uses strongly emotive language at first. He immediately moves, however, to drily list calculations of the expected costs and revenues of various prospective investments, taking into account demand and supply and sundry other elements of the international markets for copper products. Miers interrupts his unadorned summary of market details to conclude that "the inference was irresistible, that, upon the given data, an immense fortune might rapidly be made in the proposed speculation" (*TCP*, I, p. 2). The powerful allure of profits evokes visions of desire unbound, cloaked,

"To Give This Country Its True Value" 229

ironically, as an "irresistible" logical inference; facts and reason begat unreason. Miers then returns to his recitation of copper market facts and recalls how South American officials not only confirmed these, but assured him that they would provide every possible means of assistance in his enterprise. But he immediately casts doubt on the value of these pledges of support. They resemble fictions: "These tales [of the fortune to be had] were magnified by the South American deputies then in London."

Once on the ground in Rio de la Plata, Miers repeats his observation that tall tales abound in discussions about the mines. On reports of the extraordinary richness of ores in two gold mines between Cordova and San Luis, for instance, "no small degree of allowance, however, should be made for exaggeration, and a great portion of these asserted riches must be placed to the account of the marvellous" (*TCP*, I, p. 251). Miers concludes that "so many are the obstacles, delays, and vexations, and such the bad faith of these petty governments, that it is impossible to calculate with certainty on any results of mining in the region [of Famatima in Rioja]" (*TCP*, I, p. 255).

When Miers turns in the first volume to the prospects for foreigners mining in Chile, he voices similar pessimism. He couches his doubts in the language of political economy:

> Little can reasonably be expected in the way of profit from any attempts by foreigners to carry on mining operations in Chile ... Working of mines to advantage must be postponed to a very distant period, when the population has become much more dense, when proper divisions of labour are practised, and such conveniences have become common as will diminish the cost of labour, of materials, and of transport.
>
> (*TCP*, I, pp. 408–9)

Miers references, without naming them, Malthus, Smith, and, in invoking the passage of time, stadial historians. His dour evaluation says nothing about the effect the politics, history, or the morals of the Chilenos might have on their economic prospects.

Miers does an about-face in the second volume. He lays out a vision for realizing immediate, if modest profits by investing in Chilean mines over the course of two consecutive chapters entitled "Mines.–Mining". The chapter subheadings for the first of these summarize its contents. But the subheadings also contain two key conclusions Miers reached during his seven-year residence in Chile, that Chilean mines "Cannot be worked productively by Foreigners" and that "Large Capitals cannot be employed."

Miers opens the body of this chapter by vouching for its veracity. He begins by deferring to an established authority, Hall, whose *Extracts from a journal written on the coasts of Chili, Peru, and Mexico, in the years 1820, 1821, 1822*, was already in its fourth edition by 1825. Miers characterizes Hall's work as containing a "correct" description of the legally prescribed separation of the functions of financing, managing, and physically working the mines in Chile. The roles were performed by the *habilitador*, or capitalist who typically advanced supplies rather than money to the *minero* or mining proprietor, and the *trapichero*, or the miner, respectively (*TCP*, II, pp. 377–9, 388). Miers then tries to assure readers that he has taken pains to ensure that his own account is accurate, too. This despite his entanglement in a drawn-out lawsuit with a neighbor over property he wished to purchase, a frustrating experience which probably contributed to his judgment that the Chilenos had no virtues.

> My attention having necessarily been drawn to other matters, I have not had such frequent opportunities of examining, on the spot, the modes pursued by the miners, as I could have wished; but I lost no opportunities of making all the observations I could, and collecting from the most intelligent miners, and other well informed persons, all the information possible; of comparing my own observations with their communications, and their accounts with one another: the information I have thus collected is sufficiently minute and correct to be interesting, so at least I conclude, in no small degree, at a period when public attention is directed to the mining concerns of South America.
> (*TCP*, II, p. 379)

Here Miers affects a humble tone. He downplays his thoroughness and focus, and alludes to concerns that have distracted him and kept him from making as many eyewitness observations as he would have liked. On the other hand, he does point to certain particulars of his methodical attempts to obtain information from Chilenos, including the miners themselves. He takes none of what he has gathered at face value, rather conducts a careful comparative analysis to verify the credibility of accounts, his own observations included. Miers's observations emerge as part of a social process. This process is continuous, and he invites readers of *TCP* to join in and accept or reject what he relates.

Miers modestly asserts that his information is, at most, "interesting". But he has conducted lengthy inquiries, and proceeds to offer readers a taste of the epistemological and ontological shifts his views underwent during his extended residency in Chile. Error, unsurprisingly, plays a prominent role in Miers' case for his credibility, and he diligently debunks the errors of others. Some observers he judges prejudiced; others, including in one instance Hall, are simply incorrect.[38] Even "travelers of credit" have "maintained that the mountains of Chile consist almost wholly of copper ore", a claim, like all claims of the "extraordinary cuperiferous riches of the country", Miers declares an "unpardonable exaggeration" (*TCP*, II, p. 415).

Miers's tale hinges, however, on his dawning awareness of his own mistakes. His struggles to recognize and overcome these errors make manifest that Miers not only sees new things during his travels, but becomes a new (World) person. He has to let go of the prejudice shared by his countrymen

"To Give This Country Its True Value" 231

that they are superior to all others with respect to commercial knowledge and enterprise. Thus, Miers asserts that the English are wrong to believe the Chileans do not know how to mine; in fact, they do so skillfully, efficiently, and profitably:

> Our countrymen at home are evidently deceived in thinking that the Chilenos understand but little of the art of mining: they may, on the contrary, be assured that they are very skilful and efficient miners, and will not only produce the ore at the earth's surface at a lower rate than others, but that, in their rude and economical processes, they will extract the metals at a much less cost.
> (*TCP*, II, pp. 380–1)

Miers's statement marks a stark contrast with early modern European notions of mining in the Spanish New World, where "translators did not look for evidence of Indigenous knowledge, ... [and] [o]n one point they all agreed ... : Indigenous miners produced labor, not knowledge."[39] Miers's recommended cure for self-deception includes gaining "experience" and "knowledge" about the people and resources of Chile as a precondition for mining there, in order "that he might be competent to calculate with certainty how far his arrangements could be adapted to the peculiar habits he will have to contend with, and the scanty materials he will be able to command". He speaks from experience:

> I was at first deceived to a great extent, and so will all foreigners who attempt any operations in Chile: the very customs and methods which to them will appear barbarous and inefficient, will be found on better knowledge, to be grounded upon experience and reason; and to benefit by these observations, so as to apply them to their own particular views, they must so far exert their judgment as to trace them to their origin, and discover the necessities which have induced them.
> (*TCP*, II, p. 381)

Miers recognizes that his initial classification of Chilenos as mining in a manner befitting a particular state of civilization, barbarism, was incorrect. But even accurate knowledge of the Chilenos' capacities is not enough to guarantee success for foreign speculators. Miers claims that observations vital to successful mining investments will be adequate only if founded on extensive historical research on the origins of Chileno customs, habits, and ways of operating the mines.

Miers indicates that such minute analyses would prove valuable to commercial speculators. He reflects again on his own experience to derive this insight:

> On my arrival in Chile every thing appeared to be irrationally contrived and barbarously managed; but the more I became acquainted with the

> people and their customs, the more I saw of the country and its productions, the better I understood the capabilities of the land, the more I discovered ingenuity in that which I before considered barbarous, and could trace a far better adaptation of those means to the condition of the people, and the present nature of the country, than our own English notions could possibly have contrived.
>
> (*TCP*, II, pp. 381–2)

Miers's English notions about the Chilenos and mining led him astray, and he found it necessary to discard such ideas about native inferiority. His assumption of his own expertise proved false, too:

> It is the habit of an Englishman, educated in the midst of the most wonderful contrivances, and used to means adapted to a highly refined, industrious and intelligent community, to carry his notions of improvement to any foreign object which comes under his observation; and it is easier, and more gratifying to apply these notions than it is to unlearn his knowledge, and bring back his ideas to a state applicable to a more primative [sic] condition of society.
>
> (*TCP*, II, p. 382)

Miers describes a process of self-transformation that enables a commercial traveler to understand the Chilenos. Stadial classifications prove as unwieldy in the second as in the first volume of *TCP*. Chilenos, for example, while no longer barbarous, nonetheless reside in a primitive state of commercial civilization. Miers's re-evaluation of the Chilenos likely constitutes a nod to Humboldt, whose *Essai* Miers mentions only late in the second volume (*TCP*, II, p. 431). Yet Miers proposes that commercial travelers do more than augment their knowledge by accumulating information about foreign governments, religions, commercial regulations, customs, morals, manners, and environmental conditions: Miers beckons his fellow Englishmen to unlearn their Englishness in order to learn otherness.

Miers notes with distaste that English travelers and residents in Chile did not emulate this model of the ideal commercial traveler. He points out, as had his friend Graham, that English merchants in Chile routinely failed to take notice of objects of interest that were literally under their noses.

> I was surprised to find persons of considerable ability provokingly uninquisitive, and unconscious even of the existence of matters that had been incessantly under their observation. However distinguished for commercial knowledge, these deserving individuals are not those from whom may be expected any assistance in matters of speculative utility respecting the country, or any valuable statistic information.
>
> (*TCP*, II, pp. 383–4)

Again, Miers, as did Graham, found the Englishmen in Chile to be dull observers. Prospective speculators could not rely on foreign resident merchants for credible information, despite their commercial pedigrees, Commercial knowledge, then, was in and of itself insufficient for commercial speculation in Chile.

If one wishes to mine in Chile, one must also listen and persuade, according to Miers. And one must change. This dictum applies to all foreigners, whether investors, managers, or workers of mines. But Miers acknowledges how difficult it was for foreigners to undergo this transformation:

> It cannot be expected that the persons sent out from England, however competent to the practical discharge of their duties at home, will be equally so in the execution of their functions abroad, with the want of local experience, and the necessary adaptation of new habits to a new and uncivilized people. I employed a number of the most intelligent English workmen, but I found in every case, the greatest difficulty in managing them. Their efforts, their knowledge and art, most valuable at home, become useless among the Chilenos, and in the absence of their habitual resources.
>
> (*TCP*, II, pp. 382–3)

Note that Miers hardly spares Chilenos from unflattering comments with respect to mining. He remarks, for instance, that they resemble agricultural peons and "are remarkable for the same inanition, want of interest in passing events, improvident carelessness for the future, disposition to gambling, and contentedness under bodily privations" (*TCP*, II, p. 385). Thus, at present the "idle and dissolute Chilenos" are well-suited to washing gold as opposed to employing other methods to extract it because the process requires far less exertion; but "Whenever labour becomes more valuable, and greater incitements lead the uncivilized Chileno to more active employments, gold-washing will never be worth following; it is now only so because the labour of these idle persons is scarcely of any value" (*TCP*, II, p. 399). Here Miers supplies one answer to the question about value that opens this chapter; despite its scarcity labor is of almost no value in this part of the continent.

Miers directs most of his scorn at the Chilenos for their penchant for ignoring any evidence that contradicts their prior beliefs about the value of the mines; "The Chilenos are fully convinced that their copper is superior to any in the world: they cannot be dissuaded from an error current among them, that their copper contains a large proportion of gold" (*TCP*, II, p. 411). Conversations with Chilenos about mining are of dubious value as a consequence. Specifically, "there is generally so much exaggeration, so many falsehoods, and so much fabulous nonsense, current with the Chilenos, respecting their mines, that I feel disposed to give credit to little more than what has been testified by the authority of intelligent and disinterested observers" (*TCP*, II, p. 415).

Beyond reining in their incredible observations, Chilenos will have to adapt in other ways if they wish to expand mining operations in their country. This will also prove difficult. But Miers sees the unwillingness of Chilenos to countenance change as natural in the sense that every nation derives its particular character from its natural resources and national customs. "Necessity alone has been the author of national customs, and it cannot be denied that methods must vary according to the peculiar resources of the country, and the habits of the natives" (*TCP*, II, p. 382). As a result of his experience and knowledge he has gained from living among and closely observing the Chilenos, Miers insists that speculators should not make major capital investments in Chilean mines. He ties his conclusion to principles of political economy:

> Another consideration, which will operate powerfully against the success of the mining companies, is the absolute impossibility of employing any considerable capital in mining speculations, much less the immense sums contemplated in England. It will be seen from the modes adopted in the country how little capital is employed therein; and is an evident relation between the scantiness of capital, and the scantiness of population. It is clearly deducible from the simplest principles of political economy, that there the one cannot operate without the other, so as to raise the demand for labour beyond what can be supplied, must raise wages, and lessen profits.
>
> (*TCP*, II, p. 384)

Political economists had long argued that a virtuous cycle existed between capital investment and population growth in sparsely peopled areas. But investment had to be prudently and moderately applied, or else wage increases would fritter away profits. Miers concluded that prudence called for modest foreign investment of English men, money, and machines in South American mines. The South Americans should bear the bulk of the risk.

The Crisis of 1825–6: "Knaves Riding Fools" or "a Throw of the Dice"?

Miers toiled for a joint-stock association. The formation of such companies rapidly accelerated in the post-Napoleonic period as brokers and customers in London capital markets sought new outlets for investment, including recently privatized South American mines, to replace high-yielding British government debt being retired.[40] General unease and, in many cases, genuine antipathy in Britain toward joint-stock companies added piquancy to questions about what to do about South American mining ventures. Any traveler setting forth to the continent to inquire about mining investments gone sour was already enmeshed in a set of religious, moral, legal, and political debates about the status of such enterprises back home.

The use of joint-stock companies to invest in South American mines almost guaranteed principal-agent problems. Principals would have to travel far distances, or have agents travel on their behalf in order to monitor their South American representatives, and their reports would take weeks, if not months to reach London. Agents would include any one carrying out company directives in South America, such as representatives sent on behalf of the companies based in England, and South American capitalists, mine managers, and mineworkers. Principals would include shareholders and directors of the joint-stock mining associations both in South America and in England, and the company directors the agents directly reported to. And, individuals could be both principal and agent in mining ventures. Miers and other travelers fretted about the nature of contracts in the new republics in general, complaining that the inhabitants behaved in business, political, and legal realms as they did in the social realm: they would say one thing and do another, all as a matter of politesse. Graham concluded that "these South American governments seem to laugh at contracts" (*JRC*, p. 107). But the possibility that principal-agent problems in in these companies would give rise to shirking and dishonest business behavior heightened the risk of any joint-stock investment.[41]

Political economists, though cognizant of principal-agent problems in joint-stock companies, singled out uncertainty generated by the English banking system as the chief source of the fever and panic of 1825 to 1826.[42] In a February 1826 essay in *The Edinburgh Review*, McCulloch calls banking a "system that exposes the fortunes of individuals to such tremendous shocks, and goes far to render every industrious undertaking no better than a gambling speculation".[43] McCulloch contends that unpredictable fluctuations in the nation's money supply lay at the heart of "miscalculation and improvident speculation" by producers and merchants. Present-day historians and economists support this verdict. Neal, for example, lays blame on the havoc wrought by informational asymmetries in the links between English financial institutions and investors in 1825. Borrowers sought to take advantage of the fact that they knew more about the investment proposals they floated than did lenders, and lenders looking for high-quality investments increasingly shied away from the market.[44] The Bank of England exacerbated the situation by promoting "exceptional monetary ease in 1824 and into 1825, and then contraction in mid-1825, helping to bring on a payments crisis for country banks"; specifically, the Bank failed to act to ease credit despite information available to it, and not country banks, of problems in remittances from South America already in early 1825.[45] Thus, unprofitable investments in the mines did not cause the stock market plunge; on the contrary, the stock market collapse stifled development of the mines in the 1820s. This was especially true for the Chilean associations, which formed just as the stock market began its precipitous decline; silver and copper production and exports actually rose throughout the 1820s into the 1830s.[46] The memory of the crisis, however, helped dry up British investment in parts of the region until the end of the century.[47]

In "The late Crisis in the Money Market Impartially considered", a companion piece to the 1826 essay McCulloch asserts that: "nothing ... tends so much to encourage miscalculation and improvident speculation, on the part both of producers and merchants, as sudden fluctuations in the supply and value of money" ([McCulloch] 1826b: 84).[48] McCulloch's analysis recalls Edgeworth's lesson from *Practical Education*. Uncertain fluctuations in money supplied to individual children, entire classes, or to the English as a whole, produce improvident behavior. McCulloch repeats his conclusion almost word for word that, since money was prone to violent swings in its supply and value, "Its unavoidable effect is to render every industrious undertaking as much of a gambling transaction, as if its success depended on a throw of the dice."[49]

If we take what McCulloch calls an "industrious undertaking" or "investment", compare it to "speculation", and throw in "gamble" in turn, each denotes riskier and less respectable connotations than the previous. But, the meanings of investment, speculation, and gamble are confusedly jumbled up, as in McCulloch's "gambling speculation", or Francis Place's identical description of investments in South American joint-stock mining companies.[50] A safe investment may turn out, in retrospect, to have been a speculative investment, even a gamble. If we apply McCulloch's logic, uncertainty turned investments and speculations alike into gambles, and an investor may unwittingly turn out to be a speculator, maybe even a gambler.[51]

Somarriva proposes that for the period between 1810 and 1820 we should think of speculation as a key term for understanding representations of the area.[52] For contemporaries in Britain the lack of first-hand information about the region meant that what information they had was speculative, while most British traders in the region were speculators who could potentially profit from this lack of information. For others, it appeared that investments could turn into gambles before any money had actually been committed. Graham, for instance, writes that "Commercial speculations and war are only gambling on a larger scale" (*JRC*, pp. 168–9).[53] Barrow derisively refers to the speculative investments in South American mines as "sheer gambling, and the worst kind of gambling, as little is left to the ordinary chances" due to the inherent riskiness of any mining venture.[54] Even so, many investors in joint-stock companies may not have considered them gambles. But the events of 1825 and 1826 rendered the meanings of all three terms indistinguishable.

Travelers thought seriously about these issues. They could lead to "knaves riding fools", and harm the bottom line of the companies they represented. According to Miers, information mismatches between principals and agents did in fact make a material difference in the operation of South American mining ventures, as persons in this country, the best informed of the real state of Chile, and of the utter impossibility of employing any considerable sum of money in mining with the least chance of its being productive of any profit whatever, put forth proposals for raising immense sums from the credulity of persons less informed than themselves, for the purpose, as it was pretended, of working mines of gold, silver, and copper, which were to produce immense profits.

(*TCP*, II, p. 417)

As proof of this deceptive process, Miers weighs the claims put forth in prospectuses published in the first half of 1825 by the Chilian Mining Association, the Anglo-Chilian Mining Association, and the Chilian and Peruvian Mining Association. They had, respectively, nominal capitalization of £1,000,000, £1,500,000, and £1,000,000, though the actual amounts allocated, £75,000, £120,000, and £50,000, respectively, were far less.[55] Miers found the prospectuses, replete with "assertions ..., backed by great names", bore little relation to the truth, even in seemingly innocuous statements as the one from the Chilian Mining Association that in the mining districts in Chile, "The climate is healthy, labour is cheap, wood and water are generally abundant" (English 1825: 19).[56] Miers, who cloaks his critique of the associations' claims in the language of credibility, calling himself "a recorder of facts", concludes the prospectuses contain "great exaggerations, holding out delusive hopes which can never be realized" (*TCP*, II, pp. 419, 420).

The prospectuses could be classed among works composed by what Malthus's friend Clarke demeaned as those cobbled together by a "mere writer of Travels, who never himself saw what he relates". When London share prices began to tumble in the beginning of 1825, losses prompted John Diston Powles, a speculator, to commission Benjamin Disraeli to write two such works, published by John Murray; the first, *An Inquiry into the Plans, Progress, and Policy of the American Mining Companies*, appeared in March. In both of the unsigned works Disraeli, who himself speculated heavily in mining shares, touted companies whose prospectuses Miers deemed deceptive, as well as a number of other associations formed to mine in Mexico, Colombia, Brazil, and Peru. Disraeli opens the second compilation, *Lawyers and Legislators; Or, Notes on the American Mining Companies*, by asserting that unbiased reportage and logical reasoning lay behind *An Inquiry*:

In that inquiry, we did not express one single opinion respecting them [the associations' plans], until we had laid before the reader a body of information, from which, and from which alone, we drew our deductions, hazarding no opinion which was not supported by a fact, of the sufficiency of which to support our opinion, the reader was an unbiassed judge. The accuracy of our facts has never been disputed, nor has, we believe, the soundness of our deductions.[57]

Disraeli sought to soothe nervous shareholders rattled when the Lord Chancellor, the Earl of Eldon, irked by the speculation and spreading unease at the widespread losses, threatened to prosecute unincorporated joint-stock companies. Murray was also losing money in mining speculations. Thus Murray, who worked so assiduously with Graham to craft and burnish her credibility for her South American accounts, was not above publishing work by someone polishing the facts to try to furnish his own South American accounts. Despite their wide readership, however, and Disraeli's strong affirmation of the soundness of the companies, the publications failed to raise share prices.

In *An Inquiry* Disraeli uses the doctrines of political economy to interpret selections from association prospectuses in the light of travel accounts notable and obscure, including reports from association agents on the scene in the mining regions. Disraeli begins his analysis by invoking the authority of Humboldt, checked against the calculations of Raynal and Adam Smith, to provide an estimate of the "net annual produce" of the mines under their former, colonial, management.[58] Molina's work and Caldcleugh's *Travels in South America* make appearances in sections on Peru and Chile, and Disraeli rhapsodizes over the literary qualities of J.B. Von Spix's *Travels in Brazil*.[59] Disraeli also quotes extensively from the report of a Captain Garby, the Cornish superintendent of the mines for the Anglo-Mexican Association, on the state of the mines, and the areas where the application of British science and capital, such as the introduction of steam power, offered room for improvements; Cornish miners and their methods represented the acme of British expertise in mining in this period.[60] Disraeli concludes the section on the Anglo-Mexican with the report that the association, by the introduction of a new method of amalgamation, had produced more silver ore from the Guanaxuato mines in twenty-four hours "than the Spaniards were in the habit of doing in six weeks!"[61] Disraeli assures readers not only that "the government of Mexico appears to be perfectly and completely consolidated", but that there is not the slightest prospect that the Mexican government will raise the duties on gold and silver.

Disraeli paints a glowing picture of the mines. But he cuts *An inquiry* with just enough cautionary remarks, with an admixture of uncertainty, to avoid the charge of unalloyed optimism. For example, of the General South American Mining Association, Disraeli writes, that "It does not appear that any mines are engaged, nor are any reasons given, why it has been thought advisable not to embrace Mexico in the arrangements of this Company." He concludes that the associations have published reports that are "neither visionary nor deceptive", and that "In the plans of those associations, which have been very recently formed and very lately organized, we are unable to detect any circumstances, from which we can infer a disposition, either to misrepresent or to conceal".[62]

Disraeli ventures into the principles of political economy in the last third of *An inquiry* to support his deductions. At one point he tosses off a reference

"To Give This Country Its True Value" 239

to the division of labor; elsewhere he discusses at length only to dismiss contemporaries' fears that an influx of New World gold and silver would result in monetary depreciation.[63] Still longer is his political economic brief in support of joint-stock companies. He repeats one contemporary criticism of domestic joint-stock companies, that railways, docks, and water companies drive up the wages of labor and encourage population growth. When competition drives these companies out of business, immiseration is not just an issue for the individual family, but a national problem. Disraeli offers a simple solution for those opposed to the formation of such companies: vote down enabling legislation in Parliament.[64] This leads Disraeli to argue, in Smithian terms, at yet greater length against legislation to restrict the formation of joint-stock associations for foreign speculations, especially American mining companies.[65]

The Rio Plata Mining Association, one of the companies whose prospectuses Disraeli reviewed, sent Francis Bond Head to South America to investigate the causes of the company's collapse. Head, commissioned as a lieutenant in the Royal Engineers in 1811, fought at Waterloo. In 1816, he married his cousin, Julia Valenza Somerville, and the couple eventually had four children. After retiring from military service as a major in 1825, Head took a position as a mining supervisor for the Rio Plata Mining Association to manage their speculative ventures. Head captained an international crew in South America, taking "two highly-respectable captains of the Cornish mines, a French assayer, a surveyor, and three labouring miners", over a thousand miles from Buenos Aires to gold mines in San Luis and silver mines in Uspallata, leaving two groups, English and German miners, respectively, in Buenos while he took stock of the situation in the provinces.[66]

Head claims he initially designed *Rough Notes* as a report for the association directors' eyes only: "The sole object of my journey was to inspect certain mines".[67] Head asserts that "both the formation of these Companies, and their failure, have proceeded from one cause- Ignorance of the country which was to be the field of speculation" (*Rough Notes*, p. iv). Though Head felt compelled to "lay before the public, Reports, and other evidence" on the events that led to the failure of the association, he did not do so in *Rough Notes*, believing it proper to withhold proprietary information which could affect the sales of the mines (*Rough Notes*, pp. v, ix–x). The volume contains little information on South American mines and mining in the main body of the text as a result, with Head reserving most of his discussion on these topics for the penultimate chapter, "A Few General Observations Respecting the Working of Mines in South America".

Contemporaries found great value in *Rough Notes* nonetheless. It unfolds as a rollicking set of adventures, filled with vivid prose and memorable vignettes including a scene where Head recalls his joy at riding barebacked and bare naked through the pampas. Head's exploits, often dashed off in sentence fragments that mimicked his headlong rush through the pampas and over the Cordillera, earned him the nickname "Galloping Head".

The Quarterly Review essayist contrasts Head's style, "all over vivacity and good-humour, with a buoyancy of spirits rarely to be met with, always taking affairs as he finds them without murmuring", favorably with Miers's work. The latter, while containing "a much larger fund of valuable information", wearies the reader with prose "crowded with minute objects, and these so strangely huddled together".[68] On the other hand, a *Monthly Review* essayist writing on "The Pampas" faults Head for drawing too hasty conclusions about South American society from brief or missing observations. The writer complains that Head, an experienced traveler, "really appears to have landed at Buenos Ayres with all the prejudices, and forwardness, and sheer ignorance of the world, that are usually to be found only in a school – boy". The writer finds Head's glib generalizations, based on fleeting observations of individuals he had no time to converse with and the "nonchalance with which he speaks of whole communities, whose society he admits he had not time to enter, are in every respect unworthy of a gentleman"; regrettable, given his "piquante" style, though, even here Head's rough notes were occasionally "unintelligible".[69] English readers as a whole found Head's travel writing truly entertaining; *Rough Notes* became the most popular of the more than dozen or so travel narratives published on Argentina and Chile between about 1825 and 1835.[70]

In the wake of Head's botched handling of the Rebellion of 1837, the debacle that led to his recall as Lieutenant-Governor of Upper Canada in 1838, *The Westminster Review* ran a review of *Rough Notes* in which the essayist, "H.W.", calls Head to task for erring too much on the side of entertainment.[71] H.W. decries how in the public imagination the money value of a publication, measured by both the size of the contract an author could garner and subsequent sales, "an identification of merit and money", has come to override its actual literary value. Head is neither an unbiassed or methodologically sound observer, but one of "a type of the English travellers of the day, a race who have neither German accuracy nor French enlargement of views", and for whom "the past furnishes no principles for understanding the present".[72] Head, one of the "careless observers", falls short of the ideal, "a traveller by whom knowledge is extended, is a fearless statement of truth, with its features unminced and unmodified". Head and his ilk instead "speak to the prejudices of a buying class", and, in a mocking rebuke to Head's commercial mission, H.W. contends Head and his fellows "hear only the tinkle of the precious metals".[73]

But even Head's few, general comments on mining in Chile outside of "General Observations" illuminate his observational methods and deductions. These depend in no small part on the principles of political economy. His remarks on a "small establishment" for amalgamation, for example, mirror those of Miers on the efficiency of the Chilean methods in an area lacking in capital: "the works were laid out with a great deal of ingenuity, with a very happy regard to economy" (*Rough Notes*, p. 216). Head notes that, though the works did not possess many of the mechanical advantages which a large capital might have afforded them, yet they were on a plan suited to the resources of the country, and upon the whole were well adapted for the economical reduction and amalgamation of ores upon a small scale.

(*Rough Notes*, p. 217)

Pratt concludes that Head pointedly inverts the usual "value signs" of European travelers who observe and judge South America.[74] It is more accurate to state that Head simply resorts to the logic of what had become a familiar pairing of political economy and stadial theory. He elaborates on how this pairing works in *A Few Practical Arguments against the Theory of Emigration* (1828), the opening and closing of which draw heavily on his observations from his South American travels. Head had wished to publish the piece anonymously, "as an Article for a Review", but believed that he would not be able to remain "incognito", likely because of his fame and his detailed references to conditions on ground in South America.[75] Head's descriptions of the pampas, towns, and cities of Rio de la Plata, all "infant civilizations" because plentiful provisions produce non-existent or meager wants and desires among the inhabitants, soon give way to considerations on the population question and emigration from England which constitute the bulk of the essay.

Head continues to employ the figure of the traveler, this time a fictional one, as the focus of *A few practical arguments* pivots from abroad to home. He imagines a stranger arriving in England "ignorant of all its details" who would soon observe, nonetheless, that "he was in a country possessing, in the habits of its people, a mine of inexhaustible wealth" (Head 1828, p. 13).[76] The observation is notable for two reasons. First, "habits of its people" refers not only to the industriousness of the wealthy and poor alike; "every horse on the roads was straining to its utmost", and even the "steam-engines and machinery were competing with man and horse". Head taps into a theme common in contemporary foreigners' works about the English: the English were ceaselessly active. English commercial civilization unleashes purposeful energies from man, beast and machine alike, labor so obvious as to be detectable by a traveler utterly unfamiliar with England. Second, "a mine of inexhaustible wealth" may be a sly reference to his work in South America; activity represents the true lodestone for civilization, not metallic ores wrested from the earth.

Has Head offered an answer to Miers's question about what is of value in society? In *Rough Notes* Head certainly views value through the perspective of Malthus's political economy. But as he idealizes the active life of the Pampas gauchos and dozy city-dwellers in Mendoza alike, he suspends judgment of the inhabitants and their civilization until the region is more heavily populated. He writes, "It is true that the Gaucho has no luxuries, but the great feature of his character is, that he is a person without wants."

While the gaucho chooses not to participate in activities that could earn him money, or allow him to procure a more varied diet or more possessions

> In fact, he is contented with his lot; and when one reflects that, in the increasing series of human luxuries, there is no point that produces contentment, one cannot but feel that there is as much philosophy as folly in the Gaucho's determination to live without wants; and the life he leads is certainly more noble than if he was slaving from morning to night to get other food for his body or other garments to cover it. It is true he is of little service to the great cause of civilization, which is the duty of every rational being to promote; but an humble individual, living by himself in a boundless plain, cannot introduce into the vast uninhabited regions which surround him either arts or sciences: he may, therefore, without blame be permitted to leave them as he found them, and as they must remain, until population, which will create wants, devises the means of supplying them.
>
> (*Rough Notes*, pp. 22–3)

Head uses the gaucho as a foil to question the value of multiplying wants, a marker that defines commercial civilization. He clearly does not subscribe to the notion that an ascent up the stadial scale represents an unqualified good. The gaucho works tirelessly while on horseback, but requires and wants only beef and water, the clothes on his back, ground to sleep on, and, of course, his horse and its equipage. His limited desires define his independence as much as his work freely roaming the pampas. British wage work in the service of the many wants of commercial civilization, on the other hand, leaves man in the state of dependence. Notice, too, that the "great cause of civilization" entails introducing and promoting "either arts or sciences", but not "industry". Yet Head, Southey and other Romantics who inveighed against the emerging British factory system, readily cede rhetorical ground to the political economists when they assume increasing population and population density create and proliferate desires, which accompany and drive the spread of the division of labor.

As for the siesta-loving Mendozans, Head reflects, while enjoying ices as he sits alongside the Almeida, the principal walk in town,

> I used always to acknowledge, that if a man could but bear an indolent life, there can be no spot on earth where he might be more indolent and more independent that at Mendoza, for he might sleep all day and eat ices in the evening, until his hour-glass is out. Provisions are cheap, and the people who bring them quiet and civil; the climate is exhausting, and the whole population indolent – "Mais que voulez-vous?" how can the people of Mendoza be otherwise? Their situation dooms them to inactivity; – they are bounded by the Andes and the Pampas, and, with such formidable and relentless barriers around

them, what have they to do with the history, or the improvements, or the notions of the rest of the world? Their wants are very few, and nature readily supplies them, – the day is long, and therefore as soon as they have had their breakfasts, and have made a few arrangements for their supper, it is so very hot that they go to sleep, and what else could they do better?

(*Rough Notes*, pp. 70–1)

Labor represents both a chief signifier and value of European commercial civilization; indolence constitutes its opposite. But Head asks why not choose indolence if conditions permit? In fact, the environment "dooms" Mendozans to inactivity. As with the gaucho, Head asks readers to suspend judgment about the lack of participation by the townspeople in the whirl of commercial society.

Head's promotion of an anti-labor theory of value becomes more pointed in an extended passage on the silver mines at San Pedro Nolasco. The isolated and desolate location of the mines, with crosses marking the many deaths of workers and travelers who perished in the sudden snowstorms that beset the area, lead Head to muse:

The view from San Pedro Nolasco, taking it all together, is certainly the most dreadful scene which in my life I have ever witnessed; and it appeared so little adapted or intended for a human residence, that when I commenced my inspection of the lode, and of the several mines, I could not help feeling that I was going against nature, and that no sentiment but that of avarice could approve of establishing a number of fellow-creatures in a spot, which was a subject of astonishment to me how it ever was discovered.

(*Rough Notes*, p. 224)

Again, commercial activity unleashed and gave force to desires, especially greed. But this natural sentiment could lead man to commit unnatural acts. Head implicitly asks readers to ask of the mining enterprise whether the silver extracted was valuable enough to sacrifice the lives of those who labored on and in the mountain.

Head split *Rough Notes* into two parts, each fulfilling one of the two functions of travel writing, to entertain and to inform. He tucked his conclusions about the prospects for mining into "General Observations", in language political economists would find familiar. "General Observations" includes "a rough memorandum of some of the difficulties, physical, moral, and political which would probably obstruct the working of mines in the provinces of Rio de la Plata by an English association" (*Rough Notes*, pp. 277–8). The best method for speculating about the success of a mining operation in South America rests on measuring not just the value of the "produce of the mine", as difficult as that is to assay, but the costs, too.

The great distances between mines and sources of supplies, including water, for example, make provisioning difficult, and preclude the use of heavy machinery. Thus, Head concludes that "the mines are better adapted to the exertions of a few people, than to the extensive operations of an English association", a sentiment similar to that reached by Miers in Chile (*Rough Notes*, p. 278).

Those workers would have to be La Platans, initially. Head's experience indicated that the geology of the Andes was such that the Cornish miner in South America, so adept with tin and copper

> is unacquainted with the [silver] ores he is to seek. The ... ores, are by him so unnoticed, and unvalued, that the native miner has actually to point out to him the riches of the mine he has come to improve.
> (*Rough Notes*, p. 283)

This underlines Head's assertion at the opening of *Rough Notes* that "Ignorance of the country which was to be the field of speculation" was the one cause of the failure of the association. Head later explains, in "Cornish Miners in America", that the mining speculators projected their own lack of knowledge onto the South Americans: "The singular foundation on which all these Companies principally rested being the notion that the natives of America were *ignorant* of the proper mode of working their own mines."[77] The moment when Europeans understood what Miers called the "true value" of the land, and could "appreciate its actually existent available resources" had clearly not yet arrived. The English literally did not know what or who they observed.

Head appended a long note to the above anecdote in which he elaborates on his belief that the English miner's expertise at home does not translate to South American conditions, or to the demands of a mining association:

> There exists in England a natural feeling of confidence in the exertions of English workmen, but I am afraid this expectation will not be realized in South America. The Cornish miner is, I believe, one of the best-regulated workmen in England, but like all well-regulated workmen his attention has been directed to a particular object, and in proportion as he is intelligent upon that point, he is ignorant of all others. By a division of labour, which is now so well understood in England, we have goldsmiths, silversmiths, coppersmiths, whitesmiths, and blacksmiths, who are all ignorant of each other's trades; and if this is the case, why should a man whose life has been spent working copper ores, be supposed able to search in any country for silver ores? There is certainly a much greater difference and variety between the ores than there is between the metals.
> (*Rough Notes*, pp. 283–4 note)

"To Give This Country Its True Value" 245

Head blames the miner's ignorance on the extensive spread of the division of labor in England, a phenomenon and a principle which he claims are common knowledge in England by this time. Head highlights a negative aspect of the division of labor touched on by Smith, that even intelligent, "well-regulated workmen" became ignorant of anything outside their purview. The division of labor can dull the powers of observation.

Yet Smith further argued that consumers need not know details about how goods were produced in order to conduct their daily business within commercial society. Buyers had only to consider the exchange value of bread or beer. Indeed, information about all that went into the manufacture of a good was likely beyond the ken of any one individual. Head implies, however, that specific knowledge about how a good is produced is necessary for the initial spread of the division of labor to occur. How else would the parties involved in a potential transaction recognize value and thus be moved to actually make an exchange?

Head on Mining Company Principals and Agents

Head returns to common ground with political economists when he offers a peek at the future of the pampas and the provinces of Rio de la Plata. Population is key. Lack of population had led to a lack of competition and the creation of monopolies in the region. Head offers a lurid joke about monopoly and herd behavior when investors catch wind of a large capital:

> without the slightest intention to blame any individual, I must declare, that from the Atlantic to the Pacific, I found that Englishmen and foreigners alike were preparing to monopolize every article that could be required for mining purposes; and that a large English capital, belonging sometimes to A., and sometimes to B., was considered by a pack of people as a headless, unprotected carcass, which was a fair subject for universal "worry".
>
> (*Rough Notes*, pp. 287–8)

Despite his questioning of markers of value throughout *Rough Notes*, Head concludes Rio de la Plata remains uncivilized. To achieve a place among civilized nations requires a large population, industry and intelligence, "protected by the integrity and power of well-constituted governments". Only when Rio de la Plata achieves these will it take "that rank in the civilized world which is due to its climate and soil". Lack of population represents the great "desideratum" in Rio de la Plata's march toward civilization, "for until there is a certain proportion of inhabitants, the provisions of life must necessarily be easily obtained, and people will remain indolent, until necessity drives them to exertion" (*Rough Notes*, p. 297). Head echoes Malthus's optimistic take on the effect of population pressures on food supplies; it is not a positive check so much as a spur to positive action.

Head's few words in "Introduction" on how he came to compose the work indicate that he wishes readers to take his plain words as unbiased. Head admits that he meant only to amuse himself with the occasional jottings that comprise *Rough Notes*; so, if he did not set out to impart information to the general reader, why would he dissemble (*Rough Notes*, p. xii)? He concludes "Introduction" by expressing the hope that the lack of quality of his prose provides evidence that he records his observations from a disinterested position; "I trust that the rough, unpolished state in which they appear will at least be a proof that I have no other object" (*Rough Notes*, p. xii). Head ventures this statement of trust to gain the trust of readers.

Head redoubles his efforts to vouch for his credibility in *Reports Relating to the Failure of the Rio Plata Mining Association* (1827), his follow up to *Rough Notes*. Head's partial reconstruction of his deteriorating relationship with the directors of the association in *Reports* offers a clear illustration of how the mechanics of observation, representation, and interpretation in the mining sector in contemporary South America played out as principal-agent problems. The directors accused Head of failing to follow their directives, and acting against the interests of the company. These problems were themselves framed by questions about who bore liability for losses suffered by the association during 1825–6. *Reports* recounts the steps Head took to recover payment for his services to the association, monies that the directors initially refused to pay him. The dispute went to arbitration, with Head ultimately prevailing after nearly four months of proceedings.

Reports consists principally of documents from the arbitration process, accompanied by Head's commentary, as he shapes an argument supporting both his integrity and his effectiveness as an agent for the company. Hence, though Head offers distillations of his own travel observations, he presents much more in *Reports*. He appears variously as a witness, a plaintiff, an accountant estimating the savings accruing to the association as a result of his actions, as well as a collector and interpreter of the observations, letters, memoranda, testimony, and judgments of others. The latter includes Humboldt, who Head cites on several occasions on how best to interpret assays in order to determine the value of mines in Spanish America. Head does all this to buttress his case for the soundness of his methodology and judgment as an agent.[78]

Head uses the language of political economy in *Reports* to recount how political turmoil in Rio de la Plata resulted in uncertainty about exactly who had rights to the mines; uncertain property rights produced uncertain prospects for the association. The title page announces that the Rio Plata Mining Association had been "Formed under an Authority Signed by His Excellency Don Bernadino Rivadavia". But upon arrival in South America, Head found that the provincial governments in the interior of Rio de la Plata had sold or attempted to sell the rights to work the mines, which Rivadavia had promised to the association, to other companies (*Reports*, pp. 7–8; 144–6; 148). Repeated entreaties by Head failed to persuade

Rivadavia to intervene to affirm the ownership of the mines he had pledged to the association. To Head, "they [the Rio de la Plata governments] had acted in direct violation of the mining laws, and contrary to the first maxims of political economy" (*Reports*, p. 8). The maxims Head refers to are apparently those about the overriding necessity to ensure the security of property.

Head acted as an agent for the association, but was also a principal while in South America. The association granted Head powers of attorney and discretion as to how to proceed with other agents on the scene. Head frames his struggle to further the interests of the association while fulfilling his dual roles with the plaint that "In vain I looked into my written instructions for assistance, or for advice" (*Reports*, p. 37). Grosvenor Bunster, an agent for the company charged with organizing Cornish miners who continued the public campaign against Head on behalf of the association even after the arbitration ruling, repeats these very words to attack Head's authority and actions. Bunster neglects to add, however, that, in the next sentence in *Reports* Head notes that he also had been given written instructions "to vary and modify the proceedings as might appear most fit and proper for promoting the interest of the Association, according to my judgment and circumstances" (*Reports*, p. 37).[79] The directors even appointed Head "Commissioner and Inspector of the affairs of the Association in South America". Head thus acted as one principal among several in his dealings with Rivadavia; he refers to the association man in Santiago, who he tried to order about, as the directors' "agent".

Head's directors, however, treated Head strictly as an agent upon his return to London. They fobbed off responsibility for his salary to the shareholders of the association, who the directors said should determine his compensation, or whether he should receive any money at all. In effect, the directors said to Head that the shareholders, not they, were the principals. Head responded that such a shift of roles would entangle the shareholders in a conflict of interest: "the Shareholders would therefore be judges in their own cause!" (*Reports*, p. 56).

After begrudgingly agreeing to arbitration, the directors of the Rio Plata Mining Association accused Head of shirking his responsibilities. They laid ten charges against him, including failure to fulfill his duties as an agent, indeed overstepping his instructions as an agent, and, as a result, bringing about the destruction of the association (*Reports*, pp. 63–70). The final charge and Head's rebuttal illustrate a problem that typically arises in principal-agent relationships, as well as some of the liability issues faced by contemporary English joint-stock companies. The directors held that Head "*has exposed the Association to a very considerable loss of capital*"; not only that, he had "broken up a plan founded upon the calculation of an extensive reciprocity of interests" (*Reports*, p. 68, emphasis in original). The directors list some of these interlocking interests, claiming that the plan would have been carried into execution if Captain Head had adhered to his instructions, or had acted under the sanction and advice of Mr. Rivadavia, or had awaited at Buenos Aires the receipt of the advice of the agents, which crossed him on his return home, or had awaited at Buenos Aires without further instructions.

(*Reports*, p. 68)

Head retorted that part of the reason for his actions was that he had in fact acted responsibly to further the interests of the association. True, the unraveling of the association's "extensive reciprocity of interests" had led Head to bring his action against the directors. By defending his reputation, he was acting in a self-interested manner, and against the interests of the directors. That is, he sought to prove his lack of self-interest in order to serve his self-interest.

Head claimed, however, that he understood and protected the interests of the directors far more than they appreciated. Refuting the final charge by the directors, Head asserts that he had taken their potential liability for heavy losses into consideration, and had acted in the interest of the directors. He helpfully provides an estimate of the capital he had saved them:

> If I had "carried the plan into execution," which was fortunately impossible, since I could not get a single mine, the result would have been an expense of more than 100,000l., and as a proportion even of the last call upon the Shareholders remains still unpaid, this loss would have fallen upon the Directors themselves, and would have involved them in personal responsibility to a most alarming extent.
>
> (*Reports*, p. 68)

Head believed his dispute with the directors stemmed from questions about whether his professional identity would impinge on his ability to function as a commercial agent. As a newly retired military engineer, he admits that "Neither my profession, nor the habits of my life, had ever led me to be what is termed a man of business. The Directors were made perfectly aware of this before I left England" (*Reports*, p. 75). Head maintains, however, that the directors needed an individual made of sterner stuff to make unbiased observations and representations to and for the association. The directors

> were also perfectly aware, that "a steady man of business" was not the person they required. The mines were so distant from one another, and the country so wild and uncivilized, that "a steady man of business" would never have undertaken the job; and if he had started with his ledger behind him to ride across the Pampas, the hardships he would have encountered, the violence of the exercise, the kicking of the horses, and the want of food, would have soon brought him again to the sedentary habits of his life. They therefore, following the axiom

in mechanics, that what is lost in power is gained in time, determined upon putting their mercantile speculation in the hands of a military man.

(*Reports*, p. 75)

His brisk pace through the pampas had given *Rough Notes* its frisson, and greatly enhanced his value as an author. Here, he asserts that his riding skills, his forbearance under extreme discomfort, and his steeliness against the real possibility of violent death, all derived from his military experience, while not standard items on the resume of "a steady man of business", had enhanced his abilities as an observer, and, as a result, his value as an agent and principal for the association.

Head's prowess as a traveler affected his ability to compile evidence that others would deem creditworthy. A crucial element in Head's assertion to the directors that the two mine captains who had accompanied him in the inspections would give statements "unbiassed by me" about what they witnessed was the fact that Head had ridden away from them straightaway after they had finished their work, and therefore had no influence on their immediate assessments (*Reports*, pp. 42–3). Head admits that the solitary nature of his efforts also hurt his case. Members of his party could not verify all his claims because Head, pressing on, would often leave his companions behind. Here Head's military skills threatened to undercut his value as an agent.

Combined, the testimonials and the lack of testimony from members of Head's party testify to the fragility of a traveler's credibility. While Head had spectacularly established his authenticity as a travel writer in *Rough Notes*, *Reports* informs readers that different standards of proof applied in a quasi-juridical proceeding. Head recalls that his association lacked oversight of the sole individual (i.e., himself) designated to gather evidence in South America. Some other mining associations had instituted Boards of Management, typically comprised of three members, to verify observations by agents they oversaw. But the distance between the mines claimed by his association was too great for this expediency (*Reports*, pp. 223ff).

With money at stake, the arbitrators in Head's case needed more evidence than his word, no matter how entertaining. As a consequence, Head attacked the credibility of the association as part of his brief. He noted that the company prospectus included a statement from Rivadavia's chief clerk, Ignacio Nuñez, that

We can affirm, *without hyperbole*, that the first two curacies, Rinconda and Santa-Catalina, contain the greatest riches in the universe. I am going to prove it by a single assertion which is attested by *thousands* of witnesses. In its fields the gold springs up with the rains, as in others weeds.

(quoted by Head in *Reports*, p. 143; emphases in original)

According to Nuñez's statement, the sweepings of houses and mule sheds in La Plata contain "more or less gold", too (*Reports*, p. 144). Nuñez, recall, had in 1825 bemoaned European ignorance of his nation, stating that "Europe knows not my country". He himself contributed to this lack of knowledge, using the association to spread misinformation.

The steps Head took to win his case against the association can be seen as a yet another answer to the question that opens this chapter. Travelers *produced* value in South America through trustworthy observations and actions. Miers and Head use the work of British political economists as a point of departure for their travel observations; they remind us, however, that British political economy, no unified discipline, had its limits as a creator and organizer of knowledge, especially on the road. Far from assuming a set of political economic principles that applied in the same fashion, everywhere and at all times, the two travelers employ their observations to address the very nature of observation itself.

They also raise questions about contemporary ideals of economic subjectivity and agency. Both Head and Miers question the acumen of travelers motivated purely by self-interest, and uninterested in or physically unfit for exploration in this new world. Unbridled self-interested behavior can lead individuals in markets to conceal information, lie, or steal; political economists and others cited the need for well-functioning systems of justice and an internalized sense of propriety on the part of individuals to temper these tendencies. In reality, the British were heavily involved in smuggling contraband in the immediate pre- and post-revolutionary period in Chile.[80] When it came to the mines, Head observed, British capital was viewed as so much booty, too. "We have no mines, and *no chance of getting any*. The whole country, however, has its eye upon your capital" (*Reports*, p. 200; emphasis in original).

Miers concluded that he had to lose attributes of his native country, his Englishness, in order to operate effectively in South America. Head admits that if English travelers blindly applied assumptions of British political economy about, say, the workings of the division of labor, to interpret what they observe in South America, they could easily overlook "true value". Individuals from the other parts of Great Britain were not exempt from calls to cast off their national habits in order to extract value from South America. Joseph Andrews, sent to South America by the Chilian and Peruvian Mining Association, another one of the associations whose prospectuses Miers pans in *TCP*, recounts in *Journey from Buenos Ayres* (1827) how weary he grew at the many disputes between his Cornish and Welsh miners. He found the miners from Germany

> more hardy, patient, and enduring, and far less nice and punctilious about trifles. Cornishmen are intractable if put the least out of their way. They harmonize together "one and all", but not with strangers; and their dispositions and habits by no means correspond with the tried, placid tempers and dispositions of the South Americans.[81]

"To Give This Country Its True Value" 251

The English could ask the Germans to do the job. Or, they could turn to South Americans, though the natives needed to change, too. Miers and Head ultimately advised the British not to mine or own mines in South America. They might instead, as Basil Hall suggested, take up the role of the "habilitador", who Hall defines as "the mining capitalist, and his character is that of a diligent, saving man of business, very different in habits from the miner, who is generally an extravagant and improvident person".[82] One might also make loans to "habilitadores" which, while not without risk, protected creditors from the most direct risk.[83]

One might even become an entrepreneur who would draw on the best of imported and local methods. Charles Lambert worked as both an agent and a commissioner for the Chilian Mining Association, yet another one of the companies whose prospectuses Miers had disparaged. Lambert, an Anglo-French mining engineer, relied in part on the services of locals, including "the most respectable merchant", to purchase, drain, and work flooded mines in Illapel shortly after his arrival in Chile, in September 1825.[84] Lambert, whose private journal of his time in South America did not surface until 1975, came into conflict with directors who went to Chile but chose not to travel with him from the capital to the mining regions; he was eventually dismissed as an agent by his association. He went into business on his own, buying and successfully operating mines by employing a mix of local and Cornish techniques, and by navigating the shoals of post-revolutionary governance, even serving in several official posts, all the while maintaining good relations with British consular officials.[85]

While these travelers and residents mooted issues of the utility of European observation, subjectivity and agency in foreign climes as a result of the crisis of 1825–6, political economists' focus remained domestic. They correctly chose to trace the crises in value and meaning to uncertainty generated by money and the banking system, rather than the cultivation of particular British interests in South America. But the travelers indicate how accurate observations would help stabilize meaning, and could help ensure that even overseas "mercantile speculation[s]" did not turn into gambles. The recommendation of Miers and Head to prudently invest British capital in South American mining ventures hinged on such awareness. Andrews agreed with his fellow travelers on the future of British investments in South American mining ventures. He opens *Journey* with the hope that

> If these various mining companies should produce no other benefit, they at least contributed to make known to us geographically the interior of a vast continent, its vegetable and mineral productions, and the manners and habits of a people with whom it had been the policy of their former masters we should be, if at all, but superficially acquainted.
>
> (*Journey*, 1, p. vii)

Andrews derides measuring South America "by the home standard" to determine its true value (*Journey*, 1, p. ix). Yet he also decries "the un-English-like way in which some of them [the associations] were suffered to become defunct". The English, driven by greed, had taken leave of their senses; until they regained their English business savvy, they would continue to drag down "fairly established [mining]" associations, and miss out on opportunities for profit (*Journey*, 1, pp. vii–ix). He deflects blame from the Chileans, who lacked only capital. Andrews concludes that "it is not the fault of the war-exhausted South American, nor of its rich but deserted mines"; rather, the English "were too deficient in our usual skill, experience, and spirit" (*Journey*, 1, pp. viii; x–xi; xiv).

Englishness, which Miers believes should be shucked off if a traveler is to learn about the continent, contains the very characteristics that Andrews says was needed during the crisis. So, commercial travelers who left England equipped with a basic understanding of political economy return not merely with a political economic conundrum, but with a proto-anthropological one as well. How could the English outfit themselves to observe and invest in South America?

Notes

1 John Miers, *Travels in Chile and La Plata*, vols. 1 and 2 (London: Baldwin, Cradock, and Joy. 1826), vol. 1, p. 265. Hereafter referred to as *TCP*.
2 Hannah More, who had both embraced prejudice in observation and strenuously argued against travel, had, ironically enough, pointed to the same.
3 la mas útil i la mas esencial de las artes, que debe considerarse como la madre nodriza mas fecunda del jénero humano; de la que depende i resulta la verdadera felícidad pública, porque toda riqueza que no se deba a la tierra es artificial i precaria, i porque un estado bien cultivado produce los hombres por los frutos de ella i las riquezas por los hombres. (Iriberri, "Segunda Memoria", p. 303)
4 [John Barrow], "Canals and Rail-Roads", *The Quarterly Review*, 31, no. LXII (1825): 349–78 (at pp. 349, 350).
5 [Barrow], "Canals", pp. 351–3; Somarriva, "An Open Field", chapter 5.
6 See: Henry English, *A general guide to the companies formed for working foreign mines: with their prospectuses, amount of capital, number of shares, names of directors, &c., and an appendix, showing their progress since their formation ... with a table of the extent of their fluctuations in price, up to the present period* (London: Boosey & Sons, 1825), and *A complete view of the joint stock companies formed during the years 1824 and 1825* (London: Boosey & Sons, 1827); Michael P. Costeloe, *Bonds and Bondholders: British Investors and Mexico's Foreign Debt, 1824–1888* (Westport, CT: Praeger, 2003), and *Bubbles and Bonanzas: British Investors and Investments in Mexico, 1824–1860*, (Lanham, MD: Lexington Books, 2011); Sharron P. Schwartz, "Creating the Cult of 'Cousin Jack': Cornish Miners in Latin America 1812–1848 and the Development of an International Mining Labour Market" (1999), pp. 10–2. <https://projects.exeter.ac.uk/cornishlatin/Creating%20the%20Cult%20of%20Cousin%20Jack.pdf > [12 May 2015].
7 Ricardo Cicerchia, *Journey, Rediscovery and Narrative: British Travel Accounts of Argentina (1800-1850)* (London: Institute of Latin American Studies, 1998), p. 2.

"To Give This Country Its True Value" 253

8 Miers likely previews his pessimistic views on the chaotic state of governance and the harmful influence of the Catholic Church in Chile in a series of anonymous letters which appeared in the *Morning Chronicle* in 1824. Somarriva, "An Open Field", pp. 163–6.
9 Giorgio Fodor, "The Boom That Never Was? Latin American Loans in London: 1822–1825", Discussion Paper No. 5. Universita' degli Studi di Trento – Dipartimento di Economia (2002), pp. 1–45 (at pp. 26–32).
10 Francis Bond Head, *A Few Practical Arguments against the Theory of Emigration* (London: John Murray, 1828), p. 39.
11 Anon., "Obituary Notices of Fellows Deceased", *Proceedings of the Royal Society of London* 29 (1879): xxii–xxiii (at p. xxiii).
12 Somarriva, "An Open Field", pp. 187–9.
13 Political unrest forced him to leave in 1831. He then proceeded to Rio de Janeiro to take up similar duties for the Brazilian government, only returning to England for good in 1838.
14 Anon., "Miers's Travels in Chile", *The London Magazine*, 6 (1826): 119–32 (at p. 120).
15 Robert M. Will, "The Introduction of Classical Economics into Chile", *Hispanic American Historical Review*, 44, no. 1 (1964): 1–21.
16 Anon., "Travels in Chile and La Plata", *The Monthly Review*, 2 (1826): 365–74 (at p. 365).
17 Anon., "Travels in Chile and La Plata", *The Westminster Review*, 6 (1826): 202–30 (at p. 204).
18 Anon., "Travels", *The Monthly Review*, p. 372.
19 Anon., "Travels", *The Monthly Review*, pp. 365–6 (emphasis in original).
20 Anon., "Miers's Travels in Chile", *The London Magazine*, 6 (1826): 119–32 (at pp. 120, 131).
21 Anon., "Miers's Travels", pp. 120–4. The excerpt is from *TCP*, I, pp. 171–91.
22 Anon., "Travels", *The Westminster Review*, p. 208.
23 The following draws from Brian P. Cooper, "Social Classifications, Social Statistics and the 'Facts' of 'Difference' in Economics", in Drucilla K. Barker and Edith Kuiper, eds., *Toward a Feminist Philosophy of Economics* (London and New York: Routledge, 2003), pp. 161–79 (at pp. 167 ff).
24 Alexander Gillespie, *Gleanings and Remarks: Collected during Many Months of Residence at Buenos Ayres, and within the Upper Country* (Leeds: B. Dewhirst, 1818), p. ii.
25 Gillespie, *Gleanings*, p. 331.
26 Ignacio Nuñez, *An Account, Historical, Political, and Statistical, of the United Provinces of Rio de la Plata: With an Appendix, Concerning the Usurpation of Monte Video by the Portuguese and Brazilian Governments*, vol. 1 (London: R. Ackermann, 1825), p. 17.
27 Nuñez, *An Account*, p. 12.
28 Nuñez, *An Account*, pp. 294–5.
29 Nuñez, *An Account*, p. 211–3.
30 Nuñez, *An Account*, p. 213–5.
31 Somarriva, "An Open Field", pp. 87–96.
32 [James B. McCulloch], "Emigration", *The Edinburgh Review*, 47 (1828): 204–42 (at p. 209, emphases in original).
33 Somarriva, "An Open Field", pp. 71–2.
34 [John Bird Sumner], "On Malthus", *The Quarterly Review*, 17, no. 34 (1817): 369–403 (at pp. 371–2).
35 James Mill, *Elements of Political Economy* (London: Baldwin, Cradock, and Joy, 1821), pp. 33–4.

36 [Thomas Carlyle], "Signs of the Times," *The Edinburgh Review*, 49, no. 98 (1829): 439–59 (at p. 449).
37 Anon., "Travels", *The Monthly Review*, p. 366.
38 Hall writes that Chileans separated silver ores by smelting. Miers reports that Chileans used ovens not to separate ores but to roast and mechanically break them down in order to facilitate amalgamation (*TCP*, II, p. 400).
39 Bigelow, "Transatlantic Quechañol", p. 253–4.
40 Larry Neal, "The Financial Crisis of 1825 and the Restructuring of the British Financial System", *The Federal Reserve Bank of St. Louis Review*, 80 (1998): 53–76 (at p. 54).
41 Timothy L. Alborn, *Conceiving Companies: Joint-Stock Politics in Victorian England*, (London: Routledge, 1998), pp. 89, 185.
42 Smith, while skeptical of the viability of joint-stock companies formed for investment overseas, notes that profit sharing can overcome the principal-agent problems just cited (*WN* V. I. III). See also: Gary M. Anderson and Robert D. Tollison, "Adam Smith's Analysis of Joint-Stock Companies", *Journal of Political Economy*, 90, no. 6 (1982): 1237–56 (at p. 1243); James P. Henderson, "Agency or Alienation? Smith, Mill, and Marx on the Joint-Stock Company," *History of Political Economy*, 18, no.1 (1986): 111–31.
43 [James B. McCulloch], "Thoughts on Banking", *The Edinburgh Review*, 43 (1826): 263–98 (at p. 296).
44 Neal, "The Financial Crisis of 1825", p. 74.
45 Neal, "The Financial Crisis of 1825", pp. 60, 70.
46 Claudio Veliz, "Egaña, Lambert, and the Chilean Mining Associations of 1825", *The Hispanic American Historical Review*, 55, no. 4 (1975): 637–63 (at pp. 641–4).
47 John Mayo, "The Development of British Interests in Chile's Norte Chico in the Early Nineteenth Century", *The Americas*, 57, no. 3 (2001): 363–94 (at p. 373).
48 [James B. McCulloch], "The Late Crisis in the Money Market Impartially Considered [Commercial Revulsions]", *The Edinburgh Review*, 44, no. 87 (1826): 70–93 (at p. 84).
49 McCulloch], "The Late Crisis", p. 91.
50 Somarriva, "An Open Field", p. 169.
51 Brian P. Cooper, "'A Not Unreasonable Panic': Character, Confidence, and Credit in Harriet Martineau's Berkeley the Banker", *Nineteenth-Century Contexts: An Interdisciplinary Journal*, 32, no. 4 (2010): 363–84 (at p. 365); David C. Itzkowitz,,"Fair Enterprise or Extravagant Speculation: Investment, Speculation, and Gambling in Victorian England", *Victorian Studies*, 45, no. 1 (2002): 121–47; Audrey Jaffe, "Trollope in the Stock Market: Irrational Exuberance and *The Prime Minister*", *Victorian Studies*, 45, no. 1 (2002): 43–64 (at pp. 53–4).
52 Marcelo Somarriva, "A Matter of Speculation: British Representations of Argentina, Chile and Perú during the Wars of Independence", *Bulletin of Latin American Research*, 36, no. 2 (2017): 223–36.
53 For a brief discussion on the technical differences between investments and gambles, see Roger Munting, *An Economic and Social History of Gambling in Britain and the USA* (Manchester: Manchester University Press, 1996), pp. 1–3.
54 Barrow, "Canals", p. 353.
55 Veliz, "Egaña, Lambert", p. 640.
56 English, *A General Guide*, p. 19.
57 Benjamin Disraeli, *Lawyers and Legislators; Or, Notes on the American Mining Companies* (London: John Murray, 1825), pp. 1–2.
58 Benjamin Disraeli, *An Inquiry into the Plans, Progress, and Policy of the American Mining Companies*, 3rd edn. (London: John Murray, 1825), p. 10.
59 Disraeli, *An inquiry*, pp. 57–8, note.

60 Sharron P. Schwartz, "The Making of a Myth: Cornish Miners in the New World in the Early Nineteenth Century", *Cornish Studies*, 9 (2001): 105–26, and "Exporting the Industrial Revolution: The Migration of Cornish Mining Technology to Latin America in the Early Nineteenth Century", in Heidi Slettedahl Macpherson and Will Kaufman, eds., *New Perspectives in Transatlantic Studies* (New York: University Press of America, 2002), pp. 143–58
61 Disraeli, *An Inquiry*, pp. 31–4, 35.
62 Disraeli, *An Inquiry*, pp. 76–7.
63 Disraeli, *An Inquiry*, pp. 79, 82–91.
64 Disraeli, *An Inquiry*, pp. 91–4.
65 Disraeli, *An Inquiry*, pp. 94–124.
66 Anon., "Head and Miers on Buenos Ayres and Chile", *The Quarterly Review*, 35, no. 69 (1827): 114–48 (at p. 116).
67 Francis Bond Head, *Rough Notes Taken during Some Rapid Journeys across the pampas and among the Andes* (London: John Murray, 1826), p. v. Further references to *Rough Notes* are included parenthetically in the text.
68 Anon., "Head and Miers", p. 117.
69 Anon., "The Pampas", *The Monthly Review*, 3 (1826): 152–67 (at pp. 152–3, 159).
70 David T. Haberly, "Francis Bond Head and Domingo Sarmiento: A Note on the Sources of 'Facundo'", *MLN*, 120, no. 2 (2005): 287–93 (at pp. 287–8).
71 Head arrived in Toronto in January 1838 after his appointment to the position in December of the previous year. His controversial actions during the revolt of 1837 led to his removal; he spent the remainder of his years in England riding and writing travel books and other works.
72 [H.W.], "Sir Francis Head's Works", *The London and Westminster Review*, 31, no. 2 (1838): 461–7 (at p. 462).
73 [H.W.], "Sir Francis Head's Works", p. 463.
74 Pratt, *Imperial Eyes*, pp. 150–1.
75 Francis Bond Head, *A Few Practical Arguments against the Theory of Emigration* (London: John Murray, 1828), pp. 1–2, note.
76 Head, *A Few Practical Arguments*, p. 13.
77 Francis Bond Head, "Cornish Miners in America", *Descriptive Essays Contributed to the Quarterly Review*, vol. 1 (London: John Murray, 1857), pp. 1–45 (at p. 19, emphasis in original).
78 Francis Bond Head, *Reports Relating to the Failure of the Rio Plata Mining Association* (London: John Murray, 1827), pp. 155–6, 162 (note), 168–9. Further references to *Reports* are included parenthetically in the text.
79 Grosvenor Bunster, *Observations on Capt. F. B. Head's Reports, Relating to the Failure of the Rio de la Plata Mining Association*, 2nd edn. (London: E. Wilson, 1827), p. 3.
80 Mayo, "The Development of British Interests", p. 386.
81 Joseph Andrews, *Journey from Buenos Ayres: Through the Provinces of Cordova, ... etc.*, vols. 1 and 2 (London: John Murray, 1827), vol. 1, pp. 209–10. Further references to *Journey* are included parenthetically in the text.
82 Basil Hall, *Extracts from a Journal Written on the Coasts of Chili, Peru, and Mexico, in the Years 1820, 1821, 1822*, 2 vols., 3rd edn. (London: Hurst, Robinson, and Co, 1824), vol. 2, p. 49.
83 Mayo, "The Development of British Interests", pp. 382–3.
84 Mayo, "The Development of British Interests", pp. 378–9. See also, Louise Miskell, "From Copperopolis to Coquimbo: International Knowledge Networks in the Copper Industry of the 1820s", *The Welsh History Review* 27, no. 1 (2014): 92–111.
85 Mayo, "The Development of British Interests", p. 388; Veliz, "Egaña, Lambert".

7 Travels with Harriet Martineau

> An observer, to be perfectly accurate, should be himself perfect.
> Harriet Martineau, *How to Observe. Morals and Manners.* (1838b)[1]

Harriet Martineau drafted the above words on her way from England to North America in 1834, less than a decade after Miers, Head, and Andrews posed their questions about observation by travelers in parts of South America. Martineau had been preceded in her travels in the United States by her fellow Englishwoman Frances Trollope, whose account, *Domestic Manners of the Americans* (1832), aroused great consternation in America and England. Trollope and her party departed London for America in November 1827, and arrived at the mouth of the Mississippi on Christmas Day. After a brief stay in New Orleans they proceeded north by steamship, disembarking at Cincinnati in February 1828. Trollope was accompanied by three of her five children, Emily, Cecelia, and Henry, two servants, and a French artist and family friend, Auguste Hervieu. Fanny (Frances) Wright, a well-known Scottish lecturer, writer, and reformer who had published her own travel narrative on America, *Views of Society and Manners in America* (1821), and had become an American citizen in 1825, joined the group for a portion of the trip.

Trollope's husband, Thomas, a barrister, and two older sons remained in England. Thomas and their eldest son Thomas joined Trollope in November 1828, to help her establish the Cincinnati Bazaar, but soon returned to England. The Bazaar, which has been called the first shopping mall in the United States, failed, and, destitute, Trollope decided to leave America in March 1830, but did not do so immediately. Instead, she and her household made their way from Cincinnati to Virginia, visited Washington, D.C., Philadelphia, Boston, and New York City. After taking a trip up the Hudson River and across New York to Niagara Falls and Canada, the party returned to New York City, and departed for London from there in the summer of 1831.

Trollope completed *Domestic Manners* during the trans-Atlantic crossing home. She offered the work to London publishers Whittaker and Treacher

DOI: 10.4324/9781315778952-7

who, in turn, handed it over to Basil Hall whose three-volume *Travels in North America in 1827 and 1828* (1829) had also stoked controversy for his criticism of American politics and manners. Published in two volumes on 19 March 1832, *Domestic Manners* became a trans-Atlantic best-seller, quickly going through multiple editions, and making Trollope the best-known travel writer in England. Her account, stuffed with offhand, flippant, and self-deprecating remarks, rambles, but contains arresting observations about uncouth Americans, most notably the constant tobacco chewing and spitting by men. At one point, Trollope flatly declares that among Americans the "total and universal want of manners, both in males and females, is so remarkable, that I was constantly endeavouring to account for it" (*Domestic Manners*, I, p. 63).[2] She famously dismisses almost all things American with two stark declarative sentences: "I do not like them. I do not like their principles, I do not like their manners, I do not like their opinions" (*Domestic Manners*, II, p. 263).

Trollope claims her status as woman and as a stranger keeps her from adding, "I do not like their government." She earlier noted that she felt

> in no way competent to judge of the political institutions of America; and if I should occasionally make on observation on their effects, as they meet my superficial glance, they will be made in the spirit, and with the feeling of a woman, who is apt to tell what her first impressions may be, but unapt to reason back from effects to their causes. Such observations, if they be unworthy of much attention, are also obnoxious to little reproof: but there are points of which women may judge as ably as men, – all that constitutes the external of society may be fairly trusted to us.
>
> (*Domestic Manners*, I, p. 65)[3]

Trollope lists other American subjects she will not broach; thus, "With their hours of business, whether judicial or mercantile, civil or military, I have nothing to do." Apparently, women can observe effects in these spheres, but are "unapt to reason back from effects to their causes". Women's nature leads them to consider only surfaces, not depths, and only certain surfaces at that, like manners in social settings such as church-going, dining, and dances. She appears to violate her claim to avoid noticing the mercantile doings of Americans when she writes that "It is the custom for gentlemen to go to market at Cincinnati" (*Domestic Manners*, I, p. 119). See Figure 7.1. She does not stop, however, to comment on what this gendered market activity might mean for the household economy.

Further, Trollope mentions her family's American speculation only once, briefly and obliquely in *Domestic Manners*. She elides the failure of the Bazaar, the subsequent seizure of the household's goods and her reliance on the charity of others to enable the household subsist and return home. Instead, Trollope attributes the return to London to

258 *Travels with Harriet Martineau*

Figure 7.1 Man returning from the market in Cincinnati, circa 1830. Yale University.

her fears over her son's repeated bouts with the ague, writing that "our Cincinnati speculation for my son would in no way answer our expectation" (*Domestic Manners*, I, p. 252). Timothy Flint, her Cincinnati neighbor and friend, ascribes the failure of Trollope's entrepreneurial efforts to her lack of knowledge about the American market in general, "and of the proper place in which to build her Bazaar, and to her entrusting the sales to irresponsible and probably dishonest foreigners".[4] According to Flint, Trollope deigned to examine the wares of retail competitors, which consisted of "an assortment of twenty times her capital, and far more rich and expensive", only after her goods had arrived from France. She reacted, bewildered, "How could such things, she exclaimed, have found their way to the United States."

Trollope draws on a range of literary and scientific thought in *Domestic Manners* to make sense of what she did find in the United States. She mixes, among others, physiognomic theory, snippets of literary works, the picturesque, and the aesthetics of the sublime which, when describing Canada's Horseshoe Falls, she appears to cojoin with Bentham's utilitarianism:

> wonder, terror, and delight completely overwhelmed me. I wept with a strange mixture of pleasure and of pain, and certainly was, for some time, too violently affected in the physique to be capable of much pleasure: but when this emotion of the senses subsided, and I had recovered some degree of composure, my enjoyment was very great indeed.
> (*Domestic Manners*, II, p. 225)

Natural history makes only cameo appearances, in her descriptions of school curricula and museum holdings. Political economy turns up in schools, too, at girls' academies. Trollope was able to visit only one of the numerous schools dotting Cincinnati, however, so admits to having little basis for judging whether they delivered on the promise of their curriculum.[5]

Dr. Lock, "a gentleman who appears to have liberal and enlarged opinions on the subject of female education", ran the one school Trollope did observe. She speculated that if the school "produce[d] practical results proportionably excellent, the ladies of Cincinnati will probably some years hence be much improved in their powers of companionship" (*Domestic Manners*, I, p. 114). Trollope had her doubts on this last point. Domestic duties took up too much time for the free American women she observed. The combined efforts of teacher and student, endowed with the paltry offerings of "'A quarter's' mathematics, or 'two quarters'' political economy, moral philosophy, algebra, and quadratic equations, would hardly furnish a stock of these sciences as would stand the wear and tear of half a score of children, and one help" (*Domestic Manners*, I, p. 115). More generally, "household drudgery" for women, even those of the very highest classes, "precludes the possibility of their becoming elegant and enlightened companions". Household responsibilities apparently keep free American women from fulfilling one of their household responsibilities, the leisure-work of sociability (*Domestic Manners*, I, p. 218).

Trollope observes the effects wrought in society by what she saw as the circumscribed social roles of American women compared to their European counterparts. These limits, evidenced in Philadelphia by the rarity of dinner parties including both ladies and gentlemen, forestall the "salutary effects" a mixing of the sexes has on manners, which had been attested to by "both sages and men of the world" (*Domestic Manners*, II, p. 80). The education American women receive counts for little in face of these restrictions, and

> It is after marriage, and when these young attempts upon all the sciences are forgotten, that the lamentable insignificance of the American woman appears, and till this be remedied, I venture to prophesy that the tone of their drawing-rooms will not improve.
> (*Domestic Manners*, II, p. 80)

Trollope rhetorically links her vision of the future of American drawing room manners and to the Second Great Awakening. The separation of American men and women extended to religious practices; despite American professions of spirituality, only women regularly attended church on Sundays. Men did not, or so Trollope observed. This led Trollope to conclude that American women and men maintain "a division of their hours of leisure" (*Domestic Manners*, II, p. 170).

According to Trollope, a key reason that American women have little opportunity for leisure is that they have little access to money. She muses:

> Perhaps if the ladies had quite their own way, a little more relaxation would be permitted; but there is one remarkable peculiarity in their manners which precludes the possibility of any dangerous out-breaking of the kind: few ladies have any command of ready money entrusted in them.
> (*Domestic Manners*, II, p. 110)

Their lack of pocket money compounds the effects of the all-encompassing toil of their unpaid household responsibilities. Trollope's American ladies had little opportunity to purchase time for amusements, or, in her words, indulge in "dangerous out-breaking". If Trollope flirts with possibility that the women she observed in Cincinnati were slaves to their households, she fully embraces the analogy when she compares the lot of rural American women to their English sisters, declaring "if the condition of the labourer be not superior to that of the English peasant, that of his wife and daughters is incomparably worse. It is they who are indeed the slaves of the soil" (*Domestic Manners*, I, p. 166). If single women in American cities strongly dislike service work, the cause of this distaste lay in a strong desire for independence and equality. Thus, girls and young woman prefer the relative freedom of factory work over service, despite lower earnings.

If free American women lack the time and money to pursue leisure, Trollope observes that free American men prefer to pursue money as an end, rather than as a means to afford amusement. Trollope again openly puts paid to the idea that she will not cite causes, referencing, only to partially reject, the logic some American political economists use to explain this state of affairs. On the rapid growth of Cincinnati, she writes:

> Some of the native political economists assert that this rapid conversion of a bear-brake into a prosperous city, is the result of free political institutions: not being very deep in such matters, a more obvious cause suggested itself to me, in the unceasing goad which necessity applies to industry in this country, and in the absence of all resource for the idle. During nearly two years that I resided in Cincinnati or its neighbourhood, I neither saw a beggar, nor a man of sufficient fortune to permit his ceasing efforts to increase it; thus every bee in the hive is actively employed in search of that honey of Hybla, vulgarly called money; neither art, science, learning, nor pleasure, can seduce them from its pursuit.
> (*Domestic Manners*, I, pp. 60–1)

An irresistible desire for money, which Trollope renders in a trope alluding to both Mandeville and Shakespeare, serves as the object of whatever infinite desires that underlay the spread of commercial society in America. Trollope's catalogue of the causal factors behind American's pursuit of money does not simply reduce to a means to avoid poverty. Avidity, lax regulation, low taxes, lack of poor relief, a universal "spirit of enterprise", and "a *total* absence of probity, where interest is concerned", all contribute to American's attempts to slake their insatiable thirst for money (*Domestic Manners*, I, p. 61, emphasis in original).

Trollope turns her observation of national difference into a criticism of English armchair travelers' statements, and of her own previous willingness to submit to their reasonings about the constitution of economic man. She acknowledges:

> I have read much of the "few and simple wants of rational man", and I used to give a dreamy acquiescence to the reasoning that went to prove that each added want an added woe. Those who reason in a comfortable London drawing-room know little about the matter.
> (*Domestic Manners*, I, pp. 61–2)

Trollope playfully contrasts plentitude with scarcity, her many readings with the few wants of rational man. She proceeds to mix the mechanical and the anatomical as she muses, in psychological terms both sensationalist and, more specifically Benthamite, about the pleasures and comforts of society. These sensations differentiate humans, like the daydreamers in London drawing rooms, from hogs, the chief denizens of Cincinnati:

> if we analyze an hour of enjoyment, we shall find that it is made up of agreeable sensations occasioned by a thousand delicate impressions on almost as many nerves; where these nerves are sluggish from never having been awakened, external objects are less important, for they are less perceived; but where the whole machine of the human frame is in full activity, where every sense brings home to consciousness its touch of pleasure or of pain, then every object that meets the senses is important as a vehicle of happiness or misery.
> (*Domestic Manners*, I, p. 62)

Trollope gives scant space to discuss the means by which she turned her own sensations into observations, her observations into notes, and these notes, some "six hundred pages of griffonage", into *Domestic Manners* (*Domestic Manners*, II, p. 261). She offers readers a glimpse of this process, though. She recounts the 12 February 1831 solar eclipse at Alexandria, Virginia, by employing precise scientific vocabulary and measurement otherwise absent from *Domestic Manners*. The eclipse "was nearer total than any I ever saw, or ever shall see. It was completely annular at Alexandria, and the bright ring which surrounded the moon's shadow, though only 81° in breadth." Trollope continues: "During the following months I occupied myself partly in revising my notes, and arranging these pages; and partly in making myself acquainted, as much as possible, with the literature of the country." She excises what she deems much unnecessary material in which she criticizes Americans; she discovers as well that she had omitted making observations of the sort "which all scribbling travellers are expected to notice". Trollope believes, however, neither editorial choice affects the credibility of her "few pages of miscellaneous observations" (*Domestic Manners*, II, pp. 94–6).

British reviewers of *Domestic Manners* judged it in part on her political bent. Trollope, like Hall, avowedly went to America a friend of liberalism, but returned a Tory, appalled by viewing American democracy in action. A reviewer in the Tory organ *The Quarterly Review* praises Trollope's credibility, claiming that she "enjoyed unusually favourable opportunities for observation" and had captured phenomena through "an intelligent traveller's optics" which "bring life near in utter nakedness". The reviewer, having read the volumes with "instruction – we may add, with great amusement", also expressed satisfaction that Trollope fulfilled the two principal criteria for travel literature.[6] The essayist, while deeming it "impossible, or almost impossible, to draw useful inferences from the state of the one people to the practice of the other", shared Trollope's doubts about the American experiment in republicanism.[7]

The essayist in the politically radical Unitarian journal *The Monthly Repository*, however, lumps together the American accounts of Trollope and Hall, and, while excoriating both, singles out Trollope for letting her political conservatism taint her observations:

> the descriptions of the United States have been those of persons either of small intellect, and incapable, with their best efforts, of judging between that which is essential and that which is accidental, as instance Basil Hall; or, worse, those whose prejudices make their principles, and whose long-formed habits of subserviency make them fancy servility refinement, and its absence coarseness.[8]

If Hall could not discern the difference between natural and accidental causes, Trollope's prejudices, in tune with "the rancour of her dislike to republicanism", proved worse still. The 24 March 1832 review in *The Athenaeum* cites the fact that "She is an Englishwoman, and insists on weighing everything American in an English balance" as the source of Trollope's prejudice, a sentiment amplified the same day by a critic in *The Literary Gazette* who remarks that "Our own standard of habit and enjoyment is a false criterion for that of others."[9] Moreover, as *The Athenaeum's* critic and others observe, Trollope condemns American manners that had ready analogues in English society, thus appearing to be ignorant of English standards in the bargain. The *Tait's Edinburgh Magazine* critic goes further, attacking Trollope for making false statements: "Mrs. Trollope goes further [than Hall]; for, with double his quantity of spleen, she is by no means particular about the accuracy of her statements." The reviewer chides Trollope for telling "fibs"; "just as bad", she retails "unaccredited stories", and "Scarcely one of her anecdotes is given as the result of her own observation."[10]

The *Literary Gazette* review not only finds Trollope "full of prejudices", but questions the ability of *any* woman to credibly interpret what she observes. "A woman always judges by her feelings, and these feelings are often interested or disgusted by slight causes – hence, impartiality is the rarest of female merits."[11] Women's sex proves an almost insurmountable natural hindrance to their appreciation of national differences. Combined with her animus toward American republicanism, Trollope's appraisal of American habits suffers from "unfair bias".[12]

The volumes were also reviewed in *The Penny Magazine*, one of showpieces of the Society for Diffusion of Useful Knowledge (SDUK), founded in 1829 by Henry Brougham and other Whig political reformers, and published by Charles Knight in order to bring inexpensive and informative reading material to all classes of society. The piece implies that American manners should be seen through the lens of stadial history. Thus, Trollope applies a faulty methodology for making and interpreting observations:

> she shows throughout her work the ... natural error of judging of every thing by a fixed English standard, from which all her liberalism never

relieved her for a moment. Than this nothing can be less philosophical or just. Every state of society must have its peculiarities, its advantages and disadvantages (if, as regards America, we can designate domestic trifles by so important a word) attached to it, and inseparable from it ... The things after which Mrs. Trollope's heart yearned were dependent on the civilization of centuries, on the existence of a body wealthy and idle enough to be elegant in all things.[13]

The critic turns from Trollope's mistake in employing a one-size-fits-all technique to consider broader "philosophical", moral, and ethical flaws in her work. Her observations center, for instance, on American domestic trifles, objects too insignificant for a traveler to devote to "*four years*" of observation. Further, even if Trollope's volumes entertained and informed, they did not constitute "wholesome amusement or useful instruction", which the SDUK required in order to bring a work to the attention of its reading public, and mold them into better citizens. Yet *Domestic Manners* proved too popular for the leaders of the SDUK to overlook. If travelers were to observe manners, however, they should make allowance for national idiosyncrasies; the review essay is titled "National Peculiarities". To the reviewer the current state of manners in America simply reflected a particular instance in the history of the "*state of society*".[14] The reviewer suggests that, in contemporary American commercial civilization, Americans were too preoccupied with useful work to adopt manners as nice as those of the wealthy and idle English.

Trollope readily confesses the partial nature of her observations, advising readers that the "United States form a continent of almost distinct nations, and I must now, and always, be understood to speak only of that portion of them that I have seen" (*Domestic Manners*, I, p. 20). Within this constraint, she insists that she has recorded conversations as closely as possible to verbatim, writing that, "whenever I give conversations they were not made *à loisir*, but were written down immediately after they occurred, with all the verbal fidelity my memory permitted" (*Domestic Manners*, I, p. 75). J.G. Lockhart, the reviewer in *Fraser's Magazine*, seizes on Trollope's translation errors and predicts, correctly, that Americans would recoil at her barbs: "A mistake in an obscure locality will be set down as proof undeniable of ignorance of the country – a mispelt name adduced as a sure mark of the want of the powers of observation."[15] Indeed, her faulty rendering of American dialects led the essayist in *The North American Review* to conclude that "Mrs. Trollope's pure and veracious page has been sadly interpolated."[16] Flint was more direct; while he marveled at her gift for mimicry in conversation, "The slang language which she puts into the mouth of her servants, and the common people has not even the remotest smack of west country dialect. It is entirely woven, warp and woof, from Cockney and Yorkshire."[17] In sum, Americans reacted with fierce, near-universal condemnation, as captured by the scathing "Editor's Preface" to the fourth edition, reprinted in New

York, which the editor frames as "A Brief Inquiry into the Real Name and Character of the Author of this Book".[18] Convinced of "the impossibility of the book being the production of an English lady", the editor concludes that *Domestic Manners* had in fact been written by Hall, or, as the editor dubs him, "Captain All".[19]

Trollope's assertion about the limits to what women can observe, represent, and, implicitly, participate in produced dissonance, reflected in the reactions of a number of essayists who sought to take the measure of *Domestic Manners* as a philosophical statement on the Americans. *The Literary Gazette* anoints her "the philosophical lady".[20] The critic in *Blackwood's Edinburgh Magazine*, on the other hand, maintains "the wide field they [the United States] present for philosophical observation has hitherto yielded no harvest" and concludes that Trollope "is not a philosopher in petticoats".[21] Again, European philosophical travel had from its inception in the seventeenth century encouraged less prejudiced, more detached, systematic observation and analysis, self-reflection, and a cosmopolitan attitude toward difference on the part of travelers. If Trollope reveals what it means to be an Englishwoman of a certain class and political persuasion, most contemporary critics, on both sides of the Atlantic, judge her attempt to philosophically observe and describe the heretofore unknown Americans an abject failure.

Harriet Martineau's Methodologies of Observation; or, How to Observe Morals and Manners

Trollope read Hall's work in July 1830, and spends an entire chapter of *Domestic Manners* considering its reception in America. She was glad she had waited to read the volumes, believing that her curiosity about "the contents of a work so violently anathematised" helped her pursue more interesting inquiries in her conversations with Americans. She expresses approval of Hall's methods, especially his reliance on interviews with notables: he "saw the country to the greatest possible advantage" with "letters of introduction to the most distinguished individuals". In contrast to her observations, "He saw the country in full dress, and had little or no opportunity of judging it unhouselled, unanointed, unannealed, with all its imperfections on its head, as I and my family too often had" (*Domestic Manners*, II, p. 190). Trollope leaves it to readers to decide whether she or Hall presents a more accurate depiction of Americans; she invites those English sympathetic to democracy, "conscientious, but mistaken reasoners", to travel to America to "pass a few years" in order to observe the republic for themselves, and "to trace effects to their causes" (*Domestic Manners*, II, p. 192).

Martineau left England to travel to America on 9 August 1834, to do just that. She published two major works on her American travels, *Society in America* (1837) and *Retrospect of Western Travel* (1838b), each originally published in three volumes. Readers on either side of the north Atlantic eagerly awaited both: she was the international best-selling author of *Illustrations of Political Economy* (1832–4), fictions designed to instruct readers in principles of British political economy. Martineau claims, retrospectively in *Autobiography*, that she did not travel to America with any intention of writing a book about her experiences. She did so, she recalls, in order to keep her observations unbiased, freeing her from potential charges of obligation or interest. In her words, "I am sure that no traveller seeing things through author spectacles, can see them as they are: and it was not till I looked over my journal on my return that I decided to write '*Society in America*.'"[22]

Martineau composed *Illustrations* to harness details of everyday life to principles of political economy. She set loose characters all over the world, from Manchester to Ireland, from South Africa to Australia, wherever she believed the principles she wished to impart best fit real life. A "Summary of Principles illustrated in this Volume" appears after the conclusion of each tale to reinforce the political economy lessons and help readers to, in Trollope's words, "trace effects to their causes". Martineau presumes that she could accurately depict different times and places, and credibly construct fictional characters in these locations as representative types who embodied or failed to embody the principles.[23] She wrote the tales with the assistance of government documents, travel literature, and material forwarded to her by sympathetic correspondents. The tales in *Illustrations* thus evoked reactions similar to those by which contemporaries judged travel accounts: readers focused on both their entertainment and educational value.

When some carped that her characters lacked verisimilitude and her scenarios credibility, they did so not only as a means to critique Martineau's qualities as a writer of fictions, but to also question the tales' underlying political economic principles and her abilities as an observer of (the operation of those principles in) real life. Martineau, for instance, portrays the widow Katie and Ella, the main characters of two of her Malthusian tales, the Garveloch stories, as credible observers and rational reasoners. When, in "Weal and Woe in Garveloch" (1832), Martineau depicts the two women pondering whether Katie should marry Ella's brother Ronald, in light of the collapse of their (fictional) Scottish island's fishery, she writes:

> Ella and Katie, sensible and unprejudiced, and rendered quick sighted by anxiety for their children, were peculiarly qualified for seeing the truth when fairly placed before them. Their interests in Ronald, as well as in their own offspring, gave them a view of both sides of the [population] question.[24]

The geologist and political economist George Poulett Scrope bristled at Martineau's characterization of the two women. In *The Quarterly Review*, he strenuously objected, in terms a present-day standpoint epistemology theorist would recognize, that the fishing-village heroines were not unprejudiced observers, and were hardly fit to converse on political economy: "the notion of such dialogues, on such subjects, being held under such circumstances – between a couple of Highland queans, on the shores of the Hebrides, and ... in the Erse dialect, was never surpassed in the dreams of Laputa".[25] Ignore, if you can, the irony of using Swift's island in the sky to pan the realism of another fictional island. What piques Scrope are questions that had aroused the interest of European travelers and scientists for centuries: how could individuals, whether fictional or real, observe without prejudice, and then reason about what they observed?

Martineau wrote *How to Observe. Morals and Manners* (1838a) on her voyage to America in order to systematically address these questions.[26] H. Bellenden Ker and Knight commissioned Martineau for the work; in 1833, Knight, along with Brougham, had called on Martineau to write *Poor Laws and Paupers Illustrated* (1833–4), four fictional tales which depict observations reported by the Commissioners of Inquiry for the Poor Law Commission on the contemporary operation of parish relief in England. Martineau set each story in one of four different types of locales, in accordance with the classification system set out by the field investigators for the commission, covering topics following the mode of inquiry used by the commissioners: town, rural community, mining district, and fishing village.[27] Martineau later claimed that "Lord Brougham sent me all the evidence as it was delivered in by the Commissioners of Inquiry into the operation of the Poor-laws."[28]

Knight and Brougham, the Lord Chancellor and the bill's chief sponsor in the House of Lords, wished to capitalize on Martineau's popularity, and hoped the series would bolster support for the proposed New Poor Law; one number, "The Hamlets", spelled out the proposed reform, which would shift control of relief from local authorities to a new, national Poor Law Commission. Knight, appointed "publisher by Authority" for the Poor Law Commission in 1834, oversaw publication of a popular summary of the Commission's report; Martineau's series, however, proved a financial disaster. Moreover, her credibility as a disinterested, unprejudiced observer came under severe attack, especially, but hardly exclusively, in the radical press.[29] Martineau later lamented that, although she did "not repent doing those tales, because I hope and believe they were useful at a special crisis", her connection with the SDUK, Brougham, the Whig government, and the New Poor Law produced "so much mere detriment to my usefulness and my influence".[30]

Ker begins the "Advertisement" from the first, and what turned out to be the only other work completed for the subsequent SDUK series on observation, Henry Thomas De la Beche's *How to Observe. Geology* (1835), by quoting Sir John Herschel's "Discourse on the study of Natural Philosophy" on the requisites of "a perfect observer in any science". This ideal being, a male subject, needs not only extensive familiarity with the science related to the facts observed but also with "every branch of knowledge which may enable him to appreciate the effects of extraneous and disturbing causes". But Ker also welcomes the contributions of any man who is simply "well-informed". He too can add to "the general stock of knowledge" if properly trained, "if he will only observe regularly and methodically some particular class of facts, which may most excite his attention, or which his situation may best enable him to study with effect".[31] Ker recognizes a divide between expert observation and interpretation and the observation done by nonexperts. Science could still profit, however, from the work of the latter.

Ker promoted future works in the project as a "a series of hints for travellers and students, calling their attention to the points necessary for inquiry or observation in the different branches of Geology, Natural History, Agriculture, the Fine Arts, General Statistics, and Social Manners"; he cites Charles Babbage's instructions in *On the Economy of Machinery and Manufactures* (1832), published by Knight, as one of the few works to explore the issues of observation the series was meant to address.[32] Babbage, best known as a natural philosopher, mathematician, and mechanical engineer, had traveled throughout England for a decade prior to publishing his work, visiting factories to look into questions of political economy. He sought to determine how the divisions of physical and mental labors operated in specific manufacturing processes, all to facilitate the building of his "Calculating-Engine".[33] Babbage foregoes examining "all the difficult questions of *political economy* which are intimately connected with such inquiries", others having already done so (*Economy*, pp. iv, v, emphases in original). Babbage, instead, signals his intention to discuss political economy by following the example of previous traveler writers, with an eye to both entertain and inform, successively, different reading populations:

> In touching on the more abstract principles of political economy, after shortly stating the reasons on which they are founded, I have endeavoured to support them by facts and anecdotes; so that whilst young persons might be amused and instructed by the illustrations, those of more advanced judgment may find subject for meditation in the general conclusions to which they point.
>
> (*Economy*, p. vi)

Likewise, Babbage employs language familiar to readers of travel accounts when he vouches for the credibility of his observations. He admits that he "was anxious to support the principles which I have advocated by the observations of others". Appreciative of the testimony and evidence presented by committees of the House of Commons in reports on manufacturing and commerce, he "derived some additional confidence from the support they have afforded to my views" (*Economy*, pp. vi–vii).

Babbage spends a chapter, albeit a scant five pages, on his recommended methodology of observation and representation for factory visits. While he urges the immediate transcription of information, "*especially when numbers are concerned*", he admits that it is not always possible or advisable to do so; it represents "a great interruption to the examination of machinery" (*Economy*, p. 93, emphases in original). He suggests the method he himself followed: the visitor should prepare and print a list of general inquiries beforehand, including queries on the history of the factory, the ownership and control of tools, capital and work processes, as well as details on each step of manufacturing, with blanks to be filled in during the visit. Babbage includes a skeleton list as an illustration. His method includes repetitive motion, in the form of repeated travel to the same sites, as well as ongoing refinement of the work process; after the initial visit, the traveler can draw up more questions for subsequent revisits, and tailor these questions to the manufacturing methods specific to each factory (*Economy*, pp. 93–6). Babbage's travels resemble refinements to a manufacturing process, in this case work undertaken to produce credible facts and evidence.

The questions in Babbage's list are weighted heavily toward the collection of statistics. He cautions against the risk, in counting the number of operations performed per time period, that the observed, workmen, may speed up their rate of work if they know they are under observation. As correctives, one can, if possible: observe while unobserved; obtain daily output data and average these over the number of workers; and, count the number of motions of machinery per minute (*Economy*, pp. 96–7). Babbage also acknowledges, again, that ascertaining the credibility of observations is a social process, urging travelers to consult the work of others, if available, to have some idea of the range of results to expect: "advantage should always be taken of these verifications, in order to confirm the accuracy of the statements; or, in case they are discordant, to correct the apparent anomalies." Singularities represent errors to be fixed, not phenomena to be explained. Babbage explains that in some cases we may need to choose a suitable agent or multiple agents of sound judgment to gather information on our behalf; these choices help "us to determine the value of our own judgment". Babbage's factory visitors more closely approach the shape of ideal observers when they become adept at making statistical estimates; "forming an estimate of the magnitude or frequency of any object immediately previous to our applying to it measure or number, tends materially to fix our attention and to improve our judgment" (*Economy*, p. 97).

For Babbage, to see the principles of political economy in operation in manufacturing processes involves observing the principles of domestic economy. Competition will drive manufacturers to minimize costs, that is, "to attend to the principles of the domestic economy of manufactures". Thus, "*in order to succeed in a manufacture, it is necessary not merely to possess good machinery, but that the domestic economy of the factory should be most carefully regulated*" (*Economy*, pp. 99, 295, emphases in original). What is good for the individual factory is good for the nation as a whole; English success in international trade depends in no small degree "on the admirable arrangements of the domestic economy of our factories" (*Economy*, p. 302).

What Babbage means by domestic economy in manufactures depends on the scale of the operation. He approvingly reproduces an extract of testimony from an 1806 Report of the Committee of the House of Commons on the Woollen Trade on differences between large and small establishments. Where large establishments can afford the expense of costly investments, creating new products or experimenting with new means of production, smaller manufacturers cannot. There are in fact two systems of domestic economy at work in factories, dictated by the amount of capital owners and managers command, and, correspondingly, two different types of ideal behavior by owners and managers. A small-scale capitalist acts as an economist, one who "regulated" his factory in identical fashion to the self-regulation required to run a household; "diligence, economy, and prudence, are the requisites of his character, not invention, taste, and enterprise". Owners and managers of larger establishments, by way of contrast, can indulge in speculation and risk large losses in the pursuit of large profits through the development of innovative products and production processes. This definition purges capitalists and speculation of the taint of moral disapprobation, their negative association with rash and imprudent behavior. Larger manufacturers often set the standards in an industry; further, they purchase many intermediate goods used in production from smaller domestic producers. Thus, the two domestic systems in manufacturing, and the two types of economic man complement rather than compete with one another; they "are mutual aids to each other; each supplying the other's defects, and promoting the other's prosperity" (*Economy*, pp. 185–6).

Despite Babbage's nod to the vital role of domestic economy in manufacturing, to go by the pronouns employed by la Beche in *Geology*, the business of scientific observation constitutes a strictly male domain, with no "she" or "her" in sight. In Ker's words, however, individuals of indeterminate sex abound in geology, content, "to exercise the useful and highly entertaining task of collecting specimens" wherever they go. Furthermore, the travel writer's imperative to both inform and entertain, which hovers over the project he and Knight contemplate, is gendered. Ker finds this requirement exemplified in the same Barbauld story cited by Maria Graham in her reminisces about Chile: "The advantages and pleasures to be derived from accurate observation have indeed been often pointed out; and nowhere have they been better enforced than in the admirable tale '*Eyes and no Eyes*.'" Women can at least illustrate the discipline of observation and its benefits. Ker ventures, though, that perhaps "the best mode of exciting the love of observation is, by teaching 'How to Observe'", rather than through reading fiction.[34]

Ker, in another concession to amateur observers,

> determined somewhat to extend the plan, and to separate the great divisions of the field of observation, so that those whose tastes led them to

one particular branch of inquiry might not be encumbered with other parts in which they do not feel an equal interest.[35]

Taste should guide your choice of what to observe, a familiar suggestion. The acquisition of observational skills can not only convert an otherwise feckless individual into someone who can contribute something of value, it will also awaken and sharpen the amateur observer's taste: "the listless idler may be changed into an inquiring and useful observer, and may acquire the power of converting a dull and dreary road into a district teeming with interest and pleasure".[36]

Martineau opens her *How to Observe* by revisiting verities about travel accounts, these concerning the dubious credibility of travelers' observations. Thus, travelers, who Martineau uniformly refers to as men in *How to Observe*, can have little confidence drawing conclusions about morals and manners from conversations with individuals. Martineau asserts that these observations "reveal more of the mind of the observer than the observed". Even the best equipped and well-meaning traveler comes away with a mere sample, without knowing whether it is representative. The problems of observational excess and interpretational defect loom, because "the wearied mind soon finds itself overwhelmed by the multitude of unconnected or contradictory particulars, and lies passive to be run over by the crowd" (*How to Observe*, pp. 4, 5).

Martineau's cautions extend, unsurprisingly, to travel writing as a genre. She approvingly quotes a correspondent who despairs that "No books are to be so little trusted as travels." Yet, the writer continues, "Still I think travels useful. Different accounts give means of approximation to truth; and by-and-by what is fixed and essential in a people will be brought out" (*How to Observe*, p. 9). Nor do the challenges to the ability of travelers to avoid too hasty generalizations mean the individual traveler cannot contribute facts to support an impartial judgment of another society. Martineau draws an analogy between physics (and, perhaps unwittingly, the contemporary interest in applying the law of large numbers to social phenomena) and the moral sciences, calling for a "large number of observers" to accumulate enough facts so that, in time, a "cautious philosopher might draw conclusions". Thus, "no fact is without its use." Her text will serve as a guide for the traveler so that, quoting the afore-mentioned writer again, "he can infallibly aid in supplying means of securing an approximation to truth, and of bringing out 'what is fixed and essential in a people'" (*How to Observe*, pp. 9, 10). To that end, Martineau lays out methods to help travelers observe in three parts: philosophical, moral, and mechanical – "Requisites for Observation" to help prepare "the mind of the observer"; "What to Observe"; and "Mechanical Methods" for observation (*How to Observe*, p. 11).

Martineau remonstrates, in "Philosophical Requisites", how travelers could easily misconstrue facts absent fixed and essential principles, like political economy combined with stadial history, with which to interpret them. In her words, "principles ... may serve as a rallying point for his observations" (*How to Observe*, pp. 14–5). She demonstrates her point by contrasting travelers' erroneous accounts of the causes of Iberian poverty with Smith's remarks in *Wealth of Nations* on the perverse effects of New World gold and silver on the manufactures and agriculture of Spain and Portugal (*How to Observe*, pp. 28–30). Smith thus helps Martineau draw the distinction between a philosophical observer and an unphilosophical observer, even if the former is an armchair traveler and the latter an actual traveler.

Martineau continues her conjectures on Spain to show how travelers could hit upon the truth in their observations. She cites *Travels in the South of Spain* (1811), where William Jacob compares the civility, hospitality, and moral "sobriety" of the peasants he met favorably to the "the state of contempt and degradation" of the higher orders. Jacob blames the dissolution of the higher orders on "their wretched education, and their early habits of indolence and dissipation".[37] The passage Martineau quotes includes an assertion by Jacob that he proffers a credible account, "the result of the observations I have made, in which every accurate observer among our countrymen has concurred with me". Martineau concludes her textual foray into Spain by gesturing again to Smith's political economy as the proper epistemology to analyze and understand Spanish behavior.

> All this might be foreseen to be unavoidable in a country where the means of living are passively derived from abroad, and where the honour and rewards of successful industry are confined to a class of the community. The mines should bear the blame of the prevalent faults of the saucy beggars and beggarly grandees of Spain.
>
> (*How to Observe*, p. 30)

Martineau proceeds to imagine a representative feudal society which exemplifies how a social system, and in particular the "stage of society", determines the types and prevalence of virtues and vices on view in its different communities. Faced with similar questions about fundamental or even trivial aspects of human life, different societies find different ways to solve them. As a reminder to travelers to not too harshly view behaviors they observe in different nations as they move to render a "judgement of nations", Martineau insists that "the vices which exist under them will be, however mourned, leniently judged" (*How to Observe*, pp. 21, 31). These include, presumably, the Spanish peasants "laxity in matrimonial fidelity", which Jacob considers a "stain upon their character".[38]

Thus, Martineau informs readers that "Unless a traveller interprets by his sympathies what he sees, he cannot but misunderstand the greater part of that which comes under his observation" (*How to Observe*, p. 43). Sympathy not only constitutes the principal moral requisite for observation by a traveler in *How to Observe*, it drives progress, defined as ever greater societal happiness. Martineau claims that a traveler lacking the proper philosophical requisites will fail to improve both the "chance of self-advancement and mutual understanding". In turn, Martineau considers these objectives subordinate to "the relative amount of human happiness. Every element of social life derives its importance from this great consideration ... Here then is the wise traveller's aim, to be kept in view to the exclusion of prejudice, both philosophical and national" (*How to Observe*, p. 13).

Consequently, the traveler

> is to prepare himself to bring whatever he may observe to the test of some high and broad principle, and not to that of a low comparative practice. To test one people by another, is to argue within a very small segment of a circle; and the observer can only pass backwards and forwards at an equal distance from the point of truth. To test the morals and manners of a nation by a reference to the essentials of human happiness, is to strike at once to the centre, and to see things as they are.
> (*How to Observe*, p. 14)

In the chapter "Progress", Martineau describes how a traveler can divine the current state of a society; significantly, she employs just the shell of stadial histories, instructing readers to tailor observations to measure moral rather than economic progress. Justice and charity, directed to their furthest possible extent by sympathy, signify progress, and wisdom and happiness, not the delivery of ever greater material abundance, represent its endpoints. Further, Martineau claims that "All agree that if the whole race could live as brethren, society would be in the most advanced state that can be conceived of" (*How to Observe*, p. 206). What pertains to any individual nation in its peoples' efforts to recognize the equality of (and assist and raise the status of) women, the poor, the enslaved, the blind, deaf and dumb, pertains to the human race as a whole: "the more any society becomes like a band of brothers, the more powerful must be the sympathy which it will have to offer to other such bands" (*How to Observe*, p. 207).

Martineau thus expands the reach of Smith's concept of sympathy, where the impartial spectator identifies with the other and feels approval or disapproval based on the other's perspective.[39] Martineau observes that people do feel sympathy toward those they do not know, beyond the communities of gentleman in England and Great Britain: "Classes, crowds, nations of sufferers are aided and protected by strangers, powerful and at ease, who never saw an individual of the suffering thousands, and who have none but a spiritual interest in their welfare" (*How to Observe*, p. 208). Absent this principle a traveler will fail to observe signs of progress in a society.

> The traveller must be strangely careless who, in observing upon the morals of a people, omits to mark the manifestations of this principle; – to

learn what is its present strength, and what the promise of its growth. By fixing his observation on this he may learn, and no otherwise can he learn, whether the country he studies is advancing in wisdom and happiness, or whether it is stationary, or whether it is going back.

(*How to Observe*, pp. 208–9)

She devotes the final paragraph of *How to Observe* to explain that travelers will also fail to recognize and seize truth if they lack sympathy, no matter how well versed in mechanical methods and intellectual achievements.

Mechanical methods are nothing but in proportion to the power which uses them; as the intellectual accomplishments of the traveller avail him little, and may even bring him back less wise than he went out, a wanderer from truth, as well as from home, unless he sees by a light from his heart shining through the eyes of his mind. He may see, and hear, and record, and infer, and conclude for ever; and he will still not understand if his heart be idle, if he have not sympathy. Sympathy by itself may do much: with fit intellectual and mechanical aids, it cannot but make the traveller a wise man. His journey may be but for a brief year, or even month; but if, by his own sympathy, he grasps and brings home to himself the life of a fresh portion of his race, he gains a wisdom for which he will be the better for ever.

(*How to Observe*, p. 238)

As is clear from the epigraph to this chapter, Martineau, in contrast to Ker and Herschel, maintains that no one can obtain the attributes of the ideal observer, even if well-equipped with philosophical requisites, and even if they were to achieve the cosmopolitanism status of "citizen of the world" (*How to Observe*, pp. 52–7). Few contemporaries may have actually "observed" *How to Observe*. It merited only a brief mention in *The London and Westminster Review* in an essay on what songs tell us about a people, with a parenthetical aside that it was "a book that everybody who wishes to observe society well should read, as it contains many excellent remarks, though mixed with some crudities".[40] It elicited a savage assessment in *The Quarterly Review* by John Wilson Croker. Croker expresses little faith in the purpose of Ker's series, in Martineau's book in particular, in her skills as an observer, or her character. He opines that Martineau lacked the experience for giving advice to travelers, noting that she had not "been on the continent of Europe, nor indeed in any country of which English is not the vernacular language".[41]

Where Martineau asserts that "The observer must have sympathy", Croker sarcastically applauds the fact that "This circumstance ... must produce a fortunate sympathy between the teacher and the pupil, however ignorant and inexperienced the latter may be", and mocks Martineau's description of a philosophical traveler.[42] Croker truncates his "contemptuous notice", stopping at the point at which Martineau takes up the question of how to observe different religious practices. He calls her classification of religions into licentious, ascetic, and moderate practices not just "sheer nonsense", but "disgusting to all good sense and right feeling". He vents that "Miss Martineau's scrapbook" represents "the very foolishest and most unfeminine farrago we have ever met of apocryphal anecdotes, promiscuous facts, and jumbled ideas – picked at random (or at least which might be so) out of the Penny Magazine and such like depositories". He perceives only "mischievous" meaning in her work, sneers that such a system consists of "stupid and impudent impostures", and warns that *How to Observe* may be "the precursor of a course of *Martineau morality*".[43]

Julian Jackson, on the other hand, commends *How to Observe* in his own methodological work, *What to Observe; or, The Traveller's Remembrancer* (1841), an updated and translated version of his *Guide du Voyageur*, first published in 1822. Jackson was, variously, secretary, editor, and librarian to the Royal Geographical Society, and he compiled *What to Observe* in order to improve the methods travelers used to gather facts, including recommendations on the use of scientific instruments and other technologies. Over the course of roughly six hundred pages, including skeleton tables appended to the end of the document, Jackson suggests precepts for observing subjects literally ranging from A to Z, from agriculture to zoology, focusing on geography in particular.[44]

Jackson directs readers' attention in "Preface" to his hope that his work piques readers' interest. Entertaining readers remains secondary, however, to his aim of helping travelers produce useful knowledge.

> In the execution of our task we have not confined ourselves to a mere list of questions, but have endeavoured to excite a desire for useful knowledge awakening curiosity. The traveller, it is hoped, will, from a perusal of the present work see what an immense field of physical and moral research lies open to his investigation, and be encouraged to exertion by the assurance that, without being what is termed a philosopher, he may not only do much to enlarge the sphere of his own ideas, but acquire the means of communicating to others a great mass of valuable or interesting information.[45]

Jackson designed *What to Observe* not to shape the reader into a philosophical traveler, but "for general use". He hopes it will assist any traveler produce "true knowledge" about not just what to observe, but "*how* and what to observe".[46] With respect to Martineau, Jackson lists the difficulties a traveler will likely encounter when observing the morals and manners of a nation's inhabitants. Dealing with excess, parsing the innumerable "shades of difference" across societies, represents the chief obstacle to analyzing said observations. Jackson, showing his geographer's colors, ascribes these differences in part to the "indestructible influence of locality", even when comparing nations "equally civilized", such as Great Britain and France. The traveler should persevere with observations of morals and manners precisely to observe these differences: "Every nation then, having its peculiarities of morals and manners, more or less discernible, more or less natural or adventitious, it should be the business of the traveller to discover and describe them to the best of his ability."[47] The "prejudice which too often distorts truth, and the proneness to generalize from insulated facts" also hamper such a task; excess of a different sort, where "all the observations [of public and private life] made must be as numerous and as diversified as possible" makes the work more difficult still. Note that prejudice, in and of itself may not necessarily distorts facts or the truth. Yet Jackson writes that he need not take up the subject of "such paramount importance" because Martineau, "an author of acknowledged ability ... who, in her book on 'Morals and Manners,' gives the fullest instructions for the way in which these should be observed".[48]

How to Observe: Society in America

Martineau landed in New York City on 19 September 1834. She spent the next twenty-three months crisscrossing the United States.[49] She met with Americans obscure and prominent, including President Jackson and the Madisons, and visited prisons, farms, factories, and plantations, before sailing back to England on 1 August 1836. Louisa Jeffrey accompanied Martineau for much of the trip; Martineau recalls that Jeffrey,

> a lady of very superior qualifications, who was eager to travel, but not rich enough to indulge her desire, offered to go with me, as companion and helper, if I would bear her expenses. She paid her own voyages, and I the rest.

Jeffrey was not just a companion; she was a second observer for the American volumes. Martineau remembers Jeffrey glowingly, as "supremely rational", "conscientious", "able", and "amiable", and admits that "I should have made hourly mistakes but for her. She seemed to make none, – so observant, vigilant and retentive were her faculties."[50] The two women working in tandem approached more closely the ideals of a single perfect observer, albeit one embodied, textually, almost solely as Martineau; Jeffrey rarely appears in either *Society* or in *Retrospect*, and only pops up in lengthier passages years later in *Autobiography*. These omissions effectively suppress her role as translator in *Society* and *Retrospect*, and leave readers with a partial picture of Martineau's methodology of observation.[51]

Martineau enlisted Jeffrey to help collect institutional data featured in the third volume of *Society*. In addition, Jeffrey helped fill in gaps in Martineau's observations resulting from the author's disabilities. Present-day commentators argue that Martineau trims her observational methodology to take into account limitations placed on her by her significant hearing loss, which began when she was twelve.[52] Martineau did use her ear trumpet, a technological innovation first commercially produced around 1800, in making observations. But the device, while a valuable asset for intimate conversations in crowds, was less so in group discussions or group interviews. Jeffrey was able to report on these latter and more; in Martineau's words, she was "for ever on the watch to supply my want of ears, – and, I may add, my defects of memory".[53]

Martineau's argument on how the deaf are to conduct themselves, which she lays out in her 1834 "Letter to the Deaf", offers additional insights on how she views observation. The deaf, first and foremost, should seek out society; how they should behave in society "require[s] the most careful fixing of principles, and framing of methods".[54] By following her principles and methods, the deaf can turn a disability into an observational asset. Specifically, Martineau holds that for the deaf the capacity to indulge, at length, in the visual observation of people and things, "the sunset lights and shadows on the lawn to be watched, and the never-ceasing play of human countenances, [constitutes] our grand resource when we have once gained ease enough to enjoy them at leisure". Thus, "the very apparatus of the table, and the various dexterities of the servants, are matters worth observing when we [the deaf] have nothing else to do".[55] The deaf "*have* some accomplishments" in observation, and have a superior ability, because of their disability, to glimpse some truths about society:

> We are good physiognomists – good perceivers in every way, and have (if we are not idle) rather the advantage over others in the power of abstract reasoning. This union of two kinds of power, which in common cases are often cultivated at the expense of each other, puts a considerable amount of accurate knowledge within easier reach of us than of most other people.[56]

The deaf should seize the opportunities these capacities represent. "We must set ourselves to gather knowledge from whatever we see and touch, and to digest it into wisdom during the extra time which is our privilege." Those who observe and reflect well will inch ever closer to an ideal: "if we are acute and quick of observation, ... and disposed for thought, nothing is likely to prevent our going on to be wiser continually".[57] Martineau's other sensory losses, impaired taste and smell, helped contribute to her self-fashioning as a keener observer, more prone to self-reflection than if she had the full range of sensory apparatus to draw on, and more aware of the limitations of the spoken word and conversation as evidence.[58]

Martineau returns to questions about observations and evidence in the "Introduction" to *Society*. She acknowledges the checkered reputation of travel observations in citing an 1827 *Edinburgh Review* essay, "State of German Literature", published anonymously by her friend, Thomas Carlyle.

Carlyle, in a passage not quoted by Martineau, points to the obstacles foreign observers face when attempting to divine the character of societies, like the United States, that lack a well-known literature.

> A country which has no national literature, or a literature too insignificant to force its way abroad, must always be, to its neighbours, at least in every important spiritual respect, an unknown and misestimated country. Its towns may figure on our maps; its revenues, population, manufactures, political connexions, may be recorded in statistical books: but the character of the people has no symbol and no voice; we cannot know them by speech and discourse, but only by mere sight and outward observation of their manners and procedure.[59]

But to "seize a character, even that of one man, in its life and secret mechanism, requires a philosopher; to delineate it with truth and impressiveness, is work for a poet". This explains why travelers such as "a speculative half-pay captain" (perhaps a reference to Hall) fall back on preconceived notions. Prejudice bedevils even the truthful observer. Martineau quotes Carlyle:

> And so, with a few flowing strokes, [the writer] completes a picture, which, though it may not resemble any possible object, his countrymen are to take for a national portrait. Nor is the fraud so readily detected; for the character of a people has such a complexity of aspect, that even the honest observer knows not always, not perhaps after long inspection, what to determine regarding it.[60]
>
> (*Society*, I, pp. v–vi)

Travelers would enlist facts in the service of "*any* image" or narrative about an alien society in order to avoid interpretational excess (*Society*, I, pp. v–vi, emphasis in original).[61] Carlyle finds inadequate the very records that Martineau, in *How to Observe*, designates as more credible than discourse. In the chapter "What to Observe", Martineau concludes that

> To arrive at the facts of the condition of a people through the discourse of individuals, is a hopeless enterprise. The plain truth is – it is beginning at the wrong end. The grand secret of wise inquiry into Morals and Manners is to begin with the study of THINGS, using the DISCOURSE OF PERSONS as a commentary upon them. Though the facts sought by travellers relate to Persons, they may most readily be learned from Things. The eloquence of Institutions and Records, in which the action of the nation is embodied and perpetuated, is more comprehensive and more faithful than that of any variety of individual voices. The voice of a whole people goes up in the silent workings of an institution; the condition of the masses is reflected from the surface of a record.
>
> (*How to Observe*, 63–4, capitalization in original)

Martineau's "study of THINGS" should not be confused with present-day thing theory, which "is not a theory about the cultural significance of objects".[62] On the contrary, Martineau claims the representativeness of institutions and records; these things embody national character, and speak more eloquently than persons. Yet Martineau agrees with Carlyle; national literature does represent a thing. She writes in *How to Observe*: "It is clear that we cannot know the mind of a nation, any more than of an individual, by merely looking at it, without hearing any speech. National literature is national speech" (*How to Observe*, p. 138). Jackson cites this as the last word in his chapter "Literature"; curiously, for a tome devoted to educating travelers about methods to garner more accurate observations, Jackson both misquotes it as "national literature is national speech, and that without hearing this speech, we cannot judge of the mind of a nation", and misattributes it to Martineau's "excellent book on 'How to Observe Men and Manners'".[63]

When Martineau endows people with principles of British political economy in *Illustrations* it is difficult at times to discern who embodies what principles, whether characters' principles could change, or even whether they simultaneously embody contradictory principles.[64] In *How to Observe*, Martineau adopts a different epistemological position; it is easier to detect principles in action in institutions and records than in people, hence easier to tease out the workings of causal factors in things than in individuals.

Martineau read what she could about America before her trip, including the volumes of Trollope and Hall. Both had stated that they preferred to travel America without preconceived notions about what they might observe, and had consequently avoided acquainting themselves with literature on America before setting out. Martineau, despite her preparatory reading, admits her unfamiliarity with America, and, consequently claims to lack prejudice, too.

> I went with a mind, I believe, as nearly as possible unprejudiced about America, with a strong disposition to admire democratic institutions, but an entire ignorance how far the people of the United States lived up to, or fell below, their own theory. I had read whatever I could lay hold of that had been written about them; but was unable to satisfy myself that, after all, I understood anything whatever of their condition. As to knowledge of them, my mind was nearly a blank; as to opinion of their state, I did not carry the germ of one.
>
> (*Society*, I, p. x)

She did not read the first volume Alexis de Tocqueville's *De la démocratie en Amérique*, or *Democracy in America* (1835 and 1840), the most famous travel account of America to appear in this period, and a landmark in what became the discipline of political science, during her travels in America.[65] Tocqueville left for America on 2 April 1831, arrived in Newport, Rhode

Island on 9 May, and traveled through the United States until 20 February 1832. Martineau and Tocqueville took similar routes, though Tocqueville's trip was shorter in duration and included an extended foray into French-speaking Canada. Their travels shared other similarities. Americans eagerly anticipated both visitors, and though this robbed them of the possibility of observing without being observed on some occasions, it opened doors in others. Both had travel companions, in the case of Tocqueville his life-long friend, the magistrate and prison reformer Gustave de Beaumont. And while Martineau had to cope with her hearing loss, Tocqueville's and Beaumont's limited proficiency in English impeded their ability to make observations in America.

Tocqueville and Beaumont also produced *Du système pénitentaire aux États-Unis et de son application en France* (1833), translated into English and published as *On the Penitentiary System in the United States and Its Application in France* (1833), as a result of their journey. Remarks on the poor relief system in Maryland in *On the Penitentiary System* indicate Tocqueville's familiarity with Malthus's *Essay*.[66] The title speaks to the official nature of a trip commissioned by King Louis-Phillipe and sponsored by the French Ministry of Justice; Tocqueville thus employs what Martineau would later dismiss as "author spectacles". Hill notes that the pair's prison observations also suffer from informant bias: Tocqueville and Beaumont neglected to interview any prisoners; Martineau, in contrast, met with wardens, overseers, and prisoners, the last in private and without the presence of guards, in her visits to American penal institutions.[67]

This pattern repeats elsewhere. Tocqueville does report discussions with Americans other than those he met through letters of introduction or who sought out the travelers as news of their visit spread. But he looked in particular for those he considered knowledgeable, the "most enlightened" people, preferably those who spoke French. And, by recording only those conversations that accorded with his preconceived notions on a subject, Tocqueville produces accounts based almost exclusively on the words of "professional, upper-middle, and upper class males".[68] He reports no female informants in *Democracy*; Martineau, as she urges travelers in *How to Observe*, draws on a wide range of interviewees in *Society*. She pledges she will introduce readers to people anonymous and famous, including "slave-holders, colonizationists, and abolitionists; ... farmers, lawyers, merchants, professors, and clergy", slaves and Indians, the president, members of Congress, former president Madison, and former Chief Justice Marshall (*Society*, I, p. xii). In *Retrospect*, however, she acknowledges that her statement against slavery, which she made in a public meeting in Boston on Wednesday, 18 November 1835, hindered her ability to freely observe and interact with Americans as she continued her travels:

> I foresaw that every house in Boston, except those of the abolitionists, would be shut against me; that my relation to the country would be

completely changed, as I should be suddenly transformed from being a guest and an observer to being a missionary or a spy.[69]

Martineau did suffer ostracism, and more as a result of her statement, in her further travels through the northeastern and western states. But she abjured to go into much detail, save that the effects that she had foreseen "came to pass; but only for a time" (*Retrospect*, III, p. 158).

Tocqueville and Beaumont perused a number of works during the Atlantic crossing to prepare for their travels, including the *Cours complet d'économie politique* of Jean-Baptiste Say. Say's work proved fundamental to Tocqueville musings in *Democracy* (1835) on how Americans' desire for money and wealth shaped American politics, political attitudes, and institutions. Tocqueville had begun to study *Cours complet* in earnest in 1828; during the voyage to America he paid particular attention to "the first part of the work, the *considérations générales*, which discussed the purpose and method of political economy". These "influenced the method adopted in *Democracy in America* (1835), serving as a model to understand a republic on a large scale".[70] Further travel, discussions, and correspondence with British political economists such as Nassau Senior and Richard Whately, shaped Tocqueville's changing views on political economy after *Democracy* (1835). In London in 1833, Tocqueville knocked on Senior's door unannounced and introduced himself; the pair struck up a conversation, beginning a friendship that only ended upon the death of Tocqueville in 1859.[71] Senior suggested British journals that would review Tocqueville's work, with the caveats that few reviewers cared to put much thought into what they wrote, and that none would do so anonymously. Tocqueville's work inspired British economists, too. J.S. Mill wrote the first review of *Democracy* (1835) in an English journal, and the effect of *Democracy* is clearly discernible in the sections on America in Mill's *Civilization* (1836); Mill also acknowledges the influence of Tocqueville's ideas on civilization on his own in his autobiography, though Varouxakis cautions against overstating the degree to which Mill drew inspiration from *Democracy*.[72]

Tocqueville grew dissatisfied with Say's work even before 1835. He turned toward Malthus, the population principle, and, more broadly, Christian political economy, the latter especially through his reading in 1834 of the work on pauperism by the French political economist Alban de Villeneuve-Bargemont, *Économie politique chrétienne* (1834).[73] Malthus's views on philanthropy, pauperism, and self-interest colored Tocqueville's *Memoir on Pauperism* (1835), which incorporates observations from his trips to England in 1833 and 1835. Malthus's work helped Tocqueville understand the following paradoxes: as commercial civilization had advanced in Europe, unemployment increased and the lower classes regressed into a new form of barbarism, more prone to poverty, pauperism, and crime; and, as society became increasingly democratic, industrial conditions resulted in more inequality.[74]

Other elements indispensable to Tocqueville's study of government and society post-1835 include moral statistics and Jansenism, and reflect the welter of new social sciences emerging in Europe in the 1820s and 1830s. Tocqueville viewed analyses of natural laws as indivisible from issues of governance; thus, economics and politics could not be divorced from morals and religious considerations.[75] Tocqueville's definitions of the object of his analysis evolves over the course of the two volumes. In 1835 he identified this object, in the title of the third chapter, as the social state, "État Social des Anglo-Américains". He opens the chapter by claiming that

> The social state is ordinarily the result of a fact, sometimes of laws, most often of these two causes together. But once it exists, it can itself be considered the first cause of most of the laws, customs and ideas that regulate the conduct of nations; what it does not produce, it modifies.[76]

By 1840 Tocqueville had modified this object, slightly; in paratext he describes his work as the examination of "un état sociale démocratique", which emphasizes the political nature of the object.[77] Tocqueville drew on lectures by François Guizot, *Histoire générale de la civilisation en Europe* (1828) and *The Histoire de la civilisation en France* (1829 and 1830), in his search for regularities in the American social state. Guizot based his "philosophical history" on the distinction between particular and general facts. Civilization, according to Guizot, "could be understood as a general fact subject to underlying universal historical regularities", yet to understand those constants, one had to discern the particular elements of a society.[78]

Martineau too seeks to unearth general facts. Yet anecdotes shared by Americans she met also help inform her method, which, as she outlines in paratext, consists of project more expansive than political economy. She proposes to compare the "existing state of society in America with the principles on which it is professedly founded; thus testing Institutions, Morals, and Manners by an indisputable, instead of an arbitrary standard" (*Society*, I, p. viii). The American constitution enshrined the promotion of the "general welfare" (*Society*, I, p. 35). In enacting the Tariff of 1833, however, the nation failed to allow free markets in labor, capital, and trade, and thus neglected to adhere to her own "republican principles" and "her faith in the natural laws of social economy" (*Society*, II, p. 240). It is unclear what to make of Martineau's reference to social economy here. She moved toward a more favorable view of Robert Owens's work during her trip, expressing approval of the "co-operative system" system of production she witnessed in both the Shaker and Rappite communities she visited.[79] The lack of clarity lies in the shifting and porous meanings and boundaries of both political economy and social economy. Her contemporaries held a wide range of views on the relationship between political and social economy, leading Gueslin to declare that "social economy means, no more no less, another way to do political economy".[80]

Martineau complains that America had chosen to ignore the lessons of political economy, and had resorted to employing the "false principles" and failed institutions of the old order:

> Her doctrine was, and I fear still is, that she need not study political economy while she is so prosperous as at present: that political economy is for those who are under adversity. If in other cases she allows that prevention is better than cure, avoidance than reparation, why not in this? It may not yet be too late for her to be in the van of all the world in economical as in political philosophy. The old world will still be long in getting above its bad institutions. If America would free her servile class by the time the provisions of the Compromise Bill expire, and start afresh in pure economical freedom, she might yet be the first to show, by her transcendent peace and prosperity, that democratic principles are the true foundation of economical, as well as political, welfare.
> (*Society*, II, p. 241)

A society should pursue welfare as its chief object. Welfare eclipses prosperity and happiness, despite the latter being enshrined in the work of the utilitarians and announced in the American Declaration of Independence. The ends of social sciences exhibit a propensity to multiply that approaches the multiplication of the sciences themselves.

Tariff policy hardly represents the most egregious American deviation from the stated principles of the republic. Martineau introduces "Morals of Slavery", for instance, by adverting to her comparative method:

> This title is not written down in a spirit of mockery; though there appears to be a mockery somewhere, when we contrast slavery with the principles and the rule which are the test of all American institutions: the principles that all men are born free and equal; that rulers derive their just powers from the consent of the governed; and the rule of reciprocal justice. This discrepancy between principles and practice needs no more words. But the institution of slavery exists; and what we have to see is what the morals are of the society which is subject to it.
> (*Society*, II, pp. 312–3)

Martineau admits that she most likely failed to collect a representative sample of American things and words. She implies, nonetheless, that she has strenuously sought to determine whether Americans meet the ideals they set so much store by:

> It is in the highest degree improbable that my scanty gleanings in the wide field of American society should present a precisely fair sample of the whole. I can only explain that I have spared no pains to discover the truth ... and invite correction in all errors of fact.
> (*Society*, I, p. viii)

Martineau immediately launches into to the methodology she will apply to make and understand her observations in America. She only arrives at sustained travel writing of the type "after a light breakfast we proceeded early the next morning by coach to X, a pretty little village nestled in valley Y", in Part II of the first volume, after opening the work with one hundred and fifty-five pages of "Politics". She does, however, intersperse her analysis in "Politics" with short, entertaining digressions. In sharp contrast to Trollope, for instance, Martineau rhapsodizes about the beauty of Cincinnati and its environs, calling it a "glorious place", and finding that "Their vineyards, their conservatories, their fruit and flower gardens delight the eye in the gorgeous month of June" (*Society*, I, pp. 187, 189). But, even here she prioritizes trenchant observations of society. Her praise for Cincinnati appears in "Sectional Prejudice", where she notes that interstate travel by Americans does little to erase regional antipathies, and "The most mortifying instance that I witnessed of this sectional prejudice was at Cincinnati" (*Society*, I, p. 186). Lyrical passages remain secondary to her tart summaries detailing how Americans fail to measure up to their avowed devotion to democracy and justice for all. The treatment of abolitionists and free Blacks speak otherwise, and, while slavery represents the most monstrous shortcoming of the republic, she concludes "Politics" with her famous chapter, "Political Non-Existence of Women".

Martineau claims that "The position or prospects of men in a new country may best be made intelligible by accounts of what the traveller saw and heard while among them. Pictures serve the purpose better than reports." She indicates, in a sly aside, that she chose to offer select, abbreviated accounts in order to avoid the pitfall of representational excess; "My narratives, or pictures, must be but a few selected from among a multitude. My chapter would extend to a greater length than any old novel, if I were to give all I possess" (*Society*, I, p. 214). In *Retrospect* Martineau relates that

> When I finished my late work on Society in America, I had not the most remote idea of writing any thing more on the subject of the New World. I have since been strongly solicited to communicate more of my personal narrative, and of the lighter characteristics of men, and incidents of travel, than it suited my purpose to give in the other work.
>
> (*Retrospect*, I, p. v)

English readers demanded a more diverting account of her American journey than she delivered in *Society*, and Martineau happily bowed to their wishes to have "a picture of the aspect of the country, and of its men and manners. There seems no reason why such a picture should not be appended to an inquiry into the theory and practice of their society" (*Retrospect*, I, pp. v–vi). In *How to Observe*, Martineau calls manners mere manifestations of morals, and follows this analytical hierarchy within and across her American volumes. Much as she had in her ethnographic fictions that made up *Illustrations*, where chapters of tea and talk about political economy often alternate with realistic scenes from domestic and industrial life, Martineau segregates the travel writer's work of delivering both information and novelistic divertissement, largely relegating manners and entertainment to the three volumes of *Retrospect*.

In *Society*, she shifts the scene from the White Mountains of New Hampshire, to Mammoth Cave, Kentucky, thence to Cincinnati, and on to White Sulphur Springs, Virginia and environs (*Society*, I, p. 230). Here she chooses to "break off; and, instead of adding another description of the Natural Bridge to the hundred which exist, bring into contrast with life at the Virginia Springs, life in a New England farm-house", omitting whatever territory lay in between (*Society*, I, p. 260). Martineau places these vignettes, eight in total, in the long opening to Part II of *Society*, "Economy". The sketches stretch into the second volume and help illustrate just how difficult it might be to stick to the methods she outlines in *How to Observe*. She acknowledges the temptation a European traveler faces to immediately resort to principles to account for the sensations generated by observations in America. She suggests instead that travelers squelch the impulse to speculate in order to simply observe; "The traveller from the Old World to the New is apt to lose himself in reflection when he should be observing" (*Society*, I, p. 208). Yet, Martineau quickly shifts to praising the benefits of analysis. While "Too many gentlemen and ladies analyze nothing at all", if "better taught, and introduced at an early age into the world of analysis, nothing, in the whole course of education, is probably so striking to their mind". Teaching women and men how to analyze creates new subjects and agents, new observers, as "They begin a fresh existence from the day when they first obtain a glimpse into this new region of discovery" (*Society*, I, p. 209).

The discovery of analysis is similar to the discovery of the wilder regions of America by Old World travelers. There, nature and people, but nature especially, transform the nation, and a traveler's

> old experience is all reversed. He sees nothing of art in its entireness; but little of nature in her instrumentality. Nature is there the empress, not the handmaid ... It is an absorbing thing to watch the process of world-making; – both the formation of the natural and the conventional world. I witnessed both in America; and when I look back upon it now, it seems as if I had been in another planet.
> (*Society*, I, pp. 209–10)

A New World indeed. She presents, if not quite singularities, merely a sampling of American peculiarity, "sketches of some of the most remarkable parts of the country", while "hoping that a pretty distinct idea might thus be afforded of their primary resources, and of the modes of life of their inhabitants". Analytically, American country life and agriculture take precedence for Martineau over commercial society; "I have said nothing of the towns, in this connexion; town-life in America having nothing very peculiar about it, viewed in the way of general survey. The several departments of industry will now be particularly considered" (*Society*, II, p. 28). Thus, "Agriculture" is the first sector she considers in "Economy" as "The possession of land is the aim of all action, generally speaking, and the cure for all social evils, among men in the United States" (*Society*, II, pp. 30–1).

Martineau's American "Economy" bears some resemblance to the ontological union of nature and man in the work of French Physiocrats, or, to cite an epistemology, William Marshall's natural economy. Though establishing a tourist trade around Niagara Falls – "destined to be as the traditionary monsters of the ancient earth – a giant existence, to be spoken of to wondering ears in studious hours" – is far removed from *tableau économique* or an experiment with turnips on an English farm, "Land was spoken of as the unfailing resource against over manufacture; the great wealth of the nation; the grand security of every man in it" (*Society*, I, p. 211; II, p. 30). The visible effects of incursions of settlers into nature fascinates Martineau, and leads her to not only to observe but to confess that "Here was strong instigation to the exercise of analysis" (*Society*, I, p. 212). She concludes that the desire for land and the resulting prevalence of "Economy" is "natural enough in a country where political economy has never been taught by its only effectual propounder – social adversity" (*Society*, II, p. 31).

Martineau rarely uses the term "political economy" in *Society*. She does, however, repeat the charge that Americans know little of its principles. She insists that German immigrants settled in Pennsylvania "know more of political economy than their native neighbors. They show by their votes that they understand the tariff and bank questions; and they are staunch supporters of democratic principles" (*Society*, II, p. 39). Readers then and now point to Martineau's calls for egalitarianism both in America and England, albeit supporting slower adaptation in her home country, in volume three of *Society* (*Society*, III, pp. 39, 50).[81] Again, she expresses approval of the economic organization of utopian Shaker and Rappite communities she visits. Both hold all property in common, and they provide further evidence of "the produce of co-operative labour being so much greater than in a state of division into families. The truth of these last positions can be denied by none who have witnessed the working of a co-operative system" (*Society*, II, pp. 57–8). Martineau had earlier cautioned readers, however, that the "moral and economical principles of these societies ought to be most carefully distinguished by the observer" (*Society*, II, p. 55). The Shakers and Rappites, she concludes, present to the observer material wealth, built according to sound "economical principles", but, given "the badness of their moral arrangements", urges emulating the "co-operative methods of the Shakers and Rappites ... without any adoption of their spiritual pride and cruel superstition" (*Society*, II, pp. 55, 59).

Her descriptions of the communities at times test the limits of her ability to feel sympathetic, in a positive sense, toward those she observes. For instance, Shaker women, "in their frightful costume, close opaque caps, and drab gowns of the last degree of tightness and scantiness, are nothing short of disgusting" (*Society*, II, p. 60). Shaker women have been almost totally dehumanized by the conditions of their community. Martineau describes them as behaving like slaves,

> pallid and spiritless. They look far more forlorn and unnatural than the men. Their soulless stare at us, before their worship began, was almost as afflicting as that of the lowest order of slaves; and, when they danced, they were like so many galvanised corpses. I had been rather afraid of not being able to keep my countenance during this part of their worship; but there was no temptation to laugh. It was too shocking for ridicule.
>
> (*Society*, II, p. 60)

While lauding the economic output of Shaker society, Martineau finds herself repelled by a spiritual community which so warps humans that they turn into near-wraiths. The dystopia of plantation societies similarly gives rise to economic bounty yet hardly human people. Martineau describes slave quarters of an estate in the neighborhood of Montgomery, Alabama, as typical, "a part of the estate which filled me with disgust, wherever I went. It is something between a haunt of monkeys and a dwelling-place of human beings. The natural good taste, so remarkable in free negroes, is here extinguished" (*Society*, I, p. 302). Kaplan points to the disturbing and problematic aesthetics of some of Martineau's descriptions of Blacks in both *Society* and *Retrospect*. Smith's concept of sympathy equally applies to scenes that evoke disgust in an onlooker; when Martineau writes of her dread and revulsion as she observes slaves in their quarters, in the fields, or simply walking, she implies, wittingly or no, that their degradation results from causes both institutional and natural.[82]

Martineau aims her antipathy and disgust mostly at the institution of slavery. Plantation owners treated slaves like capital, and did not shy away from accumulating real corpses in their pursuit of greater efficiency and profits. Owners counted among their innovations in management slave mortgages and statistics on the depreciation of human skills, steps taken in the name of economy.[83] Martineau writes that a sugar cane plantation owner from Louisiana "stated to a sugar-refiner in New York, that it was found the best economy to *work off* the stock of negroes once in seven years" (*Society*, II, p. 53, emphases in original).

Martineau may or may not have had access to the account books of slave owners, "things" that eloquently speak to the harsh economic truths of the institution of slavery. But she avers that her status as a woman allows her access to domestic spaces, which gives her an advantage as an observer, including as an observer of slavery. Thus,

> I have seen much more of domestic life than could possibly have been exhibited to any gentleman travelling through the country. The nursery, the boudoir, the kitchen, are all excellent schools in which to learn the morals and manners of a people.
>
> (*Society*, I, p. xvi)

Domestic life produces important matters of fact. Households, places to educate children, also represent "schools" for observation for travelers. Martineau strikes a teasing, self-referential, and gendered note here. Would contemporary male travelers really desire access to domestic spaces? Could they even gain admittance to certain spaces?

Credibility proved harder to gain for women than men, even with respect to these domestic spaces. Well into the nineteenth century, readers continued to reject the revelations of Lady Mary Wortley Montagu about the non-scandalous goings-on in hammam and harem in her *The Turkish Embassy Letters* (1763), preferring more salacious reports from men who never set foot in either institution. Nor should we fall into the trap of believing social categories, of the observer and the observed, fall into simple binaries such as male/female or professional/amateur. Status and class mattered. Some American critics sniffed that Frances Trollope's observations were skewed because she had no money, hence no entrée to the more refined society to be found in major American cities; Martineau's fame allowed her to meet American leaders in private and press them on how they understood American democratic principles and American behavior. And biological sex does not map into simple binaries of gender, either. Edgar Allan Poe joked in 1843 that "gentlemen of elegant leisure are, for the most part, neither men, women, nor Harriet Martineaus".[84]

Still, Martineau expresses in paratext her belief that women travelers would not find access blocked to the public sphere in America: "as for public and professional affairs, – those may always gain full information upon such matters, who really feel an interest in them, – be they men or women" (*Society*, I, p. xvi). She found that Americans could hardly be more "frank, confiding and, affectionate", as well as "skillful and liberal in communicating information" (*Society*, I, pp. xvi, xvii). As a result, she writes, "I doubt whether a single fact that I wished to learn, or any doctrine that I desired to comprehend, was ever kept from me because I was a woman" (*Society*, I, p. xvii).

Martineau writes that conversations, not things, help reveal how exquisite politeness coexisted with the pervasive cruelty fostered by slavery in "the wilder districts of the south" (*Society*, I, p. 312). She opens the section in "Economy" on "South Country Life" by recalling how she and her party, on approaching Columbus, Georgia,

were struck with amazement at the stories we were told, and the anecdotes that were dropped, in the stage, about the recent attempts on human life in the neighbourhood; and at the number of incidents of the same kind which were the news of the day along the road. Our driver from Macon had been shot at, in attempting to carry off a young lady.
(*Society*, I, p. 286)

The frequent assaults and murders should prove rich fodder for newspapers, but these fail to report such incidences. Martineau reports that, just before she reached Mobile, Alabama, two men were burned alive "in a slow fire, in the open air, in the presence of the gentlemen of the city generally. No word was breathed of the transaction in the newspapers"; Martineau only learns of the story from a "lady of Mobile" (*Society*, II, pp. 141, 142). Likewise, legal institutions, which could oversee the apprehension, detention, and trials of suspected perpetrators of many of these crimes, barely function. Instead, gossip, facts privately circulated by women and men in the domestic sphere, proves crucial for residents and travelers alike wishing to gain a more accurate picture of a region where the "suppression of fact and opinion" characterize the public sphere (*Society*, II, p. 141).

Slavery and codes of honor undergird the science and art of Southern political economy. So does the desire for cash, as Trollope had emphasized. Presumably referring to the White population, Martineau views the new settlers as "pioneers of civilisation" entirely composed of "money-getters" (*Society*, I, p. 298). One interviewee describes the local character, again presumably of Whites, as "composed of the chivalric elements, badly combined" (*Society*, I, pp. 299–300). The mix proves deadly. It produces countless outbreaks of violence paired with near-total absence about such acts in the public records, a combination of excess and defect for observers. Martineau recalls that

> The tales of jail-breaking and rescue were numberless; and a lady of Montgomery told me that she had lived there four years, during which no time, she believed, had passed without some one's life having been attempted, either by dueling or assassination.
> (*Society*, I, p. 308)

Again, "newspapers do not insert such things" (*Society*, II, p. 146). Martineau attributes the "fearful" state of Southern frontier society to its newness: "It will be understood that I describe this region as presenting an extreme case of the material advantages and moral evils of a new settlement, under the institution of slavery".[85] Yet White inhabitants on the frontier behave in still other ways that could lead travelers to overlook their cruelty: "The most prominent relief is the hospitality, – that virtue of young society. It is so remarkable, and to the stranger so grateful, that there is danger of its blinding him to the real state of affairs" (*Society*, I, pp. 308–9).

Southern hospitality in no way ensures that Southerners would be forthcoming about conditions in the region. Yet Martineau maintains that she was able to elicit truthful testimony in the South due to the fact that her abolitionist views were known beforehand.

> My opinions of slavery were known, through the press, before I went abroad: the hospitality which was freely extended to me was offered under a full knowledge of my detestation of the system. This was a great advantage, in as much as it divested me entirely of the character of a spy, and promoted the freest discussion, wherever I went.
> (*Society*, II, pp. 147)

The unsympathetic reviewer of *Society* in the *Southern Literary Messenger* took issue with Martineau's penchant for making sweeping claims, as above; the writer questions her credibility. Thus, her hearing loss might have proven costly in discussions, hindering her ability to observe and to gather facts:

> We have heard of many intelligent persons who declined to make the lady's acquaintance while in this country, simply on account of her trumpet, and the awkwardness of such a chat in company, who, otherwise, would have been very well pleased to know her; and who might have afforded her some very useful information.[86]

Notwithstanding questions about how free Martineau's conversations actually were, she believed genteel manners could blind Southerners to the evils of slavery:

> it is impossible to sit down to reflect, with every order of human beings filling an equal space before one's mental eye, without being struck to the soul with the conviction that the state of society, and no less of individual families, is false and hollow, whether their members are aware of it or not ... they must be just before they can be generous.
> (*Society*, I, p. 309)

Beyond the immediate extension of sympathy to others, a traveler needs both spatial and temporal distance to reflect and accurately gauge the meaning of what they have observed. Martineau stresses the necessity to value each human being equally, counter to a system where Whites regard free Blacks as inferior, and Black slaves equivalent to property, worth only the price they can fetch on the market. She continues: "The severity of this truth is much softened to sympathetic persons on the spot; but it returns with awful force when they look back upon it from afar."

Nor do expressions of sympathy necessarily sway the views of other onlookers. Martineau meets a young man who had attempted to run away from his owners three different times. After contracting frostbite during his last effort, he had his legs amputated. When Martineau pities his plight, a neighbor, a woman, neither a slave owner nor American nor English by birth, scornfully asks, mystified, why the "ungrateful wretch" would keep running away from such from benevolent masters. She not only does not comprehend when Martineau replies, "He wanted to be free", but says she told him that his punishment is only what he deserved; indeed, were she his master, she would "give him no help nor nursing", but let him die (*Society*, I, pp. 309–11). As for those Southerners who agree with Martineau on the horrors of slavery,

> There was a warm sympathy between myself and very many, whose sufferings under the system caused me continual and deep sorrow, though no surprise. Neither was I surprised at their differing from me as widely as they do about the necessity of immediate action, either by resistance or flight, while often agreeing, nearly to the full, in my estimate of the evils of the present state of things.
>
> (*Society*, II, p. 147)

Martineau concludes, however, that these Southerners suffer from the same analytical blindness she had previously cited.

> To them, the moral deformity of the whole is much obscured by its nearness; while the small advantages, and slight prettinesses which it is very easy to attach to it, are prominent, and always in view. These circumstances prevented my being surprised at the candour with which they not only discussed the question, but showed me all that was to be seen of the economical management of plantations; the worst as well as the best.
>
> (*Society*, II, p. 148)

According to Martineau, slave owners' lack of distance from the plantation system does much to obscure its moral ugliness and exaggerate its faint attractions. The economy with which owners run the system seduces with its beauty, too. But, economical reckoning escapes neither Martineau's moral nor aesthetic judgment.

Martineau speculates on what would be needed to overcome this lack of observational acuity. She imagines an ideal being who would also be an ideal observer. Martineau does not identify this being as economic man or woman or child. She instead uses stadial history and work of Carlyle, harsh critic of British political economists, to focus her narrative of human progress, in which she conjectures the changing valuation of work and of the classes who perform different types of work as societies pass through the different stages. Martineau opens "Morals of Economy" with an epigraph drawn from Carlyle's *Sartor Resartus* (1836), a copy of which she picked up while in America. Carlyle asserts the impossibility of knowledge of self and others without the observation of works: "A certain inarticulate self-consciousness dwells dimly in us; which only our works can render articulate. Our works are the mirror wherein the spirit first sees its natural lineaments" (*Society*, II, p. 293). Martineau follows the epigraph by tracing a historical progression of humankind through shifts in how we regard one another and who we see as an ideal; human progress runs from worshipping kings and warriors to appreciating martyrs, poets, and artisans as the true heroes of an age (*Society*, II, p. 294)

Martineau considers men compound beings, as had Malthus in the 1798 *Essay*. Malthus's beings live forever torn between the dictates of reason and the pull of corporal desires. Their actions, never entirely rational, serve as a riposte to the eventual triumph of man's reason posited by Godwin and Condorcet (*Essay*, 1798, XIII, 3). Martineau regards individuals as beings riven by a different fissure:

> There are two aspects under which every individual man may be regarded: as a solitary being, with inherent powers, and an omnipotent will; a creator, a king, an inscrutable mystery: and again, as a being infinitely connected with all other beings, with none but derived powers, with a heavenly-directed will; a creature, a subject, a transparent medium through which the workings of principles are to be eternally revealed. Both these aspects are true, and therefore reconcilable.
> (*Society*, II, 294)

Men are both solitary and social beings, but unlike Malthus's compound beings, Martineau's can harmoniously reconcile their separate characters. Further, Martineau indicates that men have actually made progress toward this end. Martineau equates the current manifestation of the two halves of her compound beings with handwork and headwork; both "too little freedom, and too little knowledge", and too little or too much work keeps slaves, women, idle princes, and half-starved artisans from approaching their ideal state. This state deprives them of the capacity to even observe the truth (*Society*, II, pp. 295–6). Thus, mankind miscalculates human happiness and value:

> Those who have been able to get through life with the least possible work have been treated as the happiest: those who have had the largest share imposed upon them have been passively pitied as the most miserable. If the experience of the two could have been visibly or tangibly brought into comparison, the false estimate would have been long ago banished for ever from human calculations.
> (*Society*, II, p. 296)

The errors in reckoning lie in the application of an incorrect methodology, itself the consequence of failing to properly discipline mind and body.

The freedom to do "joint head-and-hand work" enables an individual to observe "the truth that lies about him; and so far, and by the only appointed method, invested him with heaven while he was upon earth" (*Society*, II, p. 298). Still, it is difficult to perceive the "inevitable" progress in "morals and manners of nations" in the Old World. Thus, "We must look to new or renovated communities to see how much has been really learned" (*Society*, II, p. 299). America is fertile ground for more clear-eyed observations.

Martineau proceeds to trace the advance of nations as they move from savagery, to barbarism and beyond. She renders a reading of stadial histories with a twist: as societies evolve, they moderate their denigration of those who perform handwork and their veneration of head-workers. She speculates that eventually, perhaps, civilization "reaches a critical period out of which must arise a new organization of society", one where these "two classes celebrate the union of thought and handicraft" (*Society*, II, pp. 299, 300, 301). Martineau uses stadial histories to conjecture forward into the future, rather than backward into the past.

Martineau asks "If, in such an era, a new nation begins its career, what should be expected from it?" (*Society*, II, p. 301). She envisions progress, but no clean break from past beliefs and institutions. Rather

> The advantage of the new nation over the old will be no more than that its individual members are more open to conviction, from being more accessible to evidence, less burdened with antique forms and institutions, and partial privileges, so called. The result will probably be that some members of the new society will follow the ancient fashion of considering work a humiliation; while, upon the whole, labour will be more honoured than it has ever been before.
> (*Society*, II, p. 302)

In volume III of *Society*, Martineau uses stadial history to emphasize that spiritual as opposed to material improvements signifies progress. She asserts, in the very first sentence, that "The degree of civilisation of any people corresponds with the exaltation of the idea which is the most prevalent among that people" (*Society*, III, p. 1). Martineau sketches an ascension up the scale of civilization as a move from a focus in savage societies on satisfying bodily wants to a state where that condition has eased, and "the love of pleasure, the love of idleness, succeeds. Then comes the desire of wealth; and next, the regard to opinion" (*Society*, III, p. 2). Again, Martineau does not emphasize modes of production as the organizing factor for her stadial taxonomy. Rather,

> The civilisation of the old world still corresponds with the low idea, that man lives in and for the outward, in and for what is around him rather than what is within him. It is still supposed, that whatever a few individuals say and do, the generality of men live for wealth, outward ease

and dignity, and, at the highest, lofty reputation. The degree of civilisation corresponds with this.

(*Society*, III, p. 1)

Martineau returns to questions about how a traveler-observer defines the degree of civilization, progress, and the ends of progress at the conclusion of *Retrospect*. She hopes that what she relates in the volumes will serve to increase sympathy between the English and Americans. But Martineau, as she had in *Society*, warns against the snares laid by sympathy for a traveler's ability to make impartial observations of another society. Finding herself in a reflective mood at Mount Auburn Cemetery in Cambridge, Massachusetts, she ruminates on the ends of her American travels. In language laden with associations between the observations made by the living and (of) the dead, she concludes that

> The profit of travel is realized at home, in the solitude of the study; and the true meaning of human life (as far as its meaning can become known to us here) is best made out from its place of rest.
>
> (*Retrospect*, III, p. 283)

A traveler realizes the benefit of travel only after stopping traveling, returning home to solitude, and achieving distance from the observed, as she had recommended in *Society*. A traveler could also reach this state of detachment by either contemplating the dead, sympathetically adopting the viewpoint of the dead, or, at the end of life's journey, being dead. Martineau continues

> While busy among strangers, one is carried away by sympathy and by prejudice from the point whence foreign society can be viewed with any thing like impartiality: one cannot but hear the mutual criminations of parties: one cannot but be perplexed by the mutual misrepresentations of fellow-citizens: one cannot but sympathize largely with all in turn, since there is a large mixture of truth in all views about which people are strongly persuaded.

In *How to Observe*, Martineau had maintained that sympathy constituted the principal moral requisite travelers needed in order to observe others. Here, recalling her remarks in *Society* about feeling "warm sympathy" with slaveholders who express anguish about the system, Martineau characterizes sympathy as an irresistible force. It buffets and captures travelers; they ally themselves with whatever prejudice their native companions hold, now this opinion now that. Sympathy thus robs a traveler of impartiality. Martineau enlarges on the value to a traveler of returning home, insisting

> It is only after sitting down alone at home that the traveller can separate the universal truth from the partial error with which he has sympathized,

and can make some approximation towards assurance as to what he has learned, and what he believes.

Sympathy also renders a traveler incapable of picking out truth from error. Only when home again, at rest, can the traveler can perform the solitary "head-work" necessary to reflect on what one has observed. Martineau persists in an elegiac mode, drawing even closer analogies between the perspective of the dead, and that of the living traveler and travel writer:

> So it is in the turmoil of life. While engaged in it, we are ignorantly persuaded, and liable therefore to be shaken from our certainty: we are disproportionately moved, and we sympathize with incompatibilities; so as to be sure of disappointment and humiliation, inflicted through our best sensibilities. In the place of retrospect we may find our repose again in contemplating our ignorance and weakness, and ascertaining the conviction and strength which they have wrought out for us.
>
> (*Retrospect*, III, pp. 283–4)

Solitary life/death affords individuals an ideal perspective. A view from the study, a place of retrospect, approaches a view from the grave, a place of repose. Presumably, the living and the dead can each pursue the truth unencumbered by earthly cares and meaner sentiments such as prejudice.

One of the most important insights a traveler can arrive at is to recognize where true value lies. The dead would tell us where to find value, if only they could speak. It is not in material possessions, but happiness: "Nothing is more conspicuous in the traveller's retrospect than the fact how little external possession has to do with happiness" (*Retrospect*, III, p. 287). A traveler will observe that

> Each class kindly pities the one below it in power and wealth: the traveller pities none but those who are wasting their energies in the exclusive pursuit of either. Generally speaking, they have all an equal endowment of the things from which happiness is really derived. They have, in pretty equal distribution, health, senses and their pleasures, homes, children, pursuits, and successes.
>
> (*Retrospect*, III, p. 287)

Martineau's is a leveling gaze. She considers abolitionists, "men and women wholly devoted to a lofty pursuit, and surrendering for it much that others most prize", to be the happiest class in America. Yet American abolitionists fit Martineau's criteria that the happiest come from "all ranks and orders of men", and share "one point of resemblance, that they have not staked their peace on anything so unreal as money or fame" (*Retrospect*, III, p. 288). Maria Edgeworth had asked David Ricardo, "are they happy?" when the two friends debated the comparative state of the English and the

Irish. Martineau asks a prospective traveler "to prepare himself to bring to whatever he may observe to a test of some high and broad principle, and not to that of a low and comparative practice". This does not contradict Edgeworth's method. Martineau insists "That to test the morals and manners of a nation by a reference to the essentials of human happiness, is to strike at once to the centre [truth], and to see things as they are" (*How to Observe*, p. 14).

Happiness carries Benthamite connotations. But Martineau chides Bentham for apparently forgetting that, though "the principles of government are to be deduced more from experience of human nature than experience of human governments, the institutions in which those principles are to be embodied must be infinitely modified by preceding circumstances" when he offers "to codify for several of the United States". She offers that "These could not, from his want of local knowledge, have been very specific; and if general, what was society to do till the lawyers had done arguing?" (*Society*, I, p. 32). Bentham, handicapped by one of the potential pitfalls of armchair travel, does not keep to his principles. The American Declaration of Independence, on the other hand, does valorize happiness. Martineau's preference for it as a true measure of value derives, perhaps, from whatever residue of sympathy she retains for her American friends and their principles. Wealth, status, and power matter less to a people dedicated, in principle, to liberty, equality, and the pursuit of happiness; hence, the abolitionists represent the American ideal. In "The Martyr Age of the United States", published in December 1838, Martineau admits that her views should be deemed "faint, partial, and imperfect", coming, as they do, from a "foreign observer".[87] Nonetheless, she concludes "A just survey of the whole can leave little doubt that the abolitionists of the United States are the greatest people now living and moving in it."[88]

Martineau Visits the East: "Knowledge in This Very Negation of Knowledge"

Martineau fell seriously ill in 1839, apparently with an ovarian cyst, and removed from London to Tynemouth in 1840 to what she thought would be her deathbed. In *Life in the Sick-Room* (1844) she offers insights from her sick-bed on how those with disabilities observe.[89] Martineau did not travel in this period, but observed others walking and playing on the beach when she peered out of her window with a telescope. The restricted number, range, and scope of observations she and her fellow shut-ins could make formed no barrier to knowledge, according to Martineau. On the contrary, they had ample time to reflect, if they chose to do so, and to gain deep insights into the human condition as a result; "it seems to me scarcely necessary to see more than the smallest sample, in order to analyze life in its entireness".[90] She repeats this sentiment in language similar to her delineation, in *How to Observe*, of the distinction between morals and manners: "We may be excluded from much observation of the outer life of men; but of the inner life, which originates and interprets the outer, it is scarcely possible that in any other circumstances we could have known so much."[91]

Martineau resumed traveling after recuperating from her illness in 1844. In the fall of 1846, while visiting friends in Liverpool, she took up their invitation to join them on a trip to Egypt, Palestine, and Sinai; the party formed part of the rising numbers of European, especially British tourists, visiting Egypt during the period from 1815 to 1850.[92] Martineau published an account of the tour, which lasted until May 1847, in *Eastern Life, Present and Past* (1848). She brought to *Eastern Life* extensive experience writing about religion, including three prize-winning essays on Christianity, Judaism, and Islam for the British and Foreign Unitarian Association. These were all printed in the Unitarian *Monthly Repository* where Martineau was the most frequent contributor from 1829 until 1832, when she turned to the task of writing *Illustrations*.[93] *Eastern Life* features Martineau's reflections on past, present, and future religious life, prompted by her observations in the region. Present-day commentators consider the work a landmark in the comparative study of religions.

Contemporary reaction, on the other hand, was decidedly mixed, even prior to publication. John Murray rejected the manuscript as "a work of infidel tendency" due to Martineau's relativism, her belief that Christianity represented a transitional phase in mankind's progress toward a more rational future, and, with that, her flirtation with outright atheism. The reviewer in *The Christian Reformer* dismisses her philosophical and theological readings and confesses "We are disappointed". Martineau writes "on subjects her knowledge of which can only be partial and obtained at second-hand", and reaches conclusions, for example, on the origin of the Pentateuch where "the utmost that an impartial reporter could assert is, that the question yet remains under dispute in the theological world".[94] The reviewer questions whether some topics should be included in a book of travel writings at all because

> in the present divided and agitated state of religious opinion, literature ought to supply a neutral ground; and if any travels should be free from sectarian and partizan theology, surely they are those which relate to the lands trodden by 'the blessed feet' of the common Christian Lord.[95]

Martineau belongs to England's "small body of cultivated pyrrhonists"; though the reviewer concedes that "In the description of scenery we think her specially successful", she is adjudged to be both partial and prejudiced. In the case of Jerusalem, "she spoils an impression by her overpowering theological prejudices", tarnishing what are ultimately "attractive volumes".[96]

The writer in *The Prospective Review*, on the other hand, unreservedly praises Martineau's use of mimesis in *Eastern Life*. Her representations prove truthful, despite their failure to convey the multitudinous details of real life:

> With regard to her descriptions – we believe there is an unanimous concession of their great excellence. They are vivid, realising and *true*. We speak of truth in the artistic sense – not as comprehending a minute representation of particulars, but as expressing the general effect of the actual scene on the observing mind.[97]

Rejecting the opinion that Martineau should have avoided controversial theological subjects in a book of travels, the reviewer reproduces a large portion of the penultimate paragraph of the main body of text in *Eastern Life*.[98] There Martineau argues for a particular form of travel writing, what one might call "how to represent", as an integral part of how to observe. A thoughtful traveler, initially described as male, needs to both describe and interpret, as well as he can, what he sees: "he must use such knowledge and reflective faculty as he has". Travelers need to do so in order to be faithful to one's self, to the public, and to truth; "When all thinkers say freely what is to them true, we shall know more of abstract and absolute truth than we have ever known yet." Travelers' fidelity to their observations and prior knowledge will allow readers or listeners (Martineau does not distinguish between speech and writing here) to judge whether they have erred or not.[99] Martineau indicates that she has applied these standards of observation and representation to herself, writing, in the last paragraph of the volumes, that "I could not have accepted the privilege of my travels without accepting also their responsibilities" (*Eastern Life*, III, pp. 334–5).

Martineau has come full circle. Already in "Preface" she highlights her concern with methods of observation, and in the main body of the text she launches her analysis of Egypt by adopting the perspective of political economy for her interpretations, viewing inhabitants through the lens of Malthus's population principle. Martineau remained largely faithful throughout *Eastern Life* to the philosophical and mechanical methods she outlines in *How to Observe*. She prepared for her eastern travels by reading as widely as she could on the region; she did not read or speak Arabic, however, but relied on dragomen as guides and translators, as well as using an Arab–English lexicon. As for other mechanical requisites, Martineau not only kept a journal, but, deviating from her previous practice, read the section covering Egypt to her traveling companions in order that she "might have the satisfaction of knowing whether they agreed in my impressions of the facts which came under our observation. About these facts there is an entire agreement between them and me" (*Eastern Life*, I, pp. v–vi). She was both limited by and able to take advantage of her gender. Men in her party, particularly Mr. Yates, who along with his wife invited Martineau on the trip, and Mr. Ewart, who joined the party in Malta, helpfully arranged for accommodations for Martineau, and set up meetings with dignitaries she would not have otherwise seen. But she was able to visit harems in Damascus and Cairo, while the men were not.

Martineau also notes how closely her own recommended methods and actual observations matched the behavior, recorded descriptions, and maps of previous travelers, and serves up praise or condemnation depending upon whether the travelers proved credible or not. She wholeheartedly commends the implied preparation, methods, and results on display in Sir J.G. Wilkinson's *Modern Egypt and Thebes* (1843): "Such almost faultless correctness requires an union of intellectual and moral powers and training which it is encouraging for those who are interested in the results of travel to contemplate" (*Eastern Life*, I, pp. vi–vii). Wilkinson's practical instructions for travelers, which appear at every stage throughout *Modern Egypt and Thebes*, and run from recommended equipage to what to pay for various services, begin in the "Preface", where he interjects that he "may here mention two things which I omitted in the body of the work". The first indicates that he has revised his instructions due to the rising numbers of European women traveling in Egypt. That is, "when Ladies are of the party, on the Nile, the boatmen should be supplied with drawers, and an order given that they never go into the water without them".[100] Martineau defers to Wilkinson and other guides, but also offers a few of her own tips for travelers, and women travelers in particular, in the "Appendix" of *Eastern Life*. Her directives acknowledge the sensibilities of women with regards to the practicalities of dressing for both comfort and, when possible, style; thus, "Brown holland is the best material for ladies' dresses; and nothing looks better, if set off with a little trimming of ribbon, which can be put on and taken off in a few minutes." She also addresses, for half a page, a fundamental question of household management, strongly urging that "No lady who values her peace on the journey, or desires any freedom of mind or movement, will take a maid … If her mistress has any foresight, or any compassion, she will leave her at home", because a servant, even if she does not miss the comforts of home, will have to be taught "to ride, – and to ride well: or she may have much to answer for" (*Eastern Life*, III, pp. 341–2). European females of a certain class considering travel to Egypt should act prudently; economy should prevail at home and abroad.

Martineau did not follow Wilkinson's lead in one key area; where *Modern Egypt and Thebes* includes numerous woodcuts, *Eastern Life* contains no illustration. Early in the same year Martineau left on her trip, illustrations famously figured in a competition that broke out among London newspapers sending correspondents across the Irish Sea to report on the famine. Advances in print technologies had enabled publishers of the dailies to include high quality engravings alongside write-ups, and tout the pictures as a vouchsafe for the credibility of their reporters' accounts.[101] The critic in *Prospective Review* reads *Eastern Life* in light of these conversations about whether illustrations add verisimilitude to travel writing. The reviewer affirms the credibility of Martineau's prose-only narrative, and couches a positive assessment in psychological terms: "Her fidelity here may be tested by comparison with the admirable sketches of Roberts. But the impression of the pen is stronger than that of the pencil, as it opens more varied sources of association." The reviewer praises Martineau's ability to capture, better than any illustration, the truth in her words about the desert light, for example, and, tellingly, for the deaf traveler, the "grand music of the everlasting cataracts" of the Nile.[102]

In her review of the work of other travelers to the region, Martineau dresses down Mrs. Romer, author of *A Pilgrimage to the Temples and Tombs of Egypt, Nubia, and Palestine in 1845–6* (1846), for transgressing a key principle of observation by travelers. Upon recalling reading that Mrs. Romer had her dragoman remove a portion of statuary from Benee Hasan in Egypt, Martineau voices her outrage: "Who will undertake to say what may be the value of any one head and shoulders in a group which may be made unintelligible by its absence!" She blanches at the additional barrier such violations present to travelers attempting to grasp both symbolic and real value in another society. "[S]cientific antiquarians" do enough harm to the search for truth when they separate objects from a group because any object is "symbolical and necessary in its own place", but "there really seems no hope left if desultory travelers are to pick and steal at their fancy from a repository where everything has its place, and is in its place" (*Eastern Life*, II, pp. 38, 39). Vandalizing antiquities in the name of science proves a disservice to science; the removal of one object from a group renders the objects incompletely legible, making it even harder for future travelers, observers, and truth seekers to determine their true value.

In *How to Observe*, Martineau suggests that the value of any single object or practice a traveler may observe may be incalculable. How does a traveler decipher what one observes? Through, again, the exercise of sympathy. Martineau writes that if a traveler "be full of sympathy, every thing he sees will be instructive, and the most important matters will be the most clearly revealed". Lacking sympathy, a traveler will find "the most important things will be hidden from him, and symbols (in which every society abounds) will be only absurd or trivial forms". Martineau insists that "The stranger will be wise to conclude, when he sees anything seriously done which appears to him insignificant or ludicrous, that there is more in it than he perceives, from deficiency of knowledge or feeling of his own" (*How to Observe*, p. 48). Martineau's censure of Romer's removal of the ancient statue's torso serves as reminder of her belief that any object, even silent stone, could speak. The statuary group represents a record, a "thing" which could, possibly, hold the key to unlocking a system or systems of meaning about ancient Egyptian society. Romer's action diminishes that possibility.

Martineau presents a sharp contrast to the conduct of Romer during her walks through Nubian dwellings, when inhabitants are absent, in order to glimpse "some notion of their household economy" (*Eastern Life*, I, p. 127). She takes inventory of Nubian household arrangements and objects, but she and her fellow travelers do not disturb them. Yet Martineau evinces no consciousness of impropriety or national prejudice, nor any breach in methodology when recounting how she and her party enter a home, during the day, without permission. Instead, her reflections on Nubian household economy lead Martineau to speculate about matters of political economy and history. She considers the environmental and institutional conditions that shape how residents of the region exercise economy. Martineau cites the encroaching desert and the "abundant evidence of willful and careless lapse" as the chief barriers to a revival of agriculture and a rebound of population in Egypt. She claims, without specifying a time period, that the population has declined from 8,000,000 to 2,500,000 people. Wilkinson estimated the population to be 1,800,000, down from 4,000,000 some "200 years ago" and 2,500,000 in 1800; he attributes the continued decline to "Plague and a Turkish system of government". Of the breakdown of the population of Cairo he remarks, in a note, that "These calculations are very uncertain."[103] Despite this statistical uncertainty, Martineau holds out hope that for Egypt "there seems no reason why it should not, with the knowledge and skill of our own time, rise to what it once was, and exceed it" (*Eastern Life*, I, p. 128). The scarcity of both arable land and raw materials for industry in Nubia, on the other hand, affords little chance of population growth there, despite the apparent ability and willingness of Nubians to work.

Martineau does not use the term population principle, or political economy either, in *Eastern Life*. But upon first contact after landing in the port city of Alexandria she moves quickly to view the size and health Egypt's population as an outcome stemming from food availability, the security of property, and, as Malthus himself had so often done, directly compares the physical appearance of Egyptians to that of England's poor. Martineau's immediate impressions of the people of Egypt, on disembarking in Alexandria in November 1846, offers a set of depressing and dehumanizing descriptions: "we had a crowd of boats about us, containing a few European gentlemen and a multitude of screaming Arabs. I know no din to be compared to it but that of a frog concert in a Carolina swamp" (*Eastern Life*, I, p. 5).

In fact, the look of the human population pleases Martineau: "I must say that I was agreeably surprised, both this morning and throughout my travels in Egypt, by the appearance of the people." They "appeared to us, there and throughout the country, sleek, well-fed and cheerful". She observes no

> want of food. I am told, and no doubt truly, that this is partly owing to the law of the Kuran by which every man is bound to share what he has, to the last mouthful, with his brother in need: but there must be enough, or nearly enough food for all, whatever be the law of distribution.
>
> (*Eastern Life*, I, p. 9)

Martineau harbors no illusions that conditions in Egypt are ideal. She invokes contemporary medico-scientific beliefs on the effects of environment on health to link the ever-present dirt in the streets of Alexandria to disease. A notice of "heaps of rubbish and hillocks of dust" gives way to a more general observation that, "About the dirt there can be no doubt; – the dirt of both dwellings and persons; and the diseases which proceed from want of cleanliness" constitute one class of misery the population endures. Further, the population could be four times larger but for "all the misgovernment and oppression that the people suffer". Still, despite the misery, the Egyptians "raise food enough to support life and health" (*Eastern Life*, I, p. 9).

When Martineau pivots to compare the physical well-being of Egyptians and her fellow English, she ventures that "I have seen more emaciated, and stunted, and depressed men, women and children in a single walk in England, than I observed from end to end of the land of Egypt" (*Eastern Life*, I, pp. 9–10). This observation leads her to remark, however, that an adequate food supply is insufficient in and of itself: "So much for the mere food question. No one will suppose that in Egypt a sufficiency of food implies, as with us, a sufficiency of some other things scarcely less important to welfare than food" (*Eastern Life*, I, p. 10). Martineau returns to the rhetorical terrain she mapped out in *How to Observe*, where national welfare and national morals, rather than money or happiness, represent the primary goals for society, and the ultimate objects of value for travelers to observe (*How to Observe*, p. 163).

Martineau returns to the language of stadial histories in describing the party's passage through the First Cataract on the Nile. She contrasts the boys and men whose physical exertions guide their boat through the rapids with the sedentary men of London:

> I felt the great peculiarity of this day to be my seeing, for the first, and probably the only time of my life, the perfection of savage faculty: and truly it is an imposing sight. The quickness of movement and apprehension, the strength and suppleness of frame, and the power of experience in all concerned this day contrasted strangely with images of the bookworm and the professional man at home, who can scarcely use their own limbs and senses, or conceive of any control over external realities.
> (*Eastern Life*, I, p. 120)

Martineau continues her comparative analysis of human development and civilization, drawing on observations she made during previous travels. Men and women in the United States constitute her real-life ideal types:

> I always thought in America, and I always shall think, that the finest specimens of human development I have seen are in the United States, where every man, however learned and meditative, can ride, drive, keep

his own horse, and roof his own dwelling: and every woman, however intellectual, can do, if necessary, all the work of her own house.
(*Eastern Life*, I, p. 120)

While every man and every woman in America can apparently do "every thing" having to do with either mind or body, Martineau presumably means her remarks to apply (mostly) to free Whites. Trade between Egypt and England would teach each nation's men how to best utilize body and mind like her idealized Americans:

> I wish that, in return for our missions to the heathen, the heathens would send missionaries to us, to train us to a grateful use of our noble natural endowments, – of our powers of sense and limb, and the functions which are involved in their activity. I am confident that our morals and our intellect would gain inestimably by it. There is no saying how much vicious propensity would be checked, and intellectual activity equalised in us by such a reciprocity with those whose gifts are at the other extreme from our own.
> (*Eastern Life*, I, p. 121)

Martineau opens her imaginary trade, a gift economy comprising the exchange of teachers between savage and commercial societies, to women when she shifts textual terrain to England from the United States. English women could easily step into their socially acceptable, valued, nay sacred occupations as teachers and missionaries. Martineau goes further still. By removing any hint of gender in the above quote, she makes space for men, women, *and* Poe's "Harriet Martineaus" to carry out these tasks.

Smith regretted that men in commercial society became softer, as trade and social intercourse sapped their martial spirit. In proposing exchanges that would reinvigorate bodies and simultaneously benefit minds, Martineau calls up a much older notion of difference, that between heathens or non-Christians and Christians, fitting for volumes devoted to reveries on religious life. Martineau's version of monogenesis is cosmopolitan; all share common physical and mental capacities and need only a proper education to take full advantage of them. Strengthening individual bodies will thereby strengthen the social body, solving at a stroke one of the paradoxes of Malthus's population principle. Ironic, that Martineau writes this as disaster unfolds in Ireland.

Martineau muddies a clear binary distinction between physically adept heathens and mentally acute Londoners. She celebrates both the physicality of the Egyptian boys and men, and their intelligence and keen awareness of their nonhuman environments.

> Throughout the four hours of our ascent, I saw incessantly that though much is done by sheer force, – by men enough pulling at a rope strong

enough, – some other requisites were quite as essential: – great forecast, great sagacity; much nice management among currents, and hidden and threatening rocks; and much knowledge of the forces and subtilties of wind and water.

(*Eastern Life*, I, p. 121)

Martineau concludes the anecdote by citing the authority of Mr. Ewart to interpret this display: "Mr. E., who has great experience in nautical affairs, said that nothing could be cleverer than the management of the whole business. He believed that the feat could be achieved nowhere else, as there are no such swimmers elsewhere" (*Eastern Life*, I, p. 123). The Egyptians embody an ideal type of human development, specific to that particular time and place. Martineau's perspective was hardly unusual among her British contemporaries. Some twenty years earlier, the reviewer of works by Miers and Head in *The Quarterly Review*, in assessing the skills of the Gauchos on the Pampas, asserts the universality of these locale-specific skills among savages: "The Gauchos are endued with a species of sagacity which, indeed, is common to all savages, and to men but little removed from a state of nature."[104]

Martineau readily admits the prevailing lack of expert, credible eye-witness testimony in Egypt; but she opens the chapter on "The Present Condition of Egypt." by explaining how adopting a perspective mixing stadial history and political economy allows one to observe and determine the material condition of the people of Egypt in the absence of facts. She quotes her journal to the effect that "one can get no reliable information from the most reliable men" in Egypt. Thus

About matters on which there ought to be no difference of statement, we meet with strange contradictions; such as the rate and amount of tax, &c. In fact, there are no data; and there is little free communication. Even a census does not help. The present census, we are told, will be a total failure – so many will bribe the officials to omit their names, because of the poll-tax.

(*Eastern Life*, II, p. 168)

Martineau concludes that "neither I nor any other traveller can give accounts of any value of the actual material condition of the people of Egypt". What is of value to Martineau and any other traveler is good information on the state of the people in the regions they cross. But Egypt lacks both reliable "things", such as a population census, and reliable discourse about these things.

Absent that information, her two pillars of what to observe, Martineau nonetheless deduces that "we have a substantial piece of knowledge in this very negation of knowledge", a cheery contrast to Miers and his contemporaries who suffered financial losses in the absence of necessary observations and "matters of fact" about South America. Clues abound in the manner in which accurate information is actively suppressed by both the government and its people:

> We know for certain that a government is bad, and that the people are unprosperous and unhappy in a country where there is a great ostentation of civilisation and improvement, side by side with mystery as to the actual working of social arrangements, and every sort of evasion on the part of the people.
> (*Eastern Life*, II, p. 168)

Martineau traces the source of the material deprivation, unhappiness, and evasion to another absence familiar to political economists:

> One thing is certain: that, in his endeavours to improve the civilisation of his people, Mohammed Alee has omitted the first step, which is essential to all substantial advance. He has given them no security of property or other rights. Moreover, he seems to be unaware that this security is the only ground of improvement. He appears never to have learned that national welfare can arise from no other basis than national industry; and that there can be no reliable national industry where no man is sure of receiving the rewards of his labour.
> (*Eastern Life*, II, p. 170)

According to Martineau, Mohammed Ali Pasha, viceroy of Egypt, fails to understand the importance of the security of property. His failure to ensure it, and obey the fundamental principle of political economy, thwarts his attempts to enact policies that would enhance the welfare of Egypt. The insecurity of property explains as well the inability of officials of the Pasha to accurately count the population via a census; people flee when government officials appear. His efforts to promote the advance of Egypt through stadial history were doomed from the start.

The Westminster and Foreign Quarterly Review essayist faults Martineau, along with other European and American travelers and observers, for holding the Pasha's government to European standards. The reviewer repeats a familiar critique of prejudiced, Eurocentric comparative analysis:

> Europeans, as incapable of getting beyond the narrowest European notions, as they are of collecting evidence, or knowing it when they have got it, constantly judge him [Pasha] as if he were a European Prince, governing a civilized and long-established European community, according to fixed laws, and with the aid of a large body of well trained European public officers. Nay, he has even incurred this obloquy in consequence of being almost the only oriental ruler whose dominions are so governed that Europeans can travel safely in them.[105]

The reviewer reinterprets the import of Martineau's acknowledgement that neither she nor anyone else knows anything of Egypt with certainty. If true, then "We must decline drawing the conclusion that the affairs of a foreign country must be going wrong because we can find out little that is certain about them".[106] The reviewer offers an alternative method:

> Having first ascertained the facts regarding Egypt and Mohammed Ali, we may either compare the country with some ideal state conceived to be perfect, or with some other Mahomedan countries. According to the first method we should doubtless find it low in the scale: according to the second it would probably stand high. But, as the ordinary traveller knows no more of other oriental countries than he knows of Egypt, he finds it easiest to draw on his imagination, and to vituperate rather than to inquire and discriminate.[107]

Martineau traveled to Egypt knowing, rather than imagining, that in 1816 Mohammed Ali Pasha had launched one of the world's first state industrialization programs, replete with monopolies and commercial restrictions. It failed. Martineau, no ordinary traveler, proceeds to employ her method of choice, comparing Egypt by its own standard, and conjectures forthwith. When Muhammad Ali Pasha called for a population census in 1845, by pronouncing that "It is therefore necessary for Us to enumerate exactly the people of Our country so that it may be a cause of its progress in civilization", Martineau, evincing little sympathy, joined others in assuming it too would fail.[108]

A population census was a relatively new institution; the British conducted their first only in 1801, and subsequent enumerations underwent extensive revisions. For Martineau, the ability of a nation to successfully undertake a population census signifies that it can mobilize state resources and retains enough trust of residents that they will cooperate with the count, generating a "thing" necessary for a nation to qualify as a civilized commercial society. Was the 1848 population census a failure? It was the first nationwide enumeration carried out in Egypt. Census registers gathered from households in Cairo, Alexandria, and numerous villages, both prior to 1848 and in the period leading up to the next nationwide census in 1882, also contain information at an individual level for a wide range of demographic and socioeconomic variables. While the Egyptian registers compiled facts in accordance with contemporaneous surveys in the central Ottoman empire, they contain information on women, whereas the other Ottoman surveys do not.[109]

Martineau also borrows a page from stadial histories to demonstrate how political economy could help her conjecture about events in Egypt's past. The application of the principle of population fills in the missing gaps in "things", official records of the Exodus as written in the Old Testament. Speculating on how many Jews departed in the section "Absence of Hebrew

Records.", Martineau concludes, using a Malthusian reckoning for the maximum rate a population could increase, that 600,000, the highest number ascribed by Mosaic history, did not in fact leave:

> It is probable that no one will contend for the accuracy of the numbers as they stand in the Mosaic history; for, taking the longest term assigned for the residence of the Hebrews in Egypt, – 430 years, – and supposing the most rapid rate of increase known in the world, their numbers could not have amounted to one-third of that assigned.
> (*Eastern Life*, I, p. 161, note)

No accurate evidence exists on the population of Egypt during the time of her visit, either. But Martineau takes it as an article of faith that it has declined. She encourages readers to look to the principles of political economy to explain the causes of population decline and subsequent stagnation in Egypt. The principles of political economy help travelers observe important aspects of Eastern life present and past, even in the absence of facts.

Conclusion: "Travel during the Last Half Century" and Economical Science

Martineau's documentation of her last overseas journey provides entry to a final look at the key themes of the present work: the evolving relationships between travel and travel writing, the observer and observation, and British political economy and other sciences. Martineau traveled over 1,200 miles through all four provinces in Ireland from late summer into autumn 1852 at the behest of Frederick Knight Hunt, editor of *The Daily News*; the paper printed twenty-seven letters in which Martineau chronicles her observations of the struggles of the Irish to recover from aftereffects of the Great Famine. These form a significant portion of her work on the Irish question, which she first addressed in fictional form in "Ireland: A Tale" (1832), one of the *Illustrations of Political Economy*, which followed a trip to Ireland in 1831; she wrote contemporaneous articles on Ireland for *Household Words*, and continued her work in *Once a Week*, *The Westminster Review*, and the American publications *New York Evening Post* and *Atlantic Monthly*, as well as other occasional pieces on Ireland for *The Daily News* until 1866.[110]

Martineau's unsigned Irish letters appeared thrice weekly in *The Daily News* in 1852. They almost always appeared on a Friday, in the same place in the paper, on page four, leading Crawford to assert that "they claim authority through their very regularity".[111] Crawford notes that Martineau begins in Ulster, the area of Ireland most familiar to English readers, and proceeds to move farther and farther away; Martineau defamiliarizes the land, taking an itinerary and a narrative path similar to her American journey where she trekked from cities on America's coast to the putatively uncivilized frontier.[112] She mentions the untapped productive possibilities in the bountiful natural resources in Ireland.[113] In Martineau's account, however, the frontier of Ireland throws up taxonomic scandals. In Galway, she labors to represent what she observes in stadial terms:

> Whatever we may find that is strange in the wild parts of Ireland, we shall hardly find anything stranger than this town of Galway. If we should encounter a wilder barbarism in remote places, it will, at least, not be jumbled together with an advanced civilization.[114]

Galway tests the limits of Martineau ability to observe, represent, and interpret using the tools of political economy. Fishermen in Claddagh, a suburb, could catch more basking sharks with better harpoons and make better bargains for the shark oil they harvest. But they persist in following less-efficient customary practices. They use antique harpoons and, though "The oil is almost inestimable as a commercial resource, if its value was understood", the "people do not understand or believe it", ignorant of the work of a local professor of chemistry attesting to its properties as exceedingly useful for lighting and medicinal purposes. The "mournfulness and vexatiousness of this perverseness" in commerce is reflected in their dwellings: "The once white walls are mossy and mouldy. The sordidness is indescribable. But infinitely worse is the inside." In one home, "kneeling at a bench, a mother and daughter, whose faces haunt us. The mother's eyes were bleared, and her hair starting like a patient's in Bedlam". Not only do the residents behave irrationally, in the sense of not acting like economists, they *are* irrational. The Claddagh fishermen even test the limits of Martineau's sympathy, the touchstone for her observational methodology. She laments that the new owner of the village hopes to persuade the fisherman to use a modern harpoon which he is sending them; "But, till this is achieved, what is to be done about those cabins? How can any man endure to call them his?"

As in *Society in America*, Martineau follows methods of observation laid out in *How to Observe*, stating that "Our business is to tell of things as they are, and not to sentimentalize about how they might be expected to be".[115] Martineau demonstrates to readers how the process of inductive reasoning works. She observes Irish life, and turns these observations of particulars into facts to build evidence for her general conclusions. In the final letter she makes deductions both retrospective and prospective. The recent terrible events in Ireland, where absentee landlordism and the pernicious effects of religious institutions exacerbated the operation of the population principle, nevertheless open the possibilities for a bright economic future:

> The miseries of Ireland, it has been often and long agreed, proceed from economical and religious causes. The worst economic maladies are in course of extirpation by a method of awful severity, but one that discloses unbounded promise. The old barriers are thrown down day by day; the country is opened to occupation and industry.[116]

Martineau published *Letters from Ireland*, reprints of the reports she sent to the *Daily News*, in December 1852, due, she claims in "Preface", to popular demand, and, implicitly, to more widely disseminate her findings among English readers. She left the letters almost entirely unaltered, save for including the date she sent the letters rather than the date published, and with each letter now constituting a discrete chapter in a single document rather than column inches in separate editions of the *Daily News*.[117] The book also allowed Martineau to publicly acknowledge what she "was rather uneasy not to be able to make [known] at the time", her debt to "members of the Dublin Statistical Society and of the Belfast Social Inquiry Society, whose tracts, before interesting to me by my own fireside, were of high value in my journey, by directing my observation and inquiries". She publicly expresses her gratitude to William Neilson Hancock in particular; in Dublin she had informed him "how freely I was using his ideas in my interpretation of Irish affairs".[118] Hancock had been the Whateley Professor of Political Economy at Trinity College, Dublin, from 1846 to 1851; he had authored *Impediments to the Prosperity of Ireland* (1850), a compilation of lectures he had delivered at Trinity in the winter 1847, in the depths of the Famine, as well as "A notice of the theory 'that there is no hope for a nation which lives on potatoes'", delivered in 1848 to the Statistical Society when he was a secretary of the organization.[119] Martineau calls on readers to "ascribe to him, and the other economists of those societies, whatever they may think valuable in my treatment of economical questions in this volume". Martineau embraces modesty, one of the ideals of the still-emerging ethos of objectivity in the social sciences, by adopting a deferential tone, and invoking and ceding authority to those who have obtained official status as statisticians and economists.

Though Martineau "was scarcely ever in reach of books" during her trip, she affirms in "Preface" that her methodological dicta, "observation, inquiry, and reflection", inform her noneconomic representations of Ireland (Martineau, 1852, p. iv).[120] She blends political economy, and, particularly, cutting asides on the noxious effects of potato cultivation, with occasionally wry sketches of scenery (noting in the first letter that just outside of Londonderry "is a proud country for the ragwort"), expressions of regret at the present inconsistent administration of justice, hope based on the spread of education, and a final jeremiad, the last letter, "The People and The Two Churches", on the baneful influence of the Catholic Church and the Church of England.[121] Thus, in the first letter Martineau references natural historians and antiquarians to reflect on features in the landscape that have or have not changed over time before delving into recent developments in the production and trade of linen, potato, pork, cattle, etc., in Lough Foyle and Newton-Limavady. The shift from an oat-based diet to one centered on Indian meal imported from America wrought positive effects on the health and appearance of the area's population; "On the whole, the change is visible enough from the old manufacturing to the modern agricultural population;

and it is very interesting to the observation of an English visitor."[122] Her letters, like travel books in miniature, both entertain and inform.

British political economy and its practitioners shape the information Martineau offers to readers. Yet she calls the science economical science, not political economy, and her friends economists, not political economists, though economist retains its earlier meaning of anyone who practices economy. These terminological changes involve not simply nominative drift but nominative indeterminacy. Martineau's friends at the Dublin Statistical Society had been alert to this issue; in the first paper read before the Society in 1848, "On the Connexion between Statistics and Political Economy", James A. Lawson, Whateley Professor of Political Economy from 1840 to 1845, and serving as secretary alongside Hancock, returns to a topic he had discussed previously, in August 1843, at the 13th meeting of the British Association for the Advancement of Science held at Cork. The minutes recorded Lawson maintaining "that statistics present nothing but a dull and barren show of figures, until united with the principles which belong to political economy". But, while statistics "afford at once the materials and the test of political economy, the latter points out the proper object of statistical inquiries, and draws conclusions for their results".[123]

In 1848 Lawson returns to the subject by stating that members of the Society had joined together "to promote the study of 'Statistical and Economical Science'". Political Economy and Economical science are evidently interchangeable at this point. But one needed to be clear about the meaning of Statistical before explaining its connection to Political Economy. Or Economical Science. Lawson had not found, however, any definition of Statistics "in any author who has written upon the subject", and had "been therefore obliged to make one, and shall be thankful to any of my friends who will correct or amend it".[124]

A decade later, in October 1858, Martineau reflects on the results of nineteenth century explorations by Europeans and Americans around the entire world. In *The Westminster Review* essay "Travel during the Last Half Century", Martineau examines the position of readers of travel narratives rather than issuing guidance to travelers making observations. She makes clear the central role political economy plays when an observer analyzes societies around the globe, noting its place in helping birth new, yet to be defined social sciences, while demonstrating how difficult it was to achieve the position of a "perfect" observer she articulated in *How to Observe*. Martineau reaches further back in time than promised in the title to the article, claiming that Richard Hakluyt's collections enhanced cosmopolitanism among its readers; the accounts "expanded and enriched the minds of readers with new imagery and associations, and liberalized their conceptions of mankind in its variety of life and ways". As for the more realistic narratives of her own day, Martineau asserts that travel had unleashed wonders no less fantastic than the sea monsters found in Hakluyt's books. These unintended if valuable consequences are recognizably political economic in nature; for instance, from little more than the exchange of "knowledge by hearsay" between populations on opposite sides of the globe, "millions would be added to both by the creative operation of commerce".[125]

Seeking out and trading with others creates more people. Martineau express no fear of Malthusian traps, a feeling keeping with the temper of the times in England. Moreover,

> Few could have imagined even how far history might be disclosed by antiquarian travel; much less could it have occurred even to the most far-sighted that interpretation would lead to prophecy, both in science and in history; that the imagination of fireside voyagers would be more richly feasted than ever, the more real the tale of travel became; and that the life of men universally would be tempered by new arts, adorned by fresh and innocent luxuries, secured by a perpetual expansion of political science, grounded on a wider and wider induction, and rendered altogether more worth having, by a spreading participation among all peoples in the special inheritance of each.
> ([Martineau], "Travel", p. 429)

The objects of trade alter the identities of those they touch, and expand the scope of their agency. Martineau repeats a stock argument of political economists in favor of foreign trade; trade softens men's manners. Indeed, Martineau claims that more commerce, combined with the increase in knowledge and the birth and advancement of new sciences produced by exploratory travels, has yielded and will continue to yield salutary physical and, in clear contrast to Hannah More, moral benefits for populations around the world:

> In conjunction with improved ethnological science, the discovery of new sources of tropical products, like cotton and sugar, will extinguish slavery. Other social wretchedness will be diminished with the expanded scope of commerce. A free trade in corn has cured a vast amount of misery and guilt already.
> ([Martineau], "Travel", p. 462)

The repeal of the Corn Laws illustrates how applying the principles of political economy literally delivers the material, moral, and spiritual goods in real life.

Political economy principles are not enough, however, to cure all social ills. For that, Martineau turns to political science and ethnology. She conducts a brief ethnological analysis, characterizing China and Japan as civilizations frozen in time, where nothing of their "faith, notions, or manners" has changed. Yet she rejects the belief that neither have anything to teach the West beyond satisfying historical curiosity. In fact, they "are a fine lesson to us, if we have but the grace to use it, against the folly of supposing that all wisdom and welfare come out of our favourite ideas and manners", and serve as a "standing rebuke of our narrowness and conceit" ([Martineau], "Travel", p. 446). Martineau asks readers to ignore the caricature represented by the photograph of Commissioner Ye Mingchen taken by the correspondent for the *Times*; they should look instead to "men who know them [the Chinese] better – to Mr. Meadows, Mr. Fortune, and American merchants, whose long residence and open minds have qualified them to judge with some fairness of men so unlike themselves" ([Martineau], "Travel", pp. 446–7). Ethnology requires careful observations by unprejudiced viewers; in this case, resident aliens provide more accurate, more realistic, portrayals of the Chinese than an actual photograph.

Her relativist ethnology contains elements of stadial histories, her cosmopolitanism gesturing toward a mildly chiding anti-Occidentalism. Still, political economy forms the foundation of Martineau's understanding of how travel transforms societies and peoples. "More demands, new products; more wants, new markets" are all the result of travel and discovery, as are all "pleasures ... thoughts and feelings" ([Martineau], "Travel", p. 463). The wonders produced by contemporary travel writing include facts disseminated by travelers which lead to "interpretation" that itself would generate "prophecy, both in science and in history". This methodological, epistemological, and ontological sorcery as well as advances in mental and material comfort had been secured by inductive political science. If trade and the political economic tools to analyze it help usher in new sciences, Martineau contributed to this process when she introduced the new science of sociology, née social physics, to Britain, translating and publishing a condensed version of Auguste Comte's *Cours de Philosophie Positive* (1839) as *The Positive Philosophy of Auguste Comte* (1853).

New forms of inquiry would have to meet certain conditions to be considered sciences. The same month that "Travel during the Last Half Century" appeared Martineau cast doubt in *The Spectator* on whether "Social Science" actually amounted to a science. She uses the interrogative in the title of her short piece, "What is 'Social Science'?", to question the purpose, objects, and, crucially, the facts pursued by attendees of the second annual meeting of The National Association for the Promotion of Social Science.

> Before they attempt to construct a science, they search into facts, collect positive knowledge, and from the relation of fact to fact they deduce the law which the human intellect is permitted to recognize as vitally governing the subject-matter of the science. In what part of the proceedings at Liverpool, in what part of any proceedings carried on by the senators taking part in those deliberations, have we had the slightest attempt towards this first step in the construction of a "science"?[126]

Martineau eventually embraced the efforts of the Association. Still, as she points out in "Travel During the Last Half Century", stubborn skepticism among readers about the truth of travel narratives had formed a barrier to acceptance of the facts that generate new sciences.

As evidence of the difficulties travel writers faced, Martineau traces how the credibility of European travelers had evolved. Late in the previous century, Grand Tourists offered little or no new information; they simply retraced the footsteps of others. Consequently "Their tours were no pleasure to people at home." Arthur Young, on the other hand, had, as part of his agricultural experimentation, produced innovations in traveling and travel writing, and

> the idea of a more edifying way of traversing foreign countries; but his social observations and economical inferences did not prepare a good reception for the more adventurous class who were about to set forth on fresh explorations of the globe.
> ([Martineau], "Travel", p. 430)

Young's write-ups of his travels provided valuable information if little entertainment; the predictably repetitive Grand Tour accounts produced little of either. Together, they dulled the imagination of readers around the turn of the century, leaving them less receptive to novel facts revealed by travelers to novel destinations.

As for readers, Martineau criticizes earlier consumers of European travel accounts who, peering out from their domestic spaces, reflexively rejected things foreign. She recounts the ridicule endured by James Bruce upon publication of *Travels to Discover the Source of the Nile* (1790):

> The mournful story of Bruce reveals, in the clearest light, the spirit of the time. It does not occur to travellers like Bruce, and like some other educated and honourable gentlemen who might be pointed out, that their accounts of what they had seen would be utterly disbelieved at home, and that they should be pronounced impostors, as soon as they had anything to relate which comfortable and conceited domestic people did not know before, and had not happened to imagine.
> ([Martineau], "Travel", p. 430)

From his position in Bombay Sir James Mackintosh had accused Bruce of "enterprising credulity"; less imaginative readers in England also regarded Bruce as a credulous rather than credible observer, and his testimony naïve rather than innocent.[127] Martineau decries the then-prevailing tendency for society to disbelieve the first eyewitness account of marvels such as Abyssinians eating beefsteak raw, a gustatory tidbit recounted by Bruce. Even imaginative readers could fall prey to national prejudice. Horace Walpole, one of Martineau's "Sceptics at Home.", had written the fantastical gothic *The Castle of Otranto* (1764) but dismissed the account of Bruce, scoffed that the findings of Sir Joseph Banks hardly merited travel at all, and justified his refusal to read accounts of Captain Cook's explorations by venting that he had seen quite enough in illustrations from the voyages, prints of the "parcel of ugly faces" of "rows of savages". Walpole committed a methodological error (and more) when he "measured all lands and peoples by the standard of home" ([Martineau], "Travel", pp. 430–2, 432).

Under the heading, "Scepticism of Ignorance", Martineau writes that such distrust upends a worthy status-based hierarchy of credibility. Gentlemen, who should be accorded the benefit of doubt, "suffer the most, because honourable people are unsuspecting, and confide in the world before it occurs to them that the world does not always reciprocate the confidence" ([Martineau], "Travel", p. 433). Although it had not entirely disappeared, such skepticism had eased considerably during the course of the century due primarily to Humboldt. He represents the living embodiment of the conquest of doubts about the credibility of travelers:

> a spirit so grave, so scientific, so unselfish, so simple and business-like, has been infused into exploratory journeying within the lifetime of the prince of modern travel, Humboldt, that it is nearly beyond the malice of the superficial and the ignorant, who can no longer spoil what they cannot appreciate.
>
> ([Martineau], "Travel", p. 435)

Yet Martineau illustrates just how hard it is for travelers to approach the ideal of Humboldt, even when equipped with the latest science, and an appreciation for the methodology of observation. While she foresees a future not dominated by Europe and America, where "Even if the prophecy of greatness moving westwards be still reverenced, the turn of Central Asia must come again", Martineau takes an emphatically blinkered, Eurocentric view of contemporary European empire-building and its accompanying exploitation and violence ([Martineau], "Travel", p. 445). Martineau approvingly notes that in the public imagination India will soon join China as a supplier of tea to Britain due in part to what she refers to simply as the "acquisition of Assam". This as the nationalist uprising in India sputtered to a close. And she can only muster a bland statement about "European plenipotentiaries recently on the spot" in China. This as the Second Opium War entered its third year ([Martineau], "Travel", p. 446).

At least Western observers could derive useful knowledge from China and Japan. Martineau bestows no such blessings on the Indigenous peoples of the Antipodes. Writing of the Australian, New Zealand, and Tasmanian colonists, Martineau enthuses that

> These organized peoples are living on territory which was but lately the domain of the savage and the wild beast. The kangaroo and the emu have almost disappeared where millions of sheep supply the finest wool

in the world; and "the diggings" have opened under the feet of the staring aborigines.

([Martineau], "Travel", p. 447)

Martineau constructs, in her grammatical parallelisms, a kinship between Aboriginal peoples and wild beasts; violence meted out by the colonists threatens the Aboriginal peoples with extermination, and the kangaroo and emu with extinction. And when Martineau switches from referring to savages to naming a people, she diminishes their status by calling them aborigines rather than Aborigines. Contemporary British readers would have been keenly aware of the savagery visited by colonists upon Aboriginal peoples, especially the genocidal warfare aimed at the Palawa on Tasmania in the 1820s and 1830s. Martineau certainly was; she set one of her *Illustrations of Political Economy*, "Homes Abroad" (1832), a Malthusian story on emigration, in Australia. The tale, in a foreshadowing of the passage above, contains a scene in which: an immigrant from Kent mistakes an Aboriginal baby for a pig; Martineau, as narrator, describes an Aboriginal man as ape-like; and Martineau, again as narrator, pronounces that an Aboriginal woman looks and acts more like a "tame monkey" than a person.[128] But Martineau mentions none of this. Here she considers the Aborigines as simply commercially unorganized savages who gawp uncomprehendingly at the gold mines of the colonists. Nor does Martineau cite any benefits flowing from or to the Aborigines from recent exploratory and commercial travel by Europeans. The latter, Britons especially, clearly profit from land, trade, and gold, so much so "that it would not be too much to say that the omission of the discovery of Australia would have retarded our progress in the proportion of centuries, and have essentially altered the aspect of society all over Europe" ([Martineau], "Travel", p. 447).

Martineau ultimately questions, however, where value lies. Like Miers, she declares that information gained from travel trumps the products of mines or any other items of trade. Thus, with Egypt, "the enlargement of our knowledge, and the value to history of the great series of Egyptian researches, are a gain which will distinguish our age more than any extension of commerce in any quarter, and to any amount" ([Martineau], "Travel", p. 451). Regarding facts that might be produced from future exploratory travel, Martineau foresees the arrival of

> more rational views of our human life than have ever been held yet, now that we can study various races of men in all stages of civilization below our own, and provide for our own further progress by the physiological studies indicated by ethnological discovery.
>
> ([Martineau], "Travel", p. 461)

Europeans constitute the "we" for whom a likely more rational future awaits. They make up the "our" in "stages of civilization below our own", too. Future civilizations will rest, however, on foundations built from facts still to be discovered, in areas yet to be explored:

> natural philosophy will still be opening new avenues to fresh regions, in which the human race may find a more and more advanced guidance in the use they may make of their planetary abode, and the purposes to which they should apply the life they lead upon it.
>
> ([Martineau], "Travel", p. 464)

Facts travel. Natural philosophy travels. Martineau and her contemporaries promoted the dissemination of information around the globe; they helped further open the world to the trade in ideas. If Martineau chose to promote other social sciences as useful epistemologies for analysis of different societies, she nonetheless insisted that the art and science of political economy serve as the foundations, timeless principles for how to observe. Martineau predicts that travelers will diffuse and adapt facts, principles, and practices in all sciences, to all points on earth. From her vantage point, travel and travel writing, and observations about travel and travel writing, open possibilities for the benefit of the entire human race.

Notes

1 Harriet Martineau, *How to Observe. Morals and Manners* (London: Charles Knight, 1838b), p. 40. Further references to *How to Observe* are included parenthetically in the text.
2 Frances Trollope, *Domestic Manners of the Americans*, vols. 1 and 2 (London: Whittaker, Treacher, & Co, 1832), I, p. 63. Further references to *Domestic Manners* are included parenthetically in the text.
3 Trollope completely abandons fencing off observations on government in the two-volume *Vienna and the Austrians; with Some Account of a Journey through Swabia, Bavaria, the Tyrol, and the Salzbourg*, vols. 1 and 2 (London: R. Bentley, 1838). In the preface, she defines her study as observations "on the simple machinery of her [Austria's] government, and its effect upon her own people" (Trollope, *Vienna and the Austrians*, I, p. iv).
4 [Timothy Flint], "Travellers in America, &c.", *The Knickerbocker: or, New-York Monthly Magazine*, 2, October (1833): 283–302 (at p. 289).
5 She also mentions that the prospectus for a "fashionable boarding-school", the "Brooklyn Collegiate Institute for Young Ladies", includes "Compend of Political Economy" as part of the final sequence in the curriculum, along with elements of natural philosophy, Horace, Tacitus, astronomy, and so forth (*Domestic Manners*, II, pp. 164–6).
6 Anon., "Domestic Manners of the Americans. By Mrs. Trollope", *The Quarterly Review*, 47, no. 93 (1832): 39–80 (at pp. 39, 40).
7 Anon., "Domestic Manners", *The Quarterly Review*, p. 40.
8 Anon., "Domestic Manners of the Americans", *Monthly Repository*, 6 (1832): 401–6 (at p. 402).
9 Anon., "Domestic Manners of the Americans", *The Athenaeum*, no. 230 (24 March 1832): 187–8 (at p. 187); Anon., "Domestic Manners of the Americans", *The Literary Gazette*, no. 792 (24 March 1832): 178–80 (at p. 178).

10 Anon., "British Writers on America", *Tait's Edinburgh Magazine*, 1, no. 2 (1832): 229–34 (at p. 232).
11 Anon., "Domestic Manners", *The Literary Gazette*, p. 178.
12 Anon., "Domestic Manners", *The Literary Gazette*, p. 179.
13 Anon., "National Peculiarities", *The Penny Magazine*, 1, no. 9 (1832): 83.
14 Anon., "National Peculiarities", *The Penny Magazine*, 1, no. 9 (1832): 83 (emphases in original).
15 [J. G. Lockhart], "Trollope and Paulding on America," *Fraser's Magazine*, 5, no. 27 (1832): 336–50 (at p. 343).
16 Anon., "Prince Pückler Muscau and Mrs. Trollope", *The North American Review*, 36, no. 78 (1833): 1–48 (at p. 14).
17 [Flint], "Travellers in America", p. 290.
18 Anon., ed., "A Brief Inquiry into the Real Name and Character of the Author of This Book", in *Domestic Manners of the Americans*, by Mrs. Trollope (London: Whittaker, Treacher, & Co., 1832), pp. iii–ix (at p. iii).
19 Anon., ed., "A Brief Inquiry", pp. iv, ix.
20 Anon., "Domestic Manners of the Americans [continued]", *The Literary Gazette*, no. 797 (28 April 1832): 262–3 (at p. 263).
21 Anon., "Domestic Manners of the Americans", *Blackwood's Edinburgh Magazine*, 31, no. 194 (1832): 829–47 (at pp. 829, 840).
22 Harriet Martineau, *Harriet Martineau's Autobiography*, 3 vols., ed. Maria Chapman (Boston: James R. Osgood and Company, 1877), I, p. 330.
23 Cooper, *Family Fictions*, chapter 4.
24 Harriet Martineau, "Weal and Woe in Garveloch" [1832], in Harriet Martineau, *Illustrations of Political Economy*, vol. 2, no. 6 (London: Charles Fox, 1834), p. 104.
25 [George Poulett Scrope], "Miss Martineau's Monthly Novels", *The Quarterly Review*, 49, no. 98 (1833): 136–52 (at p. 142).
26 If Martineau kept or even wrote up notes or drafts for *How to Observe*, none survive. She rarely made changes to her first drafts for *Illustrations*.
27 Claudia Orazem, *Political Economy and Fiction in the Early Works of Harriet Martineau* (Frankfurt: Peter Lang, 1999), p. 149.
28 Martineau, *Autobiography*, I, p. 221.
29 Gregory Vargo, "Contested Authority: Reform and Local Pressure in Harriet Martineau's Poor Law Stories", *Nineteenth-Century Gender Studies*, 3, no. 2 (2007). <https://www.ncgsjournal.com/issue32/vargo.htm> [18 June 2017].
30 Martineau, *Autobiography*, I, p. 221.
31 ["K.[er], H.B."], "Advertisement", in H. T. De la Beche, *How to Observe. Geology* (London: Charles Knight, 1835), pp. iii–vi (at p. iii).
32 "K.[er]", "Advertisement", p. iv.
33 Charles Babbage, *On the Economy of Machinery and Manufactures* (London: Charles Knight, 1832), p. iii. Further references to *Economy* are included parenthetically in the text.
34 "K.[er]", "Advertisement", p. iv.
35 "K.[er]", "Advertisement", pp. iv, v.
36 "K.[er]", "Advertisement", p. v.
37 William Jacob, *Travels in the South of Spain, in Letters Written A. D. 1809 and 1810* (London: J. Johnson and Co., 1811), pp. 338, 341.
38 Jacob, *Travels*, p. 340.
39 Lisa Pace Vetter, "Harriet Martineau on the Theory and Practice of Democracy in America", *Political Theory*, 36, no. 3 (2008): 424–55.
40 [A.C.W.], "Songs of the Metropolis", *The London and Westminster Review*, 32, no. 1 (1838): 220–41 (at p. 221).

41 [John Wilson Croker], "Miss Martineau's *Morals and Manners*", *The Quarterly Review*, 63, no. 125 (1839): 61–72 (at p. 62).
42 *How to Observe*, p. 48; [Croker], "Miss Martineau's *Morals and Manners*", pp. 62, 67–70.
43 [Croker], "Miss Martineau's *Morals and Manners*", p. 72, emphases in original.
44 Jackson hoped *What to Observe* would enhance the disciplinary status and public standing of geography. Keighren, Withers, and Bell, *Travels into Print*, p. 62.
45 Julian Jackson, *What to Observe; or, The Traveller's Remembrancer* (London: James Madden and Co., 1841), p. iii.
46 Jackson, *What to Observe*, p. iv.
47 Jackson, *What to Observe*, p. 222.
48 Jackson, *What to Observe*, pp. 222–3.
49 Martineau traveled from New York to Massachusetts, then south via Pennsylvania, through the mid-Atlantic and then to the deep South, visiting Alabama, Mississippi, and Louisiana. She returned north to Massachusetts before heading west through Illinois and Ohio.
50 Martineau, *Autobiography*, I, p. 331.
51 Eitan Bar-Yosef, "'With the Practiced Eye of a Deaf Person': Martineau's Travel Writing and the Construction of the Disabled Traveller", in Ella Dzelzianis and Cora Kaplan, eds., *Harriet Martineau: Authorship, Society, and Empire* (Manchester: Manchester University Press, 2010), pp. 165–79 (at pp. 172–4).
52 Michael R. Hill, "A Methodological Comparison of Harriet Martineau's *Society in America* (1837) and Alexis De Tocqueville's *Democracy in America* (1835–1840)", in Michael R. Hill and Susan Hoecker-Drysdale, eds., *Harriet Martineau: Theoretical and Methodological Perspectives* (New York: Routledge, 2001), pp. 59–74 (at p. 65); Mary Jo Deegan, "Making Lemonade: Harriet Martineau on Being Deaf", in Michael R. Hill and Susan Hoecker-Drysdale, eds., *Harriet Martineau: Theoretical and Methodological Perspectives* (New York: Routledge, 2001), pp. 41–58.
53 Martineau, *Autobiography*, I, p. 331.
54 Harriet Martineau, "Letter to the Deaf", *Tait's Edinburgh Magazine*, 1 (1834): 174–9 (at p. 175).
55 Martineau, "Letter to the Deaf", p. 176.
56 Martineau, "Letter to the Deaf", pp. 178–9, emphasis in original.
57 Martineau, "Letter to the Deaf", p. 179.
58 Deegan, "Making Lemonade", p. 52; Bar-Yosef, "'With the Practiced Eye of a Deaf Person'".
59 [Thomas Carlyle], "State of German Literature", *The Edinburgh Review*, 46, no. 92 (1827): 304–51 (at p. 309).
60 [Carlyle], "State of German Literature", p. 309.
61 [Carlyle], "State of German Literature", p. 309.
62 John Plotz, "Can the Sofa Speak? A Look at Thing Theory", *Criticism*, 47, no. 1 (2005): 109–18 (at p. 110).
63 Jackson, *What to Observe*, p. 392.
64 Cooper, *Family Fictions*, pp. 113–53.
65 Those who have taken up, at length, the influence of Jean-Baptiste Say, Malthus, and other British political economists on Tocqueville's views on the social sciences, as well as comparing the methodologies of *Democracy* and *Society* include: Drolet 2003a and 2003b; Swedberg 2009; McDonald 1994; Hill 2001; Vetter 2008; Craiutu 2009; and Kemple 2011.
66 Michael Drolet, "Democracy and Political Economy: Tocqueville's Thoughts on J.-B. Say and T.R. Malthus", *History of European Ideas*, 29, no. 2 (2003a): 159–81 (at p. 178).

67 Hill, "A Methodological Comparison", pp. 69–71.
68 Hill, "A Methodological Comparison", pp. 69, 71.
69 Harriet Martineau, *Retrospect of Western Travel*, 3 vols. (London: Saunders and Otley, 1838a), pp. 156–7. Further references to *Retrospect*, by volume and page number, are included parenthetically in the text.
70 They also brought *The History of North America*, by Reverend Mr. W.D. Cooper, first published in 1789, *Tableau du climat et du sol des États-Unis* (1803) by the French philosopher, orientalist, and abolitionist Constantin François de Chassebœuf, comte de Volney, who had traveled to the United States in 1795, and Hall's volumes on North America, translating that part pertaining to prisons. See Drolet, "Democracy and Political Economy", pp. 161, 168.
71 Mary C.M. Simpson, "Preface", in Mary C.M. Simpson, ed., *Correspondence & Conversations of Alexis de Tocqueville with Nassau William Senior from 1834 to 1859*, vol. 1 (London: Henry S. King & Co, 1872), pp. iii–v (at p. iii).
72 Varouxakis, Giorgios, "Guizot's Historical Works and J.S. Mill's Reception of Tocqueville", *History of Political Thought*, 20, no. 2 (1999): 292–312.
73 Drolet, "Democracy and Political Economy", pp. 173–81; Michael Drolet, *Tocqueville, Democracy and Social Reform* (New York: Palgrave Macmillan, 2003b), p. 95; Aurelian Craiutu, "What Kind of Social Scientist Was Tocqueville?", in Aurelian Craiutu and Sheldon Gellar, eds., *Conversations with Tocqueville: The Global Democratic Revolution in the Twenty-First Century* (Lanham, MD: Lexington Books, 2009), pp. 55–82 (at p. 73).
74 Richard Swedberg, *Tocqueville's Political Economy* (Princeton: Princeton University Press, 2009), pp. 126–45; Craiutu, "What Kind of Social Scientist", pp. 73–4.
75 Drolet, "Democracy and Political Economy", p. 170; Craiutu, "What Kind of Social Scientist", p. 73.
76 Alexis de Tocqueville, *De la Démocratie en Amérique*, vol. 1 (Paris: Charles Gosselin, 1835), p. 47. The original French reads:

> L'état social est ordinairement le produit d'un fait, quelquefois des lois, le plus souvent de ces deux causes réunies; mais une fois qu'il existe, on peu le considérer lui-même comme la cause première de la plupart de lois, des coutumes et des idées qui reglent la conduite des nations; ce qu'il ne produit pas, il le modifie.

77 Alexis de Tocqueville, "Avertissement." in Alexis de Tocqueville, *De la Démocratie en Amérique*, vol. 3 (Paris: Charles Gosselin, 1840), p. I.
78 Drolet, "Democracy and Political Economy", p. 169.
79 Years later Martineau recalls how her American travels helped change her views on property, political economy, and the social state:

> What I witnessed in America considerably modified my views on the subject of Property; and from that time forward I saw social modifications taking place which have already altered the tone of leading Economists, and opened a prospect of further changes which will probably work out in time a totally new social state.
>
> (*Society*, I, p. 232)

80 André Gueslin, *L'invention de l'économie sociale* (Paris, Economica, 1998), p. 1; Henri Desroche *Pour un traité d'économie sociale* (Paris: CIEM, 1983). The French liberal economist Charles Dunoyer, who authored *Nouveau traité d'économie sociale* (1830), believed social economy an extension of political economy. In his view, social economy encompasses influences on the production

of the means of existence beyond mere material inputs. Others, Christian political economists and socialists, fancied social economy a critique of and substitute for political economy. See Danièle Demoustier and Damien Rousselière, "Social Economy as Social Science and Practice: Historical Perspectives on France", Eleventh World Congress of Social Economics: "Social Economics: A Paradigm for a Global Society," Albertville, 8–11 June 2004, (2004), pp. 1–42 (at p. 3).

81 Caroline Roberts, *The Woman and the Hour: Harriet Martineau and Victorian Ideologies* (Toronto: University of Toronto Press, 2002), pp. 26–51.

82 Cora Kaplan, "Slavery, Race, History: Harriet Martineau's Ethnographic Imagination", in Ella Dzelzianis and Cora Kaplan, eds., *Harriet Martineau: Authorship, Society, and Empire* (Manchester: Manchester University Press, 2010), pp. 165–79 (at pp. 187–94).

83 Caitlin Rosenthal, *Accounting for Slavery: Masters and Management* (Cambridge, MA: Harvard University Press, 2018).

84 Edgar A. Poe, "Our Amateur Poets. No. 1.- Flaccus", *Graham's Magazine*, 22, no. 3 (1843): 195–8 (at p. 198).

85 She cites an annual profit rate of thirty-five percent for cotton-growing in Alabama during her visit (*Society*, I, p. 307).

86 Anon., "Miss Martineau on Slavery", *Southern Literary Messenger*, 3, no. 11 (1837): 641–57 (at p. 641).

87 [H.M.], "The Martyr Age of the United States", *The London and Westminster Review*, 32, no. 1 (1838): 1–32 (at pp. 1, 2).

88 [H.M.], "The Martyr Age", p. 31.

89 Nadav Gabay, "'With the Practiced Eye of a Deaf Person': Harriet Martineau, Deafness and the Scientificity of Social Knowledge", *The American Sociologist*, 50, no. 3 (2019): 335–55; Bar-Yosef, "'With the Practiced Eye of a Deaf Person'".

90 Harriet Martineau, *Life in the Sick-Room: Essays* (Boston, MA: L.C. Bowles and W. Crosby, 1844), p. 93.

91 Martineau, *Life in the Sick-Room*, p. 196.

92 Martin Anderson, "The Development of British Tourism in Egypt, 1815 to 1850", *Journal of Tourism History*, 4, no. 3 (2012): 259–79.

93 The competition was announced in 1830, and solicited essays "proving Unitarian ideas superior to those of Catholics, Jews and Moslems".

94 Anon., "Miss Martineau's Eastern Life", *The Christian Reformer, Or, Unitarian Magazine and Review*, 4, no. 43 (1848): 385–98 (at pp. 385, 387).

95 Anon., "Miss Martineau's Eastern Life", *The Christian Reformer*, p. 387.

96 Anon., "Miss Martineau's Eastern Life", *The Christian Reformer*, pp. 392, 393, 398.

97 Anon., "Miss Martineau's Eastern Life", *The Prospective Review*, 4, no. 16 (1848): 524–38 (at p. 524, emphasis in original).

98 Anon., "Miss Martineau's Eastern Life", *The Prospective Review*, p. 526.

99 Harriet Martineau, *Eastern Life, Present and Past*, 3 vols. (London: Edward Moxon, 1848), vol. III, pp. 333–4. Further references to *Eastern Life* are included parenthetically in the text by volume and page number.

100 Sir John Gardner Wilkinson, *Modern Egypt and Thebes*, vols. 1 and 2 (London: John Murray, 1843), vol. 1, p. iv.

101 Nadav Gabay, "The Political Origins of Social Science: The Cultural Transformation of the British Parliament and the Emergence of Scientific Policymaking, 1803–1857. UC San Diego (2007), pp. 348–9. <https://escholarship.org/content/qt9b48n807/qt9b48n807.pdf> [20 November 2019].

102 Anon., "Miss Martineau's Eastern Life", *The Prospective Review*, p. 524.

103 Wilkinson, *Modern Egypt and Thebes*, vol. 1, p. 257.
104 Anon., "Head and Miers on Buenos Ayres and Chile.", p. 128.
105 Anon., "Eastern Life; Present and Past.", *The Westminster and Foreign Quarterly Review*, 50, no. 96 (1848): 314–33 (at p. 316).
106 Anon., "Eastern Life; Present and Past.", p. 317.
107 Anon., "Eastern Life; Present and Past.", pp. 317–8.
108 Kenneth M. Cuno and Michael J. Reimer, "The Census Registers of Nineteenth-Century Egypt: A New Source for Social Historians", *British Journal of Middle Eastern Studies*, 24, no. 2 (1997): 193–216 (quoted at p. 213).
109 Cuno and Reimer, "The Census Registers of Nineteenth-Century Egypt"; Mohamed Salah, "A Pre-colonial Population Brought to Light: Digitization of the Nineteenth Century Egyptian Censuses", *Historical Methods: A Journal of Quantitative and Interdisciplinary History*, 46, no. 1 (2013): 5–18.
110 For a collection of Martineau's writings on Ireland, see Deborah A. Logan, ed., *Harriet Martineau and the Irish Question: Condition of Post-famine Ireland* (Lehigh: Lehigh University Press, 2011).
111 Iain Crawford, "Harriet Martineau: Travel and the Writer", in Valerie Sanders and Gaby Weiner, eds., *Harriet Martineau and the Birth of Disciplines: Nineteenth-Century Intellectual Powerhouse* (London: Routledge, 2017), pp. 171–86 (at p. 180).
112 Crawford, "Harriet Martineau: Travel and the Writer", pp. 180–1.
113 Joel Scherer, "Troubling Journey: Elite Women Travellers of Ireland and the Irish Question, 1834–1852", *Madison Historical Review*, 11 (2014): 1–16 (at pp. 7–9); Brian Conway and Michael R. Hill, "Harriet Martineau and Ireland", in Séamas Ó Síocháin, ed., *Social Thought on Ireland in the Nineteenth Century* (Dublin, Ireland: University College Dublin Press, 2009), pp. 47–66 (at p. 48).
114 Harriet Martineau, "Letters from Ireland. Letter XI", *The Daily News*, Friday, 3 September 1852b, p. 4.
115 Harriet Martineau, "Letters from Ireland, XVI", *The Daily News*, Friday, 17 September 1852c, p. 4.
116 Harriet Martineau, "Letters from Ireland, XXVII", *The Daily News*, Thursday, 14 October 1852d, p. 4.
117 The book does in fact contain at least one alteration, substituting "The worst economic mischiefs" for "The worst economic maladies" in the key passage cited above. The former suggests more human responsibility for the ills of Ireland than does the latter.
118 Harriet Martineau, *Letters from Ireland* (London: John Chapman, 1852e), p. iv.
119 William Neilson Hancock, *Impediments to the Prosperity of Ireland* (London: Simms and M'Intyre, 1850), and "A notice of the theory 'that there is no hope for a nation which lives on potatoes'", *Two Papers Read Before the Dublin Statistical Society* [1848] (Dublin: Hodges and Smith for the Dublin Statistical Society, 1854), pp. 7–10.
120 Martineau, *Letters from Ireland*, p. iv.
121 Martineau, "Letters from Ireland, I", *The Daily News*, Friday, 13 August 1852a, p. 4, and "Letters from Ireland, XXVII", p. 4.
122 Martineau, "Letters from Ireland, I", p. 4.
123 James A. Lawson, "On the Connexion between Statistics and Political Economy", *Report of the Thirteenth Meeting of the British Association for the Advancement of Science* (London: John Murray, 1844), pp. 94–5 (at pp. 94–5).
124 James A. Lawson, "On the Connexion between Statistics and Political Economy", *Papers Read before the Dublin Statistical Society* [1848] (Dublin: Alexander Thom for the Dublin Statistical Society, 1854), pp. 3–9 (at p. 3).

125 [Harriet Martineau], "Travel during the Last Half Century", *The Westminster Review*, 70 (1858): 426–65 (at p. 429). Further references to "Travel" are included parenthetically in the text.
126 [Harriet Martineau], "What Is 'Social Science'?", *The Spectator*, 31 (1858): 1119–20 (at p. 1120).
127 [Mackintosh?], "Note on 'Preliminary Discourse'", p. xxxi.
128 See Cooper, *Family Fictions*, pp. 191–2.

Bibliography

[A.C.W.], "Songs of the Metropolis", *The London and Westminster Review*, 32, no. 1 (1838): 220–41.

Adamovsky, Ezequiel, "Before Development Economics: Western Political Economy, the "Russian Case," and the First Perceptions of Economic Backwardness (from the 1760s Until the Mid-Nineteenth Century)", *Journal of the History of Economic Thought*, 32, no. 3 (2010): 349–76.

Adams, William, *The Present Operations and Future Prospects of the Mexican Mine Associations Analysed: By the Evidence of Official Documents, English and Mexican, and the National Advantages Expected from Joint Stock Companies, Considered in a Letter to the Right Hon. George Canning* (London: J. Hatchard and Son, Sherwood and Company, and J.M. Richardson, 1825).

Addison, Joseph, *Remarks on Several Parts of Italy, &c in the Years 1701, 1702, 1703* [1705] (London: J. and R. Tonson, and S. Draper, 1745).

Akel, Regina, *The Journals of Maria Graham (1785–1842)* (2007) <wrap.warwick.ac.uk/2585/> [18 April 2015].

Alborn, Timothy L., *Conceiving Companies: Joint-Stock Politics in Victorian England* (London: Routledge, 1998).

———, "Age and Empire in the Indian Census, 1871–1931", *The Journal of Interdisciplinary History*, 30, no. 1 (1999): 61–89.

———, "Boys to Men: Moral Restraint at Haileybury College", in Brian Dolan, ed., *Malthus, Medicine and Morality: "Malthusianism" after 1798* (Amsterdam: Editions Rodopi, 2000), pp. 33–55.

———, *All that Glittered: Britain's Most Precious Metal from Adam Smith to the Gold Rush* (New York: Oxford University Press, 2019).

[Allen, John], "Humboldt- *Essai Politique sur la Nouvelle Espagne*", *The Edinburgh Review*, 16, no. 21 (1810): 62–102.

Allen, Robert Carson and Ó Gráda, Cormac, "On the Road Again with Arthur Young: English, Irish, and French Agriculture during the Industrial Revolution", *The Journal of Economic History*, 48, no. 1 (1988): 93–116.

Altick, Richard D., *The English Common Reader: A Social History of the Mass Reading Public, 1800–1900* [1957] (Columbus, OH: Ohio State University Press, 1998).

Alù, Giorgia, and Hill, Sarah Patricia, "The Travelling Eye: Reading the Visual in Travel Narratives", *Studies in Travel Writing*, 22, no. 1 (2018): 1–15.

Bibliography

Amsler, Christine E., Bartlett, Robin L., and Bolton, Craig J., "Thoughts of Some British Economists on Early Limited Liability and Corporate Legislation", *History of Political Economy*, 13, no. 4 (1981): 774–93.

Anderson, Martin, "The Development of British Tourism in Egypt, 1815 to 1850", *Journal of Tourism History*, 4, no. 3 (2012): 259–79.

Anderson Gary, M. and Tollison, Robert D., "Adam Smith's Analysis of Joint-Stock Companies", *Journal of Political Economy*, 90, no. 6 (1982): 1237–56.

Andrews, Joseph, *Journey from Buenos Ayres: Through the Provinces of Cordova, ... etc.*, vols. 1 and 2 (London: John Murray, 1827).

Anon., "Preface", in Lady Mary Wortley Montagu, ed., *Letters of the Right Honourable Lady M—y W—y M—e Written during Her Travels in Europe, Asia and Africa to Persons of Distinction, Men of Letters, &c. in Different Parts of Europe*, vol. 1 [1724] (London: P. Becket and P.A. De Hondt, 1763), pp. v–xi.

———, "Carta", *Semanario de Agricultura y Artes: dirigido á los párrocos*, vol. 1 (Madrid: Real Jardin Botanico, 1797).

———, "Cooper's *Letters on the Irish Nation*", *The New London Review; or, Monthly Report of Authors and Books*, 3 (1800): 49–56.

———, "Retrospect of Domestic Literature. – Irish Politics", *The Monthly Magazine, or, British Register, Supplementary Number to the Monthly Magazine*, 10, no. 68 (1800): 597.

———, "Cooper's *Letters on the Irish Nation*", *The Anti-Jacobin Review and Magazine*, 7 (1801): 173–8.

———, "Malthus on the Principle of Population", *The British Critic and Quarterly Theological Review*, 23 (1804): 59–69.

———, "Depons [sic]- *Voyage dans l' Amerique Meridionale*", *The Edinburgh Review: Or Critical Journal*, 8, no. 16 (1806): 378–99.

———, "Depons's *Travels in South America*", *The Monthly Review, Or, Literary Journal*, 54 (1807): 351–62.

———, "M. Depons' *Travels in South America*", *The Gentleman's Magazine*, 78, Part 2 (1808): 808–15.

———, "Humboldt- *Essai Politique sur la Nouvelle Espagne*", *The Edinburgh Review*, 19, no. 37 (1811): 164–98.

———, "Graham's *Journal of a Residence in India*", *The Quarterly Review*, 8, no. 16 (1812): 406–421.

———, "Maria Graham's *Journal of a Residence in India*", *The Critical Review*, 3, no. 4 (1813): 337–46.

———, "Hannah More's New Work", *The Analectic Magazine*, 14 (1819): 429–33.

———, "Review of Hannah More's *Moral Sketches of Prevailing Opinions and Manners, Foreign and Domestic*", *The British Review, and London Critical Journal*, 14, no. 28 (1819): 458–74.

———, "Review of J.W. Cunningham's *Cautions to Continental Travellers*", *The Monthly Review*, 89 (1819): 445–6.

———, "[Review of] *Moral Sketches of Prevailing Opinions and Manners, &c., With Reflections on Prayer*", *The Gentleman's Magazine*, 89, Part 2 (1819): 434–35; 532–34.

———, "Review. More's *Moral Sketches, &c*", *The Investigator*, 1 (1820): 131–41.

———, "Review of Hannah More's *Moral Sketches of Prevailing Opinions and Manners, Foreign and Domestic*", *The Monthly Review*, 91 (1820): 164–74.

———, "Chili, Peru, &c", *The Quarterly Review*, 30, no. 60 (1824): 441–72.

——, "Graham's *Journal of a Residence in Chile*", *The Philomathic Journal*, 1 (1824): 410–421.

——, "[Review of] *Journal of a Voyage to Brazil*", *The London Literary Gazette*, 377 (1824): 227–8.

——, "Transactions of the Literary Society of Bombay", *The Quarterly Oriental Magazine, Review, and Register*, 1, no. 2 (1824): 177–235.

——, "Transactions of the Literary Society of Bombay", *The Quarterly Oriental Magazine, Review, and Register*, 2 (1824): 17–53.

——, "Continuan las Observaciones de la Víctima de las Teorías", *La Década Araucana*, 13 (1825): 320–322.

——, "Mrs. Graham's *Residence in Chile*", *Monthly Review, or Literary Journal Enlarged*, 106 (1825): 189–200.

——, "Mrs. Graham's *Voyage to Brazil*", *Monthly Review, or Literary Journal Enlarged*, 106 (1825): 180–89.

——, "Proctor's *Journey across the Cordillera of the Andes*", *Monthly Review, or Literary Journal Enlarged*, 107 (1825): 128–140.

——, "Miers's Travels in Chile", *The London Magazine*, 6 (1826): 119–32.

——, "The Pampas", *The Monthly Review*, 3 (1826): 152–67.

——, "Travels in Chile and La Plata", *The Monthly Review*, 2 (1826): 365–74.

——, "Travels in Chile and La Plata", *The Westminster Review*, 6 (1826): 202–30.

——, "Head and Miers on Buenos Ayres and Chile", *The Quarterly Review*, 35, no. 69 (1827): 114–48.

——, "Notes on the United States of America", *Blackwood's Edinburgh Magazine*, 24, no. 145 (1828): 621–38.

——, "A Brief Inquiry into the Real Name and Character of the Author of this Book", in Anon., ed., *Domestic Manners of the Americans*, by Mrs. Trollope (London: Whittaker, Treacher, & Co., 1832), pp. iii–ix.

——, "British Writers on America", *Tait's Edinburgh Magazine*, 1, no. 2 (1832): 229–34.

——, "Domestic Manners of the Americans", *Blackwood's Edinburgh Magazine*, 31, no. 194 (1832): 829–47.

——, "Domestic Manners of the Americans", *Monthly Repository*, 6 (1832): 401–6.

——, "Domestic Manners of the Americans", *The Athenaeum*, no. 230 (24 March 1832): 187–88, cont. no. 231 (31 March 1832) (1832): 204–6.

——, "Domestic Manners of the Americans", *The Literary Gazette*, no. 792 (24 March 1832): 178–80, cont. no. 797 (28 April 1832): 262–63.

——, "Domestic Manners of the Americans. By Mrs. Trollope", *The Quarterly Review*, 47, no. 93 (1832): 39–80.

——, "National Peculiarities", *The Penny Magazine*, 1, no. 9 (1832): 83.

——, "Prince Pückler Muscau and Mrs. Trollope", *The North American Review*, 36, no. 78 (1833): 1–48.

——, "Miss Martineau on Slavery", *Southern Literary Messenger*, 3(XI) (1837): 641–57.

——, "Eastern Life; Present and Past", *The Westminster and Foreign Quarterly Review*, 50, no. 96 (1848): 314–33.

——, "Miss Martineau's Eastern Life", *The Christian Reformer, Or, Unitarian Magazine and Review*, 4, no. 43 (1848): 385–98.

———, "Miss Martineau's Eastern Life", *The Prospective Review*, 4, no. 16 (1848): 524–38.

———, "Advertisement", *Transactions of the Literary Society of Bombay*, vol. 1 [1819], ed. Vishvanath Narayan Mandlik (Bombay: Bombay Education Society Press, 1877), pp. v–ix.

———, "Obituary Notices of Fellows Deceased", *Proceedings of the Royal Society of London*, 29 (1879): xxii–xxiii.

Babbage, Charles, *On the Economy of Machinery and Manufactures* (London: Charles Knight, 1832).

Bagehot, William, "Adam Smith as a Person", *Fortnightly Review*, 26 (1876): 18–42.

Bahar, Saba, "The "Value of a NAME:" The Representation of Political Economy in Maria Edgeworth's *The Absentee*", *Genre*, 35, no. 2 (2002): 283–308.

Barbauld, Anna Laetitia, "Eyes and no Eyes; or, the Art of Seeing", in John Aikin and Anna Laetitia Barbauld, eds., *Evenings at Home; or, the Juvenile Budget Opened: Consisting of a Variety of Miscellaneous Pieces*, vol. 4 (London: J. Johnson, 1794), pp. 93–109.

Barrie, David G., "Patrick Colquhoun, the Scottish Enlightenment and Police Reform in Glasgow in the Late Eighteenth Century", *Crime, Histoire & Sociétiés/Crime, History & Societies*, 12, no. 2 (2008): 59–79.

Barrow, John, *An Account of Travels into the Interior of Southern Africa, in the Years 1797 and 1798*, vols. 1 and 2 (London: T. Cadell, junior and W. Davies, 1801–1804).

———, "Canals and Rail-Roads", *The Quarterly Review*, 31, no. LXII (1825): 349–78.

Barton, Hildor Arnold, *Northern Arcadia: Travelers in Scandinavia, 1765–1815* (Carbondale, IL: Southern Illinois University Press, 1998).

Bar-Yosef, Eitan, "'With the Practiced Eye of a Deaf Person': Martineau's Travel Writing and the Construction of the Disabled Traveller", in Ella Dzelzianis and Cora Kaplan, eds., *Harriet Martineau: Authorship, Society, and Empire* (Manchester: Manchester University Press, 2010), pp. 165–79.

Batchelor, Robert K., *London: The Selden Map and the Making of a Global City, 1549–1689* (Chicago, IL: Chicago University Press, 2014).

Beatson, Alexander, *A New System of Cultivation* (London: W. Bulmer and W. Nicol, 1820).

Beaumont, J.A.B., *Travels in Buenos Ayres, and the Adjacent Provinces of the Rio de la Plata. With Observations, Intended for the Use of Persons Who Contemplate Emigrating to that Country; or, Embarking Capital in Its Affairs* (London: J. Ridgway, 1828).

Becker, Gary S., *A Treatise on the Family* (Cambridge, MA: Harvard University Press, 1981).

Bederman, Gail, "Sex, Scandal, Satire, and Population in 1798: Revisiting Malthus's First Essay", *Journal of British Studies*, 47, no. 4 (2008): 768–95.

Berlin, Ira, *Many Thousands Gone: The First Two Centuries of Slavery in North America* (Cambridge, MA: Harvard University Press, 1998).

Besomi, Daniele, "The Periodicity of Crises: A Survey of the Literature Before 1850", *Journal of the History of Economic Thought*, 32, no. 1 (2010): 85–132.

Bigelow, Allison Margaret, "Transatlantic Quechañol: Reading Race through Colonial Translations", *PMLA*, 134, no. 2 (2019): 242–59.

Black, John, "Preface by the Translator", in vol. 1, Alexander von Humboldt, ed., *Political Essay on the Kingdom of New Spain* (London: Longman, et al, 1811).
Blake, Kathleen, *Pleasures of Benthamism: Victorian Literature, Utility, Political Economy* (New York: Oxford University Press, 2009).
Boianovsky, Mauro, "Humboldt and the Economists on Natural Resources, Institutions and Underdevelopment (1752 to 1859)", *The European Journal of the History of Economic Thought*, 20, no. 1 (2013): 58–88.
Bonar, John, *Malthus and His Work* (London: Macmillan, 1885).
Bonnycastle, Sir Richard Henry, *Spanish America: Or, a Descriptive, Historical, and Geographical Account of the Dominions of Spain in the Western Hemisphere, Continental & Insular* (Philadelphia, PA: Abraham Small, 1819).
Bonnyman, Brian, *The Third Duke of Buccleuch and Adam Smith: Estate Management and Improvement in Enlightenment Scotland* (Edinburgh: Edinburgh University Press, 2014).
Bordo, Michael D., "Commentary", *The Federal Reserve Bank of St. Louis Review*, 80, no. 3 (1998): 77–82.
Bourguet, Marie-Noëlle, "A Portable World: The Notebooks of European Travellers (Eighteenth to Nineteenth Centuries)", *Intellectual History Review*, 20, no. 3 (2010): 377–400.
Bowerbank, Sylvia, "The Bastille of Nature: Wollstonecraft versus Malthus in Scandinavia", in Anka Ryall and Catherine Sandbach-Dahlström, eds., *Mary Wollstonecraft's Journey to Scandinavia: Essays* (Stockholm: Almqvist & Wicksell International, 2003), pp. 165–84.
Boyle, Robert, *Experiments and Considerations touching Colours* (London, 1664) <http://www.gutenberg.org/files/14504/14504-h/14504-h.htm#Page_151> [13 April 2020].
———, "General Heads for a Natural History of a Countrey, Great or Small, Imparted Likewise by Mr. Boyle", *Philosophical Transactions of the Royal Society*, 1 (1665–6): 186–9.
Brand, Charles, *Journal of a Voyage to Peru: A Passage across the Cordillera of the Andes in the Winter of 1827, Performed on Foot in the Snow, and a Journey across the Pampas* (London: H. Colburn, 1828).
Braun, Carlos Rodríguez, "Early Smithian Economics in the Spanish Empire: J.H. Vieytes and Colonial Policy", *The European Journal of the History of Economic Thought*, 4, no. 3 (1997): 444–54.
Bravo, Michael T., "Precision and Curiosity in Scientific Travel: James Rennell and the Orientalist Geography of the New Imperialist Age (1760–1830)", in Jás Elsner and Joan-Pau Rubiés, eds., *Voyages and Visions: Towards a Cultural History of Travel* (London: Reaktion Books, 1999), pp. 162–83.
Brickhouse, Anna, *The Unsettlement of America: Translation, Interpretation, and the Story of Don Luis de Velasco, 1560–1945* (New York: Oxford University Press, 2015).
Brock, W.H., "Humboldt and the British: A Note on the Character of British Science", *American Scientist*, 50, no. 4 (1993): 365–72.
Brown, Bill, "Thing Theory", *Critical Inquiry*, 28, no. 1 (2001): 1–22.
Brown, Matthew, ed., *Informal Empire in Latin America: Culture, Commerce, and Capital* (Malden, MA: Blackwell; John Wiley & Sons, 2009).

Browning, Webster E., "Joseph Lancaster, James Thomson, and the Lancasterian System of Mutual Instruction, with Special Reference to Hispanic America", *Hispanic American Historical Review*, 4, no. 1 (1921): 49–98.

Bruce, James, *Travels to Discover the Source of the Nile, in the Years 1768, 1769, 1770, 1771, 1772 and 1773* [1768] five volumes (London: G.G.J. and J. Robinson, 1790).

Brunt, Liam, "Rehabilitating Arthur Young", *The Economic History Review*, 56, no. 2 (2003): 265–99.

Bunster, Grosvenor, *Observations on Capt. F. B. Head's Reports, Relating to the Failure of the Rio de la Plata Mining Association*, 2nd edn (London: E. Wilson, 1827).

Burke, Peter, "The Philosopher as Traveller: Bernier's Orient", in Jaś Elsner and Joan-Pau Rubiés, eds., *Voyages and Visions: Towards a Cultural History of Travel* (London: Reaktion Books, 1999), pp. 124–37.

Bush, John, *Hibernia Curiosa* (London: W. Flexney, 1769).

Butler, Marilyn, *Maria Edgeworth: A Literary Biography* (Oxford: Clarendon, 1972).

Buttimer, Anne, "Beyond Humboldtian Science and Goethe's Way of Science: Challenges of Alexander von Humboldt's Geography", *Erdkunde. Archive for Scientific Geography*, 55, no. 2 (2001): 105–20.

———, "Bridging the Americas: Humboldtian Legacies", *Geographical Review*, 96, no. 3 (2006): vi–ix.

Cabot, Sebastian, "Ordinances for the Direction of the Intended Voyage for Cathay, Dated May, 9, 1553", [n.d.] Reprinted in Pinkerton, John, *A General Collection of the Best and Most Interesting Voyages and Travels in All Parts of the World: Many of which are Now First Translated Into English; Digested on a New Plan*, vol. I (London: Longman, Hurst, Rees, and Orme, 1808), pp. 1–7.

Cahill, David, "Colour by Numbers: Racial and Ethnic Categories in the Viceroyalty of Peru", *Journal of Latin American Studies*, 26, no. 2 (1994): 325–46.

Calaresu, Melissa, "Looking for Virgil's Tomb: The End of the Grand Tour and the Cosmopolitan Ideal: Neapolitan Critiques of French Travel Accounts (1750–1800)", in Jás Elsner And Joan-Pau Rubiés, eds., *Voyages and Visions: Towards a Cultural History of Travel* (London: Reaktion Books, 1999), pp. 138–161.

Caldcleugh, Alexander, *Travels in South America, during the Years, 1819-20-21: Containing an Account of the Present State of Brazil, Buenos Ayres, and Chile*, vols. 1 and 2 (London: J. Murray, 1825).

Canizares-Esquerra, Jorge, *How to Write the History of the New World: Histories, Epistemologies, and Identities in the Eighteenth-Century Atlantic World* (Stanford, CA: Stanford University Press, 2001).

Carey, Daniel, "Compiling Nature's History: Travellers and Travel Narratives in the Early Royal Society", *Annals of Science*, 54, no. 3 (1997): 269–92.

———, "Inquiries, Heads, and Directions: Orienting Early Modern Travel", in Judy A. Hayden, ed., *Travel Narratives, the New Science, and Literary Discourse, 1569–1750* (Burlington, VT: Ashgate, 2012), pp. 25–51.

Carey, Daniel and Jowitt, Claire, *Richard Hakluyt and Travel Writing in Early Modern Europe* (Burlington, VT: Ashgate, 2012).

[Carlyle, Thomas], "State of German Literature", *The Edinburgh Review*, 46, no. 92 (1827): 304–51.

———, "Signs of the Times", *The Edinburgh Review*, 49, no. 98 (1829): 439–59.

Chandler, James, Davidson, Arnold I., and Harootunian, Harry, eds., "Editors' Introduction: Questions of Evidence", *Critical Inquiry*, 17, no. 4 (1991): 738–40.
Chaplin, Joyce E., "Natural Philosophy and an Early Racial Idiom in North America: Comparing English and Indian Bodies", *William Mary Quarterly*, 54, no. 1 (1997): 229–52.
Cicerchia, Ricardo, *Journey, Rediscovery and Narrative: British Travel Accounts of Argentina (1800–1850)* (London: Institute of Latin American Studies, 1998).
Clark, Walter Ernest, *Josiah Tucker, Economist: A Study in the History of Economics* (New York: Columbia University, 1903).
Clarke, Edward Daniel, *Travels in Various Countries of Europe, Asia and Africa*, vol. 3 Part 1 (London: T. Cadell and W. Davies, 1819).
———, *Travels in Various Countries of Europe, Asia and Africa*, vol. 3, Part 2 (London: T. Cadell, 1823).
Colbert, Benjamin, "Bibliography of British Travel Writing, 1780–1840. The European Tour, 1814–1818 (Excluding Britain and Ireland)", *Cardiff Corvey. Reading the Romantic Text*, 13 (2004): 5–44. <http://www.cf.ac.uk/encap/corvey/articles/cc13_n01.pdf> [21 November 2016].
Colley, Linda, *Britons: Forging the Nation 1707–1837* (New Haven, CT: Yale University Press, 1992).
Colquhoun, Patrick, *A Treatise on the Police of the Metropolis* (London: H. Fry, 1796).
Conway, Brian and Hill, Michael R., "Harriet Martineau and Ireland", in Séamas Ó Síocháin, ed., *Social Thought on Ireland in the Nineteenth Century* (Dublin, Ireland: University College Dublin Press, 2009), pp. 47–66.
Cooper, Brian P., "Social Classifications, Social Statistics and the 'Facts' of 'Difference' in Economics", in Drucilla K. Barker and Edith Kuiper, eds., *Toward a Feminist Philosophy of Economics* (London and New York: Routledge, 2003), pp. 161–79.
———, *Family Fictions and Family Facts: Harriet Martineau, Adolphe Quetelet, and the Population Question in England, 1789–1859* (London and New York: Routledge, 2007).
———, "'A not Unreasonable Panic': Character, Confidence, and Credit in Harriet Martineau's Berkeley the Banker", *Nineteenth-Century Contexts: An Interdisciplinary Journal*, 32, no. 4 (2010): 363–84.
Cooper, Brian P. and Murphy, Margueritte S., "The Death of the Author at the Birth of Social Science: The Cases of Harriet Martineau and Adolphe Quetelet", *Studies in History and Philosophy of Science*, 31, no. 1 (2000): 1–36.
Cooper, George, *Letters on the Irish Nation: Written during a Visit to that Kingdom, in the Autumn of the Year 1799* (London: J. Davis for J. White, 1800).
———, *Letters on the Irish Nation: Written during a Visit to that Kingdom, in the Autumn of the Year 1799*, 2nd edn (London: J. Davis for J. White, 1801).
Cope, Douglas R., *The Limits of Racial Domination: Plebeian Society in Colonial Mexico City, 1660–1720* (Madison, WI: University of Wisconsin Press, 1994).
Costeloe, Michael P., *Bonds and Bondholders: British Investors and Mexico's Foreign Debt, 1824–1888* (Westport, CT: Praeger, 2003).
———, *Bubbles and Bonanzas: British Investors and Investments in Mexico, 1824–1860* (Lanham, MD: Lexington Books, 2011).
Coxe, William, *Travels into Poland, Russia, Sweden, and Denmark*, vol. 5 (London: T. Cadell, 1791).

Craiutu, Aurelian, "What Kind of Social Scientist Was Tocqueville?", in Aurelian Craiutu and Sheldon Gellar, eds., *Conversations with Tocqueville: The Global Democratic Revolution in the Twenty-First Century* (Lanham, MD: Lexington Books, 2009), pp. 55–82.
Crawford, Iain, "Harriet Martineau: Travel and the Writer", in Valerie Sanders and Gaby Weiner, eds., *Harriet Martineau and the Birth of Disciplines: Nineteenth-Century Intellectual Powerhouse* (London: Routledge, 2017), pp. 171–86.
Cremaschi, Sergio and Dascal, Marcelo, "Malthus and Ricardo on Economic Methodology", *History of Political Economy*, 28, no. 3 (1996): 475–511.
[Croker, John Wilson], "Miss Martineau's *Morals and Manners*", *The Quarterly Review*, 63, no. 125 (1839): 61–72.
Crowley, John E., "[Review of] *Witnessing Slavery: Art and Travel in the Age of Abolition*", *Journal of British Studies*, 59, no. 4 (2020): 966–7.
Cunha, Alexandre Mendes, "Police Science and Cameralism in Portuguese Enlightened Reformism: Economic Ideas and the Administration of the State during the Second Half of the 18th Century", *e-Journal of Portuguese History* 8 (2010) <www.scielo.oces.mctes.pt/scielo.php?pid=S1645-64322010000100003&script=sci_arttext> [27 February 2015].
Cunningham, John William, *Cautions to Continental Travellers* (London: Ellerton and Henderson, 1818).
Cuno, Kenneth M. and Reimer, Michael J., "The Census Registers of Nineteenth-Century Egypt: A New Source for Social Historians", *British Journal of Middle Eastern Studies*, 24, no. 2 (1997): 193–216.
Curran, Andrew S., *The Anatomy of Blackness: Science and Slavery in an Age of Enlightenment* (Baltimore, MD: Johns Hopkins University Press, 2011).
Cutmore, Jonathan, ed., "The Quarterly Review Archive", *Romantic Circles* (2015) https://www.rc.umd.edu/reference/qr/index/16.html. [12 October 2015].
Dalton, Susan, *Engendering the Republic of Letters: Reconnecting Public and Private Spheres* (Montreal, QC: McGill-Queen's University Press, 2003).
Daston, Lorraine, "The Ideal and Reality of the Republic of Letters", *Science in Context* 4, no. 2 (1991): 367–86.
———, "Objectivity and the Escape from Perspective", *Social Studies of Science*, 22, no. 4 (1992): 597–618.
———, "Baconian Facts, Academic Civility, and the Prehistory of Objectivity", in Alan Megill, ed., *Rethinking Objectivity* [1991] (Durham, NC: Duke University Press, 1994), pp. 37–63.
———, "The Moral Economy of Science", *Osiris* 10 (1995a): 1–24.
———, *Classical Probability in the Enlightenment* (Princeton, NJ: Princeton University Press, 1995b).
———, "On Scientific Observation", *Isis*, 99, no. 1 (2008): 97–110.
Daston, Lorraine and Galison, Peter, "The Image of Objectivity", *Representations*, 40 (1992): 81–128.
———, *Objectivity* (New York: Zone Books, 2007).
Daston, Lorraine and Lunbeck, Elizabeth, "Introduction: Observation Observed", in Lorraine Daston and Elizabeth Lunbeck, eds., *Histories of Scientific Observation* (Chicago, IL: Chicago University Press, 2011), pp. 1–9.
———, "Framing the History of Scientific Observation, 500–1800. Introduction", in Lorraine Daston and Elizabeth Lunbeck, eds., *Histories of Scientific Observation* (Chicago, IL: Chicago University Press, 2011), pp. 11–14.

Davies, Mark, *A Perambulating Paradox: British Travel Literature and the Image of Sweden, c. 1770–1865* (Lund: Lunds Universitet, 2000).
Davison, William, Devereux, Robert and Sidney, Philip, *Profitable Instructions Describing What Speciall Observations Are to Be Taken by Travellers in All Nations, States and Countries; Pleasant and Profitable* (London: Benjamin Fisher, 1633).
de Champs, Emmanuelle, *Enlightenment and Utility: Bentham in French, Bentham in France* (Cambridge: Cambridge University Press, 2015).
de Salas, Manuel, "Representación hecha al ministerio de Hacienda 10 de enero 1796", in Miguel Cruchaga, ed., *Estudio sobre la organización i la hacienda pública de Chile*, vol. 1 (Santiago: "Los Tiempos", 1878), pp. 274–90.
de Vries, Jan, "The Industrial Revolution and the Industrious Revolution", *The Journal of Economic History*, 54, no. 2 (1994): 249–70.
——, *The Industrious Revolution: Consumer Behavior and the Household Economy, 1650 to the Present* (New York: Cambridge University Press, 2008).
Deegan, Mary Jo, "Making Lemonade: Harriet Martineau on Being Deaf", in Michael R. Hill and Susan Hoecker-Drysdale, eds., *Harriet Martineau: Theoretical and Methodological Perspectives* (New York: Routledge, 2001), pp. 41–58.
Demoustier, Danièle and Rousselière, Damien, "Social Economy as Social Science and Practice: Historical Perspectives on France", *Eleventh World Congress of Social Economics: "Social Economics: A Paradigm for a Global Society"*, Albertville, 8–11 June 2004 (2004), pp. 1–42.
Denis, Andy, "Epistemology, Observed Particulars and Providentialist Assumptions: The Fact in the History of Political Economy", *Studies in History and Philosophy of Science*, Part A, 31, no. 2 (2000): 353–61.
Depons (sic), F.[R.J.], *Voyage à la partie orientale de la terre-ferme dans l'Amérique Méridionale: fait pendant les années 1801, 1802, 1803 et 1804*, 3 vols (Paris: Chez Colnet, 1806).
——, *Travels in Parts of South America, during the Years 1801, 1802, 1803 & 1804; Containing a Description of the Captain-Generalship of Carraccas, with an Account of the Laws, Commerce, and Natural Productions of that Country: As Also a View of the Customs and Manners of the Spaniards and Native Indians. An abridged English translation of* Voyage à la partie orientale de la terre-ferme dans l'Amérique Méridionale *(Paris, 1806)*. (London: Richard Phillips, 1806).
——, *Travels in Parts of South America, during the Years 1801, 1802, 1803 & 1804; Containing a Description of the Captain-Generalship of Carraccas, with an Account of the Laws, Commerce, and Natural Productions of that Country: As Also a View of the Customs and Manners of the Spaniards and Native Indians*, 2 vols. (London: Longman and Co., and Hurst, Rees, and Orme, 1807).
Depoortière, Christophe, "William Nassau Senior and David Ricardo on the Method of Political Economy", *Journal of the History of Economic Thought*, 35, no. 1 (2013): 19–42.
Desroche, Henri, *Pour un traité d'économie sociale* (Paris: CIEM, 1983).
Dimand, Robert W., "'I Have no Great Faith in Political Arithmetick'": Adam Smith and Quantitative Political Economy", in Ingrid H. Rima, ed., *Measurement, Quantification and Economic Analysis: Numeracy in Economics* (London: Routledge, 1995), pp. 22–30.
——, "Classical Political Economy and Orientalism: Nassau Senior's Eastern Tours", in Eiman Ein-Zelabdin and S. Charusheela, eds., *Post-Colonialism Meets Economics* (London: Routledge, 2004), pp. 73–90.

Dimsdale, Nicholas and Hotson, Anthony, eds., *British Financial Crises since 1825* (New York: Oxford University Press, 2014).
Disraeli, Benjamin, *An Inquiry into the Plans, Progress, and Policy of the American Mining Companies*, 3rd edn (London: John Murray, 1825a).
———, *Lawyers and Legislators; Or, Notes on the American Mining Companies* (London: John Murray, 1825b).
d'Ivernois, François, *Tableau historique et politique des pertes* (London: Baylis, 1799).
Dolan, Brian, "Malthus's Political Economy of Health: The Critique of Scandinavia in the *Essay on Population*", in Brian Dolan, ed., *Malthus, Medicine and Morality: "Malthusianism" after 1798* (Amsterdam: Editions Rodopi, 2000), pp. 9–32.
Douglas, Bronwen, *Science, Voyages, and Encounters in Oceania, 1511–1850* (New York: Palgrave Macmillan, 2014).
Drake, Michael, "Malthus on Norway", *Population Studies*, 20, no. 2 (1966): 175–96.
Driver, Felix, *Geography Militant: Cultures of Exploration and Empire* (Oxford: Blackwell, 2001).
Driver, Felix and Gilbert, David, "Imperial Cities: Overlapping Territories, Intertwined Histories", in Felix Driver and David Gilbert, eds., *Imperial Cities: Landscape, Display and Identity* (Manchester: Manchester University Press, 1999), pp. 1–20.
Drolet, Michael, "Democracy and Political Economy: Tocqueville's Thoughts on J.-B. Say and T.R. Malthus", *History of European Ideas*, 29, no. 2 (2003a): 159–81.
———, *Tocqueville, Democracy and Social Reform* (New York: Palgrave Macmillan, 2003b).
Dryjanska, Anna, "Harriet Martineau: The Forerunner of Cultural Studies", in Marcia Texler Segal and Vasilikie Demos, eds., *Advancing Gender Research from the Nineteenth to the Twenty-First Centuries* (Bingley, UK: JAI Press, 2008), pp. 63–77.
Duane, William, *A Visit to Colombia: In the Years 1822 & 1823, by Laguayra and Caracas, Over the Cordillera to Bogota, and Thence by the Magdalena to Cartagena* (Philadelphia, PA: T.H. Palmer, 1826).
Dym, Jordana, "Taking a Walk on the Wild Side: Experiencing the Spaces of Colonial Latin America", *Colonial Latin American Review*, 21, no. 1 (2012): 3–16.
Eamon, William, "From the Secrets of Nature to Public Knowledge", David C. Lundberg and Robert S. Westman, eds., *Reappraisals of the Scientific Revolution* (Cambridge: Cambridge University Press, 1990), pp. 333–66.
Edgeworth, Maria, *The Life and Letters of Maria Edgeworth*, Augustus John Cuthbert Hare, ed., vols. 1 and 2 (New York: Houghton Mifflin, 1895).
———, *Castle Rackrent* [1800] and *Ennui* [1809] (New York: Penguin Classics, 1992).
Edgeworth, Richard Lovell and Edgeworth, Maria, *Practical Education* (London: J. Johnson, 1798).
———, *The Memoirs of Richard Lovell Edgeworth*, 3rd edn (London: Richard Bentley, 1844).
[El economista], "Remitido al señor editor del eco de los andes "víctima de las teorías", *La Década Araucana*, 15 (1826): 350–2.

Elliot, John H., *The Old World and the New, 1492–1650*, 2nd edn (Cambridge: Cambridge University Press, 1992).
———, "Barbarians at the Gates", *New York Review of Books*, 53, no. 3 (2006): 36–8.
Elsner, Jaś, and Rubiés, Joan-Pau, "Introduction", in J. Elsner and Joan-Pau Rubiés, eds., *Voyages and Visions: Towards a Cultural History of Travel* (London: Reaktion Books, 1999), pp. 1–56.
English, Henry, *A General Guide to the Companies Formed for Working Foreign Mines: With Their Prospectuses, Amount of Capital, Number of Shares, Names of Directors, &c., and an Appendix, Showing Their Progress Since Their Formation... with a Table of the Extent of Their Fluctuations in Price, up to the Present Period* (London: Boosey & Sons, 1825).
———, *A Complete View of the Joint Stock Companies Formed during the Years 1824 and 1825* (London: Boosey & Sons, 1827).
Fabian, Johannes, *Out of Our Minds: Reason and Madness in the Exploration of Central Africa* (Berkeley, CA: University of California Press, 2000).
Fahnestock, Jeanne, "Accommodating Science: The Rhetorical Life of Scientific Facts", *Written Communication*, 3, no. 3 (1986): 275–96.
Fenn, Robert A., ed., "Literature," in James Mill's *Common Place Books*, vol. IV, ch. 18 (2010) <http://intellectualhistory.net/mill/cpb4ch18.html> [10 January 2017].
Fergus, Jan, *Provincial Readers in Eighteenth-Century England* (Oxford: Oxford University Press, 2006).
Ferguson, Adam, *An Essay on the History of Civil Society* (Edinburgh: A. Millar & T. Caddel, 1767).
Ferns, H.S., "Beginnings of British Investment in Argentina", *The Economic History Review*, 4, no. 3 (1952): 341–52.
———, "Britain's Informal Empire in Argentina, 1806–1914", *Past and Present*, 4 (1953): 60–75.
Ferris, Ina, *The Romantic National Tale and the Question of Ireland* (Cambridge: Cambridge University Press, 2002).
Fetter, Frank Whitson, "The Authorship of Economic Articles in the *Edinburgh Review*, 1802–47", *Journal of Political Economy*, 61, no. 3 (1953): 232–59.
Fisher, John, "Imperial 'Free Trade' and the Hispanic Economy, 1778–1796", *Journal of Latin American Studies*, 13, no. 1 (1981): 21–56.
Fjågesund, Peter and Symes, Ruth A., *The Northern Utopia: British Perceptions of Norway in the Nineteenth Century* (Amsterdam: Rodopi, 2003).
Flavell, Julie, *When London was Capital of America* (New Haven, CT: Yale University Press, 2010).
[Flint, T.] "Travellers in America, &c", *The Knickerbocker: Or, New-York Monthly Magazine*, 2, October (1833): 283–302.
Floyd-Wilson, Mary, *English Ethnicity and Race in Early Modern Drama* (Cambridge: Cambridge University Press, 2003).
Fodor, Giorgio, "The Boom that Never Was? Latin American Loans in London: 1822–1825", Discussion Paper no. 5. Universita' degli Studi di Trento - Dipartimento di Economia (2002), pp. 1–45.
Fontes da Costa, Palmira, *The Singular and the Making of Knowledge at the Royal Society of London in the Eighteenth Century* (Cambridge: Cambridge Scholars, 2009).

334 Bibliography

Forrester, David A.R., "Rational Administration, Finance and Control Accounting: The Experience of Cameralism", *Critical Perspectives on Accounting*, 1, no. 4 (1990): 285–317.

Francis, John, *Chronicles and Characters of the Stock Exchange* (London: Willoughby and Co, 1849).

Francis, John George, *Notes from a Journal Kept in Italy and Sicily* (London: Longman, Brown, Green, and Longmans, 1847).

Friedman, Michael, "History and Philosophy of Science in a New Key", *Isis*, 99, no. 1 (2008): 125–34.

Fussell, Paul, *The Norton Book of Travel* (New York: W.W. Norton, 1987).

Gabay, Nadav, "The Political Origins of Social Science: The Cultural Transformation of the British Parliament and the Emergence of Scientific Policymaking, 1803–1857". UC San Diego (2007) <https://escholarship.org/content/qt9b48n807/qt9b48n807.pdf> [20 November 2019].

———, "'With the Practiced Eye of a Deaf Person': Harriet Martineau, Deafness and the Scientificity of Social Knowledge", *The American Sociologist*, 50, no. 3 (2019): 335–55.

Gallagher, Catherine, "The Body Versus the Social Body in the Works of Thomas Malthus and Henry Mayhew", *Representations*, 14 (1986): 83–106.

———, *Nobody's Story: The Vanishing Acts of Women Writers in the Marketplace, 1670–1820* (Oxford: Clarendon, 1994).

Gallagher, Catherine and Greenblatt, Stephen, *Practicing New Historicism* (Chicago, IL: University of Chicago Press, 2000).

Gallagher, John and Robinson, Ronald, "The Imperialism of Free Trade", *Economic History Review*, 6, no. 1 (1953): 1–15.

Gamer, Michael, "Maria Edgeworth and the Romance of Real Life", *Novel*, 34, no. 2 (2001): 232–66.

Games, Allison, *The Web of Empire: English Cosmopolitans in an Age of Expansion, 1560–1660* (New York: Oxford University Press, 2008).

Gascoigne, John, "The Royal Society, Natural History and the Peoples of the 'New World(s)', 1660–1800", *The British Society for the History of Science*, 42, no. 4 (2009): 539–62.

Genette, Gérard, *Paratexts: Thresholds of Interpretation* [1987], trans. Jane E. Lewin (Cambridge: Cambridge University Press, 1997).

Gerbi, Antonello, *The Dispute of the New World. The History of a Polemic, 1750–1900* [1973], trans. Jeremy Moyle (Pittsburgh, PA: University of Pittsburgh Press, 2010).

Gillespie, Alexander, *Gleanings and Remarks: Collected during Many Months of Residence at Buenos Ayres, and within the Upper Country* (Leeds: B. Dewhirst, 1818).

Godelier, Maurice, "Malthus and Ethnography", in Jacques Dupâqier, Antoinette Fauve-Chamoux, and Eugene Grebènik, eds., *Malthus Past and Present* (London: Academic Press, 1983), pp. 125–50.

Gordon, Robert Jacob, "Fourth Journey" [From 27 June 1779 to 13 January 1780], trans. Patrick Cullinan (Johannesburg, SA: Brenthurst Library), MSS 107/3/1, from 27 June 1779 to 21 October 1779, pp. 1–59. (14 February 2017). https://www.robertjacobgordon.nl/travel-journals/fourth-journey/fourth-journey [4 June 2018].

Govier, Mark, "The Royal Society, Slavery and the Island of Jamaica: 1660–1700", *Notes and Records of the Royal Society of London*, 53, no. 2 (1999): 203–17.

Graham, Maria, *Journal of a Residence in India* [1812] (London: Longman, Hurst, Rees, Orme, and Brown, 1813).

———, *Letters on India* (London: Longman, Hurst, Rees, Orme, and Brown, 1814).

———, *Three Months Passed in the Mountains East of Rome, during the Year 1819* (London: Longman, Hurst, Rees, Orme, Brown, 1820).

———, *Journal of a Voyage to Brazil, and Residence There, during Part of the Years 1821, 1822, 1823* (London: Longman, Hurst, Rees, Orme, Brown, and Green; John Murray, 1824a).

———, *Journal of a Residence in Chile, during the Year 1822; and a Voyage from Chile to Brazil, in 1823* (London: Longman, Hurst, Rees, Orme, Brown, and Green; John Murray, 1824b).

Grapard, Ulla and Hewitson, Gillian, eds., *Robinson Crusoe's Economic Man: A Construction and Deconstruction* (London: Routledge, 2011).

Graubart, Karen B., "The Creolization of the New World: Local Forms of Identification in Urban Colonial Peru, 1560–1640", *Hispanic American Historical Review*, 89, no. 3 (2009): 471–99.

Greenblatt, Stephen, *Marvelous Possessions: The Wonder of the New World* (Chicago, IL: Chicago University Press, 1991).

Great Britain, House of Commons Select Committee on Emigration, *Third report from the Select Committee on Emigration from the United Kingdom, 1827* (London: House of Commons, 1827).

Great Britain, Parliament. House of Lords, *First and Second Reports from the Committees of the House of Lords, Appointed to Inquire into the State of the Growth, Commerce, and Consumption of Grain, and All Laws Relating Thereto: To Which Were Referred the Several Petitions Presented to the House in the Session of 1813–14, Respecting the Corn Laws* (London: J. Ridgway, 1814).

Gueslin, André, *L'invention de l'économie sociale* (Paris: Economica, 1998).

H[iggs], H[enry], "Introduction", *Political Economy Club. Founded in London, 1821. Minutes of Proceedings, etc.*, vol. 6 (London: Macmillan and Co, 1921), pp. vii–xxvi.

[H.W.], "Sir Francis Head's Works", *The London and Westminster Review*, 31, no. 2 (1838): 461–7.

Haberly, David T., "Francis Bond Head and Domingo Sarmiento: A Note on the Sources of 'Facundo'", *MLN*, 120, no. 2 (2005): 287–93.

Hacking, Ian, "Biopower and the Avalanche of Printed Numbers", *Humanities in Society*, 5 (1982): 279–95.

Haggerty, Sheryllynne, *'Merely for Money'? Business Culture in the British Atlantic, 1750–1815* (Liverpool: Liverpool University Press, 2012).

Hagglund, Betty, "From Travel Diary to Printed Book: The Indian Travel Writings of Maria Graham", *Itinérances Féminines* (2008) <www.crlv.org/viatica/septembreoctobre-2008-itin%C3%A9rances-f%C3%A9minines/travel-diary-printed-book> [30 April 2015].

———, "The Botanical Writings of Maria Graham", *Journal of Literature and Science*, 4, no. 1 (2011): 44–58. <http://www.literatureandscience.org/issues/JLS_4_1/JLS_vol_4_no_1_Hagglund.pdf> [10 October 2015].

Hall, Basil, *Extracts from a Journal Written on the Coasts of Chili, Peru, and Mexico, in the Years 1820, 1821, 1822*, 2 vols., 3rd edn (London: Hurst, Robinson, and Co, 1824).

———, *Travels in North America in 1827 and 1828*, 3 vols. (Edinburgh: Cadell and Co, 1829).

Hamlin, Christopher and Gallagher-Kamper, Kathleen, "Malthus and the Doctors: Political Economy, Medicine, and the State in England, Ireland, and Scotland, 1800–1840", in Brian Dolan, ed., *Malthus, Medicine and Morality: "Malthusianism" after 1798* (Amsterdam: Editions Rodopi, 2000), pp. 115–40.

Hancock, William Neilson, *Impediments to the Prosperity of Ireland* (London: Simms and M'Intyre, 1850).

———, "A Notice of the Theory 'That There is no Hope for a Nation Which Lives on Potatoes'", *Two Papers Read Before the Dublin Statistical Society* [1848] (Dublin: Hodges and Smith for the Dublin Statistical Society, 1854).

Harden, O. Elizabeth Mc Whorter, *Maria Edgeworth's Art of Prose Fiction* (The Hague: Mouton, 1971).

Hargraves, Neil, "Enterprise, Adventure and Industry: The Formation of 'Commercial Character' in William Robertson's History of America", *History of European Ideas*, 29, no. 1 (2003): 33–54.

Harris, Jonathan, "Bernardino Rivadavia and Benthamite 'Discipleship'", *Latin American Research Review*, 33, no. 1 (1998): 129–49.

Harris, Steven, "Networks of Travel, Correspondence, and Exchange", in Katharine Park and Lorraine Daston, eds., *Early Modern Science*, vol. 3 of the Cambridge History of Science (Cambridge: Cambridge University Press, 2006), pp. 341–62.

Hayden, Judy A., "Intersections and Cross-Fertilization", in Judy A. Hayden, ed., *Travel Narratives, the New Science, and Literary Discourse, 1569–1750* (Burlington, VT: Ashgate, 2012), pp. 1–21.

Head, Francis Bond, *Rough Notes Taken During Some Rapid Journeys across the Pampas and among the Andes* (London: John Murray, 1826).

———, *Reports Relating to the Failure of the Rio Plata Mining Association* (London: John Murray, 1827).

———, *A Few Practical Arguments against the Theory of Emigration* (London: John Murray, 1828).

———, "Cornish Miners in America", *Descriptive Essays Contributed to the Quarterly Review*, vol. 1 (London: John Murray, 1857), pp. 1–45.

Heffernan, Teresa and O'Quinn, Daniel, "Introduction", in Teresa Heffernan and Daniel O'Quinn, eds., *The Turkish Embassy Letters* [1763] by Lady Mary Wortley Montagu (Peterborough, ON: Broadview Press, 2013), pp. 11–34.

Heinowitz, R. Cole, *Spanish America and British Romanticism, 1777–1826: Rewriting Conquest* (Edinburgh: Edinburgh University Press, 2010).

Henderson, James P., "Agency or Alienation? Smith, Mill, and Marx on the Joint-Stock Company", *History of Political Economy*, 18, no. 1 (1986): 111–131.

Herbert, Christopher, *Culture and Anomie: Ethnographic Imagination in the Nineteenth Century* (Chicago, IL: University of Chicago Press, 1991).

Herder, Johann Gottfried von, *Outlines of a Philosophy of the History of Man* [1784] trans. T.O. Churchill (London: J. Johnson, 1800).

Hernández, P. M., "Translation and Reception of *The Wealth of Nations* by Spanish and Latin American Authors during Eighteenth and Nineteenth Centuries", *Open*

Journal of Social Sciences, 3, no. 5 (2015): 46–57. <http://dx.doi.org/10.4236/jss.2015.35008> [6 November 2018].
Hill, Michael R., "A Methodological Comparison of Harriet Martineau's *Society in America* (1837) and Alexis De Tocqueville's *Democracy in America* (1835–1840)", in Michael R. Hill and Susan Hoecker-Drysdale, eds., *Harriet Martineau: Theoretical and Methodological Perspectives* (New York: Routledge, 2001), pp. 59–74.
Home, Henry and Lord Kames, *Sketches of the History of Man Considerably Enlarged by the Last Additions and Corrections of the Author* [1788] 3 vols. James A. Harris, ed. (Indianapolis, IN: Liberty Fund, 2007).
Hont, István, *Jealousy of Trade: Competition and the Nation State in Historical Perspective* (Cambridge, MA: Harvard University Press, 2005).
Hooper, Glenn, "Preface", in Glenn Hooper, ed., *The Tourist's Gaze: Travellers to Ireland, 1800–2000* (Cork: Cork University Press, 2001), pp. xiii–xxx.
Höpfl, H.M., "From Savage to Scotsman: Conjectural History in the Scottish Enlightenment", *The Journal of British Studies*, 17, no. 2 (1978): 19–40.
Hoquet, Thierry, "Biologization of Race and Racialization of the Human: Bernier, Buffon, Linnaeus", in Nicolas Bancel, Thomas David, and Dominic Thomas, eds., *The Invention of Race: Scientific and Popular Representations* (New York: Routledge, 2014), pp. 17–32.
Horrocks, Ingrid, "Creating an 'Insinuating Interest': Mary Wollstonecraft's Travel Reviews and *A Short Residence*", *Studies in Travel Writing*, 19, no. 1 (2015): 1–15.
Houston, Chlöe, "'Thou Glorious Kingdome, Thou Chiefe of Empires': Persia in Early Seventeenth-Century Travel Literature", *Studies in Travel Writing*, 13, no. 2 (2009): 141–52.
Hudson, Nicholas, "From 'Nation' to 'Race': The Origin of Racial Classification in Eighteenth-Century Thought", *Eighteenth-Century Studies*, 29, no. 3 (1996): 247–264.
Huigen, Siegfried, *Knowledge and Colonialism: Eighteenth-Century Travellers in South Africa* (Leiden: Brill, 2009).
Hulmes, Peter and Youngs, Tim, eds., *The Cambridge Companion to Travel Writing* (Cambridge: Cambridge University Press, 2002).
Humboldt, Alexander von, *Essai Politique sur la Royaume de la Nouvelle-Espagne* (Paris: F. Schoell, 1811).
———, *Political Essay on the Kingdom of New Spain*, 3 vols., trans. John Black (London Longman, Hurst, Rees, Orme and Brown, 1811).
———, *Political Essay on the Kingdom of New Spain*. trans. John Black (New York: I. Riley, 1811).
———, *Political Essay on the Island of Cuba*, trans. Vera M. Kutzinski and Ottmar Ette, eds. (Chicago, IL: University of Chicago Press, 2010).
Humboldt, Alexander von and Williams, Helen M., *Personal Narrative of Travels of the Equinoctial Regions of the New Continent during Years 1799–1804*, trans. Helen Maria Williams, vol. I (London: Longman, et al, 1814).
Hundert, E.J., "Sociability and Self-Love in the Theatre of Moral Sentiments: Mandeville to Adam Smith", in Stefan Collini, Richard Whatmore, and Brian Young, eds., *Economy, Polity, and Society: British Intellectual History* (Cambridge: Cambridge University Press, 2000), pp. 31–47.
Hunt, Margaret, "Racism, Imperialism, and the Traveler's Gaze in Eighteenth-Century England", *The Journal of British Studies*, 32, no. 4 (1993): 333–357.

Hunter, J. Paul, *Before Novels: The Cultural Contexts of Eighteenth-Century English Fiction* (New York: W.W. Norton, 1990).

Iriberri, José de Cos, "Segunda Memoria leida por el mismo señor secretario en Junta de Posesión de 1ero de octubre de 1798", in Miguel Cruchaga, ed., *Estudio sobre la organización i la hacienda pública de Chile*, vol. 1 (Santiago: "Los Tiempos", 1878), pp. 303–8.

Irving, Sarah, "Public Knowledge, Natural Philosophy, and the Eighteenth-Century Republic of Letters", *Early American Literature*, 49, no. 1 (2014): 67–88.

Itzkowitz, David C., "Fair Enterprise or Extravagant Speculation: Investment, Speculation, and Gambling in Victorian England", *Victorian Studies*, 45, no. 1 (2002): 121–47.

Jackson, Julian, *What to Observe; or, The Traveller's Remembrancer* (London: James Madden and Co., 1841).

Jacob, William, *Travels in the South of Spain, in Letters Written A. D. 1809 and 1810* (London: J. Johnson and Co., 1811).

Jacobs, Michael, *The Painted Voyage: Art, Travel, and Exploration* (London: British Museum Press, 1995).

Jacques, T.C., "From Savages and Barbarians to Primitives: Africa, Social Typologies, and History in 18th-Century French Philosophy", *History and Theory*, 36, no. 2 (1997): 190–215.

Jaffe, Audrey, "Trollope in the Stock Market: Irrational Exuberance and *The Prime Minister*", *Victorian Studies*, 45, no. 1 (2002): 43–64.

Jagoe, Eva-Lynn Alicia, *The End of the World as They Knew it: Writing Experiences of the Argentine South* (Lewisburg, PA: Bucknell University Press, 2008).

James, Patricia, *Population Malthus, His Life and Times* (London: Routledge & Kegan Paul, 1979).

Jarvis, Robin, "William Beckford: Travel Writer, Travel Reader", *The Review of English Studies*, 65, no. 268 (2014): 99–117.

Jones, Calvin P., "The Spanish-American Works of Alexander von Humboldt as Viewed by Leading British Periodicals, 1800–1830", *The Americas*, 29, no. 4 (1973): 442–448.

Jones, Kristine L., "Nineteenth Century British Travel Accounts of Argentina", *Ethnohistory*, 33, no. 2 (1986): 195–211.

Jones, Richard, *An Essay on the Distribution of Wealth, and on the Sources of Taxation* (London: John Murray, 1831).

Jonsson, Fredrik Albritton, "Rival Ecologies of Global Commerce: Adam Smith and the Natural Historians", *American Historical Review*, 115, no. 5 (2010): 1342–63.

Kaplan, Cora, "Slavery, Race, History: Harriet Martineau's Ethnographic Imagination", in Ella Dzelzianis and Cora Kaplan, eds., *Harriet Martineau: Authorship, Society, and Empire* (Manchester: Manchester University Press, 2010), pp. 165–79.

Katzew, Ilona, *Casta Paintings: Images of Race in Eighteenth-Century Mexico* (New Haven, CT: Yale University Press, 2004).

Keevak, Michael, *Becoming Yellow: A Short History of Racial Thinking* (Princeton, NJ: Princeton University Press, 2011).

Keighren, Innes M. and Withers, Charles W.J., "Questions of Inscription and Epistemology in British Travelers' Accounts of Early Nineteenth-Century South America", *Annals of the Association of American Geographers*, 101, no. 6 (2011): 1331–46.

Keighren, Innes M., Withers, Charles W.J., and Bell, Bill, *Travels into Print: Exploration, Writing, and Publishing with John Murray, 1773–1859* (Chicago, IL: University of Chicago Press, 2015).

Kelly, James, "Bordering on Fact in Early Eighteenth-Century Sea Journals", in Dan Doll and Jessica Munns, eds., *Recording and Reordering: Essays on the Seventeenth- and Eighteenth-Century Diary and Journal* (Cranbury, NJ: Bucknell University Press, 2006), pp. 158–84.

Kemple, Thomas, "The Spatial Sense of Empire: Encountering Strangers with Simmel, Tocqueville and Martineau", *Journal of Classical Sociology*, 11, no. 4 (2011): 340–55.

["K.[er], H.B."], "Advertisement", in H.T. De la Beche, ed., *How to Observe. Geology* (London: Charles Knight, 1835), pp. iii–vi.

Kern, William, "Maria Edgeworth and Classical Political Economy" (n.d.) American Economic Association: Committee on the Status of Women in the Economics Profession. <https://web.archive.org/web/20110725212131/http://www.cswep.org/edgeworth.html> [10 May 2013].

Koerner, Lisbet, *Linnaeus: Nature and Nation* (Cambridge, MA: Harvard University Press, 1999).

Kowaleski-Wallace, Elizabeth, *Their Fathers' Daughters: Hannah More, Maria Edgeworth and Patriarchal Complicity* (Oxford: Oxford University Press, 1991).

Kronick, David A., *"Devant Le Deluge" and Other Essays on Early Scientific Communication* (Lanham, MD: Scarecrow Press, 2004).

Lamb, Jonathan, "Coming to Terms with What Isn't There: Early Narratives of New Holland", *Eighteenth-Century Life*, 26, no. 1 (2002): 147–55.

Lamb, Jonathan, Smith, Vanessa Jane, and Thomas, Nicholas, eds., *Exploration and Exchange: A South Seas Anthology, 1680–1900* (Chicago, IL: University of Chicago Press, 2001).

Lavoie, Amy, "Rothschild Explores Economics' Human Side", *Harvard Gazette Online* (2008) <https://news.harvard.edu/gazette/story/2008/05/rothschild-explores-economics-human-side/> [8 December 2010].

Lawson, James A., "On the Connexion between Statistics and Political Economy", *Report of the Thirteenth Meeting of the British Association for the Advancement of Science* (London: John Murray, 1844), pp. 94–5.

———, "On the Connexion between Statistics and Political Economy", *Papers Read Before the Dublin Statistical Society* [1848] (Dublin: Alexander Thom for the Dublin Statistical Society, 1854), pp. 3–9.

Lesham, Dotan, "Oikonomia Redefined", *Journal of the History of Economic Thought*, 35, no. 1 (2013): 43–61.

Levine, Joseph M. "Review [of Shapiro, Barbara J. (2000) A Culture of Fact: England, 1550–1720, Ithaca, NY: Cornell University Press]", *Albion*, 33, no. 1 (2001): 102–3.

Levy, David and Peart, Sandra J. "G. Warren Nutter's 'Traveler's Tales of the Soviet Economy'" (Unpublished paper, 2012).

———, *Escape from Democracy: The Role of Experts & the Public in Economic Policy* (Cambridge: Cambridge University Press, 2016).

Lindenfeld, David F., *The Practical Imagination: The German Sciences of State in the Nineteenth Century* (Chicago, IL: University of Chicago Press, 1997).

Lindquist, Jason Howard, A 'Pure Excess of Complexity': Tropical Surfeit, the Observing Subject, and the Text, 1773–1871 (2008) <https://search.proquest.c

om/openview/927e44e3ed239a0504a0272b2740fa9d/1?pq-origsite=gscholar&cbl=18750&diss=y> [6 July 2016].

Lipset, Seymour, ed., "Harriet Martineau's America", in Seymour Lipset, ed., *Society in America* [1837] (Garden City, NY: Anchor Books, 1962), pp. 5–42.

Livesey, James, "Free Trade and Empire in the Anglo-Irish Commercial Proposition", *Journal of British Studies*, 52, no. 1 (2013): 103–127.

Livingstone, David N., "The Moral Discourse of Climate: Historical Considerations on Race, Place and Virtue", *Journal of Historical Geography*, 17, no. 4 (1991): 413–34.

———, "Science, Text and Space: Thoughts on the Geography of Reading", *Transactions of the Institute of British Geographers*, 30, no. 4 (2005): 391–401.

Lluch, Ernest, "Cameralism beyond the Germanic World: A Note on Tribe", *History of Economic Ideas*, 5, no. 2 (1997): 85–99.

[Lockhart, J.G.], "Trollope and Paulding on America", *Fraser's Magazine*, 5, no. 27 (1832): 336–50.

Logan, Deborah A., ed., *Harriet Martineau and the Irish Question: Condition of Post-Famine Ireland* (Lehigh: Lehigh University Press, 2011).

Lopez, Nicolás Barbosa, "The Exiled Insider: The Ambivalent Reception of Maria Graham's Journal of a Voyage to Brazil (1824)", *e-Journal of Portuguese History*, 16, no. 1 (2018). <http://www.scielo.mec.pt/scielo.php?script=sci_arttext&pid=S1645-64322018000100005> [16 August 2020].

Lurquín, Tomás, "Cuarta Memoria leida por el secretario sustituto don Tomás Lurquín en Junta de Posesión de 12 de enero de 1801", in Miguel Cruchaga, ed., *Estudio sobre la organización i la hacienda pública de Chile*, vol. 1 (Santiago: "Los Tiempos", 1878), pp. 314–19.

Lux, David and Cook, Harold, "Closed Circles or Open Networks: Communicating at a Distance during the Scientific Revolution", *History of Science*, 36, no. 112 (1998): 179–211.

M.L.B., "Review of J.W. Cunningham's *Cautions to Continental Travellers*", *The Monthly Review*, 89 (August 1819): 445–6.

Maas, Harro, "Sorting Things Out: The Economist as an Armchair Observer", in Lorraine Daston and Elizabeth Lunbeck, eds., *Histories of Scientific Observation* (Chicago, IL: Chicago University Press, 2011), pp. 206–229.

MacDonald, J. Marc, "Malthus and the Philanthropists, 1764–1859: The Cultural Circulation of Political Economy, Botany, and Natural Knowledge", *Social Sciences*, MDPI, Open Access Journal, 6, no. 1 (2017): 1–33.

Macintyre, Iona, *Women and Print Culture in Post-independence Buenos Aires* (Woodbridge: Tamesis Books, 2010).

———, "Corinne in the Andes: European Advice for Women in 1820s Argentina and Chile", in Matthew Brown and Gabriel Paquette, eds., *Connections after Colonialism: Europe and Latin America in the 1820s* (Tuscaloosa, AL: University of Alabama Press, 2013), pp, 179–90.

Mackintosh, James, "A Discourse at the Opening of the Literary Society of Bombay" [1819], in Vishvanath Narayan Mandlik, ed., *Transactions of the Literary Society of Bombay*, vol. 1 (Bombay: Bombay Education Society Press, 1877), pp. xii–xxvi.

———, "Appendix A", [1819] in Vishvanath Narayan Mandlik, ed., *Transactions of the Literary Society of Bombay*, vol. 1 (Bombay: Bombay Education Society Press, 1877), pp. 305–8.

———, *Memoirs of the Life of the Right Honourable Sir James Mackintosh*, vol. 1, ed. Robert James Mackintosh (London: Edward Moxon, 1835).

[Mackintosh, James], "Note on 'Preliminary Discourse'" [1819], in Vishvanath Narayan Mandlik, ed., *Transactions of the Literary Society of Bombay*, vol 1 (Bombay: Bombay Education Society Press, 1877), pp. xxvii–xli.

Macksey, Richard, "Foreword", in *Paratexts: Thresholds of Interpretation* [1987], trans. Jane E. Lewin (Cambridge: Cambridge University Press, 1997), pp. xi–xxii.

MacLaren, I.S., "In Consideration of the Evolution of Explorers and Travellers into Authors: A Model", *Studies in Travel Writing*, 15, no. 3 (2011): 221–41.

MacRoberts, M.H. and MacRoberts, Barbara R., "Problems of Citation Analysis", *Scientometrics*, 46 (1996): 435–44.

Magnusson, Lars, *Mercantilism: The Shaping of an Economic Language* (New York: Routledge, 2002).

Malcolmson, Cristina, *Studies of Skin Color in the Early Royal Society: Boyle, Cavendish, Swift* (Burlington, VT: Ashgate, 2013).

[Malthus, Thomas Robert], *An Essay on the Principle of Population, as it Affects the Future Improvement of Society, with Remarks on the Speculations of Mr. Godwin, M. Condorcet, and Other Writers* (London: J. Johnson, 1798).

———, "Newenham and Others on the State of Ireland", *The Edinburgh Review*, 12, no. 24 (1808): 336–55.

———, "Newenham on the State of Ireland", *The Edinburgh Review*, 14, no. 27 (1809): 151–70.

Malthus, Thomas Robert, *An Essay on the Principle of Population*, 2nd edn (London: J. Johnson, 1803).

———, *A Letter to the Rt. Hon. Lord Grenville* (London: J. Johnson, 1813).

———, *Statements Respecting the East-India College, with an Appeal to Facts, in Refutation of the Charges Lately Brought against it, in the Court of Proprietors* (London: John Murray, 1817a).

———, *An Essay on the Principle of Population*, 5th edn, 3 vols. (London: John Murray, 1817b).

———, *An Essay on the Principle of Population*, 6th edn, 2 vols. (London: John Murray, 1826).

———, *Definitions in Political Economy* (London: John Murray, 1827).

———, *Principles of Political Economy*, 2nd edn [1820] (London: William Pickering, 1836).

———, *Occasional Papers of T.R. Malthus on Ireland, Population, and Political Economy, from Contemporary Journals written Anonymously and Hitherto Uncollected*, Bernard Semmel, ed. (New York: B. Franklin, 1963).

———, *The Travel Diaries of Thomas Robert Malthus*, Patricia James, ed. (London: Cambridge University Press, 1966).

———, *An Essay on the Principle of Population: Text, Sources and Background, Criticism*, Philip Appelman, ed., 2nd edn (New York: W.W. Norton & Company, 2004).

Mandell, Daniel, "Review" [of Nancy Shoemaker. *A Strange Likeness: Becoming Red and White in Eighteenth-Century North America* (New York: Oxford University Press, 2004)], *H-Atlantic, H-Net Reviews* (April 2005) <http://www.h-net.org/reviews/showrev.php?id=10476> [13 March 2018].

Mandler, Peter, "Tories and Paupers: Christian Political Economy and the Making of the New Poor Law", *Historical Journal*, 33, no. 1 (1990): 81–103.

Marcet, Jane Haldimand, *Conversations on Political Economy; in Which the Elements of that Science Are Familiarly Explained* (London: Longman, et al., 1816).

Martin, Alison, *Nature Translated: Alexander von Humboldt's Works in Nineteenth-Century Britain* (Edinburgh: Edinburgh University Press, 2018).

Martineau, Harriet, "Weal and Woe in Garveloch", [1832] in Harriet Martineau, ed., *Illustrations of Political Economy*, vol. 2, no. 6 (London: Charles Fox, 1834).

———, "Letter to the Deaf", *Tait's Edinburgh Magazine*, 1 (1834): 174–9.

———, *Society in America*, 3 vols. (London: Saunders and Otley, 1837).

———, *Retrospect of Western Travel*, 3 vols. (London: Saunders and Otley, 1838a).

———, *How to Observe. Morals and Manners* (London: Charles Knight, 1838b).

———, *Life in the Sick-Room: Essays* (Boston, MA: L.C. Bowles and W. Crosby, 1844).

———, *Eastern Life, Present and Past*, 3 vols. (London: Edward Moxon, 1848).

———, "Letters from Ireland, I", *The Daily News*, Friday, 13 August 1852a, p. 4.

———, "Letters from Ireland. Letter XI", *The Daily News*, Friday, 3 September 1852b, p. 4.

———, "Letters from Ireland, XVI", *The Daily News*, Friday, 17 September 1852c, p. 4.

———, "Letters from Ireland, XXVII", *The Daily News*, Thursday, 14 October 1852d, p. 4.

———, *Letters from Ireland* (London: John Chapman, 1852e).

———, *Harriet Martineau's Autobiography*, 3 vols, ed. Maria Chapman (Boston, MA: James R. Osgood and Company, 1877).

["H.M."], "The Martyr Age of the United States", *The London and Westminster Review*, 32, no. 1 (1838): 1–32.

[Martineau, H.], "Travel during the Last Half Century", *Westminster Review*, 70 (1858): 426–65.

———, "What is 'Social Science'?", *The Spectator*, 31 (1858): 1119–20.

Mathison, Gilbert Farquhar, *Narrative of a Visit to Brazil, Chile, Peru, and the Sandwich Islands during the Years 1821 and 1822. With Miscellaneous Remarks on the Past and Present State, and Political Prospects of Those Countries* (London: Charles Knight, 1825).

Maunder, Samuel, *The Treasury of History*, 2nd edn (London: Longman, Brown, Green, and Longmans, 1844).

Mayo, John, "The Development of British Interests in Chile's Norte Chico in the Early Nineteenth Century", *The Americas*, 57, no. 3 (2001): 363–94.

McCarthy, Kate, "Agrarian Discourse in Imperial Context: Landed Property, Scottish Stadial Theory and Indigenes in Early Colonial Australia", *Australia & New Zealand Law & History E-Journal* (2005): 60–69 <http://classic.austlii.edu.au/au/journals/ANZLawHisteJl/2005/4.pdf> [18 August 2016].

McCormick, Ted, "Political Arithmetic and Sacred History: Population Thought in the English Enlightenment, 1660–1750", *Journal of British Studies*, 52, no. 4 (2013): 829–57.

[McCulloch, James B.], "Thoughts on Banking", *The Edinburgh Review*, 43, no. 86 (1826): 263–98.

———, "The Late Crisis in the Money Market Impartially Considered [Commercial Revulsions]", *The Edinburgh Review*, 44, no. 87 (1826): 70–93.

———, "Emigration", *The Edinburgh Review*, 47, no. 93 (1828): 204–42.

McDaniel, Iain, *Adam Ferguson in the Scottish Enlightenment: The Roman Past and Europe's Future* (Cambridge, MA: Harvard University Press, 2013).

McDonald, Lynn, *The Women Founders of the Social Sciences* (Ottawa, ON: Carleton University Press, 1994).

McKeon, Michael, *Origin of the English Novel 1600–1740* (Baltimore, MD: Johns Hopkins University Press, 1987).

Marouby, Christian, "Adam Smith and the Anthropology of the Enlightenment: The "Ethnographic" Sources of Economic Progress", in Larry Wolff and Marco Cipolloni, eds., *The Anthropology of the Enlightenment* (Stanford, CA: Stanford University Press, 2007), pp. 85–102.

Marshall, William, *A Review (and Complete Abstract) of the Reports to the Board of Agriculture from the Midland Department of England* (York: Thomas Wilson and Sons, 1815).

——, *The Review and Abstract of the County Reports to the Board of Agriculture* [1808], 1st edn (York: Thomas Wilson and Sons, 1818).

Martínez, Maria Elena, *Genealogical Fictions: Limpieza de sangre, Religion, and Gender in Colonial Mexico* (Palo Alto, CA: Stanford University Press, 2008).

Mathew, W.M., "The imperialism of Free Trade: Peru, 1820–70", *The Economic History Review* 21, no. 3 (1968): 562–579.

Mayhew, Robert, "The Character of English Geography c. 1660–1800: A Textual Approach", *Journal of Historical Geography* 24, no. 4 (1998): 385–412.

Meek, Ronald L., *Social Science and the Ignoble Savage* (Cambridge: Cambridge University Press, 1976).

Miers, John, *Travels in Chile and La Plata*, 2 vols (London: Baldwin, Cradock, and Joy, 1826).

Millar, Ashley Eva, *A Singular Case: Debating China's Political Economy in the European Enlightenment* (Montreal, QC: McGill-Queen's Press, 2017).

Millar, John, *The Origin of the Distinction of Ranks*, 4th edn (London: William Blackwood, and Longman, Huest, Rees, & Orme, 1806).

Mill, James, *The History of British India*, vol. 1. (London: Baldwin, Cradock and Joy, 1817).

——, *Elements of Political Economy* (London: Baldwin, Cradock, and Joy, 1821).

——, *James Mill: Selected Economic Writings*, ed. Donald Winch (Edinburgh: Oliver and Boyd, 1966).

Mill, John Stuart, "On the Definition of Political Economy; and the Method of Investigation Proper to It", in John Stuart Mill, *Essays on Some Unsettled Questions of Political Economy* (London: John W. Parker, 1844), pp. 120–64.

——, *Principles of Political Economy*, vol. 1. (Boston, MA: C.C. Little & J. Brown, 1848).

——, *Memorandum of the Improvements in the Administration of India during the Last Thirty Years: And the Petition of the East-India Company to Parliament* (London: Allen, 1858).

Miller, David Philip and Reill Peter H., eds., *Visions of Empire: Voyages, Botany and Representations of Nature* (Cambridge: Cambridge University Press, 1996).

Miskell, Louise, "From Copperopolis to Coquimbo: International Knowledge Networks in the Copper Industry of the 1820s", *The Welsh History Review* 27, no. 1 (2014): 92–111.

["M.L.B."], "The Genoese", *Mirror of Literature, Amusement, and Instruction*, 14, no. 390 (1829): 178–80.

Mokyr, Joel, "Review [of Murphy, Antoin, ed. *Economists and the Irish Economy from the Eighteenth Century to the Present Day*. Dublin: Irish Academic Press]", *The Journal of Economic History*, 45, no. 3 (1985): 731–2.

Moloney, Pat, "Savages in the Scottish Enlightenment's History of Desire", *Journal of the History of Sexuality*, 14, no. 3 (2005): 237–265.

Montagu, Lady Mary Wortley, *The Turkish Embassy Letters* [1763], Teresa Heffernan and Daniel O'Quinn, eds. (Peterborough, ON: Broadview Press, 2013).

[Montagu, Lady Mary Wortley], *Letters of the Right Honourable Lady M—y W—y M—e Written during Her Travels in Europe, Asia and Africa to Persons of Distinction, Men of Letters, &c. in Different Parts of Europe* (London: P. Becket and P.A. De Hondt, 1763).

More, Hannah, *Slavery, a Poem* (London: T. Cadell, 1788).

———, *Moral Sketches of Prevailing Opinions and Manners, Foreign and Domestic: With Reflections on Prayer* (London: T. Cadell & W. Davies, 1819).

Morgan, Mary S., "Experimental Farming and Ricardo's Political Arithmetic of Distribution", Working Papers on the Nature of Evidence: How Well do 'Facts' Travel? 03/05 (Department of Economic History: London School of Economics, 2005).

———, "Travelling Facts", in Peter Howlett and Mary S. Morgan, eds., *How Well Do Facts Travel? The Dissemination of Reliable Knowledge* (Cambridge: Cambridge University Press, 2010), pp. 3–39.

———, *The World in the Model: How Economists Work and Think* (New York: Cambridge University Press, 2012).

Mosselmans, Bert, "Adolphe Quetelet, the Average Man and the Development of Economic Methodology", *European Journal of the History of Economic Thought*, 12, no. 4 (2005): 565–83.

Muldrew, Craig, *The Economy of Obligation: The Culture of Credit and Social Relations in Early Modern England* (New York: St. Martin's, 1999).

Munting, Roger, *An Economic and Social History of Gambling in Britain and the USA* (Manchester: Manchester University Press, 1996).

Myers, Mitzi, "Romancing the Moral Tale: Maria Edgeworth and the Problematics of Pedagogy", in James Holt, ed., *Romanticism and Children's Literature in Nineteenth-Century England* (Athens, GA: The University of Georgia Press, 1991), pp. 96–128.

———, "Daddy's Girl as Motherless Child: Maria Edgeworth and Maternal Romance; an Essay in Reassessment", in Dale Spender, ed., *Living by the Pen: Early British Women Writers* (New York: Teachers College Press, 1992), pp. 137–59.

———, "'A Peculiar Protection': Hannah More and the Cultural Politics of Blagdon Controversy", in Beth Fowkes Tobin, ed., *History, Gender, and 18th-Century Literature* (Athens, GA: University of Georgia Press, 1994), pp. 227–57.

———, "'Anecdotes from the Nursery' in Maria Edgeworth's Practical Education (1798): Learning from Children 'Abroad and at Home'", *Princeton University Library Chronicle*, 60, no. 2 (1999): 220–50.

Nagle, Thomas, *The View from Nowhere* (Oxford: Oxford University Press, 1986).

Nardin, Jane, "Hannah More and the Problem of Poverty", *Texas Studies in Literature and Language*, 43, no. 3 (2001): 267–84.

Neal, Larry, "The Financial Crisis of 1825 and the Restructuring of the British Financial System", *The Federal Reserve Bank of St. Louis Review*, 80 (1998): 53–76.

Neocleous, Mark, "Social Police and the Mechanisms of Prevention", *The British Journal of Criminology*, 40, no. 4 (2000): 710–72.

Nocia, Megan A., "The London Shopscape: Educating the Child Consumer in the Stories of Mary Wollstonecraft, Maria Edgeworth, and Mary Martha Sherwood", *Children's Literature*, 41 (2013): 28–56.

Nuñez, Ignacio, *An Account, Historical, Political, and Statistical, of the United Provinces of Rio de la Plata: With an Appendix, Concerning the Usurpation of Monte Video by the Portuguese and Brazilian Governments*, vols. 1 and 2 (London: R. Ackermann, 1825).

O'Brien, Karen, "Between Enlightenment and Stadial History: William Robertson on the History of Europe", *British Journal for Eighteenth-Century Studies*, 16, no. 1 (1993): 53–63.

———, *Narratives of Enlightenment: Cosmopolitan History from Voltaire to Gibbon* (Cambridge: Cambridge University Press, 1997).

———, *Women and Enlightenment in Eighteenth-Century Britain* (Cambridge: Cambridge University Press, 2009).

Ogborn, Miles, "Writing Travels: Power, Knowledge and Ritual on the English East India Company's Early Voyages", *Transactions of the Institute of British Geographers*, 27, no. 2 (2002): 155–71.

———, *Indian Ink: Script and Print in the Making of the English East India Company* (Chicago, IL: University of Chicago Press, 2007).

Ó Gráda, Cormac, "Malthus and the Pre-famine Economy", in Antoin Murphy, ed., *Economists and the Irish Economy from the Eighteenth Century to the Present Day* (Dublin: Irish Academic Press, 1984), pp. 75–95.

———, *Black '47 and Beyond: The Great Irish Famine in History, Economy, and Memory* (Princeton, NJ: Princeton University Press, 1999).

Olson, Richard, "Sex and Status in Scottish Enlightenment Social Science: John Millar and the Sociology of Gender Roles", *History of the Human Sciences*, 11, no. 1 (1998): 73–100.

Orazem, Claudia, *Political Economy and Fiction in the Early Works of Harriet Martineau* (Frankfurt: Peter Lang, 1999).

Ostry, Elaine, "'Social Wonders': Fancy, Science, and Technology in Dickens's Periodicals", *Victorian Periodicals Review*, 34, no. 1 (2001): 54–78.

Otis, Laura, "Science Surveys and Literature: Reflections on an Uneasy Kinship", *Isis*, 101, no. 3 (2010): 570–7.

Pagden, Anthony, "The Immobility of China: Orientalism and Occidentalism in the Enlightenment", in Larry Wolff and Marco Cipolloni, eds., *The Anthropology of the Enlightenment* (Stanford, CA: Stanford University Press, 2007), pp. 50–64.

Palmeri, Frank, "Conjectural History and the Origins of Sociology", *Studies in Eighteenth Century Culture*, 37 (2008): 1–21.

———, *State of Nature, Stages of Society: Enlightenment Conjectural History and Modern Social Discourse* (New York: Columbia University Press, 2016).

Parish, Woodbine, *Buenos Ayres, and the Provinces of the Rio de La Plata: Their Present State, Trade, and Debt* (London: John Murray, 1838).

Pearl, Jason H., "Geography and Authority in the Royal Society Instructions", in Judy A. Hayden, ed., *Travel Narratives, the New Science, and Literary Discourse, 1569–1750* (Burlington, VT: Ashgate, 2012), pp. 71–83.

Pérez-Mejía, Angela, *A Geography of Hard Times: Narratives about Travel to South America, 1780–1849*, trans. Dick Cluster (Albany, NY: State University of New York Press, 2004).

Petty, William, "A Treatise on Ireland, 1687", in Charles Henry Hull, ed., *The Economic Writings of Sir William Petty, Together with the Observations upon Bills of Mortality, More Probably by Captain John Graunt*, vol. 2 (Cambridge: Cambridge University Press, 1899), pp. 545–621.

———, *The Petty Papers: Some Unpublished Writings of Sir William Petty*, vol. 1, ed. Marquis of Lansdowne (London: Constable & Company, 1927).

Phillipson, Nicholas, "Language, Sociability, and History: Some Reflections on the Foundations of Adam Smith's Science of Man", in Stefan Collini, Richard Whatmore, and Brian Young, eds., *Economy, Polity, and Society: British Intellectual History* (Cambridge: Cambridge University Press, 2000), pp. 70–84.

Pickstone, John V., "Working Knowledges before and after Circa 1800: Practices and Disciplines in the History of Science, Technology, and Medicine", *Isis*, 98, no. 3 (2007): 489–516.

Plotz, John, "Can the Sofa Speak? A Look at Thing Theory", *Criticism*, 47, no. 1 (2005): 109–18.

Plumptre, Anne, *Narrative of a Residence in Ireland during the Summer of 1814, and that of 1815* (London: Henry Colburn, 1817).

Poe, Edgar A., "Our Amateur Poets. no. 1.- Flaccus", *Graham's Magazine*, 22, no. 3 (1843): 195–8.

Pontoppidan, Erich, *Natural History of Norway* [1751], vols. 1 and 2 (London: A. Linde, 1755).

Poovey, Mary, "Figures of Arithmetic, Figures of Speech: The Discourse of Statistics in the 1830s", *Critical Inquiry*, 19, no. 2 (1993): 256–76.

Porter, Theodore, *The Rise of Statistical Thinking, 1820–1900* (Princeton, NJ: Princeton University Press, 1986).

Pratt, Mary Louise, *Imperial Eyes: Travel Writing and Transculturation*, 2nd edn (New York: Routledge, 2008).

Prendergast, Renee, "Knowledge and Information in Economics: What Did the Classical Economists Know?" *History of Political Economy*, 39, no. 4 (2007): 679–712.

Procacci, Giovanna, *Gouverner la misère, la question sociale en France, 1789–1848* (Paris: Le Seuil, 1993).

Proctor, Robert, *Narrative of a Journey across the Cordillera of the Andes, and of a Residence in Lima, and Other Parts of Peru, in the Years 1823 and 1824* (London: Hurst, Robinson, and Company, 1825).

Pujol, Michèle, *Feminism and Anti-Feminism in Early Economic Thought* (Northampton, MA: Edward Elgar, 1992).

Puro, Edward, "Use of the Term 'Natural' in Adam Smith's Wealth of Nations", *Research in the History of Economic Thought and Methodology* 9 (1992): 73–86.

Quick, Tom, "Political Economy and Disciplinary Formation at the University of London c.1828" (n.d.) <http://www.ucl.ac.uk/bloomsbury-project/articles/0articles/quick.pdf> [4 April 2016].

["R"], "Transactions of The Statistical Society of London", *The London and Westminster Review* 31, no. 1 (1838): 45–72.

Rankine, Margaret E., "The Mexican Mining Industry in the Nineteenth Century with Special Reference to Guanajuato", *Bulletin of Latin American Research*, 11, no. 1 (1992): 29–48.

Rappaport, Joanne, *The Disappearing Mestizo: Configuring Difference in the Colonial Kingdom of Granada* (Durham, NC: Duke University Press, 2014).

Rebel, Hermann, "Reimagining the *Oikos*: Austrian Cameralism in its Social Formation", in Jay O'Brien and William Roseberry, eds., *Golden Ages, Dark Ages: Imagining the Past in Anthropology and History* (Berkeley, CA: University of California Press, 1991), pp. 48–80.

Rees Jones, Ricardo, *Bernardino Rivadavia y Su Negocio Minero: Rio de La Plata Mining Association* (Buenos Aires: Libreria Histórica, 2008).

Reilly, Terry, "Arthur Young's *Travels in France*: Historicity and the Use of Literary Forms", in Dan Doll and Jessica Munns, eds., *Recording and Reordering: Essays on the Seventeenth- and Eighteenth-Century Diary and Journal* (Cranbury, NJ: Bucknell University Press, 2006), pp. 122–36.

Reinert, Sophus, *Translating Empire: Emulation and the Origins of Political Economy* (Cambridge, MA: Harvard University Press, 2011).

Remien, Peter, "Oeconomy and Ecology in Early Modern England", *PMLA*, 132, no. 5 (2017): 1117–33.

Rendall, J., "The Condition of Women, Women's Writing, and the Empire in Nineteenth-century Britain", in Catherine Hall and Sonya O. Rose, eds., *At Home with the Empire: Metropolitan Culture and the Imperial World* (Cambridge: Cambridge University Press, 2006), pp. 101–21.

Reniers, Georges, "Malthus, the 18th Century European Explorers and the Principle of Population in Africa", *African Population Studies*, 25, no. 2 (2011): 181–193.

Roberts, Caroline, *The Woman and the Hour: Harriet Martineau and Victorian Ideologies* (Toronto, ON: University of Toronto Press, 2002).

Ricardo, David, *The Works and Correspondence of David Ricardo, vol. three Pamphlets and Papers, 1809–1811* [1951], ed. Piero Sraffa, with the collaboration of Maurice H. Dobb (Cambridge: Cambridge University Press for the Royal Economic Society, 1962).

———, *The Works and Correspondence of David Ricardo, vol. 6 Letters 1810–1815* [1951], ed. Piero Sraffa, with the collaboration of Maurice H. Dobb (Cambridge: Cambridge University Press for the Royal Economic Society, 1973a).

———, *The Works and Correspondence of David Ricardo, vol. 7 Letters 1816–1818* [1951], ed. Piero Sraffa, with the collaboration of Maurice H. Dobb (Cambridge: Cambridge University Press for the Royal Economic Society, 1973b).

———, *The Works and Correspondence of David Ricardo, vol. 9 Letters 1821–1823* [1951], ed. Piero Sraffa, with the collaboration of Maurice H. Dobb (Cambridge: Cambridge University Press for the Royal Economic Society, 1973c).

Ricoeur, Paul, *On Translation*, trans. Eileen Brennan (New York: Routledge, 2014).

Roberts, Arthur, ed., *Letters of Hannah More to Zachary Macaulay, Containing Notices of Lord Macaulay's Youth* (London: James Nisbet and Co, 1860).

Roberts, Lissa, "Practicing Oeconomy during the Second Half of the Long Eighteenth Century: An Introduction", *History and Technology*, 30, no. 3 (2014): 133–148.

Roberts, William, ed., *Memoirs of the Life and Correspondence of Mrs. Hannah More*, 2nd edn (London: R.B. Seeley and W. Burnside, 1839).

Robertson, John, *The Case for the Enlightenment: Scotland and Naples, 1680–1760* (Cambridge: Cambridge University Press, 2005).

Robertson, William, *The history of America*, Books 1–8, 3 vols.; Books 9–10. (Dublin: Whitestone, et al., 1777, 1796).

Rock, David, "Porteño Liberals and Imperialist Emissaries in the Rio de la Plata: Rivadavia and the British", in Matthew Brown and Gabriel Paquette, eds., *Connections after Colonialism: Europe and Latin America in the 1820s* (Tuscaloosa, AL: The University of Alabama Press), pp. 207–22.

Rodenas, Adriana Méndez, *Transatlantic Travels in Nineteenth-Century Latin America: European Women Pilgrims* (Lanham, MD: Bucknell University Press and Rowman & Littlefield, 2014).

Rodriguez, Julia, "Beyond Prejudice and Pride: The Human Sciences in Nineteenth- and Twentieth-Century Latin America", *ISIS*, 104, no. 4 (2013): 307–17.

Romer, Isabella Frances, *A Pilgrimage to the Temples and Tombs of Egypt, Nubia, and Palestine in 1845–6* (London: Richard Bentley, 1846).

Rosenthal, Caitlin, *Accounting for Slavery: Masters and Management* (Cambridge, MA: Harvard University Press, 2018).

Rothschild, Emma, *The Inner Life of Empires: An Eighteenth-Century History* (Princeton, NJ: Princeton University Press, 2011).

Ruigh, Deborah A., *The Sociology of Harriet Martineau in EASTERN LIFE, PRESENT AND PAST: The Foundations of the Islamic Sociology of Religion* (Lincoln, NE: University of Nebraska-Lincoln, 2012).

Rubiés, Joan-Pau, "New Worlds and Renaissance Ethnology", *History and Anthropology* 6, nos. 2–3 (1993): 157–97.

———, "Christianity and Civilization in Sixteenth Century Ethnological Discourse", in Henriette Brugge, and Joan-Pau Rubiés, eds., *Shifting Cultures: Interaction and Discourse in the Expansion of Europe* (Münster: Lit Verlag, 1995), pp. 35–60.

———, "Instructions for Travellers: Teaching the Eye to See", *History and Anthropology*, 9, nos. 2–3 (1996): 139–90.

———, *Travel and Ethnology in the Renaissance: South India through European Eyes, 1250–1625* (New York: Cambridge University Press, 2001).

———, "From the 'History of Travayle' to the History of Travel Collections: The Rise of an Early Modern Genre", in Daniel Carey and Claire Jowitt, eds., *Richard Hakluyt and Travel Writing in Early Modern Europe* (New York: Ashgate, 2012), pp. 25–41.

Rupke, Nicolaas A., *Alexander von Humboldt: A Metabiography* (Chicago, IL: University of Chicago Press, 2008).

["S.R."], "The Arctic Discoveries", *The London and Westminster Review*, 31, no. 2 (1838): 373–92.

Sacks, David Harris, "'To Deduce a Colonie': Richard Hakluyt's Godly Mission in its Contexts, c. 1580–1616", in Daniel Carey and Claire Jowitt, eds., *Richard Hakluyt and Travel Writing in Early Modern Europe* (New York: Ashgate, 2012), pp. 197–218.

Salah, Mohamed, "A Pre-Colonial Population Brought to Light: Digitization of the Nineteenth Century Egyptian Censuses", *Historical Methods: A Journal of Quantitative and Interdisciplinary History*, 46, no. 1 (2013): 5–18.

Salvatore, Ricardo D., "The Strength of Markets in Latin America's Sociopolitical Discourse, 1750–1850: Some Preliminary Observations", *Latin American Perspectives*, 26, no. 1 (1999): 22–43.

Sanders, Valerie and Weiner, Gaby, eds., *Harriet Martineau and the Birth of Disciplines: Nineteenth-Century Intellectual Powerhouse* (London: Routledge, 2017).

Schabas, Margaret, *The Natural Origins of Economics* (Chicago, IL: The University of Chicago Press, 2005).
Scherer, Joel, "Troubling Journey: Elite Women Travellers of Ireland and the Irish Question, 1834–1852", *Madison Historical Review*, 11 (2014): 1–16. <https://commons.lib.jmu.edu/cgi/viewcontent.cgi?article=1004&context=mhr> [18 September 2020].
Schmeller, Erik S., *Perceptions of Race and Nation in English and American Travel Writers, 1833–1914* (New York: Peter Lang, 2004).
Scholl, Lesa, "Mediation and Expansion: Harriet Martineau's Travels in America", *Women's History Review*, 18, no. 5 (2009): 819–33.
Schürer, Norbert, "The Impartial Spectator of Sati, 1757–84", *Eighteenth-Century Studies*, 42, no. 1 (2008): 19–44.
Schwartz, Stuart B., "Colonial Identities and the Sociedad de Castas", *Colonial Latin America Review*, 4, no. 1 (1995): 185–201.
Schwartz, Sharron P., "Creating the Cult of 'Cousin Jack': Cornish Miners in Latin America 1812–1848 and the Development of an International Mining Labour Market" (1999). <https://projects.exeter.ac.uk/cornishlatin/Creating%20the%20Cult%20of%20Cousin%20Jack.pdf> [12 May 2015].
———, "The Making of a Myth: Cornish Miners in the New World in the Early Nineteenth Century", *Cornish Studies*, 9 (2001): 105–126.
———, "Exporting the Industrial Revolution: The Migration of Cornish Mining Technology to Latin America in the Early Nineteenth Century", in Heidi Slettedahl Macpherson and Will Kaufman, eds., *New Perspectives in Transatlantic Studies* (New York: University Press of America, 2002), pp. 143–58.
[Scrope, George Poulett], "Miss Martineau's Monthly Novels", *The Quarterly Review*, 49, no. 98 (1833): 136–52.
Sebastiani, Silvia, *The Scottish Enlightenment: Race, Gender, and the Limits of Progress* (New York: Palgrave, 2013).
Semmel, Bernard, *The Rise of Free Trade Imperialism: Classical Political Economy the Empire of Free Trade and Imperialism 1750–1850* (New York: Cambridge University Press, 1970).
Senior, Nassau, *Four Introductory Lectures on Political Economy. Delivered before the University of Oxford* (London: Longman, Brown, Green, and Longmans, 1852).
Serrano, Elena, "Making *oeconomic* People: The Spanish *Magazine of Agriculture and Arts for Parish Rectors* (1797–1808)", *History and Technology*, 30, no. 3 (2014): 149–76.
Shapin, Steven, *A Social History of Truth: Civility and Science in Seventeenth-Century England* (Chicago, IL: University of Chicago Press, 1994).
———, "The Sciences of Subjectivity", *Social Studies of Science*, 42, no. 2 (2012): 170–84.
Shapin, Steven and Schaffer, Simon, *Leviathan and the Air-Pump: Hobbes, Boyle, and the Experimental Life* (Princeton, NJ: Princeton University Press, 1985).
Shapiro, Barbara J., *A Culture of Fact: England, 1550–1720* (Ithaca, NY: Cornell University Press, 2000).
Shelton, George, *Dean Tucker and 18th-Century Economics and Political Thought* (New York: Macmillan, 1981).
Shoemaker, Nancy, "How Indians Got to be Red", *The American Historical Review*, 102, no. 3 (1997): 625–44.

———, *A Strange Likeness: Becoming Red and White in Eighteenth-Century North America* (Oxford: Oxford University Press, 2004).

Simpson, David, "Touches of the Real" [Review of *Practising New Historicism* by Catherine Gallagher and Stephen Greenblatt], *London Review of Books*, 23, no. 10 (2001): 25–6.

Simpson, Mary C.M., "Preface", in Mary C.M. Simpson (ed.) *Correspondence & Conversations of Alexis de Tocqueville with Nassau William Senior from 1834 to 1859*, vol. 1 (London: Henry S. King & Co, 1872), pp. iii–v.

Sivasundaram, Sujit, *Nature and the Godly Empire: Science and the Evangelical Mission in the Pacific, 1795–1850* (New York: Cambridge University Press, 2005).

Sluyter, Andrew, "Humboldt's Mexican Texts and Landscapes", *Geographical Review*, 96, no. 3 (2006): 361–81.

———, "Traveling/Writing the Unworld with Alexander von Humboldt", *Landscapes of a New Cultural Economy of Space*, 5 (2006): 93–116.

Smith, Adam, *The Theory of Moral Sentiments* (1759), D.D. Raphael, and A.L. Macfie, eds., *Glasgow Edition of the Works and Correspondence of Adam Smith*, vol. 1 (Oxford: Oxford University Press, 1976).

———, *Lectures on Jurisprudence* (1762–3), *Glasgow Edition of the Works and Correspondence of Adam Smith*, vol. 5. R.L. Meek, D.D. Raphael, and P.G. Stein, eds. (Oxford: Oxford University Press, 1978a).

———, *An Inquiry into the Nature and Causes of the Wealth of Nations* (1776), 2 vols., *Glasgow Edition of the Works and Correspondence of Adam Smith*, vol. 3., R.H. Campbell, A.S. Skinner, and W.B. Todd, eds. (Oxford: Oxford University Press, 1978b).

———, *A Catalogue of the Library of Adam Smith*, John Bonar, ed. (London: Macmillan and Co., 1894).

Smith, John, *The Generall Historie of Virginia* (1624), in Philip L. Barbour, ed., *The Complete Works of John Smith (1580–1631)*, vol. 2 (Chapel Hill, NC: University of North Carolina Press, 1986).

Smith, John, *The Generall Historie of Virginia* (1624) <http://docsouth.unc.edu/southlit/smith/smith.html> [27 January 2013].

Somarriva, Marcelo, "'An Open Field and Fair Play': The Relationship between Britain and the Southern Cone of America, c. 1808 and 1830", Ph.D. Thesis. Department of History, University College London, 2013.

———, "A Matter of Speculation: British Representations of Argentina, Chile and Perú during the Wars of Independence", *Bulletin of Latin American Research*, 36, no. 2 (2017): 223–36.

Sockwell, W.D., "Contributions of Henry Brougham to Classical Political Economy", *History of Political Economy*, 23, no. 4 (1991): 645–673.

[Southey, R.], "Malthus on Population", *The Annual Review, and History of Literature; for 1803*, 2 (1804): 292–301.

Speake, Jennifer, ed., *Travel and Exploration: An Encyclopedia*, 3 vols. (London: Routledge, 2003).

Stagl, Justin, "The Methodising of Travel in the 16th Century: A Tale of Three Cities", *History and Anthropology*, 4, no. 2 (1990): 303–38.

———, *A History of Curiosity: The Theory of Travel, 1550–1800* (Amsterdam: Harwood Academic Publishers, 1995).

Steedman, Carolyn, "Inside, Outside, Other: Accounts of National Identity in the 19th Century", *History of the Human Sciences*, 8, no. 4 (1995): 59–76.
Stephen, Leslie, "Edgeworth, Richard Lovell", [1888] *Dictionary of National Biography, 1885–1900*, vol. 16 (London: Smith, Elder & Co. (1885–1900), pp. 383–5.
Stevenson, William Bennet, *A Historical and Descriptive Narrative of Twenty Years' Residence in South America*, 1, 2, and 3 (London: Hurst, Robinson, 1825).
Stewart, Dugald, "Account of the Life and Writings of Adam Smith, LL.D", *Transactions of The Royal Society of Edinburgh*, 3 (Part 1) (Edinburgh: Royal Society of Edinburgh, 1794), pp. 55–137.
——, *Elements of the Philosophy of the Human Mind* [1792]) vols. 1 and 2 (Albany, NY: E. and E. Hosford, 1822).
Stocking, George, *Victorian Anthropology* (New York: Free Press, 1987).
Stokes, Eric, *The English Utilitarians and India* (Oxford: Clarendon Press, 1959).
Stott, Anne, "Hannah More and the Blagdon Controversy, 1799–1802", *The Journal of Ecclesiastical History*, 51, no. 2 (2000): 319–46.
Stuurman, Siep, "François Bernier and the Invention of Racial Classification", *History Workshop Journal*, 50, no. 1 (2000): 1–21.
Summerfield, Goeffrey, *Fantasy and Reason: Children's Literature in the Eighteenth Century* (London: Methuen & Co, Ltd, 1984).
[Sumner, John Bird], "On Malthus", *The Quarterly Review*, 17, no. 34 (1817): 369–403.
Sutherland, Kathryn, "Adam Smith's Master Narrative: Women and the *Wealth of Nations*", in Stephen Copley and Kathryn Sutherland, eds., *Adam Smith's Wealth of Nations: New Interdisciplinary Essays* (Manchester: Manchester University Press, 1995), pp. 97–121.
Swedberg, Richard, *Tocqueville's Political Economy* (Princeton, NJ: Princeton University Press, 2009).
Tennenhouse, Leonard, *The Importance of Feeling English: American Literature and the British Diaspora, 1750–1850* (Princeton, NJ: Princeton University Press, 2007).
Thomas, Nicholas, *Entangled Objects: Exchange, Material Culture, and Colonialism in the Pacific* (Cambridge, MA: Harvard University Press, 1991).
Thompson, Carl, *Travel Writing* (London: Routledge, 2011).
——, "Earthquakes and Petticoats: Maria Graham, Geology, and Early Nineteenth-Century 'Polite' Science", *Journal of Victorian Culture*, 17, no. 3 (2012): 329–46.
Thompson, E.P., "Time, Work-Discipline, and Industrial Capitalism", *Past and Present*, 38 (1967): 56–97.
Thomson, James, *Letters on the Moral and Religious State of South America: Written During a Residence of Nearly Seven Years in Buenos Aires, Chile, Peru, and Colombia* (London: J. Nisbet, 1827).
Tobin, Beth Fowkes, "Arthur Young, Agriculture, and the Construction of the New Economic Man", in Beth Fowkes Tobin, ed., *History, Gemder, and 18th-Century Literature* (Athens, GA: University of Georgia Press, 1994), pp. 179–97.
Tocqueville, Alexis de, *De la Démocratie en Amérique*, vols. 1 and 3 (Paris: Charles Gosselin, 1835 and 1840).
Tribe, Keith, "Cameralism and the Science of Government", *The Journal of Modern History*, 56, no. 2 (1984): 263–284.

——, *Governing Economy: The Reformation of German Economic Discourse, 1750–1840* (Cambridge: Cambridge University Press, 1988).

——, "Professors Malthus and Jones: Political Economy at the East India College 1806–1858", *European Journal of the History of Economic Thought*, 2, no. 2 (1995): 327–54.

——, "Oeconomic history", *Studies in the History and Philosophy of Science*, Part A, 36, no. 3 (2005): 586–97.

Trifilo, S. Samuel, "Catholicism in Argentina as Viewed by Early Nineteenth-Century British Travelers", *The Americas*, 19, no. 3 (1963): 262–75.

Trollope, Frances, *Domestic Manners of the Americans*, vols. 1 and 2 (London: Whittaker, Treacher, & Co, 1832).

——, *Vienna and the Austrians; with Some Account of a Journey through Swabia, Bavaria, the Tyrol, and the Salzbourg*, vols. 1 and 2 (London: R. Bentley, 1838).

Tucker, Josiah, *A Brief Essay on the Advantages and Disadvantages, Which Respectively Attend France and Great Britain, with Regard to Trade* (1749), 2nd edn (London: Printed for T. Tyre, 1750).

——, *Reflections on the Expediency of a Law for the Naturalization of Foreign Protestants: In Two Parts*, Part 1 (London: Printed for T. Tyre, 1751).

——, "Important Queries Occasioned by the Rejection of the Late Naturalization Bill", in *A Brief Essay on the Advantages and Disadvantages Which Respectively Attend France and Great Britain, with Regard to Trade: With Some Proposals for Removing the Principal Disadvantages of Great Britain. In a New Method* (London: Printed for T. Tyre, 1753), pp. 1–48.

——, *Instructions for Travellers* [1757] (Dublin: William Watson, 1758).

Valenze, Deborah, "Malthus among the Laplanders: Reindeer Herders in the Crucible of Civilization" (Unpublished paper, 2016).

van Ittersum, Martine, "A Miracle Mirrored? The Reception of Dutch Economic and Political Thought in Europe in the Seventeenth and Eighteenth Centuries", *Low Countries Historical Review*, 127, no. 4 (2012): 83–99.

Vargo, Gregory, "Contested Authority: Reform and Local Pressure in Harriet Martineau's Poor Law Stories", *Nineteenth-Century Gender Studies*, 3, no. 2 (2007). <https://www.ncgsjournal.com/issue32/vargo.htm> [18 June 2017].

Varouxakis, Giorgios, "Guizot's Historical Works and J.S. Mill's Reception of Tocqueville", *History of Political Thought*, 20, no. 2 (1999): 292–312.

Veliz, Claudio, "Egaña, Lambert, and the Chilean Mining Associations of 1825", *The Hispanic American Historical Review*, 55, no. 4 (1975): 637–63.

Vetter, Lisa Pace, "Harriet Martineau on the Theory and Practice of Democracy in America", *Political Theory*, 36, no. 3 (2008): 424–55.

Vidal, Emeric Essex, *Picturesque Illustrations of Buenos Ayres and Monte Video, Consisting of Twenty-Four Views: Accompanied with Descriptions of the Scenery, and of the Costumes, Manners, &c., of the Inhabitants of Those Cities and Their Environs* (London: R. Ackermann, 1820).

Walls, Laura Dassow, *The Passage to Cosmos: Alexander von Humboldt and the Shaping of America* (Chicago, IL: University of Chicago Press, 2009).

Ward, Henry G., *Mexico in 1827*, vols. 1 and 2 (London: Henry Colburn, 1828).

Waterman, A.M.C., *Revolution, Economics and Religion. Christian Political Economy, 1798–1833* (Cambridge: Cambridge University Press, 1991).

Weatherall, David, *David Ricardo: A Biography* (The Hague: Martinus Nijhoff, 1976).

Weingast, Barry R., "Adam Smith's Theory of Violence and the Political-Economics of Development", National Bureau of Economics (2017). <http://www.nber.org/chapters/c13509.pdf> [29 March 2017].

Wheeler, Roxanne, *The Complexion of Race: Categories of Difference in Eighteenth-Century British Culture* (Philadelphia, PA: University of Pennsylvania Press, 2000).

Wilkinson, Sir John Gardner, *Modern Egypt and Thebes*, vols. 1 and 2 (London: John Murray, 1843).

Will, Robert M., "The Introduction of Classical Economics into Chile", *Hispanic American Historical Review*, 44, no. 1 (1964): 1–21.

Williams, Helen Maria, "Preface", in Alexander von Humboldt [and Aimé Bonpland?], *Personal Narrative of Travels of the Equinoctial Regions of the New Continent during Years 1799–1804*, vol I, trans. Helen Maria Williams (London: Longman, et. al, 1814), pp. v–xii.

Williams, John, *A Narrative of Missionary Enterprises in the South Sea Islands; with Remarks upon the Natural History of the Islands, Origin, Languages, Traditions and Usages of the Inhabitants* (London: John Snow, 1837).

Williams, William H.A, *Tourism, Landscape, and the Irish Character: British Travel Writers in Pre-Famine Ireland* (Madison, WI: University of Wisconsin Press, 2008).

Winch, Donald, *Wealth and Life: Essays on the Intellectual History of Political Economy in Britain, 1848–1914* (Cambridge: Cambridge University Press, 2009).

Winn, Peter, "British Informal Empire in Uruguay in the Nineteenth Century", *Past and Present*, 73 (1976): 100–126.

Withers, Charles W.J., "Mapping the Niger, 1798–1832: Trust, Testimony and 'Ocular Demonstration' in the Late Enlightenment", *Imago Mundi: The International Journal for the History of Cartography*, 56, no. 2 (2004): 170–93.

———, "Science, Scientific Instruments and Questions of Method in Nineteenth-Century British Geography", *Transactions of the Institute of British Geographers*, 38, no. 1 (2013): 167–79.

Wohlgemut, Esther, "Maria Edgeworth and the Question of National Identity", *Studies in English Literature, 1500-1900*, 39, no. 4 (1999): 645–58.

Wokler, Robert, "Conjectural History and Anthropology in the Enlightenment", in Christopher Fox, Roy Porter, and Robert Wokler, eds., *Inventing Human Science: Eighteenth-Century Domains* (Berkeley, CA: University of California Press, 1995), pp. 31–52.

Wolff, Larry and Cipolloni Marco, eds., *The Anthropology of the Enlightenment* (Stanford, CA: Stanford University Press, 2007).

Wolloch, Nathaniel, "The Civilizing Process, Nature, and Stadial Theory", *Eighteenth-Century Studies*, 44, no. 2 (2011): 245–59.

Wollstonecraft, Mary, *Original Stories from Real Life; with Conversations, Calculated to Regulate the Affections, and Form the Mind to Truth and Goodness* (1788) (London: J. Johnson, 1796).

———, *Letters Written during a Short Residence in Sweden, Norway, and Denmark* (London: J. Johnson, 1796).

Wulf, Andrea, *The Invention of Nature: Alexander von Humboldt's New World* (New York: Alfred A. Knopf, 2015).

Young, Arthur, *A Six Weeks Tour, Through the Southern Counties of England and Wales* (London: W. Nicoll, 1768).

———, *A Six Months Tour Through the North of England, Containing, an Account of the Present State of Agriculture, Manufactures and Population, in Several Counties of This Kingdom* (London: W. Strahan, 1771).

———, *A Tour in Ireland; with General Observations on the Present State of that Kingdom: Made in the Years 1776, 1777, and 1778. And Brought Down to the End of 1779*, vol. 2 (London: T. Cadell, 1780).

———, *The Questions of Scarcity Plainly Stated and Remedies Considered* (London: W.J. and J. Richardson and J. Wright, 1800).

Young, David, "Montesquieu's View of Despotism and His Use of Travel Literature", *The Review of Politics*, 40, no. 3 (1978): 392–405.

Ziman, J.M., "Information, Communication, Knowledge", *Nature*, 224, no. 5217 (1969): 318–24.

Zimmerer, Karl S., "Humboldt's Nodes and Modes of Interdisciplinary Environmental Science in the Andean World", *Geographical Review*, 96, no. 3 (2006): 335–60.

Index

Note: Page locators in italics denotes figure.

abolitionist 93, 106, 149, 188, 280, 284, 290, 295–6
Addison, J. 44
agricultural: backwardness 219; colony 226; concerns 78; developments 79; districts 16; divergent histories 138; estates 32; experimentation 155, 159, 200, 313; holdings 163; improvement 16, 55, 74, 154, 156; innovation 56, 74, 201; inventions 155; knowledge 78; land 56; operations 78; peons 233; poor 144; population 309; potential 71; practice 78; production 53, 65; productivity 96; products 55; reform 155; rent 154; sector 83, 178; societies 51, 56, 58; surplus 56–7; survey 75, 78; troubles 155; work 58
agriculturalist 74
Akel, R. 187
Alborn, T. L. 6–7
Allen, J. 168, 175, 179
American Declaration of Independence 283, 296
amusement 59, 63, 139, 260–2, 264
analysis 93, 125, 136–7, 154, 161, 169, 171, 181, 193, 219, 227, 236, 238, 265, 282, 284–5, 298, 316: causal 19; comparative 17, 230, 302, 305; economic 18, 93, 169, 196, 212; ethnological 311; exercise of 286; formal 160; of happiness 162; historical 18, 154; institutional 194; market 2; preliminary 160; quantitative 164; social 22–3, 169; stadial 51; statistical 98; summary of 65
Andrews, J. 10, 212–13, 250–2, 256

anthropology 4, 17, 23
antiquarianism 3, 48

Babbage, C. 268–70
Bagehot, W. 18
barbarian 16–17, 21, 33, 37, 40, 44, 51–2, 69–70, 72, 103, 116, 119, 136, 138, 217, 231, 281, 293, 308
Barbauld, A. L. 146, 197–8, 200, 270
Barrow, J. 71–4, 187, 211, 236
Becker, G. S. 101
Bederman, G. 95
Belfast Social Inquiry Society 309
Bigelow, A. M. 15, 42
Black, J. 175–6, 179
Blagdon Controversy 104
Blue Stockings Society 93
botany 3, 72, 187, 191, 214
boundaries 67–8, 92–3, 147, 162, 282; amorphous 32; epistemological 3; gendered 20; lack of 124; methodological 3; of political economy 3, 94; porous 116; religious 4
Boyle, R. 30, 38–9
British East India Company 8, 187
Bruce, J. 124, 313
Bunster, G. 247
Burke, E. 75
Bush, J. 29, 59–67, 69, 138

Cabot, S. 34–5, 37
Calaresu, M. 45
Caldcleugh, A. 238
cameralism 74, 181–2
capitalist 54, 76, 156, 230, 235, 270; conspiracy 194; greedy 54; mining

251; profits 154; small-scale 270; vanguard 21
Carlyle, T. 228, 277–9, 291–2
Cathay Company 34
Catholic 143, 198; Church 34, 64, 185, 219, 309; concerns 213; Emancipation 143–4; Europe 34; France 83; hosts 34; Irish 136; Mass 35; papist 33; paraphernalia 35; properties 7
census 304–5; nationwide 306; population 83, 116, 140, 225, 304, 306; registers 306; takers 83
Christian 33–4, 105–6, 123, 297, 303; bad 33; charity 82; domestic economy 103; education 202; England 93; life 33; political economy 93, 107, 281; sinful 33; virtue 94
Christianity 36, 297; absence of 33
civility 17, 33, 51, 53, 63, 66, 272
civilization 16–17, 20, 22, 32–3, 52, 58, 69, 101, 116, 138, 140, 174–5, 177–8, 193–4, 201, 217–18, 225–6, 231, 241–2, 281–2, 294, 302, 306, 311, 315–16; advanced 308; ancient 51; commercial 52, 54, 101, 115–16, 140, 174, 202, 222, 232, 241–3, 245, 264, 281; degree of 172, 174; growth of 221; indicators of 203; indigenous 52; infant 241; lack of 22; manufacturing 51; marker of 54, 66; past 51; progress of 22, 51; sophisticated 33; stagnant 52; superior 33
Clarke, E. D. 92, 96–7, 102–3, 146, 237
Colbert, B. 103
Coleridge, S. T. 14
colonization 15, 29, 35–6, 55, 280
Colquhoun, P. 150
Cooper, G. 59, 67–70, 137
Corn Laws 12, 311
corruption 37, 54, 80, 219
cosmopolitanism 31–2, 37, 45, 274, 312; enhanced 310; Enlightenment 32; Mediterranean 34
Costeloe, M. P. 212
Coxe, W. 95–8, 155
Crawford, I. 307
credibility 3, 9–12, 15–16, 21, 23, 30–1, 38, 47, 54, 62, 64, 66, 80, 92, 97, 104, 116, 124, 126, 141–2, 173, 195, 212, 217, 228, 230, 238, 246, 249, 262, 266–9, 288, 290, 299, 313; achieving 187; eyewitness 31; of facts 18; hierarchy of 314; ideals of 20; lacking 11; language of 237; sociology of 11; of travelers 18, 62, 249, 271, 314
Croker, J. W. 274
cultivation 13, 57, 112, 154–5, 177–8, 201, 251, 309; of manners 174
Cunningham, J. W. 3, 103, 109
curiosity 37, 59, 61–2, 135, 217, 265; awakening 275; cabinet 59; economy of 30; historical 311; literary 187; natural 67; of nature 61; public 170

d'Ivernois, F. 128–9
Daston, L. 11
Davies, M. 10
de Beaumont, G. 280–1
de Pons, F. R. J. 168–75, 177
de Salas, M. 201
Defoe, D. 13, 148
democratic 281; institutions 279; principles 283, 286, 288
deprivation: material 150, 305; sensory 151
despotism 37, 63
diplomacy 29, 35, 171
diplomats 1, 34, 170, 185
Disraeli, B. 237–9
domestic 1, 137–8, 169, 213, 251; arrangements 102, 108, 187; duties 259; economy 5–6, 13, 19–20, 66–7, 72–3, 75, 78, 92–3, 99–103, 106–7, 111–13, 138, 147, 169, 171–2, 197, 201, 204, 269; fiction 216; goods 108; happiness 102; investment 225; joint-stock companies 239; labor 101; life 102, 153, 285, 288; literati 146; market 62; people 313; relations 113; scientific communication networks 100; slaves 102; space 75, 288, 313; sphere 153, 289; traveler 59; trifles 264; tyrants 102; woman 54, 99; work 103
domesticity 107; English 111; female 109–10; French 108; universal models of 101
Drake, M. 99
Duane, W. 1
Dublin Statistical Society 309–10
Dutch East India Company 71–2

East India College 94, 121
ecology 76; history of 76; human 66; local 79

Index 357

economic man 18, 32, 79, 81–2, 261, 270, 291
Economical Society of Berne 115
economics 13, 93, 106, 108, 136, 170, 221, 282; comparative 17; feminist 5; history of 5, 17, 156; political 122; present-day 7; problems in 120
economy: civil 170; of curiosity 30; general 77–8; gift 303; household 19, 99, 257, 300–1; micro- 79; national 76; natural 32, 75–8, 286; political 1–7, 12–14, 17–20, 22–3, 29, 31–2, 45–6, 48, 50–2, 59, 62–4, 66–8, 70–2, 76–8, 83, 92–3, 96, 99–102, 107, 111, 113–15, 117–23, 125, 128, 138–9, 141, 146–9, 151–2, 154–6, 159, 162–3, 168–72, 178–9, 181, 185, 191–7, 200–2, 204, 212, 214–15, 218–20, 222, 225, 227–9, 234, 238, 240–1, 246–7, 250, 252, 259, 266–9, 272, 279, 281–3, 285–6, 289, 298, 300–1, 304–12, 316; principles of 202; rural 77–8; social 282; *see also* domestic
Edgeworth, M. 19, 135, 137, 145–63, 181, 197–8, 211, 236, 295–6
enclosure movement 65, 138, 163
Enlightenment 16, 32, 46
epistemological shift 11
epistemology 40, 92, 117, 266, 272, 286; historical 11
ethnology 3, 311–12; relativist 312
Evangelical activism 104, 110
evidence 3, 12–14, 16, 18–22, 30, 32, 43, 52, 57–8, 64–5, 92–4, 96, 115–16, 122, 125, 128, 149, 154, 157–9, 161, 163, 179, 193, 203, 231, 233, 239, 246, 249, 260, 267–9, 277, 286, 293, 305, 307–8, 313; abundant 301; actual 12; anecdotal 155; assembling 17; authentic 31; body of 96; direct 18; of experience 156, 158, 194; gathering 12; lack of 31, 51; nature of 93; partial 20; physical 10; of regularities 18; scant 92; spurious 124; statistical 99; supporting 12; from travelers 56, 93
expansion 79; of the British Empire 121; colonial 4, 30; commercial 23, 56, 70, 173; imperial 4, 23, 30; of political science 311; of rationality 172; of trade 70, 103, 171; of travel 37
exploration 16, 29, 35–6, 119, 213, 250, 310, 313–14; commercial 4; scientific 4, 23

fact: absence of 304, 307; authenticated 19, 31, 142, 154, 157, 159, 185; basic 83; conflicting 204; credibility of 12, 18, 269; detached 18; discourse of 30; economical 77, 79; environmental 19; errors of 283; established 99; gathering 15, 17, 99, 119, 141; historical 19, 153; identical 12; importance of 38; important 12; individual 83; institutional 19; insulated 18, 276; interpretation of 31, 154; irregular 39; lack of 145, 173; matters of 30, 36–7, 39, 62, 64, 126, 211, 288, 305; measurable 117; natural 39, 77, 79; novel 313; numerical 227; observing 64, 68; pertinent 8; political 19; promiscuous 275; scientific 126; social 80; statistical 22, 95, 117, 135, 143; suppression of 289; travelers' 124; truth of 30; underlying 226; unique 126
Ferguson, A. 51, 54
feudal 46, 51, 272
Flint, T. 259, 264
Francis, J. G. 6
Franklin, B. 55
French Revolution 95

Gamer, M. 153
Games, A. 34
gender studies 4, 11, 100
Genette, G. 7
geography 4, 29, 31, 35, 95, 171, 176, 182, 214, 275
geology 3, 72, 244, 268, 270
Gillespie, A. 74, 222
Gilpin, W. 4
Glorious Revolution (1688) 83
Gordon, R. J. 72–3
gothic 4, 153, 313
Graham, M. 10, 21, 169, 185–200, 202–4, 211–12, 216, 232–3, 235–6, 238, 270
Grand Tour 16, 32, 43–5, 48, 313
Great Famine 141, 307
growth 57, 261, 274; of civilization 221; of commercial civilizations 101; economic 180, 221; of the global slave trade 30; of local prejudices 152; natural 56; of political controversies 39; population 76, 98, 129, 135, 140, 143, 157, 179, 221, 225, 227, 234, 239, 301; of scientific

networks 37; in social statistics 99; stages of 51, 179; of towns and cities 56–7; unnatural 57; vegetative 64
Gueslin, A. 282

Hagglund, B. 195
Hakluyt, R. 15, 29–31, 35, 310
Hall, B. 191, 216, 229–30, 251, 257, 262–3, 265, 278–9
Hancock, W. N. 309–10
happiness 22, 46, 53, 69, 76, 94, 98, 114–17, 129–30, 135, 157, 161–4, 169, 172, 182, 192–3, 201, 203–4, 228, 262, 273–4, 283, 295–6, 302; actual 153; analysis of 162; comparative 128–9; domestic 102; greater 22, 221; human 273, 292, 296; inhabitants' 129; marker of 129; prospects of 142; public 211; pursuit of 162, 296; societal 273; superior 129; test of 129; visions of 19
Head, F. B. 10, 21, 212–13, 239–51, 304
Hill, M. R. 280
Home, H. 51
Hooper, G. 136
Huigen, S. 71–4

ideologies: emerging 109; nationalist 4; of separate spheres 6
Indigenes 33, 58, 168, 171
industrial: conditions 281; life 285; organization 22; uses 201
industry 47, 50, 73, 110, 120, 149, 170, 177–8, 180, 193, 198, 200–1, 222, 242, 245, 261, 270, 272, 286, 301, 305, 308
investment 70, 164, 170–1, 213, 221, 225, 234, 236; boom 21; capital 221, 225, 234; costly 270; foreign 225, 234; future 213; high-quality 235; joint-stock 235; mining 212–13, 231, 234; opportunities 22, 212; potential 1; proposals 235; prospective 228; prospects for 21; Royal Society 39; safe 236; scheme 22; speculative 236; timing of 157; unprofitable 235
Iriberri, J. de Cos 201, 211
Islam 34, 297

Jackson, J. 275–6, 279
Jacob, W. 272
Jews 34, 306
Jones, R. 154

Jones, W. 125
Jonsson, F. A. 16, 55–6
Judaism 297

Kalm, P. 55–6
Kaplan, C. 287
Keighren, I. M. 11

labor 57–8, 135, 159, 163, 179, 200–1, 213, 219, 231, 233, 241, 243, 282, 308; ceaseless 101; demand for 162; discernible 58; division of 11, 22, 47, 54, 99–101, 147, 199, 213, 221, 239, 242, 245, 250; domestic 101; force 100; free movement of 47; household 92, 101; market 99, 101; mental 268; paid 211; physical 268; relations 150; useful 174; wage 144, 239
Lambert, C. 251
Lawson, J. A. 310
lazzari 45
leisure and tourism studies 4
Lesham, D. 181
Linnaeus, C. 40, 55–6, 72
Literary Society of Bombay 118, 127
Livesey, J. 46
Lockhart, J. G. 264
Lurquín, T. 201

Mackintosh, J. 93, 117–21, 123–5, 128–9, 181, 186, 313
Malthus, T. R. 5, 12–14, 17, 19, 22, 51–2, 72, 83, 92–102, 105, 111–19, 121–5, 129, 136, 139–46, 154, 156–7, 159, 161, 163, 178–82, 185–6, 214, 219, 226, 229, 237, 241, 245, 266, 280–1, 292, 298, 301, 303, 307, 311, 315
management 77, 287, 304; active 155; colonial 238; crop 55; efficient 32; of empire 121; estate 155; farm 74; forestry 55; good 150; household 92, 100, 147, 299; of Irish lands 67; land 66; mis- 32; of people 55, 66; of plantations 291; prudent 182; self- 121; of testimony 30; woodland 79
Marcet, J. H. 1, 3, 5, 99, 115, 146, 189, 194
Marouby, C. 55–8
Marshall, J. 16
Marshall, W. 32, 75–80, 82, 286
Martineau, H. 22–3, 256, 265–7, 271–316
maternalism 110

Maunder, S. 7
McCulloch, J. B. 139, 226, 235–6
mercantilism 3
merchants 1, 4, 21, 30, 34–7, 47, 52, 54, 79, 96, 109, 121, 159, 171–2, 189, 193–4, 197, 219, 232–3, 235–6, 280, 312
Miers, J. 10, 21, 204, 211–22, 225–37, 240–1, 244, 250–2, 256, 304, 315
Milk-Boys 2
Mill, J. S. 17, 105, 125–7, 146, 159–60, 214, 227–8, 281
Millar, J. 51
mining association 244, 249, 252; Chilian 237, 250–1; English 212; General South American 238; joint-stock 235; Peruvian 237, 250; Rio Plata 239, 246–7
Montagu, Lady M. W. 20, 199–200, 288
moral: arrangements 286; behavior 17, 219; causes 178; concerns 83; condition 202; conduct 219; decorum 195; deformity 291; dimensions 111; disapprobation 270; discipline 157; duties 186; eighteenth century 54; energies 83; good 81, 105; hierarchy 116; history 36, 38; judgment 38, 81, 291; manifestations of 284; observation of 275–6; order 107; philosophy 3, 10, 195, 259; polluters of 93; powers 299; principles 108, 286; research 275; restraint 19, 94, 100, 121, 161, 219; sciences 119, 271; sentiments 80; sobriety 272; statistics 282; taxonomy 116; transformations 73; of travel 106; virtue 80
More, H. 19, 92–3, 102–11, 200, 311
Morellet, A. 146
Morgan, M. S. 157
Muslims 34, 123, 127

National Association for the Promotion of Social Science 312
Neal, L. 235
neo-Machiavellian 46
neo-mercantilist 16, 109, 172
New Poor Law 267
Nuñez, I. 225, 249–50

O'Brien, K. 18
Ó Gráda, C. 141

objectivity 10–12; aperspectival 11; criteria of 173; ethos of 309; mechanical 11; prehistory of 11; scientific 5, 112, 177
observation 3, 6, 9, 11, 16, 20, 22, 37–9, 41, 45, 78, 112, 116, 120, 125, 142, 158, 175, 194, 229, 232, 241, 251, 256–7, 263–5, 267–72, 274, 276–8, 288, 292, 297–8, 300, 302, 307, 309–10, 314; accurate 270; actual 97; adequate 78; careful 38, 211; contemporary 95; discipline of 270; economical 118; expert 144, 268; eyewitness 126; failings in 212; first-hand 156, 175; framework for 6; histories of 5, 10–12, 20; ideal of 152; immediate 195; implications of 32; lessons in 71; love of 270; mechanics of 246; methods of 10, 16, 198, 298, 308; nature of 124, 169, 250; objective 176; opportunities for 262; personal 41, 68, 126; philosophical 265; powers of 126, 245, 264; prejudice in 48; scientific 100, 159, 177, 270; spheres of 21; standards of 298; systematic 37, 265; universal methodology for 50; vehicles for 32; visual 277; woman of 94
Orientalism 6, 127

Palmeri, F. 17–18
paternalism 107, 110
perception: cultivated 12; power of 126
Petty, W. 44, 136, 140
pilgrimages 29, 48
Pitt, W. 46, 137
Plumptre, A. 137–9, 145
Poe, E. A. 288, 303
political: advantage 143; ailments 135; arithmetic 3, 16, 32, 74, 82–3, 118–20, 123–4, 129, 136–7, 181, 227; attitudes 281; bent 262; bodies 145; community 46; connexions 278; conservatism 263; context 8, 43; control 22, 40; controversies 39, 144; debates 235; developments 46; discourse 169; discussions 31; ecology 76; elites 191; entity 137; essays 75; events 191; exemplar 76; experience 44; geo- 21, 182; harmony 137; history 4, 36, 95, 137, 181, 196; information 21; instability 180, 213; institutions 144, 257,

261; interests 143; leaders 190–1; management 55; maneuvering 190; mismanagement 32; nature 282; needs 32; opinion 16; order 43, 105; persuasion 265; philosophers 228; philosophy 283; point of view 71; realms 235; reforms 46, 136, 263; science 279, 311–12; space 150, 227; stability 46, 181; state 138; statistics 120; status 213; tour 144; turmoil 246; uncertainty 34; union 143; welfare 283; *see also* economy, fact
Political Economy Club 160
Pontoppidan, E. 95, 97
population: agricultural 309; Amerindian 43; census 83, 116, 140, 225, 304–6; Christian 123; counts 120; decline 307; density 221, 242; distribution 119; estimates 22, 83, 136, 223, 224–5; European 182; growth 98, 129, 135, 140, 157, 179, 221, 225, 227, 234, 239, 301; Hindu 125; human 31, 76, 301; hybrid 73; Indigenous 72–3; Irish 136, 140–1, 143–4, 158, 162; lack of 200, 245; models 139; Muslim 123; phenomena 119; polyglot 40; principle 13–14, 19, 22, 52, 83, 92–5, 98, 100, 113–17, 122, 139–40, 144–5, 154, 157, 159, 161, 163, 182, 219, 226–7, 281, 298, 301, 303, 306, 308; problem 52, 225; protection of 72; redundant 113; rural 63; scanty 64; settler 73; size 56; sizeable 58; statistics 117, 182, 222, 225, 227; urban 56–7
poverty 45, 49, 53–4, 63–5, 69, 80, 83, 104–5, 113, 115, 136–8, 203–4, 220, 227–8, 261, 272, 281
Pratt, M. L. 21, 169, 241
prejudice 11, 16, 23, 45, 48, 61, 75, 93, 104, 127–8, 152–3, 168, 174, 188, 211, 215, 230, 240, 263, 265–6, 276, 278, 294–5, 297, 305; blinkers of 152; definition of 104; European 186; exclusion of 273; lack of 37, 279; local 48, 79, 152; national 16, 46, 71, 212, 301, 313; party 20; personal 20; popular 48; Protestant 143; reflexive 105; sectional 284; theological 297; without 79, 152, 267
principal-agent problem 22, 120–1, 155, 213, 235, 246

Proctor, R. 40, 216, 218
progress 18, 51–2, 57, 72, 103, 116, 154, 169, 177–8, 221, 273, 292–4, 306, 315; civil 37; of civility 51; of civilization 22, 51; commercial 226; conception of 54; economic 273; historical 292; human 291–2; inevitable 293; mankind's 297; material 17, 94, 128; mental 17; national 54; population 221; societal 17
prosperity 46–7, 49, 98, 114, 128–30, 157, 161–2, 169, 172, 176, 192–3, 202–3, 270, 283, 309
Protestant 226; children 108; clergy 143; England 83; evangelism 31; prejudice 143; radical 33

Quesnay, F. 2, 45, 47

Rappite communities 282, 286
Report of the Committee of the House of Commons on the Woollen Trade (1806) 270
republicanism 262–3
Ricardo, D. 5, 12, 19, 135, 139, 145–6, 154–63, 180, 194, 295
Ricoeur, P. 41
Rodriguez, J. 193
romantic 59, 97, 216, 242; novels 4; paradise 66; poet 177; reveries 97; subjectivity 187; subjects of nature 59
Romer, I. F. 300
Rousseau, J.-J. 2, 51, 72, 94
Royal African Company 39
Royal Society of London 15, 30, 36

savage 16–18, 21, 33, 40, 51–2, 73–4, 106, 116–17, 138, 168, 217–18, 220, 293, 303–4, 314–15; assessment 274; faculty 302; life 116–17, 218; naked 58; nations 58; race 218; societies 54, 57–8, 293; stupid 175; unorganized 315; white 106
Say, J.-B. 2, 202, 215, 281
scarcity 151, 160, 163, 181, 185, 233, 261, 301
Schwartz, S. P. 212
Scrope, G. P. 266–7
Select Committee on Emigration of the House of Commons 163
self: -advancement 273; -approval 82; -consciousness 292; -control 54, 121;

-deception 54, 231; -denial 53, 111, 151; -deprecating 257; -discipline 151; -evident 1, 105; -fashioning 277; -governance 172; -identify 43, 162; -importance 195; -interest 6, 22, 55, 80, 111, 114, 122, 172, 181, 189, 193, 197, 212–13, 248, 250, 281; knowledge of 292; -love 6, 49; -management 121; -practice 78; -professed 65; -referential 288; -reflection 37, 265, 277; -regulating 55, 270; -reinforcing 17; -rule 126; sense of 11, 107; shrinkage of 61; -sufficient 36; -transformation 232
Senior, N. 139, 281
sensory: apparatus 277; deprivation 151; losses 277
servility 54, 263
Shaker communities 282, 286–7
Shapiro, B. J. 126
Shoemaker, N. 43
slavery 39, 55, 102, 188, 280, 283–4, 288–90; alleviate 188; anti- 106; Brazilian 189; denouncing 200; domestic 102; evils of 290; extinguishing 311; horrors of 291; iconography of 188; institution of 283, 287, 289; observer of 288; of servants 102
slaves 4, 64, 66, 74, 102, 149–50, 188, 260, 280, 287, 292; African 42–3, 73; Black 290; domestic 102; freeing of 106; global trade 30; -holders 280, 294; market 188, 189–90; owners 287, 291; -produced sugar 106; purchase of 106; quarters 287; revolt 170; suffering of 188; -trading 39, 106; West Indian 150–1
Smith, A. 2, 4–5, 7, 10, 17–18, 31–2, 45–7, 51–9, 66, 68, 70, 74, 80–3, 99, 101, 120, 150, 158, 170, 172, 178–9, 181, 192, 194, 199–200, 202, 215, 229, 238–9, 245, 272–3, 287, 303
Smith, J. 33, 52
social: adversity 286; analysis 22–3, 100, 156, 169, 212; arrangements 305; beings 292; bodies 145, 147, 303; categories 288; conditions 178; connexions 222; consequence 16; development 186; evils 286; factors 80; good 181; -historical 154; ills 311; institutions 176, 179; interactions 81, 174; intercourse 303; life 95, 174, 273; machine 123;

medicine 129; networks 9; objects 102; observations 313; order 107; organization 187; phenomena 32, 163, 217, 271; physics 312; point of view 228; process 230, 269; realm 235; reproduction 75; roles 260; roots 11; scale 54; sciences 11, 23, 100, 163, 282–3, 309–10, 316; settings 257; spheres 54; state 282; statistics 93, 99; status 10, 30; system 272; wretchedness 311; *see also* economy
Society for Diffusion of Useful Knowledge (SDUK) 263–4, 267
Society for Effecting the Abolition of the African Slave Trade 106
Society for the Diffusion of Useful Knowledge 115
sociology 4, 17, 23, 312; of credibility 11
Sockwell, W. D. 17
Somarriva, M. 236
Southey, R. 187, 190, 242
stadial history 32, 51, 57–8, 117, 175, 263, 272, 291, 293, 304–5
Stevenson, W. B. 41–2, 222
Stewart, D. 18, 57, 82–3, 126, 146–7, 186
subjectivity 8, 11, 17, 45, 65, 80, 251; adaptable 34; economic 149, 250; female 107; limited 8; masculine 79; of observing 188; *see also* romantic
Sumner, J. B. 226–7
sympathy 72, 82, 111, 127, 174, 272–4, 287, 290–1, 294–6, 300, 306, 308

theological: prejudices 297; readings 297; subjects 298; world 297
Thompson, C. 191
Thomson, J. 202–3
Tobin, B. F. 79
Tocqueville, A. 279–82
trade 17, 29, 33–5, 38, 45–7, 49, 53–4, 57, 59, 69, 79, 83, 93, 103, 109–10, 157, 161, 170–1, 173, 191, 193, 196, 198–9, 215, 221, 226, 244, 282, 303, 309, 311–12, 315–16; absence of 172; barriers 172, 193; brutality of 106; calf-skin 60; cross-Channel 110; equal 192; expansion of 70, 103, 171; foreign 69, 76, 103, 107, 311; free 22, 46–7,

93, 96, 105, 169, 171–3, 191–4, 200, 202, 311; imaginary 303; international 46, 269; Irish 64; policy 194; reorganization 46; secrets 35; stock-in- 21; supporter 93; theories of 95; tourist 3, 286; treaty 172; *see also* slave
transatlantic studies 4
Tribe, K. 43
Trollope, F. 256–7, 259–66, 279, 284, 288–9
Tucker, J. 31, 40, 46–51, 95

unhappiness 204, 304

Varouxakis, G. 281
Vidal, E. E. 2, 4, 7
von Humboldt, A. 16, 20–1, 157–8, 162, 164, 169, 175–82

wage fund 5
Wakefield, Edgar 13, 79, 157
Walls, L. D. 181
Ward, H. G. 175
Weingast, B. R. 7
welfare 38, 273, 282–3, 302, 305, 312; national 302, 305
Wilberforce, W. 104, 106
Wilkinson, Sir J. G. 299, 301
Williams, H. M. 177
Wollstonecraft, M. 94–5, 98, 102, 106–7, 137, 148–9, 151

xenophobia 71

Young, A. 16, 32, 74–5, 79–80, 82–3, 138, 142–4, 148, 156–7, 313

zoology 4, 275

Printed in the United States
by Baker & Taylor Publisher Services